Twentieth Century
DRAMA

CONSULTING EDITOR:

Haskell M. Block
Brooklyn College of The City University of New York

Twentieth Century DRAMA:
England, Ireland, the United States

EDITED BY

RUBY COHN

AND

BERNARD F. DUKORE

Queens College of The City University of New York

RANDOM HOUSE / *New York*

© Copyright, 1966, by Random House, Inc.

All rights reserved under International and Pan-American Copyright Conventions. Published in New York by Random House, Inc. Library of Congress Catalog Card Number: 66-19849. Manufactured in the United States of America. Typography by Guy Fleming.

CAUTION: Professionals and amateurs are hereby warned that all the plays in this volume, being fully protected under the Copyright Laws of the United States of America, the British Commonwealth and Empire, and all other countries of the Berne, International, and Pan-American Conventions, are subject to royalty. All rights, including, but not limited to, professional, amateur, stock, motion picture, television, recitation, lecturing, public reading, radio broadcasting, publication, and the rights of translation into foreign languages are strictly reserved. Inquiries concerning these rights should be addressed to the author or agent whose name appears in the following acknowledgments. All other inquiries should be addressed to the publishers named.

MAJOR BARBARA by George Bernard Shaw. Copyright 1907, 1913, 1930, 1941 by George Bernard Shaw. Copyright 1957 by the Public Trustee as Executor of the Estate of George Bernard Shaw. Reprinted by permission of the Society of Authors and Dodd, Mead & Co.

THE PLAYBOY OF THE WESTERN WORLD by John M. Synge. Copyright 1907 and renewed 1934 by the Estate of John M. Synge. Reprinted from *The Complete Works of John M. Synge,* by permission of Random House, Inc.

THE ONLY JEALOUSY OF EMER by W. B. Yeats. Reprinted with permission of the publisher from *The Collected Plays of W. B. Yeats.* Copyright 1934, 1952 by The Macmillan Company.

MURDER IN THE CATHEDRAL by T. S. Eliot. Copyright, 1935, by Harcourt, Brace & World, Inc.; renewed, 1963, by T. S. Eliot.

AWAKE AND SING! by Clifford Odets. Copyright, 1933, 1935, by Clifford Odets; Copyright renewed, 1961, 1963, by Clifford Odets, in care of Harold Freedman, Brandt & Brandt Dramatic Department, Inc., 101 Park Ave., New York, N.Y.

OUR TOWN by Thornton Wilder. Copyright © 1938, 1957 by Thornton Wilder, in care of Harold Freedman, Brandt & Brandt Dramatic Department, Inc., 101 Park Ave., New York, N.Y. All requests for amateur rights should be addressed to Samuel French, 25 West 45th Street, New York 19, N.Y. Reprinted by permission of Harper & Row, Publishers, Inc.

THE GLASS MENAGERIE by Tennessee Williams. Copyright 1945 by Tennessee Williams and Edwina D. Williams. Reprinted from *Six Modern American Plays*, by permission of Random House, Inc.

THE ICEMAN COMETH by Eugene O'Neill. Copyright, as an unpublished work, 1940 by Eugene O'Neill. Copyright 1946 by Eugene O'Neill. Reprinted from *Plays of Eugene O'Neill*, by permission of Random House, Inc.

LOOK BACK IN ANGER by John Osborne. Reprinted by permission of S. G. Phillips, Inc. Copyright © 1957 by S. G. Phillips, Inc.

THE DUMB WAITER by Harold Pinter. Copyright © 1960 by Harold Pinter. Reprinted from *The Caretaker and The Dumb Waiter* by permission of the publisher, Grove Press, Inc.

THE ZOO STORY by Edward Albee. Reprinted from *The Zoo Story, The Sand Box and The Death of Bessie Smith* by permission of Coward-McCann, Inc. Copyright © 1960 by Edward Albee, in care of The William Morris Agency, 1740 Broadway, New York.

EMBERS by Samuel Beckett. Reprinted from *Krapp's Last Tape and Other Dramatic Pieces* by Samuel Beckett, published by Grove Press, Inc. Copyright © 1957 by Samuel Beckett, Copyright © 1958, 1959, 1960 by Grove Press, Inc.

FOREWORD

THIS ANTHOLOGY AROSE from the teaching needs of its editors, who wished to deal with a significant range of twentieth-century drama written in English. The criteria for selection were: (1) the author had to be an important playwright who has produced a corpus of work, (2) the play itself had to be a good play, and (3) the reprinting rights had to be available.

In several cases—Shaw's *Major Barbara* and Synge's *Playboy of the Western World*, for example—there is widespread agreement that the play is a twentieth-century classic. Where this is not the case, selection was dictated by copyright restrictions, editorial compromise, and/or the perhaps astigmatic viewpoint of 1965.

We envisage this anthology primarily as a textbook of contemporary dramatic literature and have therefore supplied brief introductions dealing with the author, the work, and the specific play. In the Selective Bibliographies that follow these introductions, we have confined ourselves to those works that elucidate the plays in this anthology. There are, we believe, two significant omissions, Sean O'Casey and Arthur Miller, whose plays were unavailable to us. Since we feel students should nevertheless be introduced to these playwrights, we have provided editorial material for the plays we would have selected.

We are enthusiastic about these plays, and we hope that others will share that enthusiasm.

Ruby Cohn
Bernard F. Dukore

CONTENTS

Major Barbara (1905)* · George Bernard Shaw	3
The Playboy of the Western World (1907) · John Millington Synge	91
The Only Jealousy of Emer (1919) · William Butler Yeats	147
Preface to *Juno and the Paycock* (1925)† · Sean O'Casey	165
Murder in the Cathedral (1935) · Thomas Stearns Eliot	171
Awake and Sing! (1935) · Clifford Odets	219
Our Town (1938) · Thornton Wilder	275
The Glass Menagerie (1944) · Tennessee Williams	331
The Iceman Cometh (1946) · Eugene O'Neill	403
Preface to *The Crucible* (1953)† · Arthur Miller	535
Look Back in Anger (1956) · John Osborne	541
The Dumb Waiter (1957) · Harold Pinter	617
The Zoo Story (1958)* · Edward Albee	649
Embers (1959) · Samuel Beckett	677

* Dates throughout refer to first performance or first publication, whichever is earlier, with the exception of plays by Shaw and Albee, where the dates refer to the year of completion.
† Play not included in anthology. Prefaces to O'Casey and Miller to be used with separate versions of these particular plays.

Twentieth Century

DRAMA

GEORGE BERNARD SHAW
[1856 – 1950]

❧ *The Man*

BERNARD SHAW was born before the encounter of the Monitor and the Merrimac, and died after the atomic destruction of Hiroshima and Nagasaki. He was concerned with nearly all of the major social and artistic currents of the century, from Darwinism to Fascism, from Ibsenism to Motion Pictures. His writings include political commentaries, economic treatises, religious essays, plays, novels, theater criticism, music criticism, and art criticism.

George Bernard Shaw, known also as G.B.S., later dropped his first name. His parents were Lucinda Elizabeth Gurly and George Carr Shaw, Protestants in a predominantly Catholic city. As a boy in Dublin, he hated school; as a man, he made the famous statement "He who can, does. He who cannot, teaches." Nevertheless, young Shaw liked to read; among his favorites were Shakespeare, Dickens, Bunyan, and The Bible. At the Dublin theater he saw melodramas, Shakespearean productions, and operas. Music played an important role in his development. His mother assisted George John Vandeleur Lee, a voice teacher and conductor, in his musical undertakings. In 1873 she followed Lee to London, and three years later young Shaw joined her.

He first sought literary success in fiction, and from 1879 produced a novel a year for five years. As he was later to do in the drama, he utilized conventions of the nineteenth-century novel, injecting such Shavian elements as wit, an untraditional point of view, and articulate characters aware of their intellectual and social commitments.

Before he wrote his last novel, he was converted to socialism. In 1884 he joined the newly formed Fabian Society and soon became one of its leading figures.

Shaw's playwriting career began shortly after the formation of J. T. Grein's Independent Theatre in 1891. Shaw responded to Grein's call for native playwrights by completing *Widowers' Houses* (begun in 1885 in collaboration with William Archer but soon dropped). Dealing with the problem of slum landlordism, *Widowers' Houses*, produced in 1892, was England's first modern drama. From 1904 to 1907 Harley Granville-Barker, in partnership with J. E. Vedrenne as business manager, leased the Royal Court Theatre. With Barker acting in his plays and Barker and Shaw directing them, there was a triumphant meeting of actor and playwright, which created some of Shaw's greatest successes.

❦ *The Work*

SHAW'S PLAYS are intended, through laughter, to cure abscesses in the social body. However, though he writes political and economic essays advocating socialism as the cure for England's ills, his plays generally treat the subject indirectly; in *Heartbreak House*, for example, he describes the collapse of capitalist England and allows the audience to infer the remedy.

Shaw was himself a lover of paradox, and several of the characteristics of his plays may be stated in the form of paradox. He writes of passionate people who do not have what is commonly thought of as passion; although sexual passion plays a negligible role in Shaw's comedies, his characters are obsessed by intellectual and moral passions. His plays deal with ideas but are peopled by emotional characters; he presents his ideas dramatically by drawing people whose intellectual and moral positions govern their lives, create their conflicts, and cause their deaths. Another Shavian paradox is that these apparently "talky" plays contain much action and many highly theatrical ingredients: a fugitive in a lady's bedroom, a costume party, a waltz with a lion, bombs falling, beauties in bathing suits. Shaw's "intellectual" theater is set in a framework of hi-jinks and hokum, characteristic of "unintellectual" theater.

Shavian dialogue is rhetorical, and at times operatic. One of its most distinctive features is its humor: the impudent placing of familiar phrases in unfamiliar contexts, paradox, comic irony, inversion, as well as low-comedy devices. Shaw's plays abound in pratfalls as well as wit.

5 · *Major Barbara*

❧ *The Play*

IN CONTRAST to today's significant plays, such as those of Beckett and Pinter, which generally present a "face" of obscurity and ambiguity, Shaw's plays present a "face" of the utmost clarity. Nevertheless, they have layers of meaning and significance beneath the surface; they are complex *in addition to* being clear.

The roots of all of his plays lie in traditional theater, and *Major Barbara* is no exception. Beneath the economics and religion is the familiar love story which concludes with the foundling winning the princess and gaining the kingdom. The first act of *Major Barbara* is drawing-room comedy; in the second act a brass band strikes up a rousing march while the heroine's heart is breaking; in the third, life-size, corpse-like dummies draw the audience's attention while a diabolonian character discusses the virtues of his establishment.

As is often the case with Shaw's plays, *Major Barbara* deals with conversions. There are the pretended conversions of "Snobby" Price and "Rummy" Mitchens, the potential conversion of Bill Walker, and the actual conversions of the principal members of the Undershaft family. Stephen is converted to the view that his father's business is respectable and praiseworthy. Lady Brit is converted to an acceptance of the facts that Stephen will not inherit the foundry, and that in order to keep it in the family she must marry Barbara to a foundling. Andrew Undershaft is converted to the view that Cusins is a legitimate bastard and therefore eligible to inherit the foundry. Cusins and Barbara are converted to Undershaft's doctrine of realism and power. Although they realize that the Undershaft gospel—the elimination of poverty—is the essential first step, they hope to convert the Undershaft power to their own ends. In direct opposition to Undershaft, Cusins intends to broaden the base of power by giving it to the common man. Barbara realizes that God's work cannot be done by bribery but can be accomplished only by well-fed, free human beings determined to do that work for its own sake; her endeavors at Perivale St. Andrews will be toward that end. The converted young couple will themselves try to convert.

The aims and points of view of Undershaft, Cusins, and Barbara form a mystic trinity of body, mind, and soul, which are necessary for the salvation of mankind. In *John Bull's Other Island*, written shortly before *Major Barbara*, Father Keegan speaks of several trinities in his dreams of heaven. There, the State was the Church and the Church the people, work was play and play life, the priest was the worshiper and the worshiper the worshiped, life was human and humanity divine. In large measure, these trinities are embodied by the principal trio of *Major Barbara*, who are connected to each other by several links: Undershaft is Barbara's father and will be her father-in-law, Cusins will become Undershaft and will be Barbara's husband and step-brother, Barbara is the daughter of Undershaft and will be the wife of Undershaft. The father, the adopted son, and the holy salvationist are united in what Cusins describes as a potentially heavenly city. After Barbara's Gethsemane in the second act, she undergoes an apotheosis in the third—a *"transfigured"* Barbara "has gone right up into the skies" and, to paraphrase Matthew and Mark, she becomes as a child (tugging at her mother's skirts) before entering the kingdom of heaven. Rarely simplistic, Shaw calls in the final scene of *Major Barbara* for both individual regeneration and social improvement.

Major Barbara may be called Shaw's Grecian play. One of the characters is a Greek professor who is modeled on Gilbert Murray and is nicknamed Euripides. Murray himself advised Shaw on the play and allowed him to use two passages from his translation of Euripides' *The Bacchae*. Homer is quoted and Plato paraphrased. The stories of the Greek god and the modern salvationist are connected by Undershaft. Father of Barbara, he is called Dionysus; appropriately, his wine is rich in natural alcohol, and under his influence Cusins declares himself to be possessed. His own "rebirth" at the hands of an adoptive father parallels that of the Greek god. Just as Dionysus was born twice (when Semele died in giving birth to him, Zeus saved him by enclosing the infant god in his thigh, from which he was born a second time), so the successor to the cannon foundry has a symbolic second birth upon assuming the name Andrew Undershaft. Just as Dionysus is associated with the seasonal pattern of the transition of winter to spring and the archetypal pattern of death and resurrection, so *Major Barbara* progresses from Barbara's wintry despair of the second act to her spiritual rebirth in the third.

❧ Dramatic Works

Widowers' Houses, 1892.
The Philanderer, 1893.
Mrs. Warren's Profession, 1894.
Arms and the Man, 1894.
Candida, 1895.
The Man of Destiny, 1896.
You Never Can Tell, 1897.
The Devil's Disciple, 1897.
Caesar and Cleopatra, 1898.
Captain Brassbound's Conversion, 1899.
The Admirable Bashville, 1901.
Man and Superman, 1903.
John Bull's Other Island, 1904.
How He Lied to Her Husband, 1904.
Major Barbara, 1905.
Passion, Poison, and Petrifaction, 1905.
The Doctor's Dilemma, 1906.
The Interlude at the Playhouse, 1907.
Getting Married, 1908.
The Shewing-up of Blanco Posnet, 1909.
Press Cuttings, 1909.
The Fascinating Foundling, 1909.
The Glimpse of Reality, 1909.
Misalliance, 1910.
The Dark Lady of the Sonnets, 1910.
Fanny's First Play, 1911.
Androcles and the Lion, 1912.

Overruled, 1912.
Pygmalion, 1912.
Great Catherine, 1913.
The Music-Cure, 1914.
O'Flaherty, V.C., 1915.
The Inca of Perusalem, 1916.
Augustus Does His Bit, 1916.
Annajanska, the Wild Grand Duchess (later changed to Annajanska, the Bolshevik Empress), 1917.
Heartbreak House, 1919.
Back to Methuselah, 1920.
Jitta's Atonement (adapted from the German of Siegfried Trebitsch), 1922.
Saint Joan, 1923.
The Apple Cart, 1929.
Too True to Be Good, 1931.
Village Wooing, 1933.
On the Rocks, 1933.
The Simpleton of the Unexpected Isles, 1934.
The Six of Calais, 1934.
The Millionairess, 1935.
Cymbeline Refinished, 1937.
Geneva, 1938.
In Good King Charles's Golden Days, 1939.
Buoyant Billions, 1948.
Farfetched Fables, 1948.
Shakes Versus Shav, 1949.
Why She Would Not, 1950.

❦ Selective Bibliography

Bentley, Eric. *Bernard Shaw*. New York: New Directions, 1957.
Frankel, Charles. "Efficient Power and Inefficient Virtue," in *Great Moral Dilemmas in Literature, Past and Present*, ed. R. M. MacIver. New York: Institute for Religious and Social Studies, 1956, pp. 15–23.
Henderson, Archibald. *George Bernard Shaw: Man of the Century*. New York: Appleton-Century-Crofts, 1956.
Irvine, William. *The Universe of G.B.S.* New York: Whittlesey House, 1949.
MacCarthy, Desmond. *Shaw*. London: MacGibbon and Kee, 1951.
Mander, Raymond, and Mitchenson, Joe. *Theatrical Companion to Shaw*. London: Rockliff, 1954.
Meisel, Martin. *Shaw and the Nineteenth-Century Theater*. Princeton, New Jersey: Princeton University Press, 1963.
Nethercot, Arthur H. *Men and Supermen: The Shavian Portrait Gallery*. New York: Benjamin Blom, 1966.

Major Barbara

CHARACTERS

SIR ANDREW UNDERSHAFT
LADY BRITOMART UNDERSHAFT, *his wife*
BARBARA, *his elder daughter, a Major in the Salvation Army*
SARAH, *his younger daughter*
STEPHEN, *his son*
ADOLPHUS CUSINS, *a professor of Greek in love with Barbara*
CHARLES LOMAX, *young-man-about-town engaged to Sarah*
MORRISON, *Lady Britomart's butler*
BRONTERRE O'BRIEN ("Snobby") PRICE, *a cobbler-carpenter down on his luck*
MRS ROMOLA ("Rummy") MITCHENS, *a worn-out lady who relies on the Salvation Army*
JENNY HILL, *a young Salvation Army worker*
PETER SHIRLEY, *an unemployed coal-broker*
BILL WALKER, *a bully*
MRS BAINES, *Commissioner in the Salvation Army*
BILTON, *a foreman at Perivale St Andrews*

The action of the play occurs within several days in January, 1906.

ACT I *The Library of Lady Britomart's house in Wilton Crescent, a fashionable London suburb.*

ACT II *The yard of the Salvation Army shelter in West Ham, an industrial suburb in London's East End.*

ACT III *The library in Lady Britomart's house; a parapet overlooking Perivale St Andrews, a region in Middlesex northwest of London.*

Act One

It is after dinner in January 1906, in the library in LADY BRITOMART UNDERSHAFT'S *house in Wilton Crescent. A large and comfortable settee is in the middle of the room, upholstered in dark leather. A person sitting on it (it is vacant at present) would have, on his right,* LADY BRITOMART'S *writing-table, with the lady herself busy at it; a smaller writing-table behind him on his left; the door behind him on* LADY BRITOMART'S *side; and a window with a window-seat directly on his left. Near the window is an armchair.*

LADY BRITOMART *is a woman of fifty or thereabouts, well dressed and yet careless of her dress, well bred and quite reckless of her breeding, well mannered and yet appallingly outspoken and indifferent to the opinion of her interlocutors, amiable and yet peremptory, arbitrary, and hightempered to the last bearable degree, and withal a very typical managing matron of the upper class, treated as a naughty child until she grew into a scolding mother, and finally settling down with plenty of practical ability and worldly experience, limited in the oddest way with domestic and class limitations, conceiving the universe exactly as if it were a large house in Wilton Crescent, though handling her corner of it very effectively on that assumption, and being quite enlightened and liberal as to the books in the library, the pictures on the walls, the music in the portfolios, and the articles in the papers.*

Her son, STEPHEN, *comes in. He is a gravely correct young man under 25, taking himself very seriously, but still in some awe of his mother, from childish habit and bachelor shyness rather than from any weakness of character.*

STEPHEN What's the matter?
LADY BRITOMART Presently, Stephen.

(STEPHEN *submissively walks to the settee and sits down. He takes up a liberal weekly called* The Speaker)

LADY BRITOMART Don't begin to read, Stephen. I shall require all your attention.

STEPHEN It was only while I was waiting—

LADY BRITOMART Don't make excuses, Stephen. (*He puts down* The Speaker) Now! (*She finishes her writing, rises; and comes to the settee*) I have not kept you waiting very long, I think.

STEPHEN Not at all, mother.

LADY BRITOMART Bring me my cushion. (*He takes the cushion from the chair at the desk and arranges it for her as she sits down on the settee*) Sit down. (*He sits down and fingers his tie nervously*) Don't fiddle with your tie, Stephen: there is nothing the matter with it.

STEPHEN I beg your pardon. (*He fiddles with his watch chain instead*)

LADY BRITOMART Now are you attending to me, Stephen?

STEPHEN Of course, mother.

LADY BRITOMART No: it's not of course. I want something much more than your everyday matter-of-course attention. I am going to speak to you very seriously, Stephen. I wish you would let that chain alone.

STEPHEN (*Hastily relinquishing the chain*) Have I done anything to annoy you, mother? If so, it was quite unintentional.

LADY BRITOMART (*Astonished*) Nonsense! (*With some remorse*) My poor boy, did you think I was angry with you?

STEPHEN What is it, then, mother? You are making me very uneasy.

LADY BRITOMART (*Squaring herself at him rather aggressively*) Stephen: may I ask how soon you intend to realize that you are a grown-up man, and that I am only a woman?

STEPHEN (*Amazed*) Only a—

LADY BRITOMART Don't repeat my words, please: it is a most aggravating habit. You must learn to face life seriously, Stephen. I really cannot bear the whole burden of our family affairs any longer. You must advise me: you must assume the responsibility.

STEPHEN I!

LADY BRITOMART Yes, you, of course. You were twenty-four last June. You've been at Harrow and Cambridge. You've been to India and Japan. You must know a lot of things, now; unless you have wasted your time most scandalously. Well, advise me.

STEPHEN (*Much perplexed*) You know I have never interfered in the household—

LADY BRITOMART No: I should think not. I don't want you to order the dinner.

STEPHEN I mean in our family affairs.

LADY BRITOMART Well, you must interfere now; for they are getting quite beyond me.

STEPHEN (*Troubled*) I have thought sometimes that perhaps I ought; but really, mother, I know so little about them; and what I do know is so painful—it is so impossible to mention some things to you— (*He stops, ashamed*)

LADY BRITOMART I suppose you mean your father.

STEPHEN (*Almost inaudibly*) Yes.

LADY BRITOMART My dear: we can't go on all our lives not mentioning him. Of course you were quite right not to open the subject until I asked you to; but you are old enough now to be taken into my confidence, and to help me to deal with him about the girls.

STEPHEN But the girls are all right. They are engaged.

LADY BRITOMART (*Complacently*) Yes: I have made a very good match for Sarah. Charles Lomax will be a millionaire at thirty-five. But that is ten years ahead; and in the meantime his trustees cannot under the terms of his father's will allow him more than £800 a year.

STEPHEN But the will says also that if he increases his income by his own exertions, they may double the increase.

LADY BRITOMART Charles Lomax's exertions are much more likely to decrease his income than to increase it. Sarah will have to find at least another £800 a year for the next ten years; and even then they will be as poor as church mice. And what about Barbara? I thought Barbara was going to make the most brilliant career of all of you. And what does she do? Joins the Salvation Army; discharges her maid; lives on a pound a week; and walks in one evening with a professor of Greek whom she has picked up in the street, and who pretends to be a Salvationist, and actually plays the big drum for her in public because he has fallen head over ears in love with her.

STEPHEN I was certainly rather taken aback when I heard they were engaged. Cusins is a very nice fellow, certainly: nobody would ever guess that he was born in Australia; but—

LADY BRITOMART Oh, Adolphus Cusins will make a very good husband. After all, nobody can say a word against Greek: it stamps a man at once as an educated gentleman. And my family, thank Heaven, is not a pigheaded Tory one. We are Whigs, and believe in liberty. Let snobbish people say what they please: Barbara shall marry, not the man they like, but the man *I* like.

STEPHEN Of course I was thinking only of his income. However, he is not likely to be extravagant.

LADY BRITOMART Don't be too sure of that, Stephen. I know your quiet, simple, refined, poetic people like Adolphus—quite content with the best of everything! They cost more than your extravagant people, who are always as mean as they are second rate. No: Barbara will need at least £2000 a year. You see it means two additional households. Besides, my dear, you must marry soon. I don't approve of the present fashion of philandering bachelors and late marriages; and I am trying to arrange something for you.

STEPHEN It's very good of you, mother; but perhaps I had better arrange that for myself.

LADY BRITOMART Nonsense! you are much too young to begin matchmaking: you would be taken in by some pretty little nobody. Of course I don't mean that you are not to be consulted: you know that as well as I do. (STEPHEN *closes his lips and is silent*) Now don't sulk, Stephen.

STEPHEN I am not sulking, mother. What has all this got to do with—with—with my father?

LADY BRITOMART My dear Stephen: where is the money to come from? It is easy enough for you and the other children to live on my income as long as we are in the same house; but I can't keep four families in four separate houses. You know how poor my father is: he has barely seven thousand a year now; and really, if he were not the Earl of Stevenage, he would have to give up society. He can do nothing for us. He says, naturally enough, that it is absurd that he should be asked to provide for the children of a man who is rolling in money. You see, Stephen, your father must be fabulously wealthy, because there is always a war going on somewhere.

STEPHEN You need not remind me of that, mother. I have hardly ever opened a newspaper in my life without seeing our name in it. The Undershaft torpedo! The Undershaft quick firers! The Undershaft ten inch! The Undershaft disappearing rampart gun! The Undershaft submarine! and now the Undershaft aerial battleship! At Harrow they called me the Woolwich Infant.[1] At Cambridge it was the same. A little brute at King's who was always trying to get up revivals, spoilt my Bible —your first birthday present to me—by writing under my name, "Son and heir to Undershaft and Lazarus, Death and Destruction Dealers: address, Christendom and Judea." But that was not so bad as the way I was kowtowed to everywhere because my father was making millions by selling cannons.

LADY BRITOMART It is not only the cannons, but the war loans that Lazarus arranges under cover of giving credit for the cannons. You know, Stephen, it's perfectly scandalous. Those two men, Andrew Undershaft and Lazarus, positively have Europe under their thumbs. That is why your father is able to behave as he does. He is above the

---

[1] The name of a cannon. See scenic description of Perivale St Andrews, in Act III.

law. Do you think Bismarck or Gladstone or Disraeli could have openly defied every social and moral obligation all their lives as your father has? They simply wouldn't have dared. I asked Gladstone to take it up. I asked *The Times* to take it up. I asked the Lord Chamberlain to take it up. But it was just like asking them to declare war on the Sultan. They wouldn't. They said they couldn't touch him. I believe they were afraid.

STEPHEN   What could they do? He does not actually break the law.

LADY BRITOMART   Not break the law! He is always breaking the law. He broke the law when he was born: his parents were not married.

STEPHEN   Mother! Is that true?

LADY BRITOMART   Of course it's true: that was why we separated.

STEPHEN   He married without letting you know this!

LADY BRITOMART   (*Rather taken aback by this inference*)   Oh no. To do Andrew justice, that was not the sort of thing he did. Besides, you know the Undershaft motto: Unashamed. Everybody knew.

STEPHEN   But you said that was why you separated.

LADY BRITOMART   Yes, because he was not content with being a foundling himself: he wanted to disinherit you for another foundling. That was what I couldn't stand.

STEPHEN   (*Ashamed*)   Do you mean for—for—for—

LADY BRITOMART   Don't stammer, Stephen. Speak distinctly.

STEPHEN   But this is so frightful to me, mother. To have to speak to you about such things!

LADY BRITOMART   It's not pleasant for me, either, especially if you are still so childish that you must make it worse by a display of embarrassment. It is only in the middle classes, Stephen, that people get into a state of dumb helpless horror when they find that there are wicked people in the world. In our class, we have to decide what is to be done with wicked people; and nothing should disturb our self-possession. Now ask your question properly.

STEPHEN   Mother: you have no consideration for me. For Heaven's sake either treat me as a child, as you always do, and tell me nothing at all; or tell me everything and let me take it as best I can.

LADY BRITOMART   Treat you as a child! What do you mean? It is most unkind and ungrateful of you to say such a thing. You know I have never treated any of you as children. I have always made you my companions and friends, and allowed you perfect freedom to do and say whatever you liked, so long as you liked what I could approve of.

STEPHEN   (*Desperately*)   I daresay we have been the very imperfect children of a very perfect mother; but I do beg of you to let me alone for once, and tell me about this horrible business of my father wanting to set me aside for another son.

LADY BRITOMART (*Amazed*) Another son! I never said anything of the kind. I never dreamt of such a thing. This is what comes of interrupting me.

STEPHEN But you said—

LADY BRITOMART (*Cutting him short*) Now be a good boy, Stephen, and listen to me patiently. The Undershafts are descended from a foundling in the parish of St Andrew Undershaft in the city. That was long ago, in the reign of James the First. Well, this foundling was adopted by an armorer and gunmaker. In the course of time the foundling succeeded to the business; and from some notion of gratitude, or some vow or something, he adopted another foundling, and left the business to him. And that foundling did the same. Ever since that, the cannon business has always been left to an adopted foundling named Andrew Undershaft.

STEPHEN But did they never marry? Were there no legitimate sons?

LADY BRITOMART Oh yes: they married just as your father did; and they were rich enough to buy land for their own children and leave them well provided for. But they always adopted and trained some foundling to succeed them in the business; and of course they always quarreled with their wives furiously over it. Your father was adopted in that way; and he pretends to consider himself bound to keep up the tradition and adopt somebody to leave the business to. Of course I was not going to stand that. There may have been some reason for it when the Undershafts could only marry women in their own class, whose sons were not fit to govern great estates. But there could be no excuse for passing over my son.

STEPHEN (*Dubiously*) I am afraid I should make a poor hand of managing a cannon foundry.

LADY BRITOMART Nonsense! you could easily get a manager and pay him a salary.

STEPHEN My father evidently had no great opinion of my capacity.

LADY BRITOMART Stuff, child! you were only a baby: it had nothing to do with your capacity. Andrew did it on principle, just as he did every perverse and wicked thing on principle. When my father remonstrated, Andrew actually told him to his face that history tells us of only two successful institutions: one the Undershaft firm, and the other the Roman Empire under the Antonines. That was because the Antonine emperors all adopted their successors. Such rubbish! The Stevenages are as good as the Antonines, I hope; and you are a Stevenage. But that was Andrew all over. There you have the man! Always clever and unanswerable when he was defending nonsense and wickedness: always awkward and sullen when he had to behave sensibly and decently.

STEPHEN Then it was on my account that your home life was broken up, mother. I am sorry.

LADY BRITOMART Well, dear, there were other differences. I really cannot bear an immoral man. I am not a Pharisee, I hope; and I should not have minded his merely doing wrong things: we are none of us perfect. But your father didn't exactly do wrong things: he said them and thought them: that was what was so dreadful. He really had a sort of religion of wrongness. Just as one doesn't mind men practicing immorality so long as they own that they are in the wrong by preaching morality; so I couldn't forgive Andrew for preaching immorality while he practiced morality. You would all have grown up without principles, without any knowledge of right and wrong, if he had been in the house. You know, my dear, your father was a very attractive man in some ways. Children did not dislike him; and he took advantage of it to put the wickedest ideas into their heads, and make them quite unmanageable. I did not dislike him myself: very far from it; but nothing can bridge over moral disagreement.

STEPHEN All this simply bewilders me, mother. People may differ about matters of opinion, or even about religion; but how can they differ about right and wrong? Right is right; and wrong is wrong; and if a man cannot distinguish them properly, he is either a fool or a rascal: that's all.

LADY BRITOMART (*Touched*) That's my own boy! (*She pats his cheek*) Your father never could answer that: he used to laugh and get out of it under cover of some affectionate nonsense. And now that you understand the situation, what do you advise me to do?

STEPHEN Well, what can you do?

LADY BRITOMART I must get the money somehow.

STEPHEN We cannot take money from him. I had rather go and live in some cheap place like Bedford Square or even Hampstead than take a farthing of his money.

LADY BRITOMART But after all, Stephen, our present income comes from Andrew.

STEPHEN (*Shocked*) I never knew that.

LADY BRITOMART Well, you surely didn't suppose your grandfather had anything to give me. The Stevenages could not do everything for you. We gave you social position. Andrew had to contribute something. He had a very good bargain, I think.

STEPHEN (*Bitterly*) We are utterly dependent on him and his cannons, then?

LADY BRITOMART Certainly not: the money is settled. But he provided it. So you see it is not a question of taking money from him or not: it is simply a question of how much. I don't want any more for myself.

STEPHEN Nor do I.
LADY BRITOMART But Sarah does; and Barbara does. That is, Charles Lomax and Adolphus Cusins will cost them more. So I must put my pride in my pocket and ask for it, I suppose. That is your advice, Stephen, is it not?
STEPHEN No.
LADY BRITOMART (*Sharply*) Stephen!
STEPHEN Of course if you are determined—
LADY BRITOMART I am not determined: I ask your advice; and I am waiting for it. I will not have all the responsibility thrown on my shoulders.
STEPHEN (*Obstinately*) I would die sooner than ask him for another penny.
LADY BRITOMART (*Resignedly*) You mean that I must ask him. Very well, Stephen: it shall be as you wish. You will be glad to know that your grandfather concurs. But he thinks I ought to ask Andrew to come here and see the girls. After all he must have some natural affection for them.
STEPHEN Ask him here! ! !
LADY BRITOMART Do not repeat my words, Stephen. Where else can I ask him?
STEPHEN I never expected you to ask him at all.
LADY BRITOMART Now don't tease, Stephen. Come! you see that it is necessary that he should pay us a visit, don't you?
STEPHEN (*Reluctantly*) I suppose so, if the girls cannot do without his money.
LADY BRITOMART Thank you, Stephen: I knew you would give me the right advice when it was properly explained to you. I have asked your father to come this evening. (STEPHEN *bounds from his seat*) Don't jump, Stephen: it fidgets me.
STEPHEN (*In utter consternation*) Do you mean to say that my father is coming here to-night—that he may be here at any moment?
LADY BRITOMART (*Looking at her watch*) I said nine. (*He gasps. She rises*) Ring the bell, please. (STEPHEN *goes to the smaller writing table; presses a button on it; and sits at it with his elbows on the table and his head in his hands, outwitted and overwhelmed*) It is ten minutes to nine yet; and I have to prepare the girls. I asked Charles Lomax and Adolphus to dinner on purpose that they might be here. Andrew had better see them in case he should cherish any delusions as to their being capable of supporting their wives. (*The butler enters:* LADY BRITOMART *goes behind the settee to speak to him*) Morrison: go up to the drawing-room and tell everybody to come down here at once. (MORRISON *withdraws.* LADY BRITOMART *turns to* STEPHEN) Now remem-

ber, Stephen: I shall need all your countenance and authority. (*He rises and tries to recover some vestige of these attributes*) Give me a chair, dear. (*He pushes a chair forward from the wall to where she stands, near the smaller writing table. She sits down; and he goes to the armchair, into which he throws himself*) I don't know how Barbara will take it. Ever since they made her a major in the Salvation Army she has developed a propensity to have her own way and order people about which quite cows me sometimes. It's not ladylike: I'm sure I don't know where she picked it up. Anyhow, Barbara shan't bully me; but still it's just as well that your father should be here before she has time to refuse to meet him or make a fuss. Don't look nervous, Stephen: it will only encourage Barbara to make difficulties. *I* am nervous enough, goodness knows; but I don't shew it.

(SARAH *and* BARBARA *come in with their respective young men,* CHARLES LOMAX *and* ADOLPHUS CUSINS. SARAH *is slender, bored, and mundane.* BARBARA *is robuster, jollier, much more energetic.* SARAH *is fashionably dressed:* BARBARA *is in Salvation Army uniform.* LOMAX, *a young man about town, is like many other young men about town. He is afflicted with a frivolous sense of humor which plunges him at the most inopportune moments into paroxysms of imperfectly suppressed laughter.* CUSINS *is a spectacled student, slight, thin haired, and sweet voiced, with a more complex form of* LOMAX'S *complaint. His sense of humor is intellectual and subtle, and is complicated by an appalling temper. The life-long struggle of a benevolent temperament and a high conscience against impulses of inhuman ridicule and fierce impatience has set up a chronic strain which has visibly wrecked his constitution. He is a most implacable, determined, tenacious, intolerant person who by mere force of character presents himself as—and indeed actually is—considerate, gentle, explanatory, even mild and apologetic, capable possibly of murder, but not of cruelty or coarseness. By the operation of some instinct which is not merciful enough to blind him with the illusions of love, he is obstinately bent on marrying* BARBARA. LOMAX *likes* SARAH *and thinks it will be rather a lark to marry her. Consequently he has not attempted to resist* LADY BRITOMART'S *arrangements to that end.*

All four look as if they had been having a good deal of fun in the drawing room. The girls enter first, leaving the swains outside. SARAH *comes to the settee.* BARBARA *comes in after her and stops at the door*)

BARBARA Are Cholly and Dolly to come in?

LADY BRITOMART (*Forcibly*) Barbara: I will not have Charles called

19 · *Major Barbara* [ACT ONE]

Cholly: the vulgarity of it positively makes me ill.
BARBARA It's all right, mother: Cholly is quite correct nowadays. Are they to come in?
LADY BRITOMART Yes, if they will behave themselves.
BARBARA (*Through the door*) Come in, Dolly; and behave yourself.

(BARBARA *comes to her mother's writing table.* CUSINS *enters smiling, and wanders towards* LADY BRITOMART)

SARAH (*Calling*) Come in, Cholly. (LOMAX *enters, controlling his features very imperfectly, and places himself vaguely between* SARAH *and* BARBARA)
LADY BRITOMART (*Peremptorily*) Sit down, all of you. (*They sit.* CUSINS *crosses to the window and seats himself there.* LOMAX *takes a chair.* BARBARA *sits at the writing table and* SARAH *on the settee*) I don't in the least know what you are laughing at, Adolphus. I am surprised at you, though I expected nothing better from Charles Lomax.
CUSINS (*In a remarkably gentle voice*) Barbara has been trying to teach me the West Ham Salvation March.
LADY BRITOMART I see nothing to laugh at in that; nor should you if you are really converted.
CUSINS (*Sweetly*) You were not present. It was really funny, I believe.
LOMAX Ripping.
LADY BRITOMART Be quiet, Charles. Now listen to me, children. Your father is coming here this evening.

(*General stupefaction.* LOMAX, SARAH, *and* BARBARA *rise:* SARAH *scared, and* BARBARA *amused and expectant*)

LOMAX (*Remonstrating*) Oh I say!
LADY BRITOMART You are not called on to say anything, Charles.
SARAH Are you serious, mother?
LADY BRITOMART Of course I am serious. It is on your account, Sarah, and also on Charles's. (*Silence.* SARAH *sits, with a shrug.* CHARLES *looks painfully unworthy*) I hope you are not going to object, Barbara.
BARBARA I! why should I? My father has a soul to be saved like anybody else. He's quite welcome as far as I am concerned. (*She sits on the table, and softly whistles "Onward, Christian Soldiers"*)
LOMAX (*Still remonstrant*) But really, don't you know! Oh I say!
LADY BRITOMART (*Frigidly*) What do you wish to convey, Charles?
LOMAX Well, you must admit that this is a bit thick.
LADY BRITOMART (*Turning with ominous suavity to* CUSINS) Adolphus: you are a professor of Greek. Can you translate Charles Lomax's remarks into reputable English for us?
CUSINS (*Cautiously*) If I may say so, Lady Brit, I think Charles has

rather happily expressed what we all feel. Homer, speaking of Autolycus, uses the same phrase. πυκινὸν δόμον ἐλθεῖν means a bit thick.[2]

LOMAX (*Handsomely*) Not that I mind, you know, if Sarah don't. (*He sits*)

LADY BRITOMART (*Crushingly*) Thank you. Have I your permission, Adolphus, to invite my own husband to my own house?

CUSINS (*Gallantly*) You have my unhesitating support in everything you do.

LADY BRITOMART Tush! Sarah: have you nothing to say?

SARAH Do you mean that he is coming regularly to live here?

LADY BRITOMART Certainly not. The spare room is ready for him if he likes to stay for a day or two and see a little more of you; but there are limits.

SARAH Well, he can't eat us, I suppose. I don't mind.

LOMAX (*Chuckling*) I wonder how the old man will take it.

LADY BRITOMART Much as the old woman will, no doubt, Charles.

LOMAX (*Abashed*) I didn't mean—at least—

LADY BRITOMART You didn't think, Charles. You never do; and the result is, you never mean anything. And now please attend to me, children. Your father will be quite a stranger to us.

LOMAX I suppose he hasn't seen Sarah since she was a little kid.

LADY BRITOMART Not since she was a little kid, Charles, as you express it with that elegance of diction and refinement of thought that seem never to desert you. Accordingly—er— (*Impatiently*) Now I have forgotten what I was going to say. That comes of your provoking me to be sarcastic, Charles. Adolphus: will you kindly tell me where I was.

CUSINS (*Sweetly*) You were saying that as Mr. Undershaft has not seen his children since they were babies, he will form his opinion of the way you have brought them up from their behavior to-night, and that therefore you wish us all to be particularly careful to conduct ourselves well, especially Charles.

LADY BRITOMART (*With emphatic approval*) Precisely.

LOMAX Look here, Dolly: Lady Brit didn't say that.

LADY BRITOMART (*Vehemently*) I did, Charles. Adolphus's recollection is perfectly correct. It is most important that you should be good; and I do beg you for once not to pair off into opposite corners and giggle and whisper while I am speaking to your father.

---

[2] *Pukinon domon elthein, Iliad* X, 267. Homer's line refers to the burglar Autolycus "breaking into the stoutly [thickly] built house." Cusins' quotation may refer to the criminal nature of Undershaft as capitalist, to his intrusion into Lady Britomart's house, and to the possibility that he has gone too far ("a bit thick") in making the visit.

BARBARA All right, mother. We'll do you credit. (*She comes off the table, and sits in her chair with ladylike elegance*)
LADY BRITOMART Remember, Charles, that Sarah will want to feel proud of you instead of ashamed of you.
LOMAX Oh I say! there's nothing to be exactly proud of, don't you know.
LADY BRITOMART Well, try and look as if there was.

(MORRISON, *pale and dismayed, breaks into the room in unconcealed disorder*)

MORRISON Might I speak a word to you, my lady?
LADY BRITOMART Nonsense! Shew him up.
MORRISON Yes, my lady. (*He goes*)
LOMAX Does Morrison know who it is?
LADY BRITOMART Of course. Morrison has always been with us.
LOMAX It must be a regular corker for him, don't you know.
LADY BRITOMART Is this a moment to get on my nerves, Charles, with your outrageous expressions?
LOMAX But this is something out of the ordinary, really—
MORRISON (*At the door*) The—er—Mr. Undershaft. (*He retreats in confusion*)

(ANDREW UNDERSHAFT *comes in. All rise.* LADY BRITOMART *meets him in the middle of the room behind the settee.*

ANDREW *is, on the surface, a stoutish, easygoing elderly man, with kindly patient manners, and an engaging simplicity of character. But he has a watchful, deliberate, waiting, listening face, and formidable reserves of power, both bodily and mental, in his capacious chest and long head. His gentleness is partly that of a strong man who has learnt by experience that his natural grip hurts ordinary people unless he handles them very carefully, and partly the mellowness of age and success. He is also a little shy in his present very delicate situation*)

LADY BRITOMART Good evening, Andrew.
UNDERSHAFT How d'ye do, my dear.
LADY BRITOMART You look a good deal older.
UNDERSHAFT (*Apologetically*) I am somewhat older. (*Taking her hand with a touch of courtship*) Time has stood still with you.
LADY BRITOMART (*Throwing away his hand*) Rubbish! This is your family.
UNDERSHAFT (*Surprised*) Is it so large? I am sorry to say my memory is failing very badly in some things. (*He offers his hand with paternal kindness to* LOMAX)
LOMAX (*Jerkily shaking his hand*) Ahdedoo.

UNDERSHAFT I can see you are my eldest. I am very glad to meet you again, my boy.

LOMAX (*Remonstrating*) No, but look here don't you know—(*Overcome*) Oh I say!

LADY BRITOMART (*Recovering from momentary speechlessness*) Andrew: do you mean to say that you don't remember how many children you have?

UNDERSHAFT Well, I am afraid I— They have grown so much—er. Am I making any ridiculous mistake? I may as well confess: I recollect only one son. But so many things have happened since, of course—er—

LADY BRITOMART (*Decisively*) Andrew: you are talking nonsense. Of course you have only one son.

UNDERSHAFT Perhaps you will be good enough to introduce me, my dear.

LADY BRITOMART That is Charles Lomax, who is engaged to Sarah.

UNDERSHAFT My dear sir, I beg your pardon.

LOMAX Notatall. Delighted, I assure you.

LADY BRITOMART This is Stephen.

UNDERSHAFT (*Bowing*) Happy to make your acquaintance, Mr. Stephen. Then (*Going to* CUSINS) you must be my son. (*Taking* CUSINS' *hands in his*) How are you, my young friend? (*To* LADY BRITOMART) He is very like you, my love.

CUSINS You flatter me, Mr. Undershaft. My name is Cusins: engaged to Barbara. (*Very explicitly*) That is Major Barbara Undershaft, of the Salvation Army. That is Sarah, your second daughter. This is Stephen Undershaft, your son.

UNDERSHAFT My dear Stephen, I beg your pardon.

STEPHEN Not at all.

UNDERSHAFT Mr. Cusins: I am indebted to you for explaining so precisely. (*Turning to* SARAH) Barbara, my dear—

SARAH (*Prompting him*) Sarah.

UNDERSHAFT Sarah, of course. (*They shake hands. He goes over to* BARBARA) Barbara—I am right this time, I hope.

BARBARA Quite right. (*They shake hands*)

LADY BRITOMART (*Resuming command*) Sit down, all of you. Sit down, Andrew. (*She comes forward and sits on the settee.* CUSINS *also brings his chair forward on her left.* BARBARA *and* STEPHEN *resume their seats.* LOMAX *gives his chair to* SARAH *and goes for another*)

UNDERSHAFT Thank you, my love.

LOMAX (*Conversationally, as he brings a chair forward between the writing table and the settee, and offers it to* UNDERSHAFT) Takes you some time to find out exactly where you are, don't it?

UNDERSHAFT (*Accepting the chair, but remaining standing*) That is not what embarrasses me, Mr. Lomax. My difficulty is that if I play the part of a father, I shall produce the effect of an intrusive stranger; and if I play the part of a discreet stranger, I may appear a callous father.

LADY BRITOMART There is no need for you to play any part at all, Andrew. You had much better be sincere and natural.

UNDERSHAFT (*Submissively*) Yes, my dear: I daresay that will be best. (*He sits down comfortably*) Well, here I am. Now what can I do for you all?

LADY BRITOMART You need not do anything, Andrew. You are one of the family. You can sit with us and enjoy yourself. (*A painfully conscious pause.* BARBARA *makes a face at* LOMAX, *whose too long suppressed mirth immediately explodes in agonized neighings*)

LADY BRITOMART (*Outraged*) Charles Lomax: if you can behave yourself, behave yourself. If not, leave the room.

LOMAX I'm awfully sorry, Lady Brit; but really, you know, upon my soul! (*He sits on the settee between* LADY BRITOMART *and* UNDERSHAFT, *quite overcome*)

BARBARA Why don't you laugh if you want to, Cholly? It's good for your inside.

LADY BRITOMART Barbara: you have had the education of a lady. Please let your father see that; and don't talk like a street girl.

UNDERSHAFT Never mind me, my dear. As you know, I am not a gentleman; and I was never educated.

LOMAX (*Encouragingly*) Nobody'd know it, I assure you. You look all right, you know.

CUSINS Let me advise you to study Greek, Mr. Undershaft. Greek scholars are privileged men. Few of them know Greek; and none of them know anything else; but their position is unchallengeable. Other languages are the qualifications of waiters and commercial travellers: Greek is to a man of position what the hallmark is to silver.

BARBARA Dolly: don't be insincere. Cholly: fetch your concertina and play something for us.

LOMAX (*Jumps up eagerly, but checks himself to remark doubtfully to* UNDERSHAFT) Perhaps that sort of thing isn't in your line, eh?

UNDERSHAFT I am particularly fond of music.

LOMAX (*Delighted*) Are you? Then I'll get it. (*He goes upstairs for the instrument*)

UNDERSHAFT Do you play, Barbara?

BARBARA Only the tambourine. But Cholly's teaching me the concertina.

UNDERSHAFT Is Cholly also a member of the Salvation Army?

BARBARA No: he says it's bad form to be a dissenter. But I don't despair of Cholly. I made him come yesterday to a meeting at the dock gates, and take the collection in his hat.

UNDERSHAFT (*Looks whimsically at his wife*)!!

LADY BRITOMART It is not my doing, Andrew. Barbara is old enough to take her own way. She has no father to advise her.

BARBARA Oh yes she has. There are no orphans in the Salvation Army.

UNDERSHAFT Your father there has a great many children and plenty of experience, eh?

BARBARA (*Looking at him with quick interest and nodding*) Just so. How did you come to understand that? (LOMAX *is heard at the door trying the concertina*)

LADY BRITOMART Come in, Charles. Play us something at once.

LOMAX Righto! (*He sits down in his former place, and preludes*)

UNDERSHAFT One moment, Mr Lomax, I am rather interested in the Salvation Army. Its motto might be my own: Blood and Fire.

LOMAX (*Shocked*) But not your sort of blood and fire, you know.

UNDERSHAFT My sort of blood cleanses: my sort of fire purifies.

BARBARA So do ours. Come down tomorrow to my shelter—the West Ham shelter—and see what we're doing. We're going to march to a great meeting in the Assembly Hall at Mile End. Come and see the shelter and then march with us: it will do you a lot of good. Can you play anything?

UNDERSHAFT In my youth I earned pennies, and even shillings occasionally, in the streets and in public house parlors by my natural talent for stepdancing. Later on, I became a member of the Undershaft orchestral society, and performed passably on the tenor trombone.

LOMAX (*Scandalized—putting down the concertina*) Oh I say!

BARBARA Many a sinner has played himself into heaven on the trombone, thanks to the Army.

LOMAX (*To* BARBARA, *still rather shocked*) Yes; but what about the cannon business, don't you know? (*To* UNDERSHAFT) Getting into heaven is not exactly in your line, is it?

LADY BRITOMART Charles!!!

LOMAX Well; but it stands to reason, don't it? The cannon business may be necessary and all that: we can't get on without cannons; but it isn't right, you know. On the other hand, there may be a certain amount of tosh about the Salvation Army—I belong to the Established Church myself—but still you can't deny that it's religion; and you can't go against religion, can you? At least unless you're downright immoral, don't you know.

UNDERSHAFT You hardly appreciate my position, Mr Lomax—

LOMAX (*Hastily*) I'm not saying anything against you personally—

UNDERSHAFT Quite so, quite so. But consider for a moment. Here I am, a profiteer in mutilation and murder. I find myself in a specially amiable humor just now because, this morning, down at the foundry, we blew twenty-seven dummy soldiers into fragments with a gun which formerly destroyed only thirteen.

LOMAX (*Leniently*) Well, the more destructive war becomes, the sooner it will be abolished, eh?

UNDERSHAFT Not at all. The more destructive war becomes, the more fascinating we find it. No, Mr Lomax: I am obliged to you for making the usual excuse for my trade; but I am not ashamed of it. I am not one of those men who keep their morals and their business in water-tight compartments. All the spare money my trade rivals spend on hospitals, cathedrals, and other receptacles for conscience money, I devote to experiments and researches in improved methods of destroying life and property. I have always done so; and I always shall. Therefore your Christmas card moralities of peace on earth and goodwill among men are of no use to me. Your Christianity, which enjoins you to resist not evil, and to turn the other cheek, would make me a bankrupt. My morality—my religion—must have a place for cannons and torpedoes in it.

STEPHEN (*Coldly—almost sullenly*) You speak as if there were half a dozen moralities and religions to choose from, instead of one true morality and one true religion.

UNDERSHAFT For me there is only one true morality; but it might not fit you, as you do not manufacture aerial battleships. There is only one true morality for every man; but every man has not the same true morality.

LOMAX (*Overtaxed*) Would you mind saying that again? I didn't quite follow it.

CUSINS It's quite simple. As Euripides says, one man's meat is another man's poison morally as well as physically.

UNDERSHAFT Precisely.

LOMAX Oh, that. Yes, yes, yes. True. True.

STEPHEN In other words, some men are honest and some are scoundrels.

BARBARA Bosh. There are no scoundrels.

UNDERSHAFT Indeed? Are there any good men?

BARBARA No. Not one. There are neither good men nor scoundrels: there are just children of one Father; and the sooner they stop calling one another names the better. You needn't talk to me: I know them. I've had scores of them through my hands: scoundrels, criminals, infidels, philanthropists, missionaries, county councillors, all sorts. They're all just the same sort of sinner; and there's the same salvation ready for them all.

UNDERSHAFT May I ask have you ever saved a maker of cannons?

BARBARA No. Will you let me try?
UNDERSHAFT Well, I will make a bargain with you. If I go to see you tomorrow in your Salvation Shelter, will you come the day after to see me in my cannon works?
BARBARA Take care. It may end in your giving up the cannons for the sake of the Salvation Army.
UNDERSHAFT Are you sure it will not end in your giving up the Salvation Army for the sake of cannons?
BARBARA I will take my chance of that.
UNDERSHAFT And I will take my chance of the other. (*They shake hands on it*) Where is your shelter?
BARBARA In West Ham. At the sign of the cross. Ask anybody in Canning Town. Where are your works?
UNDERSHAFT In Perivale St Andrews. At the sign of the sword. Ask anybody in Europe.
LOMAX Hadn't I better play something?
BARBARA Yes. Give us "Onward, Christian Soldiers."
LOMAX Well, that's rather a strong order to begin with, don't you know. Suppose I sing "Thou're passing hence, my brother." It's much the same tune.
BARBARA It's too melancholy. You get saved, Cholly; and you'll pass hence, my brother, without making such a fuss about it.
LADY BRITOMART Really, Barbara, you go on as if religion were a pleasant subject. Do have some sense of propriety.
UNDERSHAFT I do not find it an unpleasant subject, my dear. It is the only one that capable people really care for.
LADY BRITOMART (*Looking at her watch*) Well, if you are determined to have it, I insist on having it in a proper and respectable way. Charles: ring for prayers. (*General amazement.* STEPHEN *rises in dismay*)
LOMAX (*Rising*) Oh I say!
UNDERSHAFT (*Rising*) I am afraid I must be going.
LADY BRITOMART You cannot go now, Andrew: it would be most improper. Sit down. What will the servants think?
UNDERSHAFT My dear: I have conscientious scruples. May I suggest a compromise? If Barbara will conduct a little service in the drawing room, with Mr Lomax as organist, I will attend it willingly. I will even take part, if a trombone can be procured.
LADY BRITOMART Don't mock, Andrew.
UNDERSHAFT (*Shocked—to* BARBARA) You don't think I am mocking, my love, I hope.
BARBARA No, of course not; and it wouldn't matter if you were: half the Army came to their first meeting for a lark. (*Rising*) Come along.

(*She throws her arm round her father and sweeps him out, calling to the others from the threshold*) Come, Dolly. Come, Cholly.

(CUSINS *rises*)

LADY BRITOMART I will not be disobeyed by everybody. Adolphus: sit down. (*He does not*) Charles: you may go. You are not fit for prayers: you cannot keep your countenance.

LOMAX Oh I say! (*He goes out*)

LADY BRITOMART (*Continuing*) But you, Adolphus, can behave yourself if you choose to. I insist on your staying.

CUSINS My dear Lady Brit: there are things in the family prayer book that I couldn't bear to hear you say.

LADY BRITOMART What things, pray?

CUSINS Well, you would have to say before all the servants that we have done things we ought not to have done, and left undone things we ought to have done, and that there is no health in us. I cannot bear to hear you doing yourself such an injustice, and Barbara such an injustice. As for myself, I flatly deny it: I have done my best. I shouldn't dare to marry Barbara—I couldn't look you in the face—if it were true. So I must go to the drawing room.

LADY BRITOMART (*Offended*) Well, go. (*He starts for the door*) And remember this, Adolphus (*He turns to listen*) I have a strong suspicion that you went to the Salvation Army to worship Barbara and nothing else. And I quite appreciate the clever way in which you systematically humbug me. I have found you out. Take care Barbara doesn't. That's all.

CUSINS (*With unruffled sweetness*) Don't tell on me. (*He steals out*)

LADY BRITOMART Sarah: if you want to go, go. Anything's better than to sit there as if you wished you were a thousand miles away.

SARAH (*Languidly*) Very well, mamma. (*She goes*).

(LADY BRITOMART, *with a sudden flounce, gives way to a little gust of tears*)

STEPHEN (*Going to her*) Mother: what's the matter?

LADY BRITOMART (*Swishing away her tears with her handkerchief*) Nothing. Foolishness. You can go with him, too, if you like, and leave me with the servants.

STEPHEN Oh, you mustn't think that, mother. I—I don't like him.

LADY BRITOMART The others do. That is the injustice of a woman's lot. A woman has to bring up her children; and that means to restrain them, to deny them things they want, to set them tasks, to punish them when they do wrong, to do all the unpleasant things. And then the father, who has nothing to do but pet them and spoil them, comes in when all her work is done and steals their affection from her.

STEPHEN   He has not stolen our affection from you. It is only curiosity.

LADY BRITOMART   (*Violently*) I won't be consoled, Stephen. There is nothing the matter with me. (*She rises and goes towards the door*)

STEPHEN   Where are you going, mother?

LADY BRITOMART   To the drawing room, of course. (*She goes out.* "Onward, Christian Soldiers," *on the concertina, with tambourine accompaniment, is heard when the door opens*) Are you coming, Stephen?

STEPHEN   No. Certainly not. (*She goes. He sits down on the settee, with compressed lips and an expression of strong dislike*)

End of Act I

Act Two

The yard of the West Ham shelter of the Salvation Army is a cold place on a January morning. The building itself, an old warehouse, is newly whitewashed. Its gabled end projects into the yard in the middle, with a door on the ground floor, and another in the loft above it without any balcony or ladder, but with a pulley rigged over it for hoisting sacks. Those who come from this central gable end into the yard have the gateway leading to the street on their left, with a stone horse-trough just beyond it, and, on the right, a penthouse shielding a table from the weather. There are forms at the table; and on them are seated a man and a woman, both much down on their luck, finishing a meal of bread (one thick slice each, with margarine and golden syrup) and diluted milk.

The man, a workman out of employment, is young, agile, a talker, a poser, sharp enough to be capable of anything in reason except honesty or altruistic considerations of any kind. The woman is a commonplace old bundle of poverty and hard-worn humanity. She looks sixty and probably is forty-five. If they were rich people, gloved and muffed and well wrapped up in furs and overcoats, they would be numbed and miserable; for it is a grindingly cold, raw, January day; and a glance at the back-

ground of grimy warehouses and leaden sky visible over the whitewashed walls of the yard would drive any idle rich person straight to the Mediterranean. But these two, being no more troubled with visions of the Mediterranean than of the moon, and being compelled to keep more of their clothes in the pawnshop, and less on their persons, in winter than in summer, are not depressed by the cold: rather are they stung into vivacity, to which their meal has just now given an almost jolly turn. The man takes a pull at his mug, and then gets up and moves about the yard with his hands deep in his pockets, occasionally breaking into a stepdance.

THE WOMAN   Feel better arter your meal, sir?

THE MAN   No. Call that a meal! Good enough for you, p'raps; but wot is it to me, an intelligent workin' man?

THE WOMAN   Workin' man! Wot are you?

THE MAN   Painter.

THE WOMAN   (*Skeptically*)   Yus, I dessay.

THE MAN   Yus, you dessay! I know. Every loafer that can't do nothink calls 'isself a painter. Well, I'm a real painter: grainer, finisher, thirty-eight bob a week when I can get it.

THE WOMAN   Then why don't you go and get it?

THE MAN   I'll tell you why. Fust: I'm intelligent—fffff! it's rotten cold here (*He dances a step or two*)—yes; intelligent beyond the station o' life into which it has pleased the capitalists to call me; and they don't like a man that sees through 'em. Second, an intelligent bein' needs a doo share of 'appiness; so I drink somethink cruel when I get the chawnce. Third, I stand by my class and do as little as I can so's to leave 'arf the job for me fellow workers. Fourth, I'm fly[3] enough to know wot's inside the law and wot's outside it; and inside it I do as the capitalists do: pinch wot I can lay me 'ands on. In a proper state of society I am sober, industrious, and honest: in Rome, so to speak, I do as the Romans do. Wot's the consequence? When trade is bad —and it's rotten bad just now—and the employers 'az to sack 'arf their men, they generally start on me.

THE WOMAN   What's your name?

THE MAN   Price. Bronterre O'Brien Price.[4] Usually called Snobby Price, for short.

THE WOMAN   Snobby's a carpenter, ain't it? You said you was a painter.

PRICE   Not that kind of snob, but the genteel sort. I'm too uppish, ow-

---

[3] Shrewd.

[4] James O'Brien, a nineteenth-century Chartist who wrote socialist articles under the names "Bronterre" and "James Bronterre O'Brien."

ing to my intelligence, and my father being a Chartist and a reading, thinking man: a stationer, too. I'm none of your common hewers of wood and drawers of water; and don't you forget it. (*He returns to his seat at the table, and takes up his mug*) Wot's your name?

THE WOMAN   Rummy Mitchens, sir.

PRICE   (*Quaffing the remains of his milk to her*)   Your 'elth, Miss Mitchens.

RUMMY   (*Correcting him*)   Missis Mitchens.

PRICE   Wot! Oh Rummy, Rummy! Respectable married woman, Rummy, gittin' rescued by the Salvation Army by pretendin' to be a bad un. Same old game!

RUMMY   What am I to do? I can't starve. Them Salvation lasses is dear good girls; but the better you are, the worse they likes to think you were before they rescued you. Why shouldn't they 'av a bit o' credit, poor loves? they're worn to rags by their work. And where would they get the money to rescue us if we was to let on we're no worse than other people? You know what ladies and gentlemen are.

PRICE   Thievin' swine! Wish I 'ad their job, Rummy, all the same. Wot does Rummy stand for? Pet name p'raps?

RUMMY   Short for Romola.

PRICE   For wot!?

RUMMY   Romola. It was out of a new book.[5] Somebody me mother wanted me to grow up like.

PRICE   We're companions in misfortune, Rummy. Both of us got names that nobody cawn't pronounce. Consequently I'm Snobby and you're Rummy because Bill and Sally wasn't good enough for our parents. Such is life!

RUMMY   Who saved you, Mr Price? Was it Major Barbara?

PRICE   No: I come here on my own. I'm goin' to be Bronterre O'Brien Price, the converted painter. I know wot they like. I'll tell 'em how I blasphemed and gambled and wopped my poor old mother—

RUMMY   (*Shocked*)   Used you to beat your mother?

PRICE   Not likely. She used to beat me. No matter: you come and listen to the converted painter, and you'll hear how she was a pious woman that taught me me prayers at 'er knee, an' how I used to come home drunk and drag her out o' bed be 'er snow-white 'airs, an' lam into 'er with the poker.

RUMMY   That's what's so unfair to us women. Your confessions is just as big lies as ours: you don't tell what you really done no more than us; but you men can tell your lies right out at the meetin's and be

---

[5] The heroine of George Eliot's novel *Romola*.

made much of for it; while the sort o' confessions we 'az to make 'az to be whispered to one lady at a time. It ain't right, spite of all their piety.

PRICE Right! Do you s'pose the Army'd be allowed if it went and did right? Not much. It combs our 'air and makes us good little blokes to be robbed and put upon. But I'll play the game as good as any of 'em. I'll see somebody struck by lightnin', or hear a voice sayin' "Snobby Price: where will you spend eternity?" I'll 'ave a time of it, I tell you.

RUMMY You won't be let drink, though.

PRICE I'll take it out in gorspellin', then. I don't want to drink if I can get fun enough any other way.

(JENNY HILL, *a pale, overwrought, pretty Salvation lass of eighteen, comes in through the yard gate, leading* PETER SHIRLEY, *a half hardened, half worn-out elderly man, weak with hunger*)

JENNY (*Supporting him*) Come! pluck up. I'll get you something to eat. You'll be all right then.

PRICE (*Rising and hurrying officiously to take the old man off* JENNY's *hands*) Poor old man! Cheer up, brother: you'll find rest and peace and 'appiness 'ere. Hurry up with the food, miss: 'e's fair done. (JENNY *hurries into the shelter*) 'Ere, buck up, daddy! she's fetchin y'a thick slice o' bread'n treacle, an' a mug o' skyblue.[6] (*He seats him at the corner of the table*)

RUMMY (*Gaily*) Keep up your old 'art! Never say die!

SHIRLEY I'm not an old man. I'm only forty-six. I'm as good as ever I was. The grey patch come in my hair before I was thirty. All it wants is three pennorth o' hair dye: am I to be turned on the streets to starve for it? Holy God! I've worked ten to twelve hours a day since I was thirteen, and paid my way all through; and now am I to be thrown into the gutter and my job given to a young man that can do it no better than me because I've black hair that goes white at the first change?

PRICE (*Cheerfully*) No good jawrin' about it. You're only a jumped-up, jerked-off, 'orspittle-turned-out incurable of an ole workin' man: who cares about you? Eh? Make the thievin' swine give you a meal: they've stole many a one from you. Get a bit o' your own back. (JENNY *returns with the usual meal*) There you are, brother. Awsk a blessin' an' tuck that into you.

SHIRLEY (*Looking at it ravenously but not touching it, and crying like a child*) I never took anything before.

JENNY (*Petting him*) Come, come! the Lord sends it to you: he wasn't

[6] Watery milk, or perhaps water.

above taking bread from his friends; and why should you be? Besides, when we find you a job you can pay us for it if you like.

SHIRLEY (*Eagerly*) Yes, yes: that's true. I can pay you back: it's only a loan. (*Shivering*) Oh Lord! oh Lord! (*He turns to the table and attacks the meal ravenously*)

JENNY Well, Rummy, are you more comfortable now?

RUMMY God bless you, lovey! you've fed my body and saved my soul, haven't you? (JENNY, *touched, kisses her*) Sit down and rest a bit: you must be ready to drop.

JENNY I've been going hard since morning. But there's more work than we can do. I mustn't stop.

RUMMY Try a prayer for just two minutes. You'll work all the better after.

JENNY (*Her eyes lighting up*) Oh isn't it wonderful how a few minutes prayer revives you! I was quite lightheaded at twelve o'clock, I was so tired; but Major Barbara just sent me to pray for five minutes; and I was able to go on as if I had only just begun. (*To* PRICE) Did you have a piece of bread?

PRICE (*With unction*) Yes, miss; but I've got the piece that I value more; and that's the peace that passeth hall hannerstennin.

RUMMY (*Fervently*) Glory Hallelujah!

(BILL WALKER, *a rough customer of about 25, appears at the yard gate and looks malevolently at* JENNY)

JENNY That makes me so happy. When you say that, I feel wicked for loitering here. I must get to work again.

(*She is hurrying to the shelter, when the newcomer moves quickly up to the door and intercepts her. His manner is so threatening that she retreats as he comes at her truculently, driving her down the yard*)

BILL Aw knaow you. You're the one that took aw'y maw girl. You're the one that set 'er agen me. Well, I'm gowin' to 'ev 'er aht. Not that Aw care a carse for 'er or you: see? But Aw'll let 'er knaow; and Aw'll let you knaow. Aw'm gowin' to give her a doin' that'll teach 'er to cat aw'y from me. Nah in wiv you and tell 'er to cam aht afore Aw cam in and kick 'er aht. Tell 'er Bill Walker wants 'er. She'll knaow wot thet means; and if she keeps me witin' it'll be worse. You stop to jawr beck at me; and Aw'll stawt on you: d'ye 'eah? There's your w'y. In you gow. (*He takes her by the arm and slings her towards the door of the shelter. She falls on her hand and knee.* RUMMY *helps her up again*)

PRICE (*Rising, and venturing irresolutely towards* BILL) Easy there, mate. She ain't doin' you no 'arm.
BILL 'Oo are you callin' mite? (*Standing over him threateningly*) Youre gowin' to stend up for 'er, aw yer? Put ap your 'ends.
RUMMY (*Running indignantly to him to scold him*) Oh, you great brute— (*He instantly swings his left hand back against her face. She screams and reels back to the trough, where she sits down, covering her bruised face with her hands and rocking herself and moaning with pain*)
JENNY (*Going to her*) Oh, God forgive you! How could you strike an old woman like that?
BILL (*Seizing her by the hair so violently that she also screams, and tearing her away from the old woman*) You Gawd forgimme again and Aw'll Gawd forgive you one on the jawr thet'll stop you pryin' for a week. (*Holding her and turning fiercely on* PRICE) 'Ev you ennything to s'y agen it?
PRICE (*Intimidated*) No, matey: she ain't anything to do with me.
BILL Good job for you! Aw'd pat two meals into you and fawt you with one finger arter, you stawved cur. (*To* JENNY) Nah are you gowin' to fetch aht Mog Ebbijem; or em Aw to knock your fice off you and fetch her meself?
JENNY (*Writhing in his grasp*) Oh, please, someone go in and tell Major Barbara— (*She screams again as he wrenches her head down; and* PRICE *and* RUMMY *flee into the shelter*)
BILL You want to gow in and tell your Mijor of me, do you?
JENNY Oh, please, don't drag my hair. Let me go.
BILL Do you or down't you? (*She stifles a scream*) Yus or nao?
JENNY God give me strength—
BILL (*Striking her with his fist in the face*) Gow an' shaow her thet, and tell her if she wants one lawk it to cam and interfere with me. (JENNY, *crying with pain, goes into the shed. He goes to the form and addresses the old man*) 'Eah: finish your mess; and git aht o' maw w'y.
SHIRLEY (*Springing up and facing him fiercely, with the mug in his hand*) You take a liberty with me, and I'll smash you over the face with the mug and cut your eye out. Ain't you satisfied—young whelps like you —with takin' the bread out o' the mouths of your elders that have brought you up and slaved for you, but you must come shovin' and cheekin' and bullyin' in here, where the bread o' charity is sickenin' in our stummicks?
BILL (*Contemptuously, but backing a little*) Wot good are you, you aold palsy mag? Wot good are you?

SHIRLEY As good as you and better. I'll do a day's work agen you or any fat young soaker of your age. Go and take my job at Horrockses, where I worked for ten year. They want young men there: they can't afford to keep men over forty-five. They're very sorry—give you a character and happy to help you to get anything suited to your years—sure a steady man won't be long out of a job. Well, let 'em try you. They'll find the differ. What do you know? Not as much as how to beeyave yourself—layin' your dirty fist across the mouth of a respectable woman!

BILL Downt provowk me to l'y it acrost yours: d'ye 'eah?

SHIRLEY (*With blighting contempt*) Yes: you like an old man to hit, don't you, when you've finished with the women. I ain't seen you hit a young one yet.

BILL (*Stung*) You loy, you aold soupkitchener, you. There was a yang menn 'eah. Did Aw offer to 'itt him or did Aw not?

SHIRLEY Was he starvin' or was he not? Was he a man or only a cross-eyed thief an' a loafer? Would you hit my son-in-law's brother?

BILL 'Oo's 'ee?

SHIRLEY Todger Fairmile o' Balls Pond. Him that won £20 off the Japanese wrastler at the music hall by standin' out 17 minutes 4 seconds agen him.

BILL (*Sullenly*) Aw'm nao music 'awl wrastler. Ken he box?

SHIRLEY Yes: an' you can't.

BILL Wot! Aw cawn't, cawn't Aw? Wot's they you s'y? (*Threatening him*)

SHIRLEY (*Not budging an inch*) Will you box Todger Fairmile if I put him on to you? Say the word.

BILL (*Subsiding with a slouch*) Aw'll stend ap to enny menn alawv, if he was ten Todger Fairmawls. But Aw down't set ap to be a perfeshnal.

SHIRLEY (*Looking down on him with unfathomable disdain*) You box! Slap an old woman with the back o' your hand! You hadn't even the sense to hit her where a magistrate couldn't see the mark of it, you silly young lump of conceit and ignorance. Hit a girl in the jaw and on'y make her cry! If Todger Fairmile'd done it, she wouldn't 'a got up inside o' ten minutes, no more than you would if he got on to you. Yah! I'd set about you myself if I had a week's feedin' in me instead o' two months' starvation. (*He turns his back on him and sits down moodily at the table*)

BILL (*Following him and stooping over him to drive the taunt in*) You loy! you've the bread and treacle in you that you cam 'eah to beg.

SHIRLEY (*Bursting into tears*) Oh God! it's true: I'm only an old pauper on the scrap heap. (*Furiously*) But you'll come to it yourself; and then you'll know. You'll come to it sooner than a teetotaller like me, fillin' yourself with gin at this hour o' the mornin!

BILL Aw'm nao gin drinker, you oald lawr; bat wen Aw want to give my girl a bloomin' good 'awdin' Aw lawk to 'ev a bit o' devil in me: see? An' 'eah Aw emm, talking to a rotten aold blawter like you stead o' given' 'er wot for. (*Working himself into a rage*) Aw'm gowin' in there to fetch her aht. (*He makes vengefully for the shelter door*)

SHIRLEY You're goin' to the station on a stretcher, more likely; and they'll take the gin and the devil out of you there when they get you inside. You mind what you're about: the major here is the Earl o' Stevenage's granddaughter.

BILL (*Checked*) Garn!

SHIRLEY You'll see.

BILL (*His resolution oozing*) Well, Aw ain't dan nathin' to 'er.

SHIRLEY S'pose she said you did! who'd believe you?

BILL (*Very uneasy, skulking back to the corner of the penthouse*) Gawd! there's no jastice in this cantry. To think wot them people can do! Aw'm as good as 'er.

SHIRLEY Tell her so. It's just what a fool like you would do.

(BARBARA, *brisk and businesslike, comes from the shelter with a note book, and addresses herself to* SHIRLEY. BILL, *cowed, sits down in the corner on a form, and turns his back on them*)

BARBARA Good morning.

SHIRLEY (*Standing up and taking off his hat*) Good morning, miss.

BARBARA Sit down: make yourself at home. (*He hesitates; but she puts a friendly hand on his shoulder and makes him obey*) Now then! since you've made friends with us, we want to know all about you. Names and addresses and trades.

SHIRLEY Peter Shirley. Fitter. Chucked out two months ago because I was too old.

BARBARA (*Not at all surprised*) You'd pass still. Why didn't you dye your hair?

SHIRLEY I did. Me age come out at a coroner's inquest on me daughter.

BARBARA Steady?

SHIRLEY Teetotaller. Never out of a job before. Good worker. And sent to the knackers like an old horse!

BARBARA No matter: if you did your part God will do his.

SHIRLEY (*Suddenly stubborn*) My religion's no concern of anybody but myself.

BARBARA (*Guessing*) I know. Secularist?

SHIRLEY (*Hotly*) Did I offer to deny it?

BARBARA Why should you? My own father's a Secularist, I think. Our Father—yours and mine—fulfils himself in many ways; and I daresay he knew what he was about when he made a Secularist of you. So buck up, Peter! we can always find a job for a steady man like you. (SHIRLEY, *disarmed and a little bewildered, touches his hat. She turns from him to* BILL) What's your name?
BILL (*Insolently*) Wot's thet to you?
BARBARA (*Calmly making a note*) Afraid to give his name. Any trade?
BILL 'Oo's afride to give 'is nime? (*Doggedly, with a sense of heroically defying the House of Lords in the person of Lord Stevenage*) If you want to bring a chawge agen me, bring it. (*She waits, unruffled*) Moy nime's Bill Walker.
BARBARA (*As if the name were familiar: trying to remember how*) Bill Walker? (*Recollecting*) Oh, I know: you're the man that Jenny Hill was praying for inside just now. (*She enters his name in her note book*)
BILL 'Oo's Jenny 'Ill? And wot call 'as she to pr'y for me?
BARBARA I don't know. Perhaps it was you that cut her lip.
BILL (*Defiantly*) Yus, it was me that cat her lip. Aw ain't afride o' you.
BARBARA How could you be, since you're not afraid of God? You're a brave man, Mr Walker. It takes some pluck to do our work here; but none of us dare lift our hand against a girl like that, for fear of her father in heaven.
BILL (*Sullenly*) I want nan o' your kentin' jawr.[7] I spowse you think Aw cam 'eah to beg from you, like this demmiged lot 'eah. Not me. Aw down't want your bread and scripe[8] and ketlep.[9] Aw don't b'lieve in your Gawd, no more than you do yourself.
BARBARA (*Sunnily apologetic and ladylike, as on a new footing with him*) Oh, I beg your pardon for putting your name down, Mr Walker. I didn't understand. I'll strike it out.
BILL (*Taking this as a slight, and deeply wounded by it*) 'Eah! you let maw nime alown. Ain't it good enaff to be in your book?
BARBARA (*Considering*) Well, you see, there's no use putting down your name unless I can do something for you, is there? What's your trade?
BILL (*Still smarting*) Thets nao concern o' yours.
BARBARA Just so. (*Very businesslike*) I'll put you down as (*Writing*) the man who—struck—poor little Jenny Hill—in the mouth.
BILL (*Rising threateningly*) See 'eah. Awve 'ed enaff o' this.

[7] Canting jaw.
[8] Bread and scrape. The Salvation Army was said to put butter or lard on the bread and then "scrape" it off.
[9] Cat lap; watered milk, like that given to a cat.

BARBARA (*Quite sunny and fearless*) What did you come to us for?
BILL   Aw cam for maw gel, see? Aw cam to tike her aht o' this and to brike 'er jawr for 'er.
BARBARA (*Complacently*) You see I was right about your trade. (BILL, *on the point of retorting furiously, finds himself, to his great shame and terror, in danger of crying instead. He sits down again suddenly*) What's her name?
BILL (*Dogged*) 'Er nime's Mog Ebbijem: thet's wot her nime is.
BARBARA   Mog Habbijam! Oh, she's gone to Canning Town, to our barracks there.
BILL (*Fortified by his resentment of* MOG'S *perfidy*) Is she? (*Vindictively*) Then Aw'm gowin' to Kennintahn arter her. (*He crosses to the gate; hesitates; finally comes back at* BARBARA) Are you loyin' to me to git shat o' me?
BARBARA   I don't want to get shut of you. I want to keep you here and save your soul. You'd better stay: you're going to have a bad time today, Bill.
BILL   'Oo's gowin' to give it to me? You, p'reps?
BARBARA   Someone you don't believe in. But you'll be glad afterwards.
BILL (*Slinking off*) Aw'll gow to Kennintahn to be aht o' reach o' your tangue. (*Suddenly turning on her with intense malice*) And if Aw down't fawnd Mog there, Aw'll cam beck and do two years for you, s'elp me Gawd if Aw downt!
BARBARA (*A shade kindlier, if possible*) It's no use, Bill. She's got another bloke.
BILL   Wot!
BARBARA   One of her own converts. He fell in love with her when he saw her with her soul saved, and her face clean, and her hair washed.
BILL (*Surprised*) Wottud she wash it for, the carroty slat? It's red.
BARBARA   It's quite lovely now, because she wears a new look in her eyes with it. It's a pity you're too late. The new bloke has put your nose out of joint, Bill.
BILL   Aw'll put his nowse aht o' joint for him. Not that Aw care a carse for 'er, mawnd thet. But Aw'll teach her to drop me as if Aw was dirt. And Aw'll teach him to meddle with maw judy. Wots 'iz bleedin' nime?
BARBARA   Sergeant Todger Fairmile.
SHIRLEY (*Rising with grim joy*) I'll go with him, miss. I want to see them two meet. I'll take him to the infirmary when it's over.
BILL (*To* SHIRLEY, *with undissembled misgiving*) Is thet 'im you was speakin' on?
SHIRLEY   That's him.

BILL 'Im that wrastled in the music 'awl?
SHIRLEY The competitions at the National Sportin' Club was worth nigh a hundred a year to him. He's gev 'em up now for religion; so he's a bit fresh for want of the exercise he was accustomed to. He'll be glad to see you. Come along.
BILL Wot's 'is wight?
SHIRLEY Thirteen four.[10] (BILL's *last hope expires*)
BARBARA Go and talk to him, Bill. He'll convert you.
SHIRLEY He'll convert your head into a mashed potato.
BILL (*Sullenly*) Aw ain't afride of 'im. Aw ain't afride of ennybody. Bat 'e can lick me. She's dan me. (*He sits down moodily on the edge of the horse trough*)
SHIRLEY You ain't goin'. I thought not. (*He resumes his seat*)
BARBARA (*Calling*) Jenny!
JENNY (*Appearing at the shelter door with a plaster on the corner of her mouth*) Yes, Major.
BARBARA Send Rummy Mitchens out to clear away here.
JENNY I think she's afraid.
BARBARA (*Her resemblance to her mother flashing out for a moment*) Nonsense! she must do as she's told.
JENNY (*Calling into the shelter*) Rummy: the Major says you must come.

(JENNY *comes to* BARBARA, *purposely keeping on the side next* BILL, *lest he should suppose that she shrank from him or bore malice*)

BARBARA Poor little Jenny! Are you tired? (*Looking at the wounded cheek*) Does it hurt?
JENNY No: it's all right now. It was nothing.
BARBARA (*Critically*) It was as hard as he could hit, I expect. Poor Bill! You don't feel angry with him, do you?
JENNY Oh no, no, no: indeed I don't, Major, bless his poor heart! (BARBARA *kisses her; and she runs away merrily into the shelter.* BILL *writhes with an agonizing return of his new and alarming symptoms, but says nothing.* RUMMY MITCHENS *comes from the shelter*)
BARBARA (*Going to meet* RUMMY) Now Rummy, bustle. Take in those mugs and plates to be washed; and throw the crumbs about for the birds.

(RUMMY *takes the three plates and mugs; but* SHIRLEY *takes back his mug from her, as there is still some milk left in it*)

[10] Thirteen stone, four pounds, or 186 pounds. This probably means that Bill Walker weighs considerably less.

RUMMY There ain't any crumbs. This ain't a time to waste good bread on birds.

PRICE (*Appearing at the shelter door*) Gentleman come to see the shelter, Major. Says he's your father.

BARBARA All right. Coming. (SNOBBY *goes back into the shelter, followed by* BARBARA)

RUMMY (*Stealing across to Bill and addressing him in a subdued voice, but with intense conviction*) I'd 'av the lor of you, you flat eared pig-nosed potwalloper,[11] if she'd let me. You're no gentleman, to hit a lady in the face. (BILL, *with greater things moving in him, takes no notice*)

SHIRLEY (*Following her*) Here! in with you and don't get yourself into more trouble by talking.

RUMMY (*With hauteur*) I ain't 'ad the pleasure o' being hintroduced to you, as I can remember. (*She goes into the shelter with the plates*)

SHIRLEY That's the—

BILL (*Savagely*) Downt you talk to me, d'ye 'eah? You lea' me alown, or Aw'll do you a mischief. Aw'm not dirt under your feet, ennywy.

SHIRLEY (*Calmly*) Don't you be afeerd. You ain't such prime company that you need expect to be sought after. (*He is about to go into the shelter when* BARBARA *comes out, with* UNDERSHAFT *on her right*)

BARBARA Oh, there you are, Mr Shirley! (*Between them*) This is my father: I told you he was a Secularist, didn't I? Perhaps you'll be able to comfort one another.

UNDERSHAFT (*Startled*) A Secularist! Not the least in the world: on the contrary, a confirmed mystic.

BARBARA Sorry, I'm sure. By the way, papa, what is your religion? in case I have to introduce you again.

UNDERSHAFT My religion? Well, my dear, I am a Millionaire. That is my religion.

BARBARA Then I'm afraid you and Mr Shirley won't be able to comfort one another after all. You're not a Millionaire, are you, Peter?

SHIRLEY No; and proud of it.

UNDERSHAFT (*Gravely*) Poverty, my friend, is not a thing to be proud of.

SHIRLEY (*Angrily*) Who made your millions for you? Me and my like. What's kep' us poor? Keepin' you rich. I wouldn't have your conscience, not for all your income.

UNDERSHAFT I wouldn't have your income, not for all your conscience, Mr Shirley. (*He goes to the penthouse and sits down on a form*)

BARBARA (*Stopping* SHIRLEY *adroitly as he is about to retort*) You wouldn't think he was my father, would you, Peter? Will you go into

---

[11] The clod who rises in the middle of the night and bumps into the chamber pot, dirtying himself and waking everyone.

the shelter and lend the lasses a hand for a while: we're worked off our feet.

SHIRLEY (*Bitterly*)   Yes: I'm in their debt for a meal, ain't I?

BARBARA   Oh, not because you're in their debt, but for love of them, Peter, for love of them. (*He cannot understand, and is rather scandalized*) There! don't stare at me. In with you; and give that conscience of yours a holiday. (*Bustling him into the shelter*)

SHIRLEY (*As he goes in*)   Ah! it's a pity you never was trained to use your reason, miss. You'd have been a very taking lecturer on Secularism.

(BARBARA *turns to her father*)

UNDERSHAFT   Never mind me, my dear. Go about your work; and let me watch it for a while.

BARBARA   All right.

UNDERSHAFT   For instance, what's the matter with that outpatient over there?

BARBARA (*Looking at* BILL, *whose attitude has never changed, and whose expression of brooding wrath has deepened*)   Oh, we shall cure him in no time. Just watch. (*She goes over to* BILL *and waits. He glances up at her and casts his eyes down again, uneasy, but grimmer than ever*) It would be nice to just stamp on Mog Habbijam's face, wouldn't it, Bill?

BILL (*Starting up from the trough in consternation*)   It's a loy: Aw never said so. (*She shakes her head*) 'Oo taold you wot was in moy mawnd?

BARBARA   Only your new friend.

BILL   Wot new friend?

BARBARA   The devil, Bill. When he gets round people they get miserable, just like you.

BILL (*With a heartbreaking attempt at devil-may-care cheerfulness*)   Aw ain't miserable. (*He sits down again, and stretches his legs in an attempt to seem indifferent*)

BARBARA   Well, if you're happy, why don't you look happy, as we do?

BILL (*His legs curling back in spite of him*)   Aw'm 'eppy enaff, Aw tell you. Woy cawn't you lea' me alown? Wot 'ev I dan to you? Aw ain't smashed your fice, 'ev Aw?

BARBARA (*Softly: wooing his soul*)   It's not me that's getting at you, Bill.

BILL   'Oo else is it?

BARBARA   Somebody that doesn't intend you to smash women's faces, I suppose. Somebody or something that wants to make a man of you.

BILL (*Blustering*)   Mike a menn o' me! Ain't Aw a menn? eh? 'Oo sez Aw'm not a menn?

BARBARA   There's a man in you somewhere, I suppose. But why did he let you hit poor little Jenny Hill? That wasn't very manly of him, was it?

BILL (*Tormented*) 'Ev dan wiv it, Aw tell you. Chack it. Aw'm sick o' your Jenny 'Ill and 'er silly little fice.

BARBARA Then why do you keep thinking about it? Why does it keep coming up against you in your mind? You're not getting converted, are you?

BILL (*With conviction*) Not ME. Not lawkly.

BARBARA That's right, Bill. Hold out against it. Put out your strength. Don't let's get you cheap. Todger Fairmile said he wrestled for three nights against his salvation harder than he ever wrestled with the Jap at the music hall. He gave in to the Jap when his arm was going to break. But he didn't give in to his salvation until his heart was going to break. Perhaps you'll escape that. You havn't any heart, have you?

BILL Wot d'ye mean? Woy ain't Aw got a 'awt the sime as ennybody else?

BARBARA A man with a heart wouldn't have bashed poor little Jenny's face, would he?

BILL (*Almost crying*) Ow, will you lea' me alown? 'Ev Aw ever offered to meddle with you, that you cam neggin' and provowkin' me lawk this? (*He writhes convulsively from his eyes to his toes*)

BARBARA (*With a steady soothing hand on his arm and a gentle voice that never lets go*) It's your soul that's hurting you, Bill, and not me. We've been through it all ourselves. Come with us, Bill. (*He looks wildly round*) To brave manhood on earth and eternal glory in heaven. (*He is on the point of breaking down*) Come. (*A drum is heard in the shelter; and* BILL, *with a gasp, escapes from the spell as* BARBARA *turns quickly.* ADOLPHUS *enters from the shelter with a big drum*) Oh! there you are, Dolly. Let me introduce a new friend of mine, Mr Bill Walker. This is my bloke, Bill: Mr Cusins. (CUSINS *salutes with his drumstick*)

BILL Gowin to merry 'im?

BARBARA Yes.

BILL (*Fervently*) Gawd 'elp 'im! Gaw-aw-aw-awd 'elp 'im!

BARBARA Why? Do you think he won't be happy with me?

BILL Awve aony 'ed to stend it for a mawnin': 'e'll 'ev to stend it for a lawftawm.

CUSINS That is a frightful reflection, Mr Walker. But I can't tear myself away from her.

BILL Well, Aw ken. (*To* BARBARA) 'Eah! do you knaow where Aw'm gowin' to, and wot Aw'm gowin' to do?

BARBARA Yes: you're going to heaven; and you're coming back here before the week's out to tell me so.

BILL You loy. Aw'm gowin to Kennintahn, to spit in Todger Fairmawl's eye. Aw beshed Jenny 'Ill's fice; an nar Aw'll git me aown fice beshed and cam beck and shaow it to 'er. 'Ee'll 'itt me 'ardern Aw 'itt 'er. That'll mike us square. (*To* ADOLPHUS) Is that fair or is it not? You're a genlm'n: you oughter knaow.

BARBARA Two black eyes won't make one white one, Bill.

BILL Aw didn't awst you. Cawnt you never keep your mahth shat? Oy awst the genlm'n.

CUSINS (*Reflectively*) Yes: I think you're right, Mr Walker. Yes: I should do it. It's curious: it's exactly what an ancient Greek would have done.

BARBARA But what good will it do?

CUSINS Well, it will give Mr Fairmile some exercise; and it will satisfy Mr Walker's soul.

BILL Rot! there ain't nao sach a thing as a saoul. Ah kin you tell wevver Aw've a saoul or not? You never seen it.

BARBARA I've seen it hurting you when you went against it.

BILL (*With compressed aggravation*) If you was maw gel and took the word aht o' me mahth lawk thet, Aw'd give you sathink you'd feel 'urtin, Aw would. (*To* ADOLPHUS) You tike maw tip, mite. Stop 'er jawr; or you'll doy afoah your tawm. (*With intense expression*) Wore aht: thet's you'll be: wore aht. (*He goes away through the gate*)

CUSINS (*Looking after him*) I wonder!

BARBARA Dolly! (*Indignant, in her mother's manner*)

CUSINS Yes, my dear, it's very wearing to be in love with you. If it lasts, I quite think I shall die young.

BARBARA Should you mind?

CUSINS Not at all. (*He is suddenly softened, and kisses her over the drum, evidently not for the first time, as people cannot kiss over a big drum without practice.* UNDERSHAFT *coughs*)

BARBARA It's all right, papa, we've not forgotten you. Dolly: explain the place to papa: I havn't time. (*She goes busily into the shelter*)

> (UNDERSHAFT *and* ADOLPHUS *now have the yard to themselves.* UNDERSHAFT, *seated on a form, and still keenly attentive, looks hard at* ADOLPHUS. ADOLPHUS *looks hard at him*)

UNDERSHAFT I fancy you guess something of what is in my mind, Mr Cusins. (CUSINS *flourishes his drumsticks as if in the act of beating a lively rataplan, but makes no sound*) Exactly so. But suppose Barbara finds you out!

CUSINS You know, I do not admit that I am imposing on Barbara. I am quite genuinely interested in the views of the Salvation Army. The fact

is, I am a sort of collector of religions; and the curious thing is that I find I can believe them all. By the way, have you any religion?
UNDERSHAFT Yes.
CUSINS Anything out of the common?
UNDERSHAFT Only that there are two things necessary to Salvation.
CUSINS (*Disappointed, but polite*) Ah, the Church Catechism. Charles Lomax also belongs to the Established Church.
UNDERSHAFT The two things are—
CUSINS Baptism and—
UNDERSHAFT No. Money and gunpowder.
CUSINS (*Surprised, but interested*) That is the general opinion of our governing classes. The novelty is in hearing any man confess it.
UNDERSHAFT Just so.
CUSINS Excuse me: is there any place in your religion for honor, justice, truth, love, mercy and so forth?
UNDERSHAFT Yes: they are the graces and luxuries of a rich, strong, and safe life.
CUSINS Suppose one is forced to choose between them and money or gunpowder?
UNDERSHAFT Choose money and gunpowder; for without enough of both you cannot afford the others.
CUSINS That is your religion?
UNDERSHAFT Yes.

(*The cadence of this reply makes a full close in the conversation.* CUSINS *twists his face dubiously and contemplates* UNDERSHAFT. UNDERSHAFT *contemplates him*)

CUSINS Barbara won't stand that. You will have to choose between your religion and Barbara.
UNDERSHAFT So will you, my friend. She will find out that that drum of yours is hollow.
CUSINS Father Undershaft: you are mistaken: I am a sincere Salvationist. You do not understand the Salvation Army. It is the army of joy, of love, of courage: it has banished the fear and remorse and despair of the old hell-ridden evangelical sects: it marches to fight the devil with trumpet and drum, with music and dancing, with banner and palm, as becomes a sally from heaven by its happy garrison. It picks the waster out of the public house and makes a man of him: it finds a worm wriggling in a back kitchen, and lo! a woman! Men and women of rank too, sons and daughters of the Highest. It takes the poor professor of Greek, the most artificial and self-suppressed of human creatures, from his meal of roots, and lets loose the rhapsodist in him;

reveals the true worship of Dionysos to him; sends him down the public street drumming dithyrambs. (*He plays a thundering flourish on the drum*)

UNDERSHAFT You will alarm the shelter.

CUSINS Oh, they are accustomed to these sudden ecstasies of piety. However, if the drum worries you— (*He pockets the drumsticks; unhooks the drum; and stands it on the ground opposite the gateway*)

UNDERSHAFT Thank you.

CUSINS You remember what Euripides says about your money and gunpowder?

UNDERSHAFT No.

CUSINS (*Declaiming*)

> One and another
> In money and guns may outpass his brother;
> And men in their millions float and flow
> And seethe with a million hopes as leaven;
> And they win their will; or they miss their will;
> And their hopes are dead or are pined for still;
>   But whoe'er can know
>   As the long days go
> That to live is happy, has found his heaven.[12]

My translation: what do you think of it?

UNDERSHAFT I think, my friend, that if you wish to know, as the long days go, that to live is happy, you must first acquire money enough for a decent life, and power enough to be your own master.

CUSINS You are damnably discouraging. (*He resumes his declamation*)

> Is it so hard a thing to see
> That the spirit of God—whate'er it be—
> The law that abides and changes not, ages long,
> The Eternal and Nature-born: these things be strong?
> What else is Wisdom? What of Man's endeavor,
> Or God's high grace so lovely and so great?
> To stand from fear set free? to breathe and wait?
> To hold a hand uplifted over Fate?
> And shall not Barbara be loved for ever?[13]

---

[12] From Gilbert Murray's translation of Euripides' *The Bacchae*. In line 2, Shaw substitutes "money and guns" for "gold and power."

[13] Also from Murray's translation of *The Bacchae*. Shaw substitutes "Fate" for "Hate" in the penultimate line, and, as Cusins notes, "Barbara" for "loveliness."

UNDERSHAFT Euripides mentions Barbara, does he?
CUSINS It is a fair translation. The word means Loveliness.
UNDERSHAFT May I ask—as Barbara's father—how much a year she is to be loved for ever on?
CUSINS As Barbara's father, that is more your affair than mine. I can feed her by teaching Greek: that is about all.
UNDERSHAFT Do you consider it a good match for her?
CUSINS (*With polite obstinacy*) Mr Undershaft: I am in many ways a weak, timid, ineffectual person; and my health is far from satisfactory. But whenever I feel that I must have anything, I get it, sooner or later. I feel that way about Barbara. I don't like marriage: I feel intensely afraid of it; and I don't know what I shall do with Barbara or what she will do with me. But I feel that I and nobody else must marry her. Please regard that as settled— Not that I wish to be arbitrary; but why should I waste your time in discussing what is inevitable?
UNDERSHAFT You mean that you will stick at nothing: not even the conversion of the Salvation Army to the worship of Dionysos.
CUSINS The business of the Salvation Army is to save, not to wrangle about the name of the pathfinder. Dionysos or another: what does it matter?
UNDERSHAFT (*Rising and approaching him*) Professor Cusins: you are a young man after my own heart.
CUSINS Mr Undershaft: you are, as far as I am able to gather, a most infernal old rascal; but you appeal very strongly to my sense of ironic humor.

(UNDERSHAFT *mutely offers his hand. They shake*)

UNDERSHAFT (*Suddenly concentrating himself*) And now to business.
CUSINS Pardon me. We were discussing religion. Why go back to such an uninteresting and unimportant subject as business?
UNDERSHAFT Religion is our business at present, because it is through religion alone that we can win Barbara.
CUSINS Have you, too, fallen in love with Barbara?
UNDERSHAFT Yes, with a father's love.
CUSINS A father's love for a grown-up daughter is the most dangerous of all infatuations. I apologize for mentioning my own pale, coy, mistrustful fancy in the same breath with it.
UNDERSHAFT Keep to the point. We have to win her; and we are neither of us Methodists.
CUSINS That doesn't matter. The power Barbara wields here—the power that wields Barbara herself—is not Calvinism, not Presbyterianism, not Methodism—

UNDERSHAFT   Not Greek Paganism either, eh?
CUSINS   I admit that. Barbara is quite original in her religion.
UNDERSHAFT   (*Triumphantly*)   Aha! Barbara Undershaft would be. Her inspiration comes from within herself.
CUSINS   How do you suppose it got there?
UNDERSHAFT   (*In towering excitement*)   It is the Undershaft inheritance. I shall hand on my torch to my daughter. She shall make my converts and preach my gospel—
CUSINS   What! Money and gunpowder!
UNDERSHAFT   Yes, money and gunpowder; freedom and power; command of life and command of death.
CUSINS   (*Urbanely: trying to bring him down to earth*)   This is extremely interesting, Mr Undershaft. Of course you know that you are mad.
UNDERSHAFT   (*With redoubled force*)   And you?
CUSINS   Oh, mad as a hatter. You are welcome to my secret since I have discovered yours. But I am astonished. Can a madman make cannons?
UNDERSHAFT   Would anyone else than a madman make them? And now (*With surging energy*) question for question. Can a sane man translate Euripides?
CUSINS   No.
UNDERSHAFT   (*Seizing him by the shoulder*)   Can a sane woman make a man of a waster or a woman of a worm?
CUSINS   (*Reeling before the storm*)   Father Colossus—Mammoth Millionaire—
UNDERSHAFT   (*Pressing him*)   Are there two mad people or three in this Salvation shelter to-day?
CUSINS   You mean Barbara is as mad as we are?
UNDERSHAFT   (*Pushing him lightly off and resuming his equanimity suddenly and completely*)   Pooh, Professor! let us call things by their proper names. I am a millionaire; you are a poet; Barbara is a savior of souls. What have we three to do with the common mob of slaves and idolaters? (*He sits down again with a shrug of contempt for the mob*)
CUSINS   Take care! Barbara is in love with the common people. So am I. Have you never felt the romance of that love?
UNDERSHAFT   (*Cold and sardonic*)   Have you ever been in love with Poverty, like St Francis? Have you ever been in love with Dirt, like St Simeon? Have you ever been in love with disease and suffering, like our nurses and philanthropists? Such passions are not virtues, but the most unnatural of all the vices. This love of the common people may please an earl's granddaughter and a university professor; but I have been a common man and a poor man; and it has no romance for me. Leave it to the poor to pretend that poverty is a blessing: leave it

to the coward to make a religion of his cowardice by preaching humility: we know better than that. We three must stand together above the common people: how else can we help their children to climb up beside us? Barbara must belong to us, not to the Salvation Army.

CUSINS Well, I can only say that if you think you will get her away from the Salvation Army by talking to her as you have been talking to me, you don't know Barbara.

UNDERSHAFT My friend: I never ask for what I can buy.

CUSINS (*In a white fury*) Do I understand you to imply that you can buy Barbara?

UNDERSHAFT No; but I can buy the Salvation Army.

CUSINS Quite impossible.

UNDERSHAFT You shall see. All religious organizations exist by selling themselves to the rich.

CUSINS Not the Army. That is the Church of the poor.

UNDERSHAFT All the more reason for buying it.

CUSINS I don't think you quite know what the Army does for the poor.

UNDERSHAFT Oh, yes, I do. It draws their teeth: that is enough for me —as a man of business—

CUSINS Nonsense! It makes them sober—

UNDERSHAFT I prefer sober workmen. The profits are larger.

CUSINS —honest—

UNDERSHAFT Honest workmen are the most economical.

CUSINS —attached to their homes—

UNDERSHAFT So much the better: they will put up with anything sooner than change their shop.

CUSINS —happy—

UNDERSHAFT An invaluable safeguard against revolution.

CUSINS —unselfish—

UNDERSHAFT Indifferent to their own interests, which suits me exactly.

CUSINS —with their thoughts on heavenly things—

UNDERSHAFT (*Rising*) And not on Trade Unionism nor Socialism. Excellent.

CUSINS (*Revolted*) You really are an infernal old rascal.

UNDERSHAFT (*Indicating* PETER SHIRLEY, *who has just come from the shelter and strolled dejectedly down the yard between them*) And this is an honest man!

SHIRLEY Yes; and what 'av I got by it? (*He passes on bitterly and sits on the form, in the corner of the penthouse*)

(SNOBBY PRICE, *beaming sanctimoniously, and* JENNY HILL, *with a tambourine full of coppers, come from the shelter and go to the drum, on which* JENNY *begins to count the money*)

UNDERSHAFT (*Replying to* SHIRLEY) Oh, your employers must have got a good deal by it from first to last. (*He sits on the table, with one foot on the side form.* CUSINS, *overwhelmed, sits down on the same form nearer the shelter.* BARBARA *comes from the shelter to the middle of the yard. She is excited and a little overwrought*)

BARBARA We've just had a splendid experience meeting at the other gate in Cripp's Lane. I've hardly ever seen them so much moved as they were by your confession, Mr Price.

PRICE I could almost be glad of my past wickedness if I could believe that it would 'elp to keep hathers stright.

BARBARA So it will, Snobby. How much, Jenny?

JENNY Four and tenpence, Major.

BARBARA Oh, Snobby, if you had given your poor mother just one more kick, we should have got the whole five shillings!

PRICE If she heard you say that, miss, she'd be sorry I didn't. But I'm glad. Oh what a joy it will be to her when she hears I'm saved!

UNDERSHAFT Shall I contribute the odd twopence, Barbara? The millionaire's mite,[14] eh? (*He takes a couple of pennies from his pocket*)

BARBARA How did you make that twopence?

UNDERSHAFT As usual. By selling cannons, torpedoes, submarines, and my new patent Grand Duke hand grenade.

BARBARA Put it back in your pocket. You can't buy your Salvation here for twopence: you must work it out.

UNDERSHAFT Is twopence not enough? I can afford a little more, if you press me.

BARBARA Two million millions would not be enough. There is bad blood on your hands; and nothing but good blood can cleanse them. Money is no use. Take it away. (*She turns to* CUSINS) Dolly: you must write another letter for me to the papers. (*He makes a wry face*) Yes: I know you don't like it; but it must be done. The starvation this winter is beating us: everybody is unemployed. The General says we must close this shelter if we can't get more money. I force the collections at the meetings until I am ashamed: don't I, Snobby?

PRICE It's a fair treat to see you work it, Miss. The way you got them up from three-and-six to four-and-ten with that hymn, penny by penny and verse by verse, was a caution. Not a Cheap Jack on Mile End Waste could touch you at it.[15]

[14] Undershaft, recently called "an infernal old rascal," devilishly plays on the biblical "widow's mite," pronounced the same as "might."

[15] At the end of Mile End Road are numerous pushcart vendors; Cheap Jacks are salesmen who hound potential customers, trying to persuade them to purchase from their stalls.

BARBARA Yes; but I wish we could do without it. I am getting at last to think more of the collection than of the people's souls. And what are those hatfuls of pence and halfpence? We want thousands! tens of thousands! hundreds of thousands! I want to convert people, not to be always begging for the Army in a way I'd die sooner than beg for myself.
UNDERSHAFT (*In profound irony*) Genuine unselfishness is capable of anything, my dear.
BARBARA (*Unsuspectingly, as she turns away to take the money from the drum and put it in a cash bag she carries*) Yes, isn't it? (UNDERSHAFT *looks sardonically at* CUSINS)
CUSINS (*Aside to* UNDERSHAFT) Mephistopheles! Machiavelli!
BARBARA (*Tears coming into her eyes as she ties the bag and pockets it*) How are we to feed them? I can't talk religion to a man with bodily hunger in his eyes. (*Almost breaking down*) It's frightful.
JENNY (*Running to her*) Major, dear—
BARBARA (*Rebounding*) No: don't comfort me. It will be all right. We shall get the money.
UNDERSHAFT How?
JENNY By praying for it, of course. Mrs Baines says she prayed for it last night; and she has never prayed for it in vain: never once. (*She goes to the gate and looks out into the street*)
BARBARA (*Who has dried her eyes and regained her composure*) By the way, dad, Mrs Baines has come to march with us to our big meeting this afternoon; and she is very anxious to meet you, for some reason or other. Perhaps she'll convert you.
UNDERSHAFT I shall be delighted, my dear.
JENNY (*At the gate: excitedly*) Major! Major! here's that man back again.
BARBARA What man?
JENNY The man that hit me. Oh, I hope he's coming back to join us.

> (BILL WALKER, *with frost on his jacket, comes through the gate, his hands deep in his pockets and his chin sunk between his shoulders, like a cleaned-out gambler. He halts between* BARBARA *and the drum*)

BARBARA Hullo, Bill! Back already!
BILL (*Nagging at her*) Bin talkin' ever sence, 'ev you?
BARBARA Pretty nearly. Well, has Todger paid you out for poor Jenny's jaw?
BILL Nao 'e ain't.
BARBARA I thought your jacket looked a bit snowy.

BILL Sao it is snaowy. You want to knaow where the snaow cam from, down't you?
BARBARA Yes.
BILL Well, it cam from orf the grahnd in Pawkinses Corner in Kennintahn. It got rabbed orf be maw shaoulders: see?
BARBARA Pity you didn't rub some off with your knees, Bill! That would have done you a lot of good.
BILL (*With sour mirthless humor*) Aw was sivin' anather menn's knees at the tawm. 'E was kneelin' on moy 'ed, 'e was.
JENNY Who was kneeling on your head?
BILL Todger was. 'E was pryin' for me: pryin' camfortable wiv me as a cawpet. Sow was Mog. Sao was the aol bloomin' meetin'. Mog she sez "Ow Lawd brike is stabborn sperrit; bat down't 'urt is dear 'art." Thet was wot she said. "Downt 'urt is dear 'art"! An 'er blowk—thirteen stun four!—kneelin' wiv all is wight on me. Fanny, ain't it?
JENNY Oh no. We're so sorry, Mr Walker.
BARBARA (*Enjoying it frankly*) Nonsense! of course it's funny. Served you right, Bill! You must have done something to him first.
BILL (*Doggedly*) Aw did wot Aw said Aw'd do. Aw spit in 'is eye. 'E looks ap at the skoy and sez. " 'Ow that Aw should be fahnd worthy to be spit upon for the gospel's sike!" 'e sez; an Mog sez "Glaory 'Allelloolier!"; an' then 'e called me Braddher, and dahned me as if Aw was a kid and 'e was me mather worshin' me a Setterda nawt. Aw 'ednt jast nao shaow wiv 'im at all. 'Arf the street pr'yed; and the tather 'arf larfed fit to split theirselves. (*To* BARBARA) There! are you settisfawd nah?
BARBARA (*Her eyes dancing*) Wish I'd been there, Bill.
BILL Yus: you'd 'a got in a hextra bit 'o talk on me, wouldn't you?
JENNY I'm so sorry, Mr Walker.
BILL (*Fiercely*) Down't you gow bein' sorry for me: you've no call. Listen 'eah. Aw browk your jawr.
JENNY No, it didn't hurt me: indeed it didn't, except for a moment. It was only that I was frightened.
BILL Aw down't want to be forgive be you, or be ennybody. Wot Aw did Aw'll p'y for. Aw trawd to gat me aown jawr browk to settisfaw you—
JENNY (*Distressed*) Oh no—
BILL (*Impatiently*) Tell y' Aw did: cawnt you listen to wot's bein' taold you? All Aw got be it was being mide a sawt of in the pablic street for me pines. Well, if Aw cawnt settisfaw you one wy, Aw ken anather. Listen 'eah! Aw 'ed two quid sived agen the frost; an Aw've a pahnd of it left. A mite o' mawn last week 'ed words with the judy 'e's gowin to merry. 'E give 'er wotfor; an' 'e's bin fawnd fifteen bob.

51 · *Major Barbara* [ACT TWO]

'E 'ed a rawt to 'itt 'er cause they was gowin to be merrid; but Aw 'ednt nao rawt to 'itt you; sao put anather fawv bob on an cal it a pahnd's worth. (*He produces a sovereign*) 'Eahs the manney. Tike it; and let's 'ev no more o' your forgivin' an' pryin' and your Mijor jawrin' me. Let wot Aw dan be dan an' pide for; and let there be a end of it.

JENNY Oh, I couldn't take it, Mr Walker. But if you would give a shilling or two to poor Rummy Mitchens! you really did hurt her; and she's old.

BILL (*Contemptuously*) Not lawkly. Aw'd give her anather as soon as look at 'er. Let her 'ev the lawr o' me as she threatened! She ain't forgiven me: not mach. Wot Aw dan to 'er is not on me mawnd—wot she (*Indicating* BARBARA) mawt call on me conscience—no more than stickin' a pig. It's this Christian gime o' yours that Aw wown't 'ev pl'yed agen me: this bloomin' forgivin' an neggin' an jawrin' that mikes a menn thet sore that 'iz lawf's a burden to 'im. Aw wown't 'ev it, Aw tell you; sao tike your manney and stop thraowin' your silly beshed fice hap agen me.

JENNY Major: may I take a little of it for the Army?

BARBARA No: the Army is not to be bought. We want your soul, Bill; and we'll take nothing less.

BILL (*Bitterly*) Aw knaow. Me an' maw few shillin's is not good enaff for you. You're a earl's grendorter, you are. Nathink less than a 'andered pahnd for you.

UNDERSHAFT Come, Barbara! you could do a great deal of good with a hundred pounds. If you will set this gentleman's mind at ease by taking his pound, I will give the other ninety-nine.

(BILL, *dazed by such opulence, instinctively touches his cap*)

BARBARA Oh, you're too extravagant, papa. Bill offers twenty pieces of silver. All you need offer is the other ten. That will make the standard price to buy anybody who's for sale. I'm not; and the Army's not. (*To* BILL) You'll never have another quiet moment, Bill, until you come round to us. You can't stand out against your salvation.

BILL (*Sullenly*) Aw cawnt stend aht agen music 'awl wrastlers and awtful tangued women. Aw've offered to p'y. Aw can do no more. Tike it or leave it. There it is. (*He throws the sovereign on the drum, and sits down on the horse trough. The coin fascinates* SNOBBY PRICE, *who takes an early opportunity of dropping his cap on it*)

(MRS BAINES *comes from the shelter. She is dressed as a Salvation Army Commissioner. She is an earnest looking woman of about forty, with a caressing, urgent voice, and an appealing manner*)

BARBARA This is my father, Mrs Baines. (UNDERSHAFT *comes from the table, taking his hat off with marked civility*) Try what you can do with him. He won't listen to me, because he remembers what a fool I was when I was a baby. (*She leaves them together and chats with* JENNY)

MRS BAINES Have you been shewn over the shelter, Mr Undershaft? You know the work we're doing, of course.

UNDERSHAFT (*Very civilly*) The whole nation knows it, Mrs Baines.

MRS BAINES No, sir: the whole nation does not know it, or we should not be crippled as we are for want of money to carry our work through the length and breadth of the land. Let me tell you that there would have been rioting this winter in London but for us.

UNDERSHAFT You really think so?

MRS BAINES I know it, I remember 1886, when you rich gentlemen hardened your hearts against the cry of the poor. They broke the windows of your clubs in Pall Mall.

UNDERSHAFT (*Gleaming with approval of their method*) And the Mansion House Fund went up next day from thirty thousand pounds to seventy-nine thousand! I remember quite well.

MRS BAINES Well, won't you help me to get at the people? They won't break windows then. Come here, Price. Let me shew you to this gentleman. (PRICE *comes to be inspected*) Do you remember the window breaking?

PRICE My ole father thought it was the revolution, ma'am.

MRS BAINES Would you break windows now?

PRICE Oh no ma'am. The windows of 'eaven 'av bin opened to me. I know now that the rich man is a sinner like myself.

RUMMY (*Appearing above at the loft door*) Snobby Price!

SNOBBY Wot is it?

RUMMY Your mother's askin' for you at the other gate in Crippses Lane. She's heard about your confession. (PRICE *turns pale*)

MRS BAINES Go, Mr. Price; and pray with her.

JENNY Yon can go through the shelter, Snobby.

PRICE (*To* MR. BAINES) I couldn't face her now, ma'am, with all the weight of my sins fresh on me. Tell her she'll find her son at 'ome, waitin' for her in prayer. (*He skulks off through the gate, incidentally stealing the sovereign on his way out by picking up his cap from the drum*)

MRS BAINES (*With swimming eyes*) You see how we take the anger and the bitterness against you out of their hearts, Mr. Undershaft.

UNDERSHAFT It is certainly most convenient and gratifying to all large employers of labor, Mrs Baines.

MRS BAINES Barbara: Jenny: I have good news: most wonderful news. (JENNY *runs to her*) My prayers have been answered. I told you they would, Jenny, didn't I?
JENNY Yes, yes.
BARBARA (*Moving nearer to the drum*) Have we got money enough to keep the shelter open?
MRS BAINES I hope we shall have enough to keep all the shelters open. Lord Saxmundham has promised us five thousand pounds—
BARBARA Hooray!
JENNY Glory!
MRS BAINES —if—
BARBARA "If!" If what?
MRS BAINES —if five other gentlemen will give a thousand each to make it up to ten thousand.
BARBARA Who is Lord Saxmundham? I never heard of him.
UNDERSHAFT (*Who has pricked up his ears at the peer's name, and is now watching* BARBARA *curiously*) A new creation, my dear. You have heard of Sir Horace Bodger?
BARBARA Bodger! Do you mean the distiller? Bodger's whisky!
UNDERSHAFT That is the man. He is one of the greatest of our public benefactors. He restored the cathedral at Hakington. They made him a baronet for that. He gave half a million to the funds of his party: they made him a baron for that.
SHIRLEY What will they give him for the five thousand?
UNDERSHAFT There is nothing left to give him. So the five thousand, I should think, is to save his soul.
MRS BAINES Heaven grant it may! Oh Mr Undershaft, you have some very rich friends. Can't you help us towards the other five thousand? We are going to hold a great meeting this afternoon at the Assembly Hall in the Mile End Road. If I could only announce that one gentleman had come forward to support Lord Saxmundham, others would follow. Don't you know somebody? couldn't you? wouldn't you? (*Her eyes fill with tears*) oh, think of those poor people, Mr Undershaft: think of how much it means to them, and how little to a great man like you.
UNDERSHAFT (*Sardonically gallant*) Mrs Baines: you are irresistible. I can't disappoint you; and I can't deny myself the satisfaction of making Bodger pay up. You shall have your five thousand pounds.
MRS BAINES Thank God!
UNDERSHAFT You don't thank me?
MRS BAINES Oh sir, don't try to be cynical: don't be ashamed of being a good man. The Lord will bless you abundantly; and our prayers

will be like a strong fortification round you all the days of your life. (*With a touch of caution*) You will let me have the cheque to shew at the meeting, won't you? Jenny: go in and fetch a pen and ink. (JENNY *runs to the shelter door*)

UNDERSHAFT Do not disturb Miss Hill: I have a fountain pen. (JENNY *halts. He sits at the table and writes the cheque.* CUSINS *rises to make room for him. They all watch him silently*)

BILL (*Cynically, aside to* BARBARA, *his voice and accent horribly debased*) Wot prawce Selvytion nah?

BARBARA Stop. (UNDERSHAFT *stops writing: they all turn to her in surprise*) Mrs Baines: are you really going to take this money?

MRS BAINES (*Astonished*) Why not, dear?

BARBARA Why not! Do you know what my father is? Have you forgotten that Lord Saxmundham is Bodger the whisky man? Do you remember how we implored the County Council to stop him from writing Bodger's Whisky in letters of fire against the sky; so that the poor drink-ruined creatures on the Embankment could not wake up from their snatches of sleep without being reminded of their deadly thirst by that wicked sky sign? Do you know that the worst thing I have had to fight here is not the devil, but Bodger, Bodger, Bodger, with his whisky, his distilleries, and his tied houses?[16] Are you going to make our shelter another tied house for him, and ask me to keep it?

BILL Rotten dranken whisky it is too.

MRS BAINES Dear Barbara: Lord Saxmundham has a soul to be saved like any of us. If heaven has found the way to make a good use of his money, are we to set ourselves up against the answer to our prayers?

BARBARA I know he has a soul to be saved. Let him come down here; and I'll do my best to help him to his salvation. But he wants to send his cheque down to buy us, and go on being as wicked as ever.

UNDERSHAFT (*With a reasonableness which* CUSINS *alone perceives to be ironical*) My dear Barbara: alcohol is a very necessary article. It heals the sick—

BARBARA It does nothing of the sort.

UNDERSHAFT Well, it assists the doctor: that is perhaps a less questionable way of putting it. It makes life bearable to millions of people who could not endure their existence if they were quite sober. It enables Parliament to do things at eleven at night that no sane person would do at eleven in the morning. Is it Bodger's fault that this inestimable gift is deplorably abused by less than one per cent of the poor? (*He

---

[16] Inns or public houses owned or controlled by a distiller; the innkeeper is forced to take his liquor from (is therefore tied to) that distiller.

turns again to the table; signs the cheque; and crosses it)

MRS BAINES Barbara: will there be less drinking or more if all those poor souls we are saving come tomorrow and find the doors of our shelters shut in their faces? Lord Saxmundham gives us the money to stop drinking—to take his own business from him.

CUSINS (*Impishly*) Pure self-sacrifice on Bodger's part, clearly! Bless dear Bodger! (BARBARA *almost breaks down as Adolphus, too, fails her*)

UNDERSHAFT (*Tearing out the cheque and pocketing the book as he rises and goes past* CUSINS *to* MRS BAINES) I also, Mrs Baines, may claim a little disinterestedness. Think of my business! think of the widows and orphans! the men and lads torn to pieces with shrapnel and poisoned with lyddite! (MRS BAINES *shrinks; but he goes on remorselessly*) the oceans of blood, not one drop of which is shed in a really just cause! the ravaged crops! the peaceful peasants forced, women and men, to till their fields under the fire of opposing armies on pain of starvation! the bad blood of the fierce little cowards at home who egg on others to fight for the gratification of their national vanity! All this makes money for me: I am never richer, never busier than when the papers are full of it. Well, it is your work to preach peace on earth and goodwill to men. (MRS BAINES's *face lights up again*) Every convert you make is a vote against war. (*Her lips move in prayer*) Yet I give you this money to help you to hasten my own commercial ruin. (*He gives her the cheque*)

CUSINS (*Mounting the form in an ecstasy of mischief*) The millennium will be inaugurated by the unselfishness of Undershaft and Bodger. Oh be joyful! (*He takes the drumsticks from his pocket and flourishes them*)

MRS BAINES (*Taking the cheque*) The longer I live the more proof I see that there is an Infinite Goodness that turns everything to the work of salvation sooner or later. Who would have thought that any good could have come out of war and drink? And yet their profits are brought today to the feet of salvation to do its blessed work. (*She is affected to tears*)

JENNY (*Running to* MRS BAINES *and throwing her arms round her*) Oh dear! how blessed, how glorious it all is!

CUSINS (*In a convulsion of irony*) Let us seize this unspeakable moment. Let us march to the great meeting at once. Excuse me just an instant. (*He rushes into the shelter.* JENNY *takes her tambourine from the drum head*)

MRS BAINES Mr Undershaft: have you ever seen a thousand people fall on their knees with one impulse and pray? Come with us to the meeting. Barbara shall tell them that the Army is saved, and saved through you.

CUSINS (*Returning impetuously from the shelter with a flag and a trombone, and coming between* MRS BAINES *and* UNDERSHAFT) You will carry the flag down the first street, Mrs Baines. (*He gives her the flag*) Mr Undershaft is a gifted trombonist: he shall intone an Olympian diapason[17] to the West Ham Salvation March. (*Aside to* UNDERSHAFT, *as he forces the trombone on him*) Blow, Machiavelli, blow.
UNDERSHAFT (*Aside to him, as he takes the trombone*) The trumpet in Zion![18] (CUSINS *rushes to the drum, which he takes up and puts on.* UNDERSHAFT *continues, aloud*) I will do my best. I could vamp a bass[19] if I knew the tune.
CUSINS It is a wedding chorus from one of Donizetti's operas; but we have converted it.[20] We convert everything to good here, including Bodger. You remember the chorus. "For thee immense rejoicing—*immenso giubilo—immenso giubilo.*" (*With drum obbligato*) Rum tum ti tum tum, tum tum ti ta—
BARBARA Dolly: you are breaking my heart.
CUSINS What is a broken heart more or less here? Dionysos Undershaft has descended. I am possessed.
MRS BAINES Come, Barbara: I must have my dear Major to carry the flag with me.
JENNY Yes, yes, Major darling.

(CUSINS *snatches the tambourine out of* JENNY'S *hand and mutely offers it to* BARBARA)

BARBARA (*Coming forward a little as she puts the offer behind her with a shudder, whilst* CUSINS *recklessly tosses the tambourine back to* JENNY *and goes to the gate*) I can't come.
JENNY Not come!
MRS BAINES (*With tears in her eyes*) Barbara: do you think I am wrong to take the money?
BARBARA (*Impulsively going to her and kissing her*) No, no: God help you, dear, you must: you are saving the Army. Go; and may you have a great meeting!
JENNY But arn't you coming?

[17] The interval or consonance of the octave in Greek music.
[18] *Book of Joel*, 2:01 and 2:15. Theodore H. Gaster, in *Thespis* (New York: Doubleday, 1961), pp. 71–75, interprets *The Book of Joel* as symbolizing the seasonal pattern of death and rebirth; this relates to the Dionysian festivals, which also symbolize this pattern.
[19] Play by ear.
[20] The Salvation Army "converted" the Wedding Chorus from Donizetti's *Lucia di Lammermoor* to "I Am a Soldier, Glory to God."

BARBARA   No. (*She begins taking off the silver S brooch from her collar*)
MRS BAINES   Barbara: what are you doing?
JENNY   Why are you taking your badge off? You can't be going to leave us, Major.
BARBARA (*Quietly*)   Father: come here.
UNDERSHAFT (*Coming to her*)   My dear! (*Seeing that she is going to pin the badge on his collar, he retreats to the penthouse in some alarm*)
BARBARA (*Following him*)   Don't be frightened. (*She pins the badge on and steps back towards the table, shewing him to the others*) There! It's not much for £5000, is it?
MRS BAINES   Barbara: if you won't come and pray with us, promise me you will pray for us.
BARBARA   I can't pray now. Perhaps I shall never pray again.
MRS BAINES   Barbara!
JENNY   Major!
BARBARA (*Almost delirious*)   I can't bear any more. Quick march!
CUSINS (*Calling to the procession in the street outside*)   Off we go. Play up, there! Immenso giubilo. (*He gives the time with his drum; and the band strikes up the march, which rapidly becomes more distant as the procession moves briskly away*)
MRS BAINES   I must go, dear. You're overworked: you will be all right tomorrow. We'll never lose you. Now Jenny: step out with the old flag. Blood and Fire! (*She marches out through the gate with her flag*)
JENNY   Glory Hallelujah! (*Flourishing her tambourine and marching*)
UNDERSHAFT (*To* CUSINS, *as he marches out past him easing the slide of his trombone*)   "My ducats and my daughter"![21]
CUSINS (*Following him out*)   Money and gunpowder!
BARBARA   Drunkenness and Murder! My God: why hast thou forsaken me?[22]

(*She sinks on the form with her face buried in her hands. The march passes away into silence.* BILL WALKER *steals across to her*)

BILL (*Taunting*)   Wot prawce selvytion nah?
SHIRLEY   Don't you hit her when she's down.
BILL   She 'itt me wen aw wiz dahn. Waw shouldn't Aw git a bit o' me aown beck?
BARBARA (*Raising her head*)   I didn't take your money, Bill. (*She crosses the yard to the gate and turns her back on the two men to hide her face from them*)

[21] *The Merchant of Venice*, II, viii, 17.
[22] The last words of Christ on the cross, *Matthew* 27:46 and *Mark* 15:34. Also the beginning of Psalm 22.

BILL (*Sneering after her*) Naow, it warn't enaff for you (*Turning to the drum, he misses the money*) 'Ellow! If you ain't took it sammun else 'ez. Were's it gorn? Bly me if Jenny 'Ill didn't tike it arter all!
RUMMY (*Screaming at him from the loft*) You lie, you dirty blackguard! Snobby Price pinched it off the drum when he took up his cap. I was up here all the time an see 'im do it.
BILL Wot! Stowl maw manney! Waw didn't you call thief on him, you silly aold macker you?
RUMMY To serve you aht for 'ittin me acrost the face. It's cost y'pahnd, that 'az. (*Raising a pæan of squalid triumph*) I done you. I'm even with you. I've 'ad it aht o'y—(BILL *snatches up* SHIRLEY's *mug and hurls it at her. She slams the loft door and vanishes. The mug smashes against the door and falls in fragments*)
BILL (*Beginning to chuckle*) Tell us, aol menn, wot o'clock this mawnin' was it wen 'im as they call Snobby Prawce was sived?
BARBARA (*Turning to him more composedly, and with unspoiled sweetness*) About half past twelve, Bill. And he pinched your pound at a quarter to two. I know. Well, you can't afford to lose it. I'll send it to you.
BILL (*His voice and accent suddenly improving*) Not if Aw wiz to stawve for it. Aw ain't to be bought.
SHIRLEY Ain't you? You'd sell yourself to the devil for a pint o' beer; only there ain't no devil to make the offer.
BILL (*Unshamed*) Sao Aw would, mite, and often 'ev, cheerful. But she cawn't baw me. (*Approaching* BARBARA) You wanted maw saoul, did you? Well, you ain't got it.
BARBARA I nearly got it, Bill. But we've sold it back to you for ten thousand pounds.
SHIRLEY And dear at the money!
BARBARA No, Peter: it was worth more than money.
BILL (*Salvationproof*) It's nao good: you cawn't get rahnd me nah. Aw down't b'lieve in it; and Aw've seen tod'y that Aw was rawt. (*Going*) Sao long, aol soupkitchener! Ta, ta, Mijor Earl's Grendorter! (*Turning at the gate*) Wot prawce selvytion nah? Snobby Prawce! Ha! ha!
BARBARA (*Offering her hand*) Goodbye, Bill.
BILL (*Taken aback, half plucks his cap off; then shoves it on again defiantly*) Git aht. (BARBARA *drops her hand, discouraged. He has a twinge of remorse*) But thet's aw rawt, you knaow. Nathink pasn'l. Naow mellice. Sao long, Judy. (*He goes*)
BARBARA No malice. So long, Bill.
SHIRLEY (*Shaking his head*) You make too much of him, Miss, in your innocence.

BARBARA (*Going to him*) Peter: I'm like you now. Cleaned out, and lost my job.
SHIRLEY You've youth and hope. That's two better than me.
BARBARA I'll get you a job, Peter. That's hope for you: the youth will have to be enough for me. (*She counts her money*) I have just enough left for two teas at Lockharts,[23] a Rowton doss[24] for you, and my tram and bus home. (*He frowns and rises with offended pride. She takes his arm*) Don't be proud, Peter: it's sharing between friends. And promise me you'll talk to me and not let me cry. (*She draws him towards the gate*)
SHIRLEY Well, I'm not accustomed to talk to the like of you—
BARBARA (*Urgently*) Yes, yes: you must talk to me. Tell me about Tom Paine's books and Bradlaugh's lectures.[25] Come along.
SHIRLEY Ah, if you would only read Tom Paine in the proper spirit, Miss!
(*They go out through the gate together*)

End of Act II

Act Three

Next day after lunch LADY BRITOMART *is writing in the library in Wilton Crescent.* SARAH *is reading in the armchair near the window.* BARBARA, *in ordinary fashionable dress, pale and brooding, is on the settee.* CHARLES LOMAX *enters. He starts on seeing* BARBARA *fashionably attired and in low spirits.*

LOMAX You've left off your uniform!

BARBARA *says nothing; but an expression of pain passes over her face*)

LADY BRITOMART (*Warning him in low tones to be careful*) Charles!
LOMAX (*Much concerned, coming behind the settee and bending sympa-*

---

[23] London tearoom.

[24] A night's lodging at one of Rowton's cheap flophouses ("doss" is Cockney slang for "sleep").

[25] Charles Bradlaugh (1834–1891) was, like Thomas Paine, a celebrated freethinker.

thetically over BARBARA) I'm awfully sorry, Barbara. You know I helped you all I could with the concertina and so forth. (*Momentously*) Still, I have never shut my eyes to the fact that there is a certain amount of tosh about the Salvation Army. Now the claims of the Church of England—

LADY BRITOMART That's enough, Charles. Speak of something suited to your mental capacity.

LOMAX But surely the Church of England is suited to all our capacities.

BARBARA (*Pressing his hand*) Thank you for your sympathy, Cholly. Now go and spoon with Sarah.

LOMAX (*Dragging a chair from the writing table and seating himself affectionately by* SARAH's *side*) How is my ownest today?

SARAH I wish you wouldn't tell Cholly to do things, Barbara. He always comes straight and does them. Cholly: we're going to the works this afternoon.

LOMAX What works?

SARAH The cannon works.

LOMAX What? Your governor's shop!

SARAH Yes.

LOMAX Oh I say!

(CUSINS *enters in poor condition. He also starts visibly when he sees* BARBARA *without her uniform*)

BARBARA I expected you this morning, Dolly. Didn't you guess that?

CUSINS (*Sitting down beside her*) I'm sorry. I have only just breakfasted.

SARAH But we've just finished lunch.

BARBARA Have you had one of your bad nights?

CUSINS No: I had rather a good night: in fact, one of the most remarkable nights I have ever passed.

BARBARA The meeting?

CUSINS No: after the meeting.

LADY BRITOMART You should have gone to bed after the meeting. What were you doing?

CUSINS Drinking.

LADY BRITOMART Adolphus!
SARAH Dolly!
BARBARA Dolly!
LOMAX Oh I say!

LADY BRITOMART What were you drinking, may I ask?

CUSINS A most devilish kind of Spanish burgundy, warranted free from added alcohol: a Temperance burgundy in fact. Its richness in natural alcohol made any addition superfluous.

61 · *Major Barbara* [ACT THREE]

BARBARA   Are you joking, Dolly?
CUSINS   (*Patiently*) No. I have been making a night of it with the nominal head of this household: that is all.
LADY BRITOMART   Andrew made you drunk!
CUSINS   No: he only provided the wine. I think it was Dionysos who made me drunk. (*To* BARBARA) I told you I was possessed.
LADY BRITOMART   You're not sober yet. Go home to bed at once.
CUSINS   I have never before ventured to reproach you, Lady Brit; but how could you marry the Prince of Darkness?
LADY BRITOMART   It was much more excusable to marry him than to get drunk with him. That is a new accomplishment of Andrew's, by the way. He usen't to drink.
CUSINS   He doesn't now. He only sat there and completed the wreck of my moral basis, the rout of my convictions, the purchase of my soul. He cares for you, Barbara. That is what makes him so dangerous to me.
BARBARA   That has nothing to do with it, Dolly. There are larger loves and diviner dreams than the fireside ones. You know that, don't you?
CUSINS   Yes: that is our understanding. I know it. I hold to it. Unless he can win me on that holier ground he may amuse me for a while; but he can get no deeper hold, strong as he is.
BARBARA   Keep to that; and the end will be right. Now tell me what happened at the meeting?
CUSINS   It was an amazing meeting. Mrs Baines almost died of emotion. Jenny Hill simply gibbered with hysteria. The Prince of Darkness played his trombone like a madman: its brazen roarings were like the laughter of the damned. 117 conversions took place then and there. They prayed with the most touching sincerity and gratitude for Bodger, and for the anonymous donor of the £5000. Your father would not let his name be given.
LOMAX   That was rather fine of the old man, you know. Most chaps would have wanted the advertisement.
CUSINS   He said all the charitable institutions would be down on him like kites on a battle field if he gave his name.
LADY BRITOMART   That's Andrew all over. He never does a proper thing without giving an improper reason for it.
CUSINS   He convinced me that I have all my life been doing improper things for proper reasons.
LADY BRITOMART   Adolphus: now that Barbara has left the Salvation Army, you had better leave it too. I will not have you playing that drum in the streets.
CUSINS   Your orders are already obeyed, Lady Brit.
BARBARA   Dolly: were you ever really in earnest about it? Would you

have joined if you had never seen me?

CUSINS (*Disingenuously*) Well—er—well, possibly, as a collector of religions—

LOMAX (*Cunningly*) Not as a drummer, though, you know. You are a very clearheaded brainy chap, Dolly; and it must have been apparent to you that there is a certain amount of tosh about—

LADY BRITOMART Charles: if you must drivel, drivel like a grown-up man and not like a schoolboy.

LOMAX (*Out of countenance*) Well, drivel is drivel, don't you know, whatever a man's age.

LADY BRITOMART In good society in England, Charles, men drivel at all ages by repeating silly formulas with an air of wisdom. Schoolboys make their own formulas out of slang, like you. When they reach your age, and get political private secretaryships and things of that sort, they drop slang and get their formulas out of *The Spectator* or *The Times*. You had better confine yourself to *The Times*. You will find that there is a certain amount of tosh about *The Times*; but at least its language is reputable.

LOMAX (*Overwhelmed*) You are so awfully strong-minded, Lady Brit—

LADY BRITOMART Rubbish! (MORRISON *comes in*) What is it?

MORRISON If you please, my lady, Mr Undershaft has just drove up to the door.

LADY BRITOMART Well, let him in. (MORRISON *hesitates*) What's the matter with you?

MORRISON Shall I announce him, my lady; or is he at home here, so to speak, my lady?

LADY BRITOMART Announce him.

MORRISON Thank you, my lady. You won't mind my asking, I hope. The occasion is in a manner of speaking new to me.

LADY BRITOMART Quite right. Go and let him in.

MORRISON Thank you, my lady. (*He withdraws*)

LADY BRITOMART Children: go and get ready. (SARAH *and* BARBARA *go upstairs for their out-of-door wraps*) Charles: go and tell Stephen to come down here in five minutes: you will find him in the drawing room. (CHARLES *goes*) Adolphus: tell them to send round the carriage in about fifteen minutes. (ADOLPHUS *goes*)

MORRISON (*At the door*) Mr Undershaft.

(UNDERSHAFT *comes in*. MORRISON *goes out*)

UNDERSHAFT Alone! How fortunate!

LADY BRITOMART (*Rising*) Don't be sentimental, Andrew. Sit down. (*She sits on the settee: he sits beside her, on her left. She comes to the point before he has time to breathe*) Sarah must have £800 a year until Charles Lomax comes into his property. Barbara will need more, and need it permanently, because Adolphus hasn't any property.

UNDERSHAFT (*Resignedly*) Yes, my dear: I will see to it. Anything else? for yourself, for instance?

LADY BRITOMART   I want to talk to you about Stephen.

UNDERSHAFT (*Rather wearily*) Don't my dear. Stephen doesn't interest me.

LADY BRITOMART   He does interest me. He is our son.

UNDERSHAFT   Do you really think so? He has induced us to bring him into the world; but he chose his parents very incongruously, I think. I see nothing of myself in him, and less of you.

LADY BRITOMART   Andrew: Stephen is an excellent son, and a most steady, capable, highminded young man. You are simply trying to find an excuse for disinheriting him.

UNDERSHAFT   My dear Biddy: the Undershaft tradition disinherits him. It would be dishonest of me to leave the cannon foundry to my son.

LADY BRITOMART   It would be most unnatural and improper of you to leave it to anyone else, Andrew. Do you suppose this wicked and immoral tradition can be kept up for ever? Do you pretend that Stephen could not carry on the foundry just as well as all the other sons of the big business houses?

UNDERSHAFT   Yes: he could learn the office routine without understanding the business, like all the other sons; and the firm would go on by its own momentum until the real Undershaft—probably an Italian or a German—would invent a new method and cut him out.

LADY BRITOMART   There is nothing that any Italian or German could do that Stephen could not do. And Stephen at least has breeding.

UNDERSHAFT   The son of a foundling! Nonsense!

LADY BRITOMART   My son, Andrew! And even you may have good blood in your veins for all you know.

UNDERSHAFT   True. Probably I have. That is another argument in favor of a foundling.

LADY BRITOMART   Andrew: don't be aggravating. And don't be wicked. At present you are both.

UNDERSHAFT   This conversation is part of the Undershaft tradition, Biddy. Every Undershaft's wife has treated him to it ever since the house was founded. It is mere waste of breath. If the tradition be ever broken it will be for an abler man than Stephen.

LADY BRITOMART (*Pouting*)   Then go away.

UNDERSHAFT (*Deprecatory*)   Go away!

LADY BRITOMART   Yes: go away. If you will do nothing for Stephen, you are not wanted here. Go to your foundling, whoever he is; and look after him.

UNDERSHAFT   The fact is, Biddy—

LADY BRITOMART   Don't call me Biddy. I don't call you Andy.

UNDERSHAFT   I will not call my wife Britomart: it is not good sense. Seriously, my love, the Undershaft tradition has landed me in a difficulty. I am getting on in years; and my partner Lazarus has at last made a stand and insisted that the succession must be settled one way or the other; and of course he is quite right. You see, I haven't found a fit successor yet.

LADY BRITOMART   (*Obstinately*)   There is Stephen.

UNDERSHAFT   That's just it: all the foundlings I can find are exactly like Stephen.

LADY BRITOMART   Andrew!!

UNDERSHAFT   I want a man with no relations and no schooling: that is, a man who would be out of the running altogether if he were not a strong man. And I can't find him. Every blessed foundling nowadays is snapped up in his infancy by Barnardo homes[26] or School Board officers, or Boards of Guardians; and if he shews the least ability, he is fastened on by schoolmasters; trained to win scholarships like a racehorse; crammed with secondhand ideas; drilled and disciplined in docility and what they call good taste; and lamed for life so that he is fit for nothing but teaching. If you want to keep the foundry in the family, you had better find an eligible foundling and marry him to Barbara.

LADY BRITOMART   Ah! Barbara! Your pet! You would sacrifice Stephen to Barbara.

UNDERSHAFT   Cheerfully. And you, my dear, would boil Barbara to make soup for Stephen.

LADY BRITOMART   Andrew: this is not a question of our likings and dislikings: it is a question of duty. It is your duty to make Stephen your successor.

UNDERSHAFT   Just as much as it is your duty to submit to your husband. Come, Biddy! these tricks of the governing class are of no use with me. I am one of the governing class myself; and it is waste of time giving tracts to a missionary. I have the power in this matter; and I am not to be humbugged into using it for your purposes.

LADY BRITOMART   Andrew: you can talk my head off; but you can't change wrong into right. And your tie is all on one side. Put it straight.

---

[26] The philanthropist Thomas John Barnardo (1845–1905) founded the East End Juvenile Mission for Destitute Children, which developed into a large organization for homeless children.

Major Barbara [ACT THREE]

UNDERSHAFT (*Disconcerted*) It won't stay unless it's pinned—(*He fumbles at it with childish grimaces*)

(STEPHEN *comes in*)

STEPHEN (*At the door*) I beg your pardon. (*About to retire*)

LADY BRITOMART No: come in, Stephen. (STEPHEN *comes forward to his mother's writing table*)

UNDERSHAFT (*Not very cordially*) Good afternoon.

STEPHEN (*Coldly*) Good afternoon.

UNDERSHAFT (*To* LADY BRITOMART) He knows all about the tradition, I suppose?

LADY BRITOMART Yes. (*To* STEPHEN) It is what I told you last night, Stephen.

UNDERSHAFT (*Sulkily*) I understand you want to come into the cannon business.

STEPHEN I go into trade! Certainly not.

UNDERSHAFT (*Opening his eyes, greatly eased in mind and manner*) Oh! in that case—

LADY BRITOMART Cannons are not trade, Stephen. They are enterprise.

STEPHEN I have no intention of becoming a man of business in any sense. I have no capacity for business and no taste for it. I intend to devote myself to politics.

UNDERSHAFT (*Rising*) My dear boy: this is an immense relief to me. And I trust it may prove an equally good thing for the country. I was afraid you would consider yourself disparaged and slighted. (*He moves towards* STEPHEN *as if to shake hands with him*)

LADY BRITOMART (*Rising and interposing*) Stephen: I cannot allow you to throw away an enormous property like this.

STEPHEN (*Stiffly*) Mother: there must be an end of treating me as a child, if you please. (LADY BRITOMART *recoils, deeply wounded by his tone*) Until last night I did not take your attitude seriously, because I did not think you meant it seriously. But I find now that you left me in the dark as to matters which you should have explained to me years ago. I am extremely hurt and offended. Any further discussion of my intentions had better take place with my father, as between one man and another.

LADY BRITOMART Stephen! (*She sits down again, her eyes filling with tears*)

UNDERSHAFT (*With grave compassion*) You see, my dear, it is only the big men who can be treated as children.

STEPHEN I am sorry, mother, that you have forced me—

UNDERSHAFT (*Stopping him*) Yes, yes, yes, yes: that's all right, Stephen.

She won't interfere with you any more: your independence is achieved: you have won your latchkey. Don't rub it in; and above all, don't apologize. (*He resumes his seat*) Now what about your future, as between one man and another—I beg your pardon, Biddy: as between two men and a woman.

LADY BRITOMART (*Who has pulled herself together strongly*) I quite understand, Stephen. By all means go your own way if you feel strong enough. (STEPHEN *sits down magisterially in the chair at the writing table with an air of affirming his majority*)

UNDERSHAFT It is settled that you do not ask for the succession to the cannon business.

STEPHEN I hope it is settled that I repudiate the cannon business.

UNDERSHAFT Come, come! don't be so devilishly sulky: it's boyish. Freedom should be generous. Besides, I owe you a fair start in life in exchange for disinheriting you. You can't become prime minister all at once. Haven't you a turn for something? What about literature, art, and so forth?

STEPHEN I have nothing of the artist about me, either in faculty or character, thank Heaven!

UNDERSHAFT A philosopher, perhaps? Eh?

STEPHEN I make no such ridiculous pretension.

UNDERSHAFT Just so. Well, there is the army, the navy, the Church, the Bar. The Bar requires some ability. What about the Bar?

STEPHEN I have not studied law. And I am afraid I have not the necessary push—I believe that is the name barristers give to their vulgarity—for success in pleading.

UNDERSHAFT Rather a difficult case, Stephen. Hardly anything left but the stage, is there? (STEPHEN *makes an impatient movement*) Well, come! is there anything you know or care for?

STEPHEN (*Rising and looking at him steadily*) I know the difference between right and wrong.

UNDERSHAFT (*Hugely tickled*) You don't say so! What! no capacity for business, no knowledge of law, no sympathy with art, no pretension to philosophy; only a simple knowledge of the secret that has puzzled all the philosophers, baffled all the lawyers, muddled all the men of business, and ruined most of the artists: the secret of right and wrong. Why, man, you're a genius, a master of masters, a god! At twenty-four, too!

STEPHEN (*Keeping his temper with difficulty*) You are pleased to be facetious. I pretend to nothing more than any honorable English gentleman claims as his birthright. (*He sits down angrily*)

UNDERSHAFT Oh, that's everybody's birthright. Look at poor little Jenny

Hill, the Salvation lassie! she would think you were laughing at her if you asked her to stand up in the street and teach grammar or geography or mathematics or even drawing room dancing; but it never occurs to her to doubt that she can teach morals and religion. You are all alike, you respectable people. You can't tell me the bursting strain of a ten-inch gun, which is a very simple matter; but you all think you can tell me the bursting strain of a man under temptation. You daren't handle high explosives; but you're all ready to handle honesty and truth and justice and the whole duty of man, and kill one another at that game. What a country! What a world!

LADY BRITOMART (*Uneasily*) What do you think he had better do, Andrew?

UNDERSHAFT Oh, just what he wants to do. He knows nothing and he thinks he knows everything. That points clearly to a political career. Get him a private secretaryship to someone who can get him an Under Secretaryship; and then leave him alone. He will find his natural and proper place in the end on the Treasury Bench.

STEPHEN (*Springing up again*) I am sorry, sir, that you force me to forget the respect due to you as my father. I am an Englishman and I will not hear the Government of my country insulted. (*He thrusts his hands in his pockets, and walks angrily across to the window*)

UNDERSHAFT (*With a touch of brutality*) The government of your country! I am the government of your country: I, and Lazarus. Do you suppose that you and half a dozen amateurs like you, sitting in a row in that foolish gabble shop, can govern Undershaft and Lazarus? No, my friend: you will do what pays us. You will make war when it suits us, and keep peace when it doesn't. You will find out that trade requires certain measures when we have decided on those measures. When I want anything to keep my dividends up, you will discover that my want is a national need. When other people want something to keep my dividends down, you will call out the police and military. And in return you shall have the support and applause of my newspapers, and the delight of imagining that you are a great statesman. Government of your country! Be off with you, my boy, and play with your caucuses and leading articles and historic parties and great leaders and burning questions and the rest of your toys. I am going back to my counting house to pay the piper and call the tune.

STEPHEN (*Actually smiling, and putting his hand on his father's shoulder with indulgent patronage*) Really, my dear father, it is impossible to be angry with you. You don't know how absurd all this sounds to me. You are very properly proud of having been industrious enough to make money; and it is greatly to your credit that you have made so much of it. But it has kept you in circles where you are valued for your money and deferred to for it, instead of in the doubtless very old-fashioned and behind-the-times public school and university where I formed my habits of mind. It is natural for you think that money governs England; but you must allow me to think I know better.

UNDERSHAFT And what does govern England, pray?

STEPHEN Character, father, character.

UNDERSHAFT Whose character? Yours or mine?

STEPHEN Neither yours nor mine, father, but the best elements in the English national character.

UNDERSHAFT Stephen: I've found your profession for you. You're a born journalist. I'll start you with a hightoned weekly review. There!

(*Before* STEPHEN *can reply* SARAH, BARBARA, LOMAX, *and* CUSINS *come in ready for walking.* BARBARA *crosses the room to the window and looks out.* CUSINS *drifts amiably to the armchair.* LOMAX *remains near the door, whilst* SARAH *comes to her mother.*
STEPHEN *goes to the smaller writing table and busies himself with his letters*)

SARAH Go and get ready, mamma: the carriage is waiting. (LADY BRITOMART *leaves the room*)

UNDERSHAFT (*To* SARAH) Good day, my dear. Good afternoon, Mr Lomax.

LOMAX (*Vaguely*) Ahdedoo.

UNDERSHAFT (*To* CUSINS) Quite well after last night, Euripides, eh?

CUSINS As well as can be expected.

UNDERSHAFT That's right. (*To* BARBARA) So you are coming to see my death and devastation factory, Barbara?

BARBARA (*At the window*) You came yesterday to see my salvation factory. I promised you a return visit.

LOMAX (*Coming forward between* SARAH *and* UNDERSHAFT) You'll find it awfully interesting. I've been through the Woolwich Arsenal; and it gives you a ripping feeling of security, you know, to think of the lot of beggars we could kill if it came to fighting. (*To* UNDERSHAFT, *with sudden solemnity*) Still, it must be rather an awful reflection for you, from the religious point of view as it were. You're getting on, you know, and all that.

SARAH You don't mind Cholly's imbecility, papa, do you?

LOMAX (*Much taken aback*) Oh I say!

UNDERSHAFT Mr Lomax looks at the matter in a very proper spirit, my dear.

LOMAX Just so. That's all I meant, I assure you.

SARAH Are you coming, Stephen?

STEPHEN Well, I am rather busy—er— (*Magnanimously*) Oh well, yes: I'll come. That is, if there is room for me.
UNDERSHAFT I can take two with me in a little motor I am experimenting with for field use. You won't mind its being rather unfashionable. It's not painted yet; but it's bullet proof.
LOMAX (*Appalled at the prospect of confronting Wilton Crescent in an unpainted motor*) Oh I say!
SARAH The carriage for me, thank you. Barbara doesn't mind what she's seen in.
LOMAX I say, Dolly old chap: do you really mind the car being a guy?[27] Because of course if you do I'll go in it. Still—
CUSINS I prefer it.
LOMAX Thanks awfully, old man. Come, my ownest. (*He hurries out to secure his seat in the carriage.* SARAH *follows him*)
CUSINS (*Moodily walking across to* LADY BRITOMART'S *writing table*) Why are we two coming to this Works Department of Hell? that is what I ask myself.
BARBARA I have always thought of it as a sort of pit where lost creatures with blackened faces stirred up smoky fires and were driven and tormented by my father. Is it like that, dad?
UNDERSHAFT (*Scandalized*) My dear! It is a spotlessly clean and beautiful hillside town.
CUSINS With a Methodist chapel? Oh do say there's a Methodist chapel.
UNDERSHAFT There are two: a Primitive one and a sophisticated one. There is even an Ethical Society; but it is not much patronized, as my men are all strongly religious. In the High Explosives Sheds they object to the presence of Agnostics as unsafe.
CUSINS And yet they don't object to you!
BARBARA Do they obey all your orders?
UNDERSHAFT I never give them any orders. When I speak to one of them it is "Well, Jones, is the baby doing well? and has Mrs Jones made a good recovery?" "Nicely, thank you, sir." And that's all.
CUSINS But Jones has to be kept in order. How do you maintain discipline among your men?
UNDERSHAFT I don't. They do. You see, the one thing Jones won't stand is any rebellion from the man under him, or any assertion of social equality between the wife of the man with 4 shillings a week less than himself, and Mrs Jones! Of course they all rebel against me, theoretically. Practically, every man of them keeps the man just below him in his place. I never meddle with them. I never bully them. I don't

[27] Ridiculous-looking, laughable.

even bully Lazarus. I say that certain things are to be done; but I don't order anybody to do them. I don't say, mind you, that there is no ordering about and snubbing and even bullying. The men snub the boys and order them about; the carmen snub the sweepers; the artisans snub the unskilled laborers; the foremen drive and bully both the laborers and artisans; the assistant engineers find fault with the foremen; the chief engineers drop on the assistants; the departmental managers worry the chiefs; and the clerks have tall hats and hymnbooks and keep up the social tone by refusing to associate on equal terms with anybody. The result is a colossal profit, which comes to me.

CUSINS (*Revolted*) You really are a—well, what I was saying yesterday.

BARBARA What was he saying yesterday?

UNDERSHAFT Never mind, my dear. He thinks I have made you unhappy. Have I?

BARBARA Do you think I can be happy in this vulgar silly dress? I! who have worn the uniform. Do you understand what you have done to me? Yesterday I had a man's soul in my hand. I set him in the way of life with his face to salvation. But when we took your money he turned back to drunkenness and derision. (*With intense conviction*) I will never forgive you that. If I had a child, and you destroyed its body with your explosives—if you murdered Dolly with your horrible guns—I could forgive you if my forgiveness would open the gates of heaven to you. But to take a human soul from me, and turn it into the soul of a wolf! that is worse than any murder.

UNDERSHAFT Does my daughter despair so easily? Can you strike a man to the heart and leave no mark on him?

BARBARA (*Her face lighting up*) Oh, you are right: he can never be lost now: where was my faith?

CUSINS Oh, clever clever devil!

BARBARA You may be a devil; but God speaks through you sometimes. (*She takes her father's hands and kisses them*) You have given me back my happiness: I feel it deep down now, though my spirit is troubled.

UNDERSHAFT You have learnt something. That always feels at first as if you had lost something.

BARBARA Well, take me to the factory of death; and let me learn something more. There must be some truth or other behind all this frightful irony. Come, Dolly. (*She goes out*)

CUSINS My guardian angel! (*To* UNDERSHAFT) Avaunt! (*He follows* BARBARA)

STEPHEN (*Quietly, at the writing table*) You must not mind Cusins, father. He is a very amiable good fellow; but he is a Greek scholar and naturally a little eccentric.

UNDERSHAFT Ah, quite so. Thank you, Stephen. Thank you. (*He goes out*)

>   (STEPHEN *smiles patronizingly; buttons his coat responsibly; and crosses the room to the door.* LADY BRITOMART, *dressed for out-of-doors, opens it before he reaches it. She looks round for the others; looks at* STEPHEN; *and turns to go without a word*)

STEPHEN (*Embarrassed*) Mother—
LADY BRITOMART Don't be apologetic, Stephen. And don't forget that you have outgrown your mother. (*She goes out*)

>   (*Perivale St Andrews lies between two Middlesex hills, half climbing the northern one. It is an almost smokeless town of white walls, roofs of narrow green slates or red tiles, tall trees, domes, campaniles, and slender chimney shafts, beautifully situated and beautiful in itself. The best view of it is obtained from the crest of a slope about half a mile to the east, where the high explosives are dealt with. The foundry lies hidden in the depths between, the tops of its chimneys sprouting like huge skittles into the middle distance. Across the crest runs an emplacement of concrete, with a firestep, and a parapet which suggests a fortification, because there is a huge cannon of the obsolete Woolwich Infant pattern peering across it at the town. The cannon is mounted on an experimental gun carriage: possibly the original model of the Undershaft disappearing rampart gun alluded to by Stephen. The firestep, being a convenient place to sit, is furnished here and there with straw disc cushions; and at one place there is the additional luxury of a fur rug.*
>   BARBARA *is standing on the firestep, looking over the parapet towards the town. On her right is the cannon; on her left the end of a shed raised on piles, with a ladder of three or four steps up to the door, which opens outwards and has a little wooden landing at the threshold, with a fire bucket in the corner of the landing. Several dummy soldiers more or less mutilated, with straw protruding from their gashes, have been shoved out of the way under the landing. A few others are nearly upright against the shed; and one has fallen forward and lies, like a grotesque corpse, on the emplacement. The parapet stops short of the shed, leaving a gap which is the beginning of the path down the hill through the foundry to the town. The rug is on the firestep near this gap. Down on the emplacement behind the cannon is a trolley carrying a huge conical bombshell with a red band painted on it. Further to the right is the door of an office, which, like the sheds, is of the lightest possible construction.*

(CUSINS *arrives by the path from the town*)

BARBARA Well?

CUSINS Not a ray of hope. Everything perfect! wonderful! real! It only needs a cathedral to be a heavenly city instead of a hellish one.

BARBARA Have you found out whether they have done anything for old Peter Shirley?

CUSINS They have found him a job as gatekeeper and timekeeper. He's frightfully miserable. He calls the timekeeping brainwork, and says he isn't used to it; and his gate lodge is so splendid that he's ashamed to use the rooms, and skulks in the scullery.

BARBARA Poor Peter!

(STEPHEN *arrives from the town. He carries a field-glass*)

STEPHEN (*Enthusiastically*) Have you two seen the place? Why did you leave us?

CUSINS I wanted to see everything I was not intended to see; and Barbara wanted to make the men talk.

STEPHEN Have you found anything discreditable?

CUSINS No. They call him Dandy Andy and are proud of his being a cunning old rascal; but it's all horribly, frightfully, immorally, unanswerably perfect.

(SARAH *arrives*)

SARAH Heavens! what a place! (*She crosses to the trolley*) Did you see the nursing home!? (*She sits down on the shell*)

STEPHEN Did you see the libraries and schools!?

SARAH Did you see the ball room and the banqueting chamber in the Town Hall!?

STEPHEN Have you gone into the insurance fund, the pension fund, the building society, the various applications of cooperation!?

(UNDERSHAFT *comes from the office, with a sheaf of telegrams in his hand*)

UNDERSHAFT Well, have you seen everything? I'm sorry I was called away. (*Indicating the telegrams*) Good news from Manchuria.[28]

STEPHEN Another Japanese victory?

UNDERSHAFT Oh, I don't know. Which side wins does not concern us here. No: the good news is that the aerial battleship is a tremendous success. At the first trial it has wiped out a fort with three hundred soldiers in it.

[28] A reference to the Russo-Japanese War.

CUSINS (*From the platform*) Dummy soldiers?

UNDERSHAFT (*Striding across to* STEPHEN *and kicking the prostrate dummy brutally out of his way*) No: the real thing.

> (CUSINS *and* BARBARA *exchange glances. Then* CUSINS *sits on the step and buries his face in his hands.* BARBARA *gravely lays her hand on his shoulder. He looks up at her in whimsical desperation*)

UNDERSHAFT Well, Stephen, what do you think of the place?

STEPHEN Oh, magnificent. A perfect triumph of modern industry. Frankly, my dear father, I have been a fool: I had no idea of what it all meant: of the wonderful forethought, the power of organization, the administrative capacity, the financial genius, the colossal capital it represents. I have been repeating to myself as I came through your streets "Peace hath her victories no less renowned than War." I have only one misgiving about it all.

UNDERSHAFT Out with it.

STEPHEN Well, I cannot help thinking that all this provision for every want of your workmen may sap their independence and weaken their sense of responsibility. And greatly as we enjoyed our tea at that splendid restaurant—how they gave us all that luxury and cake and jam and cream for threepence I really cannot imagine!—still you must remember that restaurants break up home life. Look at the continent, for instance! Are you sure so much pampering is really good for the men's characters?

UNDERSHAFT Well you see, my dear boy, when you are organizing civilization you have to make up your mind whether trouble and anxiety are good things or not. If you decide that they are, then, I take it, you simply don't organize civilization; and there you are, with trouble and anxiety enough to make us all angels! But if you decide the other way, you may as well go through with it. However, Stephen, our characters are safe here. A sufficient dose of anxiety is always provided by the fact that we may be blown to smithereens at any moment.

SARAH By the way, papa, where do you make the explosives?

UNDERSHAFT In separate little sheds, like that one. When one of them blows up, it costs very little; and only the people quite close to it are killed.

> (STEPHEN, *who is quite close to it, looks at it rather scaredly, and moves away quickly to the cannon. At the same moment the door of the shed is thrown abruptly open; and a foreman in overalls and list slippers comes out on the little landing and holds the door for* LOMAX, *who appears in the doorway*)

LOMAX (*With studied coolness*) My good fellow: you needn't get into a state of nerves. Nothing's going to happen to you; and I suppose it wouldn't be the end of the world if anything did. A little bit of British pluck is what you want, old chap. (*He descends and strolls across to* SARAH)

UNDERSHAFT (*To the foreman*) Anything wrong, Bilton?

BILTON (*With ironic calm*) Gentleman walked into the high explosives shed and lit a cigaret, sir: that's all.

UNDERSHAFT Ah, quite so. (*Going over to* LOMAX) Do you happen to remember what you did with the match?

LOMAX Oh come! I'm not a fool. I took jolly good care to blow it out before I chucked it away.

BILTON The top of it was red hot inside, sir.

LOMAX Well, suppose it was! I didn't chuck it into any of your messes.

UNDERSHAFT Think no more of it, Mr Lomax. By the way, would you mind lending me your matches?

LOMAX (*Offering his box*) Certainly.

UNDERSHAFT Thanks. (*He pockets the matches*)

LOMAX (*Lecturing to the company generally*) You know, these high explosives don't go off like gunpowder, except when they're in a gun. Then they're spread loose, you can put a match to them without the least risk: they just burn quietly like a bit of paper. (*Warming to the scientific interest of the subject*) Did you know that, Undershaft? Have you ever tried?

UNDERSHAFT Not on a large scale, Mr Lomax. Bilton will give you a sample of gun cotton when you are leaving if you ask him. You can experiment with it at home. (BILTON *looks puzzled*)

SARAH Bilton will do nothing of the sort, papa. I suppose it's your business to blow up the Russians and Japs; but you might really stop short of blowing up poor Cholly. (BILTON *gives it up and retires into the shed*)

LOMAX My ownest, there is no danger. (*He sits beside her on the shell*)

(LADY BRITOMART *arrives from the town with a bouquet*)

LADY BRITOMART (*Impetuously*) Andrew: you shouldn't have let me see this place.

UNDERSHAFT Why, my dear?

LADY BRITOMART Never mind why: you shouldn't have: that's all. To think of all that (*Indicating the town*) being yours! and that you have kept it to yourself all these years!

UNDERSHAFT It does not belong to me. I belong to it. It is the Undershaft inheritance.

LADY BRITOMART It is not. Your ridiculous cannons and that noisy banging foundry may be the Undershaft inheritance; but all that plate and linen, all that furniture and those houses and orchards and gardens belong to us. They belong to me: they are not a man's business. I won't give them up. You must be out of your senses to throw them all away; and if you persist in such folly, I will call in a doctor.

UNDERSHAFT (*Stooping to smell the bouquet*) Where did you get the flowers, my dear?

LADY BRITOMART Your men presented them to me in your William Morris Labor Church.

CUSINS Oh! It needed only that. A Labor Church! (*He mounts the firestep distractedly, and leans with his elbows on the parapet, turning his back to them*)

LADY BRITOMART Yes, with Morris's words in mosaic letters ten feet high round the dome. NO MAN IS GOOD ENOUGH TO BE ANOTHER MAN'S MASTER. The cynicism of it!

UNDERSHAFT It shocked the men at first, I am afraid. But now they take no more notice of it than of the ten commandments in church.

LADY BRITOMART Andrew: you are trying to put me off the subject of the inheritance by profane jokes. Well, you shan't. I don't ask it any longer for Stephen: he has inherited far too much of your perversity to be fit for it. But Barbara has rights as well as Stephen. Why should not Adolphus succeed to the inheritance? I could manage the town for him; and he can look after the cannons, if they are really necessary.

UNDERSHAFT I should ask nothing better if Adolphus were a foundling. He is exactly the sort of new blood that is wanted in English business. But he's not a foundling; and there's an end of it. (*He makes for the office door*)

CUSINS (*Turning to them*) Not quite. (*They all turn and stare at him*) I think—Mind! I am not committing myself in any way as to my future course—but I think the foundling difficulty can be got over. (*He jumps down to the emplacement*)

UNDERSHAFT (*Coming back to him*) What do you mean?

CUSINS Well, I have something to say which is in the nature of a confession.

SARAH
LADY BRITOMART
BARBARA
STEPHEN
} Confession!

LOMAX Oh I say!

CUSINS Yes, a confession. Listen, all. Until I met Barbara I thought myself in the main an honorable, truthful man, because I wanted the approval of my conscience more than I wanted anything else. But the moment I saw Barbara, I wanted her far more than the approval of my conscience.

LADY BRITOMART Adolphus!

CUSINS It is true. You accused me yourself, Lady Brit, of joining the Army to worship Barbara; and so I did. She bought my soul like a flower at a street corner; but she bought it for herself.

UNDERSHAFT What! Not for Dionysos or another?

CUSINS Dionysos and all the others are in herself. I adored what was divine in her, and was therefore a true worshipper. But I was romantic about her too. I thought she was a woman of the people, and that a marriage with a professor of Greek would be far beyond the wildest social ambitions of her rank.

LADY BRITOMART Adolphus!!

LOMAX Oh I say!!!

CUSINS When I learnt the horrible truth—

LADY BRITOMART What do you mean by the horrible truth, pray?

CUSINS That she was enormously rich; that her grandfather was an earl; that her father was the Prince of Darkness—

UNDERSHAFT Chut!

CUSINS —and that I was only an adventurer trying to catch a rich wife, then I stooped to deceive her about my birth.

BARBARA (*Rising*) Dolly!

LADY BRITOMART Your birth! Now Adolphus, don't dare to make up a wicked story for the sake of these wretched cannons. Remember: I have seen photographs of your parents; and the Agent General for South Western Australia knows them personally and has assured me that they are most respectable married people.

CUSINS So they are in Australia; but here they are outcasts. Their marriage is legal in Australia, but not in England. My mother is my father's deceased wife's sister; and in this island I am consequently a foundling. (*Sensation*)

BARBARA Silly! (*She climbs to the cannon, and leans, listening, in the angle it makes with the parapet*)

CUSINS Is the subterfuge good enough, Machiavelli?

UNDERSHAFT (*Thoughtfully*) Biddy: this may be a way out of the difficulty.

LADY BRITOMART Stuff! A man can't make cannons any the better for being his own cousin instead of his proper self. (*She sits down on the rug with a bounce that expresses her downright contempt for their casuistry*)

UNDERSHAFT (*To* CUSINS) You are an educated man. That is against the tradition.
CUSINS Once in ten thousand times it happens that the schoolboy is a born master of what they try to teach him. Greek has not destroyed my mind: it has nourished it. Besides, I did not learn it at an English public school.
UNDERSHAFT Hm! Well, I cannot afford to be too particular: you have cornered the foundling market. Let it pass. You are eligible, Eurpides: you are eligible.
BARBARA Dolly: yesterday morning, when Stephen told us all about the tradition, you became very silent; and you have been strange and excited ever since. Were you thinking of your birth then?
CUSINS When the finger of Destiny suddenly points at a man in the middle of his breakfast, it makes him thoughtful.
UNDERSHAFT Aha! You have had your eye on the business, my young friend, have you?
CUSINS Take care! There is an abyss of moral horror between me and your accursed aerial battleships.
UNDERSHAFT Never mind the abyss for the present. Let us settle the practical details and leave your final decision open. You know that you will have to change your name. Do you object to that?
CUSINS Would any man named Adolphus—any man called Dolly!—object to be called something else?
UNDERSHAFT Good. Now, as to money! I propose to treat you handsomely from the beginning. You shall start at a thousand a year.
CUSINS (*With sudden heat, his spectacles twinkling with mischief*) A thousand! You dare offer a miserable thousand to the son-in-law of a millionaire! No, by Heavens, Machiavelli! you shall not cheat me. You cannot do without me; and I can do without you. I must have two thousand five hundred a year for two years. At the end of that time, if I am a failure, I go. But if I am a success, and stay on, you must give me the other five thousand.
UNDERSHAFT What other five thousand?
CUSINS To make the two years up to five thousand a year. The two thousand five hundred is only half pay in case I should turn out a failure. The third year I must have ten percent on the profits.
UNDERSHAFT (*Taken aback*) Ten per cent! Why, man, do you know what my profits are?
CUSINS Enormous, I hope: otherwise I shall require twenty-five per cent.
UNDERSHAFT But, Mr Cusins, this is a serious matter of business. You are not bringing any capital into the concern.
CUSINS What! no capital! Is my mastery of Greek no capital? Is my

access to the subtlest thought, the loftiest poetry yet attained by humanity, no capital? My character! my intellect! my life! my career! what Barbara calls my soul! are these no capital? Say another word; and I double my salary.

UNDERSHAFT Be reasonable—

CUSINS *(Peremptorily)* Mr Undershaft: you have my terms. Take them or leave them.

UNDERSHAFT *(Recovering himself)* Very well. I note your terms; and I offer you half.

CUSINS *(Disgusted)* Half!

UNDERSHAFT *(Firmly)* Half.

CUSINS You call yourself a gentleman; and you offer me half!!

UNDERSHAFT I do not call myself a gentleman; but I offer you half.

CUSINS This to your future partner! your successor! your son-in-law!

BARBARA You are selling your own soul, Dolly, not mine. Leave me out of the bargain, please.

UNDERSHAFT Come! I will go a step further for Barbara's sake. I will give you three fifths; but that is my last word.

CUSINS Done!

LOMAX Done in the eye! Why, *I* get only eight hundred, you know.

CUSINS By the way, Mac, I am a classical scholar, not an arithmetical one. Is three fifths more than half or less?

UNDERSHAFT More, of course.

CUSINS I would have taken two hundred and fifty. How you can succeed in business when you are willing to pay all that money to a University don who is obviously not worth a junior clerk's wages!—well! What will Lazarus say?

UNDERSHAFT Lazarus is a gentle romantic Jew who cares for nothing but string quartets and stalls at fashionable theatres. He will be blamed for your rapacity in money matters, poor fellow! as he has hitherto been blamed for mine. You are a shark of the first order, Euripides. So much the better for the firm!

BARBARA Is the bargain closed, Dolly? Does your soul belong to him now?

CUSINS No: the price is settled: that is all. The real tug of war is still to come. What about the moral question?

LADY BRITOMART There is no moral question in the matter at all, Adolphus. You must simply sell cannons and weapons to people whose cause is right and just, and refuse them to foreigners and criminals.

UNDERSHAFT *(Determinedly)* No: none of that. You must keep the true faith of an Armorer, or you don't come in here.

CUSINS What on earth is the true faith of an Armorer?

UNDERSHAFT To give arms to all men who offer an honest price for them, without respect of persons or principles: to aristocrat and republican, to Nihilist and Tsar, to Capitalist and Socialist, to Protestant and Catholic, to burglar and policeman, to black man, white man and yellow man, to all sorts and conditions, all nationalities, all faiths, all follies, all causes and all crimes. The first Undershaft wrote up in his shop IF GOD GAVE THE HAND, LET NOT MAN WITHHOLD THE SWORD. The second wrote up ALL HAVE THE RIGHT TO FIGHT: NONE HAVE THE RIGHT TO JUDGE. The third wrote up TO MAN THE WEAPON: TO HEAVEN THE VICTORY. The fourth had no literary turn; so he did not write up anything; but he sold cannons to Napoleon under the nose of George the Third. The fifth wrote up PEACE SHALL NOT PREVAIL SAVE WITH A SWORD IN HER HAND. The sixth, my master, was the best of all. He wrote up NOTHING IS EVER DONE IN THIS WORLD UNTIL MEN ARE PREPARED TO KILL ONE ANOTHER IF IT IS NOT DONE. After that, there was nothing left for the seventh to say. So he wrote up, simply, UNASHAMED.

CUSINS My good Machiavelli, I shall certainly write something up on the wall; only as I shall write it in Greek, you won't be able to read it. But as to your Armorer's faith, if I take my neck out of the noose of my own morality I am not going to put it into the noose of yours. I shall sell cannons to whom I please and refuse them to whom I please. So there!

UNDERSHAFT From the moment when you become Andrew Undershaft, you will never do as you please again. Don't come here lusting for power, young man.

CUSINS If power were my aim I should not come here for it. You have no power.

UNDERSHAFT None of my own, certainly.

CUSINS I have more power than you, more will. You do not drive this place: it drives you. And what drives the place?

UNDERSHAFT (*Enigmatically*) A will of which I am a part.

BARBARA (*Startled*) Father! Do you know what you are saying; or are you laying a snare for my soul?

CUSINS Don't listen to his metaphysics, Barbara. The place is driven by the most rascally part of society, the money hunters, the pleasure hunters, the military promotion hunters; and he is their slave.

UNDERSHAFT Not necessarily. Remember the Armorer's Faith. I will take an order from a good man as cheerfully as from a bad one. If you good people prefer preaching and shirking to buying my weapons and fighting the rascals, don't blame me. I cannot make courage and conviction. Bah! you tire me, Euripides, with your morality mongering. Ask Barbara: she understands. (*He suddenly reaches up and takes* BARBARA'S *hands, looking powerfully into her eyes*) Tell him, my love, what power really means.

BARBARA (*Hypnotized*) Before I joined the Salvation Army, I was in my own power; and the consequence was that I never knew what to do with myself. When I joined it, I had not time enough for all the things I had to do.

UNDERSHAFT (*Approvingly*) Just so. And why was that, do you suppose?

BARBARA Yesterday I should have said, because I was in the power of God. (*She resumes her self-possession, withdrawing her hands from his with a power equal to his own*) But you came and shewed me that I was in the power of Bodger and Undershaft. Today I feel—oh! how can I put it into words? Sarah: do you remember the earthquake at Cannes, when we were little children?—how little the surprise of the first shock mattered compared to the dread and horror of waiting for the second? That is how I feel in this place today. I stood on the rock I thought eternal; and without a word of warning it reeled and crumbled under me. I was safe with an infinite wisdom watching me, an army marching to Salvation with me; and in a moment, at a stroke of your pen in a cheque book, I stood alone; and the heavens were empty. That was the first shock of the earthquake: I am waiting for the second.

UNDERSHAFT Come, come, my daughter! don't make too much of your little tinpot tragedy. What do we do here when we spend years of work and thought and thousands of pounds of solid cash on a new gun or an aerial battleship that turns out just a hairsbreadth wrong after all? Scrap it. Scrap it without wasting another hour or another pound on it. Well, you have made for yourself something that you call a morality or a religion or what not. It doesn't fit the facts. Well, scrap it. Scrap it and get one that does fit. That is what is wrong with the world at present. It scraps its obsolete steam engines and dynamos; but it won't scrap its old prejudices and its old moralities and its old religions and its old political constitutions. What's the result? In machinery it does very well; but in morals and religion and politics it is working at a loss that brings it nearer bankruptcy every year. Don't persist in that folly. If your old religion broke down yesterday, get a newer and a better one for tomorrow.

BARBARA Oh how gladly I would take a better one to my soul! But you offer me a worse one. (*Turning on him with sudden vehemence*) Justify yourself: shew me some light through the darkness of this dreadful place, with its beautifully clean workshops, and respectable workmen, and model homes.

UNDERSHAFT Cleanliness and respectability do not need justification, Barbara; they justify themselves. I see no darkness here, no dreadfulness. In your Salvation shelter I saw poverty, misery, cold and hunger. You gave them bread and treacle and dreams of heaven. I give from thirty shillings a week to twelve thousand a year. They find their own dreams; but I look after the drainage.

BARBARA And their souls?

UNDERSHAFT I save their souls just as I saved yours.

BARBARA (*Revolted*) You saved my soul! What do you mean?

UNDERSHAFT I fed you and clothed you and housed you. I took care that you should have money enough to live handsomely—more than enough; so that you could be wasteful, careless, generous. That saved your soul from the seven deadly sins.

BARBARA (*Bewildered*) The seven deadly sins!

UNDERSHAFT Yes, the deadly seven. (*Counting on his fingers*) Food, clothing, firing, rent, taxes, respectability and children. Nothing can lift those seven millstones from Man's neck but money; and the spirit cannot soar until the millstones are lifted. I lifted them from your spirit. I enabled Barbara to become Major Barbara; and I saved her from the crime of poverty.

CUSINS Do you call poverty a crime?

UNDERSHAFT The worst of crimes. All the other crimes are virtues beside it: all the other dishonors are chivalry itself by comparison. Poverty blights whole cities; spreads horrible pestilences; strikes dead the very souls of all who come within sight, sound or smell of it. What you call crime is nothing: a murder here and a theft there, a blow now and a curse then: what do they matter? they are only the accidents and illnesses of life: there are not fifty genuine professional criminals in London. But there are millions of poor people, abject people, dirty people, ill fed, ill clothed people. They poison us morally and physically: they kill the happiness of society: they force us to do away with our own liberties and to organize unnatural cruelties for fear they should rise against us and drag us down into their abyss. Only fools fear crime: we all fear poverty. Pah! (*Turning on* BARBARA) you talk of your half-saved ruffian in West Ham: you accuse me of dragging his soul back to perdition. Well, bring him to me here; and I will drag his soul back again to salvation for you. Not by words and dreams; but by thirty-eight shillings a week, a sound house in a handsome street, and a permanent job. In three weeks he will have a fancy waistcoat; in three months a tall hat and a chapel sitting; before the end of the year he will shake hands with a duchess at a Primrose League[29] meeting, and

---

[29] A Conservative organization named after the favorite flower of Prime Minister Benjamin Disraeli.

join the Conservative Party.

BARBARA   And will he be the better for that?

UNDERSHAFT   You know he will. Don't be a hypocrite, Barbara. He will be better fed, better housed, better clothed, better behaved; and his children will be pounds heavier and bigger. That will be better than an American cloth mattress in a shelter, chopping firewood, eating bread and treacle, and being forced to kneel down from time to time to thank heaven for it: knee drill, I think you call it. It is cheap work converting starving men with a Bible in one hand and a slice of bread in the other. I will undertake to convert West Ham to Mahometanism on the same terms. Try your hand on my men: their souls are hungry because their bodies are full.

BARBARA   And leave the east end to starve?

UNDERSHAFT   (*His energetic tone dropping into one of bitter and brooding remembrance*)   I was an east ender. I moralized and starved until one day I swore that I would be a full-fed free man at all costs—that nothing should stop me except a bullet, neither reason nor morals nor the lives of other men. I said "Thou shalt starve ere I starve"; and with that word I became free and great. I was a dangerous man until I had my will: now I am a useful, beneficent, kindly person. That is the history of most self-made millionaires, I fancy. When it is the history of every Englishman we shall have an England worth living in.

LADY BRITOMART   Stop making speeches, Andrew. This is not the place for them.

UNDERSHAFT   (*Punctured*)   My dear: I have no other means of conveying my ideas.

LADY BRITOMART   Your ideas are nonsense. You got on because you were selfish and unscrupulous.

UNDERSHAFT   Not at all. I had the strongest scruples about poverty and starvation. Your moralists are quite unscrupulous about both: they make virtues of them. I had rather be a thief than a pauper. I had rather be a murderer than a slave. I don't want to be either; but if you force the alternative on me, then, by Heaven, I'll choose the braver and more moral one. I hate poverty and slavery worse than any other crimes whatsoever. And let me tell you this. Poverty and slavery have stood up for centuries to your sermons and leading articles: they will not stand up to my machine guns. Don't preach at them: don't reason with them. Kill them.

BARBARA   Killing. Is that your remedy for everything?

UNDERSHAFT   It is the final test of conviction, the only lever strong enough to overturn a social system, the only way of saying Must. Let six hundred and seventy fools loose in the street; and three policemen can scatter them. But huddle them together in a certain house in

Westminster; and let them go through certain ceremonies and call themselves certain names until at last they get the courage to kill; and your six hundred and seventy fools become a government. Your pious mob fills up ballot papers and imagines it is governing its masters; but the ballot paper that really governs is the paper that has a bullet wrapped up in it.

CUSINS That is perhaps why, like most intelligent people, I never vote.

UNDERSHAFT Vote! Bah! When you vote, you only change the names of the cabinet. When you shoot, you pull down governments, inaugurate new epochs, abolish old orders and set up new. Is that historically true, Mr Learned Man, or is it not?

CUSINS It is historically true. I loathe having to admit it. I repudiate your sentiments. I abhor your nature. I defy you in every possible way. Still, it is true. But it ought not to be true.

UNDERSHAFT Ought! ought! ought! ought! ought! Are you going to spend your life saying ought, like the rest of our moralists? Turn your oughts into shalls, man. Come and make explosives with me. Whatever can blow men up can blow society up. The history of the world is the history of those who had courage enough to embrace this truth. Have you the courage to embrace it, Barbara?

LADY BRITOMART Barbara, I positively forbid you to listen to your father's abominable wickedness. And you, Adolphus, ought to know better than to go about saying that wrong things are true. What does it matter whether they are true if they are wrong?

UNDERSHAFT What does it matter whether they are wrong if they are true?

LADY BRITOMART (*Rising*) Children: come home instantly. Andrew: I am exceedingly sorry I allowed you to call on us. You are wickeder than ever. Come at once.

BARBARA (*Shaking her head*) It's no use running away from wicked people, mamma.

LADY BRITOMART It is every use. It shews your disapprobation of them.

BARBARA It does not save them.

LADY BRITOMART I can see that you are going to disobey me. Sarah: are you coming home or are you not?

SARAH I daresay it's very wicked of papa to make cannons; but I don't think I shall cut him on that account.

LOMAX (*Pouring oil on the troubled waters*) The fact is, you know, there is a certain amount of tosh about this notion of wickedness. It doesn't work. You must look at facts. Not that I would say a word in favor of anything wrong; but then, you see, all sorts of chaps are always doing all sorts of things; and we have to fit them in somehow, don't you know. What I mean is that you can't go cutting everybody; and that's about what it comes to. (*Their rapt attention to his eloquence makes him nervous*) Perhaps I don't make myelf clear.

LADY BRITOMART You are lucidity itself, Charles. Because Andrew is successful and has plenty of money to give to Sarah, you will flatter him and encourage him in his wickedness.

LOMAX (*Unruffled*) Well, where the carcase is, there will the eagles be gathered, don't you know. (*To* UNDERSHAFT) Eh? What?

UNDERSHAFT Precisely. By the way, may I call you Charles?

LOMAX Delighted. Cholly is the usual ticket.

UNDERSHAFT (*To* LADY BRITOMART) Biddy—

LADY BRITOMART (*Violently*) Don't dare call me Biddy. Charles Lomax: you are a fool. Adolphus Cusins: you are a Jesuit. Stephen: you are a prig. Barbara: you are a lunatic. Andrew: you are a vulgar tradesman. Now you all know my opinion; and my conscience is clear, at all events. (*She sits down with a vehemence that the rug fortunately softens*)

UNDERSHAFT My dear: you are the incarnation of morality. (*She snorts*) Your conscience is clear and your duty done when you have called everybody names. Come, Euripides! it is getting late; and we all want to go home. Make up your mind.

CUSINS Understand this, you old demon—

LADY BRITOMART Adolphus!

UNDERSHAFT Let him alone, Biddy. Proceed, Euripides.

CUSINS You have me in a horrible dilemma. I want Barbara.

UNDERSHAFT Like all young men, you greatly exaggerate the difference between one young woman and another.

BARBARA Quite true, Dolly.

CUSINS I also want to avoid being a rascal.

UNDERSHAFT (*With biting contempt*) You lust for personal righteousness, for self-approval, for what you call a good conscience, for what Barbara calls salvation, for what I call patronizing people who are not so lucky as yourself.

CUSINS I do not: all the poet in me recoils from being a good man. But there are things in me that I must reckon with. Pity—

UNDERSHAFT Pity! The scavenger of misery.

CUSINS Well, love.

UNDERSHAFT I know. You love the needy and the outcast: you love the oppressed races, the negro, the Indian ryot, the underdog everywhere. Do you love the Japanese? Do you love the French? Do you love the English?[30]

---

[30] In other words: If you love the oppressed, do you also love the oppressors?

CUSINS No. Every true Englishman detests the English. We are the wickedest nation on earth; and our success is a moral horror.
UNDERSHAFT That is what comes of your gospel of love, is it?
CUSINS May I not love even my father-in-law?
UNDERSHAFT Who wants your love, man? By what right do you take the liberty of offering it to me? I will have your due heed and respect, or I will kill you. But your love! Damn your impertinence!
CUSINS (*Grinning*) I may not be able to control my affections, Mac.
UNDERSHAFT You are fencing, Euripides. You are weakening: your grip is slipping. Come! try your last weapon. Pity and love have broken in your hand: forgiveness is still left.
CUSINS No: forgiveness is a beggar's refuge. I am with you there: we must pay our debts.
UNDERSHAFT Well said. Come! you will suit me. Remember the words of Plato.
CUSINS (*Starting*) Plato! You dare quote Plato to me!
UNDERSHAFT Plato says, my friend, that society cannot be saved until either the Professors of Greek take to making gunpowder, or else the makers of gunpowder become Professors of Greek.[31]
CUSINS Oh, tempter, cunning tempter!
UNDERSHAFT Come! choose, man, choose.
CUSINS But perhaps Barbara will not marry me if I make the wrong choice.
BARBARA Perhaps not.
CUSINS (*Desperately perplexed*) You hear!
BARBARA Father: do you love nobody?
UNDERSHAFT I love my best friend.
LADY BRITOMART And who is that, pray?
UNDERSHAFT My bravest enemy. That is the man who keeps me up to the mark.
CUSINS You know, the creature is really a sort of poet in his way. Suppose he is a great man, after all!
UNDERSHAFT Suppose you stop talking and make up your mind, my young friend.
CUSINS But you are driving me against my nature. I hate war.
UNDERSHAFT Hatred is the coward's revenge for being intimidated. Dare you make war on war? Here are the means: my friend Mr Lomax is sitting on them.
LOMAX (*Springing up*) Oh I say! You don't mean that this thing is loaded, do you? My ownest: come off it.

[31] *The Republic*, Book V, 473.

SARAH (*Sitting placidly on the shell*) If I am to be blown up, the more thoroughly it is done the better. Don't fuss, Cholly.

LOMAX (*To* UNDERSHAFT, *strongly remonstrant*) Your own daughter, you know.

UNDERSHAFT So I see. (*To* CUSINS) Well, my friend, may we expect you here at six tomorrow morning?

CUSINS (*Firmly*) Not on any account. I will see the whole establishment blown up with its own dynamite before I will get up at five. My hours are healthy, rational hours: eleven to five.

UNDERSHAFT Come when you please: before a week you will come at six and stay until I turn you out for the sake of your health. (*Calling*) Bilton! (*He turns to* LADY BRITOMART, *who rises*) My dear: let us leave these two young people to themselves for a moment. (BILTON *comes from the shed*) I am going to take you through the gun cotton shed.

BILTON (*Barring the way*) You can't take anything explosive in here, sir.

LADY BRITOMART What do you mean? Are you alluding to me?

BILTON (*Unmoved*) No, ma'am. Mr Undershaft has the other gentleman's matches in his pocket.

LADY BRITOMART (*Abruptly*) Oh! I beg your pardon. (*She goes into the shed*)

UNDERSHAFT Quite right, Bilton, quite right: here you are. (*He gives* BILTON *the box of matches*) Come, Stephen. Come, Charles. Bring Sarah. (*He passes into the shed*)

(BILTON *opens the box and deliberately drops the matches into the fire-bucket*)

LOMAX Oh I say! (BILTON *stolidly hands him the empty box*) Infernal nonsense! Pure scientific ignorance! (*He goes in*)

SARAH Am I all right, Bilton?

BILTON You'll have to put on list slippers, miss: that's all. We've got 'em inside. (*She goes in*)

STEPHEN (*Very seriously to* CUSINS) Dolly, old fellow, think. Think before you decide. Do you feel that you are a sufficiently practical man? It is a huge undertaking, an enormous responsibility. All this mass of business will be Greek to you.

CUSINS Oh, I think it will be much less difficult than Greek.

STEPHEN Well, I just want to say this before I leave you to yourselves. Don't let anything I have said about right and wrong prejudice you against this great chance in life. I have satisfied myself that the business is one of the highest character and a credit to our country. (*Emotionally*) I am very proud of my father. I— (*Unable to proceed, he presses* CUSINS' *hand and goes hastily into the shed, followed by* BILTON)

(BARBARA *and* CUSINS, *left alone together, look at one another silently*)

CUSINS Barbara: I am going to accept this offer.
BARBARA I thought you would.
CUSINS You understand, don't you, that I had to decide without consulting you. If I had thrown the burden of the choice on you, you would sooner or later have despised me for it.
BARBARA Yes: I did not want you to sell your soul for me any more than for this inheritance.
CUSINS It is not the sale of my soul that troubles me: I have sold it too often to care about that. I have sold it for a professorship. I have sold it for an income. I have sold it to escape being imprisoned for refusing to pay taxes for hangmen's ropes and unjust wars and things that I abhor. What is all human conduct but the daily and hourly sale of our souls for trifles? What I am now selling it for is neither money nor position nor comfort, but for reality and for power.
BARBARA You know that you will have no power, and that he has none.
CUSINS I know. It is not for myself alone. I want to make power for the world.
BARBARA I want to make power for the world too; but it must be spiritual power.
CUSINS I think all power is spiritual: these cannons will not go off by themselves. I have tried to make spiritual power by teaching Greek. But the world can never be really touched by a dead language and a dead civilization. The people must have power; and the people cannot have Greek. Now the power that is made here can be wielded by all men.
BARBARA Power to burn women's houses down and kill their sons and tear their husbands to pieces.
CUSINS You cannot have power for good without having power for evil too. Even mother's milk nourishes murderers as well as heroes. This power which only tears men's bodies to pieces has never been so horribly abused as the intellectual power, the imaginative power, the poetic, religious power that can enslave men's souls. As a teacher of Greek I gave the intellectual man weapons against the common man. I now want to give the common man weapons against the intellectual man. I love the common people. I want to arm them against the lawyers, the doctors, the priests, the literary men, the professors, the artists, and the politicians, who, once in authority, are more disastrous and tyrannical than all the fools, rascals, and impostors. I want a power

simple enough for common men to use, yet strong enough to force the intellectual oligarchy to use its genius for the general good.

BARBARA   Is there no higher power than that? (*Pointing to the shell*)

CUSINS   Yes; but that power can destroy the higher powers just as a tiger can destroy a man: therefore Man must master that power first. I admitted this when the Turks and Greeks were last at war. My best pupil went out to fight for Hellas. My parting gift to him was not a copy of Plato's *Republic*, but a revolver and a hundred Undershaft cartridges. The blood of every Turk he shot—if he shot any—is on my head as well as on Undershaft's. That act committed me to this place for ever. Your father's challenge has beaten me. Dare I make war on war? I dare. I must. I will. And now, is it all over between us?

BARBARA   (*Touched by his evident dread of her answer*)   Silly baby Dolly! How could it be!

CUSINS   (*Overjoyed*)   Then you—you—you— Oh for my drum! (*He flourishes imaginary drumsticks*)

BARBARA   (*Angered by his levity*)   Take care, Dolly, take care. Oh, if only I could get away from you and from father and from it all! if I could have the wings of a dove and fly away to heaven!

CUSINS   And leave me!

BARBARA   Yes, you, and all the other naughty mischievous children of men. But I can't. I was happy in the Salvation Army for a moment. I escaped from the world into a paradise of enthusiasm and prayer and soul saving; but the moment our money ran short, it all came back to Bodger: it was he who saved our people: he, and the Prince of Darkness, my papa. Undershaft and Bodger: their hands stretch everywhere: when we feed a starving fellow creature, it is with their bread, because there is no other bread; when we tend the sick, it is in the hospitals they endow; if we turn from the churches they build, we must kneel on the stones of the streets they pave. As long as that lasts, there is no getting away from them. Turning our backs on Bodger and Undershaft is turning our backs on life.

CUSINS   I thought you were determined to turn your back on the wicked side of life.

BARBARA   There is no wicked side: life is all one. And I never wanted to shirk my share in whatever evil must be endured, whether it be sin or suffering. I wish I could cure you of middle-class ideas, Dolly.

CUSINS   (*Gasping*)   Middle cl—! A snub! A social snub to me! from the daughter of a foundling!

BARBARA   That is why I have no class, Dolly: I come straight out of the heart of the whole people. If I were middle-class I should turn my back on my father's business; and we should both live in an artistic drawing room, with you reading the reviews in one corner, and I in the other at the piano, playing Schumann: both very superior persons, and neither of us a bit of use. Sooner than that, I would sweep out the guncotton shed, or be one of Bodger's barmaids. Do you know what would have happened if you had refused papa's offer?

CUSINS I wonder!

BARBARA I should have given you up and married the man who accepted it. After all, my dear old mother has more sense than any of you. I felt like her when I saw this place—felt that I must have it—that never, never, never, could I let it go; only she thought it was the houses and the kitchen ranges and the linen and china, when it was really all the human souls to be saved: not weak souls in starved bodies, sobbing with gratitude for a scrap of bread and treacle, but fullfed, quarrelsome, snobbish, uppish creatures, all standing on their little rights and dignities, and thinking that my father ought to be greatly obliged to them for making so much money for him—and so he ought. That is where salvation is really wanted. My father shall never throw it in my teeth again that my converts were bribed with bread. (*She is transfigured*) I have got rid of the bribe of bread. I have got rid of the bribe of heaven. Let God's work be done for its own sake: the work he had to create us to do because it cannot be done except by living men and women. When I die, let him be in my debt, not I in his; and let me forgive him as becomes a woman of my rank.

CUSINS Then the way of life lies through the factory of death?

BARBARA Yes, through the raising of hell to heaven and of man to God, through the unveiling of an eternal light in the Valley of The Shadow.[32] (*Seizing him with both hands*) Oh, did you think my courage would never come back? did you believe that I was a deserter? that I, who have stood in the streets, and taken my people to my heart, and talked of the holiest and greatest things with them, could ever turn back and chatter foolishly to fashionable people about nothing in a drawing room? Never, never, never, never: Major Barbara will die with the colors. Oh! and I have my dear little Dolly boy still; and he has found me my place and my work. Glory Hallelujah! (*She kisses him*)

CUSINS My dearest: consider my delicate health. I cannot stand as much happiness as you can.

BARBARA Yes: it is not easy work being in love with me, is it? But it's good for you. (*She runs to the shed, and calls, childlike*) Mamma! Mamma! (BILTON *comes out of the shed, followed by* UNDERSHAFT) I want mamma.

[32] Psalm 23.

UNDERSHAFT She is taking off her list slippers, dear. (*He passes on to* CUSINS) Well? What does she say?
CUSINS She has gone right up into the skies.
LADY BRITOMART (*Coming from the shed and stopping on the steps, obstructing* SARAH, *who follows with* LOMAX. BARBARA *clutches like a baby at her mother's skirt*) Barbara: when will you learn to be independent and to act and think for yourself? I know as well as possible what that cry of "Mamma, Mamma," means. Always running to me!
SARAH (*Touching* LADY BRITOMART'S *ribs with her finger tips and imitating a bicycle horn*) Pip! pip!
LADY BRITOMART (*Highly indignant*) How dare you say Pip! pip! to me, Sarah? You are both very naughty children. What do you want, Barbara?
BARBARA I want a house in the village to live in with Dolly. (*Dragging at the skirt*) Come and tell me which one to take.
UNDERSHAFT (*To* CUSINS) Six o'clock tomorrow morning. Euripides.

Curtain

JOHN MILLINGTON SYNGE

[1871 – 1909]

❧ *The Man*

EDMUND JOHN MILLINGTON SYNGE (pronounced *sing*) was born in what is now a suburb of Dublin, the son of John Hatch and Kathleen, landowning members of the Protestant Anglo-Irish Ascendancy. Synge attended Trinity College, Dublin, where he became interested in Irish antiquity, and studied Gaelic and Hebrew; he also attended the Royal Irish Academy of Music, where he studied the violin, musical theory, and composition. In 1893 he went to the Continent, where he continued to study music but also wrote poetry and plays.

In 1896 in Paris he met William Butler Yeats who urged him to return to Ireland to rediscover his roots, to live among the inhabitants of the remote Aran Islands, off the west coast of Ireland, and to express their lives. Synge took this advice, eventually publishing a book about his sojourn, *The Aran Islands,* as well as using much of this background in his plays.

While attending rehearsals of his play at the Abbey Theatre, he fell in love with the actress Molly Allgood, whose stage name was Maire O'Neill. He was fifteen years older than she; he had a degree from Trinity, she a grade-school education; he came from a family of landowners, she a working-class family; he was a skeptic, she a Roman Catholic. Despite these problems—which in Dublin at the start of the century were even more formidable than they are today—they became engaged. But before they could be married, he died of cancer. He had not been able to piece together the various drafts of his final play, *Deirdre of the Sorrows*. His fiancée, Yeats, and Lady Gregory compiled from these drafts an acting version which was given its first performance the year after his death.

❧ *The Work*

THE MOST DISTINCTIVE element of Synge's plays is their language. In an age when prose drama is associated with flat, drab language, the richness of Synge's prose demands the adjective "poetic." Yet Synge's language is appropriately described by that cliché of drab dialogue, "rooted in reality." In the preface to *The Playboy of the Western World* he boasts that the entire play contains only one or two words he has not heard spoken in rural Ireland. This claim is given substance by the dialogue he records in his travel books. In writing peasant idiom, Synge has apparently done what the peasants themselves have done—used Gaelic syntax while speaking English. Although his dialogue is based on the language of the people of Western Ireland, it is more than reportage. Synge's "rich and copious" language, to use his words, is as dramatic as it is lyrical—that is, adapted to character and situation. The poetic dialogue of *Deirdre of the Sorrows* is tinted with a melancholy that would be as inappropriate to *Playboy* as Christy's exuberant flights would be to *Deirdre*. Moreover, the language of *Playboy* itself varies from character to character and changes as a single character develops. Thus, Christy's original sparse description of the murder of his father becomes an embroidered account that includes the sun emerging from behind a cloud and the father swinging at him with a scythe. His development is also reflected in his speeches to Pegeen. In the first act, after he timidly asks whether she is single, he talks not of boy and girl but of solitude: poaching rabbits alone at night, observing ducks and geese while others sleep. In the second act he is more confident and talks to her of such physical elements as "the sweetness of your voice" and "rinsing your ankles when the night is come." In the third act he is so self-confident that he relates "squeezing kisses on your puckered lips" to God, paradise, and the lamp of an angel.

Synge's people are as "rich and copious" as their words; because of this, the words come naturally from their mouths. Like his language, his characters are anchored in reality. In one of his poems, he bids farewell to the Shee (the fairy people)—the dreamy, mystic figures of Yeats' Celtic Twilight; he would rather drink, stretch lazily in a ditch, go poaching with Red Dan Philly's bitch—deal with real people of the Irish countryside. The characters in his plays—even the royal personages of *Deirdre*, which is based on Irish legend—are at home in ditches and would be at home with Red Dan Philly and his dog. Synge creates earthy characters who are so "superb and wild" that they are capable of expressing themselves in language "as fully flavoured as a nut or apple."

❦ *The Play*

SYNGE'S PLAYWRITING CAREER began stormily. When *In the Shadow of the Glen* was first performed, it was denounced as decadent, degenerate, and degrading to Irish womanhood. These attacks were mild in comparison to the abuse which greeted *Playboy*. The audience hissed, booed, and shouted, even drowning out the actors. Objects were throw onto the stage, and fights broke out in the theater between the play's supporters and its detractors. When the police removed the participants, the fights continued in the streets. In 1907, many Irish Catholics regarded the play as blasphemous, corrupt, and libelous. Christy Mahon declares that God Himself is lonely while he makes love to Pegeen. Such taboo words as "bloody" and "shift" appear frequently in the dialogue. Audience hostility was roused not only by the words but also by the reversal of accepted values. The pious Shawn is mocked for his piety; when the villagers become law-abiding, they are shown as dastardly and disloyal. The heroic Christy, on the other hand, swears and suggests a kind of freedom that is alien to the Church's asceticism.

Christy's maturation constitutes the spine of the play and recalls numerous mythic tales, from Oedipus, who kills his father and marries his mother, to the fairy-tale hero who vanquishes the mean giant and wins the princess. Like Oedipus, Christy "kills" his father; like the fairy-tale hero, he vanquishes a "mean giant." Unlike Oedipus, he revolts against his father in order not to marry a foster-mother, the Widow Casey; unlike the fairy-tale hero, he rejects the princess. The common element of the three tales is maturation through murder.

Playboy is the comic story of Christy's achieving manhood. Before he hit his father with a loy, he was lazy, frightened, and shy. Exposed to the adoration of Pegeen and the villagers, his self-confidence grows sufficiently for him to win the girl and the games. Though his status is based on a lie, his triumph is real. Elated by this triumph, he is able to turn the lie into a truth as he rises against his father with a loy. When Pegeen and the others turn against him after he strikes the blow in the backyard, he realizes that he no longer needs the approval of such people. In the first act he clings to Pegeen in fear of his father's ghost; at the end of the play he dominates his father and thanks the fickle community for having helped him gain his manhood.

But *Playboy* is not only the comedy of Christy. Christy's gain is counterpointed by Pegeen's loss. The men of the village lack color and heroism: squint-eyed Red Linahan, lame Patcheen, and her cousin Shawn Keogh. Gone are such heroes as Daneen Sullivan, who knocked out a policeman's eye. Once Christy arrives, he fills the gap. Pegeen soon breaks her engagement to Shawn in favor of the gallant newcomer. But the adventurous life that she professes to admire shocks her when it occurs before her eyes, and she turns against Christy. At the end of the play, as Christy leaves in triumph, she realizes too late that only Shawn remains for her.

A large part of *Playboy's* appeal is its comedy. Not only is its governing idea comic—the adulation of a young man because he killed his father—but its details are immensely funny: Christy declares that he did not shoot his father since he, a law-abiding man, had no license to carry a gun; Pegeen, her father, and his cronies agree that the lad who has just murdered his father would provide perfect protection for her while the men go off to get drunk; the Widow Quin asserts that she and Christy are alike, prompting him to inquire innocently whether she killed *her* father; Christy examines his face in a mirror and assesses his good looks; Christy and his father confront each other face to face, each on all fours, the son asking whether the father has come to be killed a third time.

With *Playboy*, Synge joins the ranks of the great Irish writers of English comedy. But his renown is not based solely on his comedy. As Yeats said, "Synge has in common with the great theatre of the world, with that of Greece and that of India, with the creator of Falstaff, with Racine, a delight in language, a preoccupation with individual life. He resembles them also by a preoccupation with what is lasting and noble. . ."

❧ Dramatic Works

In the Shadow of the Glen, 1903.
Riders to the Sea, 1904.
The Well of the Saints, 1905.

The Playboy of the Western World, 1907.
The Tinker's Wedding, 1908.
Deirdre of the Sorrows, 1910.

❧ Selective Bibliography

Corkery, Daniel. *Synge and Anglo-Irish Literature.* New York: Longmans, Green, 1931.
Greene, David H., and Stephens, Edward M. *J. M. Synge, 1871–1909.* New York: Collier, 1961.
Gregory, Lady Isabella Augusta. *Our Irish Theatre.* New York: Putnam's, 1913.
Modern Drama, IV (December, 1961). The entire issue is devoted to Synge and O'Casey.
Price, Alan. *Synge and Anglo-Irish Drama.* London: Methuen, 1961.
Yeats, William Butler. *Essays and Introductions.* New York: Macmillan, 1961.

The Playboy
of the Western World

A Play in Three Acts

Preface

IN WRITING *The Playboy of the Western World*, as in my other plays, I have used one or two words only that I have not heard among the country people of Ireland, or spoken in my own nursery before I could read the newspapers. A certain number of the phrases I employ I have heard also from herds and fishermen along the coast from Kerry to Mayo, or from beggar-women and ballad-singers nearer Dublin; and I am glad to acknowledge how much I owe to the folk-imagination of these fine people. Anyone who has lived in real intimacy with the Irish peasantry will know that the wildest sayings and ideas in this play are tame indeed, compared with the fancies one may hear in any little hillside cabin in Geesala, or Carraroe, or Dingle Bay. All art is a collaboration; and there is little doubt that in the happy ages of literature, striking and beautiful phrases were as ready to the story-teller's or the playwright's hand, as the rich cloaks and dresses of his time. It is probable that when the Elizabethan dramatist took his ink-horn and sat down to his work he used many phrases that he had just heard, as he sat at dinner, from his mother or his children. In Ireland, those of us who know the people have the same privilege. When I was writing *The Shadow of the Glen*, some years ago, I got more aid than any learning could have given me from a chink in the floor of the old Wicklow house where I was staying, that let me hear what was being said by the servant girls in the kitchen. This matter, I think, is of importance, for in countries where the imagination of the people, and the language they use, is rich and living, it is possible for a writer to be rich and copious in his words, and at the same time to give the reality, which is the root of all poetry, in a comprehensive and natural form. In the modern literature of towns, however, richness is found only in sonnets, or prose poems, or in one or two elaborate books that are far away from the profound and common interests of life. One has, on one side, Mallarmé and Huysmans producing this literature; and on the other, Ibsen and Zola dealing with the reality of life in joyless and pallid words. On the stage one must have reality, and one must have joy; and that is why the intellectual modern drama has failed, and people have grown sick of the false joy of the musical comedy, that has been given them in place of the rich joy found only in what is superb and wild in reality. In a good play every speech should be as fully flavoured as a nut or apple, and such speeches cannot be written by anyone who works among people who have shut their lips on poetry. In Ireland, for a few years more, we have a popular imagination that is fiery and magnificent, and tender; so that those of us who wish to write start with a chance that is not given to writers in places where the springtime of the local life has been forgotten, and the harvest is a memory only, and the straw has been turned into bricks.

J. M. S.

January 21, 1907

CHARACTERS

CHRISTOPHER MAHON

OLD MAHON, *his father, a squatter*

MICHAEL JAMES FLAHERTY, called MICHAEL JAMES (*a publican*)

MARGARET FLAHERTY, called PEGEEN MIKE, *his daughter*

SHAWN KEOGH, *her cousin, a young farmer*

WIDOW QUIN, *a woman of about thirty*

PHILLY CULLEN and JIMMY FARRELL, *small farmers*

SARA TANSEY, SUSAN BRADY, HONOR BLAKE, and NELLY, *village girls*

A BELLMAN, or *Town Crier*

SOME PEASANTS

The action takes place near a village, on a wild coast of Mayo. The first Act passes on an evening of autumn, the other two Acts on the following day.

Act One

SCENE *Country public-house or shebeen, very rough and untidy. There is a sort of counter on the right with shelves, holding many bottles and jugs, just seen above it. Empty barrels stand near the counter. At back, a little to left of counter, there is a door into the open air, then, more to the left, there is a settle with shelves above it, with more jugs, and a table beneath a window. At the left there is a large open fire place, with turf fire, and a small door into inner room.* PEGEEN, *a wild-looking but fine girl of about twenty, is writing at table. She is dressed in the usual peasant dress.*

PEGEEN (*Slowly as she writes*) Six yards of stuff for to make a yellow gown. A pair of lace boots with lengthy heels on them and brassy eyes. A hat is suited for a wedding-day. A fine tooth comb. To be sent with three barrels of porter in Jimmy Farrell's creel cart[1] on the evening of the coming Fair to Mister Michael James Flaherty. With the best compliments of this season. Margaret Flaherty.

SHAWN KEOGH (*A fat and fair young man comes in as she signs, looks round awkwardly, when he sees she is alone*) Where's himself?

PEGEEN (*Without looking at him*) He's coming. (*She directs the letter*) To Master Sheamus Mulroy, Wine and Spirit Dealer, Castlebar.

SHAWN (*Uneasily*) I didn't see him on the road.

PEGEEN How would you see him (*Licks stamp and puts it on letter*) and it dark night this half hour gone by?

SHAWN (*Turning toward the door again*) I stood a while outside wondering would I have a right to pass on or to walk in and see you, Pegeen Mike, (*Comes to fire*) and I could hear the cows breathing, and sighing in the stillness of the air, and not a step moving any place from this gate to the bridge.

PEGEEN (*Putting letter in envelope*) It's above at the cross-roads he is, meeting Philly Cullen; and a couple more are going along with him to Kate Cassidy's wake.

SHAWN (*Looking at her blankly*) And he's going that length in the dark night?

PEGEEN (*Impatiently*) He is surely, and leaving me lonesome on the

---

[1] A cart with high sides, often used for carrying livestock.

scruff of the hill. (*She gets up and puts envelope on dresser, then winds clock*) Isn't it long the nights are now, Shawn Keogh, to be leaving a poor girl with her own self counting the hours to the dawn of day?

SHAWN (*With awkward humour*) If it is, when we're wedded in a short while you'll have no call to complain, for I've little will to be walking off to wakes or weddings in the darkness of the night.

PEGEEN (*With rather scornful good humour*) You're making mighty certain, Shaneen, that I'll wed you now.

SHAWN Aren't we after making a good bargain, the way we're only waiting these days on Father Reilly's dispensation[2] from the bishops, or the Court of Rome?

PEGEEN (*Looking at him teasingly, washing up at dresser*) It's a wonder, Shaneen, the Holy Father'd be taking notice of the likes of you; for if I was him I wouldn't bother with this place where you'll meet none but Red Linahan, has a squint in his eye, and Patcheen is lame in his heel, or the mad Mulrannies were driven from California and they lost in their wits. We're a queer lot these times to go troubling the Holy Father on his sacred seat.

SHAWN (*Scandalized*) If we are, we're as good this place as another, maybe, and as good these times as we were for ever.

PEGEEN (*With scorn*) As good, is it? Where now will you meet the like of Daneen Sullivan knocked the eye from a peeler,[3] or Marcus Quin, God rest him, got six months for maiming ewes, and he a great warrant to tell[4] stories of holy Ireland till he'd have the old women shedding down tears about their feet. Where will you find the like of them, I'm saying?

SHAWN (*Timidly*) If you don't, it's a good job, maybe; for (*With peculiar emphasis on the words*) Father Reilly has small conceit[5] to have that kind walking around and talking to the girls.

PEGEEN (*Impatiently, throwing water from basin out of the door*) Stop tormenting me with Father Reilly (*Imitating his voice*) when I'm asking only what way I'll pass these twelve hours of dark, and not take my death with the fear. (*Looking out of door*)

SHAWN (*Timidly*) Would I fetch you the Widow Quin, maybe?

PEGEEN Is it the like of that murderer? You'll not, surely.

[2] Because Pegeen and Shawn are cousins, they need a papal dispensation in order to marry.
[3] A policeman, named after Sir Robert Peel (1788–1850), who organized the Royal Irish Constabulary. In London he reorganized the police who were then called bobbies, after his first name.
[4] Famous for telling.
[5] Desire.

SHAWN (*Going to her, soothingly*)   Then I'm thinking himself will stop along with you when he sees you taking on, for it'll be a long night-time with great darkness, and I'm after feeling a kind of fellow above in the furzy ditch, groaning wicked like a maddening dog, the way it's good cause you have, maybe, to be fearing now.

PEGEEN (*Turning on him sharply*)   What's that? Is it a man you seen?

SHAWN (*Retreating*)   I couldn't see him at all; but I heard him groaning out, and breaking his heart. It should have been a young man from his words speaking.

PEGEEN (*Going after him*)   And you never went near to see was he hurted or what ailed him at all?

SHAWN   I did not, Pegeen Mike. It was a dark, lonesome place to be hearing the like of him.

PEGEEN   Well, you're a daring fellow, and if they find his corpse stretched above in the dews of dawn, what'll you say then to the peelers, or the Justice of the Peace?

SHAWN (*Thunderstruck*)   I wasn't thinking of that. For the love of God, Pegeen Mike, don't let on I was speaking of him. Don't tell your father and the men is coming above; for if they heard that story, they'd have great blabbing this night at the wake.

PEGEEN   I'll maybe tell them, and I'll maybe not.

SHAWN   They are coming at the door. Will you whisht, I'm saying?

PEGEEN   Whisht yourself. (*She goes behind counter.* MICHAEL JAMES, *fat jovial publican, comes in followed by* PHILLY CULLEN, *who is thin and mistrusting, and* JIMMY FARRELL, *who is fat and amorous, about forty-five*)

MEN (*Together*)   God bless you. The blessing of God on this place.

PEGEEN   God bless you kindly.

MICHAEL (*To men who go to the counter*)   Sit down now, and take your rest. (*Crosses to* SHAWN *at the fire*) And how is it you are, Shawn Keogh? Are you coming over the sands to Kate Cassidy's wake?

SHAWN   I am not, Michael James. I'm going home the short cut to my bed.

PEGEEN (*Speaking across the counter*)   He's right too, and have you no shame, Michael James, to be quitting off for the whole night, and leaving myself lonesome in the shop?

MICHAEL (*Good-humouredly*)   Isn't it the same whether I go for the whole night or a part only? and I'm thinking it's a queer daughter you are if you'd have me crossing backward through the Stooks of the Dead Women,[6] with a drop taken.

PEGEEN   If I am a queer daughter, it's a queer father'd be leaving me

---

[6] Rocks by the shore, that resemble stooks (sheaves of oats or wheat stacked and set up to dry). In Synge's *In West Kerry*, it is explained that the place re-

lonesome these twelve hours of dark, and I piling the turf with the dogs barking, and the calves mooing, and my own teeth rattling with the fear.

JIMMY (*Flatteringly*) What is there to hurt you, and you a fine, hardy girl would knock the head of any two men in the place?

PEGEEN (*Working herself up*) Isn't there the harvest boys with their tongues red for drink, and the ten tinkers[7] is camped in the east glen, and the thousand militia—bad cess to them!— walking idle through the land. There's lots surely to hurt me, and I won't stop alone in it, let himself do what he will.

MICHAEL If you're that afeard, let Shawn Keogh stop along with you. It's the will of God, I'm thinking, himself should be seeing to you now.

(*They all turn on* SHAWN)

SHAWN (*In horrified confusion*) I would and welcome, Michael James, but I'm afeard of Father Reilly; and what at all would the Holy Father and the Cardinals of Rome be saying if they heard I did the like of that?

MICHAEL (*With contempt*) God help you! Can't you sit in by the hearth with the light lit and herself beyond in the room? You'll do that surely, for I've heard tell there's a queer fellow above, going mad or getting his death, maybe, in the gripe of the ditch, so she'd be safer this night with a person here.

SHAWN (*With plaintive despair*) I'm afeard of Father Reilly, I'm saying. Let you not be tempting me, and we near married itself.

PHILLY (*With cold contempt*) Lock him in the west room. He'll stay then and have no sin to be telling to the priest.

MICHAEL (*To* SHAWN, *getting between him and the door*) Go up now.

SHAWN (*At the top of his voice*) Don't stop me, Michael James. Let me out of the door, I'm saying, for the love of the Almighty God. Let me out. (*Trying to dodge past him*) Let me out of it, and may God grant you His indulgence in the hour of need.

MICHAEL (*Loudly*) Stop your noising, and sit down by the hearth. (*Gives him a push and goes to counter laughing*)

SHAWN (*Turning back, wringing his hands*) Oh, Father Reilly and the saints of God, where will I hide myself today? Oh, St. Joseph, and St. Patrick, and St. Brigid, and St. James, have mercy on me now! (SHAWN *turns round, sees door clear, and makes a rush for it*)

MICHAEL (*Catching him by the coat-tail*) You'd be going, is it?

---

ceived the name because a boat once landed there, with twelve dead women aboard.

[7] In Ireland traveling tinkers have a reputation as thieves and cutthroats.

SHAWN (*Screaming*) Leave me go, Michael James, leave me go, you old Pagan, leave me go, or I'll get the curse of the priests on you, and of the scarlet-coated bishops of the courts of Rome. (*With a sudden movement he pulls himself out of his coat, and disappears out of the door, leaving his coat in* MICHAEL's *hands*)

MICHAEL (*Turning round, and holding up coat*) Well, there's the coat of a Christian man. Oh, there's sainted glory this day in the lonesome west; and by the will of God I've got you a decent man, Pegeen, you'll have no call to be spying after if you've a score of young girls, maybe, weeding in your fields.

PEGEEN (*Taking up the defence of her property*) What right have you to be making game of a poor fellow for minding the priest, when it's your own fault is, not paying a penny pot-boy to stand along with me and give me courage in the doing of my work? (*She snaps the coat away from him, and goes behind counter with it*)

MICHAEL (*Taken aback*) Where would I get a pot-boy? Would you have me send the bellman[8] screaming in the streets of Castlebar?

SHAWN (*Opening the door a chink and putting in his head, in a small voice*) Michael James!

MICHAEL (*Imitating him*) What ails you?

SHAWN The queer dying fellow's beyond looking over the ditch. He's come up, I'm thinking, stealing your hens. (*Looks over his shoulder*) God help me, he's following me now, (*He runs into room*) and if he's heard what I said, he'll be having my life, and I going home lonesome in the darkness of the night.

(*For a perceptible moment they watch the door with curiosity. Someone coughs outside. Then* CHRISTY MAHON, *a slight young man, comes in very tired and frightened and dirty*)

CHRISTY (*In a small voice*) God save all here!

MEN God save you kindly.

CHRISTY (*Going to the counter*) I'd trouble you for a glass of porter, woman of the house. (*He puts down coin*)

PEGEEN (*Serving him*) You're one of the tinkers, young fellow, is beyond camped in the glen?

CHRISTY I am not; but I'm destroyed walking.

MICHAEL (*Patronizingly*) Let you come up then to the fire. You're looking famished with the cold.

CHRISTY God reward you. (*He takes up his glass and goes a little way across to the left, then stops and looks about him*) Is it often the polis do be coming into this place, master of the house?

[8] Town crier; he announces his presence by ringing a bell.

MICHAEL If you'd come in better hours, you'd have seen "Licensed for the sale of Beer and Spirits, to be consumed on the premises," written in white letters above the door, and what would the polis want spying on me, and not a decent house within four miles, the way every living Christian is a bona fide,[9] saving one widow alone?

CHRISTY (*With relief*) It's a safe house, so. (*He goes over to the fire, sighing and moaning. Then he sits down, putting his glass beside him and begins gnawing a turnip, too miserable to feel the others staring at him with curiosity*)

MICHAEL (*Going after him*) Is it yourself is fearing the polis? You're wanting, maybe?

CHRISTY There's many wanting.

MICHAEL Many surely, with the broken harvest and the ended wars. (*He picks up some stockings, etc., that are near the fire, and carries them away furtively*) It should be larceny, I'm thinking.

CHRISTY (*Dolefully*) I had it in my mind it was a different word and a bigger.

PEGEEN There's a queer lad. Were you never slapped in school, young fellow, that you don't know the name of your deed?

CHRISTY (*Bashfully*) I'm slow at learning, a middling scholar only.

MICHAEL If you're a dunce itself, you'd have a right to know that larceny's robbing and stealing. Is it for the like of that you're wanting?

CHRISTY (*With a flash of family pride*) And I the son of a strong[10] farmer (*With a sudden qualm*), God rest his soul, could have bought up the whole of your old house awhile since, from the butt of his tailpocket, and not have missed the weight of it gone.

MICHAEL (*Impressed*) If it's not stealing, it's maybe something big.

CHRISTY (*Flattered*) Aye; it's maybe something big.

JIMMY He's a wicked-looking young fellow. Maybe he followed after a young woman on a lonesome night.

CHRISTY (*Shocked*) Oh, the saints forbid, mister; I was all times a decent lad.

PHILLY (*Turning on* JIMMY) You're a silly man, Jimmy Farrell. He said his father was a farmer a while since, and there's himself now in a poor state. Maybe the land was grabbed from him, and he did what any decent man would do.

MICHAEL (*To* CHRISTY, *mysteriously*) Was it bailiffs?

CHRISTY The divil a one.[11]

[9] In Ireland taverns are licensed to sell liquor only during certain hours. However, a "bona fide traveler"—defined as one who slept more than three miles away on the previous night—may be served outside the regular hours.
[10] Prosperous.
[11] Not a one.

MICHAEL   Agents?
CHRISTY   The divil a one.
MICHAEL   Landlords?
CHRISTY   (*Peevishly*) Ah, not at all, I'm saying. You'd see the like of them stories on any little paper of a Munster town. But I'm not calling to mind any person, gentle, simple, judge or jury, did the like of me.

(*They all draw nearer with delighted curiosity*)

PHILLY   Well, that lad's a puzzle-the-world.
JIMMY   He'd beat Dan Davies' circus, or the holy missioners making sermons on the villainy of man. Try him again, Philly.
PHILLY   Did you strike golden guineas out of solder, young fellow, or shilling coins itself?
CHRISTY   I did not, mister, not sixpence nor a farthing coin.
JIMMY   Did you marry three wives maybe? I'm told there's a sprinkling have done that among the holy Luthers of the preaching north.
CHRISTY   (*Shyly*) I never married with one, let alone with a couple or three.
PHILLY   Maybe he went fighting for the Boers, the like of the man beyond, was judged to be hanged, quartered and drawn. Were you off east, young fellow, fighting bloody wars for Kruger and the freedom of the Boers?
CHRISTY   I never left my own parish till Tuesday was a week.
PEGEEN   (*Coming from counter*) He's done nothing, so. (*To* CHRISTY) If you didn't commit murder or a bad, nasty thing, or false coining, or robbery, or butchery, or the like of them, there isn't anything that would be worth your troubling for to run from now. You did nothing at all.
CHRISTY   (*His feelings hurt*) That's an unkindly thing to be saying to a poor orphaned traveller, has a prison behind him, and hanging before, and hell's gap gaping below.
PEGEEN   (*With a sign to the men to be quiet*) You're only saying it. You did nothing at all. A soft lad the like of you wouldn't slit the windpipe of a screeching sow.
CHRISTY   (*Offended*) You're not speaking the truth.
PEGEEN   (*In mock rage*) Not speaking the truth, is it? Would you have me knock the head off you with the butt of the broom?
CHRISTY   (*Twisting round on her with a sharp cry of horror*) Don't strike me. I killed my poor father, Tuesday was a week, for doing the like of that.
PEGEEN   (*With blank amazement*) Is it killed your father?
CHRISTY   (*Subsiding*) With the help of God I did surely, and that the

Holy Immaculate Mother may intercede for his soul.
PHILLY (*Retreating with* JIMMY) There's a daring fellow.
JIMMY Oh, glory be to God!
MICHAEL (*With great respect*) That was a hanging crime, mister honey. You should have had good reason for doing the like of that.
CHRISTY (*In a very reasonable tone*) He was a dirty man, God forgive him, and he getting old and crusty, the way I couldn't put up with him at all.
PEGEEN And you shot him dead?
CHRISTY (*Shaking his head*) I never used weapons. I've no license, and I'm a law-fearing man.
MICHAEL It was with a hilted knife maybe? I'm told, in the big world it's bloody knives they use.
CHRISTY (*Loudly, scandalized*) Do you take me for a slaughter-boy?
PEGEEN You never hanged him, the way Jimmy Farrell hanged his dog from the license,[12] and had it screeching and wriggling three hours at the butt of a string, and himself swearing it was a dead dog, and the peelers swearing it had life?
CHRISTY I did not then. I just riz the loy[13] and let fall the edge of it on the ridge of his skull, and he went down at my feet like an empty sack, and never let a grunt or groan from him at all.
MICHAEL (*Making a sign to* PEGEEN *to fill* CHRISTY's *glass*) And what way weren't you hanged, mister? Did you bury him then?
CHRISTY (*Considering*) Aye. I buried him then. Wasn't I digging spuds in the field?
MICHAEL And the peelers never followed after you the eleven days that you're out?
CHRISTY (*Shaking his head*) Never a one of them, and I walking forward facing hog, dog, or divil on the highway of the road.
PHILLY (*Nodding wisely*) It's only with a common week-day kind of a murderer them lads would be trusting their carcase, and that man should be a great terror when his temper's roused.
MICHAEL He should then. (*To* CHRISTY) And where was it, mister honey, that you did the deed?
CHRISTY (*Looking at him with suspicion*) Oh, a distant place, master of the house, a windy corner of high, distant hills.
PHILLY (*Nodding with approval*) He's a close man, and he's right, surely.
PEGEEN That'd be a lad with the sense of Solomon to have for a pot-boy, Michael James, if it's the truth you're seeking one at all.

[12] Because he could not afford to buy a license for the dog.
[13] A spade.

PHILLY The peelers is fearing him, and if you'd that lad in the house there isn't one of them would come smelling around if the dogs itself were lapping poteen[14] from the dung-pit of the yard.

JIMMY Bravery's a treasure in a lonesome place, and a lad would kill his father, I'm thinking, would face a foxy divil with a pitchpike on the flags of hell.

PEGEEN It's the truth they're saying, and if I'd that lad in the house, I wouldn't be fearing the loosed kharki cut-throats,[15] or the walking dead.

CHRISTY (*Swelling with surprise and triumph*) Well, glory be to God!

MICHAEL (*With deference*) Would you think well to stop here and be pot-boy, mister honey, if we gave you good wages, and didn't destroy you with the weight of work?

SHAWN (*Coming forward uneasily*) That'd be a queer kind to bring into a decent quiet household with the like of Pegeen Mike.

PEGEEN (*Very sharply*) Will you whisht? Who's speaking to you?

SHAWN (*Retreating*) A bloody-handed murderer the like of . . .

PEGEEN (*Snapping at him*) Whisht I am saying; we'll take no fooling from your like at all. (*To* CHRISTY *with a honeyed voice*) And you, young fellow, you'd have a right to stop, I'm thinking, for we'd do our all and utmost to content your needs.

CHRISTY (*Overcome with wonder*) And I'd be safe in this place from the searching law?

MICHAEL You would, surely. If they're not fearing you, itself, the peelers in this place is decent droughty poor fellows, wouldn't touch a cur dog and not give warning in the dead of night.

PEGEEN (*Very kindly and persuasively*) Let you stop a short while anyhow. Aren't you destroyed walking with your feet in bleeding blisters, and your whole skin needing washing like a Wicklow sheep?

CHRISTY (*Looking round with satisfaction*) It's a nice room, and if it's not humbugging me you are, I'm thinking that I'll surely stay.

JIMMY (*Jumps up*) Now, by the grace of God, herself will be safe this night, with a man killed his father holding danger from the door, and let you come on, Michael James, or they'll have the best stuff drunk at the wake.

MICHAEL (*Going to the door with men*) And begging your pardon, mister, what name will we call you, for we'd like to know?

CHRISTY Christopher Mahon.

MICHAEL Well, God bless you, Christy, and a good rest till we meet again when the sun'll be rising to the noon of day.

[14] Pronounced *petcheen;* illegally distilled whiskey.
[15] British soldiers, dressed in khaki.

CHRISTY God bless you all.
MEN God bless you.

(*They go out except* SHAWN, *who lingers at door*)

SHAWN (*To* PEGEEN) Are you wanting me to stop along with you and keep you from harm?
PEGEEN (*Gruffly*) Didn't you say you were fearing Father Reilly?
SHAWN There'd be no harm staying now, I'm thinking, and himself in it too.
PEGEEN You wouldn't stay when there was need for you, and let you step off nimble this time when there's none.
SHAWN Didn't I say it was Father Reilly . . .
PEGEEN Go on, then, to Father Reilly (*In a jeering tone*), and let him put you in the holy brotherhoods, and leave that lad to me.
SHAWN If I meet the Widow Quin . . .
PEGEEN Go on, I'm saying, and don't be waking this place with your noise. (*She hustles him out and bolts the door*) That lad would wear the spirits from the saints of peace. (*Bustles about, then takes off her apron and pins it up in the window as a blind.* CHRISTY *watching her timidly. Then she comes to him and speaks with bland good-humour*) Let you stretch out now by the fire, young fellow. You should be destroyed travelling.
CHRISTY (*Shyly again, drawing off his boots*) I'm tired, surely, walking wild eleven days, and waking fearful in the night. (*He holds up one of his feet, feeling his blisters, and looking at them with compassion*)
PEGEEN (*Standing beside him, watching him with delight*) You should have had great people in your family, I'm thinking, with the little, small feet you have, and you with a kind of a quality name, the like of what you'd find on the great powers and potentates of France and Spain.
CHRISTY (*With pride*) We were great surely, with wide and windy acres of rich Munster land.
PEGEEN Wasn't I telling you, and you a fine, handsome young fellow with a noble brow?
CHRISTY (*With a flash of delighted surprise*) Is it me?
PEGEEN Aye. Did you never hear that from the young girls where you come from in the west or south?
CHRISTY (*With venom*) I did not then. Oh, they're bloody liars in the naked parish where I grew a man.
PEGEEN If they are itself, you've heard it these days, I'm thinking, and you walking the world telling out your story to young girls or old.
CHRISTY I've told my story no place till this night, Pegeen Mike, and it's foolish I was here, maybe, to be talking free, but you're decent people,

I'm thinking, and yourself a kindly woman, the way I wasn't fearing you at all.

PEGEEN (*Filling a sack with straw*) You've said the like of that, maybe, in every cot and cabin where you've met a young girl on your way.

CHRISTY (*Going over to her, gradually raising his voice*) I've said it nowhere till this night, I'm telling you, for I've seen none the like of you the eleven long days I am walking the world, looking over a low ditch or a high ditch on my north or my south, into stony scattered fields, or scribes[16] of bog, where you'd see young, limber girls, and fine prancing women making laughter with the men.

PEGEEN If you weren't destroyed travelling, you'd have as much talk and streeleen,[17] I'm thinking, as Owen Roe O'Sullivan[18] or the poets of the Dingle Bay, and I've heard all times it's the poets are your like, fine fiery fellows with great rages when their temper's roused.

CHRISTY (*Drawing a little nearer to her*) You've a power of rings, God bless you, and would there be any offence if I was asking are you single now?

PEGEEN What would I want wedding so young?

CHRISTY (*With relief*) We're alike, so.

PEGEEN (*She puts sack on settle and beats it up*) I never killed my father. I'd be afeard to do that, except I was the like of yourself with blind rages tearing me within, for I'm thinking you should have had great tussling when the end was come.

CHRISTY (*Expanding with delight at the first confidential talk he has ever had with a woman*) We had not then. It was a hard woman was come over the hill, and if he was always a crusty kind when he'd a hard woman setting him on, not the divil himself or his four fathers could put up with him at all.

PEGEEN (*With curiosity*) And isn't it a great wonder that one wasn't fearing you?

CHRISTY (*Very confidentially*) Up to the day I killed my father, there wasn't a person in Ireland knew the kind I was, and I there drinking, waking, eating, sleeping, a quiet, simple, poor fellow with no man giving me heed.

PEGEEN (*Getting a quilt out of the cupboard and putting it on the sack*) It was the girls were giving you heed maybe, and I'm thinking it's most conceit you'd have to be gaming with their like.

CHRISTY (*Shaking his head, with simplicity*) Not the girls itself, and I

---

[16] Long stretches.
[17] Chatter.
[18] A strolling Irish poet of the eighteenth century.

won't tell you a lie. There wasn't anyone heeding me in that place saving only the dumb beasts of the field. (*He sits down at fire*)
PEGEEN (*With disappointment*) And I thinking you should have been living the like of a king of Norway or the Eastern world. (*She comes and sits beside him after placing bread and mug of milk on the table*)
CHRISTY (*Laughing piteously*) The like of a king, is it? And I after toiling, moiling, digging, dodging from the dawn till dusk with never a sight of joy or sport saving only when I'd be abroad in the dark night poaching rabbits on hills, for I was a divil to poach, God forgive me, (*Very naïvely*) and I near got six months for going with a dung fork and stabbing a fish.
PEGEEN And it's that you'd call sport, is it, to be abroad in the darkness with yourself alone?
CHRISTY I did, God help me, and there I'd be as happy as the sunshine of St. Martin's Day, watching the light passing the north or the patches of fog, till I'd hear a rabbit starting to screech and I'd go running in the furze. Then when I'd my full share I'd come walking down where you'd see the ducks and greese stretched sleeping on the highway of the road, and before I'd pass the dunghill, I'd hear himself snoring out, a loud lonesome snore he'd be making all times, the while he was sleeping, and he a man'd be raging all times, the while he was waking, like a gaudy officer you'd hear cursing and damning and swearing oaths.
PEGEEN Providence and Mercy, spare us all!
CHRISTY It's that you'd say surely if you seen him and he after drinking for weeks, rising up in the red dawn, or before it maybe, and going out into the yard as naked as an ash tree in the moon of May, and shying clods against the visage of the stars till he'd put the fear of death into the banbhs[19] and the screeching sows.
PEGEEN I'd be well-nigh afeared of that lad myself, I'm thinking. And there was no one in it but the two of you alone?
CHRISTY The divil a one, though he'd sons and daughters walking all great states and territories of the world, and not a one of them, to this day, but would say their seven curses on him, and they rousing up to let a cough or sneeze, maybe, in the deadness of the night.
PEGEEN (*Nodding her head*) Well, you should have been a queer lot. I never cursed my father the like of that, though I'm twenty and more years of age.
CHRISTY Then you'd have cursed mine, I'm telling you, and he a man never gave peace to any, saving when he'd get two months or three, or be locked in the asylums for battering peelers or assaulting men (*With

---

[19] Young pigs; pronounced *bannevs*.

depression) the way it was a bitter life he led me till I did up a Tuesday and halve his skull.

PEGEEN (*Putting her hand on his shoulder*)   Well, you'll have peace in this place, Christy Mahon, and none to trouble you, and it's near time a fine lad like you should have your good share of the earth.

CHRISTY   It's time surely, and I a seemly fellow with great strength in me and bravery of . . .

(*Someone knocks*)

CHRISTY (*Clinging to* PEGEEN)   Oh, glory! it's late for knocking, and this last while I'm in terror of the peelers, and the walking dead.

(*Knocking again*)

PEGEEN   Who's there?
VOICE (*Outside*)   Me.
PEGEEN   Who's me?
VOICE   The Widow Quin.
PEGEEN (*Jumping up and giving him the bread and milk*)   Go on now with your supper, and let on to be sleepy, for if she found you were such a warrant to talk, she'd be stringing gabble till the dawn of day. (*He takes bread and sits shyly with his back to the door*)
PEGEEN (*Opening door, with temper*)   What ails you, or what is it you're wanting at this hour of the night?
WIDOW QUIN (*Coming in a step and peering at* CHRISTY)   I'm after meeting Shawn Keogh and Father Reilly below, who told me of your curiosity man, and they fearing by this time he was maybe roaring, romping on your hands with drink.
PEGEEN (*Pointing to* CHRISTY)   Look now is he roaring and he stretched away drowsy with his supper and his mug of milk. Walk down and tell that to Father Reilly and to Shaneen Keogh.
WIDOW QUIN (*Coming forward*)   I'll not see them again, for I've their word to lead that lad forward for to lodge with me.
PEGEEN (*In blank amazement*)   This night, is it?
WIDOW QUIN (*Going over*)   This night. "It isn't fitting" says the priesteen,[20] "to have his likeness lodging with an orphaned girl." (*To* CHRISTY)   God save you, mister!
CHRISTY (*Shyly*)   God save you kindly.
WIDOW QUIN (*Looking at him with half-amazed curiosity*)   Well, aren't you a little smiling fellow? It should have been great and bitter torments did rouse your spirits to a deed of blood.

[20] Little priest.

CHRISTY (*Doubtfully*) It should, maybe.
WIDOW QUIN It's more than "maybe" I'm saying, and it'd soften my heart to see you sitting so simple with your cup and cake, and you fitter to be saying your catechism than slaying your da.
PEGEEN (*At counter, washing glasses*) There's talking when any'd see he's fit to be holding his head high with the wonders of the world. Walk on from this, for I'll not have him tormented and he destroyed travelling since Tuesday was a week.
WIDOW QUIN (*Peaceably*) We'll be walking surely when his supper's done, and you'll find we're great company, young fellow, when it's of the like of you and me you'd hear the penny poets[21] singing in an August Fair.
CHRISTY (*Innocently*) Did you kill your father?
PEGEEN (*Contemptuously*) She did not. She hit himself[22] with a worm pick, and the rusted poison did corrode his blood the way he never overed[23] it, and died after. That was a sneaky kind of murder did win small glory with the boys itself. (*She crosses to* CHRISTY's *left*).
WIDOW QUIN (*With good-humour*) If it didn't, maybe all knows a widow woman has buried her children and destroyed her man is a wiser comrade for a young lad than a girl, the like of you, who'd go helter-skeltering after any man would let you a wink upon the road.
PEGEEN (*Breaking out into wild rage*) And you'll say that, Widow Quin, and you gasping with the rage you had racing the hill beyond to look on his face.
WIDOW QUIN (*Laughing derisively*) Me, is it? Well, Father Reilly has cuteness to divide you now. (*She pulls* CHRISTY *up*) There's great temptation in a man did slay his da, and we'd best be going, young fellow; so rise up and come with me.
PEGEEN (*Seizing his arm*) He'll not stir. He's pot-boy in this place, and I'll not have him stolen off and kidnabbed while himself's abroad.
WIDOW QUIN It'd be a crazy pot-boy'd lodge him in the shebeen where he works by day, so you'd have a right to come on, young fellow, till you see my little houseen, a perch[24] off on the rising hill.
PEGEEN Wait till morning, Christy Mahon. Wait till you lay eyes on her leaky thatch is growing more pasture for her buck goat than her square of fields, and she without a tramp itself to keep in order her place at all.

[21] At the fair, ballads are sold for a penny.
[22] Her husband.
[23] Got over.
[24] A very short distance.

WIDOW QUIN When you see me contriving in my little gardens, Christy Mahon, you'll swear the Lord God formed me to be living lone, and that there isn't my match in Mayo for thatching, or mowing, or shearing sheep.

PEGEEN (*With noisy scorn*) It's true the Lord God formed you to contrive indeed. Doesn't the world know you reared a black lamb at your own breast, so that the Lord Bishop of Connaught felt the elements of a Christian, and he eating it after in a kidney stew? Doesn't the world know you've been seen shaving the foxy skipper from France for a threepenny bit, and a sop of grass tobacco would wring the liver from a mountain goat you'd meet leaping the hills?

WIDOW QUIN (*With amusement*) Do you hear her now, young fellow? Do you hear the way she'll be rating at your own self when a week is by?

PEGEEN (*To* CHRISTY) Don't heed her. Tell her to go into her pigsty and not plague us here.

WIDOW QUIN I'm going; but he'll come with me.

PEGEEN (*Shaking him*) Are you dumb, young fellow?

CHRISTY (*Timidly, to* WIDOW QUIN) God increase you; but I'm pot-boy in this place, and it's here I'd liefer stay.

PEGEEN (*Triumphantly*) Now you have heard him, and go on from this.

WIDOW QUIN (*Looking round the room*) It's lonesome this hour crossing the hill, and if he won't come along with me, I'd have a right maybe to stop this night with yourselves. Let me stretch out on the settle, Pegeen Mike; and himself can lie by the hearth.

PEGEEN (*Short and fiercely*) Faith, I won't. Quit off or I will send you now.

WIDOW QUIN (*Gathering her shawl up*) Well, it's a terror to be aged a score.[25] (*To* CHRISTY) God bless you now, young fellow, and let you be wary, or there's right torment will await you here if you go romancing with her like, and she waiting only, as they bade me say, on a sheepskin parchment to be wed with Shawn Keogh of Killakeen.

CHRISTY (*Going to* PEGEEN *as she bolts the door*) What's that she's after saying?

PEGEEN Lies and blather, you've no call to mind. Well, isn't Shawn Keogh an impudent fellow to send up spying on me? Wait till I lay hands on him. Let him wait, I'm saying.

CHRISTY And you're not wedding him at all?

PEGEEN I wouldn't wed him if a bishop came walking for to join us here.

CHRISTY That God in glory may be thanked for that.

PEGEEN There's your bed now. I've put a quilt upon you I'm after

---

[25] "Well, it's terrifying to be twenty years old!"

quilting a while since with my own two hands, and you'd best stretch out now for your sleep, and may God give you a good rest till I call you in the morning when the cocks will crow.

CHRISTY (*As she goes to inner room*) May God and Mary and St. Patrick bless you and reward you, for your kindly talk. (*She shuts the door behind her. He settles his bed slowly, feeling the quilt with immense satisfaction*) Well, it's a clean bed and soft with it, and it's great luck and company I've won me in the end of time—two fine women fighting for the likes of me—till I'm thinking this night wasn't I a foolish fellow not to kill my father in the years gone by.

Curtain

Act Two

SCENE, *as before. Brilliant morning light.* CHRISTY, *looking bright and cheerful, is cleaning a girl's boots.*

CHRISTY (*To himself, counting jugs on dresser*) Half a hundred beyond. Ten there. A score that's above. Eighty jugs. Six cups and a broken one. Two plates. A power of glasses. Bottles, a school-master'd be hard set to count, and enough in them, I'm thinking, to drunken all the wealth and wisdom of the County Clare. (*He puts down the boot carefully*) There's her boots now, nice and decent for her evening use, and isn't it grand brushes she has? (*He puts them down and goes by degrees to the looking-glass*) Well, this'd be a fine place to be my whole life talking out with swearing Christians, in place of my old dogs and cat, and I stalking around, smoking my pipe and drinking my fill, and never a day's work but drawing a cork an odd time, or wiping a glass, or rinsing out a shiny tumbler for a decent man. (*He takes the looking-glass from the wall and puts it on the back of a chair; then sits down in front of it and begins washing his face*) Didn't I know rightly I was handsome, though it was the divil's own mirror we had beyond, would twist a squint across an angel's brow; and I'll be growing fine from this day, the way I'll have a soft lovely skin on me and won't be the like of the clumsy young fellows do be ploughing all times in the earth and dung. (*He starts*) Is she coming again? (*He looks out*) Stranger girls. God help me, where'll I hide myself away and my long neck naked to the world? (*He looks out*) I'd best go to the room maybe till I'm dressed again. (*He gathers up his coat and the looking-glass, and runs into the inner room. The door is pushed open, and* SUSAN BRADY *looks in, and knocks on door*)

SUSAN There's nobody in it. (*Knocks again*)

NELLY (*Pushing her in and following her, with* HONOR BLAKE *and* SARA TANSEY) It'd be early for them both to be out walking the hill.

SUSAN I'm thinking Shawn Keogh was making game of us and there's no such man in it at all.

HONOR (*Pointing to straw and quilt*) Look at that. He's been sleeping there in the night. Well, it'll be a hard case[26] if he's gone off now, the way we'll never set our eyes on a man killed his father, and we after rising early and destroying ourselves running fast on the hill.

NELLY Are you thinking them's his boots?

SARA (*Taking them up*) If they are, there should be his father's track on them. Did you never read in the papers the way murdered men do bleed and drip?

SUSAN Is that blood there, Sara Tansey?

SARA (*Smelling it*) That's bog water, I'm thinking, but it's his own they are surely, for I never seen the like of them for whity mud, and red mud, and turf on them, and the fine sands of the sea. That man's been walking, I'm telling you. (*She goes down right, putting on one of his boots*)

SUSAN (*Going to window*) Maybe he's stolen off to Belmullet with the boots of Michael James, and you'd have a right so to follow after him, Sara Tansey, and you the one yoked the ass cart and drove ten miles to set your eyes on the man bit the yellow lady's nostril on the northern shore. (*She looks out*)

SARA (*Running to window with one boot on*) Don't be talking, and we fooled today. (*Putting on other boot*) There's a pair do fit me well, and I'll be keeping them for walking to the priest, when you'd be ashamed this place, going up winter and summer with nothing worth while to confess at all.

HONOR (*Who has been listening at the door*) Whisht! there's someone inside the room. (*She pushes door a chink open*) It's a man.

(SARA *kicks off boots and puts them where they were. They all stand in a line looking through chink*)

SARA I'll call him. Mister! Mister! (*He puts in his head*) Is Pegeen within?

[26] Bad luck.

CHRISTY (*Coming in as meek as a mouse, with the looking-glass held behind his back*) She's above on the cnuceen,[27] seeking the nanny goats, the way she'd have a sup of goat's milk for to colour my tea.
SARA And asking your pardon, is it you's the man killed his father?
CHRISTY (*Sidling toward the nail where the glass was hanging*) I am, God help me!
SARA (*Taking eggs she has brought*) Then my thousand welcomes to you, and I've run up with a brace of duck's eggs for your food today. Pegeen's ducks is no use, but these are the real rich sort. Hold out your hand and you'll see it's no lie I'm telling you.
CHRISTY (*Coming forward shyly, and holding out his left hand*) They're a great and weighty size.
SUSAN And I run up with a pat of butter, for it'd be a poor thing to have you eating your spuds dry, and you after running a great way since you did destroy your da.
CHRISTY Thank you kindly.
HONOR And I brought you a little cut of cake, for you should have a thin stomach on you, and you that length walking the world.
NELLY And I brought you a little laying pullet—boiled and all she is—was crushed at the fall of night by the curate's car. Feel the fat of that breast, mister.
CHRISTY It's bursting, surely. (*He feels it with the back of his hand, in which he holds the presents*)
SARA Will you pinch it? Is your right hand too sacred for to use at all? (*She slips round behind him*) It's a glass he has. Well, I never seen to this day a man with a looking-glass held to his back. Them that kills their fathers is a vain lot surely.

(*Girls giggle*)

CHRISTY (*Smiling innocently and piling presents on glass*) I'm very thankful to you all today . . .
WIDOW QUIN (*Coming in quickly, at door*) Sara Tansey, Susan Brady, Honor Blake! What in glory has you here at this hour of day?
GIRLS (*Giggling*) That's the man killed his father.
WIDOW QUIN (*Coming to them*) I know well it's the man; and I'm after putting him down in the sports below for racing, leaping, pitching, and the Lord knows what.
SARA (*Exuberantly*) That's right, Widow Quin. I'll bet my dowry that he'll lick the world.
WIDOW QUIN If you will, you'd have a right to have him fresh and

[27] Small hill, pronounced *nekeen*.

nourished in place of nursing a feast.[28] (*Taking presents*) Are you fasting or fed, young fellow?

CHRISTY   Fasting, if you please.

WIDOW QUIN (*Loudly*)   Well, you're the lot. Stir up now and give him his breakfast. (*To* CHRISTY) Come here to me (*She puts him on bench beside her while the girls make tea and get his breakfast*) and let you tell us your story before Pegeen will come, in place of grinning your ears off like the moon of May.

CHRISTY (*Beginning to be pleased*)   It's a long story; you'd be destroyed listening.

WIDOW QUIN   Don't be letting on to be shy, a fine, gamey, treacherous lad the like of you. Was it in your house beyond you cracked his skull?

CHRISTY (*Shy but flattered*)   It was not. We were digging spuds in his cold, sloping, stony, divil's patch of a field.

WIDOW QUIN   And you went asking money of him, or making talk of getting a wife would drive him from his farm?

CHRISTY   I did not, then; but there I was, digging and digging, and "You squinting idiot," says he, "let you walk down now and tell the priest you'll wed the Widow Casey in a score of days."

WIDOW QUIN   And what kind was she?

CHRISTY (*With horror*)   A walking terror from beyond the hills, and she two score and five years, and two hundredweights and five pounds in the weighing scales, with a limping leg on her, and a blinded eye, and she a woman of noted misbehaviour with the old and young.

GIRLS (*Clustering round him, serving him*)   Glory be.

WIDOW QUIN   And what did he want driving you to wed with her? (*She takes a bit of the chicken*)

CHRISTY (*Eating with growing satisfaction*)   He was letting on I was wanting a protector from the harshness of the world, and he without a thought the whole while but how he'd have her hut to live in and her gold to drink.

WIDOW QUIN   There's maybe worse than a dry hearth and a widow woman and your glass at night. So you hit him then?

CHRISTY (*Getting almost excited*)   I did not. "I won't wed her," says I, "when all know she did suckle me for six weeks when I came into the world, and she a hag this day with a tongue on her has the crows and seabirds scattered, the way they wouldn't cast a shadow on her garden with the dread of her curse."

WIDOW QUIN (*Teasingly*)   That one should be right company.

SARA (*Eagerly*)   Don't mind her. Did you kill him then?

[28] Hungry.

CHRISTY "She's too good for the like of you," says he, "and go on now or I'll flatten you out like a crawling beast has passed under a dray." "You will not if I can help it," says I. "Go on," says he, "or I'll have the divil making garters of your limbs tonight." "You will not if I can help it," says I. (*He sits up, brandishing his mug*)
SARA You were right surely.
CHRISTY (*Impressively*) With that the sun came out between the cloud and the hill, and it shining green in my face. "God have mercy on your soul," says he, lifting a scythe; "or on your own," says I, raising the loy.
SUSAN That's a grand story.
HONOR He tells it lovely.
CHRISTY (*Flattered and confident, waving bone*) He gave a drive with the scythe, and I gave a lep to the east. Then I turned around with my back to the north, and I hit a blow on the ridge of his skull, laid him stretched out, and he split to the knob of his gullet. (*He raises the chicken bone to his Adam's apple*)
GIRLS (*Together*) Well, you're a marvel! Oh, God bless you! You're the lad surely!
SUSAN I'm thinking the Lord God sent him this road to make a second husband to the Widow Quin, and she with a great yearning to be wedded, though all dread her here. Lift him on her knee, Sara Tansey.
WIDOW QUIN Don't tease him.
SARA (*Going over to dresser and counter very quickly, and getting two glasses and porter*) You're heroes surely, and let you drink a supeen with your arms linked like the outlandish lovers in the sailor's song. (*She links their arms and gives them the glasses*) There now. Drink a health to the wonders of the western world, the pirates, preachers, poteen-makers, with the jobbing jockies;[29] parching peelers, and the juries fill their stomachs selling judgments of the English law. (*Brandishing the bottle*)
WIDOW QUIN That's a right toast, Sara Tansey. Now, Christy.

> (*They drink with their arms linked, he drinking with his left hand, she with her right. As they are drinking,* PEGEEN MIKE *comes in with a milk can and stands aghast. They all spring away from* CHRISTY. *He goes down left.* WIDOW QUIN *remains seated*)

PEGEEN (*Angrily, to* SARA) What is it you're wanting?
SARA (*Twisting her apron*) An ounce of tobacco.
PEGEEN Have you tuppence?

---

[29] Poteen-peddlers, bootleggers.

SARA I've forgotten my purse.
PEGEEN Then you'd best be getting it and not fooling us here. (*To the* WIDOW QUIN, *with more elaborate scorn*) And what is it you're wanting, Widow Quin?
WIDOW QUIN (*Insolently*) A penn'orth of starch.
PEGEEN (*Breaking out*) And you without a white shift[30] or a shirt in your whole family since the drying of the flood. I've no starch for the like of you, and let you walk on now to Killamuck.
WIDOW QUIN (*Turning to* CHRISTY, *as she goes out with the girls*) Well, you're mighty huffy this day, Pegeen Mike, and, you young fellow, let you not forget the sports and racing when the noon is by.

(*They go out*)

PEGEEN (*Imperiously*) Fling out that rubbish and put them cups away. (CHRISTY *tidies away in great haste*) Shove in the bench by the wall. (*He does so*) And hang that glass on the nail. What disturbed it at all?
CHRISTY (*Very meekly*) I was making myself decent only, and this a fine country for young lovely girls.
PEGEEN (*Sharply*) Whisht your talking of girls. (*Goes to counter, right*)
CHRISTY Wouldn't any wish to be decent in a place . . .
PEGEEN Whisht I'm saying.
CHRISTY (*Looks at her face for a moment with great misgivings, then as a last effort, takes up a loy, and goes toward her, with feigned assurance*) It was with a loy the like of that I killed my father.
PEGEEN (*Still sharply*) You've told me that story six times since the dawn of day.
CHRISTY (*Reproachfully*) It's a queer thing you wouldn't care to be hearing it and them girls after walking four miles to be listening to me now.
PEGEEN (*Turning around astonished*) Four miles!
CHRISTY (*Apologetically*) Didn't himself say there were only four bona fides living in the place?
PEGEEN It's bona fides by the road they are, but that lot came over the river lepping the stones.[31] It's not three perches when you go like that, and I was down this morning looking on the papers the post-boy does have in his bag. (*With meaning and emphasis*) For there was great news this day, Christopher Mahon. (*She goes into room left*)
CHRISTY (*Suspiciously*) Is it news of my murder?
PEGEEN (*Inside*) Murder, indeed.

[30] Slip.
[31] Leaping over the stepping-stones in the water.

CHRISTY (*Loudly*)   A murdered da?
PEGEEN (*Coming in again and crossing right*)   There was not, but a story filled half a page of the hanging of a man. Ah, that should be a fearful end, young fellow, and it worst of all for a man who destroyed his da, for the like of him would get small mercies, and when it's dead he is, they'd put him in a narrow grave, with cheap sacking wrapping him round, and pour down quicklime on his head, the way you'd see a woman pouring any frish-frash from a cup.
CHRISTY (*Very miserably*)   Oh, God help me. Are you thinking I'm safe? You were saying at the fall of night, I was shut of jeopardy and I here with yourselves.
PEGEEN (*Severely*)   You'll be shut of jeopardy in no place if you go talking with a pack of wild girls the like of them do be walking abroad with the peelers, talking whispers at the fall of night.
CHRISTY (*With terror*)   And you're thinking they'd tell?
PEGEEN (*With mock sympathy*)   Who knows, God help you.
CHRISTY (*Loudly*)   What joy would they have to bring hanging to the likes of me?
PEGEEN   It's queer joys they have, and who knows the thing they'd do, if it'd make the green stones cry itself to think of you swaying and swiggling at the butt of a rope, and you with a fine, stout neck, God bless you! the way you'd be a half an hour, in great anguish, getting your death.
CHRISTY (*Getting his boots and putting them on*)   If there's that terror of them, it'd be best, maybe, I went on wandering like Esau or Cain and Abel on the sides of Neifin or the Erris plain.
PEGEEN (*Beginning to play with him*)   It would, maybe, for I've heard the Circuit Judges this place is a heartless crew.
CHRISTY (*Bitterly*)   It's more than Judges this place is a heartless crew. (*Looking up at her*) And isn't it a poor thing to be starting again and I a lonesome fellow will be looking out on women and girls the way the needy fallen spirits do be looking on the Lord?
PEGEEN   What call have you to be that lonesome when there's poor girls walking Mayo in their thousands now?
CHRISTY (*Grimly*)   It's well you know what call I have. It's well you know it's a lonesome thing to be passing small towns with the lights shining sideways when the night is down, or going in strange places with a dog noising before you and a dog noising behind, or drawn to the cities where you'd hear a voice kissing and talking deep love in every shadow of the ditch, and you passing on with an empty, hungry stomach failing from your heart.
PEGEEN   I'm thinking you're an odd man, Christy Mahon. The oddest

walking fellow I ever set my eyes on to this hour today.

CHRISTY What would any be but odd men and they living lonesome in the world?

PEGEEN I'm not odd, and I'm my whole life with my father only.

CHRISTY (*With infinite admiration*) How would a lovely handsome woman the like of you be lonesome when all men should be thronging around to hear the sweetness of your voice, and the little infant children should be pestering your steps I'm thinking, and you walking the roads.

PEGEEN I'm hard set to know what way a coaxing fellow the like of yourself should be lonesome either.

CHRISTY Coaxing?

PEGEEN Would you have me think a man never talked with the girls would have the words you've spoken today? It's only letting on you are to be lonesome, the way you'd get around me now.

CHRISTY I wish to God I was letting on; but I was lonesome all times, and born lonesome, I'm thinking, as the moon of dawn. (*Going to door*)

PEGEEN (*Puzzled by his talk*) Well, it's a story I'm not understanding at all why you'd be worse than another, Christy Mahon, and you a fine lad with the great savagery to destroy your da.

CHRISTY It's little I'm understanding myself, saving only that my heart's scalded this day, and I am going off stretching out the earth between us, the way I'll not be waking near you another dawn of the year till the two of us do arise to hope or judgment with the saints of God, and now I'd best be going with my wattle[32] in my hand, for hanging is a poor thing (*Turning to go*), and it's little welcome only is left me in this house today.

PEGEEN (*Sharply*) Christy! (*He turns round*) Come here to me. (*He goes toward her*) Lay down that switch and throw some sods on the fire. You're pot-boy in this place, and I'll not have you mitch off[33] from us now.

CHRISTY You were saying I'd be hanged if I stay.

PEGEEN (*Quite kindly at last*) I'm after going down and reading the fearful crimes of Ireland for two weeks or three, and there wasn't a word of your murder. (*Getting up and going over to the counter*) They've likely not found the body. You're safe so with ourselves.

CHRISTY (*Astonished, slowly*) It's making game of me you were, (*Following her with fearful joy*) and I can stay so, working at your side, and I not lonesome from this mortal day.

[32] Twig (used as a walking-stick).
[33] Sneak away.

PEGEEN   What's to hinder you from staying, except the widow woman or the young girls would inveigle you off?
CHRISTY   (*With rapture*)   And I'll have your words from this day filling my ears, and that look is come upon you meeting my two eyes, and I watching you loafing around in the warm sun, or rinsing your ankles when the night is come.
PEGEEN   (*Kindly, but a little embarrassed*)   I'm thinking you'll be a loyal young lad to have working around, and if you vexed me a while since with your leaguing with the girls, I wouldn't give a thraneen[34] for a lad hadn't a mighty spirit in him and a gamey heart.

(SHAWN KEOGH *runs in carrying a cleeve*[35] *on his back, followed by the* WIDOW QUIN)

SHAWN   (*To* PEGEEN)   I was passing below, and I seen your mountainy sheep eating cabbages in Jimmy's field. Run up or they'll be bursting surely.
PEGEEN   Oh, God mend them! (*She puts a shawl over her head and runs out*)
CHRISTY   (*Looking from one to the other. Still in high spirits*)   I'd best go to her aid maybe. I'm handy with ewes.
WIDOW QUIN   (*Closing the door*)   She can do that much, and there is Shaneen has long speeches for to tell you now. (*She sits down with an amused smile*)
SHAWN   (*Taking something from his pocket and offering it to* CHRISTY)   Do you see that, mister?
CHRISTY   (*Looking at it*)   The half of a ticket to the Western States![36]
SHAWN   (*Trembling with anxiety*)   I'll give it to you and my new hat (*Pulling it out of hamper*); and my breeches with the double seat (*Pulling it off*); and my new coat is woven from the blackest shearings for three miles around (*Giving him the coat*); I'll give you the whole of them, and my blessing, and the blessing of Father Reilly itself, maybe, if you'll quit from this and leave us in the peace we had till last night at the fall of dark.
CHRISTY   (*With a new arrogance*)   And for what is it you're wanting to get shut of me?
SHAWN   (*Looking to the* WIDOW *for help*)   I'm a poor scholar with middling faculties to coin a lie, so I'll tell you the truth, Christy Mahon. I'm wedding with Pegeen beyond, and I don't think well of having a clever fearless man the like of you dwelling in her house.

[34] A small piece of thread (therefore worthless).
[35] A basket.
[36] The United States.

CHRISTY (*Almost pugnaciously*)   And you'd be using bribery for to banish me?

SHAWN (*In an imploring voice*)   Let you not take it badly, mister honey, isn't beyond the best place for you where you'll have golden chains and shiny coats and you riding upon hunters with the ladies of the land. (*He makes an eager sign to the* WIDOW QUIN *to come to help him*)

WIDOW QUIN (*Coming over*)   It's true for him, and you'd best quit off and not have that poor girl setting her mind on you, for there's Shaneen thinks she wouldn't suit you though all is saying that she'll wed you now.

(CHRISTY *beams with delight*)

SHAWN (*In terrified earnest*)   She wouldn't suit you, and she with the devil's own temper the way you'd be strangling one another in a score of days. (*He makes the movement of strangling with his hands*) It's the like of me only that she's fit for, a quiet simple fellow wouldn't raise a hand upon her if she scratched itself.

WIDOW QUIN (*Putting* SHAWN'S *hat on* CHRISTY)   Fit them clothes on you anyhow, young fellow, and he'd maybe loan them to you for the sports. (*Pushing him toward inner door*) Fit them on and you can give your answer when you have them tried.

CHRISTY (*Beaming, delighted with the clothes*)   I will then. I'd like herself to see me in them tweeds and hat. (*He goes into room and shuts the door*)

SHAWN (*In great anxiety*)   He'd like herself to see them. He'll not leave us, Widow Quin. He's a score of divils in him the way it's well nigh certain he will wed Pegeen.

WIDOW QUIN (*Jeeringly*)   It's true all girls are fond of courage and do hate the like of you.

SHAWN (*Walking about in desperation*)   Oh, Widow Quin, what'll I be doing now? I'd inform again him, but he'd burst from Kilmainham[37] and he'd be sure and certain to destroy me. If I wasn't so God-fearing, I'd near have courage to come behind him and run a pike into his side. Oh, it's a hard case to be an orphan and not to have your father that you're used to, and you'd easy kill and make yourself a hero in the sight of all. (*Coming up to her*) Oh, Widow Quin, will you find me some contrivance when I've promised you a ewe?

WIDOW QUIN   A ewe's a small thing, but what would you give me if I did wed him and did save you so?

SHAWN (*With astonishment*)   You?

---

[37] Dublin jail.

WIDOW QUIN Aye. Would you give me the red cow you have and the mountainy ram, and the right of way across your rye path, and a load of dung at Michaelmas, and turbary[38] upon the western hill?

SHAWN (*Radiant with hope*) I would surely, and I'd give you the wedding-ring I have, and the loan of a new suit, the way you'd have him decent on the wedding-day. I'd give you two kids for your dinner, and a gallon of poteen, and I'd call the piper on the long car to your wedding from Crossmolina or from Ballina. I'd give you . . .

WIDOW QUIN That'll do so, and let you whisht, for he's coming now again.

(CHRISTY *comes in very natty in the new clothes.* WIDOW QUIN *goes to him admiringly*)

WIDOW QUIN If you seen yourself now, I'm thinking you'd be too proud to speak to us at all, and it'd be a pity surely to have your like sailing from Mayo to the Western World.

CHRISTY (*As proud as a peacock*) I'm not going. If this is a poor place itself, I'll make myself contented to be lodging here.

(WIDOW QUIN *makes a sign to* SHAWN *to leave them*)

SHAWN Well, I'm going measuring the race-course while the tide is low, so I'll leave you the garments and my blessing for the sports today. God bless you! (*He wriggles out*)

WIDOW QUIN (*Admiring* CHRISTY) Well, you're mighty spruce, young fellow. Sit down now while you're quiet till you talk with me.

CHRISTY (*Swaggering*) I'm going abroad on the hillside for to seek Pegeen.

WIDOW QUIN You'll have time and plenty for to seek Pegeen, and you heard me saying at the fall of night the two of us should be great company.

CHRISTY From this out I'll have no want of company when all sorts is bringing me their food and clothing, (*He swaggers to the door, tightening his belt*) the way they'd set their eyes upon a gallant orphan cleft his father with one blow to the breeches belt. (*He opens door, then staggers back*) Saints of glory! Holy angels from the throne of light!

WIDOW QUIN (*Going over*) What ails you?

CHRISTY It's the walking spirit of my murdered da!

WIDOW QUIN (*Looking out*) Is it that tramper?

CHRISTY (*Wildly*) Where'll I hide my poor body from that ghost of hell?

[38] The right to dig turf on another's land.

(*The door is pushed open, and old* MAHON *appears on threshold.* CHRISTY *darts in behind door*)

WIDOW QUIN (*In great amusement*) God save you, my poor man.

MAHON (*Gruffly*) Did you see a young lad passing this way in the early morning or the fall of night?

WIDOW QUIN You're a queer kind to walk in not saluting at all.[39]

MAHON Did you see the young lad?

WIDOW QUIN (*Stiffly*) What kind was he?

MAHON An ugly young streeler[40] with a murderous gob[41] on him, and a little switch in his hand. I met a tramper seen him coming this way at the fall of night.

WIDOW QUIN There's harvest hundreds do be passing these days for the Sligo boat. For what is it you're wanting him, my poor man?

MAHON I want to destroy him for breaking the head on me with the clout of a loy. (*He takes off a big hat, and shows his head in a mass of bandages and plaster, with some pride*) It was he did that, and amn't I a great wonder to think I've traced him ten days with that rent in my crown?

WIDOW QUIN (*Taking his head in both hands and examining it with extreme delight*) That was a great blow. And who hit you? A robber maybe?

MAHON It was my own son hit me, and he the divil a robber, or anything else, but a dirty, stuttering lout.

WIDOW QUIN (*Letting go his skull and wiping her hands in her apron*) You'd best be wary of a mortified[42] scalp, I think they call it, lepping around with that wound in the splendour of the sun. It was a bad blow surely, and you should have vexed him fearful to make him strike that gash in his da.

MAHON Is it me?

WIDOW QUIN (*Amusing herself*) Aye. And isn't it a great shame when the old and hardened do torment the young?

MAHON (*Raging*) Torment him, is it? And I after holding out with the patience of a martyred saint till there's nothing but destruction on, and I'm driven out in my old age with none to aid me.

WIDOW QUIN (*Greatly amused*) It's a sacred wonder the way that wickedness will spoil a man.

MAHON My wickedness, is it? Amn't I after saying it is himself has me

---

[39] Not greeting.
[40] Stroller, vagrant who tells fanciful stories.
[41] Face (literally, *mouth*).
[42] Gangrenous; dying.

destroyed, and he a lier on walls, a talker of folly, a man you'd see stretched the half of the day in the brown ferns with his belly to the sun.

WIDOW QUIN Not working at all?

MAHON The divil a work, or if he did itself, you'd see him raising up a haystack like the stalk of a rush, or driving our last cow till he broke her leg at the hip, and when he wasn't at that he'd be fooling over little birds he had—finches and felts[43]—or making mugs at his own self in the bit of a glass we had hung on the wall.

WIDOW QUIN (*Looking at* CHRISTY) What way was he so foolish? It was running wild after the girls maybe?

MAHON (*With a shout of derision*) Running wild, is it? If he seen a red petticoat coming swinging over the hill, he'd be off to hide in the sticks, and you'd see him shooting out his sheep's eyes between the little twigs and the leaves, and his two ears rising like a hare looking out through a gap. Girls, indeed!

WIDOW QUIN It was drink maybe?

MAHON And he a poor fellow would get drunk on the smell of a pint. He'd a queer rotten stomach, I'm telling you, and when I gave him three pulls from my pipe a while since, he was taken with contortions till I had to send him in the ass cart to the females' nurse.

WIDOW QUIN (*Clasping her hands*) Well, I never till this day heard tell of a man the like of that!

MAHON I'd take a mighty oath you didn't surely, and wasn't he the laughing joke of every female woman where four baronies meet, the way the girls would stop their weeding if they seen him coming the road to let a roar at him, and call him the looney of Mahon's.

WIDOW QUIN I'd give the world and all to see the like of him. What kind was he?

MAHON A small low fellow.

WIDOW QUIN And dark?

MAHON Dark and dirty.

WIDOW QUIN (*Considering*) I'm thinking I seen him.

MAHON (*Eagerly*) An ugly young blackguard.

WIDOW QUIN A hideous, fearful villain, and the spit[44] of you.

MAHON What way is he fled?

WIDOW QUIN Gone over the hills to catch a coasting steamer to the north or south.

MAHON Could I pull up on him now?

[43] Thrushes.
[44] Spitting image.

WIDOW QUIN If you'll cross the sands below where the tide is out, you'll be in it as soon as himself, for he had to go round ten miles by the top of the bay. (*She points to the door*) Strike down by the head beyond and then follow on the roadway to the north and east.

(MAHON *goes abruptly*)

WIDOW QUIN (*Shouting after him*) Let you give him a good vengeance when you come up with him, but don't put yourself in the power of the law, for it'd be a poor thing to see a judge in his black cap reading out his sentence on a civil warrior the like of you. (*She swings the door to and looks at* CHRISTY, *who is cowering in terror, for a moment, then she bursts into a laugh*) Well, you're the walking Playboy[45] of the Western World, and that's the poor man you had divided to his breeches belt.

CHRISTY (*Looking out: then, to her*) What'll Pegeen say when she hears that story? What'll she be saying to me now?

WIDOW QUIN She'll knock the head of you, I'm thinking, and drive you from the door. God help her to be taking you for a wonder, and you a little schemer making up the story you destroyed your da.

CHRISTY (*Turning to the door, nearly speechless with rage, half to himself*) To be letting on he was dead, and coming back to his life, and following after me like an old weasel tracing a rat, and coming in here laying desolation between my own self and the fine women of Ireland, and he a kind of carcase that you'd fling upon the sea ...

WIDOW QUIN (*More soberly*) There's talking for a man's one only son.

CHRISTY (*Breaking out*) His one son, is it? May I meet him with one tooth and it aching, and one eye to be seeing seven and seventy divils in the twists of the road, and one old timber leg on him to limp into the scalding grave. (*Looking out*) There he is now crossing the strands, and that the Lord God would send a high wave to wash him from the world.

WIDOW QUIN (*Scandalized*) Have you no shame? (*Putting her hand on his shoulder and turning him round*) What ails you? Near crying, is it?

CHRISTY (*In despair and grief*) Amn't I after seeing the lovelight of the star of knowledge shining from her brow, and hearing words would put you thinking on the holy Brigid speaking to the infant saints, and now she'll be turning again, and speaking hard words to me, like an old woman with a spavindy[46] ass she'd have, urging on a hill.

WIDOW QUIN There's poetry talk for a girl you'd see itching and scratch-

---

[45] Used ironically, in the sense of a hoaxer. At the end of the play, the word will be used literally.
[46] Lame.

ing, and she with a stale stink of poteen on her from selling in the shop.

CHRISTY (*Impatiently*) It's her like is fitted to be handling merchandise in the heavens above, and what'll I be doing now, I ask you, and I a kind of wonder was jilted by the heavens when a day was by.

(*There is a distant noise of girls' voices.* WIDOW QUIN *looks from window and comes to him, hurriedly*)

WIDOW QUIN You'll be doing like myself, I'm thinking, when I did destroy my man, for I'm above many's the day, odd times in great spirits, abroad in the sunshine, darning a stocking or stitching a shift; and odd times again looking out on the schooners, hookers, trawlers is sailing the sea, and I thinking on the gallant hairy fellows are drifting beyond, and myself long years living alone.

CHRISTY (*Interested*) You're like me, so.

WIDOW QUIN I am your like, and it's for that I'm taking a fancy to you, and I with my little houseen above where there'd be myself to tend you, and none to ask were you a murderer or what at all.

CHRISTY And what would I be doing if I left Pegeen?

WIDOW QUIN I've nice jobs you could be doing, gathering shells to make a whitewash for our hut within, building up a little goose-house, or stretching a new skin on an old curragh[47] I have, and if my hut is far from all sides, it's there you'll meet the wisest old men, I tell you, at the corner of my wheel, and it's there yourself and me will have great times whispering and hugging. . . .

VOICES (*Outside, calling far away*) Christy! Christy Mahon! Christy!

CHRISTY Is it Pegeen Mike?

WIDOW QUIN It's the young girls, I'm thinking, coming to bring you to the sports below, and what is it you'll have me to tell them now?

CHRISTY Aid me for to win Pegeen. It's herself only that I'm seeking now. (WIDOW QUIN *gets up and goes to window*) Aid me for to win her, and I'll be asking God to stretch a hand to you in the hour of death, and lead you short cuts through the Meadows of Ease, and up the floor of Heaven to the Footstool of the Virgin's Son.

WIDOW QUIN There's praying.

VOICES (*Nearer*) Christy! Christy Mahon!

CHRISTY (*With agitation*) They're coming. Will you swear to aid and save me for the love of Christ?

WIDOW QUIN (*Looks at him for a moment*) If I aid you, will you swear to give me a right of way I want, and a mountainy ram, and a load of dung at Michaelmas, the time that you'll be master here?

CHRISTY I will, by the elements and stars of night.

---

[47] A small boat made of hoops and covered with horsehide or tarpaulin.

WIDOW QUIN   Then we'll not say a word of the old fellow, the way Pegeen won't know your story till the end of time.
CHRISTY   And if he chances to return again?
WIDOW QUIN   We'll swear he's a maniac and not your da. I could take an oath I seen him raving on the sands today.

(*Girls run in*)

SUSAN   Come on to the sports below. Pegeen says you're to come.
SARA TANSEY   The lepping's beginning, and we've a jockey's suit to fit upon you for the mule race on the sands below.
HONOR   Come on, will you?
CHRISTY   I will then if Pegeen's beyond.
SARA TANSEY   She's in the boreen[48] making game of Shaneen Keogh.
CHRISTY   Then I'll be going to her now. (*He runs out followed by the girls*)
WIDOW QUIN   Well, if the worst comes in the end of all, it'll be great game to see there's none to pity him but a widow woman, the like of me, has buried her children and destroyed her man. (*She goes out*)

Curtain

Act Three

SCENE   As before. Later in the day. JIMMY *comes in, slightly drunk.*

JIMMY (*Calls*)   Pegeen! (*Crosses to inner door*) Pegeen Mike! (*Comes back again into the room*) Pegeen! (PHILLY *comes in in the same state*) (*To* PHILLY) Did you see herself?
PHILLY   I did not; but I sent Shawn Keogh with the ass cart for to bear him home. (*Trying cupboards which are locked*) Well, isn't he a nasty man to get into such staggers[49] at a morning wake? and isn't herself the divil's daughter for locking,[50] and she so fussy after that young gaffer,[51]

[48] Lane.
[49] To get so drunk that he cannot walk straight.
[50] Locking up the whiskey.
[51] Farmer, yokel. In Christy's final speech, he calls himself a "gaffer," meaning a leader. His progress is from the former meaning to the latter.

you might take your death with drought and none to heed you?
JIMMY   It's little wonder she'd be fussy, and he after bringing bankrupt ruin on the roulette man, and the trick-o'-the-loop man, and breaking the nose of the cockshot-man, and winning all in the sports below, racing, lepping, dancing, and the Lord knows what! He's right luck, I'm telling you.
PHILLY   If he has, he'll be rightly hobbled yet, and he not able to say ten words without making a brag of the way he killed his father, and the great blow he hit with the loy.
JIMMY   A man can't hang by his own informing, and his father should be rotten by now.

(*Old* MAHON *passes window slowly*)

PHILLY   Supposing a man's digging spuds in that field with a long spade, and supposing he flings up the two halves of that skull, what'll be said then in the papers and the courts of law?
JIMMY   They'd say it was an old Dane, maybe, was drowned in the flood. (*Old* MAHON *comes in and sits down near door listening*) Did you never hear tell of the skulls they have in the city of Dublin, ranged out like blue jugs in a cabin of Connaught?
PHILLY   And you believe that?
JIMMY   (*Pugnaciously*)   Didn't a lad see them and he after coming from harvesting in the Liverpool boat? "They have them there," says he, "making a show of the great people there was one time walking the world. White skulls and black skulls and yellow skulls, and some with full teeth, and some haven't only but one."
PHILLY   It was no lie, maybe, for when I was a young lad there was a graveyard beyond the house with the remnants of a man who had thighs as long as your arm. He was a horrid man, I'm telling you, and there was many a fine Sunday I'd put him together for fun, and he with shiny bones, you wouldn't meet the like of these days in the cities of the world.
MAHON   (*Getting up*)   You wouldn't, is it? Lay your eyes on that skull, and tell me where and when there was another the like of it, is splintered only from the blow of a loy.
PHILLY   Glory be to God! And who hit you at all?
MAHON   (*Triumphantly*)   It was my own son hit me. Would you believe that?
JIMMY   Well, there's wonders hidden in the heart of man!
PHILLY   (*Suspiciously*)   And what way was it done?
MAHON   (*Wandering about the room*)   I'm after walking hundreds and long scores of miles, winning clean beds and the fill of my belly four times in the day, and I doing nothing but telling stories of that naked

truth. (*He comes to them a little aggressively*) Give me a supeen[52] and I'll tell you now.

(WIDOW QUIN *comes in and stands aghast behind him. He is facing* JIMMY *and* PHILLY, *who are on the left*)

JIMMY Ask herself beyond. She's the stuff hidden in her shawl.

WIDOW QUIN (*Coming to* MAHON *quickly*) You here, is it? You didn't go far at all?

MAHON I seen the coasting steamer passing, and I got a drought upon me and a cramping leg, so I said, "The divil go along with him," and turned again. (*Looking under her shawl*) And let you give me a supeen, for I'm destroyed travelling since Tuesday was a week.

WIDOW QUIN (*Getting a glass, in a cajoling tone*) Sit down then by the fire and take your ease for a space. You've a right to be destroyed indeed, with your walking, and fighting, and facing the sun. (*Giving him poteen from a stone jar she has brought in*) There now is a drink for you, and may it be to your happiness and length of life.

MAHON (*Taking glass greedily and sitting down by fire*) God increase you!

WIDOW QUIN (*Taking men to the right stealthily*) Do you know what? That man's raving from his wound today, for I met him a while since telling a rambling tale of a tinker had him destroyed. Then he heard of Christy's deed, and he up and says it was his son had cracked his skull. O, isn't madness a fright, for he'll go killing someone yet, and he thinking it's the man has struck him so?

JIMMY (*Entirely convinced*) It's a fright, surely. I knew a party was kicked in the head by a red mare, and he went killing horses a great while, till he eat the insides of a clock and died after.

PHILLY (*With suspicion*) Did he see Christy?

WIDOW QUIN He didn't. (*With a warning gesture*) Let you not be putting him in mind of him, or you'll be likely summoned if there's murder done. (*Looking round at* MAHON) Whisht! He's listening. Wait now till you hear me taking him easy and unravelling all. (*She goes to* MAHON) And what way are you feeling, mister? Are you in contentment now?

MAHON (*Slightly emotional from his drink*) I'm poorly only, for it's a hard story the way I'm left today, when it was I did tend him from his hour of birth, and he a dunce never reached his second book, the way he'd come from school, many's the day, with his legs lamed under him, and he blackened with his beatings like a tinker's ass. It's a hard

---

[52] Little sup, little drink (of whiskey).

story, I'm saying, the way some do have their next and nighest raising up a hand of murder on them, and some is lonesome getting their death with lamentation in the dead of night.

WIDOW QUIN (*Not knowing what to say*) To hear you talking so quiet, who'd know you were the same fellow we seen pass today?

MAHON I'm the same surely. The wrack and ruin of three score years; and it's a terror to live that length, I tell you, and to have your sons going to the dogs against you, and you wore out scolding them, and skelping them, and God knows what.

PHILLY (*To* JIMMY) He's not raving. (*To* WIDOW QUIN) Will you ask him what kind was his son?

WIDOW QUIN (*To* MAHON, *with a peculiar look*) Was your son that hit you a lad of one year and a score maybe, a great hand at racing and lepping and licking the world?

MAHON (*Turning on her with a roar of rage*) Didn't you hear me say he was the fool of men, the way from this out he'll know the orphan's lot with old and young making game of him and they swearing, raging, kicking at him like a mangy cur.

(*A great burst of cheering outside, some way off*)

MAHON (*Putting his hands to his ears*) What in the name of God do they want roaring below?

WIDOW QUIN (*With the shade of a smile*) They're cheering a young lad, the champion Playboy of the Western World.

(*More cheering*)

MAHON (*Going to window*) It'd split my heart to hear them, and I with pulses in my brain-pan for a week gone by. Is it racing they are?

JIMMY (*Looking from door*) It is then. They are mounting him for the mule race will be run upon the sands. That's the playboy on the winkered mule.[53]

MAHON (*Puzzled*) That lad, is it? If you said it was a fool he was, I'd have laid a mighty oath he was the likeness of my wandering son (*Uneasily, putting his hand to his head*) Faith, I'm thinking I'll go walking for to view the race.

WIDOW QUIN (*Stopping him, sharply*) You will not. You'd best take the road to Belmullet, and not be dilly-dallying in this place where there isn't a spot you could sleep.

PHILLY (*Coming forward*) Don't mind her. Mount there on the bench and you'll have a view of the whole. They're hurrying before the tide

---

[53] A mule with blinders or blinkers.

will rise, and it'd be near over if you went down the pathway through the crags below.

MAHON (*Mounts on bench,* WIDOW QUIN *beside him*) That's a right view again the edge of the sea. They're coming now from the point. He's leading. Who is he at all?

WIDOW QUIN He's the champion of the world, I tell you, and there isn't a hop'orth isn't falling lucky to his hands today.

PHILLY (*Looking out, interested in the race*) Look at that. They're pressing him now.

JIMMY He'll win it yet.

PHILLY Take your time, Jimmy Farrell. It's too soon to say.

WIDOW QUIN (*Shouting*) Watch him taking the gate. There's riding.

JIMMY (*Cheering*) More power to the young lad!

MAHON He's passing the third.

JIMMY He'll lick them yet!

WIDOW QUIN He'd lick them if he was running races with a score itself.

MAHON Look at the mule he has, kicking the stars.

WIDOW QUIN There was a lep! (*Catching hold of* MAHON *in her excitement*) He's fallen! He's mounted again! Faith, he's passing them all!

JIMMY Look at him skelping her!⁵⁴

PHILLY And the mountain girls hooshing him on!

JIMMY It's the last turn! The post's cleared for them now!

MAHON Look at the narrow place. He'll be into the bogs! (*With a yell*) Good rider! He's through it again!

JIMMY He's neck and neck!

MAHON Good boy to him! Flames, but he's in!

(*Great cheering, in which all join*)

MAHON (*With hesitation*) What's that? They're raising him up. They're coming this way. (*With a roar of rage and astonishment*) It's Christy! by the stars of God! I'd know his way of spitting and he astride the moon.

(*He jumps down and makes for the door, but* WIDOW QUIN *catches him and pulls him back*)

WIDOW QUIN Stay quiet, will you. That's not your son. (*To Jimmy*) Stop him, or you'll get a month for the abetting of manslaughter and be fined as well.

JIMMY I'll hold him.

MAHON (*Struggling*) Let me out! Let me out, the lot of you! till I have my vengeance on his head today.

⁵⁴ Slapping (to make the mule go faster).

WIDOW QUIN (*Shaking him, vehemently*) That's not your son. That's a man is going to make a marriage with the daughter of this house, a place with fine trade, with a license, and with poteen too.

MAHON (*Amazed*) That man marrying a decent and a moneyed girl! Is it mad yous are? Is it in a crazyhouse for females that I'm landed now?

WIDOW QUIN It's mad yourself is with the blow upon your head. That lad is the wonder of the Western World.

MAHON I seen it's my son.

WIDOW QUIN You seen that you're mad. (*Cheering outside*) Do you hear them cheering him in the zigzags of the road? Aren't you after saying that your son's a fool, and how would they be cheering a true idiot born?

MAHON (*Getting distressed*) It's maybe out of reason that that man's himself. (*Cheering again*) There's none surely will go cheering him. Oh, I'm raving with a madness that would fright the world! (*He sits down with his hand to his head*) There was one time I seen ten scarlet divils letting on they'd cork my spirit in a gallon can; and one time I seen rats as big as badgers sucking the life blood from the butt of my lug;[55] but I never till this day confused that dribbling idiot with a likely man. I'm destroyed surely.

WIDOW QUIN And who'd wonder when it's your brain-pan that is gaping now?

MAHON Then the blight of the sacred drought upon myself and him, for I never went mad to this day, and I not three weeks with the Limerick girls drinking myself silly, and parlatic[56] from the dusk to dawn. (*To* WIDOW QUIN, *suddenly*) Is my visage astray?

WIDOW QUIN It is then. You're a sniggering maniac, a child could see.

MAHON (*Getting up more cheerfully*) Then I'd best be going to the union beyond, and there'll be a welcome before me, I tell you (*With great pride*), and I a terrible and fearful case, the way that there I was one time, screeching in a straitened waistcoat, with seven doctors writing out my sayings in a printed book. Would you believe that?

WIDOW QUIN If you're a wonder itself, you'd best be hasty, for them lads caught a maniac one time and pelted the poor creature till he ran out, raving and foaming, and was drowned in the sea.

MAHON (*With philosophy*) It's true mankind is the divil when your head's astray. Let me out now and I'll slip down the boreen, and not see them so.

[55] My earlobe.
[56] Paralyzed (paralytic).

WIDOW QUIN (*Showing him out*) That's it. Run to the right, and not a one will see.

(*He runs off*)

PHILLY (*Wisely*) You're at some gaming, Widow Quin; but I'll walk after him and give him his dinner and a time to rest, and I'll see then if he's raving or as sane as you.

WIDOW QUIN (*Annoyed*) If you go near that lad, let you be wary of your head, I'm saying. Didn't you hear him telling he was crazed at times?

PHILLY I heard him telling a power; and I'm thinking we'll have right sport, before night will fall. (*He goes out*)

JIMMY Well, Philly's a conceited and foolish man. How could that madman have his senses and his brain-pan slit? I'll go after them and see him turn on Philly now.

(*He goes;* WIDOW QUIN *hides poteen behind counter. Then hubbub outside*)

VOICES There you are! Good jumper! Grand lepper! Darlint boy! He's the racer! Bear him on, will you!

(CHRISTY *comes in, in jockey's dress, with* PEGEEN MIKE, SARA, *and other girls, and men*)

PEGEEN (*To crowd*) Go on now and don't destroy him and he drenching with sweat. Go along, I'm saying, and have your tug-of-warring till he's dried his skin.

CROWD Here's his prizes! A bagpipes! A fiddle was played by a poet in the years gone by! A flat and three-thorned blackthorn would lick the scholars out of Dublin town!

CHRISTY (*Taking prizes from the men*) Thank you kindly, the lot of you. But you'd say it was little only I did this day if you'd seen me a while since striking my one single blow.

TOWN CRIER (*Outside, ringing a bell*) Take notice, last event of this day! Tug-of-warring on the green below! Come on, the lot of you! Great achievements for all Mayo men!

PEGEEN Go on, and leave him for to rest and dry. Go on, I tell you, for he'll do no more. (*She hustles crowd out;* WIDOW QUIN *following them*)

MEN (*Going*) Come on, then. Good luck for the while!

PEGEEN (*Radiantly, wiping his face with her shawl*) Well, you're the lad, and you'll have great times from this out when you could win that wealth of prizes, and you sweating in the heat of noon!

CHRISTY (*Looking at her with delight*) I'll have great times if I win the crowning prize I'm seeking now, and that's your promise that you'll wed me in a fortnight, when our banns is called.

PEGEEN (*Backing away from him*) You've right daring to go ask me that, when all knows you'll be starting to some girl in your own townland, when your father's rotten in four months, or five.

CHRISTY (*Indignantly*) Starting from you, is it? (*He follows her*) I will not, then, and when the airs is warming in four months, or five, it's then yourself and me should be pacing Neifin in the dews of night, the times sweet smells do be rising, and you'd see a little shiny new moon, maybe, sinking on the hills.

PEGEEN (*Looking at him playfully*) And it's that kind of a poacher's love you'd make, Christy Mahon, on the sides of Neifin, when the night is down?

CHRISTY It's little you'll think if my love's a poacher's, or an earl's itself, when you'll feel my two hands stretched around you, and I squeezing kisses on your puckered lips, till I'd feel a kind of pity for the Lord God in all ages sitting lonesome in his golden chair.

PEGEEN That'll be right fun, Christy Mahon, and any girl would walk her heart out before she'd meet a young man was your like for eloquence, or talk, at all.

CHRISTY (*Encouraged*) Let you wait, to hear me talking, till we're astray in Erris, when Good Friday's by, drinking a sup from a well, and making mighty kisses with our wetted mouths, or gaming in a gap of sunshine, with yourself stretched back unto your necklace, in the flowers of the earth.

PEGEEN (*In a lower voice, moved by his tone*) I'd be nice so, is it?

CHRISTY (*With rapture*) If the mitred bishops seen you that time, they'd be the like of the holy prophets, I'm thinking, do be straining the bars of Paradise to lay eyes on the Lady Helen of Troy, and she abroad, pacing back and forward, with a nosegay in her golden shawl.

PEGEEN (*With real tenderness*) And what is it I have, Christy Mahon, to make me fitting entertainment for the like of you, that has such poet's talking, and such bravery of heart?

CHRISTY (*In a low voice*) Isn't there the light of seven heavens in your heart alone, the way you'll be an angel's lamp to me from this out, and I abroad in the darkness, spearing salmons in the Owen, or the Carrowmore?

PEGEEN If I was your wife, I'd be along with you those nights, Christy Mahon, the way you'd see I was a great hand at coaxing bailiffs, or coining funny nicknames for the stars of night.

CHRISTY You, is it? Taking your death in the hailstones, or in the fogs of dawn.

PEGEEN   Yourself and me would shelter easy in a narrow bush, (*With a qualm of dread*) but we're only talking, maybe, for this would be a poor, thatched place to hold a fine lad is the like of you.

CHRISTY   (*Putting his arm around her*)   If I wasn't a good Christian, it's on my naked knees I'd be saying my prayers and paters to every jackstraw you have roofing your head, and every stony pebble is paving the laneway to your door.

PEGEEN   (*Radiantly*)   If that's the truth, I'll be burning candles from this out to the miracles of God that have brought you from the south today, and I, with my gowns bought ready, the way that I can wed you, and not wait at all.

CHRISTY   It's miracles, and that's the truth. Me there toiling a long while, and walking a long while, not knowing at all I was drawing all times nearer to this holy day.

PEGEEN   And myself, a girl, was tempted often to go sailing the seas till I'd marry a Jew-man, with ten kegs of gold, and I not knowing at all there was the like of you drawing nearer, like the stars of God.

CHRISTY   And to think I'm long years hearing women talking that talk, to all bloody fools, and this the first time I've heard the like of your voice talking sweetly for my own delight.

PEGEEN   And to think it's me is talking sweetly, Christy Mahon, and I the fright of seven townlands for my biting tongue. Well, the heart's a wonder; and, I'm thinking, there won't be our like in Mayo, for gallant lovers, from this hour, today. (*Drunken singing is heard outside*) There's my father coming from the wake, and when he's had his sleep we'll tell him, for he's peaceful then. (*They separate*)

MICHAEL   (*Singing outside*)

>   The jailor and the turnkey
>   They quickly ran us down,
>   And brought us back as prisoners
>   Once more to Cavan town.

(*He comes in supported by* SHAWN)

>   There we lay bewailing
>   All in a prison bound. . . .

(*He see* CHRISTY. *Goes and shakes him drunkenly by the hand, while* PEGEEN *and* SHAWN *talk on the left*)

MICHAEL   (*To* CHRISTY)   The blessing of God and the holy angels on your head, young fellow. I hear tell you're after winning all in the sports below; and wasn't it a shame I didn't bear you along with me to Kate

Cassidy's wake, a fine, stout lad, the like of you, for you'd never see the match of it for flows of drink, the way when we sunk her bones at noonday in her narrow grave, there were five men, aye, and six men, stretched out retching speechless on the holy stones.

CHRISTY (*Uneasily, watching* PEGEEN) Is that the truth?

MICHAEL It is then, and aren't you a louty schemer to go burying your poor father unbeknownst when you'd a right to throw him on the crupper[57] of a Kerry mule and drive him westwards, like holy Joseph in the days gone by, the way we could have given him a decent burial, and not have him rotting beyond, and not a Christian drinking a smart drop to the glory of his soul?

CHRISTY (*Gruffly*) It's well enough he's lying, for the likes of him.

MICHAEL (*Slapping him on the back*) Well, aren't you a hardened slayer? It'll be a poor thing for the household man where you go sniffing for a female wife; and (*Pointing to* SHAWN) look beyond at that shy and decent Christian I have chosen for my daughter's hand, and I after getting the gilded dispensation this day for to wed them now.

CHRISTY And you'll be wedding them this day, is it?

MICHAEL (*Drawing himself up*) Aye. Are you thinking, if I'm drunk itself, I'd leave my daughter living single with a little frisky rascal is the like of you?

PEGEEN (*Breaking away from* SHAWN) Is it the truth the dispensation's come?

MICHAEL (*Triumphantly*) Father Reilly's after reading it in gallous[58] Latin, and "It's come in the nick of time," says he; "so I'll wed them in a hurry, dreading that young gaffer who'd capsize the stars."

PEGEEN (*Fiercely*) He's missed his nick of time, for it's that lad, Christy Mahon, that I'm wedding now.

MICHAEL (*Loudly with horror*) You'd be making him a son to me, and he wet and crusted with his father's blood?

PEGEEN Aye. Wouldn't it be a bitter thing for a girl to go marrying the like of Shaneen, and he a middling kind of a scarecrow, with no savagery or fine words in him at all?

MICHAEL (*Gasping and sinking on a chair*) Oh, aren't you a heathen daughter to go shaking the fat of my heart, and I swamped and drownded with the weight of drink? Would you have them turning on me the way that I'd be roaring to the dawn of day with the wind upon my heart? Have you not a word to aid me, Shaneen? Are you not jealous at all?

---

[57] Rump.
[58] Long-winded and impressive-sounding.

SHAWN (*In great misery*) I'd be afeard to be jealous of a man did slay his da.
PEGEEN Well, it'd be a poor thing to go marrying your like. I'm seeing there's a world of peril for an orphan girl, and isn't it a great blessing I didn't wed you, before himself came walking from the west or south?
SHAWN It's a queer story you'd go picking a dirty tramp up from the highways of the world.
PEGEEN (*Playfully*) And you think you're a likely beau to go straying along with, the shiny Sundays of the opening year, when it's sooner on a bullock's liver you'd put a poor girl thinking than on the lily or the rose?
SHAWN And have you no mind of my weight of passion, and the holy dispensation, and the drift of heifers I am giving, and the golden ring?
PEGEEN I'm thinking you're too fine for the like of me, Shawn Keogh of Killakeen, and let you go off till you'd find a radiant lady with droves of bullocks on the plains of Meath, and herself bedizened in the diamond jewelries of Pharaoh's ma. That'd be your match, Shaneen. So God save you now! (*She retreats behind* CHRISTY)
SHAWN Won't you hear me telling you . . . ?
CHRISTY (*With ferocity*) Take yourself from this, young fellow, or I'll maybe add a murder to my deeds today.
MICHAEL (*Springing up with a shriek*) Murder is it? Is it mad yous are? Would you go making murder in this place, and it piled with poteen for our drink tonight? Go on to the foreshore if it's fighting you want, where the rising tide will wash all traces from the memory of man. (*Pushing* SHAWN *toward* CHRISTY)
SHAWN (*Shaking himself free, and getting behind* MICHAEL) I'll not fight him, Michael James. I'd liefer live a bachelor, simmering in passions to the end of time, than face a lepping savage the like of him has descended from the Lord knows where. Strike him yourself, Michael James, or you'll lose my drift of heifers and my blue bull from Sneem.
MICHAEL Is it me fight him, when it's father-slaying he's bred to now? (*Pushing* SHAWN) Go on, you fool, and fight him now.
SHAWN (*Coming forward a little*) Will I strike him with my hand?
MICHAEL Take the loy is on your western side.
SHAWN I'd be afeared of the gallows if I struck him with that.
CHRISTY (*Taking up the loy*) Then I'll make you face the gallows or quit off from this.

(SHAWN *flies out of the door*)

CHRISTY Well, fine weather be after him (*Going to* MICHAEL, *coaxingly*) and I'm thinking you wouldn't wish to have that quaking blackguard in your house at all. Let you give us your blessing and hear her swear her faith to me, for I'm mounted on the springtide of the stars of luck, the way it'll be good for any to have me in the house.

PEGEEN (*At the other side of* MICHAEL) Bless us now, for I swear to God I'll wed him, and I'll not renege.

MICHAEL (*Standing up in the centre, holding on to both of them*) It's the will of God, I'm thinking, that all should win an easy or a cruel end, and it's the will of God that all should rear up lengthy families for the nurture of the earth. What's a single man, I ask you, eating a bit in one house and drinking a sup in another, and he with no place of his own, like an old braying jackass strayed upon the rocks? (*To* CHRISTY) It's many would be in dread to bring your like into their house for to end them, maybe, with a sudden end; but I'm a decent man of Ireland, and I liefer face the grave untimely and I seeing a score of grandsons growing up little gallant swearers by the name of God, than go peopling my bedside with puny weeds the like of what you'd breed, I'm thinking, out of Shaneen Keogh. (*He joins their hands*) A daring fellow is the jewel of the world, and a man did split his father's middle with a single clout, should have the bravery of ten, so may God and Mary and St. Patrick bless you, and increase you from this mortal day.

CHRISTY AND PEGEEN Amen, O Lord!

(*Hubbub outside*)
(*Old* MAHON *rushes in, followed by all the crowd, and* WIDOW QUIN. *He makes a rush at* CHRISTY, *knocks him down and begins to beat him*)

PEGEEN (*Dragging back his arm*) Stop that, will you? Who are you at all?

MAHON His father, God forgive me!

PEGEEN (*Drawing back*) Is it rose from the dead?

MAHON Do you think I look so easy quenched with the tap of a loy? (*Beats* CHRISTY *again*)

PEGEEN (*Glaring at* CHRISTY) And it's lies you told, letting on you had him slitted, and you nothing at all.

CHRISTY (*Catching* MAHON'S *stick*) He's not my father. He's a raving maniac would scare the world. (*Pointing to* WIDOW QUIN) Herself knows it is true.

CROWD You're fooling Pegeen! The Widow Quin seen him this day, and you likely knew! You're a liar!

CHRISTY (*Dumbfounded*) It's himself was a liar, lying stretched out with an open head on him, letting on he was dead.

MAHON Weren't you off racing the hills before I got my breath with the start I had seeing you turn on me at all?

PEGEEN And to think of the coaxing glory we had given him, and he after doing nothing but hitting a soft blow and chasing northward in a sweat of fear. Quit off from this.

CHRISTY (*Piteously*) You've seen my doings this day, and let you save me from the old man; for why would you be in such a scorch of haste to spur me to destruction now?

PEGEEN It's there your treachery is spurring me, till I'm hard set to think you're the one I'm after lacing in my heart-strings half-an-hour gone by. (*To* MAHON) Take him on from this, for I think bad the world should see me raging for a Munster liar, and the fool of men.

MAHON Rise up now to retribution, and come on with me.

CROWD (*Jeeringly*) There's the playboy! There's the lad thought he'd rule the roost in Mayo. Slate[59] him now, mister.

CHRISTY (*Getting up in shy terror*) What is it drives you to torment me here, when I'd asked the thunders of the might of God to blast me if I ever did hurt to any saving only that one single blow.

MAHON (*Loudly*) If you didn't, you're a poor good-for-nothing, and isn't it by the like of you the sins of the whole world are committed?

CHRISTY (*Raising his hands*) In the name of the Almighty God....

MAHON Leave troubling the Lord God. Would you have him sending down droughts, and fevers, and the old hen and the cholera morbus?[60]

CHRISTY (*To* WIDOW QUIN) Will you come between us and protect me now?

WIDOW QUIN I've tried a lot, God help me, and my share is done.

CHRISTY (*Looking round in desperation*) And I must go back into my torment is it, or run off like a vagabond straying through the unions[61] with the dusts of August making mudstains in the gullet of my throat, or the winds of March blowing on me till I'd take an oath I felt them making whistles of my ribs within?

SARA Ask Pegeen to aid you. Her like does often change.

CHRISTY I will not then, for there's torment in the splendour of her like, and she a girl any moon of midnight would take pride to meet, facing southwards on the heaths of Keel. But what did I want crawling forward to scorch my understanding at her flaming brow?

PEGEEN (*To* MAHON, *vehemently, fearing she will break into tears*) Take him on from this or I'll set the young lads to destroy him here.

MAHON (*Going to him, shaking his stick*) Come on now if you wouldn't have the company to see you skelped.[62]

PEGEEN (*Half laughing, through her tears*) That's it, now the world

[59] Thrash.
[60] Flu and stomach pains.
[61] Wandering from one workhouse to another.
[62] Beaten.

will see him pandied,[63] and he an ugly liar was playing off the hero, and the fright of men.
CHRISTY (*To* MAHON, *very sharply*) Leave me go!
CROWD That's it. Now, Christy. If them two set fighting, it will lick the world.
MAHON (*Making a grab at* CHRISTY) Come here to me.
CHRISTY (*More threateningly*) Leave me go, I'm saying.
MAHON I will maybe, when your legs is limping, and your back is blue.
CROWD Keep it up, the two of you. I'll back the old one. Now the playboy.
CHRISTY (*In low and intense voice*) Shut your yelling, for if you're after making a mighty man of me this day by the power of a lie, you're setting me now to think if it's a poor thing to be lonesome, it's worse maybe to go mixing with the fools of earth.

(MAHON *makes a movement toward him*)

CHRISTY (*Almost shouting*) Keep off . . . lest I do show a blow unto the lot of you would set the guardian angels winking in the clouds above.
(*He swings round with a sudden rapid movement and picks up a loy*)
CROWD (*Half frightened, half amused*) He's going mad! Mind yourselves! Run from the idiot!
CHRISTY If I am an idiot, I'm after hearing my voice this day saying words would raise the topknot on a poet in a merchant's town. I've won your racing, your lepping, and . . .
MAHON Shut your gullet and come on with me.
CHRISTY I'm going, but I'll stretch you first.

(*He runs at old* MAHON *with the loy, chases him out of the door, followed by crowd and* WIDOW QUIN. *There is a great noise outside, then a yell, and dead silence for a moment.* CHRISTY *comes in, half dazed, and goes to fire*)

WIDOW QUIN (*Coming in, hurriedly, and going to him*) They're turning again you. Come on, or you'll be hanged, indeed.
CHRISTY I'm thinking, from this out, Pegeen'll be giving me praises the same as in the hours gone by.
WIDOW QUIN (*Impatiently*) Come by the back-door. I'd think bad to have you stifled on the gallows tree.
CHRISTY (*Indignantly*) I will not, then. What good'd be my life-time, if I left Pegeen?
WIDOW QUIN Come on, and you'll be no worse than you were last night; and you with a double murder this time to be telling to the girls.

[63] Struck on the palm of the hand.

CHRISTY I'll not leave Pegeen Mike.
WIDOW QUIN (*Impatiently*) Isn't there the match of her in every parish public, from Binghamstown onto the plain of Meath? Come on, I tell you, and I'll find you finer sweethearts at each waning moon.
CHRISTY It's Pegeen I'm seeking only, and what'd I care if you brought me a drift of chosen females, standing in their shifts itself, maybe, from this place to the Eastern World?
SARA (*Runs in, pulling off one of her petticoats*) They're going to hang him. (*Holding out petticoat and shawl*) Fit these upon him, and let him run off to the east.
WIDOW QUIN He's raving now; but we'll fit them on him, and I'll take him, in the ferry, to the Achill boat.
CHRISTY (*Struggling feebly*) Leave me go, will you? When I'm thinking of my luck today, for she will wed me surely, and I a proven hero in the end of all.

(*They try to fasten petticoat round him*)

WIDOW QUIN Take his left hand, and we'll pull him now. Come on, young fellow.
CHRISTY (*Suddenly starting up*) You'll be taking me from her? You're jealous, is it, of her wedding me? Go on from this. (*He snatches up a stool, and threatens them with it*)
WIDOW QUIN (*Going*) It's in the mad-house they should put him, not in jail, at all. We'll go by the back-door, to call the doctor, and we'll save him so.

(*She goes out, with* SARA, *through inner room. Men crowd in the doorway.* CHRISTY *sits down again by the fire*)

MICHAEL (*In a terrified whisper*) Is the old lad killed surely?
PHILLY I'm after feeling the last gasps quitting his heart.

(*They peer in at* CHRISTY)

MICHAEL (*With a rope*) Look at the way he is. Twist a hangman's knot on it, and slip it over his head, while he's not minding at all.
PHILLY Let you take it, Shaneen. You're the soberest of all that's here.
SHAWN Is it me to go near him, and he the wickedest and worst with me? Let you take it, Pegeen Mike.
PEGEEN Come on, so.

(*She goes forward with the others, and they drop the double hitch over his head*)

CHRISTY What ails you?

SHAWN (*Triumphantly, as they pull the rope tight on his arms*) Come on to the peelers, till they stretch you now.
CHRISTY Me!
MICHAEL If we took pity on you, the Lord God would, maybe, bring us ruin from the law today, so you'd best come easy, for hanging is an easy and a speedy end.
CHRISTY I'll not stir. (*To* PEGEEN) And what is it you'll say to me, and I after doing it this time in the face of all?
PEGEEN I'll say, a strange man is a marvel, with his mighty talk; but what's a squabble in your backyard, and the blow of a loy, have taught me that there's a great gap between a gallous story and a dirty deed. (*To* MEN) Take him on from this, or the lot of us will be likely put on trial for his deed today.
CHRISTY (*With horror in his voice*) And it's yourself will send me off, to have a horny-fingered hangman hitching his bloody slip-knots at the butt of my ear.
MEN (*Pulling rope*) Come on, will you?

(*He is pulled down on the floor*)

CHRISTY (*Twisting his legs round the table*) Cut the rope, Pegeen, and I'll quit the lot of you, and live from this out, like the madmen of Keel, eating muck and green weeds, on the faces of the cliffs.
PEGEEN And leave us to hang, is it, for a saucy liar, the like of you? (*To* MEN) Take him on, out from this.
SHAWN Pull a twist on his neck, and squeeze him so.
PHILLY Twist yourself. Sure he cannot hurt you, if you keep your distance from his teeth alone.
SHAWN I'm afeard of him. (*To* PEGEEN) Lift a lighted sod, will you, and scorch his leg.
PEGEEN (*Blowing the fire, with a bellows*) Leave go now, young fellow, or I'll scorch your shins.
CHRISTY You're blowing for to torture me. (*His voice rising and growing stronger*) That's your kind, is it? Then let the lot of you be wary, for, if I've to face the gallows, I'll have a gay march down, I tell you, and shed the blood of some of you before I die.
SHAWN (*In terror*) Keep a good hold, Philly. Be wary, for the love of God. For I'm thinking he would liefest wreak his pains on me.
CHRISTY (*Almost gaily*) If I do lay my hands on you, it's the way you'll be at the fall of night, hanging as a scarecrow for the fowls of hell. Ah, you'll have a gallous jaunt I'm saying, coaching out through Limbo with my father's ghost.
SHAWN (*To* PEGEEN) Make haste, will you? Oh, isn't he a holy terror,

and isn't it true for Father Reilly, that all drink's a curse that has the lot of you so shaky and uncertain now?

CHRISTY   If I can wring a neck among you, I'll have a royal judgment looking on the trembling jury in the courts of law. And won't there be crying out in Mayo the day I'm stretched upon the rope with ladies in their silks and satins snivelling in their lacy kerchiefs, and they rhyming songs and ballads on the terror of my fate? (*He squirms round on the floor and bites* SHAWN's *leg*)

SHAWN (*Shrieking*)   My leg's bit on me. He's the like of a mad dog, I'm thinking, the way that I will surely die.

CHRISTY (*Delighted with himself*)   You will then, the way you can shake out hell's flags of welcome for my coming in two weeks or three, for I'm thinking Satan hasn't many have killed their da in Kerry, and in Mayo too.

(*Old* MAHON *comes in behind on all fours and looks on unnoticed*)

MEN (*To* PEGEEN)   Bring the sod, will you?

PEGEEN (*Coming over*)   God help him so. (*Burns his leg*)

CHRISTY (*Kicking and screaming*)   O, glory be to God! (*He kicks loose from the table, and they all drag him toward the door*)

JIMMY (*Seeing old* MAHON)   Will you look what's come in?

(*They all drop* CHRISTY *and run left*)

CHRISTY (*Scrambling on his knees face to face with old* MAHON)   Are you coming to be killed a third time, or what ails you now?

MAHON   For what is it they have you tied?

CHRISTY   They're taking me to the peelers to have me hanged for slaying you.

MICHAEL (*Apologetically*)   It is the will of God that all should guard their little cabins from the treachery of law, and what would my daughter be doing if I was ruined or was hanged itself?

MAHON (*Grimly, loosening* CHRISTY)   It's little I care if you put a bag on her back, and went picking cockles till the hour of death; but my son and myself will be going our own way, and we'll have great times from this out telling stories of the villainy of Mayo, and the fools is here. (*To* CHRISTY, *who is freed*) Come on now.

CHRISTY   Go with you, is it? I will then, like a gallant captain with his heathen slave. Go on now and I'll see you from this day stewing my oatmeal and washing my spuds, for I'm master of all fights from now. (*Pushing* MAHON) Go on, I'm saying.

MAHON   Is it me?

CHRISTY Not a word out of you. Go on from this.
MAHON (*Walking out and looking back at* CHRISTY *over his shoulder*) Glory be to God! (*With a broad smile*) I am crazy again! (*Goes*)
CHRISTY Ten thousand blessings upon all that's here, for you've turned me a likely gaffer in the end of all, the way I'll go romancing through a romping lifetime from this hour to the dawning of the judgment day. (*He goes out*)
MICHAEL By the will of God, we'll have peace now for our drinks. Will you draw the porter, Pegeen?
SHAWN (*Going up to her*) It's a miracle Father Reilly can wed us in the end of all, and we'll have none to trouble us when his vicious bite is healed.
PEGEEN (*Hitting him a box on the ear*) Quit my sight. (*Putting her shawl over her head and breaking out into wild lamentations*) Oh, my grief, I've lost him surely. I've lost the only Playboy of the Western World.

Curtain

WILLIAM BUTLER YEATS
[1865 – 1939]

❦ *The Man*

BORN into an intellectual Anglo-Irish family, son of an able painter and brother of a great one, William Butler Yeats thought at first of a career in the visual arts, but soon turned to literature. His earliest work drew upon Irish myth. From the first, he wrote both poetry and drama; *Wanderings of Oisin* (1889), a book of poems, was intended to express the pagan soul of Ireland; *The Countess Cathleen* (1892), a five-act play, was intended to express its Christian charity (as well as to provide a dramatic vehicle for Maud Gonne, with whom Yeats had fallen in love). Yeats was to woo Maud Gonne passionately for over two decades, and she was to thread through his works for the rest of his life.

After meeting Lady Gregory in 1897, Yeats worked for the foundation of an Irish theater, which became a reality in 1899, significantly named the Irish Literary Theatre. When the organization dissolved, Yeats joined forces with the actors, William and Frank Fay, to form the Irish National Theatre Society, which gave its first performance in 1902. In 1904, funds from English Miss Horniman permitted them to rent the Abbey Theatre in Dublin, for which Yeats wrote plays. Disillusioned, however, by the riots at the 1907 performance of Synge's *The Playboy of the Western World*, Yeats ceased to write for the Abbey, though he remained on its Board of Directors into the 1920's.

In 1917, having unsuccessfully proposed to both Maud Gonne (by then a widow) and her daughter, he married Georgie Hyde-Lees. For a time he served as Senator in the Irish Free State. Although he received the Nobel Prize in 1923, most critics agree that his finest poetry was written after that date.

❧ The Work

WIDELY HAILED as the greatest modern poet to write in English, Yeats has only recently received recognition as a playwright. There are several possible explanations—the difficulty of his plays, their brevity, their unfamiliar form, and their apparent lack of action. Increasingly, however, scholars are stressing the integral unity of Yeats' poetry and his drama.

His early plays drew upon Irish legend for subject matter, and upon a Decadent-Symbolist idiom for language. Unlike the tragic characters of Greek myth, his Irish heroes move in a Celtic twilight, so that these plays are richer in atmosphere than in action. Later, Yeats continued to explore Irish legend and history, but he also drew upon Classical and Christian sources. Like his poetry, Yeats' drama moved toward increased complexity and condensation; the verse line of his plays, like his poems, became increasingly irregular and musical.

The dramatic innovation usually associated with Yeats is his adaptation of the Japanese Noh play to his own needs, but he had already achieved a comparable structural simplicity, scenic economy, and interior action in *On Baile's Strand* (1904). Like the Noh play of Ghosts, Yeats' Plays for Dancers, and several of his subsequent plays, turn upon a meeting of man and ghost—a meeting that culminates in a new self-awareness that resembles an Aristotelian recognition, though in Yeats' plays the recognition is sometimes rendered through dance rather than words. One of the greatest workmen of words, Yeats did not believe that "words alone are certain good" in the theater. Always he wrote plays for presentation; always he was aware of actor, stage, and audience. And it is for this reason that he was especially enthusiastic about the masks, music, and dance of the Noh.

❧ The Play

OF YEATS' *Four Plays for Dancers* two draw upon the Cuchulain legend. *The Only Jealousy of Emer* is the second of these, the fourth of Yeats' five Cuchulain plays. There are three versions of the play, the first and

149 · The Only Jealousy of Emer

third (here printed) in verse, and the second in prose, retitled *Fighting the Waves*. As in the other dance plays, the stage is bare, the action is framed by Musicians, who chant Yeats' difficult lyrics as they fold and unfold the cloth that takes the place of the curtain of Western drama. The tension between the rhymed lines of the Musicians and the blank verse of the main action is almost all that is left of the Irish source of Yeats' play. In that source, a young and vigorous Cuchulain undertakes to shoot birds for Eithne Inguba, who has no other role in the story. He shoots a white bird, who proves to be Fand, and he is enchanted into a trance for a year, while his spirit lives in fairyland. When Cuchulain's wife, Emer, comes to claim him, Fand recognizes her prior claim, and nobly gives him up.

Yeats has decreased the theatrical importance of Fand, and increased that of Eithne Inguba. First and foremost, however, he converts a Cuchulain legend into a drama about Emer. And Yeats adds to the poignancy of her situation by shifting the time of the story, so that Cuchulain and Emer are not young and godlike, but humanly middle-aged.

Though *The Only Jealousy of Emer* was written only a few months after *At the Hawk's Well*, its action follows directly upon that of *On Baile's Strand*. In that play, Cuchulain, half-crazed with grief at killing his son, runs out to fight the sea. When the action of *The Only Jealousy of Emer* begins, Cuchulain's body lies upon the stage "in his graveclothes." Cuchulain is still hovering between life and death, and Emer seeks to revive him by any possible means, even the love of his young mistress, Eithne Inguba. However, the kiss of the lovely young woman calls back, not Cuchulain himself but his outward form, temporarily inhabited by Bricriu, "maker of discord." In this supernatural presence, all Cuchulain loved must flee; ironically, Eithne Inguba is thus forced to leave, but Cuchulain's wife, Emer, faces Bricriu and bargains for her husband's life.

Emer's all-too-human choice is entirely of Yeats' invention, and it is a choice between two evils: either she must lose Cuchulain to immortal Fand, allowing him to die; or she can save his life by renouncing any hope of his love. As in a play within the play, Bricriu shows her the wooing of Cuchulain by Fand, and Emer hears the rhymed lyrics that connect the interpolated scene with the framing lyrics. In spite of his memories of Emer, Cuchulain responds to Fand, and it is only Emer's "I renounce Cuchulain's love for ever" that restores him to life—and to the arms of

Eithne Inguba. The dramatic irony introduced by Yeats may be readily seen if we compare his ending with that of Lady Gregory: "From the moment he [Cuchulain] drank that drink, he did not remember Fand, and all the things he had done. And they gave a drink of forgetfulness to Emer as well, that she might forget her jealousy, for the state she was in was no better than his own. And after that, Manannan shook his cloak between Cuchulain and Fand, the way they should never meet one another again." In Yeats' drama, on the contrary, we feel that both Fand and Emer will remember forever.

T. S. Eliot has commented on the many levels of meaning in the dramas of Shakespeare:

> For the simplest auditors there is the plot, for the more thoughtful the character and conflict of character, for the more literary the words and phrasing, for the more musically sensitive the rhythm, and for auditors of greater sensitiveness and understanding a meaning which reveals itself gradually. And I do not believe that the classification of audience is so clear-cut as this; but rather that the sensitiveness of every auditor is acted upon by all these elements at once, though in different degrees of consciousness.

Similarly, the plays of Yeats have appealed at several levels, and *The Only Jealousy of Emer* has been responsible for many times its length in critical exegesis. It has been related not only to Irish mythology and Japanese Noh drama, but also to the Italian Renaissance and to Yeats' own eclectic philosophy as set forth in *A Vision*. And yet, for all its several sources, its dramatic impact is achieved with immediacy. Again it is T. S. Eliot who best sums it up: "So with the Cuchulain of *The Hawk's Well*, the Cuchulain, Emer and Eithne of *The Only Jealousy of Emer*; the myth is not presented for its own sake, but as a vehicle for a situation of universal meaning."

❧ *Dramatic Works*

The Countess Cathleen, 1892.
The Land of Heart's Desire, 1894.
The Shadowy Waters, 1900.
Cathleen Ni Houlihan, 1902.

Where There Is Nothing, 1902.
The Hour-Glass (prose version), 1903.
The Pot of Broth, 1904.

The King's Threshold, 1904.
On Baile's Strand, 1904.
Deirdre, 1907.
The Unicorn from the Stars, 1908 (Developed from Where There Is Nothing).
The Green Helmet, 1910.
At the Hawk's Well, 1917.
The Dreaming of the Bones, 1917.
The Only Jealousy of Emer, 1919.
Calvary, 1920.
The Player Queen, 1922.
The Cat and the Moon, 1926.

Sophocles' King Oedipus, 1928.
The Resurrection, 1931.
Sophocles' Oedipus at Colonus, 1934.
The Words upon the Window-Pane, 1934.
The King of the Great Clock Tower, 1935.
A Full Moon in March, 1935.
The Herne's Egg, 1938.
Purgatory, 1939.
The Death of Cuchulain, 1939.

Selective Bibliography

Bentley, Eric. "Yeats as a Playwright." *Kenyon Review*, X, 2 (Spring, 1948); reprinted in Hall and Steinmann, *The Permanence of Yeats*. New York: Macmillan, 1950; and Bentley, *In Search of Theater*. New York: Vintage, 1953.

Bjersby, Birgit. *The Cuchulain Legend in the Works of W. B. Yeats*. Dublin: Hodges, Figgis, 1950.

Gregory, Lady. *Cuchulain of Muirthemme*. New York: Scribner's, 1902.

Modern Drama, VII (December, 1964). The entire issue is devoted to Yeats.

Parkinson, Thomas. "The Later Plays of W. B. Yeats," in *Modern Drama: Essays in Criticism*, ed. Travis Bogard and William I. Oliver. New York: Oxford University Press, 1965.

Pearce, D. R. "Yeats' Last Plays: An Interpretation," *ELH*, XVIII (1951).

Ure, Peter. *Yeats the Playwright*. New York: Barnes and Noble, 1963.

Vendler, Helen H. *Yeats' Vision and the Later Plays*. Cambridge, Mass.: Harvard University Press, 1962.

Wilson, F. A. C. *Yeats' Iconography*. New York: Macmillan, 1960.

The Only Jealousy of Emer

PERSONS IN THE PLAY

THREE MUSICIANS, *their faces made up to resemble masks*

THE GHOST OF CUCHULAIN, *wearing a mask*

THE FIGURE OF CUCHULAIN, *wearing a mask*

EMER
EITHNE INGUBA
} *masked, or their faces made up to resemble masks*

WOMAN OF THE SIDHE, *wearing a mask*

Enter MUSICIANS; *who are dressed and made up as in "At the Hawk's Well."*[1] *They have the same musical instruments, which can either be already upon the stage or be brought in by the* FIRST MUSICIAN *before he stands in the centre with the cloth between his hands, or by a player when the cloth has been unfolded. The stage as before can be against the wall of any room, and the same black cloth can be used as in "At the Hawk's Well."*

(*Song for the folding and unfolding of the cloth*)

FIRST MUSICIAN   A woman's beauty is like a white
Frail bird, like a white sea-bird alone
At daybreak after stormy night
Between two furrows upon the ploughed land:
A sudden storm, and it was thrown
Between dark furrows upon the ploughed land.

---

[1] Yeats' first play in the Noh form, in which Cuchulain appears as a young man.

The Only Jealousy of Emer

How many centuries spent
The sedentary soul
In toils of measurement
Beyond eagle or mole,
Beyond hearing or seeing,
Or Archimedes'[2] guess,
To raise into being
That loveliness?

A strange, unserviceable thing,
A fragile, exquisite, pale shell,
That the vast troubled waters bring
To the loud sands before day has broken.
The storm arose and suddenly fell
Amid the dark before day had broken.
What death? what discipline?
What bonds no man could unbind,
Being imagined within
The labyrinth of the mind,
What pursuing or fleeing,
What wounds, what bloody press,
Dragged into being
This loveliness?

(*When the cloth is folded again the* MUSICIANS *take their place against the wall. The folding of the cloth shows on one side of the stage the curtained bed or litter on which lies a man in his grave-clothes. He wears an heroic mask. Another man with exactly similar clothes and mask crouches near the front.* EMER *is sitting beside the bed*)

FIRST MUSICIAN (*Speaking*)   I call before the eyes a roof
With cross-beams darkened by smoke;
A fisher's net hangs from a beam,
A long oar lies against the wall.
I call up a poor fisher's house;
A man lies dead or swooning,
That amorous man,
That amorous, violent man, renowned Cuchulain,
Queen Emer at his side.
At her own bidding all the rest have gone;

---

[2] Greek mathematician and inventor, who lived in Sicily during the third century B.C.

But now one comes on hesitating feet,
Young Eithne Inguba, Cuchulain's mistress.
She stands a moment in the open door.
Beyond the open door the bitter sea,
The shining, bitter sea, is crying out,
(*Singing*) White shell, white wing!
I will not choose for my friend
A frail, unserviceable thing
That drifts and dreams, and but knows
That waters are without end
And that wind blows.

EMER (*Speaking*) Come hither, come sit down beside the bed;
You need not be afraid, for I myself
Sent for you, Eithne Inguba.

EITHNE INGUBA   No, Madam,
I have too deeply wronged you to sit there.

EMER Of all the people in the world we two,
And we alone, may watch together here,
Because we have loved him best.

EITHNE INGUBA   And is he dead?

EMER Although they have dressed him out in his grave-clothes
And stretched his limbs, Cuchulain is not dead;
The very heavens when that day's at hand,
So that his death may not lack ceremony,
Will throw out fires, and the earth grow red with blood.
There shall not be a scullion but foreknows it
Like the world's end.

EITHNE INGUBA   How did he come to this?

EMER Towards noon in the assembly of the kings
He met with one who seemed a while most dear.
The kings stood round; some quarrel was blown up;
He drove him out and killed him on the shore
At Baile's tree,[3] and he who was so killed
Was his own son begot on some wild woman
When he was young, or so I have heard it said;
And thereupon, knowing what man he had killed,
And being mad with sorrow, he ran out;
And after, to his middle in the foam,
With shield before him and with sword in hand,
He fought the deathless sea. The kings looked on

[3] Subject of Yeats' 1904 drama *On Baile's Strand*.

The Only Jealousy of Emer

And not a king dared stretch an arm, or even
Dared call his name, but all stood wondering
In that dumb stupor like cattle in a gale,
Until at last, as though he had fixed his eyes
On a new enemy, he waded out
Until the water had swept over him;
But the waves washed his senseless image up
And laid it at this door.

EITHNE INGUBA How pale he looks!

EMER He is not dead.

EITHNE INGUBA You have not kissed his lips
Nor laid his head upon your breast.

EMER It may be
An image has been put into his place,
A sea-borne log bewitched into his likeness,
Or some stark horseman grown too old to ride
Among the troops of Manannan, Son of the Sea,
Now that his joints are stiff.

EITHNE INGUBA Cry out his name.
All that are taken from our sight, they say,
Loiter amid the scenery of their lives
For certain hours or days, and should he hear
He might, being angry, drive the changeling out.

EMER It is hard to make them hear amid their darkness,
And it is long since I could call him home;
I am but his wife, but if you cry aloud
With the sweet voice that is so dear to him
He cannot help but listen.

EITHNE INGUBA He loves me best,
Being his newest love, but in the end
Will love the woman best who loved him first
And loved him through the years when love seemed lost.

EMER I have that hope, the hope that some day somewhere
We'll sit together at the hearth again.

EITHNE INGUBA Women like me, the violent hour passed over,
Are flung into some corner like old nut-shells.
Cuchulain, listen.

EMER No, not yet, for first
I'll cover up his face to hide the sea;
And throw new logs upon the hearth and stir
The half-burnt logs until they break in flame.
Old Manannan's unbridled horses come

Out of the sea, and on their backs his horsemen;
But all the enchantments of the dreaming foam
Dread the hearth-fire.

(*She pulls the curtains of the bed so as to hide the sick man's face, that the actor may change his mask unseen. She goes to one side of the platform and moves her hand as though putting logs on a fire and stirring it into a blaze. While she makes these movements the* MUSICIANS *play, marking the movements with drum and flute perhaps.*

Having finished she stands beside the imaginary fire at a distance from Cuchulain and Eithne Inguba)

                Call on Cuchulain now.
EITHNE INGUBA   Can you not hear my voice?
EMER   Bend over him;
Call out dear secrets till you have touched his heart,
If he lies there; and if he is not there,
Till you have made him jealous.
EITHNE INGUBA   Cuchulain, listen.
EMER   Those words sound timidly; to be afraid
Because his wife is but three paces off,
When there is so great need, were but to prove
The man that chose you made but a poor choice:
We're but two women struggling with the sea.
EITHNE INGUBA   O my beloved, pardon me, that I
Have been ashamed. I thrust my shame away.
I have never sent a message or called out,
Scarce had a longing for your company
But you have known and come; and if indeed
You are lying there, stretch out your arms and speak;
Open your mouth and speak, for to this hour
My company has made you talkative.
What ails your tongue, or what has closed your ears?
Our passion had not chilled when we were parted
On the pale shore under the breaking dawn.
He cannot speak: or else his ears are closed
And no sound reaches him.
EMER   Then kiss that image;
The pressure of your mouth upon his mouth
May reach him where he is.
EITHNE INGUBA (*Starting back*)   It is no man.
I felt some evil thing that dried my heart
When my lips touched it.

The Only Jealousy of Emer

EMER   No, his body stirs;
  The pressure of your mouth has called him home;
  He has thrown the changeling out.
EITHNE INGUBA (*Going further off*)   Look at that arm;
  That arm is withered to the very socket.
EMER (*Going up to the bed*)   What do you come for; and from where?
FIGURE OF CUCHULAIN   I have come
  From Manannan's court upon a bridleless horse.
EMER   What one among the Sidhe has dared to lie
  Upon Cuchulain's bed and take his image?
FIGURE OF CUCHULAIN   I am named Bricriu—not the man—that Bricriu,
  Maker of discord among gods and men,
  Called Bricriu of the Sidhe.
EMER   Come for what purpose?
FIGURE OF CUCHULAIN (*Sitting up, parting curtain and showing its distorted face, as Eithne Inguba goes out*) I show my face, and everything he loves
  Must fly away.
EMER   You people of the wind
  Are full of lying speech and mockery:
  I have not fled your face.
FIGURE OF CUCHULAIN   You are not loved.
EMER   And therefore have no dread to meet your eyes
  And to demand him of you.
FIGURE OF CUCHULAIN   For that I have come.
  You have but to pay the price and he is free.
EMER   Do the Sidhe bargain?
FIGURE OF CUCHULAIN   When they would free a captive
  They take in ransom a less valued thing.
  The fisher, when some knowledgeable man
  Restores to him his wife, or son, or daughter,
  Knows he must lose a boat or net, or it may be
  The cow that gives his children milk; and some
  Have offered their own lives. I do not ask
  Your life, or any valuable thing;
  You spoke but now of the mere chance that some day
  You'd be the apple of his eye again
  When old and ailing, but renounce that chance
  And he shall live again.
EMER   I do not question
  But you have brought ill-luck on all he loves;
  And now, because I am thrown beyond your power

Unless your words are lies, you come to bargain.
FIGURE OF CUCHULAIN   You loved your mastery, when but newly married,
And I love mine for all my withered arm;
You have but to put yourself into that power
And he shall live again.
EMER   No, never, never.
FIGURE OF CUCHULAIN   You dare not be accursed, yet he has dared.
EMER   I have but two joyous thoughts, two things I prize,
A hope, a memory, and now you claim that hope.
FIGURE OF CUCHULAIN   He'll never sit beside you at the hearth
Or make old bones, but die of wounds and toil
On some far shore or mountain, a strange woman
Beside his mattress.
EMER   You ask for my one hope
That you may bring your curse on all about him.
FIGURE OF CUCHULAIN   You've watched his loves and you have not been jealous,
Knowing that he would tire, but do those tire
That love the Sidhe? Come closer to the bed
That I may touch your eyes and give them sight.

(*He touches her eyes with his left hand, the right being withered*)

EMER [*seeing the crouching* GHOST OF CUCHULAIN]   My husband is there.
FIGURE OF CUCHULAIN   I have dissolved the dark
That hid him from your eyes, but not that other
That's hidden you from his.
EMER   O husband, husband!
FIGURE OF CUCHULAIN   He cannot hear—being shut off, a phantom
That can neither touch, nor hear, nor see;
The longing and the cries have drawn him hither.
He heard no sound, heard no articulate sound;
They could but banish rest, and make him dream,
And in that dream, as do all dreaming shades
Before they are accustomed to their freedom,
He has taken his familiar form; and yet
He crouches there not knowing where he is
Or at whose side he is crouched.

(A WOMAN OF THE SIDHE *has entered and stands a little inside the door*)

EMER   Who is this woman?
FIGURE OF CUCHULAIN   She has hurried from the Country-under-Wave

And dreamed herself into that shape that he
May glitter in her basket; for the Sidhe
Are dexterous fishers and they fish for men
With dreams upon the hook.

EMER   And so that woman
Has hid herself in this disguise and made
Herself into a lie.

FIGURE OF CUCHULAIN   A dream is body;
The dead move ever towards a dreamless youth
And when they dream no more return no more;
And those more holy shades that never lived
But visit you in dreams.

EMER   I know her sort.
They find our men asleep, weary with war,
Lap them in cloudy hair or kiss their lips;
Our men awake in ignorance of it all,
But when we take them in our arms at night
We cannot break their solitude.

(She draws a knife from her girdle)

FIGURE OF CUCHULAIN   No knife
Can wound that body of air. Be silent; listen;
I have not given you eyes and ears for nothing.

(The WOMAN OF THE SIDHE moves round the crouching GHOST OF CUCHULAIN at front of stage in a dance that grows gradually quicker, as he slowly awakes. At moments she may drop her hair upon his head, but she does not kiss him. She is accompanied by string and flute and drum. Her mask and clothes must suggest gold or bronze or brass or silver, so that she seems more an idol than a human being. This suggestion may be repeated in her movements. Her hair, too, must keep the metallic suggestion)

GHOST OF CUCHULAIN   Who is it stands before me there
Shedding such light from limb and hair
As when the moon, complete at last
With every labouring crescent past,
And lonely with extreme delight,
Flings out upon the fifteenth night?[4]

WOMAN OF THE SIDHE   Because I long I am not complete.
What pulled your hands about your feet,
Pulled down your head upon your knees,

―――――――
[4] In Yeats' system, the moon is full at its fifteenth phase, and Yeats associated this phase with extraordinary beauty.

And hid your face?
GHOST OF CUCHULAIN   Old memories:
A woman in her happy youth
Before her man had broken troth,
Dead men and women. Memories
Have pulled my head upon my knees.
WOMAN OF THE SIDHE   Could you that have loved many a woman
That did not reach beyond the human,
Lacking a day to be complete,
Love one that, though her heart can beat,
Lacks it but by an hour or so?
GHOST OF CUCHULAIN   I know you now, for long ago
I met you on a cloudy hill
Beside old thorn-trees and a well.
A woman danced and a hawk flew,
I held out arms and hands; but you,
That now seem friendly, fled away,
Half woman and half bird of prey.[5]
WOMAN OF THE SIDHE   Hold out your arms and hands again;
You were not so dumbfounded when
I was that bird of prey, and yet
I am all woman now.
GHOST OF CUCHULAIN   I am not
The young and passionate man I was,
And though that brilliant light surpass
All crescent forms, my memories
Weigh down my hands, abash my eyes.
WOMAN OF THE SIDHE   Then kiss my mouth. Though memory
Be beauty's bitterest enemy
I have no dread, for at my kiss
Memory on the moment vanishes:
Nothing but beauty can remain.
GHOST OF CUCHULAIN   And shall I never know again
Intricacies of blind remorse?
WOMAN OF THE SIDHE   Time shall seem to stay his course;
When your mouth and my mouth meet
All my round shall be complete
Imagining all its circles run;
And there shall be oblivion
Even to quench Cuchulain's drouth,

[5] Subject of Yeats' drama, *At the Hawk's Well*.

The Only Jealousy of Emer

Even to still that heart.
GHOST OF CUCHULAIN   Your mouth!

(They are about to kiss, he turns away)

O Emer, Emer!
WOMAN OF THE SIDHE   So then it is she
  Made you impure with memory.
GHOST OF CUCHULAIN   O Emer, Emer, there we stand;
  Side by side and hand in hand
  Tread the threshold of the house
  As when our parents married us.
WOMAN OF THE SIDHE   Being among the dead you love her
  That valued every slut above her
  While you still lived.
GHOST OF CUCHULAIN   O my lost Emer!
WOMAN OF THE SIDHE   And there is not a loose-tongued schemer
  But could draw you, if not dead,
  From her table and her bed.
  But what could make you fit to wive
  With flesh and blood, being born to live
  Where no one speaks of broken troth,
  For all have washed out of their eyes
  Wind-blown dirt of their memories
  To improve their sight?
GHOST OF CUCHULAIN   Your mouth, your mouth!

(She goes out followed by GHOST OF CUCHULAIN*)*

FIGURE OF CUCHULAIN   Cry out that you renounce his love; make haste
  And cry that you renounce his love for ever.
EMER   No, never will I give that cry.
FIGURE OF CUCHULAIN   Fool, fool!
  I am Fand's enemy come to thwart her will,
  And you stand gaping there. There is still time.
  Hear how the horses trample on the shore,
  Hear how they trample! She has mounted up.
  Cuchulain's not beside her in the chariot.
  There is still a moment left; cry out, cry out!
  Renounce him, and her power is at an end.
  Cuchulain's foot is on the chariot-step.
  Cry——
EMER   I renounce Cuchulain's love for ever.

(*The* FIGURE OF CUCHULAIN *sinks back upon the bed, half-drawing the curtain.* EITHNE INGUBA *comes in and kneels by bed*)

EITHNE INGUBA   Come to me, my beloved, it is I.
I, Eithne Inguba. Look! He is there.
He has come back and moved upon the bed.
And it is I that won him from the sea,
That brought him back to life.
EMER   Cuchulain wakes.

(*The figure turns round. It once more wears the heroic mask*)

CUCHULAIN   Your arms, your arms! O Eithne Inguba,
I have been in some strange place and am afraid.

(*The* FIRST MUSICIAN *comes to the front of stage, the others from each side, and unfold the cloth singing*)

(*Song for the unfolding and folding of the cloth*)

MUSICIANS   Why does your heart beat thus?
Plain to be understood,
I have met in a man's house
A statue of solitude,
Moving there and walking;
Its strange heart beating fast
For all our talking.
O still that heart at last.

O bitter reward
Of many a tragic tomb!
And we though astonished are dumb
Or give but a sigh and a word,
A passing word.

Although the door be shut
And all seem well enough,
Although wide world hold not
A man but will give you his love
The moment he has looked at you,
He that has loved the best
May turn from a statue
His too human breast.

O bitter reward

The Only Jealousy of Emer

Of many a tragic tomb!
And we though astonished are dumb
Or give but a sigh and a word,
A passing word.

What makes your heart so beat?
What man is at your side?
When beauty is complete
Your own thought will have died
And danger not be diminished;
Dimmed at three-quarter light,
When moon's round is finished
The stars are out of sight.

O bitter reward
Of many a tragic tomb!
And we though astonished are dumb
Or give but a sigh and a word,
A passing word.

(When the cloth is folded again the stage is bare)

SEAN O'CASEY
[1880 – 1964]

❧ *The Man*

SEAN O'CASEY was the last of thirteen children (eight of whom had already died in infancy). Belonging to a poor Protestant family in Catholic Dublin, he grew up in deprivation and squalor. Early interested in acting, he played amateur roles in the plays of Shakespeare and Boucicault; only several years later did he learn to read, spending his meager earnings on books by Shakespeare, Dickens, Scott, Balzac, Ruskin, Byron, Shelley, Keats, Goldsmith, Sheridan. At the turn of the century, he became interested in Irish nationalism and taught himself Gaelic, changing his name from John Casey to Sean O'Cathasaigh. Being a self-educated laborer, he had no contact with upper-class, intellectually oriented Nationalists like Lady Gregory and Yeats. To further the cause of labor, he wrote political ballads and tendentious essays. His first book celebrated the martyrdom of Thomas Ashe, a labor hero killed in the Easter Rebellion.

Nearly forty before he turned to drama, O'Casey was determined to have a play accepted by the famed Abbey Theatre, and succeeded with his fourth manuscript, *Shadow of a Gunman*. On the last night of its three-night run, the Abbey Theatre was completely sold out, and the following year, O'Casey's *Juno and the Paycock* saved the Abbey from bankruptcy. Nevertheless, when his *The Plough and the Stars* (named for the banner of the Irish Citizen Army) was performed in 1926, there was a riot in the Abbey Theatre, and the police had to restore order. As in the *Playboy* riots, Yeats came forward to defend the artist, addressing his countrymen with scorn:

You have disgraced yourselves again. Is this to be an ever-recurring celebration of the arrival of Irish genius? Synge first and then O'Casey. The news of the happenings of the past few minutes will go from country to country. Dublin has once more rocked the cradle of genius. From such a scene in this theatre went forth the fame of Synge. Equally the fame of O'Casey is born here tonight. This is his apotheosis.

And yet, both temperamentally and environmentally, O'Casey was alienated from the Abbey Theatre directors who produced his plays. Invited to London to receive a prize for *Juno*, O'Casey was befriended by men like Shaw and Augustus John, in striking contrast to his reception at home; he decided to live in London. His hostility toward Ireland was increased when the Abbey Theatre rejected his next play, *The Silver Tassie*.

In voluntary exile, O'Casey partially re-Anglicized his name to Sean O'Casey. Under that name, he wrote more plays and a six-volume autobiography. Though his relations with England were never as stormy as with Ireland, he was contemptuous of Shaftesbury Avenue Drama, and he incurred the enmity of James Agate, London's most influential theater critic. In accordance with his labor sympathies, he became an outspoken champion of Soviet Russia, and this served to alienate him further from a largely middle-class theater world. Cut off from contact with the theater, he wrote his last plays for publication.

Like other Irish expatriates, O'Casey continued his stormy relationship with his native land. In 1955 Cyril Cusack produced *The Bishop's Bonfire* at the Gaiety Theatre in Dublin, to the hissing and booing of the audience. The English critic Kenneth Tynan wrote on that occasion: "At the first night of Mr. O'Casey's *Bishop's Bonfire* there were more stage Irishmen in the house than in the cast." In 1958 an International Theatre Festival was planned in Dublin, featuring three Irish plays: a dramatized version of Joyce's *Ulysses*, Beckett's *All That Fall*, and O'Casey's *The Drums of Father Ned*. Largely in objection to O'Casey, the Archbishop of Dublin declined to open the festival with the customary celebration of the Mass, and the Festival Committee rejected O'Casey's play when he refused to allow alterations "to make it suitable for the Dublin public." Beckett thereupon supported O'Casey by withdrawing his own play.

❧ The Work

MOST CRITICS divide O'Casey's dramas into the pre-exile and the post-exile plays, the former largely realistic in style, and the latter variously influenced by expressionistic techniques. O'Casey's first three full-length plays, focusing on the Irish Civil War, provide a bitter and anti heroic view of war. All three plays contain a blend of the comic and the bitter, and rapid transitions from laughter to tears.

Even in *The Silver Tassie* O'Casey used certain expressionistic techniques in a largely realistic antiwar play, but in all subsequent plays he indulged freely in generalized characters, fantastic staging, symbolic settings. In his plays written during the Depression and World War II, O'Casey, like his German models, wrote morality plays in a social context, defending the underdog against oppressive forces. Starting with *Purple Dust*, however, and even more so in his last plays, O'Casey neglects social evils to sing rollicking if dissonant paeans to the uninhibited joy of living, but for all their exuberance there has been some doubt as to their viability as drama.

What is common to all of O'Casey's plays is their distinctive idiom, and it may be remembered that he, like Shaw, another creator of distinctive theatrical idiom, was nearly forty when he turned to drama. Like Synge, however, O'Casey's language is more clearly Irish, drawing upon Gaelic locutions. But whereas Synge's dramatic language is based on peasant speech, that of O'Casey is distinctly urban. He exhibits a love of puns, polysyllables, sound play, extravagant imagery, and flamboyant rhetoric. Shakespearean and biblical rhythms often sound in O'Casey's writing, but into them he injects pungent Dublin slang. A simple pledge of abstinence is announced by Fluther in *The Plough and the Stars*: "You could stan' where you're stannin' chantin', 'Have a glass o' malt, Fluther; Fluther, have a glass o' malt,' till th' bells would be ringin' th' ould year out an' th' New Year in, an' you'd have as much chance o' movin' Fluther as a tune on a tin whistle would move a deaf man an' he dead." Or in *Cock-a-Doodle Dandy* a Rough Fellow makes a pass at a girl: "Arra, what winsome wind blew such a flower into this dread, dhried-up desert? Deirdre come to life again, not to sorrow, but to dance! If Eve was as you are, no wondher Adam fell, for a lass like you could shutther th' world away with a kiss!"

❧ *The Play*

A MORE EXACT TITLE for O'Casey's play would have been *Juno vs. the Paycock*, for the basic conflict in the play is between Mrs. Boyle's courageous responsibility and Captain Boyle's comic irresponsibility. O'Casey's achievement has been to turn a stock comedy couple into tragic material. The title suggests the mock-heroic, and this harrassed mother of the Dublin slums seems to be a mock-heroic version of the Roman goddess of domesticity, who was traditionally associated with peacocks. Other resonances of Roman comedy types are Captain Boyle as the braggart soldier and his friend Joxer as the parasite. By the end of the play, the mythical material has been substantiated, for Juno Boyle emerges as a heroic figure, saying of her unborn grandchild, whose father will not acknowledge him, "It'll have what's far betther—it'll have two mothers."

Written in 1924, with the Irish Civil War fresh in people's minds, *Juno* brought to the theater a merciless picture of the cruelty of the war; the pathetic heroics of Johnny Boyle are contrasted with his mother's realism:

> JOHNNY (*boastfully*) I'd do it agen, ma, I'd do it agen; for a principle's a principle.
> MRS. BOYLE Ah, you lost your best principle, me boy, when you lost your arm; them's the only sort o' principles that's any good to a workin' man.

Using a traditional three-act structure, O'Casey spurns climactic curtain lines and expected resolutions. The stale device of a legacy is exposed dramatically *as* a stale device, and its loss does not bring about the expected reform of Captain Boyle. Nor does Mary Boyle's reading save her from the scheming English lawyer. Johnny Boyle's pathetic fears prove more justified than his pathetic heroics. Comedy and pathos follow swiftly upon each other, in ironic counterpoint; the joyous festivities of Act II are interrupted by Mrs. Tancred's lament for her dead son. Using the same words, Juno laments Johnny's death toward the end of Act III, and this is followed by a drunk scene. In Act III, when her son is dead, her daughter pregnant and abandoned, the legacy a fraud, and her apartment stripped bare, Juno utters a passionate prayer of peace and love. With her rhetoric still ringing on the empty stage, the Paycock and his friend shuffle in drunkenly. The drunk scene is a virtual repetition of the first act drunk scene, but in the light of tragic events, the comedy has become grotesque; the Captain reiterates his favorite pronouncement: "th' whole worl's . . . in a terr . . . ible state o' . . . chassis!" And chaos is what the audience sees, as the two men stumble in the apartment stripped of furniture and family.

❧ Dramatic Works

Shadow of a Gunman, 1923.
Kathleen Listens In, 1923.
Nannie's Night Out, 1924.
Juno and the Paycock, 1924.
The Plough and the Stars, 1926.
The Silver Tassie, 1928.
Within the Gates, 1933.
The End of the Beginning, 1934.
A Pound on Demand, 1934.
The Star Turns Red, 1940.
Purple Dust, 1940.
Red Roses for Me, 1943.

Oak Leaves and Lavender, 1946.
Cock-a-Doodle Dandy, 1949.
The Hall of Healing, 1951.
Baltimore Story, 1951.
Time to Go, 1951.
The Bishop's Bonfire, 1955.
The Drums of Father Ned, 1960.
Behind the Green Curtains, 1961.
Figuro in the Night, 1961.
The Moon Shines on Kylenamoe, 1961.

❧ Selective Bibliography

Cowasjee, Saros. *Sean O'Casey: The Man Behind the Plays.* London: St. Martin's Press, 1964.

Hogan, Robert. *The Experiments of Sean O'Casey.* New York: St. Martin's Press, 1960.

Krause, David. *Sean O'Casey, The Man and His Work.* New York: Macmillan, 1960.

Modern Drama IV (December, 1961). The entire issue is devoted to Synge and O'Casey.

Ritchie, Harry M. "The Influence of Melodrama in the Early Plays of Sean O'Casey," *Modern Drama* V (1962).

Rollins, Ronald G. "Sean O'Casey's Mental Pilgrimage," *Arizona Quarterly* XVII (1961).

THOMAS STEARNS ELIOT
[1888 – 1965]

❦ *The Man*

THOUGH BORN IN St. Louis, T. S. Eliot was a descendant of New England families who emigrated from England to Massachusetts in the seventeenth century. Educated largely at Harvard, he worked toward a doctoral degree in philosophy. Planning to continue his studies at the University of Marburg in Germany, he shifted to Oxford at the outbreak of World War I. His first book of poems, *Prufrock and Other Observations*, appeared in 1917, though the title poem dates from his Harvard years.

After World War I, Eliot continued to live in Europe, but though his *Waste Land* (1922) came to be the theme song of the Lost Generation, he never joined American expatriates in Paris. Instead, he worked at Lloyds Bank in London, then subsequently for the publishers Faber and Faber, as he wrote poetry and criticism. In 1927 he became a British subject, and in 1932 made his first trip back to America after eighteen years, as Harvard's Charles Eliot Norton Professor of Poetry. In 1934, the same year he announced himself a royalist in politics, a classicist in literature, and an Anglo-Catholic in religion, he first turned his hand to theater, contributing verse choruses to a pageant play *The Rock*. This venture inspired Eliot to write his own play for the 1935 Canterbury Festival, about St. Thomas à Becket, killed at Canterbury. Aside from *Four Quartets* (1943), Eliot's last works have been in the dramatic medium. Eliot was awarded the Nobel Prize in 1958, the year of his last publication.

❧ *The Work*

T. S. ELIOT belongs to the tradition of English poet-critics, whose highlights are Jonson, Dryden, Coleridge, and Arnold. Though he turned to drama relatively late in his career, Eliot was much earlier interested in the problem of contemporary verse drama. Not only did he insist that all great poetry was dramatic, but he experimented with *Fragments of an Aristophanic Melodrama.* In his "Dialogue on Dramatic Poetry" he maintained that the greatest drama would always be poetic, and in his own first poetic drama, he used a historical setting to justify the verse.

When he turned from historical to contemporary subjects, Eliot delineated his dramatic principles in a humorous letter to Ezra Pound; among them is "But IF you can keep the bloody audience's attention engaged, then you can perform any monkey tricks you like when they ain't looking, and it's what you do behind the audience's back so to speak that makes your play IMMORTAL for a while." Eliot sought to perform the "monkey trick" of obliquely portraying the role of a Christian in a contemporary society that has lost all but vestigial traces of Christianity.

Eliot's last four plays share a contemporary setting and a source in Greek tragedy. For these plays, Eliot invented a flexible verse line based on three strong stresses and a fluctuating caesura. *The Family Reunion* and *The Cocktail Party,* in spite of their contemporaneity, resemble *Murder in the Cathedral* in treating of a saint, a special soul. *The Cocktail Party,* however, deals also with the ordinary Chamberlaynes, and comparably ordinary people are found in *The Confidential Clerk* and *The Elder Statesman.* Cumulatively then, Eliot dramatizes lives of saints, and those of more common mortals who derive meaning from the martyrdom of the saints. As his characters become progressively less distinguished in each successive play, so his lyricism is reduced to the patently prosaic. That this master of the English language should have stripped it so bare is itself a kind of martyrdom, and it is ironic that among broad audiences of ambivalent religious allegiance, *Murder in the Cathedral,* Eliot's most obviously religious and poetic play, is also his most popular.

🌿 The Play

IN DRAMATIZING the martyrdom of St. Thomas à Becket, Eliot followed Tennyson, but unlike his predecessor (or his successors, Fry's *Curtmantle* and Anouilh's *Becket*), Eliot pares away anecdotal and decorative material, so as to focus on the final catastrophe—Becket's martyrdom. Like Greek tragedy, *Murder in the Cathedral* is formed of episodes separated by choral odes, and Eliot makes full use of the Chorus. Like the medieval morality play, Eliot's drama contains biblical echoes; *Murder in the Cathedral*, like Everyman, is a drama of victory over temptation. Thomas' temptations resemble those of Christ in the desert—sensual appetite, divinity, and martyrdom. In an ironic twist, Eliot has the Fourth Tempter address Thomas in the very words Thomas used to the Women of Canterbury; it is at that moment that Thomas achieves his victory over temptation, though he does not enunciate it until after the choral ode: "The last temptation is the greatest treason:/ To do the right deed for the wrong reason."

In the Interlude between the two acts, Eliot converts the theater audience into a congregation for Thomas' sermon. Various critics have remarked on the brilliance with which he adapts the modern theater to its old religious function, and yet the theatrical experience dominates the religious. In Part II, as well, Eliot uses the theater as a cathedral, for the Knights pound at the back door, then make their way down the aisle, to desecrate the altar by the murder. The assassination itself is swift, silent, and invisible to the audience, but the Chorus of Women reflect the terrible act through the violence of their imagery.

The prose rationalizations of the Knights have been compared to the final scene of Shaw's *Saint Joan*, and in both plays the saint looms all the larger against satiric prose of the world's pragmatic viewpoint. Eliot's Becket triumphs morally over the Knights as well as the Tempters (who are usually played by the same actors). Even the Priests who defend Thomas succumb to practical measures and a limited viewpoint. The martyrdom of Thomas is finally understood only by the Chorus of once frightened women. Intuitively, they accept the marytrdom by which they are redeemed.

E. Martin Browne, the play's first producer, has remarked on the variations of the verse:

> The most superficial level, that of the quarrels between Becket and the Knights, is rhymed doggerel. . . . More subtle, and sometimes rather crabbed, is a four-stress rhyming verse for the Tempters who dramatise the tortuous progress of Becket's inner struggle. . . . There is an easy, near-blank-verse for dialogue with the Priests and Women. . . . And for the Chorus, a very varied series of forms, from the three-stress lines of the women's domestic talk . . . to the long complexes of pleading or of praise.

Browne neglects to mention the hymnal background and the prose of interlude and finale. Moreover, this rhythmic variation is quite subtle, subordinated to the dramatic movement, which is like a pendulum between the martyrdom of Thomas and its effect upon the Women of Canterbury; it is through them that Thomas' life is fulfilled, and through him that they are fulfilled.

As David Jones summarizes the final lines:

> the recurrent images of the play (the Waste Land, the seasons, beasts and birds, the everyday tasks, the blood of redemption) are gathered together and resolved in a significant pattern. They all fit together in the scheme of God's Providence: by the blood of redemption fertility is restored to the Waste Land so that the rhythm of the seasons can remain undisturbed, the natural order can be preserved, men can perform their seasonal tasks and give articulate praise not just for themselves, but for the beasts as well, and all creatures are secured in their ordained places, fulfilling their role in "the eternal design."

❧ *Dramatic Works*

Sweeney Agonistes, 1926.
The Rock, 1934.
Murder in the Cathedral, 1935.
The Family Reunion, 1939.

The Cocktail Party, 1949.
The Confidential Clerk, 1953.
The Elder Statesman, 1958.

❧ Selective Bibliography

Adair, Patricia. "Mr. Eliot's *Murder in the Cathedral*," *The Cambridge Journal*, IV (November, 1950).

Browne, E. Martin. "The Dramatic Verse of T. S. Eliot," in *T. S. Eliot: A Symposium*, ed. Richard March and Tambimuttu. Chicago: Regnery, 1948.

Fergusson, Francis. *The Idea of a Theater*. New York: Doubleday, 1953.

Jones, David E. *The Plays of T. S. Eliot*. Toronto: University of Toronto Press, 1960.

Peter, John. "*Murder in the Cathedral*," *Sewanee Review*, LXI (Spring, 1953).

Smith, Carol H. *T. S. Eliot's Dramatic Theory and Practice*. Princeton: Princeton University Press, 1963.

Smith, Grover. *T. S. Eliot's Poetry and Plays*. Chicago: University of Chicago Press, 1960.

Murder in the Cathedral

THIS play was written for production (in an abbreviated form) at the Canterbury Festival, June 1935. For help in its construction I am much indebted to Mr. E. Martin Browne, the producer, and to Mr. Rupert Doone; and for incidental criticisms, to Mr. F. V. Morley, and Mr. John Hayward.
April 1935

In the second edition a chorus was substituted for the introits which, in the first edition, constituted the opening of Part II. To this third edition the introits have been added as an appendix, and may be used instead of that chorus in productions of the play.

At the suggestion of Mr. E. Martin Browne, I have in Part II reassigned most of the lines formerly attributed to the Fourth Knight. When, as was originally intended, the parts of the Tempters are doubled with those of the Knights, the advantage of these alterations should be obvious.
June 1937

In this fourth edition certain further rearrangements and deletions have been made, which have been found advisable by experiment in the course of production.
March 1938   T. S. E.

Part I

CHARACTERS

A CHORUS OF WOMEN OF CANTER- ARCHBISHOP THOMAS BECKET
BURY

THREE PRIESTS OF THE CATHEDRAL FOUR TEMPTERS

A MESSENGER ATTENTANTS

The Scene is the Archbishop's Hall, on December 2nd, 1170.

CHORUS Here let us stand, close by the cathedral. Here let us wait.
Are we drawn by danger? Is it the knowledge of safety, that draws our feet
Towards the cathedral? What danger can be
For us, the poor, the poor women of Canterbury? What tribulation
With which we are not already familiar? There is no danger
For us, and there is no safety in the cathedral. Some presage of an act
Which our eyes are compelled to witness, has forced our feet
Towards the cathedral. We are forced to bear witness.

Since golden October declined into sombre November
And the apples were gathered and stored, and the land became brown sharp points of death in a waste of water and mud,
The New Year waits, breathes, waits, whispers in darkness.
While the labourer kicks off a muddy boot and stretches his hand to the fire,
The New Year waits, destiny waits for the coming.
Who has stretched out his hand to the fire and remembered the Saints at All Hallows,
Remembered the martyrs and saints who wait? And who shall
Stretch out his hand to the fire, and deny his master? Who shall be warm
By the fire, and deny his master?

Seven years and the summer is over,
Seven years since the Archbishop left us,
He who was always kind to his people.
But it would not be well if he should return.
King rules or barons rule;
We have suffered various oppression,
But mostly we are left to our own devices,
And we are content if we are left alone.
We try to keep our households in order;
The merchant, shy and cautious, tries to compile a little fortune,
And the labourer bends to his piece of earth, earth-colour, his own colour,
Preferring to pass unobserved.
Now I fear disturbance of the quiet seasons:
Winter shall come bringing death from the sea,
Ruinous spring shall beat at our doors,
Root and shoot shall eat our eyes and our ears,
Disastrous summer burn up the beds of our streams
And the poor shall wait for another decaying October.
Why should the summer bring consolation
For autumn fires and winter fogs?
What shall we do in the heat of summer
But wait in barren orchards for another October?
Some malady is coming upon us. We wait, we wait,
And the saints and martyrs wait, for those who shall be martyrs and saints.
Destiny waits in the hand of God, shaping the still unshapen:
I have seen these things in a shaft of sunlight.
Destiny waits in the hand of God, not in the hands of statesmen
Who do, some well, some ill, planning and guessing,
Having their aims which turn in their hands in the pattern of time.
Come, happy December, who shall observe you, who shall preserve you?
Shall the Son of Man be born again in the litter of scorn?
For us, the poor, there is no action,
But only to wait and to witness.

(*Enter* PRIESTS)

FIRST PRIEST   Seven years and the summer is over.
Seven years since the Archbishop left us.
SECOND PRIEST   What does the Archbishop do, and our Sovereign Lord the Pope
With the stubborn King and the French King

In ceaseless intrigue, combinations,
In conference, meetings accepted, meetings refused,
Meetings unended or endless
At one place or another in France?

THIRD PRIEST I see nothing quite conclusive in the art of temporal government,
But violence, duplicity and frequent malversation.
King rules or barons rule:
The strong man strongly and the weak man by caprice.
They have but one law, to seize the power and keep it,
And the steadfast can manipulate the greed and lust of others,
The feeble is devoured by his own.

FIRST PRIEST Shall these things not end
Until the poor at the gate
Have forgotten their friend, their Father in God, have forgotten
That they had a friend?

(*Enter* MESSENGER)

MESSENGER Servants of God, and watchers of the temple,
I am here to inform you, without circumlocution:
The Archbishop is in England, and is close outside the city.
I was sent before in haste
To give you notice of his coming, as much as was possible,
That you may prepare to meet him.

FIRST PRIEST What, is the exile ended, is our Lord Archbishop
Reunited with the King? What reconciliation
Of two proud men?

THIRD PRIEST What peace can be found
To grow between the hammer and the anvil?

SECOND PRIEST Tell us,
Are the old disputes at an end, is the wall of pride cast down
That divided them? Is it peace or war?

FIRST PRIEST Does he come
In full assurance, or only secure
In the power of Rome, the spiritual rule,
The assurance of right, and the love of the people?

MESSENGER You are right to express a certain incredulity.
He comes in pride and sorrow, affirming all his claims,
Assured, beyond doubt, of the devotion of the people,
Who receive him with scenes of frenzied enthusiasm,
Lining the road and throwing down their capes,
Strewing the way with leaves and late flowers of the season.

The streets of the city will be packed to suffocation,
And I think that his horse will be deprived of its tail,
A single hair of which becomes a precious relic.
He is at one with the Pope, and with the King of France,
Who indeed would have liked to detain him in his kingdom:
But as for our King, that is another matter.
FIRST PRIEST   But again, is it war or peace?
MESSENGER   Peace, but not the kiss of peace.
A patched up affair, if you ask my opinion.
And if you ask me, I think the Lord Archbishop
Is not the man to cherish any illusions,
Or yet to diminish the least of his pretensions.
If you ask my opinion, I think that this peace
Is nothing like an end, or like a beginning.
It is common knowledge that when the Archbishop
Parted from the King, he said to the King,
My Lord, he said, I leave you as a man
Whom in this life I shall not see again.
I have this, I assure you, on the highest authority;
There are several opinions as to what he meant,
But no one considers it a happy prognostic.

(*Exit*)

FIRST PRIEST   I fear for the Archbishop, I fear for the Church,
I know that the pride bred of sudden prosperity
Was but confirmed by bitter adversity.
I saw him as Chancellor, flattered by the King,
Liked or feared by courtiers, in their overbearing fashion,
Despised and despising, always isolated,
Never one among them, always insecure;
His pride always feeding upon his own virtues,
Pride drawing sustenance from impartiality,
Pride drawing sustenance from generosity,
Loathing power given by temporal devolution,
Wishing subjection to God alone.
Had the King been greater, or had he been weaker
Things had perhaps been different for Thomas.
SECOND PRIEST   Yet our lord is returned. Our lord has come back to
   his own again.
We have had enough of waiting, from December to dismal December.
The Archbishop shall be at our head, dispelling dismay and doubt.
He will tell us what we are to do, he will give us our orders, instruct us.

Our Lord is at one with the Pope, and also the King of France.
We can lean on a rock, we can feel a firm foothold
Against the perpetual wash of tides of balance of forces of barons and landholders.
The rock of God is beneath our feet. Let us meet the Archbishop with cordial thanksgiving:
Our lord, our Archbishop returns. And when the Archbishop returns
Our doubts are dispelled. Let us therefore rejoice,
I say rejoice, and show a glad face for his welcome.
I am the Archbishop's man. Let us give the Archbishop welcome!
THIRD PRIEST   For good or ill, let the wheel turn.
The wheel has been still, these seven years, and no good.
For ill or good, let the wheel turn.
For who knows the end of good or evil?
Until the grinders cease
And the door shall be shut in the street,
And all the daughters of music shall be brought low.
CHORUS   Here is no continuing city, here is no abiding stay.
Ill the wind, ill the time, uncertain the profit, certain the danger.
O late late late, late is the time, late too late, and rotten the year;
Evil the wind, and bitter the sea, and grey the sky, grey grey grey.
O Thomas, return, Archbishop; return, return to France.
Return. Quickly. Quietly. Leave us to perish in quiet.
You come with applause, you come with rejoicing, but you come bringing death into Canterbury:
A doom on the house, a doom on yourself, a doom on the world.

We do not wish anything to happen.
Seven years we have lived quietly,
Succeeded in avoiding notice,
Living and partly living.
There have been oppression and luxury,
There have been poverty and licence,
There has been minor injustice.
Yet we have gone on living,
Living and partly living.
Sometimes the corn has failed us,
Sometimes the harvest is good,
One year is a year of rain,
Another a year of dryness,
One year the apples are abundant,
Another year the plums are lacking.

Yet we have gone on living,
Living and partly living.
We have kept the feasts, heard the masses,
We have brewed beer and cyder,
Gathered wood against the winter,
Talked at the corner of the fire,
Talked at the corners of streets,
Talked not always in whispers,
Living and partly living.

We have seen births, deaths and marriages,
We have had various scandals,
We have been afflicted with taxes,
We have had laughter and gossip,
Several girls have disappeared
Unaccountably, and some not able to.
We have all had our private terrors,
Our particular shadows, our secret fears.
But now a great fear is upon us, a fear not of one but of many,
A fear like birth and death, when we see birth and death alone
In a void apart. We
Are afraid in a fear which we cannot know, which we cannot face, which none understands,
And our hearts are torn from us, our brains unskinned like the layers of an onion, our selves are lost lost
In a final fear which none understands. O Thomas Archbishop,
O Thomas our Lord, leave us and leave us be, in our humble and tarnished frame of existence, leave us; do not ask us
To stand to the doom on the house, the doom on the Archbishop, the doom on the world.
Archbishop, secure and assured of your fate, unaffrayed among the shades, do you realise what you ask, do you realise what it means
To the small folk drawn into the pattern of fate, the small folk who live among small things,
The strain on the brain of the small folk who stand to the doom of the house, the doom of their lord, the doom of the world?
O Thomas, Archbishop, leave us, leave us, leave sullen Dover, and set sail for France. Thomas our Archbishop still our Archbishop even in France. Thomas Archbishop, set the white sail between the grey sky and the bitter sea, leave us, leave us for France.

SECOND PRIEST   What a way to talk at such a juncture!
You are foolish, immodest and babbling women.

Do you not know that the good Archbishop
Is likely to arrive at any moment?
The crowds in the streets will be cheering and cheering,
You go on croaking like frogs in the treetops:
But frogs at least can be cooked and eaten.
Whatever you are afraid of, in your craven apprehension,
Let me ask you at the least to put on pleasant faces,
And give a hearty welcome to our good Archbishop.

(*Enter* THOMAS)

THOMAS Peace. And let them be, in their exaltation.
They speak better than they know, and beyond your understanding.
They know and do not know, what it is to act or suffer.
They know and do not know, that action is suffering
And suffering is action. Neither does the agent suffer
Nor the patient act. But both are fixed
In an eternal action, an eternal patience
To which all must consent that it may be willed
And which all must suffer that they may will it,
That the pattern may subsist, for the pattern is the action
And the suffering, that the wheel may turn and still
Be forever still.

SECOND PRIEST O my Lord, forgive me, I did not see you coming,
Engrossed by the chatter of these foolish women.
Forgive us, my Lord, you would have had a better welcome
If we had been sooner prepared for the event.
But your Lordship knows that seven years of waiting,
Seven years of prayer, seven years of emptiness,
Have better prepared our hearts for your coming,
Than seven days could make ready Canterbury.
However, I will have fires laid in all your rooms
To take the chill off our English December,
Your Lordship now being used to a better climate.
Your Lordship will find your rooms in order as you left them.

THOMAS And will try to leave them in order as I find them.
I am more than grateful for all your kind attentions.
These are small matters. Little rest in Canterbury
With eager enemies restless about us.
Rebellious bishops, York, London, Salisbury,
Would have intercepted our letters,
Filled the coast with spies and sent to meet me
Some who hold me in bitterest hate.

By God's grace aware of their prevision
I sent my letters on another day,
Had fair crossing, found at Sandwich
Broc, Warenne, and the Sheriff of Kent,
Those who had sworn to have my head from me
Only John, the Dean of Salisbury,
Fearing for the King's name, warning against treason,
Made them hold their hands. So for the time
We are unmolested.

FIRST PRIEST　　　　　　　　But do they follow after?
THOMAS　For a little time the hungry hawk
Will only soar and hover, circling lower,
Waiting excuse, pretence, opportunity.
End will be simple, sudden, God-given.
Meanwhile the substance of our first act
Will be shadows, and the strife with shadows.
Heavier the interval than the consummation.
All things prepare the event. Watch.

(Enter FIRST TEMPTER*)*

FIRST TEMPTER　You see, my Lord, I do not wait upon ceremony:
Here I have come, forgetting all acrimony,
Hoping that your present gravity
Will find excuse for my humble levity
Remembering all the good time past.
Your Lordship won't despise an old friend out of favour?
Old Tom, gay Tom, Becket of London,
Your Lordship won't forget that evening on the river
When the King, and you and I were all friends together?
Friendship should be more than biting Time can sever.
What, my Lord, now that you recover
Favour with the King, shall we say that summer's over
Or that the good time cannot last?
Fluting in the meadows, viols in the hall,
Laughter and apple-blossom floating on the water,
Singing at nightfall, whispering in chambers,
Fires devouring the winter season,
Eating up the darkness, with wit and wine and wisdom!
Now that the King and you are in amity,
Clergy and laity may return to gaiety,
Mirth and sportfulness need not walk warily.
THOMAS　You talk of seasons that are past. I remember

Not worth forgetting.
TEMPTER   And of the new season.
Spring has come in winter. Snow in the branches
Shall float as sweet as blossoms. Ice along the ditches
Mirror the sunlight. Love in the orchard
Send the sap shooting. Mirth matches melancholy.
THOMAS We do not know very much of the future
Except that from generation to generation
The same things happen again and again.
Men learn little from others' experience.
But in the life of one man, never
The same time returns. Sever
The cord, shed the scale. Only
The fool, fixed in his folly, may think
He can turn the wheel on which he turns.
TEMPTER My Lord, a nod is as good as a wink.
A man will often love what he spurns.
For the good times past, that are come again
I am your man.
THOMAS   Not in this train
Look to your behaviour. You were safer
Think of penitence and follow your master.
TEMPTER Not at this gait!
If you go so fast, others may go faster.
Your Lordship is too proud!
The safest beast is not the one that roars most loud,
This was not the way of the King our master!
You were not used to be so hard upon sinners
When they were your friends. Be easy, man!
The easy man lives to eat the best dinners.
Take a friend's advice. Leave well alone,
Or your goose may be cooked and eaten to the bone.
THOMAS You come twenty years too late.
TEMPTER Then I leave you to your fate.
I leave you to the pleasures of your higher vices,
Which will have to be paid for at higher prices.
Farewell, my Lord, I do not wait upon ceremony,
I leave as I came, forgetting all acrimony,
Hoping that your present gravity
Will find excuse for my humble levity.
If you will remember me, my Lord, at your prayers,
I'll remember you at kissing-time below the stairs.

THOMAS Leave-well-alone, the springtime fancy,
So one thought goes whistling down the wind.
The impossible is still temptation.
The impossible, the undesirable,
Voices under sleep, waking a dead world,
So that the mind may not be whole in the present.

(*Enter* SECOND TEMPTER)

SECOND TEMPTER Your Lordship has forgotten me, perhaps. I will remind you.
We met at Clarendon, at Northampton,
And last at Montmirail, in Maine. Now that I have recalled them,
Let us but set these not too pleasant memories
In balance against other, earlier
And weightier ones: those of the Chancellorship.
See how the late ones rise! You, master of policy
Whom all acknowledged, should guide the state again.

THOMAS Your meaning?

TEMPTER   The Chancellorship that you resigned
When you were made Archbishop—that was a mistake
On your part—still may be regained. Think, my Lord,
Power obtained grows to glory,
Life lasting, a permanent possession.
A templed tomb, monument of marble.
Rule over men reckon no madness.

THOMAS To the man of God what gladness?

TEMPTER   Sadness
Only to those giving love to God alone.
Shall he who held the solid substance
Wander waking with deceitful shadows?
Power is present. Holiness hereafter.

THOMAS Who then?

TEMPTER   The Chancellor. King and Chancellor.
King commands. Chancellor richly rules.
This is a sentence not taught in the schools.
To set down the great, protect the poor,
Beneath the throne of God can man do more?
Disarm the ruffian, strengthen the laws,
Rule for the good of the better cause,
Dispensing justice make all even,
Is thrive on earth, and perhaps in heaven.

THOMAS What means?

TEMPTER   Real power
  Is purchased at price of a certain submission.
  Your spiritual power is earthly perdition.
  Power is present, for him who will wield.
THOMAS   Who shall have it?
TEMPTER   He who will come.
THOMAS   What shall be the month?
TEMPTER   The last from the first.
THOMAS   What shall we give for it?
TEMPTER   Pretence of priestly power.
THOMAS   Why should we give it?
TEMPTER   For the power and the glory.
THOMAS   No!
TEMPTER   Yes! Or bravery will be broken,
  Cabined in Canterbury, realmless ruler,
  Self-bound servant of a powerless Pope,
  The old stag, circled with hounds.
THOMAS   No!
TEMPTER   Yes! men must manœuvre. Monarchs also,
  Waging war abroad, need fast friends at home.
  Private policy is public profit;
  Dignity still shall be dressed with decorum.
THOMAS   You forget the bishops
  Whom I have laid under excommunication.
TEMPTER   Hungry hatred
  Will not strive against intelligent self-interest.
THOMAS   You forget the barons. Who will not forget
  Constant curbing of petty privilege.
TEMPTER   Against the barons
  Is King's cause, churl's cause, Chancellor's cause.
THOMAS   No! shall I, who keep the keys
  Of heaven and hell, supreme alone in England,
  Who bind and loose, with power from the Pope,
  Descend to desire a punier power?
  Delegate to deal the doom of damnation,
  To condemn kings, not serve among their servants,
  Is my open office. No! Go.
TEMPTER   Then I leave you to your fate.
  Your sin soars sunward, covering kings' falcons.
THOMAS   Temporal power, to build a good world,
  To keep order, as the world knows order.
  Those who put their faith in worldly order

Not controlled by the order of God,
In confident ignorance, but arrest disorder,
Make it fast, breed fatal disease,
Degrade what they exalt. Power with the King—
I *was* the King, his arm, his better reason.
But what was once exaltation
Would now be only mean descent.

(*Enter* THIRD TEMPTER)

THIRD TEMPTER   I am an unexpected visitor.
THOMAS   I expected you.
TEMPTER   But not in this guise, or for my present purpose.
THOMAS   No purpose brings surprise.
TEMPTER   Well, my Lord,
I am no trifler, and no politician.
To idle or intrigue at court
I have no skill. I am no courtier.
I know a horse, a dog, a wench;
I know how to hold my estates in order,
A country-keeping lord who minds his own business.
It is we country lords who know the country
And we who know what the country needs.
It is our country. We care for the country.
We are the backbone of the nation.
We, not the plotting parasites
About the King. Excuse my bluntness:
I am a rough straightforward Englishman.
THOMAS   Proceed straight forward.
TEMPTER   Purpose is plain.
Endurance of friendship does not depend
Upon ourselves, but upon circumstance.
But circumstance is not undetermined.
Unreal friendship may turn to real
But real friendship, once ended, cannot be mended.
Sooner shall enmity turn to alliance.
The enmity that never knew friendship
Can sooner know accord.
THOMAS   For a countryman
You wrap your meaning in as dark generality
As any courtier
TEMPTER   This is the simple fact!
You have no hope of reconciliation

With Henry the King. You look only
To blind assertion in isolation.
That is a mistake.
THOMAS   O Henry, O my King!
TEMPTER   Other friends
May be found in the present situation.
King in England is not all-powerful;
King is in France, squabbling in Anjou;
Round him waiting hungry sons.
We are for England. We are in England.
You and I, my Lord, are Normans.
England is a land for Norman
Sovereignty. Let the Angevin
Destroy himself, fighting in Anjou.
He does not understand us, the English barons.
We are the people.
THOMAS   To what does this lead?
TEMPTER   To a happy coalition
Of intelligent interests.
THOMAS   But what have you—
If you do speak for barons—
TEMPTER   For a powerful party
Which has turned its eyes in your direction—
To gain from you, your Lordship asks.
For us, Church favour would be an advantage,
Blessing of Pope powerful protection
In the fight for liberty. You, my Lord,
In being with us, would fight a good stroke
At once, for England and for Rome,
Ending the tyrannous jurisdiction
Of king's court over bishop's court,
Of king's court over baron's court.
THOMAS   Which I helped to found.
TEMPTER   Which you helped to found.
But time past is time forgotten.
We expect the rise of a new constellation.
THOMAS   And if the Archbishop cannot trust the King,
How can he trust those who work for King's undoing?
TEMPTER   Kings will allow no power but their own;
Church and people have good cause against the throne.
THOMAS   If the Archbishop cannot trust the Throne,
He has good cause to trust none but God alone.

I ruled once as Chancellor
And men like you were glad to wait at my door.
Not only in the court, but in the field
And in the tilt-yard I made many yield.
Shall I who ruled like an eagle over doves
Now take the shape of a wolf among wolves?
Pursue your treacheries as you have done before:
No one shall say that I betrayed a king.

TEMPTER Then, my Lord, I shall not wait at your door.
And I well hope, before another spring
The King will show his regard for your loyalty.

THOMAS To make, then break, this thought has come before,
The desperate exercise of failing power.
Samson in Gaza[1] did no more.
But if I break, I must break myself alone.

(*Enter* FOURTH TEMPTER)

FOURTH TEMPTER Well done, Thomas, your will is hard to bend.
And with me beside you, you shall not lack a friend.

THOMAS Who are you? I expected
Three visitors, not four.

TEMPTER Do not be surprised to receive one more.
Had I been expected, I had been here before.
I always precede expectation.

THOMAS   Who are you?

TEMPTER As you do not know me, I do not need a name,
And, as you know me, that is why I come.
You know me, but have never seen my face.
To meet before was never time or place.

THOMAS Say what you come to say.

TEMPTER   It shall be said at last.
Hooks have been baited with morsels of the past.
Wantonness is weakness. As for the King,
His hardened hatred shall have no end.
You know truly, the King will never trust
Twice, the man who has been his friend.
Borrow use cautiously, employ
Your services as long as you have to lend.
You would wait for trap to snap
Having served your turn, broken and crushed.

---

[1] *Judges* 13:1–24.

As for barons, envy of lesser men
Is still more stubborn than king's anger.
Kings have public policy, barons private profit,
Jealousy raging possession of the fiend.
Barons are employable against each other;
Greater enemies must kings destroy.

THOMAS   What is your counsel?
TEMPTER   Fare forward to the end.
All other ways are closed to you
Except the way already chosen.
But what is pleasure, kingly rule,
Or rule of men beneath a king,
With craft in corners, stealthy stratagem,
To general grasp of spiritual power?
Man oppressed by sin, since Adam fell—
You hold the keys of heaven and hell.
Power to bind and loose: bind, Thomas, bind,
King and bishop under your heel.
King, emperor, bishop, baron, king:
Uncertain mastery of melting armies,
War, plague, and revolution,
New conspiracies, broken pacts;
To be master or servant within an hour,
This is the course of temporal power.
The Old King shall know it, when at last breath,
No sons, no empire, he bites broken teeth.
You hold the skein: wind, Thomas, wind
The thread of eternal life and death.
You hold this power, hold it.
THOMAS   Supreme, in this land?
TEMPTER   Supreme, but for one.
THOMAS   That I do not understand.
TEMPTER   It is not for me to tell you how this may be so;
I am only here, Thomas, to tell you what you know.
THOMAS   How long shall this be?
TEMPTER   Save what you know already, ask nothing of me.
But think, Thomas, think of glory after death.
When king is dead, there's another king,
And one more king is another reign.
King is forgotten, when another shall come:
Saint and Martyr rule from the tomb.

Think, Thomas, think of enemies dismayed,
Creeping in penance, frightened of a shade;
Think of pilgrims, standing in line
Before the glittering jewelled shrine,
From generation to generation
Bending the knee in supplication,
Think of the miracles, by God's grace,
And think of your enemies, in another place.

THOMAS   I have thought of these things.

TEMPTER   That is why I tell you.
Your thoughts have more power than kings to compel you.
You have also thought, sometimes at your prayers,
Sometimes hesitating at the angles of stairs,
And between sleep and waking, early in the morning,
When the bird cries, have thought of further scorning.
That nothing lasts, but the wheel turns,
The nest is rifled, and the bird mourns;
That the shrine shall be pillaged, and the gold spent,
The jewels gone for light ladies' ornament,
The sanctuary broken, and its stores
Swept into the laps of parasites and whores.
When miracles cease, and the faithful desert you.
And men shall only do their best to forget you.
And later is worse, when men will not hate you
Enough to defame or to execrate you,
But pondering the qualities that you lacked
Will only try to find the historical fact.
When men shall declare that there was no mystery
About this man who played a certain part in history.

THOMAS   But what is there to do? What is left to be done?
Is there no enduring crown to be won?

TEMPTER   Yes, Thomas, yes; you have thought of that too.
What can compare with glory of Saints
Dwelling forever in presence of God?
What earthly glory, of king or emperor,
What earthly pride, that is not poverty
Compared with richness of heavenly grandeur?
Seek the way of martyrdom, make yourself the lowest
On earth, to be high in heaven.
And see far off below you, where the gulf is fixed,
Your persecutors, in timeless torment,
Parched passion, beyond expiation.

THOMAS No!
  Who are you, tempting with my own desires?
  Others have come, temporal tempters,
  With pleasure and power at palpable price.
  What do you offer? What do you ask?
TEMPTER I offer what you desire. I ask
  What you have to give. Is it too much
  For such a vision of eternal grandeur?
THOMAS Others offered real goods, worthless
  But real. You only offer
  Dreams to damnation.
TEMPTER You have often dreamt them.
THOMAS Is there no way, in my soul's sickness,
  Does not lead to damnation in pride?
  I well know that these temptations
  Mean present vanity and future torment.
  Can sinful pride be driven out
  Only by more sinful? Can I neither act nor suffer
  Without perdition?
TEMPTER You know and do not know, what it is to act or suffer.
  You know and do not know, that action is suffering,
  And suffering action. Neither does the agent suffer
  Nor the patient act. But both are fixed
  In an eternal action, an eternal patience
  To which all must consent that it may be willed
  And which all must suffer that they may will it,
  That the pattern may subsist, that the wheel may turn and still
  Be forever still.
CHORUS There is no rest in the house. There is no rest in the street.
  I hear restless movement of feet. And the air is heavy and thick.
  Thick and heavy the sky. And the earth presses up against our feet.
  What is the sickly smell, the vapour? The dark green light from a cloud
    on a withered tree? The earth is heaving to parturition of issue
    of hell. What is the sticky dew that forms on the back of my hand?
THE FOUR TEMPTERS Man's life is a cheat and a disappointment;
  All things are unreal,
  Unreal or disappointing:
  The Catherine wheel,[2] the pantomime cat,
  The prizes given at the children's party,

[2] A firework named after the shape of St. Catherine's instrument of martyrdom.

The prize awarded for the English Essay,
The scholar's degree, the statesman's decoration.
All things become less real, man passes
From unreality to unreality.
This man is obstinate, blind, intent
On self-destruction.
Passing from deception to deception,
From grandeur to grandeur to final illusion,
Lost in the wonder of his own greatness,
The enemy of society, enemy of himself.

THE THREE PRIESTS O Thomas my Lord do not fight the intractable tide,
Do not sail the irresistible wind; in the storm,
Should we not wait for the sea to subside, in the night
Abide the coming of day, when the traveller may find his way,
The sailor lay course by the sun?

CHORUS, PRIESTS and TEMPTERS *alternately*
C. Is it the owl that calls, or a signal between the trees?
P. Is the window-bar made fast, is the door under lock and bolt?
T. Is it rain that taps at the window, is it wind that pokes at the door?
C. Does the torch flame in the hall, the candle in the room?
P. Does the watchman walk by the wall?
T. Does the mastiff prowl by the gate?
C. Death has a hundred hands and walks by a thousand ways.
P. He may come in the sight of all, he may pass unseen unheard.
T. Come whispering through the ear, or a sudden shock on the skull.
C. A man may walk with a lamp at night, and yet be drowned in a ditch.
P. A man may climb the stair in the day, and slip on a broken step
T. A man may sit at meat, and feel the cold in his groin.

CHORUS We have not been happy, my Lord, we have not been too happy.
We are not ignorant women, we know what we must expect and not expect.
We know of oppression and torture,
We know of extortion and violence,
Destitution, disease,
The old without fire in winter,
The child without milk in summer,
Our labour taken away from us,
Our sins made heavier upon us.
We have seen the young man mutilated,

The torn girl trembling by the mill-stream.
And meanwhile we have gone on living,
Living and partly living,
Picking together the pieces,
Gathering faggots at nightfall,
Building a partial shelter,
For sleeping, and eating and drinking and laughter.

God gave us always some reason, some hope; but now a new terror has soiled us, which none can avert, none can avoid, flowing under our feet and over the sky;
Under doors and down chimneys, flowing in at the ear and the mouth and the eye.
God is leaving us, God is leaving us, more pang, more pain than birth or death.
Sweet and cloying through the dark air
Falls the stifling scent of despair;
The forms take shape in the dark air:
Puss-purr of leopard, footfall of padding bear,
Palm-pat of nodding ape, square hyaena waiting
For laughter, laughter, laughter. The Lords of Hell are here.
They curl round you, lie at your feet, swing and wing through the dark air.
O Thomas Archbishop, save us, save us, save yourself that we may be saved;
Destroy yourself and we are destroyed.

THOMAS Now is my way clear, now is the meaning plain:
Temptation shall not come in this kind again.
The last temptation is the greatest treason:
To do the right deed for the wrong reason.
The natural vigour in the venial sin
Is the way in which our lives begin.
Thirty years ago, I searched all the ways
That lead to pleasure, advancement and praise.
Delight in sense, in learning and in thought,
Music and philosophy, curiosity,
The purple bullfinch in the lilac tree,
The tilt-yard skill, the strategy of chess,
Love in the garden, singing to the instrument,
Were all things equally desirable.
Ambition comes when early force is spent

And when we find no longer all things possible.
Ambition comes behind and unobservable.
Sin grows with doing good. When I imposed the King's law
In England, and waged war with him against Toulouse,
I beat the barons at their own game. I
Could then despise the men who thought me most contemptible,
The raw nobility, whose manners matched their fingernails.
While I ate out of the King's dish
To become servant of God was never my wish.
Servant of God has chance of greater sin
And sorrow, than the man who serves a king.
For those who serve the greater cause may make the cause serve them,
Still doing right: and striving with political men
May make that cause political, not by what they do
But by what they are. I know
What yet remains to show you of my history
Will seem to most of you at best futility,
Senseless self-slaughter of a lunatic,
Arrogant passion of a fanatic.
I know that history at all times draws
The strangest consequence from remotest cause.
But for every evil, every sacrilege,
Crime, wrong, oppression and the axe's edge,
Indifference, exploitation, you, and you,
And you, must all be punished. So must you.
I shall no longer act or suffer, to the sword's end.
Now my good Angel, whom God appoints
To be my guardian, hover over the swords' points.

Interlude

The ARCHBISHOP *preaches in the Cathedral on Christmas Morning, 1170.*

'Glory to God in the highest, and on earth peace to men of good will.' *The fourteenth verse of the second chapter of the Gospel according to Saint Luke.* In the Name of the Father, and of the Son, and of the Holy Ghost. Amen.

Dear children of God, my sermon this Christmas morning will be a very short one. I wish only that you should meditate in your hearts the deep meaning and mystery of our masses of Christmas Day. For whenever Mass is said, we re-enact the Passion and Death of Our Lord; and on this Christmas Day we do this in celebration of His Birth. So that at the same moment we rejoice in His coming for the salvation of men, and offer again to God His Body and Blood in sacrifice, oblation and satisfaction for the sins of the whole world. It was in this same night that has just passed, that a multitude of the heavenly host appeared before the shepherds at Bethlehem, saying 'Glory to God in the highest, and on earth peace to men of good will'; at this same time of all the year that we celebrate at once the Birth of Our Lord and His Passion and Death upon the Cross. Beloved, as the World sees, this is to behave in a strange fashion. For who in the World will both mourn and rejoice at once and for the same reason? For either joy will be overborne by mourning, or mourning will be cast out by joy; so it is only in these our Christian mysteries that we can rejoice and mourn at once for the same reason. Now think for a moment about the meaning of this word 'peace.' Does it seem strange to you that the angels should have announced Peace, when ceaselessly the world has been stricken with War and the fear of War? Does it seem to you that the angelic voices were mistaken, and that the promise was a disappointment and a cheat?

Reflect now, how Our Lord Himself spoke of Peace. He said to His disciples, 'My peace I leave with you, my peace I give unto you.' Did He mean peace as we think of it: the kingdom of England at peace with its neighbours, the barons at peace with the King, the householder counting over his peaceful gains, the swept hearth, his best wine for a friend at the table, his wife singing to the children? Those men His disciples knew no such things: they went forth to journey afar, to suffer by land and sea, to know torture, imprisonment, disappointment, to suffer death by martyrdom. What then did He mean? If you ask that, remember then that He said also, 'Not as the world gives, give I unto you.' So then, He gave to His disciples peace, but not peace as the world gives.

Consider also one thing of which you have probably never thought. Not only do we at the feast of Christmas celebrate at once Our Lord's Birth and His Death: but on the next day we celebrate the martyrdom of His first martyr, the blessed Stephen. Is it an accident, do you think, that the day of the first martyr follows immediately the day of the Birth of Christ? By no means. Just as we rejoice and mourn at once, in the Birth and in the Passion of Our Lord; so also, in a smaller figure, we both rejoice and mourn in the death of martyrs. We mourn, for the sins of the world that has martyred them; we rejoice, that another soul is numbered among the Saints in Heaven, for the glory of God and for the salvation of men.

Beloved, we do not think of a martyr simply as a good Christian who has been killed because he is a Christian: for that would be solely to mourn. We do not think of him simply as a good Christian who has been elevated to the company of the Saints: for that would be simply to rejoice: and neither our mourning nor our rejoicing is as the world's is. A Christian martyrdom is never an accident, for Saints are not made by accident. Still less is a Christian martyrdom the effect of a man's will to become a Saint, as a man by willing and contriving may become a ruler of men. A martyrdom is always the design of God, for His love of men, to warn them and to lead them, to bring them back to His ways. It is never the design of man; for the true martyr is he who has become the instrument of God, who has lost his will in the will of God, and who no longer desires anything for himself, not even the glory of being a martyr. So thus as on earth the Church mourns and rejoices at once, in a fashion that the world cannot understand; so in Heaven the Saints are most high, having made themselves most low, and are seen, not as we see them, but in the light of the Godhead from which they draw their being.

I have spoken to you to-day, dear children of God, of the martyrs of the past, asking you to remember especially our martyr of Canterbury, the blessed Archbishop Elphege; because it is fitting, on Christ's birth day, to remember what is that Peace which He brought; and because, dear children, I do not think I shall ever preach to you again; and because it is possible that in a short time you may have yet another martyr, and that one perhaps not the last. I would have you keep in your hearts these words that I say, and think of them at another time. In the Name of the Father, and of the Son, and of the Holy Ghost. Amen.

Part II

CHARACTERS

THREE PRIESTS
FOUR KNIGHTS
ARCHBISHOP THOMAS BECKET
CHORUS OF WOMEN OF CANTERBURY
ATTENDANTS

The first scene is in the Archbishop's Hall, the second scene is in the Cathedral, on December 29th, 1170.

Murder in the Cathedral [PART II]

CHORUS Does the bird sing in the South?
Only the sea-bird cries, driven inland by the storm.
What sign of the spring of the year?
Only the death of the old: not a stir, not a shoot, not a breath.
Do the days begin to lengthen?
Longer and darker the day, shorter and colder the night.
Still and stifling the air: but a wind is stored up in the East.
The starved crow sits in the field, attentive; and in the wood
The owl rehearses the hollow note of death.
What signs of a bitter spring?
The wind stored up in the East.
What, at the time of the birth of Our Lord, at Christmastide,
Is there not peace upon earth, goodwill among men?
The peace of this world is always uncertain, unless men keep the peace of God.
And war among men defiles this world, but death in the Lord renews it,
And the world must be cleaned in the winter, or we shall have only
A sour spring, a parched summer, an empty harvest.
Between Christmas and Easter what work shall be done?
The ploughman shall go out in March and turn the same earth
He has turned before, the bird shall sing the same song.
When the leaf is out on the tree, when the elder and may
Burst over the stream, and the air is clear and high,
And voices trill at windows, and children tumble in front of the door,
What work shall have been done, what wrong
Shall the bird's song cover, the green tree cover, what wrong
Shall the fresh earth cover? We wait, and the time is short
But waiting is long.

(*Enter the* FIRST PRIEST *with a banner of St. Stephen borne before him. The lines sung are in italics*)

FIRST PRIEST Since Christmas a day: and the day of St. Stephen, First Martyr.
Princes moreover did sit, and did witness falsely against me.
A day that was always most dear to the Archbishop Thomas.
And he kneeled down and cried with a loud voice:
Lord, lay not this sin to their charge.
Princes moreover did sit.
(*Introit of St. Stephen is heard*)

(*Enter the* SECOND PRIEST, *with a banner of St. John the Apostle borne before him*)

SECOND PRIEST   Since St. Stephen a day: and the day of St. John the
        Apostle.
In the midst of the congregation he opened his mouth.
That which was from the beginning, which we have heard,
Which we have seen with our eyes, and our hands have handled
Of the word of life; that which we have seen and heard
Declare we unto you.
In the midst of the congregation.
   (*Introit of St. John is heard*)

   (*Enter the* THIRD PRIEST, *with a banner of the Holy Innocents borne before him*)

THIRD PRIEST   Since St. John the Apostle a day: and the day of the
        Holy Innocents.
Out of the mouth of very babes, O God.
As the voice of many waters, of thunder, of harps,
They sung as it were a new song.
The blood of thy saints have they shed like water,
And there was no man to bury them. Avenge, O Lord,
The blood of thy saints. In Rama, a voice heard, weeping.
Out of the mouth of very babes, O God!

   (*The* PRIESTS *stand together with the banners behind them*)

FIRST PRIEST   Since the Holy Innocents a day: the fourth day from
        Christmas.
THE THREE PRIESTS   *Rejoice we all, keeping holy day.*
FIRST PRIEST   As for the people, so also for himself, he offereth for
        sins.
He lays down his life for the sheep.
THE THREE PRIESTS   *Rejoice we all, keeping holy day.*
FIRST PRIEST   To-day?
SECOND PRIEST   To-day, what is to-day? For the day is half gone.
FIRST PRIEST   To-day, what is to-day? But another day, the dusk of
        the year.
SECOND PRIEST   To-day, what is to-day? Another night, and another dawn.
THIRD PRIEST   What day is the day that we know that we hope for
        or fear for?
Every day is the day we should fear from or hope from. One moment
Weighs like another. Only in retrospection, selection,
We say, that was the day. The critical moment
That is always now, and here. Even now, in sordid particulars
The eternal design may appear.

(*Enter the* FOUR KNIGHTS. *The banners disappear*)

FIRST KNIGHT Servants of the King.
FIRST PRIEST   And known to us.
  You are welcome. Have you ridden far?
FIRST KNIGHT Not far to-day, but matters urgent
  Have brought us from France. We rode hard,
  Took ship yesterday, landed last night,
  Having business with the Archbishop.
SECOND KNIGHT Urgent business.
THIRD KNIGHT   From the King.
SECOND KNIGHT By the King's order.
FIRST KNIGHT   Our men are outside.
FIRST PRIEST You know the Archbishop's hospitality.
  We are about to go to dinner.
  The good Archbishop would be vexed
  If we did not offer you entertainment
  Before your business. Please dine with us.
  Your men shall be looked after also.
  Dinner before business. Do you like roast pork?
FIRST KNIGHT Business before dinner. We will roast your pork
  First, and dine upon it after.
SECOND KNIGHT We must see the Archbishop.
THIRD KNIGHT   Go, tell the Archbishop
  We have no need of his hospitality.
  We will find our own dinner.
FIRST PRIEST (*To* ATTENDANT) Go, tell His Lordship.
FOURTH KNIGHT   How much longer will you keep us waiting?

   (*Enter* THOMAS)

THOMAS (*To* PRIESTS) However certain our expectation
  The moment foreseen may be unexpected
  When it arrives. It comes when we are
  Engrossed with matters of other urgency.
  On my table you will find
  The papers in order, and the documents signed.

   (*To* KNIGHTS)

  You are welcome, whatever your business may be.
  You say, from the King?
FIRST KNIGHT   Most surely from the King.
  We must speak with you alone.

THOMAS (*To priests*)   Leave us then alone.
  Now what is the matter?
FIRST KNIGHT   This is the matter.
THE THREE KNIGHTS   You are the Archbishop in revolt against the King;
  in rebellion to the King and the law of the land;
  You are the Archbishop who was made by the King; whom he set in your place to carry out his command.
  You are his servant, his tool, and his jack,
  You wore his favours on your back,
  You had your honours all from his hand; from him you had the power, the seal and the ring.
  This is the man who was the tradesman's son: the backstairs brat who was born in Cheapside;
  This is the creature that crawled upon the King; swollen with blood and swollen with pride.
  Creeping out of the London dirt,
  Crawling up like a louse on your shirt,
  The man who cheated, swindled, lied; broke his oath and betrayed his King.
THOMAS   This is not true.
  Both before and after I received the ring
  I have been a loyal subject to the King.
  Saving my order, I am at his command,
  As his most faithful vassal in the land.
FIRST KNIGHT   Saving your order! let your order save you—
  As I do not think it is like to do.
  Saving your ambition is what you mean,
  Saving your pride, envy and spleen.
SECOND KNIGHT   Saving your insolence and greed.
  Won't you ask us to pray to God for you, in your need?
THIRD KNIGHT   Yes, we'll pray for you!
FIRST KNIGHT   Yes, we'll pray for you!
THE THREE KNIGHTS   Yes, we'll pray that God may help you!
THOMAS   But, gentlemen, your business
  Which you said so urgent, is it only
  Scolding and blaspheming?
FIRST KNIGHT   That was only
  Our indignation, as loyal subjects.
THOMAS   Loyal? To whom?
FIRST KNIGHT   To the King!
SECOND KNIGHT   The King!
THIRD KNIGHT   The King!

THE THREE KNIGHTS   God bless him!
THOMAS   Then let your new coat of loyalty be worn
    Carefully, so it get not soiled or torn.
    Have you something to say?
FIRST KNIGHT   By the King's command.
    Shall we say it now?
SECOND KNIGHT   Without delay,
    Before the old fox is off and away.
THOMAS   What you have to say
    By the King's command—if it be the King's command—
    Should be said in public. If you make charges,
    Then in public I will refute them.
FIRST KNIGHT   No! here and now!

(*They make to attack him, but the* PRIESTS *and* ATTENDANTS
return and quietly interpose themselves)

THOMAS   Now and here!
FIRST KNIGHT   Of your earlier misdeeds I shall make no mention.
    They are too well known. But after dissension
    Had ended, in France, and you were endued
    With your former privilege, how did you show your gratitude?
    You had fled from England, not exiled
    Or threatened, mind you; but in the hope
    Of stirring up trouble in the French dominions.
    You sowed strife abroad, you reviled
    The King to the King of France, to the Pope,
    Raising up against him false opinions.
SECOND KNIGHT   Yet the King, out of his charity,
    And urged by your friends, offered clemency,
    Made a pact of peace, and all dispute ended
    Sent you back to your See as you demanded.
THIRD KNIGHT   And burying the memory of your transgressions
    Restored your honours and your possessions.
    All was granted for which you sued:
    Yet how, I repeat, did you show your gratitude?
FIRST KNIGHT   Suspending those who had crowned the young prince,
    Denying the legality of his coronation.
SECOND KNIGHT   Binding with the chains of anathema.
THIRD KNIGHT   Using every means in your power to evince
    The King's faithful servants, every one who transacts
    His business in his absence, the business of the nation.
FIRST KNIGHT   These are the facts.

Say therefore if you will be content
To answer in the King's presence. Therefore were we sent.
THOMAS   Never was it my wish
To uncrown the King's son, or to diminish
His honour and power. Why should he wish
To deprive my people of me and keep me from my own
And bid me sit in Canterbury, alone?
I would wish him three crowns rather than one,
And as for the bishops, it is not my yoke
That is laid upon them, or mine to revoke.
Let them go to the Pope. It was he who condemned them.
FIRST KNIGHT   Through you they were suspended.
SECOND KNIGHT   By you be this amended.
THIRD KNIGHT   Absolve them.
FIRST KNIGHT   Absolve them.
THOMAS   I do not deny
That this was done through me. But it is not I
Who can loose whom the Pope has bound.
Let them go to him, upon whom redounds
Their contempt towards me, their contempt towards the Church
   shown.
FIRST KNIGHT   Be that as it may, here is the King's command:
That you and your servants depart from this land.
THOMAS   If that *is* the King's command, I will be bold
To say: seven years were my people without
My presence; seven years of misery and pain.
Seven years a mendicant on foreign charity
I lingered abroad: seven years is no brevity.
I shall not get those seven years back again.
Never again, you must make no doubt,
Shall the sea run between the shepherd and his fold.
FIRST KNIGHT   The King's justice, the King's majesty,
You insult with gross indignity;
Insolent madman, whom nothing deters
From attainting his servants and ministers.
THOMAS   It is not I who insult the King,
And there is higher than I or the King.
It is not I, Becket from Cheapside,
It is not against me, Becket, that you strive.
It is not Becket who pronounces doom,
But the Law of Christ's Church, the judgement of Rome.
FIRST KNIGHT   Priest, you have spoken in peril of your life.

SECOND KNIGHT   Priest, you have spoken in danger of the knife.
THIRD KNIGHT   Priest, you have spoken treachery and treason.
THE THREE KNIGHTS   Priest! traitor, confirmed in malfeasance.
THOMAS   I submit my cause to the judgement of Rome.
  But if you kill me, I shall rise from my tomb
  To submit my cause before God's throne.

(*Exit*)

FOURTH KNIGHT   Priest! monk! and servant! take, hold, detain,
  Restrain this man, in the King's name.
FIRST KNIGHT   Or answer with your bodies.
SECOND KNIGHT   Enough of words.
THE FOUR KNIGHTS   We come for the King's justice, we come with swords.

(*Exeunt*)

CHORUS   I have smelt them, the death-bringers, senses are quickened
  By subtile forebodings; I have heard
  Fluting in the night-time, fluting and owls, have seen at noon
  Scaly wings slanting over, huge and ridiculous. I have tasted
  The savour of putrid flesh in the spoon. I have felt
  The heaving of earth at nightfall, restless, absurd. I have heard
  Laughter in the noises of beasts that make strange noises: jackal, jackass, jackdaw; the scurrying noise of mouse and jerboa; the laugh of the loon, the lunatic bird. I have seen
  Grey necks twisting, rat tails twining, in the thick light of dawn. I have eaten
  Smooth creatures still living, with the strong salt taste of living things under sea; I have tasted
  The living lobster, the crab, the oyster, the whelk and the prawn; and they live and spawn in my bowels, and my bowels dissolve in the light of dawn. I have smelt
  Death in the rose, death in the hollyhock, sweet pea, hyacinth, primrose and cowslip. I have seen
  Trunk and horn, tusk and hoof, in odd places;
  I have lain on the floor of the sea and breathed with the breathing of the sea-anemone, swallowed with ingurgitation of the sponge. I have lain in the soil and criticised the worm. In the air
  Flirted with the passage of the kite, I have plunged with the kite and cowered with the wren. I have felt
  The horn of the beetle, the scale of the viper, the mobile hard insensitive skin of the elephant, the evasive flank of the fish. I have smelt
  Corruption in the dish, incense in the latrine, the sewer in the incense,

the smell of sweet soap in the woodpath, a hellish sweet scent in
the woodpath, while the ground heaved. I have seen
Rings of light coiling downwards, descending
To the horror of the ape. Have I not known, not known
What was coming to be? It was here, in the kitchen, in the passage,
In the mews in the barn in the byre in the market-place
In our veins our bowels our skulls as well
As well as in the plottings of potentates
As well as in the consultations of powers.
What is woven on the loom of fate
What is woven in the councils of princes
Is woven also in our veins, our brains,
Is woven like a pattern of living worms
In the guts of the women of Canterbury.

I have smelt them, the death-bringers; now is too late
For action, too soon for contrition.
Nothing is possible but the shamed swoon
Of those consenting to the last humiliation.
I have consented, Lord Archbishop, have consented.
Am torn away, subdued, violated,
United to the spiritual flesh of nature,
Mastered by the animal powers of spirit,
Dominated by the lust of self-demolition,
By the final utter uttermost death of spirit,
By the final ecstasy of waste and shame,
O Lord Archbishop, O Thomas Archbishop, forgive us, forgive us, pray
for us that we may pray for you, out of our shame.

(*Enter* THOMAS)

THOMAS Peace, and be at peace with your thoughts and visions.
These things had to come to you and you to accept them.
This is your share of the eternal burden,
The perpetual glory. This is one moment,
But know that another
Shall pierce you with a sudden painful joy
When the figure of God's purpose is made complete.
You shall forget these things, toiling in the household,
You shall remember them, droning by the fire,
When age and forgetfulness sweeten memory
Only like a dream that has often been told
And often been changed in the telling. They will seem unreal.
Human kind cannot bear very much reality.

(*Enter* PRIESTS)

PRIESTS (*Severally*) My Lord, you must not stop here. To the minster.
Through the cloister. No time to waste. They are coming back, armed.
To the altar, to the altar.
THOMAS All my life they have been coming, these feet. All my life
I have waited. Death will come only when I am worthy,
And if I am worthy, there is no danger.
I have therefore only to make perfect my will.
PRIESTS My Lord, they are coming. They will break through presently.
You will be killed. Come to the altar.
Make haste, my Lord. Don't stop here talking. It is not right.
What shall become of us, my Lord, if you are killed; what shall become
of us?
THOMAS Peace! be quiet! remember where you are, and what is happening;
No life here is sought for but mine,
And I am not in danger: only near to death.
PRIESTS My Lord, to vespers! You must not be absent from vespers.
You must not be absent from the divine office. To vespers. Into the
cathedral!
THOMAS Go to vespers, remember me at your prayers.
They shall find the shepherd here; the flock shall be spared.
I have had a tremour of bliss, a wink of heaven, a whisper,
And I would no longer be denied; all things
Proceed to a joyful consummation.
PRIESTS Seize him! force him! drag him!
THOMAS Keep your hands off!
PRIESTS To vespers! Hurry.

(*They drag him off. While the* CHORUS *speak, the scene is
changed to the cathedral*)

CHORUS (*While a* DIES IRÆ *is sung in Latin by a choir in the distance*)
Numb the hand and dry the eyelid,
Still the horror, but more horror
Than when tearing in the belly.

Still the horror, but more horror
Than when twisting in the fingers,
Than when splitting in the skull.

More than footfall in the passage,
More than shadow in the doorway,

More than fury in the hall.

The agents of hell disappear, the human, they shrink and dissolve
Into dust on the wind, forgotten, unmemorable; only is here
The white flat face of Death, God's silent servant,
And behind the face of Death the Judgement
And behind the Judgement the Void, more horrid than active shapes of hell;
Emptiness, absence, separation from God;
The horror of the effortless journey, to the empty land
Which is no land, only emptiness, absence, the Void,
Where those who were men can no longer turn the mind
To distraction, delusion, escape into dream, pretence,
Where the soul is no longer deceived, for there are no objects, no tones,
No colours, no forms to distract, to divert the soul
From seeing itself, foully united forever, nothing with nothing,
Not what we call death, but what beyond death is not death,
We fear, we fear. Who shall then plead for me,
Who intercede for me, in my most need?

Dead upon the tree, my Saviour,
Let not be in vain Thy labour;
Help me, Lord, in my last fear.

Dust I am, to dust am bending,
From the final doom impending
Help me, Lord, for death is near.

(*In the cathedral.* THOMAS *and* PRIESTS)

PRIESTS Bar the door. Bar the door.
 The door is barred.
 We are safe. We are safe.
 They dare not break in.
 They cannot break in. They have not the force.
 We are safe. We are safe.
THOMAS Unbar the doors! throw open the doors!
 I will not have the house of prayer, the church of Christ,
 The sanctuary, turned into a fortress.
 The Church shall protect her own, in her own way, not
 As oak and stone; stone and oak decay,
 Give no stay, but the Church shall endure.
 The church shall be open, even to our enemies. Open the door!

PRIEST My Lord! these are not men, these come not as men come, but
Like maddened beasts. They come not like men, who
Respect the sanctuary, who kneel to the Body of Christ,
But like beasts. You would bar the door
Against the lion, the leopard, the wolf or the boar,
Why not more
Against beasts with the souls of damned men, against men
Who would damn themselves to beasts. My Lord! My Lord!
THOMAS You think me reckless, desperate and mad.
You argue by results, as this world does,
To settle if an act be good or bad.
You defer to the fact. For every life and every act
Consequence of good and evil can be shown.
And as in time results of many deeds are blended
So good and evil in the end become confounded.
It is not in time that my death shall be known;
It is out of time that my decision is taken
If you call that decision
To which my whole being gives entire consent.
I give my life
To the Law of God above the Law of Man.
Unbar the door! unbar the door!
We are not here to triumph by fighting, by stratagem, or by resistance,
Not to fight with beasts as men. We have fought the beast
And have conquered. We have only to conquer
Now, by suffering. This is the easier victory.
Now is the triumph of the Cross, now
Open the door! I command it. OPEN THE DOOR!

(*The door is opened. The* KNIGHTS *enter, slightly tipsy*)

PRIESTS This way, my Lord! Quick. Up the stair. To the roof.
To the crypt. Quick. Come. Force him.
KNIGHTS Where is Becket, the traitor to the King?
Where is Becket, the meddling priest?
Come down Daniel to the lions' den,
Come down Daniel for the mark of the beast.

Are you washed in the blood of the Lamb?
Are you marked with the mark of the beast?
Come down Daniel to the lions' den,
Come down Daniel and join in the feast.

Where is Becket the Cheapside brat?
Where is Becket the faithless priest?
Come down Daniel to the lions' den,
Come down Daniel and join in the feast.

THOMAS It is the just man who
Like a bold lion, should be without fear.
I am here.
No traitor to the King. I am a priest,
A Christian, saved by the blood of Christ,
Ready to suffer with my blood.
This is the sign of the Church always,
The sign of blood. Blood for blood.
His blood given to buy my life,
My blood given to pay for His death,
My death for His death.

FIRST KNIGHT Absolve all those you have excommunicated.
SECOND KNIGHT Resign the powers you have arrogated.
THIRD KNIGHT Restore to the King the money you appropriated.
FIRST KNIGHT Renew the obedience you have violated.

THOMAS For my Lord I am now ready to die,
That His Church may have peace and liberty.
Do with me as you will, to your hurt and shame;
But none of my people, in God's name,
Whether layman or clerk, shall you touch.
This I forbid.

KNIGHTS Traitor! traitor! traitor!

THOMAS You, Reginald, three times traitor you:
Traitor to me as my temporal vassal,
Traitor to me as your spiritual lord,
Traitor to God in desecrating His Church.

FIRST KNIGHT No faith do I owe to a renegade,
And what I owe shall now be paid.

THOMAS Now to Almighty God, to the Blessed Mary ever Virgin, to the blessed John the Baptist, the holy apostles Peter and Paul, to the blessed martyr Denys, and to all the Saints, I commend my cause and that of the Church.

(*While the* KNIGHTS *kill him, we hear the* CHORUS)

CHORUS Clear the air! clean the sky! wash the wind! take stone from stone and wash them.
The land is foul, the water is foul, our beasts and ourselves defiled with blood.

A rain of blood has blinded my eyes. Where is England? Where is Kent? Where is Canterbury?
O far far far far in the past; and I wander in a land of barren boughs: if I break them, they bleed; I wander in a land of dry stones: if I touch them they bleed.
How how can I ever return, to the soft quiet seasons?
Night stay with us, stop sun, hold season, let the day not come, let the spring not come.
Can I look again at the day and its common things, and see them all smeared with blood, through a curtain of falling blood?
We did not wish anything to happen.
We understood the private catastrophe,
The personal loss, the general misery,
Living and partly living;
The terror by night that ends in daily action,
The terror by day that ends in sleep;
But the talk in the market-place, the hand on the broom,
The night-time heaping of the ashes,
The fuel laid on the fire at daybreak,
These acts marked a limit to our suffering.
Every horror had its definition,
Every sorrow had a kind of end:
In life there is not time to grieve long.
But this, this is out of life, this is out of time,
An instant eternity of evil and wrong.
We are soiled by a filth that we cannot clean, united to supernatural vermin,
It is not we alone, it is not the house, it is not the city that is defiled,
But the world that is wholly foul.
Clear the air! clean the sky! wash the wind! take the stone from the stone, take the skin from the arm, take the muscle from the bone, and wash them. Wash the stone, wash the bone, wash the brain, wash the soul, wash them wash them!

(*The* KNIGHTS, *having completed the murder, advance to the front of the stage and address the audience*)

FIRST KNIGHT   We beg you to give us your attention for a few moments. We know that you may be disposed to judge unfavourably of our action. You are Englishmen, and therefore you believe in fair play: and when you see one man being set upon by four, then your sympathies are all with the underdog. I respect such feelings, I share them. Nevertheless, I appeal to your sense of honour. You are English.

men, and therefore will not judge anybody without hearing both sides of the case. That is in accordance with our long-established principle of Trial by Jury. I am not myself qualified to put our case to you. I am a man of action and not of words. For that reason I shall do no more than introduce the other speakers, who, with their various abilities, and different points of view, will be able to lay before you the merits of this extremely complex problem. I shall call upon our eldest member to speak first, my neighbour in the country: Baron William de Traci.

THIRD KNIGHT   I am afraid I am not anything like such an experienced speaker as my old friend Reginald Fitz Urse would lead you to believe. But there is one thing I should like to say, and I might as well say it at once. It is this: in what we have done, and whatever you may think of it, we have been perfectly disinterested. (*The other* KNIGHTS: 'HEAR! HEAR!') *We* are not getting anything out of this. We have much more to lose than to gain. We are four plain Englishmen who put our country first. I dare say that we didn't make a very good impression when we came in just now. The fact is that we knew we had taken on a pretty stiff job; I'll only speak for myself, but I had drunk a good deal—I am not a drinking man ordinarily—to brace myself up for it. When you come to the point, it does go against the grain to kill an Archbishop, especially when you have been brought up in good Church traditions. So if we seemed a bit rowdy, you will understand why it was; and for my part I am awfully sorry about it. We realised this was our duty, but all the same we had to work ourselves up to it. And, as I said, *we* are not getting a penny out of this. We know perfectly well how things will turn out. King Henry—God bless him—will have to say, for reasons of state, that he never meant this to happen; and there is going to be an awful row; and at the best we shall have to spend the rest of our lives abroad. And even when reasonable people come to see that the Archbishop *had* to be put out of the way—and personally I had a tremendous admiration for him—you must have noticed what a good show he put up at the end—they won't give *us* any glory. No, we have done for ourselves, there's no mistake about that. So, as I said at the beginning, please give us at least the credit for being completely disinterested in this business. I think that is about all I have to say.

FIRST KNIGHT   I think we will all agree that William de Traci has spoken well and has made a very important point. The gist of his argument is this: that we have been completely disinterested. But our act itself needs more justification than that; and you must hear our other speakers. I shall next call upon Hugh de Morville, who has made a special study of statecraft and constitutional law. Sir Hugh de Morville.

SECOND KNIGHT   I should like first to recur to a point that was very well put by our leader, Reginald Fitz Urse: that you are Englishmen, and therefore your sympathies are always with the underdog. It is the English spirit of fair play. Now the worthy Archbishop, whose good qualities I very much admired, has throughout been presented as the underdog. But is this really the case? I am going to appeal not to your emotions but to your reason. You are hard-headed sensible people, as I can see, and not to be taken in by emotional clap-trap. I therefore ask you to consider soberly: what were the Archbishop's aims? And what are King Henry's aims? In the answer to these questions lies the key to the problem.

The King's aim has been perfectly consistent. During the reign of the late Queen Matilda and the irruption of the unhappy usurper Stephen, the kingdom was very much divided. Our King saw that the one thing needful was to restore order: to curb the excessive powers of local government, which were usually exercised for selfish and often for seditious ends, and to reform the legal system. He therefore intended that Becket, who had proved himself an extremely able administrator —no one denies that—should unite the offices of Chancellor and Archbishop. Had Becket concurred with the King's wishes, we should have had an almost ideal State: a union of spiritual and temporal administration, under the central government. I knew Becket well, in various official relations; and I may say that I have never known a man so well qualified for the highest rank of the Civil Service. And what happened? The moment that Becket, at the King's instance, had been made Archbishop, he resigned the office of Chancellor, he became more priestly than the priests, he ostentatiously and offensively adopted an ascetic manner of life, he affirmed immediately that there was a higher order than that which our King, and he as the King's servant, had for so many years striven to establish; and that—God knows why —the two orders were incompatible.

You will agree with me that such interference by an Archbishop offends the instincts of a people like ours. So far, I know that I have your approval: I read it in your faces. It is only with the measures we have had to adopt, in order to set matters to rights, that you take issue. No one regrets the necessity for violence more than we do. Unhappily, there are times when violence is the only way in which social justice can be secured. At another time, you would condemn an Archbishop by vote of Parliament and execute him formally as a traitor, and no one would have to bear the burden of being called murderer. And at a later time still, even such temperate measures as these would become unnecessary. But, if you have now arrived at a just subordination of the pretensions of the Church to the welfare of the State, remember that it is we who took the first step. We have been instrumental in bringing about the state of affairs that you approve. We have served your interests; we merit your applause; and if there is any guilt whatever in the matter, you must share it with us.

FIRST KNIGHT Morville has given us a great deal to think about. It seems to me that he has said almost the last word, for those who have been able to follow his very subtle reasoning. We have, however, one more speaker, who has I think another point of view to express. If there are any who are still unconvinced, I think that Richard Brito, coming as he does of a family distinguished for its loyalty to the Church, will be able to convince them. Richard Brito.

FOURTH KNIGHT The speakers who have preceded me, to say nothing of our leader, Reginald Fitz Urse, have all spoken very much to the point. I have nothing to add along their particular lines of argument. What I have to say may be put in the form of a question: *Who killed the Archbishop?* As you have been eye-witnesses of this lamentable scene, you may feel some surprise at my putting it in this way. But consider the course of events. I am obliged, very briefly, to go over the ground traversed by the last speaker. While the late Archbishop was Chancellor, no one, under the King, did more to weld the country together, to give it the unity, the stability, order, tranquillity, and justice that it so badly needed. From the moment he became Archbishop, he completely reversed his policy; he showed himself to be utterly indifferent to the fate of the country, to be, in fact, a monster of egotism. This egotism grew upon him, until it became at last an undoubted mania. I have unimpeachable evidence to the effect that before he left France he clearly prophesied, in the presence of numerous witnesses, that he had not long to live, and that he would be killed in England. He used every means of provocation; from his conduct, step by step, there can be no inference except that he had determined upon a death by martyrdom. Even at the last, he could have given us reason: you have seen how he evaded our questions. And when he had deliberately exasperated us beyond human endurance, he could still have easily escaped; he could have kept himself from us long enough to allow our righteous anger to cool. That was just what he did not wish to happen; he insisted, while we were still inflamed with wrath, that the doors should be opened. Need I say more? I think, with these facts before you, you will unhesitatingly render a verdict of Suicide while of Unsound Mind. It is the only charitable verdict you can give, upon one who was, after all, a great man.

FIRST KNIGHT Thank you, Brito, I think that there is no more to be said; and I suggest that you now disperse quietly to your homes. Please be careful not to loiter in groups at street corners, and do nothing that might provoke any public outbreak.

(*Exeunt* KNIGHTS)

FIRST PRIEST O father, father, gone from us, lost to us,
How shall we find you, from what far place
Do you look down on us? You now in Heaven,
Who shall now guide us, protect us, direct us?
After what journey through what further dread
Shall we recover your presence? When inherit
Your strength? The Church lies bereft,
Alone, desecrated, desolated, and the heathen shall build on the ruins,
Their world without God. I see it. I see it.
THIRD PRIEST No. For the Church is stronger for this action,
Triumphant in adversity. It is fortified
By persecution: supreme, so long as men will die for it.
Go, weak sad men, lost erring souls, homeless in earth or heaven.
Go where the sunset reddens the last grey rock
Of Brittany, or the Gates of Hercules.[3]
Go venture shipwreck on the sullen coasts
Where blackamoors make captive Christian men;
Go to the northern seas confined with ice
Where the dead breath makes numb the hand, makes dull the brain;
Find an oasis in the desert sun,
Go seek alliance with the heathen Saracen,
To share his filthy rites, and try to snatch
Forgetfulness in his libidinous courts,
Oblivion in the fountain by the date-tree;
Or sit and bite your nails in Aquitaine.
In the small circle of pain within the skull
You still shall tramp and tread one endless round
Of thought, to justify your action to yourselves,
Weaving a fiction which unravels as you weave,
Pacing forever in the hell of make-believe
Which never is belief: this is your fate on earth
And we must think no further of you.
FIRST PRIEST   O my lord
The glory of whose new state is hidden from us,
Pray for us of your charity.

[3] Gibraltar.

SECOND PRIEST   Now in the sight of God
    Conjoined with all the saints and martyrs gone before you,
    Remember us.
THIRD PRIEST   Let our thanks ascend
    To God, who has given us another Saint in Canterbury.
CHORUS (*While a* Te Deum *is sung in Latin by a choir in the distance*)
    We praise Thee, O God, for Thy glory displayed in all the creatures of the earth,
    In the snow, in the rain, in the wind, in the storm; in all of Thy creatures, both the hunters and the hunted.
    For all things exist only as seen by Thee, only as known by Thee, all things exist
    Only in Thy light, and Thy glory is declared even in that which denies Thee; the darkness declares the glory of light.
    Those who deny Thee could not deny, if Thou didst not exist; and their denial is never complete, for if it were so, they would not exist.
    They affirm Thee in living; all things affirm Thee in living; the bird in the air, both the hawk and the finch; the beast on the earth, both the wolf and the lamb; the worm in the soil and the worm in the belly.
    Therefore man, whom Thou hast made to be conscious of Thee, must consciously praise Thee, in thought and in word and in deed.
    Even with the hand to the broom, the back bent in laying the fire, the knee bent in cleaning the hearth, we, the scrubbers and sweepers of Canterbury,
    The back bent under toil, the knee bent under sin, the hands to the face under fear, the head bent under grief,
    Even in us the voices of seasons, the snuffle of winter, the song of spring, the drone of summer, the voices of beasts and of birds, praise Thee.
    We thank Thee for Thy mercies of blood, for Thy redemption by blood. For the blood of Thy martyrs and saints
    Shall enrich the earth, shall create the holy places.
    For wherever a saint has dwelt, wherever a martyr has given his blood for the blood of Christ,
    There is holy ground, and the sanctity shall not depart from it
    Though armies trample over it, though sightseers come with guide-books looking over it;
    From where the western seas gnaw at the coast of Iona,
    To the death in the desert, the prayer in forgotten places by the broken imperial column,
    From such ground springs that which forever renews the earth

Though it is forever denied. Therefore, O God, we thank Thee
Who hast given such blessing to Canterbury.

Forgive us, O Lord, we acknowledge ourselves as type of the common man,
Of the men and women who shut the door and sit by the fire;
Who fear the blessing of God, the loneliness of the night of God, the surrender required, the deprivation inflicted;
Who fear the injustice of men less than the justice of God;
Who fear the hand at the window, the fire in the thatch, the fist in the tavern, the push into the canal,
Less than we fear the love of God.
We acknowledge our trespass, our weakness, our fault; we acknowledge
That the sin of the world is upon our heads; that the blood of the martyrs and the agony of the saints
Is upon our heads.
Lord, have mercy upon us.
Christ, have mercy upon us.
Lord, have mercy upon us.
Blessed Thomas, pray for us.

CLIFFORD ODETS
[1906 — 1963]

❦ *The Man*

THOUGH BORN IN PHILADELPHIA, Clifford Odets early became familiar with the Bronx, New York, where his family settled when he was twelve. Interested in acting, he played roles in a neighborhood theater group, a church theater, and radio programs. In 1930 he became a charter member of the Group Theatre, as an actor.

While the country at large reeled from the economic blows of the Depression, the members of the Group Theatre dedicated themselves to building an ensemble, through studying the methods and philosophy of the Russian director, Stanislavsky. The name *Group* Theatre summarized the basic attitude: there were to be no stars, for the theatrical community was to function as a group. Among the Group's founders were people who were to dominate the New York theater for decades afterwards—Harold Clurman, Lee Strasberg, Cheryl Crawford, Stella Adler, John Garfield, Franchot Tone. Oriented toward such social playwrights as Sidney Kingsley, Maxwell Anderson, Paul Green, and Irwin Shaw, the Group helped develop Odets' social consciousness.

In 1935 the Group Theatre staged four Odets plays, but in spite of this and a certain celebrity as the darling of the Left, Odets was still earning very little when Hollywood began to lure him. The financial failure of his fourth play, *Paradise Lost*, caused him to accept a Hollywood contract so as to enable the play to continue its run. While in Hollywood, Odets retained his loyalty to the Group. For them he wrote *Golden Boy*, *Rocket to the Moon*, and *Night Music*. A 1938 revival of *Awake and*

Sing! resulted in the financial rewards that were lacking in 1935. But by 1940, neither the Group nor Odets himself had the money to produce his *Clash by Night*. When Billy Rose became the angel, Odets and the Group had no further connection, and the Group dissolved within a few months.

After *Clash by Night*, Odets wrote three plays, *The Big Knife* (1949), *The Country Girl* (1949), and *The Flowering Peach* (1954). Living mainly in Hollywood, he also wrote movies and had become interested in writing for television when he died of cancer.

❦ *The Work*

THE BULK OF ODETS' DRAMA was written during the 1930's, and he is sometimes viewed as the representative playwright of a socially conscious era. The shift in dramatic sensibility between the 1930's and 1950's has been tersely summarized as the shift from *Waiting for Lefty* (in which Lefty never comes because the union organizer has been shot) to *Waiting for Godot* (in which Godot never comes because waiting is the human condition).

In 1935, however, *Waiting for Godot* was still uncreated, and *Waiting for Lefty* was widely hailed as "barricade dramatics." The play is intellectually and emotionally simple, for the world of the play divides cleanly and allegorically into the evil representatives of Capitalism and the noble, oppressed Workers. In subsequent Odets plays, this agitprop tendency is subdued. Psychological insight modifies social analysis, and finally comes to replace it. For though Odets exploded on the Depression scene as a proletarian writer, he is the forerunner of Tennessee Williams as well as Arthur Miller. Like most bourgeois playwrights, Odets often builds his dramas around a family—the Bergers in *Awake and Sing!*, the Gordons in *Paradise Lost*, the Bonapartes in *Golden Boy*, the Wilenskis in *Clash by Night*, and the family of biblical Noah in *Flowering Peach*. Odets comes full circle in the corpus of his drama, from the biblical injunction of *Awake and Sing!* to the adaptation of biblical myth in *Flowering Peach*.

In an interesting critical article Arthur Miller, Odets' successor as a "family" playwright, makes this suggestion: "the language of the family is the language of the private life—prose. The language of society, the language of the public life, is verse." And Odets, though he thought and spoke of himself as a social playwright, wrote prose in Miller's sense. Like O'Casey before him, and Wesker after him, Odets could capture the vigorous, often bitter, rhythms of urban speech. That such rhythms—stemming from a native Yiddish—have been used with greater skill by novelists like Bellow, Roth, and Malamud should not deafen us to Odets' distinctive and pioneering contribution—in the form of dramatic dialogue.

❦ *The Play*

WHEN *Awake and Sing!* opened in 1935, it was respectfully but reservedly treated by both conservative and radical reviewers; Brooks Atkinson wrote in *The New York Times:* "Although [Odets] is very much awake, he does not sing with the ease and clarity of a man who has mastered his score. Although his dialogue has uncommon strength, his drama in the first two acts is wanting in the ordinary fluidity of a play. . . . To this student of the arts *Awake and Sing!* is inexplicably deficient in plain theatre emotion." The *Daily Worker* found it inferior to *Waiting for Lefty,* calling it "a comedown for the Group Theatre, an unimportant play whichever way you look at it." These reservations on both sides arise because the drama is not simplistic, and cannot be reduced to "plain theatre emotion," or propaganda.

In this realistic presentation of a Jewish middle-class family hit by the Depression, the Bible *and* Marx contribute to the idiom; there is compassion for youth *and* age, weakness *and* strength, tenderness *and* terror. The Berger household is portrayed as a miniature society; Uncle Morty is its capitalist and Jake its Marxist; Hennie is a white-collar worker and Ralph a factory worker; Myron has begun professional training and Moe exploits the rackets. But for all Odets' careful social planning, the human relationships achieve a more immediate impact. Ideologically, capitalist Uncle Morty should be the villain, but he is dramatically underplayed to his sister Bessie. By her strength and resolution, she is the villain in her conformity to materialistic standards. And yet, her villainy is selfless; she defends her family even at the cost of destroying its individual members.

Though the drama is centered on the Berger family, that family is constantly threatened by dissolution. The precarious situation of the family is emphasized by explicit comment from its members. Rich Uncle Morty thinks that "to raise a family nowadays you must be a damn fool." But ruthless Bessie counters, "a woman who don't raise a family—a girl—should jump overboard. What's she good for?" She scolds, "I raise a family they should have respect." And Jake, as a prelude to his abolition of the family through suicide, declares, "This is a house? Marx said it—abolish such families."

But in spite of Odets' Marxist beliefs, the abolition of the family insures no paradise, no panacea. Moe may dream of orange groves, Myron of winning the Irish Sweepstakes, and Ralph of mail planes, but Bessie smashes Jake's record of Caruso singing "O Paradiso." And it is Bessie who dominates family life; her commands and complaints reverberate through the claustrophobic Berger apartment.

Through the authenticity of his dialogue, Odets renders stock family types convincing—henpecked husband, unmarried and pregnant daughter, and selfless suicide. All characters speak crisply, even sensitive Ralph: "It's like a zoo in this house." When rich Uncle Morty paraphrases the old proverb about blood and water, family dissolution is imminent: "In the long run common sense is thicker than love." In the climate of common sense, love jumps off the roof. But despite the title of the play, can we be sure that Jacob's death will redeem his grandson? *Awake and Sing!* is a command rather than a *fait accompli*. Does Jacob's sacrifice result in Ralph's new birth, because the latter proclaims it? Though Ralph speaks of a new communion with his fellow workers, he deserts the orphan Blanche when she needs him most. Moe and Hennie will build their new life at the expense of an invalid and an infant. Jacob is a martyr who dies so that his grandson may lead a new life that is not printed on dollar bills, but his legacy is the dollar bills of an insurance policy. However, Ralph rejects this legacy, appropriately giving the dollars to Bessie, whose life they symbolize. As his own legacy, Ralph accepts Jacob's books: "His books, I got them too—the pages ain't cut in half of them." The uncut pages indicate Jacob's inability fully to explore and profit from his books, whereas Ralph's intention is to do just that. Jacob could only dream and listen to records, but because Ralph is able to reject his grandfather's materialistic legacy, he may yet wake up and sing.

❧ Dramatic Works

Waiting for Lefty, 1935.
Till the Day I Die, 1935.
Awake and Sing!, 1935.
Paradise Lost, 1935.
I Can't Sleep, 1936.
Golden Boy, 1937.
Rocket to the Moon, 1938.
Silent Partner, 1939.

Night Music, 1940.
Clash by Night, 1941.
The Russian People (from the Russian of Konstantin Simonov), 1942.
The Big Knife, 1949.
The Country Girl, 1949.
The Flowering Peach, 1954.

❧ Selective Bibliography

Clurman, Harold. *The Fervent Years.* New York: Knopf, 1945.
Downer, Alan S. *Fifty Years of American Drama, 1900–1950.* Chicago: Regnery, 1951.
Dusenbury, Winifred L. *The Theme of Loneliness in Modern American Drama.* Gainesville: University of Florida Press, 1960.
Lawson, John Howard. *Theory and Technique of Playwriting.* New York: Hill and Wang, 1960.
Rabkin, Gerald. *Drama and Commitment.* Bloomington: University of Indiana Press, 1964.
Shuman, R. Baird. *Clifford Odets.* New York: Twayne, 1962.
Warshow, Robert. "Clifford Odets: Poet of the Jewish Middle Class," *Essays in the Modern Drama,* ed. Morris Freedman (Boston: Heath, 1964).

Awake and Sing!

THE CHARACTERS OF THE PLAY

All of the characters in Awake and Sing! share a fundamental activity: a struggle for life amidst petty conditions.

BESSIE BERGER, as she herself states, is not only the mother in this home but also the father. She is constantly arranging and taking care of her family. She loves life, likes to laugh, has great resourcefulness and enjoys living from day to day. A high degree of energy accounts for her quick exasperation at ineptitude. She is a shrewd judge of realistic qualities in people in the sense of being able to gauge quickly their effectiveness. In her eyes all of the people in the house are equal. She is naïve and quick in emotional response. She is afraid of utter poverty. She is proper according to her own standards, which are fairly close to those of most middle-class families. She knows that when one lives in the jungle one must look out for the wild life.

MYRON, her husband, is a born follower. He would like to be a leader. He would like to make a million dollars. He is not sad or ever depressed. Life is an even sweet event to him, but the "old days" were sweeter yet. He has a dignified sense of himself. He likes people. He likes everything. But he is heartbroken without being aware of it.

HENNIE is a girl who has had few friends, male or female. She is proud of her body. She won't ask favors. She travels alone. She is fatalistic about being trapped, but will escape if possible. She is self-reliant in the best sense. Till the day she dies she will be faithful to a loved man. She inherits her mother's sense of humor and energy.

RALPH is a boy with a clean spirit. He wants to know, wants to learn. He is ardent, he is romantic, he is sensitive. He is naïve too. He is trying to find why so much dirt must be cleared away before it is possible to "get to first base."

JACOB, too, is trying to find a right path for himself and the others. He is aware of justice, of dignity. He is an observer of the others, compares their activities with his real and ideal sense of life. This produces a reflective nature. In this home he is a constant boarder. He is a sentimental idealist with no power to turn ideal to action.
With physical facts—such as housework—he putters. But as a barber he demonstrates the flair of an artist. He is an old Jew with living eyes in his tired face.

UNCLE MORTY is a successful American business man with five good senses. Something sinister comes out of the fact that the lives of others seldom touch him deeply. He holds to his own line of life. When he is generous he wants others to be aware of it. He is pleased by attention—a rich relative to the BERGER family. He is a shrewd judge of material values. He will die unmarried. Two and two make four, never five with him. He can blink in the sun for hours, a fat tomcat. Tickle him, he laughs. He lives in a penthouse with a real Japanese butler to serve him. He sleeps with dress models, but not from his own showrooms. He plays cards for hours on end. He smokes expensive cigars. He sees every Mickey Mouse cartoon that appears. He is a 32-degree Mason. He is really deeply intolerant finally.

MOE AXELROD lost a leg in the war. He seldom forgets that fact. He has killed two men in extramartial activity. He is mordant, bitter. Life has taught him a disbelief in everything, but he will fight his way through. He seldom shows his feelings: fights against his own sensitivity. He has been everywhere and seen everything. All he wants is HENNIE. He is very proud. He scorns the inability of others to make their way in life, but he likes people for whatever good qualities they possess. His passionate outbursts come from a strong but contained emotional mechanism.

SAM FEINSCHREIBER wants to find a home. He is a lonely man, a foreigner in a strange land, hypersensitive about this fact, conditioned by the humiliation of not making his way alone. He has a sense of others laughing at him. At night he gets up and sits alone in the dark. He hears acutely all the small sounds of life. He might have been a poet in another time and place. He approaches his wife as if he were always offering her a delicate flower. Life is a high chill wind weaving itself around his head.

SCHLOSSER, the janitor, is an overworked German whose wife ran away with another man and left him with a young daughter who in turn ran away and joined a burlesque show as chorus girl. The man suffers rheumatic pains. He has lost his identity twenty years before.

THE SCENE *Exposed on the stage are the dining room and adjoining front room of the* BERGER *apartment. These two rooms are typically furnished. There is a curtain between them. A small door off the front room leads to* JACOB'S *room. When his door is open one sees a picture of Sacco and Vanzetti on the wall and several shelves of books. Stage left of this door presents the entrance to the foyer hall of the apartment. The two other bedrooms of the apartment are off this hall, but not necessarily shown.*

Stage left of the dining room presents a swinging door which opens on the kitchen.

The entire action takes place in an apartment in the Bronx, New York City.

Awake and sing, ye that dwell in dust:
ISAIAH—26:19

Act One

TIME *The present (the middle 1930's); the family finishing supper.*

RALPH Where's advancement down the place? Work like crazy! Think they see it? You'd drop dead first.

MYRON Never mind, son, merit never goes unrewarded. Teddy Roosevelt used to say——

HENNIE It rewarded you—thirty years a haberdashery clerk! (JACOB *laughs*)

RALPH All I want's a chance to get to first base!

HENNIE That's all?

RALPH Stuck down in that joint on Fourth Avenue—a stock clerk in a silk house! Just look at Eddie. I'm as good as he is—pulling in two-fifty a week for forty-eight minutes a day. A headliner, his name in all the papers.

JACOB That's what you want, Ralphie? Your name in the paper?

RALPH I wanna make up my own mind about things . . . be something! Didn't I want to take up tap dancing, too?

BESSIE So take lessons. Who stopped you?

RALPH On what?

BESSIE On what? Save money.

RALPH Sure, five dollars a week for expenses and the rest in the house. I can't save even for shoe laces.
BESSIE You mean we shouldn't have food in the house, but you'll make a jig on the street corner?
RALPH I mean something.
BESSIE You also mean something when you studied on the drum, Mr. Smartie!
RALPH I don't know. . . . Every other day to sit around with the blues and mud in your mouth.
MYRON That's how it is—life is like that—a cake-walk.
RALPH What's it get you?
HENNIE A four-car funeral.
RALPH What's it for?
JACOB What's it for? If this life leads to a revolution it's a good life. Otherwise it's for nothing.
BESSIE Never mind, Pop! Pass me the salt.
RALPH It's crazy—all my life I want a pair of black and white shoes and can't get them. It's crazy!
BESSIE In a minute I'll get up from the table. I can't take a bite in my mouth no more.
MYRON (*Restraining her*) Now, Momma, just don't excite yourself——
BESSIE I'm so nervous I can't hold a knife in my hand.
MYRON Is that a way to talk, Ralphie? Don't Momma work hard enough all day? (BESSIE *allows herself to be reseated*)
BESSIE On my feet twenty-four hours?
MYRON On her feet——
RALPH (*Jumps up*) What do I do—go to night-clubs with Greta Garbo? Then when I come home can't even have my own room? Sleep on a day-bed in the front room! (*Choked, he exits to front room*)
BESSIE He's starting up that stuff again. (*Shouts to him*) When Hennie here marries you'll have her room—I should only live to see the day.
HENNIE Me, too. (*They settle down to serious eating*)
MYRON This morning the sink was full of ants. Where they come from I just don't know. I thought it was coffee grounds . . . and then they began moving.
BESSIE You gave the dog eat?
JACOB I gave the dog eat. (HENNIE *drops a knife and picks it up again*)
BESSIE You got dropsy tonight.
HENNIE Company's coming.
MYRON You can buy a ticket for fifty cents and win fortunes. A man came in the store—it's the Irish Sweepstakes.
BESSIE What?

MYRON   Like a raffle, only different. A man came in——
BESSIE   Who spends fifty-cent pieces for Irish raffles? They threw out a family on Dawson Street today. All the furniture on the sidewalk. A fine old woman with gray hair.
JACOB   Come eat, Ralph.
MYRON   A butcher on Beck Street won eighty thousand dollars.
BESSIE   Eighty thousand dollars! You'll excuse my expression, you're bughouse!
MYRON   I seen it in the paper—on one ticket—765 Beck Street.
BESSIE   Impossible!
MYRON   He did . . . yes he did. He says he'll take his old mother to Europe . . . an Austrian——
HENNIE   Europe . . .
MYRON   Six per cent on eighty thousand—forty-eight hundred a year.
BESSIE   I'll give you money. Buy a ticket in Hennie's name. Say, you can't tell—lightning never struck us yet. If they win on Beck Street we could win on Longwood Avenue.
JACOB   (*Ironically*)   If it rained pearls—who would work?
BESSIE   Another county heard from. (RALPH *enters and silently seats himself*)
MYRON   I forgot, Beauty—Sam Feinschreiber sent you a present. Since I brought him for supper he just can't stop talking about you.
HENNIE   What's that "mockie"[1] bothering about? Who needs him?
MYRON   He's a very lonely boy.
HENNIE   So I'll sit down and bust out crying " 'cause he's lonely."
BESSIE   (*Opening candy*)   He'd marry you one two three.
HENNIE   Too bad about him.
BESSIE   (*Naïvely delighted*)   Chocolate peanuts.
HENNIE   Loft's week-end special, two for thirty-nine.
BESSIE   You could think about it. It wouldn't hurt.
HENNIE   (*Laughing*)   To quote Moe Axelrod, "Don't make me laugh."
BESSIE   Never mind laughing. It's time you already had in your head a serious thought. A girl twenty-six don't grow younger. When I was your age it was already a big family with responsibilities.
HENNIE   (*Laughing*)   Maybe that's what ails you, Mom.
BESSIE   Don't you feel well?
HENNIE   'Cause I'm laughing? I feel fine. It's just funny—that poor guy sending me presents 'cause he loves me.
BESSIE   I think it's very, very nice.
HENNIE   Sure . . . swell!

---

[1] A derogatory term for a foreign-born Jew.

BESSIE   Mrs. Marcus' Rose is engaged to a Brooklyn boy, a dentist. He came in his car today. A little dope should get such a boy. (*Finished with the meal,* BESSIE, MYRON *and* JACOB *rise. Both* HENNIE *and* RALPH *sit silently at the table, he eating. Suddenly she rises*)
HENNIE   Tell you what, Mom. I saved for a new dress, but I'll take you and Pop to the Franklin. Don't need a dress. From now on I'm planning to stay in nights. Hold everything!
BESSIE   What's the matter—a bedbug bit you suddenly?
HENNIE   It's a good bill—Belle Baker. Maybe she'll sing "Eli, Eli."
BESSIE   We was going to a movie.
HENNIE   Forget it. Let's go.
MYRON   I see in the papers (*As he picks his teeth*) Sophie Tucker took off twenty-six pounds. Fearful business with Japan.
HENNIE   Write a book, Pop! Come on, we'll go early for good seats.
MYRON   Moe said you had a date with him for tonight.
BESSIE   Axelrod?
HENNIE   I told him no, but he don't believe it. I'll tell him no for the next hundred years, too.
MYRON   Don't break appointments, Beauty, and hurt people's feelings. (BESSIE *exits*)
HENNIE   His hands got free wheeling. (*She exits*)
MYRON   I don't know ... people ain't the same. N-O. The whole world's changing right under our eyes. Presto! No manners. Like the great Italian lover in the movies. What was the name? The Sheik. ... No one remembers? (*Exits shaking his head*)
RALPH   (*Unmoving at the table*)   Jake ...
JACOB   Noo?
RALPH   I can't stand it.
JACOB   There's an expression—"strong as iron you must be."
RALPH   It's a cock-eyed world.
JACOB   Boys like you could fix it some day. Look on the world, not on yourself so much. Every country with starving millions, no? In Germany and Poland a Jew couldn't walk in the street. Everybody hates, nobody loves.
RALPH   I don't get all that.
JACOB   For years, I watched you grow up. Wait! You'll graduate from my university. (*The others enter, dressed*)
MYRON   (*Lighting*)   Good cigars now for a nickel.
BESSIE   (*To* JACOB)   After take Tootsie on the roof. (*To* RALPH) What'll you do?
RALPH   Don't know.
BESSIE   You'll see the boys around the block?

RALPH I'll stay home every night!
MYRON Momma don't mean for you——
RALPH I'm flying to Hollywood by plane, that's what I'm doing.

(*Doorbell rings.* MYRON *answers it*)

BESSIE I don't like my boy to be seen with those tramps on the corner.
MYRON (*Without*) Schlosser's here, Momma, with the garbage can.
BESSIE Come in here, Schlosser. (*Sotto voce*) Wait, I'll give him a piece of my mind. (MYRON *ushers in* SCHLOSSER *who carries a garbage can in each hand*) What's the matter, the dumbwaiter's broken again?
SCHLOSSER Mr. Wimmer sends new ropes next week. I got a sore arm.
BESSIE He should live so long, your Mr. Wimmer. For seven years already he's sending new ropes. No dumbwaiter, no hot water, no steam—— In a respectable house, they don't allow such conditions.
SCHLOSSER In a decent house dogs are not running to make dirty the hallway.
BESSIE Tootsie's making dirty? Our Tootsie's making dirty in the hall?
SCHLOSSER (*To* JACOB) I tell you yesterday again. You must not leave her——
BESSIE (*Indignantly*) Excuse me! Please don't yell on an old man. He's got more brains in his finger than you got—I don't know where. Did you ever see—he should talk to you an old man?
MYRON Awful.
BESSIE From now on we don't walk up the stairs no more. You keep it so clean we'll fly in the windows.
SCHLOSSER I speak to Mr. Wimmer.
BESSIE Speak! Speak! Tootsie walks behind me like a lady any time, any place. So good-bye. . . . good-bye, Mr. Schlosser.
SCHLOSSER I tell you dot—I verk verry hard here. My arms is. . . . (*Exits in confusion*)
BESSIE Tootsie should lay all day in the kitchen maybe. Give him back if he yells on you. What's funny?
JACOB (*Laughing*) Nothing.
BESSIE Come. (*Exits*)
JACOB Hennie, take care. . . .
HENNIE Sure.
JACOB Bye-bye. (HENNIE *exits.* MYRON *pops head back in door*)
MYRON Valentino! That's the one! (*He exits*)
RALPH I never in my life even had a birthday party. Every time I went and cried in the toilet when my birthday came.
JACOB (*Seeing* RALPH *remove his tie*) You're going to bed?
RALPH No, I'm putting on a clean shirt.

JACOB Why?
RALPH I got a girl. . . . Don't laugh!
JACOB Who laughs? Since when?
RALPH Three weeks. She lives in Yorkville with an aunt and uncle. A bunch of relatives, but no parents.
JACOB An orphan girl—tch, tch.
RALPH But she's got me! Boy, I'm telling you I could sing! Jake, she's like stars. She's so beautiful you look at her and cry! She's like French words! We went to the park the other night. Heard the last band concert.
JACOB Music. . . .
RALPH (*Stuffing shirt in trousers*) It got cold and I gave her my coat to wear. We just walked along like that, see, without a word, see. I never was so happy in all my life. It got late . . . we just sat there. She looked at me—you know what I mean, how a girl looks at you—right in the eyes? "I love you," she says, "Ralph." I took her home. . . . I wanted to cry. That's how I felt!
JACOB It's a beautiful feeling.
RALPH You said a mouthful!
JACOB Her name is——
RALPH Blanche.
JACOB A fine name. Bring her sometimes here.
RALPH She's scared to meet Mom.
JACOB Why?
RALPH You know Mom's not letting my sixteen bucks out of the house if she can help it. She'd take one look at Blanche and insult her in a minute—a kid who's got nothing.
JACOB Boychick!
RALPH What's the diff?
JACOB It's no difference—a plain bourgeois prejudice—but when they find out a poor girl—it ain't so kosher.
RALPH They don't have to know I've got a girl.
JACOB What's in the end?
RALPH Out I go! I don't mean maybe!
JACOB And then what?
RALPH Life begins.
JACOB What life?
RALPH Life with my girl. Boy, I could sing when I think about it! Her and me together—that's a new life!
JACOB Don't make a mistake! A new death!
RALPH What's the idea?
JACOB Me, I'm the idea! Once I had in *my* heart a dream, a vision, but

came marriage and then you forget. Children come and you forget because——
RALPH   Don't worry, Jake.
JACOB   Remember, a woman insults a man's soul like no other thing in the whole world!
RALPH   Why get so excited? No one——
JACOB   Boychick, wake up! Be something! Make your life something good. For the love of an old man who sees in your young days his new life, for such love take the world in your two hands and make it like new. Go out and fight so life shouldn't be printed on dollar bills. A woman waits.
RALPH   Say, I'm no fool!
JACOB   From my heart I hope not. In the meantime—— (*Bell rings*)
RALPH   See who it is, will you? (*Stands off*) Don't want Mom to catch me with a clean shirt.
JACOB   (*Calls*) Come in. (*Sotto voce*) Moe Axelrod. (MOE *enters*)
MOE   Hello, girls, how's your whiskers? (*To* RALPH) All dolled up. What's it, the weekly visit to the cat house?
RALPH   Please mind your business.
MOE   Okay, sweetheart.
RALPH   (*Taking a hidden dollar from a book*)   If Mom asks where I went——
JACOB   I know. Enjoy yourself.
RALPH   Bye-bye. (*He exits*)
JACOB   Bye-bye.
MOE   Who's home?
JACOB   Me.
MOE   Good. I'll stick around a few minutes. Where's Hennie?
JACOB   She went with Bessie and Myron to a show.
MOE   She what?!
JACOB   You had a date?
MOE   (*Hiding his feelings*)   Here—I brought you some halavah.
JACOB   Halavah? Thanks. I'll eat a piece after.
MOE   So Ralph's got a dame? Hot stuff—a kid can't even play a card game.
JACOB   Moe, you're a no-good, a bum of the first water. To your dying day you won't change.
MOE   Where'd you get that stuff, a no-good?
JACOB   But I like you.
MOE   Didn't I go fight in France for democracy? Didn't I get my goddam leg shot off in that war the day before the armistice? Uncle Sam give me the Order of the Purple Heart, didn't he? What'd you mean, a no-good?
JACOB   Excuse me.

MOE If you got an orange I'll eat an orange.
JACOB No orange. An apple.
MOE No oranges, huh?—what a dump!
JACOB Bessie hears you once talking like this she'll knock your head off.
MOE Hennie went with, huh? She wantsa see me squirm, only I don't squirm for dames.
JACOB You came to see her?
MOE What for? I got a present for our boy friend, Myron. He'll drop dead when I tell him his gentle horse galloped in fifteen to one. He'll die.
JACOB It really won? The first time I remember.
MOE Where'd they go?
JACOB A vaudeville by the Franklin.
MOE What's special tonight?
JACOB Someone tells a few jokes . . . and they forget the street is filled with starving beggars.
MOE What'll they do—start a war?
JACOB I don't know.
MOE You oughta know. What the hell you got all the books for?
JACOB It needs a new world.
MOE That's why they had the big war—to make a new world, they said—safe for democracy. Sure every big general laying up in a Paris hotel with a half dozen broads pinned on his mustache. Democracy! I learned a lesson.
JACOB An imperial war. You know what this means?
MOE Sure, I know everything!
JACOB By money men the interests must be protected. Who gave you such a rotten haircut? Please (*Fishing in his vest pocket*) give me for a a cent a cigarette. I didn't have since yesterday——
MOE (*Giving one*) Don't make me laugh. (*A cent passes back and forth between them,* MOE *finally throwing it over his shoulder*) Don't look so tired all the time. You're a wow—always sore about something.
JACOB And you?
MOE You got one thing—you can play pinochle. I'll take you over in a game. Then you'll have something to be sore on.
JACOB Who'll wash dishes? (MOE *takes deck from buffet drawer*)
MOE Do 'em after. Ten cents a deal.
JACOB Who's got ten cents?
MOE I got ten cents. I'll lend it to you.
JACOB Commence.
MOE (*Shaking cards*) The first time I had my hands on a pack in two days. Lemme shake up these cards. I'll make 'em talk. (JACOB *goes to his room where he puts on a Caruso record*)

JACOB You should live so long.
MOE Ever see oranges grow? I know a certain place—— One summer I laid under a tree and let them fall right in my mouth.
JACOB (*Off, the music is playing; the card game begins*) From "L'Africana" . . . a big explorer comes on a new land—"O Paradiso." From act four this piece. Caruso stands on the ship and looks on a Utopia. You hear? "Oh paradise! Oh paradise on earth! Oh blue sky, oh fragrant air——"
MOE Ask him does he see any oranges? (BESSIE, MYRON *and* HENNIE *enter*)
JACOB You came back so soon?
BESSIE Hennie got sick on the way.
MYRON Hello, Moe. . . . (MOE *puts cards back in pocket*)
BESSIE Take off the phonograph, Pop. (*To* HENNIE) Lay down . . . I'll call the doctor. You should see how she got sick on Prospect Avenue. Two weeks already she don't feel right.
MYRON Moe . . . ?
BESSIE Go to bed, Hennie.
HENNIE I'll sit here.
BESSIE Such a girl I never saw! Now you'll be stubborn?
MYRON It's for your own good, Beauty. Influenza——
HENNIE I'll sit here.
BESSIE You ever seen a girl should say no to everything. She can't stand on her feet, so——
HENNIE Don't yell in my ears. I hear. Nothing's wrong. I ate tuna fish for lunch.
MYRON Canned goods. . . .
BESSIE Last week you also ate tuna fish?
HENNIE Yeah, I'm funny for tuna fish. Go to the show—have a good time.
BESSIE I don't understand what I did to God He blessed me with such children. From the whole world——
MOE (*Coming to aid of* HENNIE) For Chris' sake don't kibitz[2] so much!
BESSIE You don't like it?
MOE (*Aping*) No, I don't like it.
BESSIE That's too bad, Axelrod. Maybe it's better by your cigar-store friends. Here we're different people.
MOE Don't gimme that cigar store line, Bessie. I walked up five flights—
BESSIE To take out Hennie. But my daughter ain't in your class, Axelrod.

---

[2] Meddle (Yiddish).

MOE   To see Myron.
MYRON   Did he, did he, Moe?
MOE   Did he what?
MYRON   "Sky Rocket"?
BESSIE   You bet on a horse!
MOE   Paid twelve and a half to one.
MYRON   There! You hear that, Momma? Our horse came in. You see, it happens, and twelve and a half to one. Just look at that!
MOE   What the hell, a sure thing. I told you.
BESSIE   If Moe said a sure thing, you couldn't bet a few dollars instead of fifty cents?
JACOB   (*Laughs*)   Aie, aie, aie.
MOE   (*At his wallet*)   I'm carrying six hundred "plunks" in big denominations.
BESSIE   A banker!
MOE   Uncle Sam sends me ninety a month.
BESSIE   So you save it?
MOE   Run it up. Run-it-up-Axelrod, that's me.
BESSIE   The police should know how.
MOE   (*Shutting her up*)   All right, all right—— Change twenty, sweetheart.
MYRON   Can you make change?
BESSIE   Don't be crazy.
MOE   I'll meet a guy in Goldman's restaurant. I'll meet 'im and come back with change.
MYRON   (*Figuring on paper*)   You can give it to me tomorrow in the store.
BESSIE   (*Acquisitive*)   He'll come back, he'll come back!
MOE   Lucky I bet some bucks myself. (*In derision to* HENNIE) Let's step out tomorrow night, Par-a-dise. (*Thumbs his nose at her, laughs mordantly and exits*)
MYRON   Oh, that's big percentage. If I picked a winner every day. . . .
BESSIE   Poppa, did you take Tootsie on the roof?
JACOB   All right.
MYRON   Just look at that—a cake walk. We can make——
BESSIE   It's enough talk. I got a splitting headache. Hennie, go in bed. I'll call Dr. Cantor.
HENNIE   I'll sit here . . . and don't call that old Ignatz 'cause I won't see him.
MYRON   If you get sick Momma can't nurse you. You don't want to go to a hospital.
JACOB   She don't look sick, Bessie, it's a fact.

BESSIE She's got fever. I see in her eyes, so he tells me no. Myron, call Dr. Cantor. (MYRON *picks up phone, but* HENNIE *grabs it from him*)
HENNIE I don't want any doctor. I ain't sick. Leave me alone.
MYRON Beauty, it's for your own sake.
HENNIE Day in and day out pestering. Why are you always right and no one else can say a word?
BESSIE When you have your own children——
HENNIE I'm not sick! Hear what I say? I'm not sick! Nothing's the matter with me! I don't want a doctor. (BESSIE *is watching her with slow progressive understanding*)
BESSIE What's the matter?
HENNIE Nothing, I told you!
BESSIE You told me, but—— (*A long pause of examination follows*)
HENNIE See much?
BESSIE Myron, put down the . . . the . . . (*He slowly puts the phone down*) Tell me what happened. . . .
HENNIE Brooklyn Bridge fell down.
BESSIE (*Approaching*) I'm asking a question. . . .
MYRON What's happened, Momma?
BESSIE Listen to me!
HENNIE What the hell are you talking?
BESSIE Poppa—take Tootsie on the roof.
HENNIE (*Holding* JACOB *back*) If he wants he can stay here.
MYRON What's wrong, Momma?
BESSIE (*Her voice quivering slightly*) Myron, your fine Beauty's in trouble. Our society lady. . . .
MYRON Trouble? I don't under—is it——?
BESSIE Look in her face. (*He looks, understands and slowly sits in a chair, utterly crushed*) Who's the man?
HENNIE The Prince of Wales.
BESSIE My gall is busting in me. In two seconds——
HENNIE (*In a violent outburst*) Shut up! Shut up! I'll jump out the window in a minute! Shut up! (*Finally she gains control of herself, says in a low, hard voice*) You don't know him.
JACOB Bessie. . . .
BESSIE He's a Bronx boy?
HENNIE From out of town.
BESSIE What do you mean?
HENNIE From out of town!!
BESSIE A long time you know him? You were sleeping by a girl from the office Saturday nights? You slept good, my lovely lady. You'll go to him . . . he'll marry you.

HENNIE   That's what you say.
BESSIE   That's what I say! He'll do it, take *my* word he'll do it!
HENNIE   Where? (*To* JACOB) Give her the letter. (JACOB *does so*)
BESSIE   What? (*Reads*) "Dear sir: In reply to your request of the 14th inst., we can state that no Mr. Ben Grossman has ever been connected with our organization . . ." You don't know where he is?
HENNIE   No.
BESSIE   (*Walks back and forth*) Stop crying like a baby, Myron.
MYRON   It's like a play on the stage. . . .
BESSIE   To a mother you couldn't say something before. I'm old-fashioned—like your friends I'm not smart—I don't eat chop suey and run around Coney Island with tramps. (*She walks reflectively to buffet, picks up a box of candy, puts it down, says to* MYRON) Tomorrow night bring Sam Feinschreiber for supper.
HENNIE   I won't do it.
BESSIE   You'll do it, my fine beauty, you'll do it!
HENNIE   I'm not marrying a poor foreigner like him. Can't even speak an English word. Not me! I'll go to my grave without a husband.
BESSIE   You don't say! We'll find for you somewhere a millionaire with a pleasure boat. He's going to night school, Sam. For a boy only three years in the country he speaks very nice. In three years he put enough in the bank, a good living.
JACOB   This is serious?
BESSIE   What then? I'm talking for my health? He'll come tomorrow night for supper. By Saturday they're engaged.
JACOB   Such a thing you can't do.
BESSIE   Who asked your advice?
JACOB   Such a thing——
BESSIE   Never mind!
JACOB   The lowest from the low!
BESSIE   Don't talk! I'm warning you! A man who don't believe in God—with crazy ideas——
JACOB   So bad I never imagined you could be.
BESSIE   Maybe if you didn't talk so much it wouldn't happen like this. You with your ideas—I'm a mother. I raise a family they should have respect.
JACOB   Respect? (*Spits*) Respect! For the neighbors' opinion! You insult me, Bessie!
BESSIE   Go in your room, Poppa. Every job he ever had he lost because he's got a big mouth. He opens his mouth and the whole Bronx could fall in. Everybody said it——
MYRON   Momma, they'll hear you down the dumbwaiter.

BESSIE   A good barber not to hold a job a week. Maybe you never heard charity starts at home. You never heard it, Pop?
JACOB   All you know, I heard, and more yet. But Ralph you don't make like you. Before you do it, I'll die first. He'll find a girl. He'll go in a fresh world with her. This is a house? Marx said it—abolish such families.
BESSIE   Go in your room, Poppa.
JACOB   Ralph you don't make like you!
BESSIE   Go lay in your room with Caruso and the books together.
JACOB   All right!
BESSIE   Go in the room!
JACOB   Some day I'll come out, I'll—— (*Unable to continue, he turns, looks at* HENNIE, *goes to his door and there says with an attempt at humor*) Bessie, some day you'll talk to me so fresh . . . I'll leave the house for good! (*He exits*)
BESSIE   (*Crying*)   You ever in your life seen it? He should dare! He should just dare say in the house another word. Your gall could bust from such a man. (*Bell rings,* MYRON *goes*) Go to sleep now. It won't hurt.
HENNIE   Yeah? (MOE *enters, a box in his hand.* MYRON *follows and sits down*)
MOE   (*Looks around first—putting box on table*)   Cake. (*About to give* MYRON *the money, he turns instead to* BESSIE) Six fifty, four bits change . . . come on, hand over half a buck. (*She does so. Of* MYRON) Who bit him?
BESSIE   We're soon losing our Hennie, Moe.
MOE   Why? What's the matter?
BESSIE   She made her engagement.
MOE   Zat so?
BESSIE   Today it happened . . . he asked her.
MOE   Did he? Who? Who's the corpse?
BESSIE   It's a secret.
MOE   In the bag, huh?
HENNIE   Yeah. . . .
BESSIE   When a mother gives away an only daughter it's no joke. Wait, when you'll get married you'll know. . . .
MOE   (*Bitterly*)   Don't make me laugh—when I get married! What I thinka women? Take 'em all, cut 'em in little pieces like a herring in Greek salad. A guy in France had the right idea—dropped his wife in a bathtub fulla acid. (*Whistles*) Sss, down the pipe! Pfft—not even a corset button left!
MYRON   Corsets don't have buttons.
MOE   (*To* HENNIE)   What's the great idea? Gone big time, Paradise?

Christ, it's suicide! Sure, kids you'll have, gold teeth, get fat, big in the tangerines——
HENNIE   Shut your face!
MOE   Who's it—some dope pullin' down twenty bucks a week? Cut your throat, sweetheart. Save time.
BESSIE   Never mind your two cents, Axelrod.
MOE   I say what I think—that's me!
HENNIE   That's you—a lousy fourflusher who'd steal the glasses off a blind man.
MOE   Get hot!
HENNIE   My God, do I need it—to listen to this mutt shoot his mouth off?
MYRON   Please. . . .
MOE   Now wait a minute, sweetheart, wait a minute. I don't have to take that from you.
BESSIE   Don't yell at her!
HENNIE   For two cents I'd spit in your eye.
MOE   (*Throwing coin to table*)   Here's two bits. (HENNIE *looks at him and then starts across the room*)
BESSIE   Where are you going?
HENNIE   (*Crying*)   For my beauty nap, Mussolini. Wake me up when it's apple blossom time in Normandy. (*Exits*)
MOE   Pretty, pretty—a sweet gal, your Hennie. See the look in her eyes?
BESSIE   She don't feel well. . . .
MYRON   Canned goods. . . .
BESSIE   So don't start with her.
MOE   Like a battleship she's got it. Not like other dames—shove 'em and they lay. Not her. I got a yen for her and I don't mean a Chinee coin.
BESSIE   Listen, Axelrod, in my house you don't talk this way. Either have respect or get out.
MOE   When I think about it . . . maybe I'd marry her myself.
BESSIE   (*Suddenly aware of* MOE)   You could—— What do you mean, Moe?
MOE   You ain't sunburnt—you heard me.
BESSIE   Why don't you, Moe? An old friend of the family like you. It would be a blessing on all of us.
MOE   You said she's engaged.
BESSIE   But maybe she don't know her own mind. Say, it's——
MOE   I need a wife like a hole in the head. . . . What's to know about women, I know. Even if I asked her. She won't do it! A guy with one leg—it gives her the heebie-jeebies. I know what she's looking for. An arrow-collar guy, a hero, but with a wad of jack. Only the two don't

go together. But I got what it takes . . . plenty, and more where it comes from. (*Breaks off, snorts and rubs his knee. A pause. In his room* JACOB *puts on Caruso singing the lament from "The Pearl Fishers."*)

BESSIE　It's right—she wants a millionaire with a mansion on Riverside Drive. So go fight City Hall. Cake?

MOE　Cake.

BESSIE　I'll make tea. But one thing—she's got a fine boy with a business brain. Caruso! (*Exits into the front room and stands in the dark, at the window*)

MOE　No wet smack . . . a fine girl. . . . She'll burn that guy out in a month. (MOE *retrieves the quarter and spins it on the table*)

MYRON　I remember that song . . . beautiful. Nora Bayes sang it at the old Proctor's Twenty-third Street—"When It's Apple Blossom Time in Normandy."

MOE　She wantsa see me crawl—my head on a plate she wants! A snowball in hell's got a better chance. (*Out of sheer fury he spins the quarter in his fingers*)

MYRON　(*As his eyes slowly fill with tears*)　Beautiful . . .

MOE　Match you for a quarter. Match you for any goddam thing you got. (*Spins the coin viciously*) What the hell kind of house is this it ain't got an orange!!

Slow Curtain

Act Two / SCENE ONE

One year later, a Sunday afternoon. The front room. JACOB *is giving his son* MORDECAI (UNCLE MORTY) *a haircut, newspapers spread around the base of the chair,* MOE *is reading a newspaper, leg propped on a chair.* RALPH, *in another chair, is spasmodically reading a paper.* UNCLE MORTY *reads colored jokes. Silence, then* BESSIE *enters.*

BESSIE　Dinner's in half an hour, Morty.

MORTY　(*Still reading jokes*)　I got time.

BESSIE　A duck. Don't get hair on the rug, Pop. (*Goes to window and pulls down shade*) What's the matter the shade's up to the ceiling?

JACOB (*Pulling it up again*) Since when do I give a haircut in the dark? (*He mimics her tone*)
BESSIE When you're finished, pull it down. I like my house to look respectable. Ralphie, bring up two bottles seltzer from Weiss.
RALPH I'm reading the paper.
BESSIE Uncle Morty likes a little seltzer.
RALPH I'm expecting a phone call.
BESSIE Noo, if it comes you'll be back. What's the matter? (*Gives him money from apron pocket*) Take down the old bottles.
RALPH (*To* JACOB) Get that call if it comes. Say I'll be right back. (JACOB *nods assent*)
MORTY (*Giving change from vest*) Get grandpa some cigarettes.
RALPH Okay. (*Exits*)
JACOB What's new in the paper, Moe?
MOE Still jumping off the high buildings like flies—the big shots who lost all their coconuts. Pfft!
JACOB Suicides?
MOE Plenty can't take it—good in the break, but can't take the whip in the stretch.
MORTY (*Without looking up*) I saw it happen Monday in my building. My hair stood up how they shoveled him together—like a pancake—a bankrupt manufacturer.
MOE No brains.
MORTY Enough . . . all over the sidewalk.
JACOB If someone said five-ten years ago I couldn't make for myself a living, I wouldn't believe——
MORTY Duck for dinner?
BESSIE The best Long Island duck.
MORTY I like goose.
BESSIE A duck is just like a goose, only better.
MORTY I like a goose.
BESSIE The next time you'll be for Sunday dinner I'll make a goose.
MORTY (*Sniffs deeply*) Smells good. I'm a great boy for smells.
BESSIE Ain't you ashamed? Once in a blue moon he should come to an only sister's house.
MORTY Bessie, leave me live.
BESSIE You should be ashamed!
MORTY Quack quack!
BESSIE No, better to lay around Mecca Temple playing cards with the Masons.
MORTY (*With good nature*) Bessie, don't you see Pop's giving me a haircut?

BESSIE   You don't need no haircut. Look, two hairs he took off.
MORTY   Pop likes to give me a haircut. If I said no he don't forget for a year, do you, Pop? An old man's like that.
JACOB   I still do an A-1 job.
MORTY   (*Winking*)   Pop cuts hair to fit the face, don't you, Pop?
JACOB   For sure, Morty. To each face a different haircut. Custom built, no ready made. A round face needs special——
BESSIE   (*Cutting him short*)   A graduate from the B.M.T.[3] (*Going*) Don't forget the shade. (*The phone rings. She beats* JACOB *to it*) Hello? Who is it, please? . . . Who is it, please? . . . Miss Hirsch? No, he ain't here. . . . No, I couldn't say when. (*Hangs up sharply*)
JACOB   For Ralph?
BESSIE   A wrong number. (JACOB *looks at her and goes back to his job*)
JACOB   Excuse me!
BESSIE   (*To* MORTY)   Ralphie took another cut down the place yesterday.
MORTY   Business is bad. I saw his boss Harry Glicksman Thursday. I bought some velvets . . . they're coming in again.
BESSIE   Do something for Ralphie down there.
MORTY   What can I do? I mentioned it to Glicksman. He told me they squeezed out half the people. . . . (MYRON *enters dressed in apron*)
BESSIE   What's gonna be the end? Myron's working only three days a week now.
MYRON   It's conditions.
BESSIE   Hennie's married with a baby . . . money just don't come in. I never saw conditions should be so bad.
MORTY   Times'll change.
MOE   The only thing'll change is my underwear.
MORTY   These last few years I got my share of gray hairs. (*Still reading jokes without having looked up once*) Ha, ha, ha—Popeye the sailor ate spinach and knocked out four bums.
MYRON   I'll tell you the way I see it. The country needs a great man now—a regular Teddy Roosevelt.
MOE   What this country needs is a good five-cent earthquake.
JACOB   So long labor lives it should increase private gain——
BESSIE   (*To* JACOB)   Listen, Poppa, go talk on the street corner. The government'll give you free board the rest of your life.
MORTY   I'm surprised. Don't I send a five-dollar check for Pop every week?
BESSIE   You could afford a couple more and not miss it.
MORTY   Tell me jokes. Business is so rotten I could just as soon lay all day in the Turkish bath.

---

[3] Brooklyn Manhattan Transit, a New York subway system.

MYRON Why'd I come in here? (*Puzzled, he exits*)
MORTY (*To* MOE) I hear the bootleggers still do business, Moe.
MOE Wake up! I kissed bootlegging bye-bye two years back.
MORTY For a fact? What kind of racket is it now?
MOE If I told you, you'd know something. (HENNIE *comes from bedroom*)
HENNIE Where's Sam?
BESSIE Sam? In the kitchen.
HENNIE (*Calls*) Sam. Come take the diaper.
MORTY How's the Mickey Louse? Ha, ha, ha. . . .
HENNIE Sleeping.
MORTY Ah, that's life to a baby. He sleeps—gets it in the mouth—sleeps some more. To raise a family nowadays you must be a damn fool.
BESSIE Never mind, never mind, a woman who don't raise a family—a girl—should jump overboard. What's she good for? (*To* MOE—*to change the subject*) Your leg bothers you bad?
MOE It's okay, sweetheart.
BESSIE (*To* MORTY) It hurts him every time it's cold out. He's got four legs in the closet.
MORTY Four wooden legs?
MOE Three.
MORTY What's the big idea?
MOE Why not? Uncle Sam gives them out free.
MORTY Say, maybe if Uncle Sam gave out less legs we could balance the budget.
JACOB Or not have a war so they wouldn't have to give out legs.
MORTY Shame on you, Pop. Everybody knows war is necessary.
MOE Don't make me laugh. Ask me—the first time you pick up a dead one in the trench—then you learn war ain't so damn necessary.
MORTY Say, you should kick. The rest of your life Uncle Sam pays you ninety a month. Look, not a worry in the world.
MOE Don't make me laugh. Uncle Sam can take his *seventy* bucks and—— (*Finishes with a gesture*) Nothing good hurts. (*He rubs his stump*)
HENNIE Use a crutch, Axelrod. Give the stump a rest.
MOE Mind your business, Feinschreiber.
BESSIE It's a sensible idea.
MOE Who asked you?
BESSIE Look, he's ashamed.
MOE So's your Aunt Fanny.
BESSIE (*Naïvely*) Who's got an Aunt Fanny? (*She cleans a rubber plant's leaves with her apron*)
MORTY It's a joke!

MOE   I don't want my paper creased before I read it. I want it fresh. Fifty times I said that.
BESSIE   Don't get so excited for a five-cent paper—our star boarder.
MOE   And I don't want no one using my razor either. Get it straight. I'm not buying ten blades a week for the Berger family. (*Furious, he limps out*)
BESSIE   Maybe I'm using his razor too.
HENNIE   Proud!
BESSIE   You need luck with plants. I didn't clean off the leaves in a month.
MORTY   You keep the house like a pin and I like your cooking. Any time Myron fires you, come to me, Bessie. I'll let the butler go and you'll be my housekeeper. I don't like Japs so much—sneaky.
BESSIE   Say, you can't tell. Maybe any day I'm coming to stay. (HENNIE *exits*)
JACOB   Finished.
MORTY   How much, Ed. Pinaud? (*Disengages self from chair*)
JACOB   Five cents.
MORTY   Still five cents for a haircut to fit the face?
JACOB   Prices don't change by me. (*Takes a dollar*) I can't change——
MORTY   Keep it. Buy yourself a Packard.[4] Ha, ha, ha.
JACOB   (*Taking large envelope from pocket*) Please, you'll keep this for me. Put it away.
MORTY   What is it?
JACOB   My insurance policy. I don't like it should lay around where something could happen.
MORTY   What could happen?
JACOB   Who knows, robbers, fire . . . they took next door. Fifty dollars from O'Reilly.
MORTY   Say, lucky a Berger didn't lose it.
JACOB   Put it downtown in the safe. Bessie don't have to know.
MORTY   It's made out to Bessie?
JACOB   No, to Ralph.
MORTY   To Ralph?
JACOB   He don't know. Some day he'll get three thousand.
MORTY   You got good years ahead.
JACOB   Behind. (RALPH *enters*)
RALPH   Cigarettes. Did a call come?
JACOB   A few minutes. She don't let me answer it.
RALPH   Did Mom say I was coming back?

[4] Expensive automobile.

JACOB No. (MORTY *is back at new jokes*)
RALPH She starting that stuff again? (BESSIE *enters*) A call come for me?
BESSIE (*Waters pot from milk bottle*) A wrong number.
JACOB Don't say a lie, Bessie.
RALPH Blanche said she'd call me at two—was it her?
BESSIE I said a wrong number.
RALPH Please, Mom, if it was her tell me.
BESSIE You call me a liar next. You got no shame—to start a scene in front of Uncle Morty. Once in a blue moon he comes——
RALPH What's the shame? If my girl calls I wanna know it.
BESSIE You made enough mish mosh with her until now.
MORTY I'm surprised, Bessie. For the love of Mike tell him yes or no.
BESSIE I didn't tell him? No!
MORTY (*To* RALPH) No! (RALPH *goes to a window and looks out*)
BESSIE Morty, I didn't say before—he runs around steady with a girl.
MORTY Terrible. Should he run around with a foxie-woxie?
BESSIE A girl with no parents.
MORTY An orphan?
BESSIE I could die from shame. A year already he runs around with her. He brought her once for supper. Believe me, she didn't come again, no!
RALPH Don't think I didn't ask her.
BESSIE You hear? You raise them and what's in the end for all your trouble?
JACOB When you'll lay in a grave, no more trouble. (*Exits*)
MORTY Quack quack!
BESSIE A girl like that he wants to marry. A skinny consumptive-looking . . . six months already she's not working—taking charity from an aunt. You should see her. In a year she's dead on his hands.
RALPH You'd cut her throat if you could.
BESSIE That's right! Before she'd ruin a nice boy's life I would first go to prison. Miss Nobody should step in the picture and I'll stand by with my mouth shut.
RALPH Miss Nobody! Who am I? Al Jolson?[5]
BESSIE Fix your tie!
RALPH I'll take care of my own life.
BESSIE You'll take care? Excuse my expression, you can't even wipe your nose yet! He'll take care!
MORTY (*To* BESSIE) I'm surprised. Don't worry so much, Bessie. When it's time to settle down he won't marry a poor girl, will you?

[5] Popular singer and movie star.

In the long run common sense is thicker than love. I'm a great boy for live and let live.

BESSIE   Sure, it's easy to say. In the meantime he eats out my heart. You know I'm not strong.

MORTY   I know . . . a pussy cat . . . ha, ha, ha.

BESSIE   You got money and money talks. But without the dollar who sleeps at night?

RALPH   I been working for years, bringing in money here—putting it in your hand like a kid. All right, I can't get my teeth fixed. All right, that a new suit's like trying to buy the Chrysler Building. You never in your life bought me a pair of skates even—things I died for when I was a kid. I don't care about that stuff, see. Only just remember I pay some of the bills around here, just a few . . . and if my girl calls me on the phone I'll talk to her any time I please. (*He exits.* HENNIE *applauds*)

BESSIE   Don't be so smart, Miss America! (*To* MORTY) He didn't have skates! But when he got sick, a twelve-year-old boy, who called a big specialist for the last $25 in the house? Skates!

JACOB   (*Just in. Adjusts window shade*)   It looks like snow today.

MORTY   It's about time—winter.

BESSIE   Poppa here could talk like Samuel Webster, too, but it's just talk. He should try to buy a two-cent pickle in the Burland Market without money.

MORTY   I'm getting an appetite.

BESSIE   Right away we'll eat. I made chopped liver for you.

MORTY   My specialty!

BESSIE   Ralph should only be a success like you, Morty. I should only live to see the day when he rides up to the door in a big car with a chauffeur and a radio. I could die happy, believe me.

MORTY   Success she says. She should see how we spend thousands of dollars making up a winter line and winter don't come—summer in January. Can you beat it?

JACOB   Don't live, just make success.

MORTY   Chopped liver—ha!

JACOB   Ha! (*Exits*)

MORTY   When they start arguing, I don't hear. Suddenly I'm deaf. I'm a great boy for the practical side. (*He looks over to* HENNIE *who sits rubbing her hands with lotion*)

HENNIE   Hands like a raw potato.

MORTY   What's the matter? You don't look so well . . . no pep.

HENNIE   I'm swell.

MORTY   You used to be such a pretty girl.

HENNIE   Maybe I got the blues. You can't tell.

247 · *Awake and Sing!* [ACT TWO, *Scene One*]

MORTY   You could stand a new dress.
HENNIE That's not all I could stand.
MORTY   Come down to the place tomorrow and pick out a couple from the "eleven-eighty" line. Only don't sing me the blues.
HENNIE Thanks. I need some new clothes.
MORTY   I got two thousand pieces of merchandise waiting in the stock room for winter.
HENNIE I never had anything from life. Sam don't help.
MORTY   He's crazy about the kid.
HENNIE Crazy is right. Twenty-one a week he brings in—a nigger don't have it so hard. I wore my fingers off on an Underwood for six years. For what? Now I wash baby diapers. Sure, I'm crazy about the kid too. But half the night the kid's up. Try to sleep. You don't know how it is, Uncle Morty.
MORTY   No, I don't know. I was born yesterday. Ha, ha, ha. Some day I'll leave you a little nest egg. You like eggs? Ha?
HENNIE When? When I'm dead and buried?
MORTY   No, when *I'm* dead and buried. Ha, ha, ha.
HENNIE You should know what I'm thinking.
MORTY   Ha, ha, ha, I know (MYRON *enters*)
MYRON   I never take a drink. I'm just surprised at myself, I——
MORTY   I got a pain. Maybe I'm hungry.
MYRON   Come inside, Morty. Bessie's got some schnapps.
MORTY   I'll take a drink. Yesterday I missed the Turkish bath.
MYRON   I get so bitter when I take a drink, it just surprises me.
MORTY   Look how fat. Say, you live once. . . . Quack, quack. (*Both exit.* MOE *stands silently in the doorway*)
SAM   (*Entering*) I'll make Leon's bottle now!
HENNIE No, let him sleep, Sam. Take away the diaper. (*He does. Exits*)
MOE   (*Advancing into the room*) That your husband?
HENNIE Don't you know?
MOE   Maybe he's a nurse you hired for the kid—it looks it—how he tends it. A guy comes howling to your old lady every time you look cock-eyed. Does he sleep with you?
HENNIE Don't be so wise!
MOE   (*Indicating newspaper*) Here's a dame strangled her hubby with wire. Claimed she didn't like him. Why don't you brain Sam with an ax some night?
HENNIE Why don't you lay an egg, Axelrod?
MOE   I laid a few in my day, Feinschreiber. Hard-boiled ones too.
HENNIE Yeah?
MOE   Yeah. You wanna know what I see when I look in your eyes?

HENNIE   No.
MOE   Ted Lewis playing the clarinet—some of those high crazy notes! Christ, you coulda had a guy with some guts instead of a cluck stands around boilin' baby nipples.
HENNIE   Meaning you?
MOE   Meaning me, sweetheart.
HENNIE   Think you're pretty good.
MOE   You'd know if I slept with you again.
HENNIE   I'll smack your face in a minute.
MOE   You do and I'll break your arm. (*Holds up paper*) Take a look. (*Reads*) "Ten-day luxury cruise to Havana." That's the stuff you coulda had. Put up at ritzy hotels, frenchie soap, champagne. Now you're tied down to "Snake-Eye" here. What for? What's it get you? . . . a 2 x 4 flat on 108th Street . . . a pain in the bustle it gets you.
HENNIE   What's it to you?
MOE   I know you from the old days. How you like to spend it! What I mean! Lizard-skin shoes, perfume behind the ears. . . . You're in a mess, Paradise! Paradise—that's a hot one—yah, crazy to eat a knish at your own wedding.
HENNIE   I get it—you're jealous. You can't get me.
MOE   Don't make me laugh.
HENNIE   Kid Jailbird's been trying to make me for years. You'd give your other leg. I'm hooked? Maybe, but you're in the same boat. Only it's worse for you. I don't give a damn no more, but you gotta yen makes you——
MOE   Don't make me laugh.
HENNIE   Compared to you I'm sittin' on top of the world.
MOE   You're losing your looks. A dame don't stay young forever.
HENNIE   You're a liar. I'm only twenty-four.
MOE   When you comin' home to stay?
HENNIE   Wouldn't you like to know?
MOE   I'll get you again.
HENNIE   Think so?
MOE   Sure, whatever goes up comes down. You're easy—you remember —two for a nickel—a pushover! (*Suddenly she slaps him. They both seem stunned*) What's the idea?
HENNIE   Go on . . . break my arm.
MOE   (*As if saying "I love you"*)   Listen, lousy.
HENNIE   Go on, do something!
MOE   Listen——
HENNIE   You're so damn tough!
MOE   You like me. (*He takes her*)

HENNIE Take your hand off! (*Pushes him away*) Come around when it's a flood again and they put you in the ark with the animals. Not even then—if you was the last man!
MOE Baby, if you had a dog I'd love the dog.
HENNIE Gorilla! (*Exits.* RALPH *enters*)
RALPH Were you here before?
MOE (*Sits*) What?
RALPH When the call came for me?
MOE What?
RALPH The call came. (JACOB *enters*)
MOE (*Rubbing his leg*) No.
JACOB Don't worry, Ralphie, she'll call back.
RALPH Maybe not. I think somethin's the matter.
JACOB What?
RALPH I don't know. I took her home from the movie last night. She asked me what I'd think if she went away.
JACOB Don't worry, she'll call again.
RALPH Maybe not, if Mom insulted her. She gets it on both ends, the poor kid. Lived in an orphan asylum most of her life. They shove her around like an empty freight train.
JACOB After dinner go see her.
RALPH Twice they kicked me down the stairs.
JACOB Life should have some dignity.
RALPH Every time I go near the place I get heart failure. The uncle drives a bus. You oughta see him—like Babe Ruth.
MOE Use your brains. Stop acting like a kid who still wets the bed. Hire a room somewhere—a club room for two members.
RALPH Not that kind of proposition, Moe.
MOE Don't be a bush leaguer all your life.
RALPH Cut it out!
MOE (*On a sudden upsurge of emotion*) Ever sleep with one? Look at 'im blush.
RALPH You don't know her.
MOE I seen her—the kind no one sees undressed till the undertaker works on her.
RALPH Why give me the needles all the time? What'd I ever do to you?
MOE Not a thing. You're a nice kid. But grow up! In life there's two kinds—the men that's sure of themselves and the ones who ain't! It's time you quit being a selling-plater[6] and got in the first class.

---

[6] An inferior horse.

JACOB And you, Axelrod?
MOE (*To* JACOB) Scratch your whiskers! (*To* RALPH) Get independent. Get what-it-takes and be yourself. Do what you like.
RALPH Got a suggestion? (MORTY *enters, eating*)
MOE Sure, pick out a racket. Shake down the coconuts. See what that does.
MORTY We know what it does—puts a pudding on your nose! Sing Sing![7] Easy money's against the law. Against the law don't win. A racket is illegitimate, no?
MOE It's all a racket—from horse racing down. Marriage, politics, big business—everybody plays cops and robbers. You, you're a racketeer yourself.
MORTY Who? Me? Personally I manufacture dresses.
MOE Horse feathers!
MORTY (*Seriously*) Don't make such remarks to me without proof. I'm a great one for proof. That's why I made a success in business. Proof—put up or shut up, like a game of cards. I heard this remark before—a rich man's a crook who steals from the poor. Personally, I don't like it. It's a big lie!
MOE If you don't like it, buy yourself a fife and drum—and go fight your own war.
MORTY Sweatshop talk. Every Jew and Wop in the shop eats my bread and behind my back says, "a sonofabitch." I started from a poor boy who worked on an ice wagon for two dollars a week. Pop's right here—he'll tell you. I made it honest. In the whole industry nobody's got a better name.
JACOB It's an exception, such success.
MORTY Ralph can't do the same thing?
JACOB No, Morty, I don't think. In a house like this he don't realize even the possibilities of life. Economics comes down like a ton of coal on the head.
MOE Red rover, red rover, let Jacob come over!
JACOB In my day the propaganda was for God. Now it's for success. A boy don't turn around without having shoved in him he should make success.
MORTY Pop, you're a comedian, a regular Charlie Chaplin.
JACOB He dreams all night of fortunes. Why not? Don't it say in the movies he should have a personal steamship, pajamas for fifty dollars a pair and a toilet like a monument? But in the morning he wakes up and for ten dollars he can't fix the teeth. And millions more worse

[7] New York State Penitentiary.

off in the mills of the South—starvation wages. The blood from the worker's heart. (MORTY *laughs loud and long*) Laugh, laugh . . . tomorrow not.
MORTY   A real, a real Boob McNutt[8] you're getting to be.
JACOB   Laugh, my son. . . .
MORTY   Here is the North, Pop.
JACOB   North, south, it's one country.
MORTY   The country's all right. A duck quacks in every pot!
JACOB   You never heard how they shoot down men and women which ask a better wage? Kentucky 1932?
MORTY   That's a pile of chopped liver, Pop. (BESSIE *and others enter*)
JACOB   Pittsburgh, Passaic, Illinois—slavery—it begins where success begins in a competitive system. (MORTY *howls with delight*)
MORTY   Oh, Pop, what are you bothering? Why? Tell me why? Ha, ha, ha. I bought you a phonograph . . . stick to Caruso.
BESSIE   He's starting up again.
MORTY   Don't bother with Kentucky. It's full of moonshiners.
JACOB   Sure, sure——
MORTY   You don't know practical affairs. Stay home and cut hair to fit the face.
JACOB   It says in the Bible how the Red Sea opened and the Egyptians went in and the sea rolled over them. (*Quotes two lines of Hebrew*) In this boy's life a Red Sea will happen again. I see it!
MORTY   I'm getting sore, Pop, with all this sweatshop talk.
BESSIE   He don't stop a minute. The whole day, like a phonograph.
MORTY   I'm surprised. Without a rich man you don't have a roof over your head. You don't know it?
MYRON   Now you can't bite the hand that feeds you.
RALPH   Let him alone—he's right!
BESSIE   Another county heard from.
RALPH   It's the truth. It's——
MORTY   Keep quiet, snotnose!
JACOB   Be sure, charity, a bone for an old dog. But in Russia an old man don't take charity so his eyes turn black in his head. In Russia they got Marx.
MORTY   (*Scoffingly*)   Who's Marx?
MOE   An outfielder for the Yanks. (MORTY *howls with delight*)
MORTY   Ha, ha, ha, it's better than the jokes. I'm telling you. This is Uncle Sam's country. Put it in your pipe and smoke it.
BESSIE   Russia, he says! Read the papers.

[8] A comic-strip character.

SAM Here is opportunity.
MYRON People can't believe in God in Russia. The papers tell the truth, they do.
JACOB So you believe in God . . . you got something for it? You! You worked for all the capitalists. You harvested the fruit from your labor? You got God! But the past comforts you? The present smiles on you, yes? It promises you the future something? Did you found a piece of earth where you could live like a human being and die with the sun on your face? Tell me, yes, tell me. I would like to know myself. But on these questions, on this theme—the struggle for existence—you can't make an answer. The answer I see in your face . . . the answer is your mouth can't talk. In this dark corner you sit and you die. But abolish private property!
BESSIE *(Settling the issue)* Noo, go fight City Hall!
MORTY He's drunk!
JACOB I'm studying from books a whole lifetime.
MORTY That's what it is—he's drunk. What the hell does all that mean?
JACOB If you don't know, why should I tell you?
MORTY *(Triumphant at last)* You see? Hear him? Like all those nuts, don't know what they're saying.
JACOB I know, I know.
MORTY Like Boob McNutt you know! Don't go in the park, Pop—the squirrels'll get you. Ha, ha, ha.
BESSIE Save your appetite, Morty. *(To MYRON)* Don't drop the duck.
MYRON We're ready to eat, Momma.
MORTY *(To JACOB)* Shame on you. It's your second childhood.

(Now they file out. MYRON first with the duck, the others behind him)

BESSIE Come eat. We had enough for one day. *(Exits)*
MORTY Ha, ha, ha. Quack, quack. *(Exits)*

(JACOB sits there trembling and deeply humiliated. MOE approaches him and thumbs the old man's nose in the direction of the dining room)

MOE Give 'em five. *(Takes his hand away)* They got you pasted on the wall like a picture, Jake. *(He limps out to seat himself at the table in the next room)*
JACOB Go eat, boychick. *(RALPH comes to him)* He gives me eat, so I'll climb in a needle. One time I saw an old horse in summer . . . he wore a straw hat . . . the ears stuck out on top. An old horse for hire. Give me back my young days . . give me fresh blood . . . arms . . .

give me—— (*The telephone rings. Quickly* RALPH *goes to it.* JACOB *pulls the curtains and stands there, a sentry on guard*)
RALPH Hello? . . . Yeah, I went to the store and came right back, right after you called. (*Looks at* JACOB)
JACOB Speak, speak. Don't be afraid they'll hear.
RALPH I'm sorry if Mom said something. You know how excitable Mom is . . . Sure! What? . . . Sure, I'm listening. . . . Put on the radio, Jake. (JACOB *does so. Music comes in and up, a tango, grating with an insistent nostalgic pulse. Under the cover of the music* RALPH *speaks more freely*) Yes . . . yes . . . What's the matter? Why're you crying? What happened? (*To* JACOB) She's putting her uncle on. Yes? . . . Listen, Mr. Hirsch, what're you trying to do? What's the big idea? Honest to God. I'm in no mood for joking! Lemme talk to her! Gimme Blanche! (*Waits*) Blanche? What's this? Is this a joke? Is that true? I'm coming right down! I know, but—— You wanna do that? . . . I know, but—— I'm coming down . . . tonight! Nine o'clock . . . sure . . . sure . . . sure. . . . (*Hangs up*)
JACOB What happened?
MORTY (*Enters*) Listen, Pop. I'm surprised you didn't—— (*He howls, shakes his head in mock despair, exits*)
JACOB Boychick, what?
RALPH I don't get it straight. (*To* JACOB) She's leaving. . . .
JACOB Where?
RALPH Out West—— To Cleveland.
JACOB Cleveland?
RALPH . . . In a week or two. Can you picture it? It's a put-up job. But they can't get away with that.
JACOB We'll find something.
RALPH Sure, the angels of heaven'll come down on her uncle's cab and whisper in his ear.
JACOB Come eat. . . . We'll find something.
RALPH I'm meeting her tonight, but I know—— (BESSIE *throws open the curtain between the two rooms and enters*)
BESSIE Maybe we'll serve for you a special blue plate supper in the garden?
JACOB All right, all right. (BESSIE *goes over to the window, levels the shade and on her way out, clicks off the radio*)
MORTY (*Within*) Leave the music, Bessie. (*She clicks it on again, looks at them, exits*)
RALPH I know . . .
JACOB Don't cry, boychick. (*Goes over to* RALPH) Why should you make like this? Tell me why you should cry, just tell me. . . . (JACOB

takes RALPH *in his arms and both, trying to keep back the tears, trying fearfully not to be heard by the others in the dining room, begin crying*) You mustn't cry. . . . (*The tango twists on. Inside the clatter of dishes and the clash of cutlery sound.* MORTY *begins to howl with laughter*)

Curtain

Act Two / SCENE TWO

That night. The dark dining room.

At rise: JACOB *is heard in his lighted room, reading from a sheet, declaiming aloud as if to an audience.*

JACOB They are there to remind us of the horrors—under those crosses lie hundreds of thousands of workers and farmers who murdered each other in uniform for the greater glory of capitalism. (*Comes out of his room.*) The new imperialist war will send millions to their death, will bring prosperity to the pocket of the capitalist—aie, Morty—and will bring only greater hunger and misery to the masses of workers and farmers. The memories of the last world slaughter are still vivid in our minds. (*Hearing a noise he quickly retreats to his room.* RALPH *comes in from the street. He sits with hat and coat on.* JACOB *tentatively opens door and asks*) Ralphie?

RALPH It's getting pretty cold out.

JACOB (*Enters room fully, cleaning hair clippers*) We should have steam till twelve instead of ten. Go complain to the Board of Health.

RALPH It might snow.

JACOB It don't hurt . . . extra work for men.

RALPH When I was a kid I laid awake at nights and heard the sounds of trains . . . far-away lonesome sounds . . . boats going up and down the river. I used to think of all kinds of things I wanted to do. What was it, Jake? Just a bunch of noise in my head?

JACOB (*Waiting for news of the girl*) You wanted to make for yourself a certain kind of world.

RALPH I guess I didn't. I'm feeling pretty, pretty low.

255 · *Awake and Sing!* [ACT TWO, Scene Two]

JACOB You're a young boy and for you life is all in front like a big mountain. You got feet to climb.
RALPH I don't know how.
JACOB So you'll find out. Never a young man had such opportunity like today. He could make history.
RALPH Ten P.M. and all is well. Where's everybody?
JACOB They went.
RALPH Uncle Morty too?
JACOB Hennie and Sam he drove down.
RALPH I saw her.
JACOB (*Alert and eager*) Yes, yes, tell me.
RALPH I waited in Mount Morris Park till she came out. So cold I did a buck'n wing[9] to keep warm. She's scared to death.
JACOB They made her?
RALPH Sure. She wants to go. They keep yelling at her—they want her to marry a millionaire, too.
JACOB You told her you love her?
RALPH Sure. "Marry me," I said. "Marry me tomorrow." On sixteen bucks a week. On top of that I had to admit Mom'd have Uncle Morty get me fired in a second. . . . Two can starve as cheap as one!
JACOB So what happened?
RALPH I made her promise to meet me tomorrow.
JACOB Now she'll go in the West?
RALPH I'd fight the whole goddam world with her, but not her. No guts. The hell with her. If she wantsa go—all right—I'll get along.
JACOB For sure, there's more important things than girls. . . .
RALPH You said a mouthful . . . and maybe I don't see it. She'll see what I can do. No one stops me when I get going. . . . (*Near to tears, he has to stop.* JACOB *examines his clippers very closely*)
JACOB Electric clippers never do a job like by hand.
RALPH Why won't Mom let us live here?
JACOB Why? Why? Because in a society like this today people don't love. Hate!
RALPH Gee, I'm no bum who hangs around pool parlors. I got the stuff to go ahead. I don't know what to do.
JACOB Look on me and learn what to do, boychick. Here sits an old man polishing tools. You think maybe I'll use them again! Look on this failure and see for seventy years he talked, with good ideas, but only in the head. It's enough for me now I should see your happiness. This is why I tell you—DO! Do what is in your heart and you carry in

[9] Tap-dance step.

yourself a revolution. But you should act. Not like me. A man who had golden opportunities but drank instead a glass tea. No. . . . (*A pause of silence*)

RALPH (*Listening*) Hear it? The Boston air mail plane. Ten minutes late. I get a kick the way it cuts across the Bronx every night. (*The bell rings:* SAM, *excited, disheveled, enters*)

JACOB You came back so soon?

SAM Where's Mom?

JACOB Mom? Look on the chandelier.

SAM Nobody's home?

JACOB Sit down. Right away they're coming. You went in the street without a tie?

SAM Maybe it's a crime.

JACOB Excuse me.

RALPH You had a fight with Hennie again?

SAM She'll fight once . . . some day. . . . (*Lapses into silence*)

JACOB In my day the daughter came home. Now comes the son-in-law.

SAM Once too often she'll fight with me, Hennie. I mean it. I mean it like anything. I'm a person with a bad heart. I sit quiet, but inside I got a——

RALPH What happened?

SAM I'll talk to Mom. I'll see Mom.

JACOB Take an apple.

SAM Please . . . he tells me apples.

RALPH Why hop around like a billiard ball?

SAM Even in a joke she should dare say it.

JACOB My grandchild said something?

SAM To my father in the old country they did a joke . . . I'll tell you: One day in Odessa he talked to another Jew on the street. They didn't like it, they jumped on him like a wild wolf.

RALPH Who?

SAM Cossacks. They cut off his beard. A Jew without a beard! He came home—I remember like yesterday how he came home and went in bed for two days. He put like this the cover on his face. No one should see. The third morning he died.

RALPH From what?

SAM From a broken heart. . . . Some people are like this. Me too. I could die like this from shame.

JACOB Hennie told you something?

SAM Straight out she said it—like a lightning from the sky. The baby ain't mine. She said it.

RALPH Don't be a dope.

JACOB For sure, a joke.
RALPH She's kidding you.
SAM She should kid a policeman, not Sam Feinschreiber. Please . . . you don't know her like me. I wake up in the nighttime and she sits watching me like I don't know what. I make a nice living from the store. But it's no use—she looks for a star in the sky. I'm afraid like anything. You could go crazy from less even. What I shall do I'll ask Mom.
JACOB "Go home and sleep," she'll say. "It's a bad dream."
SAM It don't satisfy me more, such remarks, when Hennie could kill in the bed. (JACOB *laughs*) Don't laugh. I'm so nervous—look, two times I weighed myself on the subway station. (*Throws small cards to table*)
JACOB (*Examining one*) One hundred and thirty-eight—also a fortune. (*Turns it and reads*) "You are inclined to deep thinking, and have a high admiration for intellectual excellence and inclined to be very exclusive in the selection of friends." Correct! I think maybe you got mixed up in the wrong family, Sam. (MYRON *and* BESSIE *now enter*)
BESSIE Look, a guest! What's the matter? Something wrong with the baby? (*Waits*)
SAM No.
BESSIE Noo?
SAM (*In a burst*) I wash my hands from everything.
BESSIE Take off your coat and hat. Have a seat. Excitement don't help. Myron, make tea. You'll have a glass tea. We'll talk like civilized people. (MYRON *goes*) What is it, Ralph, you're all dressed up for a party? (*He looks at her silently and exits. To* SAM) We saw a very good movie, with Wallace Beery. He acts like life, very good.
MYRON (*Within*) Polly Moran too.
BESSIE Polly Moran too—a woman with a nose from here to Hunts Point, but a fine player. Poppa, take away the tools and the books.
JACOB All right. (*Exits to his room*)
BESSIE Noo, Sam, why do you look like a funeral?
SAM I can't stand it. . . .
BESSIE Wait. (*Yells*) You took up Tootsie on the roof.
JACOB (*Within*) In a minute.
BESSIE What can't you stand?
SAM She said I'm a second fiddle in my own house.
BESSIE Who?
SAM Hennie. In the second place, it ain't my baby, she said.
BESSIE What? What are you talking? (MYRON *enters with dishes*)
SAM From her own mouth. It went like a knife in my heart.
BESSIE Sam, what're you saying?

SAM Please, I'm making a story? I fell in the chair like a dead.
BESSIE Such a story you believe?
SAM I don't know.
BESSIE How you don't know?
SAM She told me even the man.
BESSIE Impossible!
SAM I can't believe myself. But she said it. I'm a second fiddle, she said. She made such a yell everybody heard for ten miles.
BESSIE Such a thing Hennie should say—impossible!
SAM What should I do? With my bad heart such a remark kills.
MYRON Hennie don't feel well, Sam. You see, she——
BESSIE What then?—a sick girl. Believe me, a mother knows. Nerves. Our Hennie's got a bad temper. You'll let her she says anything. She takes after me—nervous. (*To* MYRON) You ever heard such a remark in all your life? She should make such a statement! Bughouse.
MYRON The little one's been sick all these months. Hennie needs a rest. No doubt.
BESSIE Sam don't think she means it——
MYRON Oh, I know he don't, of course——
BESSIE I'll say the truth, Sam. We didn't half the time understand her ourselves. A girl with her own mind. When she makes it up, wild horses wouldn't change her.
SAM She don't love me.
BESSIE This is sensible, Sam?
SAM Not for a nickel.
BESSIE What do you think? She married you for your money? For your looks? You ain't no John Barrymore, Sam. No, she liked you.
SAM Please, not for a nickel. (JACOB *stands in the doorway*)
BESSIE We stood right here the first time she said it. "Sam Feinschreiber's a nice boy," she said it, "a boy he's got good common sense, with a business head." Right here she said it, in this room. You sent her two boxes of candy together, you remember?
MYRON Loft's candy.
BESSIE This is when she said it. What do you think?
MYRON You were just the only boy she cared for.
BESSIE So she married you. Such a world . . . plenty of boy friends she had, believe me!
JACOB A popular girl. . . .
MYRON Y-e-s.
BESSIE I'll say it plain out—Moe Axelrod offered her plenty—a servant, a house . . . she don't have to pick up a hand.
MYRON Oh, Moe? Just wild about her. . . .

SAM   Moe Axelrod? He wanted to——
BESSIE   But she didn't care. A girl like Hennie you don't buy. I should never live to see another day if I'm telling a lie.
SAM   She was kidding me.
BESSIE   What then? You shouldn't be foolish.
SAM   The baby looks like my family. He's got Feinschreiber eyes.
BESSIE   A blind man could see it.
JACOB   Sure . . . sure. . . .
SAM   The baby looks like me. Yes. . . .
BESSIE   You could believe me.
JACOB   Any day. . . .
SAM   But she tells me the man. She made up his name too?
BESSIE   Sam, Sam, look in the phone book—a million names.
MYRON   Tom, Dick and Harry. (JACOB *laughs quietly, soberly*)
BESSIE   Don't stand around, Poppa. Take Tootsie on the roof. And you don't let her go under the water tank.
JACOB   Schmah Yisroeal.[10] Behold! (*Quietly laughing he goes back into his room, closing the door behind him*)
SAM   I won't stand he should make insults. A man eats out his——
BESSIE   No, no, he's an old man—a second childhood. Myron, bring in the tea. Open a jar of raspberry jelly. (MYRON *exits*)
SAM   Mom, you think——?
BESSIE   I'll talk to Hennie. It's all right.
SAM   Tomorrow, I'll take her by the doctor. (RALPH *enters*)
BESSIE   Stay for a little tea.
SAM   No, I'll go home. I'm tired. Already I caught a cold in such weather. (*Blows his nose*)
MYRON   (*Entering with stuffs*)   Going home?
SAM   I'll go in bed. I caught a cold.
MYRON   Teddy Roosevelt used to say, "When you have a problem, sleep on it."
BESSIE   My Sam is no problem.
MYRON   I don't mean . . . I mean he said——
BESSIE   Call me tomorrow, Sam.
SAM   I'll phone supper time. Sometime I think there's something funny about me. (MYRON *sees him out. In the following pause Caruso is heard singing within*)
BESSIE   A bargain! Second fiddle. By me he don't even play in the orchestra—a man like a mouse. Maybe she'll lay down and die 'cause he makes a living?

[10] "Hear, O Israel," a Jewish prayer.

RALPH   Can I talk to you about something?
BESSIE What's the matter—I'm biting you?
RALPH   It's something about Blanche.
BESSIE Don't tell me.
RALPH   Listen now——
BESSIE I don't wanna know.
RALPH   She's got no place to go.
BESSIE I don't want to know.
RALPH   Mom, I love this girl. . . .
BESSIE So go knock your head against the wall.
RALPH   I want her to come here. Listen, Mom, I want you to let her live here for a while.
BESSIE You got funny ideas, my son.
RALPH   I'm as good as anyone else. Don't I have some rights in the world? Listen, Mom, if I don't do something, she's going away. Why don't you do it? Why don't you let her stay here for a few weeks? Things'll pick up. Then we can——
BESSIE Sure, sure. I'll keep her fresh on ice for a wedding day. That's what you want?
RALPH   No, I mean you should——
BESSIE Or maybe you'll sleep here in the same bed without marriage. (JACOB *stands in his doorway, dressed*)
RALPH   Don't say that, Mom. I only mean. . . .
BESSIE What you mean, I know . . . and what I mean I also know. Make up your mind. For your own good, Ralphie. If she dropped in the ocean I don't lift a finger.
RALPH   That's all, I suppose.
BESSIE With me it's one thing—a boy should have respect for his own future. Go to sleep, you look tired. In the morning you'll forget.
JACOB   "Awake and sing, ye that dwell in dust, and the earth shall cast out the dead." It's cold out?
MYRON   Oh, yes.
JACOB   I'll take up Tootsie now.
MYRON   (*Eating bread and jam*) He come on us like the wild man of Borneo, Sam. I don't think Hennie was fool enough to tell him the truth like that.
BESSIE Myron! (*A deep pause*)
RALPH   What did he say?
BESSIE Never mind.
RALPH   I heard him. I heard him. You don't needa tell me.
BESSIE Never mind.
RALPH   You trapped that guy.
BESSIE Don't say another word.

RALPH Just have respect? That's the idea?
BESSIE Don't say another word. I'm boiling over ten times inside.
RALPH You won't let Blanche here, huh. I'm not sure I want her. You put one over on that little shrimp. The cat's whiskers, Mom?
BESSIE I'm telling you something!
RALPH I got the whole idea. I get it so quick my head's swimming. Boy, what a laugh! I suppose you know about this, Jake?
JACOB Yes.
RALPH Why didn't you do something?
JACOB I'm an old man.
RALPH What's that got to do with the price of bonds? Sits around and lets a thing like that happen! You make me sick too.
MYRON (*After a pause*) Let me say something, son.
RALPH Take your hand away! Sit in a corner and wag your tail. Keep on boasting you went to law school for two years.
MYRON I want to tell you——
RALPH You never in your life had a thing to tell me.
BESSIE (*Bitterly*) Don't say a word. Let him, let him run and tell Sam. Publish in the papers, give a broadcast on the radio. To him it don't matter nothing his family sits with tears pouring from the eyes. (*To* JACOB) What are you waiting for? I didn't tell you twice already about the dog? You'll stand around with Caruso and make a bughouse. It ain't enough all day long. Fifty times I told you I'll break every record in the house. (*She brushes past him, breaks the records, comes out*) The next time I say something you'll maybe believe it. Now maybe you learned a lesson. (*Pause*)
JACOB (*Quietly*) Bessie, new lessons . . . not for an old dog. (MOE *enters*)
MYRON You didn't have to do it, Momma.
BESSIE Talk better to your son, Mr. Berger! Me, I don't lay down and die for him and Poppa no more. I'll work like a nigger? For what? Wait, the day comes when you'll be punished. When it's too late you'll remember how you sucked away a mother's life. Talk to him, tell him how I don't sleep at night. (*Bursts into tears and exits*)
MOE (*Sings*) "Good-by to all your sorrows. You never hear them talk about the war, in the land of Yama Yama. . . ."
MYRON Yes, Momma's a sick woman, Ralphie.
RALPH Yeah?
MOE We'll be out of the trenches by Christmas. Putt, putt, putt . . . here, stinker. . . . (*Picks up Tootsie, a small, white poodle that just then enters from the hall*) If there's reincarnation in the next life I wanna be a dog and lay in a fat lady's lap. Barrage over? How 'bout a little pinochle, Pop?

JACOB Nnno.
RALPH (*Taking dog*) I'll take her up. (*Conciliatory*)
JACOB No, I'll do it. (*Takes dog*)
RALPH (*Ashamed*) It's cold out.
JACOB I was cold before in my life. A man sixty-seven. . . . (*Strokes the dog*) Tootsie is my favorite lady in the house. (*He slowly passes across the room and exits. A settling pause*)
MYRON She cried all last night—Tootsie—I heard her in the kitchen like a young girl.
MOE Tonight I could do something. I got a yen . . . I don't know.
MYRON (*Rubbing his head*) My scalp is impoverished.
RALPH Mom bust all his records.
MYRON She didn't have to do it.
MOE Tough tit! Now I can sleep in the morning. Who the hell wantsa hear a wop air his tonsils all day long!
RALPH (*Handling the fragment of a record*) "O Paradiso!"
MOE (*Gets cards*) It's snowing out, girls.
MYRON There's no more big snows like in the old days. I think the whole world's changing. I see it, right under our very eyes. No one hardly remembers any more when we used to have gaslight and all the dishes had little fishes on them.
MOE It's the system, girls.
MYRON I was a little boy when it happened—the Great Blizzard. It snowed three days without a stop that time. Yes, and the horse cars stopped. A silence of death was on the city and little babies got no milk . . . they say a lot of people died that year.
MOE (*Singing as he deals himself cards*)

> "Lights are blinking while you're drinking,
> That's the place where the good fellows go.
> Good-by to all your sorrows,
> You never hear them talk about the war,
> In the land of Yama Yama
> Funicalee, funicala, funicalo. . . ."

MYRON What can I say to you, Big Boy?
RALPH Not a damn word.
MOE (*Goes "ta ra ta ra" throughout*)
MYRON I know how you feel about all those things, I know.
RALPH Forget it.
MYRON And your girl. . . .
RALPH Don't soft soap me all of a sudden.
MYRON I'm not foreign born. I'm an American, and yet I never got close to you. It's an American father's duty to be his son's friend.

263 · *Awake and Sing!* [ACT TWO, Scene Two]

RALPH   Who said that—Teddy R.?
MOE   (*Dealing cards*)   You're breaking his heart, *Litvak*.[11]
MYRON   It just happened the other day. The moment I began losing my hair I just knew I was destined to be a failure in life . . . and when I grew bald I was. Now isn't that funny, Big Boy?
MOE   It's a pisscutter!
MYRON   I believe in Destiny.
MOE   You get what-it-takes. Then they don't catch you with your pants down. (*Sings out*) Eight of clubs. . . .
MYRON   I really don't know. I sold jewelry on the road before I married. It's one thing to—— Now here's a thing the druggist gave me. (*Reads*) "The Marvel Cosmetic Girl of Hollywood is going on the air. Give this charming little radio singer a name and win five thousand dollars. If you will send——"
MOE   Your old man still believes in Santy Claus.
MYRON   Someone's got to win. The government isn't gonna allow everything to be a fake.
MOE   It's a fake. There ain't no prizes. It's a fake.
MYRON   It says——
RALPH   (*Snatching it*)   For Christ's sake, Pop, forget it. Grow up. Jake's right—everybody's crazy. It's like a zoo in this house. I'm going to bed.
MOE   In the land of Yama Yama. . . . (*Goes on with "ta ra"*)
MYRON   Don't think life's easy with Momma. No, but she means for your good all the time. I tell you she does, she——
RALPH   Maybe, but I'm going to bed. (*Downstairs doorbell rings violently*)
MOE   (*Ring*)   Enemy barrage begins on sector eight seventy-five.
RALPH   That's downstairs.
MYRON   We ain't expecting anyone this hour of the night.
MOE   "Lights are blinking while you're drinking, that's the place where the good fellows go. Good-by to ta ra tara ra," etc.
RALPH   I better see who it is.
MYRON   I'll tick the button. (*As he starts, the apartment doorbell begins ringing, followed by large knocking.* MYRON *goes out*)
RALPH   Who's ever ringing means it. (*A loud excited voice outside*)
MOE   "In the land of Yama Yama, Funicalee, funicalo, funic——"

(MYRON *enters followed by* SCHLOSSER *the janitor.* BESSIE *cuts in from the other side*)

BESSIE   Who's ringing like a lunatic?
RALPH   What's the matter?

[11] Literally "Lithuanian"; here used mockingly.

MYRON Momma. . . .
BESSIE Noo, what's the matter? (*Downstairs bell continues*)
RALPH What's the matter?
BESSIE Well, well . . . ?
MYRON Poppa. . . .
BESSIE What happened?
SCHLOSSER He shlipped maybe in de snow.
RALPH Who?
SCHLOSSER (*To* BESSIE) Your fadder fall off de roof. . . . Ja. (*A dead pause.* RALPH *then runs out*)
BESSIE (*Dazed*) Myron. . . . Call Morty on the phone . . . call him. (MYRON *starts for phone*) No. I'll do it myself. I'll . . . do it. (MYRON *exits*)
SCHLOSSER (*Standing stupidly*) Since I was in dis country . . . I was pudding out de ash can . . . The snow is vet. . . .
MOE (*To* SCHLOSSER) Scram. (SCHLOSSER *exits*)

(BESSIE *goes blindly to the phone, fumbles and gets it.* MOE *sits quietly, slowly turning cards over, but watching her*)

BESSIE He slipped. . . .
MOE (*Deeply moved*) Slipped?
BESSIE I can't see the numbers. Make it, Moe, make it. . . .
MOE Make it yourself. (*He looks at her and slowly goes back to his game of cards with shaking hands*)
BESSIE Riverside 7— . . . (*Unable to talk she dials slowly. The dial whizzes on*)
MOE Don't . . . make me laugh. . . . (*He turns over cards*)

Curtain

Act Three

A *week later in the dining room.* MORTY, BESSIE *and* MYRON *eating. Sitting in the front room is* MOE *marking a "dope sheet," but really listening to the others.*

BESSIE You're sure he'll come tonight—the insurance man?

MORTY Why not? I shtupped[12] him a ten-dollar bill. Everything's hot delicatessen.
BESSIE Why must he come so soon?
MORTY Because you had a big expense. You'll settle once and for all. I'm a great boy for making hay while the sun shines.
BESSIE Stay till he'll come, Morty. . . .
MORTY No, I got a strike downtown. Business don't stop for personal life. Two times already in the past week those bastards threw stink bombs in the showroom. Wait! We'll give them strikes—in the *kishkas*[13] we'll give them. . . .
BESSIE I'm a woman. I don't know about policies. Stay till he comes.
MORTY Bessie—sweetheart, leave me live.
BESSIE I'm afraid, Morty.
MORTY Be practical. They made an investigation. Everybody knows Pop had an accident. Now we'll collect.
MYRON Ralphie don't know Papa left the insurance in his name.
MORTY It's not his business. And I'll tell him.
BESSIE The way he feels. (*Enter* RALPH *into front room*) He'll do something crazy. He thinks Papa jumped off the roof.
MORTY Be practical, Bessie. Ralphie will sign when I tell him. Everything is peaches and cream.
BESSIE Wait for a few minutes. . . .
MORTY Look, I'll show you in black on white what the policy says. For God's sake, leave me live! (*Angrily exits to kitchen. In parlor,* MOE *speaks to* RALPH *who is reading a letter*)
MOE What's the letter say?
RALPH Blanche won't see me no more, she says. I couldn't care very much, she says. If I didn't come like I said. . . . She'll phone before she leaves.
MOE She don't know about Pop?
RALPH She won't ever forget me she says. Look what she sends me . . . a little locket on a chain . . . if she calls I'm out.
MOE You mean it?
RALPH For a week I'm trying to go in his room. I guess he'd like me to have it, but I can't. . . .
MOE Wait a minute! (*Crosses over*) They're trying to rook you—a freeze-out.
RALPH Who?
MOE That bunch stuffin' their gut with hot pastrami. Morty in par-

[12] Bribed.
[13] Literally, intestines; here used ironically.

ticular. Jake left the insurance—three thousand dollars—for you.
RALPH For me?
MOE Now you got wings, kid. Pop figured you could use it. That's why. . . .
RALPH That's why what?
MOE It ain't the only reason he done it.
RALPH He done it?
MOE You think a breeze blew him off? (HENNIE *enters and sits*)
RALPH I'm not sure what I think.
MOE The insurance guy's coming tonight. Morty "shtupped" him.
RALPH Yeah?
MOE I'll back you up. You're dead on your feet. Grab a sleep for yourself.
RALPH No!
MOE Go on! (*Pushes boy into room*)
SAM (*Whom* MORTY *has sent in for the paper*) Morty wants the paper.
HENNIE So?
SAM You're sitting on it. (*Gets paper*) We could go home now, Hennie! Leon is alone by Mrs. Strasberg a whole day.
HENNIE Go on home if you're so anxious. A full tub of diapers is waiting.
SAM Why should you act this way?
HENNIE 'Cause there's no bones in ice cream. Don't touch me.
SAM Please, what's the matter. . . .
MOE She don't like you. Plain as the face on your nose. . . .
SAM To me, my friend, you talk a foreign language.
MOE A quarter you're lousy. (SAM *exits*) Gimme a buck, I'll run it up to ten.
HENNIE Don't do me no favors.
MOE Take a chance. (*Stopping her as she crosses to doorway*)
HENNIE I'm a pushover.
MOE I say lotsa things. You don't know me.
HENNIE I know you—when you knock 'em down you're through.
MOE (*Sadly*) You still don't know me.
HENNIE I know what goes in your wise-guy head.
MOE Don't run away. . . . I ain't got hydrophobia. Wait. I want to tell you. . . . I'm leaving.
HENNIE Leaving?
MOE Tonight. Already packed.
HENNIE Where?
MORTY (*As he enters followed by the others*) My car goes through snow like a dose of salts.
BESSIE Hennie, go eat. . . .

Awake and Sing! [ACT THREE]

MORTY   Where's Ralphie?
MOE   In his new room. (*Moves into dining room*)
MORTY   I didn't have a piece of hot pastrami in my mouth for years.
BESSIE   Take a sandwich, Hennie. You didn't eat all day. . . . (*At window*) A whole week it rained cats and dogs.
MYRON   Rain, rain, go away. Come again some other day. (*Puts shawl on her*)
MORTY   Where's my gloves?
SAM   (*Sits on stool*) I'm sorry the old man lays in the rain.
MORTY   Personally, Pop was a fine man. But I'm a great boy for an honest opinion. He had enough crazy ideas for a regiment.
MYRON   Poppa never had a doctor in his whole life. . . . (*Enter* RALPH)
MORTY   He had Caruso. Who's got more from life?
BESSIE   Who's got more? . . .
MYRON   And Marx he had.

(MYRON *and* BESSIE *sit on sofa*)

MORTY   Marx! Some say Marx is the new God today. Maybe I'm wrong. Ha, ha, ha. . . . Personally I counted my ten million last night. . . . I'm sixteen cents short. So tomorrow I'll go to Union Square and yell no equality in the country! Ah, it's a new generation.
RALPH   You said it!
MORTY   What's the matter, Ralphie? What are you looking funny?
RALPH   I hear I'm left insurance and the man's coming tonight.
MORTY   Poppa didn't leave no insurance for you.
RALPH   What?
MORTY   In your name he left it—but not for you.
RALPH   It's my name on the paper.
MORTY   Who said so?
RALPH   (*To his mother*) The insurance man's coming tonight?
MORTY   What's the matter?
RALPH   I'm not talking to you. (*To his mother*) Why?
BESSIE   I don't know why.
RALPH   He don't come in this house tonight.
MORTY   That's what *you* say.
RALPH   I'm not talking to you, Uncle Morty, but I'll tell you, too, he don't come here tonight when there's still mud on a grave. (*To his mother*) Couldn't you give the house a chance to cool off?
MORTY   Is this a way to talk to your mother?
RALPH   Was that a way to talk to your father?
MORTY   Don't be so smart with me, Mr. Ralph Berger!
RALPH   Don't be so smart with *me*.

MORTY What'll you do? I say he's coming tonight. Who says no?
MOE (*Suddenly, from the background*) Me.
MORTY Take a back seat, Axelrod. When you're in the family——
MOE I got a little document here. (*Produces paper*) I found it under his pillow that night. A guy who slips off a roof don't leave a note before he does it.
MORTY (*Starting for* MOE *after a horrified silence*) Let me see this note.
BESSIE Morty, don't touch it!
MOE Not if you crawled.
MORTY It's a fake. Poppa wouldn't——
MOE Get the insurance guy here and we'll see how——(*The bell rings*) Speak of the devil. . . . Answer it, see what happens. (MORTY *starts for the ticker*)
BESSIE Morty, don't!
MORTY (*Stopping*) Be practical, Bessie.
MOE Sometimes you don't collect on suicides if they know about it.
MORTY You should let. . . . You should let him. . . . (*A pause in which* ALL *seem dazed. Bell rings insistently*)
MOE Well, we're waiting.
MORTY Give me the note.
MOE I'll give you the head off your shoulders.
MORTY Bessie, you'll stand for this? (*Points to* RALPH) Pull down his pants and give him with a strap.
RALPH (*As bell rings again*) How about it?
BESSIE Don't be crazy. It's not my fault. Morty said he should come tonight. It's not nice so soon. I didn't——
MORTY I said it? Me?
BESSIE Who then?
MORTY You didn't sing a song in my ear a whole week to settle quick?
BESSIE I'm surprised. Morty, you're a big liar.
MYRON Momma's telling the truth, she is!
MORTY Lissen. In two shakes of a lamb's tail, we'll start a real fight and then nobody won't like nobody. Where's my fur gloves? I'm going downtown. (*To* SAM) You coming? I'll drive you down.
HENNIE (*To* SAM, *who looks questioningly at her*) Don't look at me. Go home if you want.
SAM If you're coming soon, I'll wait.
HENNIE Don't do me any favors. Night and day he pesters me.
MORTY You made a cushion——sleep!
SAM I'll go home. I know . . . to my worst enemy I don't wish such a life——
HENNIE Sam, keep quiet.

SAM (*Quietly; sadly*) No more free speech in America? (*Gets his hat and coat*) I'm a lonely person. Nobody likes me.
MYRON I like you, Sam.
HENNIE (*Going to him gently; sensing the end*) Please go home, Sam. I'll sleep here. . . . I'm tired and nervous. Tomorrow I'll come home. I love you . . . I mean it. (*She kisses him with real feeling*)
SAM I would die for you. . . . (SAM *looks at her. Tries to say something, but his voice chokes up with a mingled feeling. He turns and leaves the room*)
MORTY A bird in the hand is worth two in the bush. Remember I said it. Good night. (*Exits after* SAM) (HENNIE *sits depressed.* BESSIE *goes up and looks at the picture calendar again.* MYRON *finally breaks the silence*)
MYRON Yesterday a man wanted to sell me a saxophone with pearl buttons. But I——
BESSIE It's a beautiful picture. In this land, nobody works. . . . Nobody worries. . . . Come to bed, Myron. (*Stops at the door, and says to* RALPH) Please don't have foolish ideas about the money.
RALPH Let's call it a day.
BESSIE It belongs for the whole family. You'll get your teeth fixed——
RALPH And a pair of black and white shoes?
BESSIE Hennie needs a vacation. She'll take two weeks in the mountains and I'll mind the baby.
RALPH I'll take care of my own affairs.
BESSIE A family needs for a rainy day. Times is getting worse. Prospect Avenue, Dawson, Beck Street—every day furniture's on the sidewalk.
RALPH Forget it, Mom.
BESSIE Ralphie, I worked too hard all my years to be treated like dirt. It's no law we should be stuck together like Siamese twins. Summer shoes you didn't have, skates you never had, but I bought a new dress every week. A lover I kept—Mr. Gigolo! Did I ever play a game of cards like Mrs. Marcus? Or was Bessie Berger's children always the cleanest on the block?! Here I'm not only the mother, but also the father. The first two years I worked in a stocking factory for six dollars while Myron Berger went to law school. If I didn't worry about the family who would? On the calendar it's a different place, but here without a dollar you don't look the world in the eye. Talk from now to next year—this is life in America.
RALPH Then it's wrong. It don't make sense. If life made you this way, then it's wrong!
BESSIE Maybe you wanted me to give up twenty years ago. Where would you be now? You'll excuse my expression—a bum in the park!

RALPH I'm not blaming you, Mom. Sink or swim—I see it. But it can't stay like this.
BESSIE My foolish boy. . . .
RALPH No, I see every house lousy with lies and hate. He said it, Grandpa— Brooklyn hates the Bronx. Smacked on the nose twice a day. But boys and girls can get ahead like that, Mom. We don't want life printed on dollar bills, Mom!
BESSIE So go out and change the world if you don't like it.
RALPH I will! And why? 'Cause life's different in my head. Gimme the earth in two hands. I'm strong. There . . . hear him? The air mail off to Boston. Day or night, he flies away, a job to do. That's us and it's no time to die. (*The airplane sound fades off as* MYRON *gives alarm clock to* BESSIE *which she begins to wind*)
BESSIE "Mom, what does she know? She's old-fashioned!" But I'll tell you a big secret: My whole life I wanted to go away too, but with children a woman stays home. A fire burned in *my* heart too, but now it's too late. I'm no spring chicken. The clock goes and Bessie goes. Only my machinery can't be fixed. (*She lifts a button: the alarm rings on the clock; she stops it, says "Good night" and exits*)
MYRON I guess I'm no prize bag. . . .
BESSIE (*From within*) Come to bed, Myron.
MYRON (*Tears page off calendar*) Hmmm. . . . (*Exits to her*)
RALPH Look at him, draggin' after her like an old shoe.
MOE Punch drunk. (*Phone rings*) That's for me. (*At phone*) Yeah? . . . Just a minute. (*To* RALPH) Your girl . . .
RALPH Jeez, I don't know what to say to her.
MOE Hang up? (RALPH *slowly takes phone*)
RALPH Hello. . . . Blanche, I wish. . . . I don't know what to say. . . . Yes . . . Hello? . . . (*Puts phone down*) She hung up on me . . .
MOE Sorry?
RALPH No girl means anything to me until . . .
MOE Till when?
RALPH Till I can take care of her. Till we don't look out on an airshaft. Till we can take the world in two hands and polish off the dirt.
MOE That's a big order.
RALPH Once upon a time I thought I'd drown to death in bolts of silk and velour. But I grew up these last few weeks. Jake said a lot.
MOE Your memory's okay?
RALPH But take a look at this. (*Brings armful of books from* JACOB'S *room—dumps them on table*) His books, I got them too—the pages ain't cut in half of them.
MOE Perfect.
RALPH Does it prove something? Damn tootin'! A ten-cent nail-file cuts

them. Uptown, downtown, I'll read them on the way. Get a big lamp over the bed. (*Picks up one*) My eyes are good. (*Puts book in pocket*) Sure, inventory tomorrow. Coletti to Driscoll to Berger—that's how we work. It's a team down the warehouse. Driscoll's a show-off, a wiseguy, and Joe talks pigeons day and night. But they're like me, looking for a chance to get to first base too. Joe razzed me about my girl. But he don't know why. I'll tell him. Hell, he might tell me something I don't know. Get teams together all over. Spit on your hands and get to work. And with enough teams together maybe we'll get steam in the warehouse so our fingers don't freeze off. Maybe we'll fix it so life won't be printed on dollar bills.

MOE Graduation Day.

RALPH (*Starts for door of his room, stops*) Can I have . . . Grandpa's note?

MOE Sure you want it?

RALPH Please— (MOE *gives it*) It's blank!

MOE (*Taking note back and tearing it up*) That's right.

RALPH Thanks! (*Exits*)

MOE The kid's a fighter! (*To* HENNIE) Why are you crying?

HENNIE I never cried in my life. (*She is now*)

MOE (*Starts for door. Stops*) You told Sam you love him. . . .

HENNIE If I'm sore on life, why take it out on him?

MOE You won't forget me to your dyin' day—I was the first guy. Part of your insides. You won't forget. I wrote my name on you—indelible ink!

HENNIE One thing I won't forget—how you left me crying on the bed like I was two for a cent!

MOE Listen, do you think——

HENNIE Sure. Waits till the family goes to the open air movie. He brings me perfume. . . . He grabs my arms——

MOE You won't forget me!

HENNIE How you left the next week?

MOE So I made a mistake. For Chris' sake, don't act like the Queen of Roumania!

HENNIE Don't make me laugh!

MOE What the hell do you want, my head on a plate?! Was my life so happy? Chris', my old man was a bum. I supported the whole damn family—five kids and Mom. When they grew up they beat it the hell away like rabbits. Mom died. I went to the war; got clapped down like a bedbug; woke up in a room without a leg. What the hell do you think, anyone's got it better than you? I never had a home either. I'm lookin' too!

HENNIE So what?!

MOE So you're it—you're home for me, a place to live! That's the whole parade, sickness, eating out your heart! Sometimes you meet a girl—she stops it—that's love. . . . So take a chance! Be with me, Paradise. What's to lose?

HENNIE My pride!

MOE (*Grabbing her*) What do you want? Say the word—I'll tango on a dime. Don't gimme ice when your heart's on fire!

HENNIE Let me go! (*He stops her*)

MOE WHERE?!!

HENNIE What do you want, Moe, what do you want?

MOE You!

HENNIE You'll be sorry you ever started——

MOE You!

HENNIE Moe, lemme go—— (*Trying to leave*) I'm getting up early—lemme go.

MOE No! . . . I got enough fever to blow the whole damn town to hell. (*He suddenly releases her and half stumbles backwards. Forces himself to quiet down*) You wanna go back to him? Say the word. I'll know what to do. . . .

HENNIE (*Helplessly*) Moe, I don't know what to say.

MOE Listen to me.

HENNIE What?

MOE Come away. A certain place where it's moonlight and roses. We'll lay down, count stars. Hear the big ocean making noise. You lay under the trees. Champagne flows like—— (*Phone rings.* MOE *finally answers the telephone*) Hello? . . . Just a minute. (*Looks at* HENNIE)

HENNIE Who is it?

MOE Sam.

HENNIE (*Starts for phone, but changes her mind*) I'm sleeping. . . .

MOE (*In phone*) She's sleeping. . . . (*Hangs up. Watches* HENNIE *who slowly sits*) He wants you to know he got home O.K. . . . What's on your mind?

HENNIE Nothing.

MOE Sam?

HENNIE They say it's a palace on those Havana boats.

MOE What's on your mind?

HENNIE (*Trying to escape*) Moe, I don't care for Sam—I never loved him——

MOE But your kid—?

HENNIE All my life I waited for this minute.

MOE (*Holding her*) Me too. Made believe I was talkin' just bedroom golf, but you and me forever was what I meant! Christ, baby, there's one life to live! Live it!

HENNIE Leave the baby?
MOE Yeah!
HENNIE I can't. . . .
MOE You can!
HENNIE No. . . .
MOE But you're not sure!
HENNIE I don't know.
MOE Make a break or spend the rest of your life in a coffin.
HENNIE Oh God, I don't know where I stand.
MOE Don't look up there. Paradise, you're on a big boat headed south. No more pins and needles in your heart, no snake juice squirted in your arm. The whole world's green grass and when you cry it's because you're happy.
HENNIE Moe, I don't know. . . .
MOE Nobody knows, but you do it and find out. When you're scared the answer's zero.
HENNIE You're hurting my arm.
MOE The doctor said it—cut off your leg to save your life! And they done it—one thing to get another. (*Enter* RALPH)
RALPH I didn't hear a word, but do it, Hennie, do it!
MOE Mom can mind the kid. She'll go on forever, Mom. We'll send money back, and Easter eggs.
RALPH I'll be here.
MOE Get your coat . . . get it.
HENNIE Moe!
MOE I know . . . but get your coat and hat and kiss the house good-bye.
HENNIE The man I love. . . . (MYRON *entering*) I left my coat in Mom's room. (*Exits*)
MYRON Don't wake her up, Beauty. Momma fell asleep as soon as her head hit the pillow. I can't sleep. It was a long day. Hmmm. (*Examines his tongue in buffet mirror*) I was reading the other day a person with a thick tongue is feeble-minded. I can do anything with my tongue. Make it thick, flat. No fruit in the house lately. Just a lone apple. (*He gets apple and paring knife and starts paring*) Must be something wrong with me—I say I won't eat but I eat. (HENNIE *enters dressed to go out*) Where you going, little Red Riding Hood?
HENNIE Nobody knows, Peter Rabbit.
MYRON You're looking very pretty tonight. You were a beautiful baby too. 1910, that was the year you was born. The same year Teddy Roosevelt come back from Africa.
HENNIE Gee, Pop; you're such a funny guy.
MYRON He was a boisterous man, Teddy. Good night. (*He exits, paring apple*)

RALPH When I look at him, I'm sad. Let me die like a dog, if I can't get more from life.
HENNIE Where?
RALPH Right here in the house! My days won't be for nothing. Let Mom have the dough. I'm twenty-two and kickin'! I'll get along. Did Jake die for us to fight about nickels? No! "Awake and sing," he said. Right here he stood and said it. The night he died, I saw it like a thunderbolt! I saw he was dead and I was born! I swear to God, I'm one week old! I want the whole city to hear it—fresh blood, arms. We got 'em. We're glad we're living.
MOE I wouldn't trade you for two pitchers and an outfielder. Hold the fort!
RALPH So long.
MOE So long.

(They go and RALPH *stands full and strong in the doorway seeing them off as the curtain slowly falls)*

Curtain

THORNTON WILDER
[1897 –]

❦ *The Man*

THORNTON NIVEN WILDER, son of Amos Parker Wilder, a devout Congregationalist, and Isabella Thornton Niven, daughter of a Presbyterian minister, was interested in the theater almost from childhood. By the time he entered Oberlin College in 1915 he had written several "three minute plays," some of which were later published in *The Angel That Troubled the Waters and Other Plays*. He completed his undergraduate studies at Yale, and in 1921 began a teaching job at Lawrenceville School, near Princeton, New Jersey. He received an A.M. degree from Princeton University in 1926.

Wilder first achieved fame as a novelist. He won his first Pulitzer Prize for *The Bridge of San Luis Rey* (1927). In 1931 *The Long Christmas Dinner and Other Plays in One Act* was published. The title play, together with *Pullman Car Hiawatha* and *The Happy Journey*, utilized theatrical concepts that were to be developed in *Our Town* and *The Skin of Our Teeth*. In 1938 two of his major plays were performed, *Our Town* and *The Merchant of Yonkers*. The former was a huge success and earned him his second Pulitzer Prize. The latter—based on Johann Nestroy's century-old *Einen Jux will er sich Machen*, which was itself based on John Oxenford's *A Day Well Spent*—lasted less than a month on Broadway. In 1941 World War II began, and in 1942 Wilder enlisted in the Air Force. Later that year *The Skin of Our Teeth*—which drew on James Joyce's *Finnegans Wake*— was performed. For this play—which deals with the survival of the human race (the Antrobus, or *anthropos*, family) by the skin of its teeth through the ice age, the flood, and war—Wilder received his third Pulitzer Prize. In 1954 his slightly revised *Merchant of Yonkers,* now called *The Matchmaker,* was a hit at the Edinburgh Festival, and the following year in London and New York, in a production directed by Tyrone Guthrie; ten years later it became a successful musical, *Hello, Dolly.* Recently, Wilder has been working on two cycles of plays, *The Seven Ages of Man* and *The Seven Deadly Sins. Infancy* and *Childhood* from the former cycle and *Someone from Assisi* from the latter were produced at New York's Circle in the Square in 1962 under the collective title *Plays for Bleeker Street.*

❧ *The Work*

ALTHOUGH THE POINT OF VIEW of Thornton Wilder's plays is different from that of most contemporary dramatists, his stagecraft is in the vanguard of current theater practice. Like Shaw—and unlike Beckett—Wilder's attitude is not one of despair but of affirmation. In *Our Town* he celebrates the seemingly trivial elements of life. *The Matchmaker* abounds in infectious high spirits. In *The Skin of Our Teeth* the birth of a child is sufficient reason for the universe to have been set in motion. In contrast to the absurdist viewpoint, Wilder feels that man is at home in the universe. He consistently relates the individual human being to the cosmos. In *The Skin of Our Teeth* Antrobus begins his address at an Atlantic City Convention with the words "Fellow-mammals, fellow-vertebrates, fellow-humans." In *Pullman Car Hiawatha* the Hours, the Archangels, and the Planets sing and speak over sleeping-car passengers in a railroad train.

Wilder's vision of man's position in the cosmos determines his theatrical practices. Because of conventions of the nonrealistic theater, he says in "Some Thoughts on Playwriting," the specific may become generalized: if Juliet, for example, moves about in a realistic room, one receives the impression that the events of the play happened only to her, in that place, in that time; whereas if she is placed on a bare stage, the events are released from the particular and Juliet becomes every girl in love, in any time and in all places. Wilder uses the theater as a means of abstracting the fundamental experience from the immediate situation.

While the physical presence of the actor creates immediacy and reality, his unreal milieu tends to neutralize the details and emphasize the essential. In *Pullman Car Hiawatha*, *The Happy Journey*, and *Our Town* he uses a bare stage and pantomime to provide a balance to particularized, realistic characterization and actions. In *The Matchmaker* there are asides and obvious farce techniques. In *The Skin of Our Teeth*, which juxtaposes modern suburbia and prehistory, the walls of the setting tilt precariously and then correct themselves, or they fly up into the air; an actress complains of her lines; a scene is rehearsed by people with scripts in their hands because the regular actors have taken sick. In short, Wilder treats the stage as a stage and presents not theater as a slice of life but reality as a theatrical event.

❧ *The Play*

In *Our Town* Wilder takes cliché situations and makes them both fresh and distinctive. A play that emphasizes the wonders and beauty of the most ordinary elements of daily living may seem to be out of harmony with contemporary literature. However, one must not identify Wilder's ideas with the more sentimental statements of his characters. Emily expects men to be perfect and George expects girls to be perfect, but there is no indication that the author shares their views. Mrs. Soames sighs that life was wonderful, but Simon Stimson bitterly questions that statement in the very next line. Nor does Stimson have the last word. Although he denounces life as cruel, ignorant, and blind, Mrs. Gibbs reminds him that this is not the whole truth. Wilder is larger than any of his characters. *Our Town* is not a demonstration that rural life is quaint and completely happy. There are worms in the apple, a cloud behind the silver lining. Grover's Corners does have a jail. It does drive a man with an artistic temperament to drink and ultimately to suicide. The newsboy, recipient of a scholarship to M.I.T., is killed in World War I. In earlier versions of *Our Town* (not included in the present text), the Stage Manager informs us that although Christianity forbids killings, one is allowed to kill not only animals but also human beings if it is done in war or in government punishings. The Stage Manager in the role of The Minister confesses to us that he does not know whether he believes in marriage. Although *Our*

Town deals with human beings who are essentially good, it is not a "goody-goody" play.

The details of human behavior are rendered with acute accuracy. One can go through scene after scene charting the thoughts of the characters between the lines and beneath the lines, revealing nuances in even ordinary moments—the newsboy having an "adult" talk wth Doc Gibbs, George employing teen-age strategy to persuade Emily to help him with his homework, Emily working up the courage to ask her mother if she is pretty, Emily influencing George not to leave town to go to school, etc. However, the details exist within a larger framework, and one of the wonders of the play is that the details of behavior and the overall pattern are seen almost simultaneously. Throughout, there is a tension between apparent opposites. The lives are small but are part of a vast pattern. A man-made institution (marriage) is part of nature.

The play's physical production, too, has this tension. An actor realistically stirs coffee, but there is neither cup nor spoon. The characters are orientated to a specific time and place, but there are no physical scenic details to set that time and place: there are no props, and the locale is simply a stage. Realism is at once present in the small and absent in the large.

The small is continually related to the large. The first act, we are told, may be called "The Daily Life," the second "Love and Marriage," and we see that the third deals with Death. Part of the opening action includes birth: Doc Gibbs returns from having delivered twins. From birth, through marriage, to death. In the beginning we are introduced to the town in statistical terms; in the end we see the eternal. The Stage Manager relates Grover's Corners to past civilizations and to future civilizations, to the surrounding countryside and to evolution. Rebecca, at the end of the first act, relates the individual to the town and to the divine as she quotes the address on Jane Crofut's letter, which starts with her name, goes through the county and state, and ends with "the Mind of God." But none of this is self-conscious: Rebecca's elaborate description of the letter is followed by "the postman brought it just the same." Although Wilder deals with the simple life, he does not do so simplistically. Not only is the simple presented in terms of the infinite, but the infinite is presented simply.

❧ Dramatic Works

St. Francis Lake, 1915.
Flamingo Red, 1916.
Brother Fire, 1916.
A Christmas Interlude, 1916.
Proserpina and the Devil, 1916.
The Angel on the Ship, 1917.
The Message and Jehanne, 1917.
That Other Fanny Otcott (later Fanny Otcott), 1918.
The Penny That Beauty Spent, 1919.
The Walled City, 1919.
Not for Leviathan (later Leviathan), 1919.
Childe Roland to the Dark Tower Came, 1919.
The Trumpet Shall Sound, 1920.
And the Sea Shall Give Up Its Dead, 1923.
Nascuntur Poetea, 1928.
Centaurs, 1928.
Now the Servant's Name Was Malchus, 1928.
Mozart and the Gray Steward, 1928.
Hast Thou Considered My Servant Job?, 1928.
The Flight into Egypt, 1928.
The Angel That Troubled the Waters, 1928.

The Long Christmas Dinner, 1931.
Queens of France, 1931.
Pullman Car Hiawatha, 1931.
Love, and How To Cure It, 1931.
Such Things Only Happen in Books, 1931.
The Happy Journey to Trenton and Camden, 1931.
Lucrece (from Le viol de Lucrèce, by André Obey), 1932.
A Doll's House (from Ibsen's play), 1937.
Our Town, 1938.
The Merchant of Yonkers, 1938.
The Skin of Our Teeth, 1942.
Our Century, 1947.
The Victors (from Morts sans sépulture, by Jean-Paul Sartre), 1948.
The Matchmaker (a slightly revised version of The Merchant of Yonkers), 1954.
The Alcestiad (called A Life in the Sun at its première), 1955.
The Wreck of the 5:25, 1957.
Berniece, 1957.
Plays for Bleeker Street (Infancy, Childhood, and Someone from Assisi), 1962.

❦ Selective Bibliography

Burbank, Rex. *Thornton Wilder*. New York: Twayne, 1961.
Fergusson, Francis. *The Human Image in Dramatic Literature*. Garden City: Doubleday Anchor, 1957. (See essay entitled "Three Allegorists: Brecht, Wilder, and Eliot.")
Goldstein, Malcolm. *The Art of Thornton Wilder*. Lincoln: University of Nebraska Press, 1965.
Hewitt, Barnard. "Thornton Wilder Says 'Yes,'" *Tulane Drama Review*, IV (December, 1959).
Kosok, Heinz. "Thornton Wilder: A Bibliography of Criticism," *Twentieth Century Literature*, IX (July, 1963).
Wilder, Thornton. "Some Thoughts About Playwriting." This essay has been printed in several collections, one of the more readily available of which is *Playwrights on Playwriting*, ed. Toby Cole. New York: Hill and Wang, 1961.

Our Town

A Play in Three Acts

CHARACTERS *(in the order of their appearance)*

STAGE MANAGER
DR. GIBBS
JOE CROWELL
HOWIE NEWSOME
MRS. GIBBS
MRS. WEBB
GEORGE GIBBS
REBECCA GIBBS
WALLY WEBB
EMILY WEBB
PROFESSOR WILLARD

MR. WEBB
WOMAN IN THE BALCONY
MAN IN THE AUDITORIUM
LADY IN THE BOX
SIMON STIMSON
MRS. SOAMES
CONSTABLE WARREN
SI CROWELL
THREE BASEBALL PLAYERS
SAM CRAIG
JOE STODDARD

The entire play takes place in Grover's Corners, New Hampshire.

Act One

No curtain.
No scenery.
The audience, arriving, sees an empty stage in half-light.
Presently the STAGE MANAGER, hat on and pipe in mouth, enters and begins placing a table and three chairs downstage left, and a table and three chairs downstage right. He also places a low bench at the corner of what will be the Webb house, left.
"Left" and "right" are from the point of view of the actor facing the audience. "Up" is toward the back wall.
As the house lights go down he has finished setting the stage and leaning against the right proscenium pillar watches the late arrivals in the audience.
When the auditorium is in complete darkness he speaks:

STAGE MANAGER This play is called "Our Town." It was written by Thornton Wilder; produced and directed by A. . . . (or: produced by A. . . . ; directed by B. . . .). In it you will see Miss C. . . . ; Miss D. . . . ; Miss E. . . . ; and Mr. F. . . . ; Mr. G. . . . ; Mr. H. . . . ; and many others. The name of the town is Grover's Corners, New Hampshire—just across the Massachusetts line: latitude 42 degrees 40 minutes; longitude 70 degrees 37 minutes. The First Act shows a day in our town. The day is May 7, 1901. The time is just before dawn.

(*A rooster crows*)

The sky is beginning to show some streaks of light over in the East there, behind our mount'in.
The morning star always gets wonderful bright the minute before it has to go,—doesn't it?

(*He stares at it for a moment, then goes upstage*)

Well, I'd better show you how our town lies. Up here—

(*That is: parallel with the back wall*)

is Main Street. Way back there is the railway station; tracks go that way. Polish Town's across the tracks, and some Canuck families.

(*Toward the left*)

Over there is the Congregational Church; across the street's the Presbyterian.
Methodist and Unitarian are over there.
Baptist is down in the holla' by the river.
Catholic Church is over beyond the tracks.
Here's the Town Hall and Post Office combined; jail's in the basement.
Bryan once made a speech from these very steps here.
Along here's a row of stores. Hitching posts and horse blocks in front of them. First automobile's going to come along in about five years—belonged to Banker Cartwright, our richest citizen . . . lives in the big white house up on the hill.
Here's the grocery store and here's Mr. Morgan's drugstore. Most everybody in town manages to look into those two stores once a day.
Public School's over yonder. High School's still farther over.
Quarter of nine mornings, noontimes, and three o'clock afternoons, the hull town can hear the yelling and screaming from those schoolyards.

(*He approaches the table and chairs downstage right*)

This is our doctor's house,—Doc Gibbs'. This is the back door.

(*Two arched trellises, covered with vines and flowers, are pushed out, one by each proscenium pillar*)

There's some scenery for those who think they have to have scenery. This is Mrs. Gibbs' garden. Corn . . . peas . . . beans . . . hollyhocks . . . heliotrope . . . and a lot of burdock.

(*Crosses the stage*)

In those days our newspaper come out twice a week—the Grover's Corners *Sentinel*—and this is Editor Webb's house.
And this is Mrs. Webb's garden.
Just like Mrs. Gibbs', only it's got a lot of sunflowers, too.

(*He looks upward, center stage*)

Right here . . .'s a big butternut tree.

(*He returns to his place by the right proscenium pillar and looks at the audience for a minute*)

Nice town, y'know what I mean?
Nobody very remarkable ever come out of it, s'far as we know.
The earliest tombstones in the cemetery up there on the mountain say 1670–1680—they're Grovers and Cartwrights and Gibbses and

Herseys—same names as are around here now.
Well, as I said: it's about dawn.
The only lights on in town are in a cottage over by the tracks where a Polish mother's just had twins. And in the Joe Crowell house, where Joe Junior's getting up so as to deliver the paper. And in the depot, where Shorty Hawkins is gettin' ready to flag the 5:45 for Boston.

(A *train whistle is heard. The* STAGE MANAGER *takes out his watch and nods*)

Naturally, out in the country—all around—there've been lights on for some time, what with milkin's and so on. But town people sleep late. So—another day's begun.
There's Doc Gibbs comin' down Main Street now, comin' back from that baby case. And here's his wife comin' downstairs to get breakfast.

(MRS. GIBBS, *a plump, pleasant woman in the middle thirties, comes "downstairs" right. She pulls up an imaginary window shade in her kitchen and starts to make a fire in her stove*)

Doc Gibbs died in 1930. The new hospital's named after him.
Mrs. Gibbs died first—long time ago, in fact. She went out to visit her daughter, Rebecca, who married an insurance man in Canton, Ohio, and died there—pneumonia—but her body was brought back here. She's up in the cemetery there now—in with a whole mess of Gibbses and Herseys—she was Julia Hersey 'fore she married Doc Gibbs in the Congregational Church over there.
In our town we like to know the facts about everybody.
There's Mrs. Webb, coming downstairs to get her breakfast, too.
—That's Doc Gibbs. Got that call at half past one this morning.
And there comes Joe Crowell, Jr., delivering Mr. Webb's *Sentinel*.

(DR. GIBBS *has been coming along Main Street from the left. At the point where he would turn to approach his house, he stops, sets down his—imaginary—black bag, takes off his hat, and rubs his face with fatigue, using an enormous handkerchief.* MRS. WEBB, *a thin, serious, crisp woman, has entered her kitchen, left, tying on an apron. She goes through the motions of putting wood into a stove, lighting it, and preparing breakfast. Suddenly,* JOE CROWELL, JR., *eleven, starts down Main Street from the right, hurling imaginary newspapers into doorways*)

JOE CROWELL, JR. Morning, Doc Gibbs.
DR. GIBBS Morning, Joe.
JOE CROWELL, JR. Somebody been sick, Doc?
DR. GIBBS No. Just some twins born over in Polish Town.

JOE CROWELL, JR. Do you want your paper now?
DR. GIBBS Yes, I'll take it.—Anything serious goin' on in the world since Wednesday?
JOE CROWELL, JR. Yessir. My schoolteacher, Miss Foster, 's getting married to a fella over in Concord.
DR. GIBBS I declare.—How do you boys feel about that?
JOE CROWELL, JR. Well, of course, it's none of my business—but I think if a person starts out to be a teacher, she ought to stay one.
DR. GIBBS How's your knee, Joe?
JOE CROWELL, JR. Fine, Doc, I never think about it at all. Only like you said, it always tells me when it's going to rain.
DR. GIBBS What's it telling you today? Goin' to rain?
JOE CROWELL, JR. No, sir.
DR. GIBBS Sure?
JOE CROWELL, JR. Yessir.
DR. GIBBS Knee ever make a mistake?
JOE CROWELL, JR. No, sir.

(JOE *goes off.* DR. GIBBS *stands reading his paper*)

STAGE MANAGER Want to tell you something about that boy Joe Crowell there. Joe was awful bright—graduated from high school here, head of his class. So he got a scholarship to Massachusetts Tech. Graduated head of his class there, too. It was all wrote up in the Boston paper at the time. Goin' to be a great engineer, Joe was. But the war broke out and he died in France.—All that education for nothing.
HOWIE NEWSOME (*Off left*) Giddap, Bessie! What's the matter with you today?
STAGE MANAGER Here comes Howie Newsome, deliverin' the milk.

(HOWIE NEWSOME, *about thirty, in overalls, comes along Main Street from the left, walking beside an invisible horse and wagon and carrying an imaginary rack with milk bottles. The sound of clinking milk bottles is heard. He leaves some bottles at Mrs. Webb's trellis, then, crossing the stage to Mrs. Gibbs', he stops center to talk to Dr. Gibbs*)

HOWIE NEWSOME Morning, Doc.
DR. GIBBS Morning, Howie.
HOWIE NEWSOME Somebody sick?
DR. GIBBS Pair of twins over to Mrs. Goruslawski's.
HOWIE NEWSOME Twins, eh? This town's gettin' bigger every year.
DR. GIBBS Goin' to rain, Howie?
HOWIE NEWSOME No, no. Fine day—that'll burn through. Come on, Bessie.

DR. GIBBS Hello Bessie. (*He strokes the horse, which has remained up center*) How old is she, Howie?
HOWIE NEWSOME Going on seventeen. Bessie's all mixed up about the route ever since the Lockharts stopped takin' their quart of milk every day. She wants to leave 'em a quart just the same—keeps scolding me the hull trip. (*He reaches* MRS. GIBBS' *back door. She is waiting for him*)
MRS. GIBBS Good morning, Howie.
HOWIE NEWSOME Morning, Mrs. Gibbs. Doc's just comin' down the street.
MRS. GIBBS Is he? Seems like you're late today.
HOWIE NEWSOME Yes. Somep'n went wrong with the separator. Don't know what 'twas. (*He passes* DR. GIBBS *up center*) Doc!
DR. GIBBS Howie!
MRS. GIBBS (*Calling upstairs*) Children! Children! Time to get up.
HOWIE NEWSOME Come on, Bessie! (*He goes off right*)
MRS. GIBBS George! Rebecca!

(DR. GIBBS *arrives at his back door and passes through the trellis into his house*)

MRS. GIBBS Everything all right, Frank?
DR. GIBBS Yes. I declare—easy as kittens.
MRS. GIBBS Bacon'll be ready in a minute. Set down and drink your coffee. You can catch a couple hours' sleep this morning, can't you?
DR. GIBBS Hm! . . . Mrs. Wentworth's coming at eleven. Guess I know what it's about, too. Her stummick ain't what it ought to be.
MRS. GIBBS All told, you won't get more'n three hours' sleep. Frank Gibbs, I don't know what's goin' to become of you. I do wish I could get you to go away someplace and take a rest. I think it would do you good.
MRS. WEBB Emileeee! Time to get up! Wally! Seven o'clock!
MRS. GIBBS I declare, you got to speak to George. Seems like something's come over him lately. He's no help to me at all. I can't even get him to cut me some wood.
DR. GIBBS (*Washing and drying his hands at the sink.* MRS. GIBBS *is busy at the stove*) Is he sassy to you?
MRS GIBBS No. He just whines! All he thinks about is that baseball—George! Rebecca! You'll be late for school.
DR. GIBBS M-m-m . . .
MRS. GIBBS George!
DR. GIBBS George, look sharp!
GEORGE'S VOICE Yes, Pa!

DR. GIBBS (*As he goes off the stage*) Don't you hear your mother calling you? I guess I'll go upstairs and get forty winks.
MRS. WEBB Walleee! Emileee! You'll be late for school! Walleee! You wash yourself good or I'll come up and do it myself.
REBECCA GIBBS' VOICE Ma! What dress shall I wear?
MRS. GIBBS Don't make a noise. Your father's been out all night and needs his sleep. I washed and ironed the blue gingham for you special.
REBECCA Ma, I hate that dress.
MRS. GIBBS Oh, hush-up-with-you.
REBECCA Every day I go to school dressed like a sick turkey.
MRS. GIBBS Now, Rebecca, you always look *very* nice.
REBECCA Mama, George's throwing soap at me.
MRS. GIBBS I'll come and slap the both of you,—that's what I'll do.

(*A factory whistle sounds. The* CHILDREN *dash in and take their places at the tables. Right,* GEORGE, *about sixteen, and* REBECCA, *eleven. Left,* EMILY *and* WALLY, *same ages. They carry strapped schoolbooks*)

STAGE MANAGER We've got a factory in our town too—hear it? Makes blankets. Cartwrights own it and it brung 'em a fortune.
MRS. WEBB Children! Now I won't have it. Breakfast is just as good as any other meal and I won't have you gobbling like wolves. It'll stunt your growth,—that's a fact. Put away your book, Wally.
WALLY Aw, Ma! By ten o'clock I got to know all about Canada.
MRS. WEBB You know the rule's well as I do—no books at table. As for me, I'd rather have my children healthy than bright.
EMILY I'm both, Mama: you know I am. I'm the brightest girl in school for my age. I have a wonderful memory.
MRS. WEBB Eat your breakfast.
WALLY I'm bright, too, when I'm looking at my stamp collection.
MRS. GIBBS I'll speak to your father about it when he's rested. Seems to me twenty-five cents a week's enough for a boy your age. I declare I don't know how you spend it all.
GEORGE Aw, Ma,—I gotta lotta things to buy.
MRS. GIBBS Strawberry phosphates—that's what you spend it on.
GEORGE I don't see how Rebecca comes to have so much money. She has more'n a dollar.
REBECCA (*Spoon in mouth, dreamily*) I've been saving it up gradual.
MRS. GIBBS Well, dear, I think it's a good thing to spend some every now and then.
REBECCA Mama, do you know what I love most in the world—do you?—Money.

MRS. GIBBS Eat your breakfast.
THE CHILDREN Mama, there's first bell.—I gotta hurry.—I don't want any more.—I gotta hurry.

The CHILDREN *rise, seize their books and dash out through the trellises. They meet, down center, and chattering, walk to Main Street, then turn left. The* STAGE MANAGER *goes off, unobtrusively, right*)

MRS. WEBB Walk fast, but you don't have to run. Wally, pull up your pants at the knee. Stand up straight, Emily.
MRS. GIBBS Tell Miss Foster I send her my best congratulations—can you remember that?
REBECCA Yes, Ma.
MRS. GIBBS You look real nice, Rebecca. Pick up your feet.
ALL Good-by.

(Mrs. *Gibbs fills her apron with food for the chickens and comes down to the footlights*)

MRS. GIBBS Here, chick, chick, chick.
No, go away, you. Go away.
Here, chick, chick, chick.
What's the matter with *you?* Fight, fight, fight,—that's all you do. Hm . . . *you* don't belong to me. Where'd you come from?

(*She shakes her apron*)

Oh, don't be so scared. Nobody's going to hurt you.

(MRS. WEBB *is sitting on the bench by her trellis, stringing beans*[1])

Good morning, Myrtle. How's your cold?
MRS. WEBB Well, I still get that tickling feeling in my throat. I told Charles I didn't know as I'd go to choir practice tonight. Wouldn't be any use.
MRS. GIBBS Have you tried singing over your voice?
MRS. WEBB Yes, but somehow I can't do that and stay on the key. While I'm resting myself I thought I'd string some of these beans.
MRS. GIBBS (*Rolling up her sleeves as she crosses the stage for a chat*) Let me help you. Beans have been good this year.
MRS. WEBB I've decided to put up forty quarts if it kills me. The children say they hate 'em, but I notice they're able to get 'em down all winter.

[1] Removing the strings from string beans.

(*Pause. Brief sound of chickens cackling*)
MRS. GIBBS Now, Myrtle. I've got to tell you something, because if I don't tell somebody I'll burst.
MRS. WEBB Why, Julia Gibbs!
MRS. GIBBS Here, give me some more of those beans. Myrtle, did one of those secondhand-furniture men from Boston come to see you last Friday?
MRS. WEBB No-o.
MRS. GIBBS Well, he called on me. First I thought he was a patient wantin' to see Dr. Gibbs. 'N he wormed his way into my parlor, and, Myrtle Webb, he offered me three hundred and fifty dollars for Grandmother Wentworth's highboy, as I'm sitting here!
MRS. WEBB Why, Julia Gibbs!
MRS. GIBBS He did! That old thing! Why, it was so big I didn't know where to put it and I almost give it to Cousin Hester Wilcox.
MRS. WEBB Well, you're going to take it, aren't you?
MRS. GIBBS I don't know.
MRS. WEBB You don't know—three hundred and fifty dollars! What's come over you?
MRS. GIBBS Well, if I could get the Doctor to take the money and go away someplace on a real trip, I'd sell it like that.—Y'know, Myrtle, it's been the dream of my life to see Paris, France.—Oh, I don't know. It sounds crazy, I suppose, but for years I've been promising myself that if we ever had the chance—
MRS. WEBB How does the Doctor feel about it?
MRS. GIBBS Well, I did beat about the bush a little and said that if I got a legacy—that's the way I put it—I'd make him take me somewhere.
MRS. WEBB M-m-m . . . What did he say?
MRS. GIBBS You know how he is. I haven't heard a serious word out of him since I've known him. No, he said, it might make him discontented with Grover's Corners to go traipsin' about Europe; better let well enough alone, he says. Every two years he makes a trip to the battlefields of the Civil War and that's enough treat for anybody, he says.
MRS. WEBB Well, Mr. Webb just *admires* the way Dr. Gibbs knows everything about the Civil War. Mr. Webb's a good mind to give up Napoleon and move over to the Civil War, only Dr. Gibbs being one of the greatest experts in the country just makes him despair.
MRS. GIBBS It's a fact! Dr. Gibbs is never so happy as when he's at Antietam or Gettysburg. The times I've walked over those hills, Myrtle, stopping at every bush and pacing it all out, like we were going to buy it.

MRS. WEBB Well, if that secondhand man's really serious about buyin' it, Julia, you sell it. And then you'll get to see Paris, all right. Just keep droppin' hints from time to time—that's how I got to see the Atlantic Ocean, y'know.

MRS. GIBBS Oh, I'm sorry I mentioned it. Only it seems to me that once in your life before you die you ought to see a country where they don't talk in English and don't even want to.

(*The* STAGE MANAGER *enters briskly from the right. He tips his hat to the ladies, who nod their heads*)

STAGE MANAGER Thank you, ladies. Thank you very much.

MRS. GIBBS *and* MRS. WEBB *gather up their things, return into their homes and disappear*)

Now we're going to skip a few hours.
But first we want a little more information about the town, kind of a scientific account, you might say.
So I've asked Professor Willard of our State University to sketch in a few details of our past history here.
Is Professor Willard here?

(PROFESSOR WILLARD, *a rural savant, pince-nez on a wide satin ribbon, enters from the right with some notes in his hand*)

May I introduce Professor Willard of our State University.
A few brief notes, thank you, Professor,—unfortunately our time is limited.

PROFESSOR WILLARD Grover's Corners . . . let me see . . . Grover's Corners lies on the old Pleistocene granite of the Appalachian range. I may say it's some of the oldest land in the world. We're very proud of that. A shelf of Devonian basalt crosses it with vestiges of Mesozoic shale, and some sandstone outcroppings; but that's all more recent: two hundred, three hundred million years old.
Some highly interesting fossils have been found . . . I may say: unique fossils . . . two miles out of town, in Silas Peckham's cow pasture. They can be seen at the museum in our University at any time—that is, at any reasonable time. Shall I read some of Professor Gruber's notes on the meteorological situation—mean precipitation, et cetera?

STAGE MANAGER Afraid we won't have time for that, Professor. We might have a few words on the history of man here.

PROFESSOR WILLARD Yes . . . anthropological data: Early Amerindian stock. Cotahatchee tribes . . . no evidence before the tenth century of this era . . . hm . . . now entirely disappeared . . . possible traces in three families. Migration toward the end of the seventeenth century of English brachiocephalic blue-eyed stock . . . for the most part. Since then some Slav and Mediterranean—

STAGE MANAGER   And the population, Professor Willard?

PROFESSOR WILLARD   Within the town limits: 2,640.

STAGE MANAGER   Just a moment, Professor. (*He whispers into the* PROFESSOR'S *ear*)

PROFESSOR WILLARD   Oh, yes, indeed?—The population, *at the moment*, is 2,642. The Postal District brings in 507 more, making a total of 3,149.—Mortality and birth rates: constant.—By MacPherson's gauge: 6.032.

STAGE MANAGER   Thank you very much, Professor. We're all very much obliged to you, I'm sure.

PROFESSOR WILLARD   Not at all, sir; not at all.

STAGE MANAGER   This way, Professor, and thank you again.

(*Exit* PROFESSOR WILLARD)

Now the political and social report: Editor Webb.—Oh, Mr. Webb?

(MRS. WEBB *appears at her back door*)

MRS. WEBB   He'll be here in a minute. . . . He just cut his hand while he was eatin' an apple.

STAGE MANAGER   Thank you, Mrs. Webb.

MRS. WEBB   Charles! Everybody's waitin'.

(*Exit* MRS. WEBB)

STAGE MANAGER   Mr. Webb is Publisher and Editor of the Grover's Corners *Sentinel*. That's our local paper, y'know.

(MR. WEBB *enters from his house, pulling on his coat. His finger is bound in a handkerchief*)

MR. WEBB   Well . . . I don't have to tell you that we're run here by a Board of Selectmen.—All males vote at the age of twenty-one. Women vote indirect. We're lower middle class: sprinkling of professional men . . . ten per cent illiterate laborers. Politically, we're eighty-six per cent Republicans; six per cent Democrats; four per cent Socialists; rest, indifferent.
Religiously, we're eighty-five per cent Protestants; twelve per cent Catholics; rest, indifferent.

STAGE MANAGER   Have you any comments, Mr. Webb?

MR. WEBB   Very ordinary town, if you ask me. Little better behaved than most. Probably a lot duller. But our young people here seem to like it well enough. Ninety per cent of 'em graduating from high school settle down right here to live—even when they've been away to college.

STAGE MANAGER Now, is there anyone in the audience who would like to ask Editor Webb anything about the town?

WOMAN IN THE BALCONY Is there much drinking in Grover's Corners?

MR. WEBB Well, ma'am, I wouldn't know what you'd call *much*. Satiddy nights the farmhands meet down in Ellery Greenough's stable and holler some. We've got one or two town drunks, but they're always having remorses every time an evangelist comes to town. No, ma'am, I'd say likker ain't a regular thing in the home here, except in the medicine chest. Right good for snake bite, y'know—always was.

BELLIGERENT MAN AT BACK OF AUDITORIUM Is there no one in town aware of—

STAGE MANAGER Come forward, will you, where we can all hear you— What were you saying?

BELLIGERENT MAN Is there no one in town aware of social injustice and industrial inequality?

MR. WEBB Oh, yes, everybody is—somethin' terrible. Seems like they spend most of their time talking about who's rich and who's poor.

BELLIGERENT MAN Then why don't they do something about it? (*He withdraws without waiting for an answer*)

MR. WEBB Well, I dunno. . . . I guess we're all hunting like everybody else for a way the diligent and sensible can rise to the top and the lazy and quarrelsome can sink to the bottom. But it ain't easy to find. Meanwhile, we do all we can to help those that can't help themselves and those that can we leave alone.—Are there any other questions?

LADY IN A BOX Oh, Mr. Webb? Mr. Webb, is there any culture or love of beauty in Grover's Corners?

MR. WEBB Well, ma'am, there ain't much—not in the sense you mean. Come to think of it, there's some girls that play the piano at High School Commencement; but they ain't happy about it. No, ma'am, there isn't much culture; but maybe this is the place to tell you that we've got a lot of pleasures of a kind here: we like the sun comin' up over the mountain in the morning, and we all notice a good deal about the birds. We pay a lot of attention to them. And we watch the change of the seasons; yes, everybody knows about them. But those other things—you're right, ma'am,—there ain't much.—*Robinson Crusoe* and the Bible; and Handel's "Largo," we all know that; and Whistler's "Mother"—those are just about as far as we go.

LADY IN A BOX So I thought. Thank you, Mr. Webb.

STAGE MANAGER Thank you, Mr. Webb.

(MR. WEBB *retires*)

Now, we'll go back to the town. It's early afternoon. All 2,642 have had their dinners and all the dishes have been washed.

(MR. WEBB, *having removed his coat, returns and starts pushing a lawn mower to and fro beside his house*)

There's an early-afternoon calm in our town: a buzzin' and a hummin' from the school buildings; only a few buggies on Main Street—the horses dozing at the hitching posts; you all remember what it's like. Doc Gibbs is in his office, tapping people and making them say "ah." Mr. Webb's cuttin' his lawn over there; one man in ten thinks it's a privilege to push his own lawn mower.
No, sir. It's later than I thought. There are the children coming home from school already.

(*Shrill girls' voices are heard, off left.* EMILY *comes along Main Street, carrying some books. There are some signs that she is imagining herself to be a lady of startling elegance*)

EMILY   I can't, Lois. I've got to go home and help my mother. I promised.
MR. WEBB   Emily, walk simply. Who do you think you are today?
EMILY   Papa, you're terrible. One minute you tell me to stand up straight and the next minute you call me names. I just don't listen to you. (*She gives him an abrupt kiss*)
MR. WEBB   Golly, I never got a kiss from such a great lady before.

(*He goes out of sight.* EMILY *leans over and picks some flowers by the gate of her house.* GEORGE GIBBS *comes careening down Main Street. He is throwing a ball up to dizzying heights, and waiting to catch it again. This sometimes requires his taking six steps backward. He bumps into an* OLD LADY *invisible to us*)

GEORGE   Excuse me, Mrs. Forrest.
STAGE MANAGER (*As* MRS. FORREST)   Go out and play in the fields, young man. You got no business playing baseball on Main Street.
GEORGE   Awfully sorry, Mrs. Forrest.—Hello, Emily.
EMILY   H'lo.
GEORGE   You made a fine speech in class.
EMILY   Well ... I was really ready to make a speech about the Monroe Doctrine, but at the last minute Miss Corcoran made me talk about the Louisiana Purchase instead. I worked an awful long time on both of them.
GEORGE   Gee, it's funny, Emily. From my window up there I can just see your head nights when you're doing your homework over in your room.

EMILY Why, can you?
GEORGE You certainly do stick to it, Emily. I don't see how you can sit still that long. I guess you like school.
EMILY Well, I always feel it's something you have to go through.
GEORGE Yeah.
EMILY I don't mind it really. It passes the time.
GEORGE Yeah.—Emily, what do you think? We might work out a kinda telegraph from your window to mine; and once in a while you could give me a kinda hint or two about one of those algebra problems. I don't mean the answers, Emily, of course not . . . just some little hint . . .
EMILY Oh, I think *hints* are allowed.—So—ah—if you get stuck, George, you whistle to me; and I'll give you some hints.
GEORGE Emily, you're just naturally bright, I guess.
EMILY I figure that it's just the way a person's born.
GEORGE Yeah. But, you see, I want to be a farmer, and my Uncle Luke says whenever I'm ready I can come over and work on his farm and if I'm any good I can just gradually have it.
EMILY You mean the house and everything?

(*Enter* MRS. WEBB *with a large bowl and sits on the bench by her trellis*)

GEORGE Yeah. Well, thanks . . . I better be getting out to the baseball field. Thanks for the talk, Emily.—Good afternoon, Mrs. Webb.
MRS. WEBB Good afternoon, George.
GEORGE So long, Emily.
EMILY So long, George.
MRS. WEBB Emily, come and help me string these beans for the winter. George Gibbs let himself have a real conversation, didn't he? Why, he's growing up. How old would George be?
EMILY I don't know.
MRS. WEBB Let's see. He must be almost sixteen.
EMILY Mama, I made a speech in class today and I was very good.
MRS. WEBB You must recite it to your father at supper. What was it about?
EMILY The Louisiana Purchase. It was like silk off a spool. I'm going to make speeches all my life.—Mama, are these big enough?
MRS. WEBB Try and get them a little bigger if you can.
EMILY Mama, will you answer me a question, serious?
MRS. WEBB Seriously, dear—not serious.
EMILY Seriously,—will you?
MRS. WEBB Of course, I will.

EMILY Mama, am I good looking?
MRS. WEBB Yes, of course you are. All my children have got good features. I'd be ashamed if they hadn't.
EMILY Oh, Mama, that's not what I mean. What I mean is: am I pretty?
MRS. WEBB I've already told you, yes. Now that's enough of that. You have a nice young pretty face. I never heard of such foolishness.
EMILY Oh, Mama, you never tell us the truth about anything.
MRS. WEBB I *am* telling you the truth.
EMILY Mama, were *you* pretty?
MRS. WEBB Yes, I was, if I do say it. I was the prettiest girl in town next to Mamie Cartwright.
EMILY But, Mama, you've got to say *some*thing about me. Am I pretty enough . . . to get anybody . . . to get people interested in me?
MRS. WEBB Emily, you make me tired. Now stop it. You're pretty enough for all normal purposes.—Come along now and bring that bowl with you.
EMILY Oh, Mama, you're no help at all.
STAGE MANAGER Thank you. Thank you! That'll do. We'll have to interrupt again here. Thank you, Mrs. Webb; thank you, Emily.

(MRS. WEBB *and* EMILY *withdraw*)

There are some more things we want to explore about this town.

(*He comes to the center of the stage. During the following speech the lights gradually dim to darkness, leaving only a spot on him*)

I think this is a good time to tell you that the Cartwright interests have just begun building a new bank in Grover's Corners—had to go to Vermont for the marble, sorry to say. And they've asked a friend of mine what they should put in the cornerstone for people to dig up . . . a thousand years from now. . . . Of course, they've put in a copy of the *New York Times* and a copy of Mr. Webb's *Sentinel*. . . . We're kind of interested in this because some scientific fellas have found a way of painting all that reading matter with a glue—a silicate glue—that'll make it keep a thousand—two thousand years.
We're putting in a Bible . . . and the Constitution of the United States—and a copy of William Shakespeare's plays. What do you say, folks? What do you think?
Y'know—Babylon once had two million people in it, and all we know about 'em is the names of the kings and some copies of wheat contracts . . . and contracts for the sale of slaves. Yet every night all those

families sat down to supper, and the father came home from his work, and the smoke went up the chimney,—same as here. And even in Greece and Rome, all we know about the *real* life of the people is what we can piece together out of the joking poems and the comedies they wrote for the theatre back then.

So I'm going to have a copy of this play put in the cornerstone and the people a thousand years from now'll know a few simple facts about us—more than the Treaty of Versailles and the Lindbergh flight. See what I mean?

So—people a thousand years from now—this is the way we were in the provinces north of New York at the beginning of the twentieth century.—This is the way we were: in our growing up and in our marrying and in our living and in our dying.

(*A choir partially concealed in the orchestra pit has begun singing "Blessed Be the Tie That Binds."* SIMON STIMSON *stands directing them. Two ladders have been pushed onto the stage; they serve as indication of the second story in the Gibbs and Webb houses.* GEORGE *and* EMILY *mount them, and apply themselves to their schoolwork.* DR. GIBBS *has entered and is seated in his kitchen reading*)

Well!—good deal of time's gone by. It's evening.

You can hear choir practice going on in the Congregational Church. The children are at home doing their schoolwork.

The day's running down like a tired clock.

SIMON STIMSON   Now look here, everybody. Music come into the world to give pleasure.—Softer! Softer! Get it out of your heads that music's only good when it's loud. You leave loudness to the Methodists. You couldn't beat 'em, even if you wanted to. Now again. Tenors!

GEORGE   Hssst! Emily!
EMILY   Hello.
GEORGE   Hello!
EMILY   I can't work at all. The moonlight's so *terrible.*
GEORGE   Emily, did you get the third problem?
EMILY   Which?
GEORGE   The *third?*
EMILY   Why, yes, George—that's the easiest of them all.
GEORGE   I don't see it. Emily, can you give me a hint?
EMILY   I'll tell you one thing: the answer's in yards.
GEORGE   ! ! ! In yards? How do you mean?
EMILY   In *square* yards.
GEORGE   Oh . . . in square yards.

EMILY Yes, George, don't you see?
GEORGE Yeah.
EMILY In square yards of *wallpaper*.
GEORGE Wallpaper,—oh, I see. Thanks a lot, Emily.
EMILY You're welcome. My, isn't the moonlight *terrible?* And choir practice going on.—I think if you hold your breath you can hear the train all the way to Contoocook. Hear it?
GEORGE M-m-m—What do you know!
EMILY Well, I guess I better go back and try to work.
GEORGE Good night, Emily. And thanks.
EMILY Good night, George.
SIMON STIMSON Before I forget it: how many of you will be able to come in Tuesday afternoon and sing at Fred Hersey's wedding?—show your hands. That'll be fine; that'll be right nice. We'll do the same music we did for Jane Trowbridge's last month.—Now we'll do: "Art Thou Weary; Art Thou Languid?" It's a question, ladies and gentlemen, make it talk. Ready.
DR. GIBBS Oh, George, can you come down a minute?
GEORGE Yes, Pa. (*He descends the ladder*)
DR. GIBBS Make yourself comfortable, George; I'll only keep you a minute. George, how old are you?
GEORGE I? I'm sixteen, almost seventeen.
DR. GIBBS What do you want to do after school's over?
GEORGE Why, you know, Pa. I want to be a farmer on Uncle Luke's farm.
DR. GIBBS You'll be willing, will you, to get up early and milk and feed the stock . . . and you'll be able to hoe and hay all day?
GEORGE Sure, I will. What are you . . . what do you mean, Pa?
DR. GIBBS Well, George, while I was in my office today I heard a funny sound . . . and what do you think it was? It was your mother chopping wood. There you see your mother—getting up early; cooking meals all day long; washing and ironing;—and still she has to go out in the back yard and chop wood. I suppose she just got tired of asking you. She just gave up and decided it was easier to do it herself. And you eat her meals, and put on the clothes she keeps nice for you, and you run off and play baseball,—like she's some hired girl we keep around the house but that we don't like very much. Well, I knew all I had to do was call your attention to it. Here's a handkerchief, son. George, I've decided to raise your spending money twenty-five cents a week. Not, of course, for chopping wood for your mother, because that's a present you give her, but because you're getting older—and I imagine there are lots of things you must find to do with it.

GEORGE Thanks, Pa.
DR. GIBBS Let's see—tomorrow's your payday. You can count on it—Hmm. Probably Rebecca'll feel she ought to have some more too. Wonder what could have happened to your mother. Choir practice never was as late as this before.
GEORGE It's only half past eight, Pa.
DR. GIBBS I don't know why she's in that old choir. She hasn't any more voice than an old crow. . . . Traipsin' around the streets at this hour of the night . . . Just about time you retired, don't you think?
GEORGE Yes, Pa. (GEORGE *mounts to his place on the ladder*)

(*Laughter and good nights can be heard on stage left and presently* MRS. GIBBS, MRS. SOAMES *and* MRS. WEBB *come down Main Street. When they arrive at the corner of the stage they stop*)

MRS. SOAMES Good night, Martha. Good night, Mr. Foster.
MRS. WEBB I'll tell Mr. Webb; I *know* he'll want to put it in the paper.
MRS. GIBBS My, it's late!
MRS. SOAMES Good night, Irma.
MRS. GIBBS Real nice choir practice, wa'n't it? Myrtle Webb! Look at that moon, will you! Tsk-tsk-tsk. Potato weather, for sure.

(*They are silent a moment, gazing up at the moon*)

MRS. SOAMES Naturally I didn't want to say a word about it in front of those others, but now we're alone—really, it's the worst scandal that ever was in this town!
MRS. GIBBS What?
MRS. SOAMES Simon Stimson!
MRS. GIBBS Now, Louella!
MRS. SOAMES But, Julia! To have the organist of a church *drink* and *drunk* year after year. You know he was drunk tonight.
MRS. GIBBS Now, Louella! We all know about Mr. Stimson, and we all know about the troubles he's been through, and Dr. Ferguson knows too, and if Dr. Ferguson keeps him on there in his job the only thing the rest of us can do is just not to notice it.
MRS. SOAMES *Not to notice it!* But it's getting worse.
MRS. WEBB No, it isn't, Louella. It's getting better. I've been in that choir twice as long as you have. It doesn't happen anywhere near so often. . . . My, I hate to go to bed on a night like this.—I better hurry. Those children'll be sitting up till all hours. Good night, Louella.

(*They all exchange good nights. She hurries downstage, enters her house and disappears*)

MRS. GIBBS Can you get home safe, Louella?

MRS. SOAMES   It's as bright as day. I can see Mr. Soames scowling at the window now. You'd think we'd been to a dance the way the menfolk carry on.

(*More good nights.* MRS. GIBBS *arrives at her home and passes through the trellis into the kitchen*)

MRS. GIBBS   Well, we had a real good time.
DR. GIBBS   You're late enough.
MRS. GIBBS   Why, Frank, it ain't any later 'n usual.
DR. GIBBS   And you stopping at the corner to gossip with a lot of hens.
MRS. GIBBS   Now, Frank, don't be grouchy. Come out and smell the heliotrope in the moonlight.

(*They stroll out arm in arm along the footlights*)

Isn't that wonderful? What did you do all the time I was away?
DR. GIBBS   Oh, I read—as usual. What were the girls gossiping about tonight?
MRS. GIBBS   Well, believe me, Frank—there is something to gossip about.
DR. GIBBS   Hmm! Simon Stimson far gone, was he?
MRS. GIBBS   Worst I've ever seen him. How'll that end, Frank? Dr. Ferguson can't forgive him forever.
DR. GIBBS   I guess I know more about Simon Stimson's affairs than anybody in this town. Some people ain't made for small-town life. I don't know how that'll end; but there's nothing we can do but just leave it alone. Come, get in.
MRS. GIBBS   No, not yet . . . Frank, I'm worried about you.
DR. GIBBS   What are you worried about?
MRS. GIBBS   I think it's my duty to make plans for you to get a real rest and change. And if I get that legacy, well, I'm going to insist on it.
DR. GIBBS   Now, Julia, there's no sense in going over that again.
MRS. GIBBS   Frank, you're just *unreasonable!*
DR. GIBBS   (*Starting into the house*)   Come on, Julia, it's getting late. First thing you know you'll catch cold. I gave George a piece of my mind tonight. I reckon you'll have your wood chopped for a while anyway. No, no, start getting upstairs.
MRS. GIBBS   Oh, dear. There's always so many things to pick up, seems like. You know, Frank, Mrs. Fairchild always locks her front door every night. All those people up that part of town do.
DR. GIBBS   (*Blowing out the lamp*)   They're all getting citified, that's the trouble with them. They haven't got nothing fit to burgle and everybody knows it.

(*They disappear.* REBECCA *climbs up the ladder beside* GEORGE)

GEORGE Get out, Rebecca. There's only room for one at this window. You're always spoiling everything.
REBECCA Well, let me look just a minute.
GEORGE Use your own window.
REBECCA I did, but there's no moon there. . . . George, do you know what I think, do you? I think maybe the moon's getting nearer and nearer and there'll be a big 'splosion.
GEORGE Rebecca, you don't know anything. If the moon were getting nearer, the guys that sit up all night with telescopes would see it first and they'd tell about it, and it'd be in all the newspapers.
REBECCA George, is the moon shining on South America, Canada and half the whole world?
GEORGE Well—prob'ly is.

(*The* STAGE MANAGER *strolls on. Pause. The sound of crickets is heard*)

STAGE MANAGER Nine thirty. Most of the lights are out. No, there's Constable Warren trying a few doors on Main Street. And here comes Editor Webb, after putting his newspaper to bed.

(MR. WARREN, *an elderly policeman, comes along Main Street from the right,* MR. WEBB *from the left*)

MR. WEBB Good evening, Bill.
CONSTABLE WARREN Evenin', Mr. Webb.
MR. WEBB Quite a moon!
CONSTABLE WARREN Yepp.
MR. WEBB All quiet tonight?
CONSTABLE WARREN Simon Stimson is rollin' around a little. Just saw his wife movin' out to hunt for him so I looked the other way—there he is now.

(SIMON STIMSON *comes down Main Street from the left, only a trace of unsteadiness in his walk*)

MR. WEBB Good evening, Simon . . . Town seems to have settled down for the night pretty well. . . .

(SIMON STIMSON *comes up to him and pauses a moment and stares at him, swaying slightly*)

Good evening . . . Yes, most of the town's settled down for the night, Simon. . . . I guess we better do the same. Can I walk along a ways with you?

(SIMON STIMSON *continues on his way without a word and disappears at the right*)

Good night.
CONSTABLE WARREN   I don't know how that's goin' to end, Mr. Webb.
MR. WEBB   Well, he's seen a peck of trouble, one thing after another. . . . Oh, Bill . . . if you see my boy smoking cigarettes, just give him a word, will you? He thinks a lot of you, Bill.
CONSTABLE WARREN   I don't think he smokes no cigarettes, Mr. Webb. Leastways, not more'n two or three a year.
MR. WEBB   Hm . . . I hope not.—Well, good night, Bill.
CONSTABLE WARREN   Good night, Mr. Webb. (*Exit*)
MR. WEBB   Who's that up there? Is that you, Myrtle?
EMILY   No, it's me, Papa.
MR. WEBB   Why aren't you in bed?
EMILY   I don't know. I just can't sleep yet, Papa. The moonlight's so *won*-derful. And the smell of Mrs. Gibbs' heliotrope. Can you smell it?
MR. WEBB   Hm . . . Yes. Haven't any troubles on your mind, have you, Emily?
EMILY   *Troubles,* Papa? No.
MR. WEBB   Well, enjoy yourself, but don't let your mother catch you. Good night, Emily.
EMILY   Good night, Papa.

(MR. WEBB *crosses into the house, whistling "Blessed Be the Tie That Binds" and disappears*)

REBECCA   I never told you about that letter Jane Crofut got from her minister when she was sick. He wrote Jane a letter and on the envelope the address was like this: It said: Jane Crofut; The Crofut Farm; Grover's Corners; Sutton County; New Hampshire; United States of America.
GEORGE   What's funny about that?
REBECCA   But listen, it's not finished: the United States of America; Continent of North America; Western Hemisphere; the Earth; the Solar System; the Universe; the Mind of God[2]—that's what it said on the envelope.
GEORGE   What do you know!
REBECCA   And the postman brought it just the same.
GEORGE   What do you know!
STAGE MANAGER   That's the end of the First Act, friends. You can go and smoke now, those that smoke.

---

[2] Cf. *Portrait of the Artist as a Young Man* by James Joyce: "Stephen Dedalus, Class of Elements, Clongowes Wood College, Sallins, County Kildare, Ireland, Europe, The World, The Universe."

Act Two

The tables and chairs of the two kitchens are still on the stage. The ladders and the small bench have been withdrawn. The STAGE MANAGER *has been at his accustomed place watching the audience return to its seats.*

STAGE MANAGER   Three years have gone by.
Yes, the sun's come up over a thousand times.
Summers and winters have cracked the mountains a little bit more and the rains have brought down some of the dirt.
Some babies that weren't even born before have begun talking regular sentences already; and a number of people who thought they were right young and spry have noticed that they can't bound up a flight of stairs like they used to, without their heart fluttering a little.
All that can happen in a thousand days.
Nature's been pushing and contriving in other ways, too: a number of young people fell in love and got married.
Yes, the mountain got bit away a few fractions of an inch; millions of gallons of water went by the mill; and here and there a new home was set up under a roof.
Almost everybody in the world gets married,—you know what I mean? In our town there aren't hardly any exceptions. Most everybody in the world climbs into their graves married.
The First Act was called the Daily Life. This act is called Love and Marriage. There's another act coming after this: I reckon you can guess what that's about.
So:
It's three years later. It's 1904.
It's July 7th, just after High School Commencement.
That's the time most of our young people jump up and get married.
Soon as they've passed their last examinations in solid geometry and Cicero's Orations, looks like they suddenly feel themselves fit to be married.
It's early morning. Only this time it's been raining. It's been pouring and thundering.
Mrs. Gibbs' garden, and Mrs. Webb's here: drenched.
All those bean poles and pea vines: drenched.

All yesterday over there on Main Street, the rain looked like curtains being blown along.
Hm . . . it may begin again any minute.
There! You can hear the 5:45 for Boston.

(MRS. GIBBS *and* MRS. WEBB *enter their kitchen and start the day as in the First Act*)

And there's Mrs. Gibbs and Mrs. Webb come down to make breakfast, just as though it were an ordinary day. I don't have to point out to the women in my audience that those ladies they see before them, both of those ladies cooked three meals a day—one of 'em for twenty years, the other for forty—and no summer vacation. They brought up two children apiece, washed, cleaned the house,—and *never a nervous breakdown.*

It's like what one of those Middle West poets said: You've got to love life to have life, and you've got to have life to love life. . . .
It's what they call a vicious circle.

HOWIE NEWSOME (*Off stage left*)   Giddap, Bessie!
STAGE MANAGER   Here comes Howie Newsome delivering the milk. And there's Si Crowell delivering the papers like his brother before him.

(SI CROWELL *has entered hurling imaginary newspapers into doorways;* HOWIE NEWSOME *has come along Main Street with Bessie*)

SI CROWELL   Morning, Howie.
HOWIE NEWSOME   Morning, Si.—Anything in the papers I ought to know?
SI CROWELL   Nothing much, except we're losing about the best baseball pitcher Grover's Corners ever had—George Gibbs.
HOWIE NEWSOME   Reckon he is.
SI CROWELL   He could hit and run bases, too.
HOWIE NEWSOME   Yep. Mighty fine ball player.—Whoa! Bessie! I guess I can stop and talk if I've a mind to!
SI CROWELL   I don't see how he could give up a thing like that just to get married. Would you, Howie?
HOWIE NEWSOME   Can't tell, Si. Never had no talent that way.

(CONSTABLE WARREN *enters. They exchange good mornings*)

You're up early, Bill.
CONSTABLE WARREN   Seein' if there's anything I can do to prevent a flood. River's been risin' all night.
HOWIE NEWSOME   Si Crowell's all worked up here about George Gibbs' retiring from baseball.

CONSTABLE WARREN   Yes, sir; that's the way it goes. Back in '84 we had a player, Si—even George Gibbs couldn't touch him. Name of Hank Todd. Went down to Maine and become a parson. Wonderful ball player.—Howie, how does the weather look to you?
HOWIE NEWSOME   Oh, 'tain't bad. Think maybe it'll clear up for good.

(CONSTABLE WARREN *and* SI CROWELL *continue on their way.* HOWIE NEWSOME *brings the milk first to Mrs. Gibbs' house. She meets him by the trellis*)

MRS. GIBBS   Good morning, Howie. Do you think it's going to rain again?
HOWIE NEWSOME   Morning, Mrs. Gibbs. It rained so heavy, I think maybe it'll clear up.
MRS. GIBBS   Certainly hope it will.
HOWIE NEWSOME   How much did you want today?
MRS. GIBBS   I'm going to have a houseful of relations, Howie. Looks to me like I'll need three-a-milk and two-a-cream.
HOWIE NEWSOME   My wife says to tell you we both hope they'll be very happy, Mrs. Gibbs. Know they *will*.
MRS. GIBBS   Thanks a lot, Howie. Tell your wife I hope she gits there to the wedding.
HOWIE NEWSOME   Yes, she'll be there; she'll be there if she kin. (HOWIE NEWSOME *crosses to* MRS. WEBB'S *house*) Morning, Mrs. Webb.
MRS. WEBB   Oh, good morning, Mr. Newsome. I told you four quarts of milk, but I hope you can spare me another.
HOWIE NEWSOME   Yes'm . . . and the two of cream.
MRS. WEBB   Will it start raining again, Mr. Newsome?
HOWIE NEWSOME   Well. Just sayin' to Mrs. Gibbs as how it may lighten up. Mrs. Newsome told me to tell you as how we hope they'll both be very happy, Mrs. Webb. Know they *will*.
MRS. WEBB   Thank you, and thank Mrs. Newsome and we're counting on seeing you at the wedding.
HOWIE NEWSOME   Yes, Mrs. Webb. We hope to git there. Couldn't miss that. Come on, Bessie. (*Exit* HOWIE NEWSOME)

(DR. GIBBS *descends in shirt sleeves, and sits down at his breakfast table*)

DR. GIBBS   Well, Ma, the day has come. You're losin' one of your chicks.
MRS. GIBBS   Frank Gibbs, don't you say another word. I feel like crying every minute. Sit down and drink your coffee.
DR. GIBBS   The groom's up shaving himself—only there ain't an awful lot to shave. Whistling and singing, like he's glad to leave us.—Every now and then he says "I do" to the mirror, but it don't sound convincing to me.

MRS. GIBBS I declare, Frank, I don't know how he'll get along. I've arranged his clothes and seen to it he's put warm things on,—Frank! they're too *young*. Emily won't think of such things. He'll catch his death of cold within a week.
DR. GIBBS I was remembering my wedding morning, Julia.
MRS. GIBBS Now don't start that, Frank Gibbs.
DR. GIBBS I was the scaredest young fella in the State of New Hampshire. I thought I'd make a mistake for sure. And when I saw you comin' down that aisle I thought you were the prettiest girl I'd ever seen, but the only trouble was that I'd never seen you before. There I was in the Congregational Church marryin' a total stranger.
MRS. GIBBS And how do you think I felt!—Frank, weddings are perfectly awful things. Farces,—that's what they are! (*She puts a plate before him*) Here, I've made something for you.
DR. GIBBS Why, Julia Hersey—French toast!
MRS. GIBBS 'Tain't hard to make and I had to do *something*.

(*Pause.* DR. GIBBS *pours on the syrup*)

DR. GIBBS How'd you sleep last night, Julia?
MRS. GIBBS Well, I heard a lot of the hours struck off.
DR. GIBBS Ye-e-s! I get a shock every time I think of George setting out to be a family man—that great gangling thing!—I tell you Julia, there's nothing so terrifying in the world as a *son*. The relation of father and son is the darndest, awkwardest—
MRS. GIBBS Well, mother and daughter's no picnic, let me tell you.
DR. GIBBS They'll have a lot of troubles, I suppose, but that's none of our business. Everybody has a right to their own troubles.
MRS. GIBBS (*At the table, drinking her coffee, meditatively*) Yes . . . people are meant to go through life two by two. 'Tain't natural to be lonesome.

(*Pause.* DR. GIBBS *starts laughing*)

DR. GIBBS Julia, do you know one of the things I was scared of when I married you?
MRS. GIBBS Oh, go along with you!
DR. GIBBS I was afraid we wouldn't have material for conversation more'n'd last us a few weeks.

(*Both laugh*)

I was afraid we'd run out and eat our meals in silence, that's a fact.— Well, you and I been conversing for twenty years now without any noticeable barren spells.

MRS. GIBBS Well,—good weather, bad weather—'tain't very choice, but I always find something to say. (*She goes to the foot of the stairs*) Did you hear Rebecca stirring around upstairs?

DR. GIBBS No. Only day of the year Rebecca hasn't been managing everybody's business up there. She's hiding in her room.—I got the impression she's crying.

MRS. GIBBS Lord's sakes!—This has got to stop.—Rebecca! Rebecca! Come and get your breakfast.

(GEORGE *comes rattling down the stairs, very brisk*)

GEORGE Good morning, everybody. Only five more hours to live. (*Makes the gesture of cutting his throat, and a loud "k-k-k," and starts through the trellis*)

MRS. GIBBS George Gibbs, where are you going?

GEORGE Just stepping across the grass to see my girl.

MRS. GIBBS Now, George! You put on your overshoes. It's raining torrents. You don't go out of this house without you're prepared for it.

GEORGE Aw, Ma. It's just a *step!*

MRS. GIBBS George! You'll catch your death of cold and cough all through the service.

DR. GIBBS George, do as your mother tells you! (DR. GIBBS *goes upstairs*)

(GEORGE *returns reluctantly to the kitchen and pantomimes putting on overshoes*)

MRS. GIBBS From tomorrow on you can kill yourself in all weathers, but while you're in my house you'll live wisely, thank you.—Maybe Mrs. Webb isn't used to callers at seven in the morning.—Here, take a cup of coffee first.

GEORGE Be back in a minute. (*He crosses the stage, leaping over the puddles*) Good morning, Mother Webb.

MRS. WEBB Goodness! You frightened me!—Now, George, you can come in a minute out of the wet, but you know I can't ask you in.

GEORGE Why not—?

MRS. WEBB George, you know's well as I do: the groom can't see his bride on his wedding day, not until he sees her in church.

GEORGE Aw!—that's just a superstition.—Good morning, Mr. Webb.

(*Enter* MR. WEBB)

MR. WEBB Good morning, George.

GEORGE Mr. Webb, you don't believe in that superstition, do you?

MR. WEBB There's a lot of common sense in some superstitions, George. (*He sits at the table, facing right*)

MRS. WEBB Millions have folla'd it, George, and you don't want to be the first to fly in the face of custom.
GEORGE How is Emily?
MRS. WEBB She hasn't waked up yet. I haven't heard a sound out of her.
GEORGE Emily's *asleep!!!*
MRS. WEBB No wonder! We were up 'til all hours, sewing and packing. Now I'll tell you what I'll do; you set down here a minute with Mr. Webb and drink this cup of coffee; and I'll go upstairs and see she doesn't come down and surprise you. There's some bacon, too; but don't be long about it.

(*Exit* MRS. WEBB. *Embarrassed silence.* MR. WEBB *dunks doughnuts in his coffee. More silence*)

MR. WEBB (*Suddenly and loudly*) Well, George, how are you?
GEORGE (*Startled, choking over his coffee*) Oh, fine, I'm fine. (*Pause*) Mr. Webb, what sense could there be in a superstition like that?
MR. WEBB Well, you see,—on her wedding morning a girl's head's apt to be full of . . . clothes and one thing and another. Don't you think that's probably it?
GEORGE Ye-e-s. I never thought of that.
MR. WEBB A girl's apt to be a mite nervous on her wedding day. (*Pause*)
GEORGE I wish a fellow could get married without all that marching up and down.
MR. WEBB Every man that's ever lived has felt that way about it, George; but it hasn't been any use. It's the womenfolk who've built up weddings, my boy. For a while now the women have it all their own. A man looks pretty small at a wedding, George. All those good women standing shoulder to shoulder making sure that the knot's tied in a mighty public way.
GEORGE But . . . you *believe* in it, don't you, Mr. Webb?
MR. WEBB (*With alacrity*) Oh, yes; oh, *yes*. Don't you misunderstand me, my boy. Marriage is a wonderful thing,—wonderful thing. And don't you forget that, George.
GEORGE No, sir.—Mr. Webb, how old were you when you got married?
MR. WEBB Well, you see: I'd been to college and I'd taken a little time to get settled. But Mrs. Webb—she wasn't much older than what Emily is. Oh, age hasn't much to do with it, George,—not compared with . . . uh . . . other things.
GEORGE What were you going to say, Mr. Webb?
MR. WEBB Oh, I don't know.—Was I going to say something? (*Pause*) George, I was thinking the other night of some advice my father gave me when I got married. Charles, he said, Charles, start out early show-

ing who's boss, he said. Best thing to do is to give an order, even if it don't make sense; just so she'll learn to obey. And he said: if anything about your wife irritates you—her conversation, or anything—just get up and leave the house. That'll make it clear to her, he said. And, oh, yes! he said never, *never* let your wife know how much money you have, never.

GEORGE Well, Mr. Webb . . . I don't think I could . . .

MR. WEBB So I took the opposite of my father's advice and I've been happy ever since. And let that be a lesson to you, George, never to ask advice on personal matters.—George, are you going to raise chickens on your farm?

GEORGE What?

MR. WEBB Are you going to raise chickens on your farm?

GEORGE Uncle Luke's never been much interested, but I thought—

MR. WEBB A book came into my office the other day, George, on the Philo System of raising chickens. I want you to read it. I'm thinking of beginning in a small way in the back yard, and I'm going to put an incubator in the cellar—

(*Enter* MRS. WEBB)

MRS. WEBB Charles, are you talking about that old incubator again? I thought you two'd be talking about things worth while.

MR. WEBB (*Bitingly*) Well, Myrtle, if you want to give the boy some good advice, I'll go upstairs and leave you alone with him.

MRS. WEBB (*Pulling* GEORGE *up*) George, Emily's got to come downstairs and eat her breakfast. She sends you her love but she doesn't want to lay eyes on you. Good-by.

GEORGE Good-by. (GEORGE *crosses the stage to his own home, bewildered and crestfallen. He slowly dodges a puddle and disappears into his house*)

MR. WEBB Myrtle, I guess you don't know about that older superstition.

MRS. WEBB What do you mean, Charles?

MR. WEBB Since the cave men: no bridegroom should see his father-in-law on the day of the wedding, or near it. Now remember that.

(*Both leave the stage*)

STAGE MANAGER Thank you very much, Mr. and Mrs. Webb.—Now I have to interrupt again here. You see, we want to know how all this began—this wedding, this plan to spend a lifetime together. I'm awfully interested in how big things like that begin.

You know how it is: you're twenty-one or twenty-two and you make some decisions; then whisssh! you're seventy: you've been a lawyer for

fifty years, and that white-haired lady at your side has eaten over fifty thousand meals with you.
How do such things begin?
George and Emily are going to show you now the conversation they had when they first knew that . . . that . . . as the saying goes . . . they were meant for one another.
But before they do it I want you to try and remember what it was like to have been very young.
And particularly the days when you were first in love; when you were like a person sleepwalking, and you didn't quite see the street you were in, and didn't quite hear everything that was said to you.
You're just a little bit crazy. Will you remember that, please?
Now they'll be coming out of high school at three o'clock. George has just been elected President of the Junior Class, and as it's June, that means he'll be President of the Senior Class all next year. And Emily's just been elected Secretary and Treasurer.
I don't have to tell you how important that is.

(*He places a board across the backs of two chairs, which he takes from those at the Gibbs family's table. He brings two high stools from the wings and places them behind the board. Persons sitting on the stools will be facing the audience. This is the counter of Mr. Morgan's drugstore. The sounds of young people's voices are heard off left*)

Yepp,—there they are coming down Main Street now.

(EMILY, *carrying an armful of—imaginary—schoolbooks, comes along Main Street from the left*)

EMILY I can't, Louise. I've got to go home. Good-by. Oh, Ernestine! Ernestine! Can you come over tonight and do Latin? Isn't that Cicero the worst thing—! Tell your mother you *have* to. G'by. G'by, Helen. G'by, Fred.

(GEORGE, *also carrying books, catches up with her*)

GEORGE Can I carry your books home for you, Emily?
EMILY (*Coolly*) Why . . . uh . . . Thank you. It isn't far. (*She gives them to him*)
GEORGE Excuse me a minute, Emily.—Say, Bob, if I'm a little late, start practice anyway. And give Herb some long high ones.
EMILY Good-by, Lizzy.
GEORGE Good-by, Lizzy.—I'm awfully glad you were elected, too, Emily.
EMILY Thank you.

(*They have been standing on Main Street, almost against the back wall. They take the first steps toward the audience when* GEORGE *stops and says*)

GEORGE Emily, why are you mad at me?
EMILY I'm not mad at you.
GEORGE You've been treating me so funny lately.
EMILY Well, since you ask me, I might as well say it right out, George,— (*She catches sight of a teacher passing*) Good-by, Miss Corcoran.
GEORGE Good-by, Miss Corcoran.—Wha—what is it?
EMILY (*Not scoldingly; finding it difficult to say*) I don't like the whole change that's come over you in the last year. I'm sorry if that hurts your feelings, but I've got to—tell the truth and shame the devil.
GEORGE A *change?*—Wha—what do you mean?
EMILY Well, up to a year ago I used to like you a lot. And I used to watch you as you did everything . . . because we'd been friends so long . . . and then you began spending all your time at *baseball* . . . and you never stopped to speak to anybody any more. Not even to your own family you didn't . . . and, George, it's a fact, you've got awful conceited and stuck-up, and all the girls say so. They may not say so to your face, but that's what they say about you behind your back, and it hurts me to hear them say it, but I've got to agree with them a little. I'm sorry if it hurts your feelings . . . but I can't be sorry I said it.
GEORGE I . . . I'm glad you said it, Emily. I never thought that such a thing was happening to me. I guess it's hard for a fella not to have faults creep into his character.

(*They take a step or two in silence, then stand still in misery*)

EMILY I always expect a man to be perfect and I think he should be.
GEORGE Oh . . . I don't think it's possible to be perfect, Emily.
EMILY Well, my *father* is, and as far as I can see *your* father is. There's no reason on earth why you shouldn't be, too.
GEORGE Well, I feel it's the other way round. That men aren't naturally good; but girls are.
EMILY Well, you might as well know right now that I'm not perfect. It's not as easy for a girl to be perfect as a man, because we girls are more— more—nervous.—Now I'm sorry I said all that about you. I don't know what made me say it.
GEORGE Emily,—
EMILY Now I can see it's not the truth at all. And I suddenly feel that it isn't important, anyway.

311 · *Our Town* [ACT TWO]

GEORGE Emily . . . would you like an ice-cream soda, or something, before you go home?
EMILY Well, thank you. . . . I would.

(*They advance toward the audience and make an abrupt right turn, opening the door of Morgan's drugstore. Under strong emotion,* EMILY *keeps her face down.* GEORGE *speaks to some passers-by*)

GEORGE Hello, Stew,—how are you?—Good afternoon, Mrs. Slocum.

(*The* STAGE MANAGER, *wearing spectacles and assuming the role of Mr. Morgan, enters abruptly from the right and stands between the audience and the counter of his soda fountain*)

STAGE MANAGER Hello, George. Hello, Emily.—What'll you have?—Why, Emily Webb,—what you been crying about?
GEORGE (*He gropes for an explanation*) She . . . she just got an awful scare, Mr. Morgan. She almost got run over by that hardware-store wagon. Everybody says that Tom Huckins drives like a crazy man.
STAGE MANAGER (*Drawing a drink of water*) Well, now! You take a drink of water, Emily. You look all shook up. I tell you, you've got to look both ways before you cross Main Street these days. Gets worse every year.—What'll you have?
EMILY I'll have a strawberry phosphate, thank you, Mr. Morgan.
GEORGE No, no, Emily. Have an ice-cream soda with me. Two strawberry ice-cream sodas, Mr. Morgan.
STAGE MANAGER (*Working the faucets*) Two strawberry ice-cream sodas, yes sir. Yes, sir. There are a hundred and twenty-five horses in Grover's Corners this minute I'm talking to you. State Inspector was in here yesterday. And now they're bringing in these auto-mo-biles, the best thing to do is to just stay home. Why, I can remember when a dog could go to sleep all day in the middle of Main Street and nothing come along to disturb him. (*He sets the imaginary glasses before them*) There they are. Enjoy 'em. (*He sees a customer, right*) Yes, Mrs. Ellis. What can I do for you? (*He goes out right*)
EMILY They're so expensive.
GEORGE No, no,—don't you think of that. We're celebrating our election. And then do you know what else I'm celebrating?
EMILY N-no.
GEORGE I'm celebrating because I've got a friend who tells me all the things that ought to be told me.
EMILY George, *please* don't think of that. I don't know why I said it. It's not true. You're—

GEORGE No, Emily, you stick to it. I'm glad you spoke to me like you did. But you'll *see*: I'm going to change so quick—you bet I'm going to change. And, Emily, I want to ask you a favor.
EMILY What?
GEORGE Emily, if I go away to State Agriculture College next year, will you write me a letter once in a while?
EMILY I certainly will. I certainly will, George . . .

(*Pause. They start sipping the sodas through the straws*)

It certainly seems like being away three years you'd get out of touch with things. Maybe letters from Grover's Corners wouldn't be so interesting after a while. Grover's Corners isn't a very important place when you think of all—New Hampshire; but I think it's a very nice town.
GEORGE The day wouldn't come when I wouldn't want to know everything that's happening here. I know *that's* true, Emily.
EMILY Well, I'll try to make my letters interesting. (*Pause*)
GEORGE Y'know, Emily, whenever I meet a farmer I ask him if he thinks it's important to go to Agriculture School to be a good farmer.
EMILY Why, George—
GEORGE Yeah, and some of them say that it's even a waste of time. You can get all those things, anyway, out of the pamphlets the government sends out. And Uncle Luke's getting old,—he's about ready for me to start in taking over his farm tomorrow, if I could.
EMILY My!
GEORGE And, like you say, being gone all that time . . . in other places and meeting other people . . . Gosh, if anything like that can happen I don't want to go away. I guess new people aren't any better than old ones. I'll bet they almost never are. Emily . . . I feel that you're as good a friend as I've got. I don't need to go and meet the people in other towns.
EMILY But, George, maybe it's very important for you to go and learn all that about—cattle judging and soils and those things. . . . Of course, I don't know.
GEORGE (*After a pause, very seriously*) Emily, I'm going to make up my mind right now. I won't go. I'll tell Pa about it tonight.
EMILY Why, George, I don't see why you have to decide right now. It's a whole year away.
GEORGE Emily, I'm glad you spoke to me about that . . . that fault in my character. What you said was right; but there was *one* thing wrong in it, and that was when you said that for a year I wasn't noticing people, and . . . you, for instance. Why, you say you were watching me when I did everything . . . I was doing the same about you all the

time. Why, sure,—I always thought about you as one of the chief people I thought about. I always made sure where you were sitting on the bleachers, and who you were with, and for three days now I've been trying to walk home with you; but something's always got in the way. Yesterday I was standing over against the wall waiting for you, and you walked home with *Miss Corcoran.*

EMILY George! . . . Life's awful funny! How could I have known that? Why, I thought—

GEORGE Listen, Emily, I'm going to tell you why I'm not going to Agriculture School. I think that once you've found a person that you're very fond of . . . I mean a person who's fond of you, too, and likes you enough to be interested in your character . . . Well, I think that's just as important as college is, and even more so. That's what I think.

EMILY I think it's awfully important, too.

GEORGE Emily.

EMILY Y-yes, George.

GEORGE Emily, if I *do* improve and make a big change . . . would you be . . . I mean: *could* you be . . .

EMILY I . . . I am now; I always have been.

GEORGE (*Pause*) So I guess this is an important talk we've been having.

EMILY Yes . . . yes.

GEORGE (*Takes a deep breath and straightens his back*) Wait just a minute and I'll walk you home. (*With mounting alarm he digs into his pockets for the money. The* STAGE MANAGER *enters, right.* GEORGE, *deeply embarrassed, but direct, says to him*) Mr. Morgan, I'll have to go home and get the money to pay you for this. It'll only take me a minute.

STAGE MANAGER (*Pretending to be affronted*) What's that? George Gibbs, do you mean to tell me—!

GEORGE Yes, but I had reasons, Mr. Morgan.—Look, here's my gold watch to keep until I come back with the money.

STAGE MANAGER That's all right. Keep your watch. I'll trust you.

GEORGE I'll be back in five minutes.

STAGE MANAGER I'll trust you ten years, George,—not a day over.— Got all over your shock, Emily?

EMILY Yes, thank you, Mr. Morgan. It was nothing.

GEORGE (*Taking up the books from the counter*) I'm ready.

(*They walk in grave silence across the stage and pass through the trellis at the Webbs' back door and disappear. The* STAGE MANAGER *watches them go out, then turns to the audience, removing his spectacles*)

STAGE MANAGER Well,— (*He claps his hands as a signal*) Now we're ready to get on with the wedding.

> (*He stands waiting while the set is prepared for the next scene.* STAGEHANDS *remove the chairs, tables and trellises from the Gibbs and Webb houses. They arrange the pews for the church in the center of the stage. The congregation will sit facing the back wall. The aisle of the church starts at the center of the back wall and comes toward the audience. A small platform is placed against the back wall on which the* STAGE MANAGER *will stand later, playing the minister. The image of a stained-glass window is cast from a lantern slide upon the back wall. When all is ready the* STAGE MANAGER *strolls to the center of the stage, down front, and, musingly, addresses the audience*)

There are a lot of things to be said about a wedding; there are a lot of thoughts that go on during a wedding.

We can't get them all into one wedding, naturally, and especially not into a wedding at Grover's Corners, where they're awfully plain and short.

In this wedding I play the minister. That gives me the right to say a few more things about it.

For a while now, the play gets pretty serious.

Y'see, some churches say that marriage is a sacrament. I don't quite know what that means, but I can guess. Like Mrs. Gibbs said a few minutes ago: People were made to live two-by-two.

This is a good wedding, but people are so put together that even at a good wedding there's a lot of confusion way down deep in people's minds and we thought that that ought to be in our play, too.

The real hero of this scene isn't on the stage at all, and you know who that is. It's like what one of those European fellas said: every child born into the world is nature's attempt to make a perfect human being. Well, we've seen nature pushing and contriving for some time now. We all know that nature's interested in quantity; but I think she's interested in quality, too,—that's why I'm in the ministry.

And don't forget all the other witnesses at this wedding,—the ancestors. Millions of them. Most of them set out to live two-by-two, also. Millions of them.

Well, that's all my sermon. 'Twan't very long, anyway.

> (*The organ starts playing Handel's "Largo." The congregation streams into the church and sits in silence. Church bells are heard.* MRS. GIBBS *sits in the front row, the first seat on the aisle, the right section; next to her are* REBECCA *and* DR. GIBBS. *Across the aisle* MRS. WEBB, WALLY *and* MR. WEBB. *A small choir takes*

its place, facing the audience under the stained-glass window.
MRS. WEBB, *on the way to her place, turns back and speaks to the audience*)

MRS. WEBB I don't know why on earth I should be crying. I suppose there's nothing to cry about. It came over me at breakfast this morning; there was Emily eating her breakfast as she's done for seventeen years and now she's going off to eat it in someone's else's house. I suppose that's it.
And Emily! She suddenly said: I can't eat another mouthful, and she put her head down on the table and *she* cried.

(*She starts toward her seat in the church, but turns back and adds*)

Oh, I've got to say it: you know, there's something downright cruel about sending our girls out into marriage this way.
I hope some of her girl friends have told her a thing or two. It's cruel, I know, but I couldn't bring myself to say anything. I went into it blind as a bat myself.

(*In half-amused exasperation*)

The whole world's wrong, that's what's the matter.
There they come.

(*She hurries to her place in the pew.* GEORGE *starts to come down the right aisle of the theatre, through the audience. Suddenly* THREE MEMBERS *of his baseball team appear by the right proscenium pillar and start whistling and catcalling to him. They are dressed for the ball field*)

THE BASEBALL PLAYERS Eh, George, George! Hast—yaow! Look at him, fellas—he looks scared to death. Yaow! George, don't look so innocent, you old geezer. We know what you're thinking. Don't disgrace the team, big boy. Whoo-oo-oo.

STAGE MANAGER All right! All right! That'll do. That's enough of that.

(*Smiling, he pushes them off the stage. They lean back to shout a few more catcalls*)

There used to be an awful lot of that kind of thing at weddings in the old days,—Rome, and later. We're more civilized now,—so they say.

(*The choir starts singing "Love Divine, All Love Excelling—."*
GEORGE *has reached the stage. He stares at the congregation a moment, then takes a few steps of withdrawal, toward the right*

proscenium pillar. His mother, from the front row, seems to have felt his confusion. She leaves her seat and comes down the aisle quickly to him)

MRS. GIBBS George! George! What's the matter?
GEORGE Ma, I don't want to grow old. Why's everybody pushing me so?
MRS. GIBBS Why, George . . . you wanted it.
GEORGE No, Ma, listen to me—
MRS. GIBBS No, no, George,—you're a man now.
GEORGE Listen, Ma,—for the last time I ask you . . . All I want to do is to be a fella—
MRS. GIBBS George! If anyone should hear you! Now stop. Why, I'm ashamed of you!
GEORGE (*He comes to himself and looks over the scene*) What? Where's Emily?
MRS. GIBBS (*Relieved*) George! You gave me such a turn.
GEORGE Cheer up, Ma. I'm getting married.
MRS. GIBBS Let me catch my breath a minute.
GEORGE (*Comforting her*) Now, Ma, you save Thursday nights. Emily and I are coming over to dinner every Thursday night . . . you'll see. Ma, what are you crying for? Come on; we've got to get ready for this.

(MRS. GIBBS, *mastering her emotion, fixes his tie and whispers to him. In the meantime,* EMILY, *in white and wearing her wedding veil, has come through the audience and mounted onto the stage. She too draws back, frightened, when she sees the congregation in the church. The choir begins: "Blessed Be the Tie That Binds"*)

EMILY I never felt so alone in my whole life. And George over there, looking so . . . ! I *hate* him. I wish I were dead. Papa! Papa!
MR. WEBB (*Leaves his seat in the pews and comes toward her anxiously*) Emily! Emily! Now don't get upset. . . .
EMILY But, Papa,—I don't want to get married. . . .
MR. WEBB Sh—sh—Emily. Everything's all right.
EMILY Why can't I stay for a while just as I am? Let's go away,—
MR. WEBB No, no, Emily. Now stop and think a minute.
EMILY Don't you remember that you used to say,—all the time you used to say—all the time: that I was *your* girl! There must be lots of places we can go to. I'll work for you. I could keep house.
MR. WEBB Sh . . . You mustn't think of such things. You're just nervous, Emily. (*He turns and calls*) George! George! Will you come here a

minute? (*He leads her toward George*)
Why you're marrying the best young fellow in the world. George is a fine fellow.
EMILY But Papa,—

(MRS. GIBBS *returns unobtrusively to her seat*. MR. WEBB *has one arm around his daughter. He places his hand on* GEORGE'S *shoulder*)

MR. WEBB I'm giving away my daughter, George. Do you think you can take care of her?
GEORGE Mr. Webb, I want to . . . I want to try. Emily, I'm going to do my best. I love you, Emily. I need you.
EMILY Well, if you love me, help me. All I want is someone to love me.
GEORGE I will, Emily. Emily, I'll try.
EMILY And I mean for *ever*. Do you hear? For ever and ever.

(*They fall into each other's arms. The March from* Lohengrin *is heard. The* STAGE MANAGER, *as* CLERGYMAN, *stands on the box, up center*)

MR. WEBB Come, they're waiting for us. Now you know it'll be all right. Come quick.

(GEORGE *slips away and takes his place beside the* STAGE MANAGER-CLERGYMAN. EMILY *proceeds up the aisle on her father's arm*)

STAGE MANAGER Do you, George, take this woman, Emily, to be your wedded wife, to have . . .

(MRS. SOAMES *has been sitting in the last row of the congregation. She now turns to her neighbors and speaks in a shrill voice. Her chatter drowns out the rest of the clergyman's words*)

MRS. SOAMES Perfectly lovely wedding! Loveliest wedding I ever saw. Oh, I do love a good wedding, don't you? Doesn't she make a lovely bride?
GEORGE I do.
STAGE MANAGER Do you, Emily, takes this man, George, to be your wedded husband,—

(*Again his further words are covered by those of* MRS. SOAMES)

MRS. SOAMES Don't know *when* I've seen such a lovely wedding. But I always cry. Don't know why it is, but I always cry. I just like to see young people happy, don't you? Oh, I think it's lovely.

(*The ring. The kiss. The stage is suddenly arrested into silent tableau. The* STAGE MANAGER, *his eyes on the distance, as though to himself*)

STAGE MANAGER   I've married over two hundred couples in my day. Do I believe in it?
I don't know.
M. . . . marries N. . . . millions of them.
The cottage, the go-cart, the Sunday-afternoon drives in the Ford, the first rheumatism, the grandchildren, the second rheumatism, the deathbed, the reading of the will,—

(*He now looks at the audience for the first time, with a warm smile that removes any sense of cynicism from the next line*)

Once in a thousand times it's interesting.
—Well, let's have Mendelssohn's "Wedding March"!

(*The organ picks up the March. The* BRIDE *and* GROOM *come down the aisle, radiant, but trying to be very dignified*)

MRS. SOAMES   Aren't they a lovely couple? Oh, I've never been to such a nice wedding. I'm sure they'll be happy. I always say: *happiness*, that's the great thing! The important thing is to be happy.

(*The* BRIDE *and* GROOM *reach the steps leading into the audience. A bright light is thrown upon them. They descend into the auditorium and run up the aisle joyously*)

STAGE MANAGER   That's all the Second Act, folks. Ten minutes' intermission.

Curtain

Act Three

During the intermission the audience has seen the STAGEHANDS arranging the stage. On the right-hand side, a little right of the center, ten or twelve ordinary chairs have been placed in three openly spaced rows facing the audience.
These are graves in the cemetery.

319 · *Our Town* [ACT THREE]

Toward the end of the intermission the ACTORS *enter and take their places. The front row contains: toward the center of the stage, an empty chair; then* MRS. GIBBS; SIMON STIMSON.
The second row contains, among others, MRS. SOAMES.
The third row has WALLY WEBB.
The dead do not turn their heads or their eyes to right or left, but they sit in a quiet without stiffness. When they speak their tone is matter-of-fact, without sentimentality and, above all, without lugubriousness.
The STAGE MANAGER *takes his accustomed place and waits for the house lights to go down.*

STAGE MANAGER This time nine years have gone by, friends—summer, 1913.
Gradual changes in Grover's Corners. Horses are getting rarer.
Farmers coming into town in Fords.
Everybody locks their house doors now at night. Ain't been any burglars in town yet, but everybody's heard about 'em.
You'd be surprised, though—on the whole, things don't change much around here.
This is certainly an important part of Grover's Corners. It's on a hilltop—a windy hilltop—lots of sky, lots of clouds,—often lots of sun and moon and stars.
You come up here, on a fine afternoon and you can see range on range of hills—awful blue they are—up there by Lake Sunapee and Lake Winnipesaukee . . . and way up, if you've got a glass, you can see the White Mountains and Mt. Washington—where North Conway and Conway is. And, of course, our favorite mountain, Mt. Monadnock, 's right here—and all these towns that lie around it: Jaffrey, 'n East Jaffrey, 'n Peterborough, 'n Dublin; and (*Then pointing down in the audience*) there, quite a ways down, is Grover's Corners. Yes, beautiful spot up here. Mountain laurel and li-lacks. I often wonder why people like to be buried in Woodlawn[3] and Brooklyn when they might pass the same time up here in New Hampshire.
Over there— (*Pointing to stage left*) are the old stones,—1670, 1680. Strong-minded people that come a long way to be independent. Summer people walk around there laughing at the funny words on the tombstones . . . it don't do any harm. And genealogists come up from Boston—get paid by city people for looking up their ancestors. They want to make sure they're Daughters of the American Revolution and of the *Mayflower*. . . . Well, I guess that don't do any harm,

---

[3] Woodlawn Cemetery is in the Bronx, New York. These references may have been written for the Broadway production.

either. Wherever you come near the human race, there's layers and layers of nonsense. . . .
Over there are some Civil War veterans. Iron flags on their graves . . . New Hampshire boys . . . had a notion that the Union ought to be kept together, though they'd never seen more than fifty miles of it themselves. All they knew was the name, friends—the United States of America. The United States of America. And they went and died about it. This here is the new part of the cemetery. Here's your friend Mrs. Gibbs. 'N let me see—Here's Mr. Stimson, organist at the Congregational Church. And Mrs. Soames who enjoyed the wedding so— you remember? Oh, and a lot of others. And Editor Webb's boy, Wallace, whose appendix burst while he was on a Boy Scout trip to Crawford Notch.
Yes, an awful lot of sorrow has sort of quieted down up here. People just wild with grief have brought their relatives up to this hill. We all know how it is . . . and then time . . . and sunny days . . . and rainy days . . . 'n snow . . . We're all glad they're in a beautiful place and we're coming up here ourselves when our fit's over.
Now there are some things we all know, but we don't take'm out and look at'm very often. We all know that *something* is eternal. And it ain't houses and it ain't names, and it ain't earth, and it ain't even the stars . . . everybody knows in their bones that *something* is eternal, and that something has to do with human beings. All the greatest people ever lived have been telling us that for five thousand years and yet you'd be surprised how people are always losing hold of it. There's something way down deep that's eternal about every human being. (*Pause*)
You know as well as I do that the dead don't stay interested in us living people for very long. Gradually, gradually, they lose hold of the earth . . . and the ambitions they had . . . and the pleasures they had . . . and the things they suffered . . . and the people they loved.
They get weaned away from earth—that's the way I put it,—weaned away.
And they stay here while the earth part of 'em burns away, burns out; and all that time they slowly get indifferent to what's goin' on in Grover's Corners.
They're waitin'. They're waitin' for something that they feel is comin'. Something important, and great. Aren't they waitin' for the eternal part in them to come out clear?
Some of the things they're going to say maybe'll hurt your feelings— but that's the way it is: mother 'n daughter . . . husband 'n wife . . . enemy 'n enemy . . . money 'n miser . . . all those terribly important

things kind of grow pale around here. And what's left when memory's gone, and your identity, Mrs. Smith?

(*He looks at the audience a minute, then turns to the stage*)

Well! There are some *living* people. There's Joe Stoddard, our undertaker, supervising a new-made grave. And here comes a Grover's Corners boy, that left town to go out West.

(JOE STODDARD *has hovered about in the background.* SAM CRAIG *enters left, wiping his forehead from the exertion. He carries an umbrella and strolls front*)

SAM CRAIG Good afternoon, Joe Stoddard.

JOE STODDARD Good afternoon, good afternoon. Let me see now: do I know you?

SAM CRAIG I'm Sam Craig.

JOE STODDARD Gracious sakes' alive! Of all people! I should'a knowed you'd be back for the funeral. You've been away a long time, Sam.

SAM CRAIG Yes, I've been away over twelve years. I'm in business out in Buffalo now, Joe. But I was in the East when I got news of my cousin's death, so I thought I'd combine things a little and come and see the old home. You look well.

JOE STODDARD Yes, yes, can't complain. Very sad, our journey today, Samuel.

SAM CRAIG Yes.

JOE STODDARD Yes, yes. I always say I hate to supervise when a young person is taken. They'll be here in a few minutes now. I had to come here early today—my son's supervisin' at the home.

SAM CRAIG (*Reading stones*) Old Farmer McCarty, I used to do chores for him—after school. He had the lumbago.

JOE STODDARD Yes, we brought Farmer McCarty here a number of years ago now.

SAM CRAIG (*Staring at* MRS. GIBBS' *knees*) Why, this is my Aunt Julia . . . I'd forgotten that she'd . . . of course, of course.

JOE STODDARD Yes, Doc Gibbs lost his wife two-three years ago . . . about this time. And today's another pretty bad blow for him, too.

MRS. GIBBS (*To* SIMON STIMSON: *in an even voice*) That's my sister Carey's boy, Sam . . . Sam Craig.

SIMON STIMSON I'm always uncomfortable when *they're* around.

MRS. GIBBS Simon.

SAM CRAIG Do they choose their own verses much, Joe?

JOE STODDARD No . . . not usual. Mostly the bereaved pick a verse.

SAM CRAIG Doesn't sound like Aunt Julia. There aren't many of those

Hersey sisters left now. Let me see: where are . . . I wanted to look at my father's and mother's . . .

JOE STODDARD   Over there with the Craigs . . . Avenue F.

SAM CRAIG   (*Reading* SIMON STIMSON'S *epitaph*)   He was organist at church, wasn't he?—Hm, drank a lot, we used to say.

JOE STODDARD   Nobody was supposed to know about it. He'd seen a peck of trouble. (*Behind his hand*) Took his own life, y' know?

SAM CRAIG   Oh, did he?

JOE STODDARD   Hung himself in the attic. They tried to hush it up, but of course it got around. He chose his own epy-taph. You can see it there. It ain't a verse exactly.

SAM CRAIG   Why, it's just some notes of music—what is it?

JOE STODDARD   Oh, I wouldn't know. It was wrote up in the Boston papers at the time.

SAM CRAIG   Joe, what did she die of?

JOE STODDARD   Who?

SAM CRAIG   My cousin.

JOE STODDARD   Oh, didn't you know? Had some trouble bringing a baby into the world. 'Twas her second, though. There's a little boy 'bout four years old.

SAM CRAIG   (*Opening his umbrella*)   The grave's going to be over there?

JOE STODDARD   Yes, there ain't much more room over here among the Gibbses, so they're opening up a whole new Gibbs section over by Avenue B. You'll excuse me now. I see they're comin'.

(*From left to center, at the back of the stage, comes a procession.* FOUR MEN *carry a casket, invisible to us. All the rest are under umbrellas. One can vaguely see:* DR. GIBBS, GEORGE, *the* WEBBS, *etc. They gather about a grave in the back center of the stage, a little to the left of center*)

MRS. SOAMES   Who is it, Julia?

MRS. GIBBS   (*Without raising her eyes*)   My daughter-in-law, Emily Webb.

MRS. SOAMES   (*A little surprised, but no emotion*)   Well, I declare! The road up here must have been awful muddy. What did she die of, Julia?

MRS. GIBBS   In childbirth.

MRS. SOAMES   Childbirth. (*Almost with a laugh*) I'd forgotten all about that. My, wasn't life awful— (*With a sigh*) and wonderful.

SIMON STIMSON   (*With a sideways glance*)   Wonderful, was it?

MRS. GIBBS   Simon! Now, remember!

MRS. SOAMES   I remember Emily's wedding. Wasn't it a lovely wedding!

And I remember her reading the class poem at Graduation Exercises. Emily was one of the brightest girls ever graduated from High School. I've heard Principal Wilkins say so time after time. I called on them at their new farm, just before I died. Perfectly beautiful farm.

A WOMAN FROM AMONG THE DEAD It's on the same road we lived on.
A MAN AMONG THE DEAD Yepp, right smart farm.

(They subside. The group by the grave starts singing "Blessed Be the Tie That Binds")

A WOMAN AMONG THE DEAD I always liked that hymn. I was hopin' they'd sing a hymn.

(Pause. Suddenly EMILY *appears from among the umbrellas. She is wearing a white dress. Her hair is down her back and tied by a white ribbon like a little girl. She comes slowly, gazing wonderingly at the dead, a little dazed. She stops halfway and smiles faintly. After looking at the mourners for a moment, she walks slowly to the vacant chair beside* MRS. GIBBS *and sits down)*

EMILY *(To them all, quietly, smiling)* Hello.
MRS. SOAMES Hello, Emily.
A MAN AMONG THE DEAD Hello, M's Gibbs.
EMILY *(Warmly)* Hello, Mother Gibbs.
MRS. GIBBS Emily.
EMILY Hello. *(With surprise)* It's raining. *(Her eyes drift back to the funeral company)*
MRS. GIBBS Yes . . . They'll be gone soon, dear. Just rest yourself.
EMILY It seems thousands and thousands of years since I . . . Papa remembered that that was my favorite hymn. Oh, I wish I'd been here a long time. I don't like being new here.—How do you do, Mr. Stimson?
SIMON STIMSON How do you do, Emily.

*(*EMILY *continues to look about her with a wondering smile; as though to shut out from her mind the thought of the funeral company she starts speaking to* MRS. GIBBS *with a touch of nervousness)*

EMILY Mother Gibbs, George and I have made that farm into just the best place you ever saw. We thought of you all the time. We wanted to show you the new barn and a great long ce-ment drinking fountain for the stock. We bought that out of the money you left us.
MRS. GIBBS I did?
EMILY Don't you remember, Mother Gibbs—the legacy you left us? Why, it was over three hundred and fifty dollars.

MRS. GIBBS   Yes, yes, Emily.
EMILY   Well, there's a patent device on the drinking fountain so that it never overflows, Mother Gibbs, and it never sinks below a certain mark they have there. It's fine. (*Her voice trails off and her eyes return to the funeral group*) It won't be the same to George without me, but it's a lovely farm. (*Suddenly she looks directly at* MRS. GIBBS) Live people don't understand, do they?
MRS. GIBBS   No, dear—not very much.
EMILY   They're sort of shut up in little boxes, aren't they? I feel as though I knew them last a thousand years ago . . . My boy is spending the day at Mrs. Carter's. (*She sees* MR. CARTER *among the dead*) Oh, Mr. Carter, my little boy is spending the day at your house.
MR. CARTER   Is he?
EMILY   Yes, he loves it there.—Mother Gibbs, we have a Ford, too. Never gives any trouble. I don't drive, though. Mother Gibbs, when does this feeling go away?—Of being . . . one of *them*? How long does it . . . ?
MRS. GIBBS   Sh! dear. Just wait and be patient.
EMILY   (*With a sigh*)   I know.—Look, they're finished. They're going
MRS. GIBBS   Sh—.

  (*The umbrellas leave the stage.* DR. GIBBS *has come over to his wife's grave and stands before it a moment.* EMILY *looks up at his face.* MRS. GIBBS *does not raise her eyes*)

EMILY   Look! Father Gibbs is bringing some of my flowers to you. He looks just like George, doesn't he? Oh, Mother Gibbs, I never realized before how troubled and how . . . how in the dark live persons are. Look at him. I loved him so. From morning till night, that's all they are—troubled.

  (DR. GIBBS *goes off*)

THE DEAD   Little cooler than it was.—Yes, that rain's cooled it off a little. Those northeast winds always do the same thing, don't they? If it isn't a rain, it's a three-day blow.—

  (A *patient calm falls on the stage. The* STAGE MANAGER *appears at his proscenium pillar, smoking.* EMILY *sits up abruptly with an idea*)

EMILY   But, Mother Gibbs, one can go back; one can go back there again . . . into living. I feel it. I know it. Why just then for a moment I was thinking about . . . about the farm . . . and for a minute I *was* there, and my baby was on my lap as plain as day.
MRS. GIBBS   Yes, of course you can.

EMILY   I can go back there and live all those days over again . . . why not?

MRS. GIBBS   All I can say is, Emily, don't.

EMILY   (*She appeals urgently to the* STAGE MANAGER)   But it's true, isn't it? I can go and live . . . back there . . . again.

STAGE MANAGER   Yes, some have tried—but they soon come back here.

MRS. GIBBS   Don't do it, Emily.

MRS. SOAMES   Emily, don't. It's not what you think it'd be.

EMILY   But I won't live over a sad day. I'll choose a happy one—I'll choose the day I first knew that I loved George. Why should that be painful?

(*They are silent. Her question turns to the* STAGE MANAGER)

STAGE MANAGER   You not only live it; but you watch yourself living it.

EMILY   Yes?

STAGE MANAGER   And as you watch it, you see the thing that they—down there—never know. You see the future. You know what's going to happen afterwards.

EMILY   But is that—painful? Why?

MRS. GIBBS   That's not the only reason why you shouldn't do it, Emily. When you've been here longer you'll see that our life here is to forget all that, and think only of what's ahead, and be ready for what's ahead. When you've been here longer you'll understand.

EMILY   (*Softly*)   But, Mother Gibbs, how can I *ever* forget that life? It's all I know. It's all I had.

MRS. SOAMES   Oh, Emily. It isn't wise. Really, it isn't.

EMILY   But it's a thing I must know for myself. I'll choose a happy day, anyway.

MRS. GIBBS   *No!*—At least, choose an unimportant day. Choose the least important day in your life. It will be important enough.

EMILY   (*To herself*)   Then it can't be since I was married; or since the baby was born. (*To the* STAGE MANAGER *eagerly*)   I can choose a birthday at least, can't I?—I choose my twelfth birthday.

STAGE MANAGER   All right. February 11th, 1899. A Tuesday.—Do you want any special time of day?

EMILY   Oh, I want the whole day.

STAGE MANAGER   We'll begin at dawn. You remember it had been snowing for several days; but it had stopped the night before, and they had begun clearing the roads. The sun's coming up.

EMILY   (*With a cry; rising*)   There's Main Street . . . why, that's Mr. Morgan's drugstore before he changed it! . . . And there's the livery stable.

(*The stage at no time in this act has been very dark; but now the left half of the stage gradually becomes very bright—the brightness of a crisp winter morning.* EMILY *walks toward Main Street*)

STAGE MANAGER   Yes, it's 1899. This is fourteen years ago.
EMILY   Oh, that's the town I knew as a little girl. And, *look*, there's the old white fence that used to be around our house. Oh, I'd forgotten that! Oh, I love it so! Are they inside?
STAGE MANAGER   Yes, your mother'll be coming downstairs in a minute to make breakfast.
EMILY   (*Softly*)   Will she?
STAGE MANAGER   And you remember: your father had been away for several days; he came back on the early-morning train.
EMILY   No . . . ?
STAGE MANAGER   He'd been back to his college to make a speech—in western New York, at Clinton.
EMILY   Look! There's Howie Newsome. There's our policeman. But he's *dead*; he *died*.

(*The voices of* HOWIE NEWSOME, CONSTABLE WARREN *and* JOE CROWELL, JR., *are heard at the left of the stage.* EMILY *listens in delight*)

HOWIE NEWSOME   Whoa, Bessie!—Bessie! 'Morning, Bill.
CONSTABLE WARREN   Morning, Howie.
HOWIE NEWSOME   You're up early.
CONSTABLE WARREN   Been rescuin' a party; darn near froze to death, down by Polish Town thar. Got drunk and lay out in the snowdrifts. Thought he was in bed when I shook'm.
EMILY   Why, there's Joe Crowell. . . .
JOE CROWELL   Good morning, Mr. Warren. 'Morning, Howie.

(MRS. WEBB *has appeared in her kitchen, but* EMILY *does not see her until she calls*)

MRS. WEBB   Chil-*dren!* Wally! Emily! . . . Time to get up.
EMILY   Mama, I'm here! Oh! how young Mama looks! I didn't know Mama was ever that young.
MRS. WEBB   You can come and dress by the kitchen fire, if you like; but hurry.

(HOWIE NEWSOME *has entered along Main Street and brings the milk to* MRS. WEBB'S *door*)

Good morning, Mr. Newsome. Whhhh—it's cold.
HOWIE NEWSOME   Ten below by my barn, Mrs. Webb.

MRS. WEBB Think of it! Keep yourself wrapped up. (*She takes her bottles in, shuddering*)
EMILY (*With an effort*) Mama, I can't find my blue hair ribbon anywhere.
MRS. WEBB Just open your eyes, dear, that's all. I laid it out for you special—on the dresser, there. If it were a snake it would bite you.
EMILY Yes, yes . . .

(*She puts her hand on her heart.* MR. WEBB *comes along Main Street, where he meets* CONSTABLE WARREN. *Their movements and voices are increasingly lively in the sharp air*)

MR. WEBB Good morning, Bill.
CONSTABLE WARREN Good morning, Mr. Webb. You're up early.
MR. WEBB Yes, just been back to my old college in New York State. Been any trouble here?
CONSTABLE WARREN Well, I was called up this mornin' to rescue a Polish fella—darn near froze to death he was.
MR. WEBB We must get it in the paper.
CONSTABLE WARREN 'Twan't much.
EMILY (*Whispers*) Papa.

(MR. WEBB *shakes the snow off his feet and enters his house.* CONSTABLE WARREN *goes off, right*)

MR. WEBB Good morning, Mother.
MRS. WEBB How did it go, Charles?
MR. WEBB Oh, fine, I guess. I told'm a few things.—Everything all right here?
MRS. WEBB Yes—can't think of anything that's happened, special. Been right cold. Howie Newsome says it's ten below over to his barn.
MR. WEBB Yes, well, it's colder than that at Hamilton College. Students' ears are falling off. It ain't Christian.—Paper have any mistakes in it?
MRS. WEBB None that I noticed. Coffee's ready when you want it.

(*He starts upstairs*)

Charles! Don't forget; it's Emily's birthday. Did you remember to get her something?
MR. WEBB (*Patting his pocket*) Yes, I've got something here. (*Calling up the stairs*) Where's my girl? Where's my birthday girl? (*He goes off left*)
MRS. WEBB Don't interrupt her now, Charles. You can see her at breakfast. She's slow enough as it is. Hurry up, children! It's seven o'clock. Now, I don't want to call you again.
EMILY (*Softly, more in wonder than in grief*) I can't bear it. They're

so young and beautiful. Why did they ever have to get old? Mama, I'm here. I'm grown up. I love you all, everything.—I can't look at everything hard enough. (*She looks questioningly at the* STAGE MANAGER, *saying or suggesting:* "*Can I go in?*" *He nods briefly. She crosses to the inner door to the kitchen, left of her mother, and as though entering the room, says, suggesting the voice of a girl of twelve*) Good morning, Mama.

MRS. WEBB (*Crossing to embrace and kiss her; in her characteristic matter-of-fact manner*) Well, now, dear, a very happy birthday to my girl and many happy returns. There are some surprises waiting for you on the kitchen table.

EMILY Oh, Mama, you *shouldn't* have. (*She throws an anguished glance at the* STAGE MANAGER) I can't—I can't.

MRS. WEBB (*Facing the audience, over her stove*) But birthday or no birthday, I want you to eat your breakfast good and slow. I want you to grow up and be a good strong girl. That in the blue paper is from your Aunt Carrie; and I reckon you can guess who brought the postcard album. I found it on the doorstep when I brought in the milk— George Gibbs . . . must have come over in the cold pretty early . . . right nice of him.

EMILY (*To herself*) Oh, George! I'd forgotten that. . . .

MRS. WEBB Chew that bacon good and slow. It'll help keep you warm on a cold day.

EMILY (*With mounting urgency*) Oh, Mama, just look at me one minute as though you really saw me. Mama, fourteen years have gone by. I'm dead. You're a grandmother, Mama. I married George Gibbs, Mama. Wally's dead, too. Mama, his appendix burst on a camping trip to North Conway. We felt just terrible about it—don't you remember? But, just for a moment now we're all together. Mama, just for a moment we're happy. *Let's look at one another.*

MRS. WEBB That in the yellow paper is something I found in the attic among your grandmother's things. You're old enough to wear it now, and I thought you'd like it.

EMILY And this is from you. Why, Mama, it's just lovely and it's just what I wanted. It's beautiful!

(*She flings her arms around her mother's neck. Her* MOTHER *goes on with her cooking, but is pleased*)

MRS. WEBB Well, I hoped you'd like it. Hunted all over. Your Aunt Norah couldn't find one in Concord, so I had to send all the way to Boston. (*Laughing*) Wally has something for you, too. He made it at manual-training class and he's very proud of it. Be sure you make a big fuss about it.—Your father has a surprise for you, too; don't know what it is myself. Sh—here he comes.

MR. WEBB (*Off stage*)   Where's my girl? Where's my birthday girl?

EMILY (*In a loud voice to the* STAGE MANAGER)   I can't. I can't go on. It goes so fast. We don't have time to look at one another.

(*She breaks down sobbing. The lights dim on the left half of the stage.* MRS. WEBB *disappears*)

I didn't realize. So all that was going on and we never noticed. Take me back—up the hill—to my grave. But first: Wait! One more look. Good-by, Good-by, world. Good-by, Grover's Corners . . . Mama and Papa. Good-by to clocks ticking . . . and Mama's sunflowers. And food and coffee. And new-ironed dresses and hot baths . . . and sleeping and waking up. Oh, earth, you're too wonderful for anybody to realize you.

(*She looks toward the* STAGE MANAGER *and asks abruptly, through her tears*)

Do any human beings ever realize life while they live it?—every, every minute?

STAGE MANAGER   No. (*Pause*) The saints and poets, maybe—they do some.

EMILY   I'm ready to go back. (*She returns to her chair beside* MRS. GIBBS. *Pause*)

MRS. GIBBS   Were you happy?

EMILY   No . . . I should have listened to you. That's all human beings are! Just blind people.

MRS. GIBBS   Look, it's clearing up. The stars are coming out.

EMILY   Oh, Mr. Stimson, I should have listened to them.

SIMON STIMSON (*With mounting violence; bitingly*)   Yes, now you know. Now you know! That's what it was to be alive. To move about in a cloud of ignorance; to go up and down trampling on the feelings of those . . . of those about you. To spend and waste time as though you had a million years. To be always at the mercy of one self-centered passion, or another. Now you know—that's the happy existence you wanted to go back to. Ignorance and blindness.

MRS. GIBBS (*Spiritedly*)   Simon Stimson, that ain't the whole truth and you know it. Emily, look at that star. I forget its name.

A MAN AMONG THE DEAD   My boy Joel was a sailor,—knew 'em all. He'd set on the porch evenings and tell 'em all by name. Yes, sir, wonderful!

ANOTHER MAN AMONG THE DEAD   A star's mighty good company.

A WOMAN AMONG THE DEAD   Yes. Yes, 'tis.

SIMON STIMSON   Here's one of *them* coming.
THE DEAD   That's funny. 'Tain't no time for one of them to be here.—Goodness sakes.
EMILY   Mother Gibbs, it's George.
MRS. GIBBS   Sh, dear. Just rest yourself.
EMILY   It's George.

(GEORGE *enters from the left, and slowly comes toward them*)

A MAN FROM AMONG THE DEAD   And my boy, Joel, who knew the stars—he used to say it took millions of years for that speck o' light to git to the earth. Don't seem like a body could believe it, but that's what he used to say—millions of years.

(GEORGE *sinks to his knees then falls full length at* EMILY's *feet*)

A WOMAN AMONG THE DEAD   Goodness! That ain't no way to behave!
MRS. SOAMES   He ought to be home.
EMILY   Mother Gibbs?
MRS. GIBBS   Yes, Emily?
EMILY   They don't understand, do they?
MRS. GIBBS   No, dear. They don't understand.

(*The* STAGE MANAGER *appears at the right, one hand on a dark curtain which he slowly draws across the scene. In the distance a clock is heard striking the hour very faintly*)

STAGE MANAGER   Most everybody's asleep in Grover's Corners. There are a few lights on: Shorty Hawkins, down at the depot, has just watched the Albany train go by. And at the livery stable somebody's setting up late and talking.—Yes, it's clearing up. There are the stars—doing their old, old crisscross journeys in the sky. Scholars haven't settled the matter yet, but they seem to think there are no living beings up there. Just chalk . . . or fire. Only this one is straining away, straining away all the time to make something of itself. The strain's so bad that every sixteen hours everybody lies down and gets a rest. (*He winds his watch*) Hm. . . . Eleven o'clock in Grover's Corners.—You get a good rest, too. Good night.

TENNESSEE WILLIAMS
[1911 –]

❦ *The Man*

THOMAS LANIER WILLIAMS, later called Tennessee, was born in Mississippi. In 1918, his parents—Cornelius Coffin and Edwina Dakin, daughter of an Episcopal rector—moved to St. Louis. Tom had difficulty adjusting to the harsh, ugly, large city, where extremes of wealth and poverty were more glaring than in the small Mississippi town. The boys at school mocked his southern accent and manners. He was small and weak for his age, and for a time one of his legs was paralyzed; his schoolmates called him "sissy" because he could not participate in their games. He and his sister Rose drew closer together, and he began to write. Cornelius Coffin, disappointed that his son was not a "he-man," contemptuously called him "Miss Nancy" and scorned his writings as an effeminate waste of time.

In 1929 he entered the University of Missouri, where he won writing prizes and failed R.O.T.C. His father pulled him out of school just before his senior year and got him a sixty-five-dollar-a-month job in a warehouse. A regimen of working by day and writing by night resulted, two years later, in a nervous breakdown. He recuperated at his grandparents' home in Tennessee. Subsidized by his grandparents, he returned to school in autumn, 1935—this time Washington University in St. Louis. While there, he wrote plays for a little theater group called The Mummers. In 1937 he was off to the University of Iowa to study playwriting. In 1938 he received his B.A. and went to New Orleans to write.

In 1939 *Story* magazine printed "A Field of Blue Children," the first published work to carry his new name, Tennessee. That year he submitted four one-act plays for a contest held by the Group Theatre. He won a special prize of one hundred dollars and was brought to the attention of Audrey Wood, who became—and still is—his agent. Miss Wood was instrumental in getting him a Rockefeller grant for playwriting. This enabled him to complete *Battle of Angels*, which was produced in 1940 by the Theatre Guild; the play contains adultery, nymphomania, lynching, murder with a blowtorch, and a portrait of Jesus resembling the play's sexually active hero. *Battle of Angels* closed in Boston. It did not reach New York until seventeen years later, when it was rewritten as *Orpheus Descending*. In 1943 Audrey Wood got him a job writing for MGM in Hollywood. While on salary, he wrote a screenplay called *The Gentleman Caller*, but the studio was not interested. When his contract expired, he turned it into a play, *The Glass Menagerie*.

The Glass Menagerie opened in Chicago on December 26, 1944. Three months later the play opened in New York, where it won the Drama Critics' Circle Award as the best American play for that season. Although begun on MGM time, the motion picture rights were sold not to MGM but to its competitor, Warner Brothers. Two other plays earned Williams two more awards from the Drama Critics' Circle, *A Streetcar Named Desire* and *Cat on a Hot Tin Roof*; for these same plays he won two Pulitzer Prizes.

❧ *The Work*

LIKE OTHER WRITERS of the Southern Renaissance, Williams explores the tense, emotional isolation of the social misfit. Although he experienced the Depression and was aware of the cleavage between rich and poor, although he experienced the boredom of routine factory work, and although his apprentice plays displayed a social commitment common to the dramas of the 1930's, his mature work shows little concern for social issues. Instead of becoming the poet laureate of the world of social oppression and machine age drudgery, he became the poet laureate of the lonely, fragile, poetic soul threatened or destroyed by this world.

His mature plays are of a piece; *The Glass Menagerie* contains themes and techniques that are repeated or expanded in other works.

Williams contrasts the realistic and the romantic temperament, a contrast that takes the form of American go-getterism and fragile sensitivity, coarse brutality and neurotic gentility, Pan and the Puritan. The romantic, with whom Williams usually sympathizes, is often crushed by the brutal world; sometimes he is prey to the ravages of time. Though *The Glass Menagerie* is an exception, violence abounds in Williams' plays, which contain rape, cannibalism, and castration. Although some regard such violence as a repellent defect, others see it as the quality of a superb melodramatist; one might call Williams the John Webster of American drama.

In Williams' plays the tension between realism and nonrealism is manifested both in the staging techniques and the dialogue. Williams rightly regards himself as a poet of the theater. Although some poetic effects are achieved by stylized scenery, others are achieved linguistically. Some critics, however, feel that he achieves his best poetry through realistic dialogue, and that when he abandons realism in an effort to be poetic, his dialogue becomes self-conscious and pretentious.

❦ *The Play*

PART OF THE INTEREST IN *The Glass Menagerie* is the play's autobiographical aspect. Not only do the characters resemble Williams' family, but he has given the narrator his own first name, which writers rarely do. Like the fictional Tom, he worked in the warehouse of a shoe factory for sixty-five dollars a month, wrote poetry, and used movies as a way of escaping reality. Although his father was not "a telephone man who fell in love with long distances" and did not desert his family, he was a traveling salesman. His mother, like Amanda, was a southern belle, a member of the D.A.R.—and she even confiscated his copy of D. H. Lawrence's *Lady Chatterley's Lover*. His sister Rose, like Laura, was shy and withdrawn; she too had an unfortunate experience at secretarial school and owned a collection of glass animals. But *The Glass Menagerie* is more than a *pièce à clef*.

Although this play deals with the subjects discussed earlier, it also—and perhaps primarily—deals with the problem of illusion and reality. Laura retreats from reality and escapes into a world of artificial glass animals who, like herself, have a delicate beauty but are extremely fragile. Tom talks of coping with reality, but his actions are as evasive as his sister's. Instead of facing the problems of an aging mother and an unmarried sister, he goes to the movies, drinks, and finally deserts them. Amanda, on the other hand, talks a good deal about the romantic past but is the only member of the trio who attempts to deal realistically with the present situation. Finally, there is the Gentleman Caller, kin to Willy Loman, victim of The American Dream, clinging tenaciously to the illusion that social poise is the key to success. Although he is apparently successful in dealing with reality, he betrays his insecurities and fears. Not only—to rephrase the famous quip about Falstaff—is Jim O'Connor himself frustrated but he is the source of frustration in others. At the beginning of the play Tom describes him as "the long delayed but always expected something that we live for." A familiar subject of modern drama, from Odets' *Waiting for Lefty* to Beckett's *Waiting for Godot*, is the anticipated arrival of someone or something which will provide a form of salvation to those who are waiting for him or it. Although the "expected something" usually does not arrive, the Gentleman Caller does; however, his arrival not only provides no solution to the problems of Amanda and her daughter, but after his departure their desperation and isolation are intensified.

Symbolic of Laura's isolation and fragility is her glass menagerie, the most prominent symbolic element of the setting. Other elements of the setting reinforce the mood of desperation and loneliness. The picture of the smiling father who deserted his family suggests the path the son will take. The very words "fire escape," say the stage directions, carry an element of "accidental poetic truth"; Tom dashes there to flee from "the slow and implacable fires of human desperation." Across the alley is the Paradise Dance Hall, which offers a temporary paradise to its customers. However, Tom, the disengaged poet, is not one of these customers; he does not enter this paradise but looks at it from a distance.

In *The Glass Menagerie*, Williams fuses character and symbol, prose and lyricism, realism and stylization. His first major success, *Menagerie* displays the poetic realism so characteristic of its author.

❧ Dramatic Works

Cairo, Shanghai, Bombay! (Prologue and Epilogue by Bernice Dorothy Shapiro), 1935.
The Magic Tower, 1936.
Headlines, 1936.
Candles to the Sun, 1937.
The Fugitive Kind, 1937.
Me, Vashya!, 1937.
Spring Storm, 1938.
Not About Nightingales, 1938.
The Lady of Larkspur Lotion, 1939.
The Long Goodbye, 1940.
Battle of Angels, 1940.
Moony's Kid Don't Cry, 1940.
The Case of the Crushed Petunias, 1941.
I Rise in Flame, Cried the Phoenix, 1941.
Stairs to the Roof, 1942.
You Touched Me (with Donald Windham), 1943.
The Purification, 1944.
The Glass Menagerie, 1944.
Twenty-seven Wagons Full of Cotton, 1945.
The Last of My Solid Gold Watches, 1945.
Portrait of a Madonna, 1945.
Auto-Da-Fé, 1945.
Lord Byron's Love Letter, 1945.
The Strangest Kind of Romance, 1945.
Hello From Bertha, 1945.
This Property Is Condemned, 1945.
The Long Stay Cut Short, or the Unsatisfactory Supper, 1946.
A Streetcar Named Desire, 1947.
Ten Blocks on the Camino Real, 1948.
The Dark Room, 1948.
Summer and Smoke, 1948.
The Rose Tattoo, 1950.
Camino Real, 1953.
Talk to Me Like the Rain, 1953.
Something Unspoken, 1953.
Cat on a Hot Tin Roof, 1955.
Orpheus Descending, 1957.
Suddenly Last Summer, 1957.
The Enemy: Time, 1959.
Sweet Bird of Youth, 1959.
Period of Adjustment, 1960.
The Night of the Iguana, 1962.
The Milk Train Doesn't Stop Here Anymore, 1963.
Slapstick Tragedy (The Mutilated and Gnädiges Fraulein), 1965.

❦ Selective Bibliography

Jones, Robert Emmet. "Tennessee Williams' Early Heroines," *Modern Drama*, II (December, 1959).

Nelson, Benjamin. *Tennessee Williams: The Man and His Work*. New York: Obolensky, 1961.

Popkin, Henry. "The Plays of Tennessee Williams," *Tulane Drama Review*, IV (March, 1960).

Stein, Roger B. "*The Glass Menagerie* Revisited: Catastrophe Without Violence," *Western Humanities Review*, XVIII (Spring, 1964).

Tischler, Nancy M. *Tennessee Williams: Rebellious Puritan*. New York: Citadel, 1961.

Williams, Edwina Dakin, as told to Lucy Freeman. *Remember Me to Tom*. New York: Putnam, 1963.

The Author's Production Notes

Being a "memory play," *The Glass Menagerie* can be presented with unusual freedom of convention. Because of its considerably delicate or tenuous material, atmospheric touches and subtleties of direction play a particularly important part. Expressionism and all other unconventional techniques in drama have only one valid aim, and that is a closer approach to truth. When a play employs unconventional techniques, it is not, or certainly shouldn't be, trying to escape its responsibility of dealing with reality, or interpreting experience, but is actually or should be attempting to find a closer approach, a more penetrating and vivid expression of things as they are. The straight realistic play with its genuine frigidaire and authentic ice-cubes, its characters that speak exactly as its audience speaks, corresponds to the academic landscape and has the same virtue of a photographic likeness. Everyone should know nowadays the unimportance of the photographic in art: that truth, life, or reality is an organic thing which the poetic imagination can represent or suggest, in essence, only through transformation, through changing into other forms than those which were merely present in appearance.

These remarks are not meant as a preface only to this particular play.

They have to do with a conception of a new, plastic theatre which must take the place of the exhausted theatre of realistic conventions if the theatre is to resume vitality as a part of our culture.

THE SCREEN DEVICE

There is *only one important difference between the original and acting version of the play* and that is the *omission* in the latter of the device which I tentatively included in my *original* script. This device was the use of a screen on which were projected magic-lantern slides bearing images or titles. I do not regret the omission of this device from the present Broadway production. The extraordinary power of Miss Taylor's performance made it suitable to have the utmost simplicity in the physical production. But I think it may be interesting to some readers to see how this device was conceived. So I am putting it into the published manuscript. These images and legends, projected from behind, were cast on a section of wall between the front-room and dining-room areas, which should be indistinguishable from the rest when not in use.

The purpose of this will probably be apparent. It is to give accent to certain values in each scene. Each scene contains a particular point (or several) which is structurally the most important. In an episodic play, such as this, the basic structure or narrative line may be obscured from the audience; the effect may seem fragmentary rather than architectural. This may not be the fault of the play so much as a lack of attention in the audience. The legend or image upon the screen will strengthen the effect of what is merely allusion in the writing and allow the primary point to be made more simply and lightly than if the entire responsibility were on the spoken lines. Aside from this structural value, I think the screen will have a definite emotional appeal, less definable but just as important. An imaginative producer or director may invent many other uses for this device than those indicated in the present script. In fact the possibilities of the device seem much larger to me than the instance of this play can possibly utilize.

THE MUSIC

Another extra-literary accent in this play is provided by the use of music. A single recurring tune, "The Glass Menagerie," is used to give emotional emphasis to suitable passages. This tune is like circus music, not when you are on the grounds or in the immediate vicinity of the parade, but when you are at some distance and very likely thinking of something else. It seems under those circumstances to continue almost interminably and it weaves in and out of your preoccupied consciousness; then it is the lightest, most delicate music in the world and perhaps the saddest. It expresses the surface vivacity of life with the underlying strain of immutable and inexpressible sorrow. When you look at a piece of delicately spun glass you think of two things: how beautiful it is and how easily it can be broken. Both of those ideas should be woven into the recurring tune, which dips in and out of the play as if it were carried on a wind that changes. It serves as a thread of connection and allusion between the narrator with his separate point in time and space and the subject of his story. Between each episode it returns as reference to the emotion, nostalgia, which is the first condition of the play. It is primarily Laura's music and therefore comes out most clearly when the play focuses upon her and the lovely fragility of glass which is her image.

THE LIGHTING

The lighting in the play is not realistic. In keeping with the atmosphere of memory, the stage is dim. Shafts of light are focused on selected areas or actors, sometimes in contradistinction to what is the apparent center. For instance, in the quarrel scene between Tom and Amanda, in which Laura has no active part, the clearest pool of light is on her figure. This is also true of the supper scene, when her silent figure on the sofa should remain the visual center. The light upon Laura should be distinct from the others, having a peculiar pristine clarity such as light used in early religious portraits of female saints or madonnas. A certain correspondence to light in religious paintings, such as El Greco's, where the figures are radiant in atmosphere that is relatively dusky, could be effectively used throughout the play. (It will also permit a more effective use of the screen.) A free, imaginative use of light can be of enormous value in giving a mobile, plastic quality to plays of a more or less static nature.

The Glass Menagerie

CHARACTERS

AMANDA WINGFIELD, *the mother*
A little woman of great but confused vitality clinging frantically to another time and place. Her characterization must be carefully created, not copied from type. She is not paranoiac, but her life is paranoia. There is much to admire in Amanda, and as much to love and pity as there is to laugh at. Certainly she has endurance and a kind of heroism, and though her foolishness makes her unwittingly cruel at times, there is tenderness in her slight person.

LAURA WINGFIELD, *her daughter*
Amanda, having failed to establish contact with reality, continues to live vitally in her illusions, but Laura's situation is even graver. A childhood illness has left her crippled, one leg slightly shorter than the other, and held in a brace. This defect need not be more than suggested on the stage. Stemming from this, Laura's separation increases till she is like a piece of her own glass collection, too exquisitely fragile to move from the shelf.

TOM WINGFIELD, *her son*
And the narrator of the play. A poet with a job in a warehouse. His nature is not remorseless, but to escape from a trap he has to act without pity.

JIM O'CONNOR, *the gentleman caller*
A nice, ordinary, young man.

SCENES

SCENE   An Alley in St. Louis.
PART I   Preparation for a Gentleman Caller
PART II   The Gentleman Calls
TIME   Now [c. 1944] and the Past.

Scene One

The Wingfield apartment is in the rear of the building, one of those vast hive-like conglomerations of cellular living-units that flower as warty growths in overcrowded urban centers of lower middle-class populations and are symptomatic of the impulse of this largest and fundamentally enslaved section of American society to avoid fluidity and differentiation and to exist and function as one interfused mass of automatism.

The apartment faces an alley and is entered by a fire escape, a structure whose name is a touch of accidental poetic truth, for all of these huge buildings are always burning with the slow and implacable fires of human desperation. The fire escape is included in the set—that is, the landing of it and steps descending from it.

The scene is memory and is therefore nonrealistic. Memory takes a lot of poetic license. It omits some details; others are exaggerated, according to the emotional value of the articles it touches, for memory is seated predominantly in the heart. The interior is therefore rather dim and poetic.
At the rise of the curtain, the audience is faced with the dark, grim rear wall of the Wingfield tenement. This building, which runs parallel to the footlights, is flanked on both sides by dark, narrow alleys which run into murky canyons of tangled clotheslines, garbage cans, and the sinister latticework of neighboring fire escapes. It is up and down these side alleys that exterior entrances and exits are made, during the play. At the end of TOM's opening commentary, the dark tenement wall slowly reveals (by the means of a transparency) the interior of the ground floor Wingfield apartment.

Downstage is the living room, which also serves as a sleeping room for LAURA, the sofa unfolding to make her bed. Upstage, center, and divided by a wide arch or second proscenium with transparent faded portieres (or second curtain), is the dining room. In an old-fashioned what-not in the living room are seen scores of transparent glass animals. A blown-up photograph of the father hangs on the wall of the living room, facing the audience, to the left of the archway. It is the face of a very handsome young man in a doughboy's[1] First World War cap. He is gallantly smiling, ineluctably smiling, as if to say, "I will be smiling forever."

The audience hears and sees the opening scene in the dining room through both the transparent fourth wall of the building and the transparent gauze portieres of the dining-room arch. It is during this revealing scene that the fourth wall slowly ascends, out of sight. This transparent exterior wall is not brought down again until the very end of the play, during TOM's speech.

The narrator is an undisguised convention of the play. He takes whatever license with dramatic convention is convenient to his purposes.

TOM enters dressed as a merchant sailor from alley, stage left, and strolls across the front of the stage to the fire escape. There he stops and lights a cigarette. He addresses the audience.

TOM Yes, I have tricks in my pocket, I have things up my sleeve. But I am the opposite of a stage magician. He gives you illusion that has the appearance of truth. I give you truth in the pleasant disguise of illusion.

To begin with, I turn back time. I reverse it to that quaint period, the thirties, when the huge middle class of America was matriculating in a school for the blind. Their eyes had failed them, or they had failed their eyes, and so they were having their fingers pressed forcibly down on the fiery Braille alphabet of a dissolving economy.

In Spain there was revolution. Here there was only shouting and confusion.

In Spain there was Guernica.[2] Here there were disturbances of labor, sometimes pretty violent, in otherwise peaceful cities such as Chicago, Cleveland, Saint Louis . . .

This is the social background of the play.

(MUSIC)

The play is memory.

Being a memory play, it is dimly lighted, it is sentimental, it is not realistic.

In memory everything seems to happen to music. That explains the fiddle in the wings.

I am the narrator of the play, and also a character in it.

The other characters are my mother, Amanda, my sister, Laura,

[1] American infantryman.

[2] During the Spanish Civil War the city of Guernica was heavily bombarded by Franco's forces.

and a gentleman caller who appears in the final scenes.

He is the most realistic character in the play, being an emissary from a world of reality that we were somehow set apart from.

But since I have a poet's weakness for symbols, I am using this character also as a symbol; he is the long delayed but always expected something that we live for.

There is a fifth character in the play who doesn't appear except in this larger-than-life-size photograph over the mantel.

This is our father who left us a long time ago.

He was a telephone man who fell in love with long distances; he gave up his job with the telephone company and skipped the light fantastic out of town . . .

The last we heard of him was a picture post-card from Mazatlan, on the Pacific coast of Mexico, containing a message of two words— "Hello— Good-bye!" and no address.

I think the rest of the play will explain itself. . . .

(AMANDA's *voice becomes audible through the portieres*)

(LEGEND ON SCREEN: "OÙ SONT LES NEIGES"[3])

(*He divides the portieres and enters the upstage area*)

(AMANDA *and* LAURA *are seated at a drop-leaf table. Eating is indicated by gestures without food or utensils.* AMANDA *faces the audience,* TOM *and* LAURA *are seated in profile. The interior has lit up softly and through the scrim we see* AMANDA *and* LAURA *seated at the table in the upstage area*)

AMANDA (*Calling*) Tom?

TOM Yes, Mother.

AMANDA We can't say grace until you come to the table!

TOM Coming, Mother. (*He bows slightly and withdraws, reappearing a few moments later in his place at the table*)

AMANDA (*To her son*) Honey, don't *push* with your *fingers*. If you have to push with something, the thing to push with is a crust of bread. And chew—chew! Animals have sections in their stomachs which enable them to digest food without mastication, but human beings are supposed to chew their food before they swallow it down. Eat food leisurely, son, and really enjoy it. A well-cooked meal has lots of delicate flavors that have to be held in the mouth for appreciation. So chew your food and give your salivary glands a chance to function!

---

[3] "Where are the snows [of yesteryear]?" From François Villon's "Ballade of Dead Ladies."

The Glass Menagerie [Scene One]

(TOM *deliberately lays his imaginary fork down and pushes his chair back from the table*)

TOM I haven't enjoyed one bite of this dinner because of your constant directions on how to eat it. It's you that make me rush through meals with your hawk-like attention to every bite I take. Sickening—spoils my appetite—all this discussion of—animals' secretion—salivary glands—mastication!

AMANDA (*Lightly*) Temperament like a Metropolitan star! (*He rises and crosses downstage*) You're not excused from the table.

TOM I'm getting a cigarette.

AMANDA You smoke too much.

(LAURA *rises*)

LAURA I'll bring in the blanc mange.

(*He remains standing with his cigarette by the portieres during the following*)

AMANDA (*Rising*) No, sister, no, sister—you be the lady this time and I'll be the darky.

LAURA I'm already up.

AMANDA Resume your seat, little sister—I want you to stay fresh and pretty—for gentlemen callers!

LAURA I'm not expecting any gentlemen callers.

AMANDA (*Crossing out to kitchenette. Airily*) Sometimes they come when they are least expected! Why, I remember one Sunday afternoon in Blue Mountain— (*Enters kitchenette*)

TOM I know what's coming!

LAURA Yes. But let her tell it.

TOM Again?

LAURA She loves to tell it.

(AMANDA *returns with bowl of dessert*)

AMANDA One Sunday afternoon in Blue Mountain—your mother received—*seventeen!*—gentlemen callers! Why, sometimes there weren't chairs enough to accommodate them all. We had to send the nigger over to bring in folding chairs from the parish house.

TOM (*Remaining at portieres*) How did you entertain those gentlemen callers?

AMANDA I understood the art of conversation!

TOM I bet you could talk.

AMANDA Girls in those days *knew* how to talk, I can tell you.

TOM Yes?

(IMAGE: AMANDA AS A GIRL ON A PORCH, GREETING CALLERS)

AMANDA They knew how to entertain their gentlemen callers. It wasn't enough for a girl to be possessed of a pretty face and a graceful figure—although I wasn't slighted in either respect. She also needed to have a nimble wit and a tongue to meet all occasions.

TOM What did you talk about?

AMANDA Things of importance going on in the world! Never anything coarse or common or vulgar. (*She addresses* TOM *as though he were seated in the vacant chair at the table though he remains by portieres. He plays this scene as though he held the book*) My callers were gentlemen—all! Among my callers were some of the most prominent young planters of the Mississippi Delta—planters and sons of planters!

(TOM *motions for music and a spot of light on* AMANDA)

(*Her eyes lift, her face glows, her voice becomes rich and elegiac*)

(SCREEN LEGEND: "OÙ SONT LES NEIGES")

There was young Champ Laughlin who later became vice-president of the Delta Planters Bank.

Hadley Stevenson who was drowned in Moon Lake and left his widow one hundred and fifty thousand in Government bonds.

There were the Cutrere brothers, Wesley and Bates. Bates was one of my bright particular beaux! He got in a quarrel with that wild Wainwright boy. They shot it out on the floor of Moon Lake Casino. Bates was shot through the stomach. Died in the ambulance on his way to Memphis. His widow was also well-provided for, came into eight or ten thousand acres, that's all. She married him on the rebound—never loved her—carried my picture on him the night he died!

And there was that boy that every girl in the Delta had set her cap for! That beautiful, brilliant young Fitzhugh boy from Greene County!

TOM What did he leave his widow?

AMANDA He never married! Gracious, you talk as though all of my old admirers had turned up their toes to the daisies!

TOM Isn't this the first you've mentioned that still survives?

AMANDA That Fitzhugh boy went North and made a fortune—came to be known as the Wolf of Wall Street! He had the Midas touch, whatever he touched turned to gold!

And I could have been Mrs. Duncan J. Fitzhugh, mind you! But—I picked your *father!*

LAURA (*Rising*) Mother, let me clear the table.

AMANDA No, dear, you go in front and study your typewriter chart. Or practice your shorthand a little. Stay fresh and pretty!—It's almost time for our gentlemen callers to start arriving. (*She flounces girlishly toward the kitchenette*) How many do you suppose we're going to entertain this afternoon?

(TOM *throws down the paper and jumps up with a groan*)

LAURA (*Alone in the dining room*) I don't believe we're going to receive any, Mother.

AMANDA (*Reappearing, airily*) What? No one—not one? You must be joking! (LAURA *nervously echoes her laugh. She slips in a fugitive manner through the half-open portieres and draws them gently behind her. A shaft of very clear light is thrown on her face against the faded tapestry of the curtains.* MUSIC: "THE GLASS MENAGERIE" UNDER FAINTLY. *Lightly*) Not one gentleman caller? It can't be true! There must be a flood, there must have been a tornado!

LAURA It isn't a flood, it's not a tornado, Mother. I'm just not popular like you were in Blue Mountain. . . . (TOM *utters another groan.* LAURA *glances at him with a faint, apologetic smile. Her voice catching a little*) Mother's afraid I'm going to be an old maid.

(*The Scene Dims Out with "Glass Menagerie" Music*)

Scene Two

"*Laura, Haven't You Ever Liked Some Boy?*"

On the dark stage the screen is lighted with the image of blue roses.

Gradually LAURA's figure becomes apparent and the screen goes out.

The music subsides.

LAURA *is seated in the delicate ivory chair at the small clawfoot table.*

She wears a dress of soft violet material for a kimono—her hair tied back from her forehead with a ribbon.

She is washing and polishing her collection of glass.

AMANDA *appears on the fire-escape steps. At the sound of her ascent,* LAURA *catches her breath, thrusts the bowl of ornaments away and seats herself stiffly before the diagram of the typewriter keyboard as though it held her spellbound.*

Something has happened to AMANDA. *It is written in her face as she climbs to the landing: a look that is grim and hopeless and a little absurd.*

She has on one of those cheap or imitation velvety-looking cloth coats with imitation fur collar. Her hat is five or six years old, one of those dreadful cloche hats that were worn in the late twenties and she is clasping an enormous black patent-leather pocketbook with nickel clasps and initials. This is her full-dress outfit, the one she usually wears to the D.A.R.[4]

Before entering she looks through the door.

She purses her lips, opens her eyes very wide, rolls them upward and shakes her head.

Then she slowly lets herself in the door. Seeing her mother's expression LAURA *touches her lips with a nervous gesture.*

LAURA   Hello, Mother, I was— (*She makes a nervous gesture toward the chart on the wall.* AMANDA *leans against the shut door and stares at* LAURA *with a martyred look*)

AMANDA   Deception? Deception? (*She slowly removes her hat and gloves, continuing the sweet suffering stare. She lets the hat and gloves fall on the floor—a bit of acting*)

LAURA (*Shakily*)   How was the D.A.R. meeting? (AMANDA *slowly opens her purse and removes a dainty white handkerchief which she shakes out delicately and delicately touches to her lips and nostrils*) Didn't you go to the D.A.R. meeting, Mother?

AMANDA (*Faintly, almost inaudibly*)   —No—No. (*Then more forcibly*) I did not have the strength—to go to the D.A.R. In fact, I did not have the courage! I wanted to find a hole in the ground and hide myself in it forever! (*She crosses slowly to the wall and removes the diagram of the typewriter keyboard. She holds it in front of her for a second, staring at it sweetly and sorrowfully—then bites her lips and tears it in two pieces*)

[4] Daughters of the American Revolution.

LAURA (*Faintly*) Why did you do that, Mother? (AMANDA *repeats the same procedure with the chart of the Gregg Alphabet*) Why are you—
AMANDA Why? Why? How old are you, Laura?
LAURA Mother, you know my age.
AMANDA I thought that you were an adult; it seems that I was mistaken. (*She crosses slowly to the sofa and sinks down and stares at* LAURA)
LAURA Please don't stare at me, Mother. (AMANDA *closes her eyes and lowers her head. Count ten*)
AMANDA What are we going to do, what is going to become of us, what is the future? (*Count ten*)
LAURA Has something happened, Mother? (AMANDA *draws a long breath and takes out the handkerchief again. Dabbing process*) Mother, has—something happened?
AMANDA I'll be all right in a minute, I'm just bewildered— (*Count five*)—by life. . . .
LAURA Mother, I wish that you would tell me what's happened!
AMANDA As you know, I was supposed to be inducted into my office at the D.A.R. this afternoon. (IMAGE: A SWARM OF TYPEWRITERS) But I stopped off at Rubicam's Business College to speak to your teachers about your having a cold and ask them what progress they thought you were making down there.
LAURA Oh. . . .
AMANDA I went to the typing instructor and introduced myself as your mother. She didn't know who you were. Wingfield, she said. We don't have any such student enrolled at the school!

I assured her she did, that you had been going to classes since early in January.

"I wonder," she said, "if you could be talking about that terribly shy little girl who dropped out of school after only a few days' attendance?"

"No," I said, "Laura, my daughter, has been going to school every day for the past six weeks!"

"Excuse me," she said. She took the attendance book out and there was your name, unmistakably printed, and all the dates you were absent until they decided that you had dropped out of school.

I still said, "No, there must have been some mistake! There must have been some mix-up in the records!"

And she said, "No—I remember her perfectly now. Her hands shook so that she couldn't hit the right keys! The first time we gave a speed-test, she broke down completely—was sick at the stomach and almost had to be carried into the wash-room! After that morning she never showed up any more. We phoned the house but never got any answer"—

while I was working at Famous and Barr, I suppose, demonstrating those— Oh!
I felt so weak I could barely keep on my feet!
I had to sit down while they got me a glass of water!
Fifty dollars' tuition, all of our plans—my hopes and ambitions for you—just gone up the spout, just gone up the spout like that.

(LAURA *draws a long breath and gets awkwardly to her feet. She crosses to the victrola and winds it up*)

What are you doing?
LAURA   Oh! (*She releases the handle and returns to her seat*)
AMANDA   Laura, where have you been going when you've gone out pretending that you were going to business college?
LAURA   I've just been going out walking.
AMANDA   That's not true.
LAURA   It is. I just went walking.
AMANDA   Walking? Walking? In winter? Deliberately courting pneumonia in that light coat? Where did you walk to, Laura?
LAURA   All sorts of places—mostly in the park.
AMANDA   Even after you'd started catching that cold?
LAURA   It was the lesser of two evils, Mother. (IMAGE: WINTER SCENE IN PARK) I couldn't go back up. I—threw up—on the floor!
AMANDA   From half past seven till after five every day you mean to tell me you walked around in the park, because you wanted to make me think that you were still going to Rubicam's Business College?
LAURA   It wasn't as bad as it sounds. I went inside places to get warmed up.
AMANDA   Inside where?
LAURA   I went in the art museum and the bird-houses at the Zoo. I visited the penguins every day! Sometimes I did without lunch and went to the movies. Lately I've been spending most of my afternoons in the Jewel-box, that big glass house where they raise the tropical flowers.
AMANDA   You did all this to deceive me, just for deception? (LAURA *looks down*) Why?
LAURA   Mother, when you're disappointed, you get that awful suffering look on your face, like the picture of Jesus' mother in the museum!
AMANDA   Hush!
LAURA   I couldn't face it.

(*Pause. A whisper of strings*)

(LEGEND: "THE CRUST OF HUMILITY")

AMANDA (*Hopelessly fingering the huge pocketbook*) So what are we going to do the rest of our lives? Stay home and watch the parades go by? Amuse ourselves with the glass menagerie, darling? Eternally play those worn-out phonograph records your father left as a painful reminder of him?

We won't have a business career—we've given that up because it gave us nervous indigestion! (*Laughs wearily*) What is there left but dependency all our lives? I know so well what becomes of unmarried women who aren't prepared to occupy a position. I've seen such pitiful cases in the South—barely tolerated spinsters living upon the grudging patronage of sister's husband or brother's wife!—stuck away in some little mouse-trap of a room—encouraged by one in-law to visit another—little birdlike women without any nest—eating the crust of humility all their life!

Is that the future that we've mapped out for ourselves?
I swear it's the only alternative I can think of!
It isn't a very pleasant alternative, is it?
Of course—some girls *do marry*.

(LAURA *twists her hands nervously*)

Haven't you ever liked some boy?
LAURA Yes. I liked one once. (*Rises*) I came across his picture a while ago.
AMANDA (*With some interest*) He gave you his picture?
LAURA No, it's in the year-book.
AMANDA (*Disappointed*) Oh—a high-school boy.

(SCREEN IMAGE: JIM AS HIGH-SCHOOL HERO BEARING A SILVER CUP)

LAURA Yes. His name was Jim. (LAURA *lifts the heavy annual from the claw-foot table*) Here he is in *The Pirates of Penzance*.
AMANDA (*Absently*) The what?
LAURA The operetta the senior class put on. He had a wonderful voice and we sat across the aisle from each other Mondays, Wednesdays, and Fridays in the Aud. Here he is with the silver cup for debating! See his grin?
AMANDA (*Absently*) He must have had a jolly disposition.
LAURA He used to call me—Blue Roses.

(IMAGE: BLUE ROSES)

AMANDA Why did he call you such a name as that?
LAURA When I had that attack of pleurosis—he asked me what was the

matter when I came back. I said pleurosis—he thought that I said Blue Roses! So that's what he always called me after that. Whenever he saw me, he'd holler, "Hello, Blue Roses!" I didn't care for the girl that he went out with. Emily Meisenbach. Emily was the best-dressed girl at Soldan. She never struck me, though, as being sincere. . . . It says in the Personal Section—they're engaged. That's—six years ago! They must be married by now.

AMANDA Girls that aren't cut out for business careers usually wind up married to some nice man. (*Gets up with a spark of revival*) Sister, that's what you'll do!

(LAURA *utters a startled, doubtful laugh. She reaches quickly for a piece of glass*)

LAURA But, Mother—
AMANDA Yes? (*Crossing to photograph*)
LAURA (*In a tone of frightened apology*) I'm—crippled!

(IMAGE: SCREEN)

AMANDA Nonsense! Laura, I've told you never, never to use that word. Why, you're not crippled, you just have a little defect—hardly noticeable, even! When people have some slight disadvantage like that, they cultivate other things to make up for it—develop charm—and vivacity —and—*charm!* That's all you have to do! (*She turns again to the photograph*)

One thing your father had *plenty of*—was *charm!*

(TOM *motions to the fiddle in the wings*)

(*The Scene Fades Out with Music*)

Scene Three

LEGEND ON SCREEN: "AFTER THE FIASCO—"

TOM *speaks from the fire-escape landing.*

TOM After the fiasco at Rubicam's Business College, the idea of getting a gentleman caller for Laura began to play a more and more important part in Mother's calculations.

The Glass Menagerie [Scene Three]

It became an obsession. Like some archetype of the universal unconscious, the image of the gentleman caller haunted our small apartment. . . .

(IMAGE: YOUNG MAN AT DOOR WITH FLOWERS)

An evening at home rarely passed without some allusion to this image, this specter, this hope. . . .

Even when he wasn't mentioned, his presence hung in Mother's preoccupied look and in my sister's frightened, apologetic manner—hung like a sentence passed upon the Wingfields!

Mother was a woman of action as well as words.

She began to take logical steps in the planned direction.

Late that winter and in the early spring—realizing that extra money would be needed to properly feather the nest and plume the bird—she conducted a vigorous campaign on the telephone, roping in subscribers to one of those magazines for matrons called *The Homemaker's Companion,* the type of journal that features the serialized sublimations of ladies of letters who think in terms of delicate cuplike breasts, slim, tapering waists, rich, creamy thighs, eyes like wood-smoke in autumn, fingers that soothe and caress like strains of music, bodies as powerful as Etruscan sculpture.

(SCREEN IMAGE: GLAMOR MAGAZINE COVER)

(AMANDA *enters with phone on long extension cord. She is spotted in the dim stage*)

AMANDA Ida Scott? This is Amanda Wingfield!
We *missed* you at the D.A.R. last Monday!
I said to myself: She's probably suffering with that sinus condition! How is that sinus condition?
Horrors! Heaven have mercy!—You're a Christian martyr, yes, that's what you are, a Christian martyr!
Well, I just now happened to notice that your subscription to the *Companion's* about to expire! Yes, it expires with the next issue, honey! —just when that wonderful new serial by Bessie Mae Hopper is getting off to such an exciting start. Oh, honey, it's something that you can't miss! You remember how *Gone With the Wind* took everybody by storm? You simply couldn't go out if you hadn't read it. All everybody *talked* was Scarlett O'Hara. Well, this is a book that critics already compare to *Gone With the Wind.* It's the *Gone With the Wind* of the post-World War generation!—What?—Burning?—Oh, honey, don't let them burn, go take a look in the oven and I'll hold the wire! Heavens—I think she's hung up!

DIM OUT

(LEGEND ON SCREEN: "YOU THINK I'M IN LOVE WITH CONTINENTAL SHOEMAKERS?")

(*Before the stage is lighted, the violent voices of* TOM *and* AMANDA *are heard*)

(*They are quarreling behind the portieres. In front of them stands* LAURA *with clenched hands and panicky expression*)

(*A clear pool of light on her figure throughout this scene*)

TOM What in Christ's name am I—
AMANDA (*Shrilly*) Don't you use that—
TOM Supposed to do!
AMANDA Expression! Not in my—
TOM Ohhh!
AMANDA Presence! Have you gone out of your senses?
TOM I have, that's true, *driven* out!
AMANDA What is the matter with you, you—big—big—*idiot!*
TOM Look!—I've got *no* thing, no single thing—
AMANDA Lower your voice!
TOM In my life here that I can call my *own!* Everything is—
AMANDA Stop that shouting!
TOM Yesterday you confiscated my books! You had the nerve to—
AMANDA I took that horrible novel back to the library—yes! That hideous book by that insane Mr. Lawrence.[5] (TOM *laughs wildly*) I cannot control the output of diseased minds or people who cater to them— (TOM *laughs still more wildly*) BUT I WON'T ALLOW SUCH FILTH BROUGHT INTO MY HOUSE! No, no, no, no, no!
TOM House, house! Who pays rent on it, who makes a slave of himself to—
AMANDA (*Fairly screeching*) Don't you DARE to—
TOM No, no, I mustn't say things! I've got to just—
AMANDA Let me tell you—
TOM I don't want to hear any more! (*He tears the portieres open. The upstage area is lit with a turgid smoky red glow*).

(AMANDA's *hair is in metal curlers and she wears a very old bathrobe, much too large for her slight figure, a relic of the faithless Mr. Wingfield. An upright typewriter and a wild disarray of manuscripts is on the drop-leaf table. The quarrel was probably*

---

[5] D. H. Lawrence (1885–1930), English novelist, author of *Lady Chatterley's Lover*, and other novels.

precipitated by AMANDA's *interruption of his creative labor. A chair lying overthrown on the floor. Their gesticulating shadows are cast on the ceiling by the fiery glow*)

AMANDA You *will* hear more, you—
TOM No, I won't hear more, I'm going out!
AMANDA You come right back in—
TOM Out, out, out! Because I'm—
AMANDA Come back here, Tom Wingfield! I'm not through talking to you!
TOM Oh, go—
LAURA (*Desperately*) —Tom!
AMANDA You're going to listen, and no more insolence from you! I'm at the end of my patience!

(*He comes back toward her*)

TOM What do you think I'm at? Aren't I supposed to have any patience to reach the end of, Mother? I know, I know. It seems unimportant to you, what I'm *doing*—what I *want* to do—having a little *difference* between them! You don't think that—
AMANDA I think you've been doing things that you're ashamed of. That's why you act like this. I don't believe that you go every night to the movies. Nobody goes to the movies night after night. Nobody in their right minds goes to the movies as often as you pretend to. People don't go to the movies at nearly midnight, and movies don't let out at two A.M. Come in stumbling. Muttering to yourself like a maniac! You get three hours' sleep and then go to work. Oh, I can picture the way you're doing down there. Moping, doping, because you're in no condition!
TOM (*Wildly*) No, I'm in no condition!
AMANDA What right have you got to jeopardize your job? Jeopardize the security of us all? How do you think we'd manage if you were—
TOM Listen! You think I'm crazy *about the warehouse?* (*He bends fiercely toward her slight figure*) You think I'm in love with the Continental Shoemakers? You think I want to spend fifty-five *years* down there in that—*celotex interior!* with—*fluorescent—tubes!* Look! I'd rather somebody picked up a crowbar and battered out my brains—than go back mornings! I *go!* Every time you come in yelling that God damn "*Rise and Shine!*" "*Rise and Shine!*" I say to myself, "How *lucky dead* people are!" But I get up. I *go!* For sixty-five dollars a month I give up all that I dream of doing and being *ever!* And you say self—*self's* all I ever think of. Why, listen, if self is what I thought of, Mother, I'd be where he is—GONE! (*Pointing to father's picture*) As

far as the system of transportation reaches! (*He starts past her. She grabs his arm*) Don't grab at me, Mother!

AMANDA Where are you going?

TOM I'm going to the *movies!*

AMANDA I don't believe that lie!

TOM (*Crouching toward her, overtowering her tiny figure. She backs away, gasping*) I'm going to opium dens! Yes, opium dens, dens of vice and criminals' hang-outs, Mother. I've joined the Hogan gang, I'm a hired assassin, I carry a tommy-gun in a violin case! I run a string of cat-houses in the Valley! They call me Killer, Killer Wingfield, I'm leading a double-life, a simple, honest warehouse worker by day, by night a dynamic *czar* of the *underworld*, Mother. I go to gambling casinos, I spin away fortunes on the roulette table! I wear a patch over one eye and a false mustache, sometimes I put on green whiskers. On those occasions they call me—*El Diablo!* Oh, I could tell you things to make you sleepless! My enemies plan to dynamite this place. They're going to blow us all sky-high some night! I'll be glad, very happy, and so will you! You'll go up, up on a broomstick, over Blue Mountain with seventeen gentlemen callers! You ugly—babbling old—*witch*. . . . (*He goes through a series of violent, clumsy movements, seizing his overcoat, lunging to the door, pulling it fiercely open. The women watch him, aghast. His arm catches in the sleeve of the coat as he struggles to pull it on. For a moment he is pinioned by the bulky garment. With an outraged groan he tears the coat off again, splitting the shoulder of it, and hurls it across the room. It strikes against the shelf of* LAURA'S *glass collection, there is a tinkle of shattering glass.* LAURA *cries out as if wounded*)

(MUSIC. LEGEND: "THE GLASS MENAGERIE")

LAURA (*Shrilly*) My glass!—menagerie. . . . (*She covers her face and turns away*)

(*But* AMANDA *is still stunned and stupefied by the "ugly witch" so that she barely notices this occurrence. Now she recovers her speech*)

AMANDA (*In an awful voice*) I won't speak to you—until you apologize! (*She crosses through portieres and draws them together behind her.* TOM *is left with* LAURA. LAURA *clings weakly to the mantel with her face averted.* TOM *stares at her stupidly for a moment. Then he crosses to shelf. Drops awkwardly on his knees to collect the fallen glass, glancing at* LAURA *as if he would speak but couldn't*)

(*"The Glass Menagerie" Steals in as the Scene Dims Out*)

Scene Four

The interior is dark. Faint light in the alley.

A deep-voiced bell in a church is tolling the hour of five as the scene commences.

TOM *appears at the top of the alley. After each solemn boom of the bell in the tower, he shakes a little noise-maker or rattle as if to express the tiny spasm of man in contrast to the sustained power and dignity of the Almighty. This and the unsteadiness of his advance make it evident that he has been drinking.*

As *he climbs the few steps to the fire-escape landing light steals up inside.* LAURA *appears in nightdress, observing* TOM'S *empty bed in the front room.*

TOM *fishes in his pockets for door key, removing a motley assortment of articles in the search, including a perfect shower of movie-ticket stubs and an empty bottle. At last he finds the key, but just as he is about to insert it, it slips from his fingers. He strikes a match and crouches below the door.*

TOM (*Bitterly*) One crack—and it falls through!

(LAURA *opens the door*)

LAURA   Tom, Tom, what are you doing?
TOM   Looking for a door key.
LAURA   Where have you been all this time?
TOM   I have been to the movies.
LAURA   All this time at the movies?
TOM   There was a very long program. There was a Garbo picture and a Mickey Mouse and a travelogue and a newsreel and a preview of coming attractions. And there was an organ solo and a collection for the milk-fund—simultaneously—which ended up in a terrible fight between a fat lady and an usher!
LAURA (*Innocently*)   Did you have to stay through everything?
TOM   Of course! And, oh, I forgot! There was a big stage show! The headliner on this stage show was Malvolio the Magician. He performed wonderful tricks, many of them, such as pouring water back and forth

between pitchers. First it turned to wine and then it turned to beer and then it turned to whiskey. I know it was whiskey it finally turned into because he needed somebody to come up out of the audience to help him, and I came up—both shows! It was Kentucky Straight Bourbon. A very generous fellow, he gave souvenirs. (*He pulls from his back pocket a shimmering rainbow-colored scarf*) He gave me this. This is his magic scarf. You can have it, Laura. You wave it over a canary cage and you get a bowl of gold-fish. You wave it over the gold-fish bowl and they fly away canaries. . . . But the wonderfullest trick of all was the coffin trick. We nailed him into a coffin and he got out of the coffin without removing one nail. (*He has come inside*) There is a trick that would come in handy for me—get me out of this 2 by 4 situation! (*Flops onto bed and starts removing shoes*)

LAURA Tom—Shhh!
TOM What're you shushing me for?
LAURA You'll wake up Mother.
TOM Goody, goody! Pay 'er back for all those "Rise an' Shines." (*Lies down, groaning*) You know it don't take much intelligence to get yourself into a nailed-up coffin, Laura. But who in hell ever got himself out of one without removing one nail?

(*As if in answer, the father's grinning photograph lights up*)

SCENE DIMS OUT

(*Immediately following: The church bell is heard striking six. At the sixth stroke the alarm clock goes off in* AMANDA'S *room, and after a few moments we hear her calling: "Rise and Shine! Rise and Shine! Laura, go tell your brother to rise and shine!"*)

TOM (*Sitting up slowly*) I'll rise—but I won't shine.

(*The light increases*)

AMANDA Laura, tell your brother his coffee is ready.

(LAURA *slips into front room*)

LAURA Tom!—It's nearly seven. Don't make Mother nervous. (*He stares at her stupidly. Beseechingly*) Tom, speak to Mother this morning. Make up with her, apologize, speak to her!
TOM She won't to me. It's her that started not speaking.
LAURA If you just say you're sorry she'll start speaking.
TOM Her not speaking—is that such a tragedy?
LAURA Please—please!
AMANDA (*Calling from kitchenette*) Laura, are you going to do what I

357 · *The Glass Menagerie* [Scene Four]

asked you to do, or do I have to get dressed and go out myself?
LAURA   Going, going—soon as I get on my coat! (*She pulls on a shapeless felt hat with nervous, jerky movement, pleadingly glancing at* TOM. *Rushes awkwardly for coat. The coat is one of* AMANDA'S, *inaccurately made-over, the sleeves too short for* LAURA) Butter and what else?
AMANDA (*Entering upstage*)   Just butter. Tell them to charge it.
LAURA   Mother, they make such faces when I do that.
AMANDA Sticks and stones can break our bones, but the expression on Mr. Garfinkel's face won't harm us! Tell your brother his coffee is getting cold.
LAURA   (*At door*)   Do what I asked you, will you, will you, Tom?

(*He looks sullenly away*)

AMANDA   Laura, go now or just don't go at all!
LAURA   (*Rushing out*)   Going—going! (*A second later she cries out.* TOM *springs up and crosses to door.* AMANDA *rushes anxiously in.* TOM *opens the door*)
TOM   Laura?
LAURA   I'm all right. I slipped, but I'm all right.
AMANDA (*Peering anxiously after her*)   If anyone breaks a leg on those fire-escape steps, the landlord ought to be sued for every cent he possesses! (*She shuts door. Remembers she isn't speaking and returns to other room*)

   (As TOM *enters listlessly for his coffee, she turns her back to him and stands rigidly facing the window on the gloomy gray vault of the areaway. Its light on her face with its aged but childish features is cruelly sharp, satirical as a Daumier print*[6])

   (MUSIC UNDER: "AVE MARIA")

   (TOM *glances sheepishly but sullenly at her averted figure and slumps at the table. The coffee is scalding hot; he sips it and gasps and spits it back in the cup. At his gasp,* AMANDA *catches her breath and half turns. Then catches herself and turns back to window*)

   (TOM *blows on his coffee, glancing sidewise at his mother. She clears her throat.* TOM *clears his. He starts to rise. Sinks back down again, scratches his head, clears his throat again.* AMANDA *coughs.* TOM *raises his cup in both hands to blow on it, his eyes staring over the rim of it at his mother for several moments. Then he slowly sets the cup down and awkwardly and hesitantly rises from the chair*)

[6] Honoré Daumier (1808–1879), French painter and caricaturist.

TOM (*Hoarsely*) Mother. I—I apologize, Mother. (AMANDA *draws a quick, shuddering breath. Her face works grotesquely. She breaks into childlike tears*) I'm sorry for what I said, for everything that I said, I didn't mean it.
AMANDA (*Sobbingly*) My devotion has made me a witch and so I make myself hateful to my children!
TOM No, you *don't*.
AMANDA I worry so much, don't sleep, it makes me nervous!
TOM (*Gently*) I understand that.
AMANDA I've had to put up a solitary battle all these years. But you're my right-hand bower! Don't fall down, don't fail!
TOM (*Gently*) I try, Mother.
AMANDA (*With great enthusiasm*) Try and you will SUCCEED! (*The notion makes her breathless*) Why, you—you're just *full* of natural endowments! Both my children—they're *unusual* children! Don't you think I know it? I'm so—*proud!* Happy and—feel I've—so much to be thankful for but— Promise me one thing, Son!
TOM What, Mother?
AMANDA Promise, Son, you'll—never be a drunkard!
TOM (*Turns to her grinning*) I will never be a drunkard, Mother.
AMANDA That's what frightened me so, that you'd be drinking! Eat a bowl of Purina!
TOM Just coffee, Mother.
AMANDA Shredded wheat biscuit?
TOM No. No, Mother, just coffee.
AMANDA You can't put in a day's work on an empty stomach. You've got ten minutes—don't gulp! Drinking too-hot liquids makes cancer of the stomach. . . . Put cream in.
TOM No, thank you.
AMANDA To cool it.
TOM No! No, thank you, I want it black.
AMANDA I know, but it's not good for you. We have to do all that we can to build ourselves up. In these trying times we live in, all that we have to cling to is—each other. . . . That's why it's so important to —Tom, I—I sent out your sister so I could discuss something with you. If you hadn't spoken I would have spoken to you. (*Sits down*)
TOM (*Gently*) What is it, Mother, that you want to discuss?
AMANDA *Laura!*

(TOM *puts his cup down slowly*)

(LEGEND ON SCREEN: "LAURA")

(MUSIC: "THE GLASS MENAGERIE")

TOM —Oh—Laura . . .
AMANDA (*Touching his sleeve*) You know how Laura is. So quiet but —still water runs deep! She notices things and I think she—broods about them. (TOM *looks up*) A few days ago I came in and she was crying.
TOM What about?
AMANDA You.
TOM Me?
AMANDA She has an idea that you're not happy here.
TOM What gave her that idea?
AMANDA What gives her any idea? However, you do act strangely. I—I'm not criticizing, understand *that*! I know your ambitions do not lie in the warehouse, that like everybody in the whole wide world—you've had to—make sacrifices, but—Tom—Tom—life's not easy, it calls for—Spartan endurance! There's so many things in my heart that I cannot describe to you! I've never told you but I—*loved* your father. . . .
TOM (*Gently*) I know that, Mother.
AMANDA And you—when I see you taking after his ways! Staying out late—and—well, you *had* been drinking the night you were in that—terrifying condition! Laura says that you hate the apartment and that you go out nights to get away from it! Is that true, Tom?
TOM No. You say there's so much in your heart that you can't describe to me. That's true of me, too. There's so much in my heart that I can't describe to *you*! So let's respect each other's—
AMANDA But, why—*why*, Tom—are you always so *restless*? Where do you *go* to, nights?
TOM I—go to the movies.
AMANDA Why do you go to the movies so much, Tom?
TOM I go to the movies because—I like adventure. Adventure is something I don't have much of at work, so I go to the movies.
AMANDA But, Tom, you go to the movies *entirely* too *much*!
TOM I like a lot of adventure.

(AMANDA *looks baffled, then hurt. As the familiar inquisition resumes he becomes hard and impatient again.* AMANDA *slips back into her querulous attitude toward him*)

(IMAGE ON SCREEN: SAILING VESSEL WITH JOLLY ROGER)

AMANDA Most young men find adventure in their careers.
TOM Then most young men are not employed in a warehouse.

AMANDA The world is full of young men employed in warehouses and offices and factories.
TOM Do all of them find adventure in their careers?
AMANDA They do or they do without it! Not everybody has a craze for adventure.
TOM Man is by instinct a lover, a hunter, a fighter, and none of those instincts are given much play at the warehouse!
AMANDA Man is by instinct! Don't quote instinct to me! Instinct is something that people have got away from! It belongs to animals! Christian adults don't want it!
TOM What do Christian adults want, then, Mother?
AMANDA Superior things! Things of the mind and the spirit! Only animals have to satisfy instincts! Surely your aims are somewhat higher than theirs! Than monkeys—pigs—
TOM I reckon they're not.
AMANDA You're joking! However, that isn't what I wanted to discuss.
TOM (*Rising*) I haven't much time.
AMANDA (*Pushing his shoulders*) Sit down.
TOM You want me to punch in red at the warehouse, Mother?
AMANDA You have five minutes. I want to talk about Laura.

(LEGEND: "PLANS AND PROVISIONS")

TOM All right! What about Laura?
AMANDA We have to be making some plans and provisions for her. She's older than you, two years, and nothing has happened. She just drifts along doing nothing. It frightens me terribly how she just drifts along.
TOM I guess she's the type that people call home girls.
AMANDA There's no such type, and if there is, it's a pity! That is, unless the home is hers, with a husband!
TOM What?
AMANDA Oh, I can see the handwriting on the wall as plain as I see the nose in front of my face! It's terrifying!
  More and more you remind me of your father! He was out all hours without explanation!—Then *left!* Good-bye!
  And me with the bag to hold. I saw that letter you got from the Merchant Marine. I know what you're dreaming of. I'm not standing here blindfolded.
  Very well, then. Then *do* it!
  But not till there's somebody to take your place.
TOM What do you mean?
AMANDA I mean that as soon as Laura has got somebody to take care

of her, married, a home of her own, independent—why, then you'll be free to go wherever you please, on land, on sea, whichever way the wind blows you!

But until that time you've got to look out for your sister. I don't say me because I'm old and don't matter! I say for your sister because she's young and dependent.

I put her in business college—a dismal failure! Frightened her so it made her sick at the stomach.

I took her over to the Young People's League at the church. Another fiasco. She spoke to nobody, nobody spoke to her. Now all she does is fool with those pieces of glass and play those worn-out records. What kind of a life is that for a girl to lead?

TOM What can I do about it?
AMANDA Overcome selfishness!

Self, self, self is all that you ever think of!

(TOM *springs up and crosses to get his coat. It is ugly and bulky. He pulls on a cap with earmuffs*)

Where is your muffler? Put your wool muffler on!

(*He snatches it angrily from the closet and tosses it around his neck and pulls both ends tight*)

Tom! I haven't said what I had in mind to ask you.
TOM I'm too late to—
AMANDA (*Catching his arm—very importunately. Then shyly*)   Down at the warehouse, aren't there some—nice young men?
TOM No!
AMANDA There *must* be—*some* . . .
TOM Mother—(*Gesture*)
AMANDA Find out one that's clean-living—doesn't drink and—ask him out for sister!
TOM What?
AMANDA For *sister*! To *meet*! Get *acquainted*!
TOM (*Stamping to door*)   Oh, my go-osh!
AMANDA Will you? (*He opens door. Imploringly*) Will you? (*He starts down*) Will you? *Will* you, dear?
TOM (*Calling back*)   YES!

(AMANDA *closes the door hesitantly and with a troubled but faintly hopeful expression*)

(SCREEN IMAGE: GLAMOR MAGAZINE COVER)

(*Spot* AMANDA *at phone*)

AMANDA Ella Cartwright? This is Amanda Wingfield!
How are you, honey?
How is that kidney condition? (*Pause*)
Horrors! (*Pause*)
You're a Christian martyr, yes, honey, that's what you are, a Christian martyr!
Well, I just now happened to notice in my little red book that your subscription to the *Companion* has just run out! I knew that you wouldn't want to miss out on the wonderful serial starting in this new issue. It's by Bessie Mae Hopper, the first thing she's written since *Honeymoon for Three*.
Wasn't that a strange and interesting story? Well, this one is even lovelier, I believe. It has a sophisticated, society background. It's all about the horsey set on Long Island!

(*Fade Out*)

Scene Five

LEGEND ON SCREEN: "ANNUNCIATION." *Fade with music.*

It is early dusk of a spring evening. Supper has just been finished in the Wingfield apartment. AMANDA *and* LAURA *in light-colored dresses are removing dishes from the table, in the upstage area, which is shadowy, their movements formalized almost as a dance or ritual, their moving forms as pale and silent as moths.*

TOM, *in white shirt and trousers, rises from the table and crosses toward the fire-escape.*

AMANDA (*As he passes her*) Son, will you do me a favor?
TOM What?
AMANDA Comb your hair! You look so pretty when your hair is combed! (TOM *slouches on sofa with evening paper. Enormous caption* "Franco Triumphs") There is only one respect in which I would like you to emulate your father.
TOM What respect is that?
AMANDA The care he always took of his appearance. He never allowed himself to look untidy. (*He throws down the paper and crosses to fire-escape*) Where are you going?

363 · *The Glass Menagerie* [Scene Five]

TOM   I'm going out to smoke.
AMANDA   You smoke too much. A pack a day at fifteen cents a pack. How much would that amount to in a month? Thirty times fifteen is how much, Tom? Figure it out and you will be astounded at what you could save. Enough to give you a night-school course in accounting at Washington U! Just think what a wonderful thing that would be for you, Son!

(TOM *is unmoved by the thought*)

TOM   I'd rather smoke. (*He steps out on landing, letting the screen door slam*)
AMANDA   (*Sharply*)   I know! That's the tragedy of it. . . . (*Alone, she turns to look at her husband's picture*)

(DANCE MUSIC: "ALL THE WORLD IS WAITING FOR THE SUNRISE!")

TOM   (*To the audience*)   Across the alley from us was the Paradise Dance Hall. On evenings in spring the windows and doors were open and the music came outdoors. Sometimes the lights were turned out except for a large glass sphere that hung from the ceiling. It would turn slowly about and filter the dusk with delicate rainbow colors. Then the orchestra played a waltz or a tango, something that had a slow and sensuous rhythm. Couples would come outside, to the relative privacy of the alley. You could see them kissing behind ash-pits and telephone poles.
   This was the compensation for lives that passed like mine, without any change or adventure.
   Adventure and change were imminent in this year. They were waiting around the corner for all these kids.
   Suspended in the mist over Berchtesgaden,[7] caught in the folds of Chamberlain's umbrella—[8]
   In Spain there was Guernica!
   But here there was only hot swing music and liquor, dance halls, bars, and movies, and sex that hung in the gloom like a chandelier and flooded the world with brief, deceptive rainbows. . . .
   All the world was waiting for bombardments!

(AMANDA *turns from the picture and comes outside*)

[7] Adolf Hitler's retreat in the Bavarian Mountains.
[8] Neville Chamberlain, England's Prime Minister before World War II, made several efforts to appease Hitler—an appeasement that came to be symbolized by the umbrella he always carried with him.

AMANDA (*Sighing*) A fire-escape landing's a poor excuse for a porch. (*She spreads a newspaper on a step and sits down, gracefully and demurely as if she were settling into a swing on a Mississippi veranda*) What are you looking at?
TOM   The moon.
AMANDA   Is there a moon this evening?
TOM   It's rising over Garfinkel's Delicatessen.
AMANDA   So it is! A little silver slipper of a moon. Have you made a wish on it yet?
TOM   Um-hum.
AMANDA   What did you wish for?
TOM   That's a secret.
AMANDA   A secret, huh? Well, I won't tell mine either. I will be just as mysterious as you.
TOM   I bet I can guess what yours is.
AMANDA   Is my head so transparent?
TOM   You're not a sphinx.
AMANDA   No, I don't have secrets. I'll tell you what I wished for on the moon. Success and happiness for my precious children! I wish for that whenever there's a moon, and when there isn't a moon, I wish for it, too.
TOM   I thought perhaps you wished for a gentleman caller.
AMANDA   Why do you say that?
TOM   Don't you remember asking me to fetch one?
AMANDA   I remember suggesting that it would be nice for your sister if you brought home some nice young man from the warehouse. I think that I've made that suggestion more than once.
TOM   Yes, you have made it repeatedly.
AMANDA   Well?
TOM   We are going to have one.
AMANDA   W*hat?*
TOM   A gentleman caller!

(THE ANNUNCIATION IS CELEBRATED WITH MUSIC)

(AMANDA *rises*)

(IMAGE ON SCREEN: CALLER WITH BOUQUET)

AMANDA   You mean you have asked some nice young man to come over?
TOM   Yep. I've asked him to dinner.
AMANDA   You really did?
TOM   I did!
AMANDA   You did, and did he—*accept?*

TOM   He did!
AMANDA   Well, well—well, well! That's—lovely!
TOM   I thought that you would be pleased.
AMANDA   It's definite, then?
TOM   Very definite.
AMANDA   Soon?
TOM   Very soon.
AMANDA   For heaven's sake, stop putting on and tell me some things, will you?
TOM   What things do you want me to tell you?
AMANDA   *Naturally* I would like to know when he's *coming!*
TOM   He's coming tomorrow.
AMANDA   *Tomorrow?*
TOM   Yep. Tomorrow.
AMANDA   But, Tom!
TOM   Yes, Mother?
AMANDA   Tomorrow gives me no time!
TOM   Time for what?
AMANDA   Preparations! Why didn't you phone me at once, as soon as you asked him, the minute that he accepted? Then, don't you see, I could have been getting ready!
TOM   You don't have to make any fuss.
AMANDA   Oh, Tom, Tom, Tom, of course I have to make a fuss! I want things nice, not sloppy! Not thrown together. I'll certainly have to do some fast thinking, won't I?
TOM   I don't see why you have to think at all.
AMANDA   You just don't know. We can't have a gentleman caller in a pig-sty! All my wedding silver has to be polished, the monogrammed table linen ought to be laundered! The windows have to be washed and fresh curtains put up. And how about clothes? We have to *wear* something, don't we?
TOM   Mother, this boy is no one to make a fuss over!
AMANDA   Do you realize he's the first young man we've introduced to your sister?
     It's terrible, dreadful, disgraceful that poor little sister has never received a single gentleman caller! Tom, come inside! (*She opens the screen door*)
TOM   What for?
AMANDA   I want to ask you some things.
TOM   If you're going to make such a fuss, I'll call it off, I'll tell him not to come!
AMANDA   You certainly won't do anything of the kind. Nothing offends

people worse than broken engagements. It simply means I'll have to work like a Turk! We won't be brilliant, but we will pass inspection. Come on inside. (TOM *follows, groaning*) Sit down.

TOM Any particular place you would like me to sit?

AMANDA Thank heavens I've got that new sofa! I'm also making payments on a floor lamp I'll have sent out! And put the chintz covers on, they'll brighten things up! Of course I'd hoped to have these walls repapered. . . . What is the young man's name?

TOM His name is O'Connor.

AMANDA That, of course, means fish—tomorrow is Friday! I'll have that salmon loaf—with Durkee's dressing! What does he do? He works at the warehouse?

TOM Of course! How else would I—

AMANDA Tom, he—doesn't drink?

TOM Why do you ask me that?

AMANDA Your father *did!*

TOM Don't get started on that!

AMANDA He *does* drink, then?

TOM Not that I know of!

AMANDA Make sure, be certain! The last thing I want for my daughter's a boy who drinks!

TOM Aren't you being a little bit premature? Mr. O'Connor has not yet appeared on the scene!

AMANDA But will tomorrow. To meet your sister, and what do I know about his character? Nothing! Old maids are better off than wives of drunkards!

TOM Oh, my God!

AMANDA Be still!

TOM (*Leaning forward to whisper*) Lots of fellows meet girls whom they don't marry!

AMANDA Oh, talk sensibly, Tom—and don't be sarcastic! (*She has gotten a hairbrush*)

TOM What are you doing?

AMANDA I'm brushing that cow-lick down!

What is this young man's position at the warehouse?

TOM (*Submitting grimly to the brush and the interrogation*) This young man's position is that of a shipping clerk, Mother.

AMANDA Sounds to me like a fairly responsible job, the sort of job *you* would be in if you just had more *get-up*.

What is his salary? Have you any idea?

TOM I would judge it to be approximately eighty-five dollars a month.

AMANDA Well—not princely, but—

TOM Twenty more than I make.
AMANDA Yes, how well I know! But for a family man, eighty-five dollars a month is not much more than you can just get by on. . . .
TOM Yes, but Mr. O'Connor is not a family man.
AMANDA He might be, mightn't he? Some time in the future?
TOM I see. Plans and provisions.
AMANDA You are the only young man that I know of who ignores the fact that the future becomes the present, the present the past, and the past turns into everlasting regret if you don't plan for it!
TOM I will think that over and see what I can make of it.
AMANDA Don't be supercilious with your mother! Tell me some more about this—what do you call him?
TOM James D. O'Connor. The D. is for Delaney.
AMANDA Irish on *both* sides! *Gracious!* And doesn't drink?
TOM Shall I call him up and ask him right this minute?
AMANDA The only way to find out about those things is to make discreet inquiries at the proper moment. When I was a girl in Blue Mountain and it was suspected that a young man drank, the girl whose attentions he had been receiving, if any girl *was*, would sometimes speak to the minister of his church, or rather her father would if her father was living, and sort of feel him out on the young man's character. That is the way such things are discreetly handled to keep a young woman from making a tragic mistake!
TOM Then how did you happen to make a tragic mistake?
AMANDA That innocent look of your father's had everyone fooled! He *smiled*—the world was *enchanted!*
No girl can do worse than put herself at the mercy of a handsome appearance!
I hope that Mr. O'Connor is not too good-looking.
TOM No, he's not too good-looking. He's covered with freckles and hasn't too much of a nose.
AMANDA He's not right-down homely, though?
TOM Not right-down homely. Just medium homely, I'd say.
AMANDA Character's what to look for in a man.
TOM That's what I've always said, Mother.
AMANDA You've never said anything of the kind and I suspect you would never give it a thought.
TOM Don't be so suspicious of me.
AMANDA At least I hope he's the type that's up and coming.
TOM I think he really goes in for self-improvement.
AMANDA What reason have you to think so?
TOM He goes to night school.

AMANDA (*Beaming*) Splendid! What does he do, I mean study?
TOM Radio engineering and public speaking!
AMANDA Then he has visions of being advanced in the world!
   Any young man who studies public speaking is aiming to have an executive job some day!
   And radio engineering? A thing for the future!
   Both of these facts are very illuminating. Those are the sort of things that a mother should know concerning any young man who comes to call on her daughter. Seriously or—not.
TOM One little warning. He doesn't know about Laura. I didn't let on that we had dark ulterior motives. I just said, why don't you come and have dinner with us? He said okay and that was the whole conversation.
AMANDA I bet it was! You're eloquent as an oyster.
   However, he'll know about Laura when he gets here. When he sees how lovely and sweet and pretty she is, he'll thank his lucky stars he was asked to dinner.
TOM Mother, you mustn't expect too much of Laura.
AMANDA What do you mean?
TOM Laura seems all those things to you and me because she's ours and we love her. We don't even notice she's crippled any more.
AMANDA Don't say crippled! You know that I never allow that word to be used!
TOM But face facts, Mother. She is and—that's not all—
AMANDA What do you mean "not all"?
TOM Laura is very different from other girls.
AMANDA I think the difference is all to her advantage.
TOM Not quite all—in the eyes of others—strangers—she's terribly shy and lives in a world of her own and those things make her seem a little peculiar to people outside the house.
AMANDA Don't say peculiar.
TOM Face the facts. She is.

(THE DANCE-HALL MUSIC CHANGES TO A TANGO THAT HAS A MINOR AND SOMEWHAT OMINOUS TONE)

AMANDA In what way is she peculiar—may I ask?
TOM (*Gently*) She lives in a world of her own—a world of—little glass ornaments, Mother. . . . (*Gets up.* AMANDA *remains holding brush, looking at him, troubled*) She plays old phonograph records and—that's about all— (*He glances at himself in the mirror and crosses to door*)
AMANDA (*Sharply*) Where are you going?

TOM I'm going to the movies. (*Out screen door*)
AMANDA Not to the movies, every night to the movies! (*Follows quickly to screen door*) I don't believe you always go to the movies! (*He is gone.* AMANDA *looks worriedly after him for a moment. Then vitality and optimism return and she turns from the door. Crossing to portieres*) Laura! Laura! (LAURA *answers from kitchenette*)
LAURA Yes, Mother.
AMANDA Let those dishes go and come in front! (LAURA *appears with dish towel. Gaily*) Laura, come here and make a wish on the moon!

(SCREEN IMAGE: MOON)

LAURA (*Entering*) Moon—moon?
AMANDA A little silver slipper of a moon. Look over your left shoulder, Laura, and make a wish!

(LAURA *looks faintly puzzled as if called out of sleep.* AMANDA *seizes her shoulders and turns her at an angle by the door*)

Now!
Now, darling, *wish!*
LAURA What shall I wish for, Mother?
AMANDA (*Her voice trembling and her eyes suddenly filling with tears*) Happiness! Good fortune!

(*The violin rises and the stage dims out*)

(*The Curtain Falls*)

Scene Six

(IMAGE: HIGH SCHOOL HERO)

TOM And so the following evening I brought Jim home to dinner. I had known Jim slightly in high school. In high school Jim was a hero. He had tremendous Irish good nature and vitality with the scrubbed and polished look of white chinaware. He seemed to move in a continual spotlight. He was a star in basketball, captain of the debating club, president of the senior class and the glee club, and he sang the male lead in the annual light operas. He was always running or bounding, never just walking. He seemed always at the point of defeating the law of gravity. He was shooting with such velocity through his adolescence that you would logically expect him to arrive at nothing short of the White House by the time he was thirty. But Jim apparently ran into more interference after his graduation from Soldan. His speed had definitely slowed. Six years after he left high school he was holding a job that wasn't much better than mine.

(IMAGE: CLERK)

He was the only one at the warehouse with whom I was on friendly terms. I was valuable to him as someone who could remember his former glory, who had seen him win basketball games and the silver cup in debating. He knew of my secret practice of retiring to a cabinet of the wash-room to work on poems when business was slack in the warehouse. He called me Shakespeare. And while the other boys in the warehouse regarded me with suspicious hostility, Jim took a humorous attitude toward me. Gradually his attitude affected the others, their hostility wore off and they also began to smile at me as people smile at an oddly fashioned dog who trots across their path at some distance.

I knew that Jim and Laura had known each other at Soldan, and I had heard Laura speak admiringly of his voice. I didn't know if Jim remembered her or not. In high school Laura had been as unobtrusive as Jim had been astonishing. If he did remember Laura, it was not as my sister, for when I asked him to dinner, he grinned and said, "You know, Shakespeare, I never thought of you as having folks!"

He was about to discover that I did. . . .

(LIGHT UP STAGE)

(LEGEND ON SCREEN: "THE ACCENT OF A COMING FOOT")

(*Friday evening. It is about five o'clock of a late spring evening which comes "scattering poems in the sky"*)

(*A delicate lemony light is in the Wingfield apartment*)

(*Amanda has worked like a Turk in preparation for the gentleman caller. The results are astonishing. The new floor lamp with its rose-silk shade is in place, a colored paper lantern conceals the broken light fixture in the ceiling, new billowing white curtains are at the windows, chintz covers are on chairs and sofa, a pair of new sofa pllows make their initial appearance*)

(*Open boxes and tissue paper are scattered on the floor*)

(LAURA *stands in the middle with lifted arms while* AMANDA *crouches before her, adjusting the hem of the new dress, devout* and ritualistic. The dress is colored and designed by memory. The arrangement of LAURA's hair is changed; it is softer and more becoming. A fragile, unearthly prettiness has come out in LAURA: she is like a piece of translucent glass touched by light, given a momentary radiance, not actual, not lasting)

AMANDA (*Impatiently*) Why are you trembling?
LAURA Mother, you've made me so nervous!
AMANDA How have I made you nervous?
LAURA By all this fuss! You make it seem so important!
AMANDA I don't understand you, Laura. You couldn't be satisfied with just sitting home, and yet whenever I try to arrange something for you, you seem to resist it.

(*She gets up*)

Now take a look at yourself.
No, wait! Wait just a moment—I have an idea!
LAURA What is it now?

(AMANDA *produces two powder puffs which she wraps in handkerchiefs and stuffs in* LAURA's *bosom*)

LAURA Mother, what are you doing?
AMANDA They call them "Gay Deceivers"!
LAURA I won't wear them!
AMANDA You will!
LAURA Why should I?
AMANDA Because, to be painfully honest, your chest is flat.
LAURA You make it seem like we were setting a trap.
AMANDA All pretty girls are a trap, a pretty trap, and men expect them to be.

(LEGEND: "A PRETTY TRAP")

Now look at yourself, young lady. This is the prettiest you will ever be!
I've got to fix myself now! You're going to be surprised by your mother's appearance! (*She crosses through portieres, humming gaily*)

(LAURA *moves slowly to the long mirror and stares solemnly at herself*)

(*A wind blows the white curtains inward in a slow, graceful motion and with a faint, sorrowful sighing*)

AMANDA (*Off stage*) It isn't dark enough yet. (*She turns slowly before the mirror with a troubled look*)

(LEGEND ON SCREEN: "THIS IS MY SISTER: CELEBRATE HER WITH STRINGS!" MUSIC)

AMANDA (*Laughing, off*) I'm going to show you something. I'm going to make a spectacular appearance!
LAURA   What is it, Mother?
AMANDA   Possess your soul in patience—you will see! Something I've resurrected from that old trunk! Styles haven't changed so terribly much after all. . . .

(*She parts the portieres*)

Now just look at your mother!

(*She wears a girlish frock of yellowed voile with a blue silk sash. She carries a bunch of jonquils—the legend of her youth is nearly revived. Feverishly*)

This is the dress in which I led the cotillion. Won the cakewalk twice at Sunset Hill, wore one spring to the Governor's ball in Jackson!
See how I sashayed around the ballroom, Laura?

(*She raises her skirt and does a mincing step around the room*)

I wore it on Sundays for my gentlemen callers! I had it on the day I met your father—
I had malaria fever all that spring. The change of climate from East Tennessee to the Delta—weakened resistance—I had a little temperature all the time—not enough to be serious—just enough to make me restless and giddy!—Invitations poured in—parties all over the Delta!—"Stay in bed," said Mother, "you have fever!"—but I just wouldn't—I took quinine but kept on going, going!—Evenings, dances!—Afternoons, long, long rides! Picnics—lovely!—So lovely, that country in May—All lacy with dogwood, literally flooded with jonquils!—That was the spring I had the craze for jonquils. Jonquils became an absolute obsession. Mother said, "Honey, there's no more room for jonquils." And still I kept on bringing in more jonquils. Whenever, wherever I saw them, I'd say, "Stop! Stop! I see jonquils!" I made the young men help me gather the jonquils! It was a joke, Amanda and her jonquils! Finally there were no more vases to hold them, every available space was filled with jonquils. No vases to hold them? All right, I'll hold them myself! And then I—(*She stops in front of the picture.* MUSIC) met your father!
Malaria fever and jonquils and then—this—boy. . . .

(*She switches on the rose-colored lamp*)
I hope they get here before it starts to rain.

(*She crosses upstage and places the jonquils in bowl on table*)
I gave your brother a little extra change so he and Mr. O'Connor could take the service car home.
LAURA (*With altered look*)   What did you say his name was?
AMANDA   O'Connor.
LAURA   What is his first name?
AMANDA   I don't remember. Oh, yes, I do. It was—Jim!

(LAURA *sways slightly and catches hold of a chair*)

(LEGEND ON SCREEN: "NOT JIM!")

LAURA (*Faintly*)   Not—Jim.
AMANDA   Yes, that was it, it was Jim! I've never known a Jim that wasn't nice!

(MUSIC: OMINOUS)

LAURA   Are you sure his name is Jim O'Connor?
AMANDA   Yes. Why?
LAURA   Is he the one that Tom used to know in high school?
AMANDA   He didn't say so. I think he just got to know him at the warehouse.
LAURA   There was a Jim O'Connor we both knew in high school—(*Then, with effort*) If that is the one that Tom is bringing to dinner—you'll have to excuse me, I won't come to the table.
AMANDA   What sort of nonsense is this?
LAURA   You asked me once if I'd ever liked a boy. Don't you remember I showed you this boy's picture?
AMANDA   You mean the boy you showed me in the year book?
LAURA   Yes, that boy.
AMANDA   Laura, Laura, were you in love with that boy?
LAURA   I don't know. Mother. All I know is I couldn't sit at the table if it was him!
AMANDA   It won't be him! It isn't the least bit likely. But whether it is or not, you will come to the table. You will not be excused.
LAURA   I'll have to be, Mother.
AMANDA   I don't intend to humor your silliness, Laura. I've had too much from you and your brother, both!
   So just sit down and compose yourself till they come. Tom has forgotten his key so you'll have to let them in, when they arrive.

LAURA (*Panicky*)   Oh, Mother—*you* answer the door!
AMANDA (*Lightly*)   I'll be in the kitchen—busy!
LAURA   Oh, Mother, please answer the door, don't make me do it!
AMANDA (*Crossing into kitchenette*)   I've got to fix the dressing for the salmon. Fuss, fuss—silliness!—over a gentleman caller!

(*Door swings shut.* LAURA *is left alone*)

(LEGEND: "TERROR!")

(*She utters a low moan and turns off the lamp—sits stiffly on the edge of the sofa, knotting her fingers together*)

(LEGEND ON SCREEN: "THE OPENING OF A DOOR!")

(TOM *and* JIM *appear on the fire-escape steps and climb to landing. Hearing their approach,* LAURA *rises with a panicky gesture. She retreats to the portieres*)

(*The doorbell.* LAURA *catches her breath and touches her throat. Low drums*)

AMANDA (*Calling*)   Laura, sweetheart! The door!

(LAURA *stares at it without moving*)

JIM   I think we just beat the rain.
TOM   Uh-huh. (*He rings again, nervously.* JIM *whistles and fishes for a cigarette*)
AMANDA (*Very, very gaily*)   Laura, that is your brother and Mr O'Connor! Will you let them in, darling?

(LAURA *crosses toward kitchenette door*)

LAURA (*Breathlessly*)   Mother—you go to the door!

(AMANDA *steps out of kitchenette and stares furiously at* LAURA. *She points imperiously at the door*)

LAURA   Please, please!
AMANDA (*In a fierce whisper*)   What is the matter with you, you silly thing?
LAURA (*Desperately*)   Please, you answer it, *please!*
AMANDA   I told you I wasn't going to humor you, Laura. Why have you chosen this moment to lose your mind?
LAURA   Please, please, please, you go!
AMANDA   You'll have to go to the door because I can't!
LAURA (*Despairingly*)   I can't either!
AMANDA   *Why?*
LAURA   I'm *sick!*

AMANDA I'm sick, too—of your nonsense! Why can't you and your brother be normal people? Fantastic whims and behavior!

(TOM *gives a long ring*)

Preposterous goings on! Can you give me one reason—(*Calls out lyrically*) COMING! JUST ONE SECOND!—why you should be afraid to open a door? Now you answer it, Laura!

LAURA Oh, oh, oh . . . (*She returns through the portieres. Darts to the victrola and winds it frantically and turns it on*)

AMANDA Laura Wingfield, you march right to that door!

LAURA Yes—yes, Mother!

(*A faraway, scratchy rendition of "Dardanella" softens the air and gives her strength to move through it. She slips to the door and draws it cautiously open*)
(TOM *enters with the caller,* JIM O'CONNOR)

TOM Laura, this is Jim. Jim, this is my sister, Laura.

JIM (*Stepping inside*) I didn't know that Shakespeare had a sister!

LAURA (*Retreating stiff and trembling from the door*) How—how do you do?

JIM (*Heartily extending his hand*) Okay!

(LAURA *touches it hesitantly with hers*)

JIM Your hand's *cold*, Laura!

LAURA Yes, well—I've been playing the victrola. . . .

JIM Must have been playing classical music on it! You ought to play a little hot swing music to warm you up!

LAURA Excuse me—I haven't finished playing the victrola. . . .

(*She turns awkwardly and hurries into the front room. She pauses a second by the victrola. Then catches her breath and darts through the portieres like a frightened deer*)

JIM (*Grinning*) What was the matter?

TOM Oh—with Laura? Laura is—terribly shy.

JIM Shy, huh? It's unusual to meet a shy girl nowadays. I don't believe you ever mentioned you had a sister.

TOM Well, now you know. I have one. Here is the *Post Dispatch*. You want a piece of it?

JIM Uh-huh.

TOM What piece? The comics?

JIM Sports! (*Glances at it*) Ole Dizzy Dean[9] is on his bad behavior.

[9] Baseball pitcher for the St. Louis Cardinals.

TOM (*Disinterest*) Yeah? (*Lights cigarette and crosses back to fire-escape door*)
JIM   Where are *you* going?
TOM   I'm going out on the terrace.
JIM   (*Goes after him*) You know, Shakespeare—I'm going to sell you a bill of goods!
TOM   What goods?
JIM   A course I'm taking.
TOM   Huh?
JIM   In public speaking! You and me, we're not the warehouse type.
TOM   Thanks—that's good news.
   But what has public speaking got to do with it?
JIM   It fits you for—executive positions!
TOM   Awww.
JIM   I tell you it's done a helluva lot for me.

(IMAGE: EXECUTIVE AT DESK)

TOM   In what respect?
JIM   In every! Ask yourself what is the difference between you an' me and men in the office down front? Brains?—No!—Ability?—No! Then what? Just one little thing—
TOM   What is that one little thing?
JIM   Primarily it amounts to—social poise! Being able to square up to people and hold your own on any social level!
AMANDA   (*Off stage*)   Tom?
TOM   Yes, Mother?
AMANDA   Is that you and Mr. O'Connor?
TOM   Yes, Mother.
AMANDA   Well, you just make yourselves comfortable in there.
TOM   Yes, Mother.
AMANDA   Ask Mr. O'Connor if he would like to wash his hands.
JIM   Aw, no—no—thank you—I took care of that at the warehouse. Tom—
TOM   Yes?
JIM   Mr. Mendoza was speaking to me about you.
TOM   Favorably?
JIM   What do you think?
TOM   Well—
JIM   You're going to be out of a job if you don't wake up.
TOM   I am waking up—
JIM   You show no signs.
TOM   The signs are interior.

(IMAGE ON SCREEN: THE SAILING VESSEL WITH JOLLY ROGER AGAIN)

TOM I'm planning to change. (*He leans over the rail speaking with quiet exhilaration. The incandescent marquees and signs of the first-run movie houses light his face from across the alley. He looks like a voyager*) I'm right at the point of committing myself to a future that doesn't include the warehouse and Mr. Mendoza or even a night-school course in public speaking.
JIM What are you gassing about?
TOM I'm tired of the movies.
JIM Movies!
TOM Yes, movies! Look at them— (*A wave toward the marvels of Grand Avenue*) All of those glamorous people—having adventures—hogging it all, gobbling the whole thing up! You know what happens? People go to the *movies* instead of *moving!* Hollywood characters are supposed to have all the adventures for everybody in America, while everybody in America sits in a dark room and watches them have them! Yes, until there's a war. That's when adventure becomes available to the masses! *Everyone's* dish, not only Gable's![10] Then the people in the dark room come out of the dark room to have some adventures themselves—Goody, goody!—It's our turn now, to go to the South Sea Island—to make a safari—to be exotic, far-off!—But I'm not patient. I don't want to wait till then. I'm tired of the *movies* and I am *about to move!*
JIM (*Incredulously*) Move?
TOM Yes.
JIM When?
TOM Soon!
JIM Where? Where?

(THEME THREE MUSIC SEEMS TO ANSWER THE QUESTION, WHILE TOM THINKS IT OVER. HE SEARCHES AMONG HIS POCKETS)

TOM I'm starting to boil inside. I know I seem dreamy, but inside—well, I'm boiling!—Whenever I pick up a shoe, I shudder a little thinking how short life is and what I am doing!—Whatever that means, I know it doesn't mean shoes—except as something to wear on a traveler's feet! (*Finds paper*) Look—
JIM What?
TOM I'm a member.
JIM (*Reading*) The Union of Merchant Seamen.

---

[10] Clark Gable, popular movie star.

TOM I paid my dues this month, instead of the light bill.
JIM You will regret it when they turn the lights off.
TOM I won't be here.
JIM How about your mother?
TOM I'm like my father. The bastard son of a bastard! See how he grins? And he's been absent going on sixteen years!
JIM You're just talking, you drip. How does your mother feel about it?
TOM Shhh!—Here comes Mother! Mother is not acquainted with my plans!
AMANDA (*Enters portieres*) Where are you all?
TOM On the terrace, Mother.

(*They start inside. She advances to them.* TOM *is distinctly shocked at her appearance. Even* JIM *blinks a little. He is making his first contact with girlish Southern vivacity and in spite of the night-school course in public speaking is somewhat thrown off the beam by the unexpected outlay of social charm*)

(*Certain responses are attempted by* JIM *but are swept aside by* AMANDA'S *gay laughter and chatter.* TOM *is embarrassed but after the first shock* JIM *reacts very warmly, grins and chuckles, is altogether won over*)

(IMAGE: AMANDA AS A GIRL)

AMANDA (*Coyly smiling, shaking her girlish ringlets*) Well, well, well, so this is Mr. O'Connor. Introductions entirely unnecessary. I've heard so much about you from my boy. I finally said to him, Tom—good gracious!—why don't you bring this paragon to supper? I'd like to meet this nice young man at the warehouse!—Instead of just hearing him sing your praises so much!

I don't know why my son is so stand-offish—that's not Southern behavior!

Let's sit down and—I think we could stand a little more air in here! Tom, leave the door open. I felt a nice fresh breeze a moment ago. Where has it gone to?

Mmm, so warm already! And not quite summer, even. We're going to burn up when summer really gets started.

However, we're having—we're having a very light supper. I think light things are better fo' this time of year. The same as light clothes are. Light clothes an' light food are what warm weather calls fo'. You know our blood gets so thick during th' winter—it takes a while fo' us to *adjust* ou'selves!—when the season changes . . .

It's come so quick this year. I wasn't prepared. All of a sudden—

heavens! Already summer!—I ran to the trunk an' pulled out this light dress— Terribly old! Historical almost! But feels so good—so good an' co-ol, y' know. . . .

TOM Mother—
AMANDA Yes, honey?
TOM How about—supper?
AMANDA Honey, you go ask Sister if supper is ready! You know that Sister is in full charge of supper!
Tell her you hungry boys are waiting for it.

(*To* JIM)

Have you met Laura?
JIM She—
AMANDA Let you in? Oh, good, you've met already! It's rare for a girl as sweet an' pretty as Laura to be domestic! But Laura is, thank heavens, not only pretty but also very domestic. I'm not at all. I never was a bit. I never could make a thing but angel-food cake. Well, in the South we had so many servants. Gone, gone, gone. All vestige of gracious living! Gone completely! I wasn't prepared for what the future brought me. All of my gentlemen callers were sons of planters and so of course I assumed that I would be married to one and raise my family on a large piece of land with plenty of servants. But man proposes— and woman accepts the proposal!—To vary that old, old saying a little bit—I married no planter! I married a man who worked for the telephone company!—That gallantly smiling gentleman over there! (*Points to the picture*) A telephone man who—fell in love with long-distance!—Now he travels and I don't even know where!—But what am I going on for about my—tribulations?
Tell me yours—I hope you don't have any!
Tom?
TOM (*Returning*) Yes, Mother?
AMANDA Is supper nearly ready?
TOM It looks to me like supper is on the table.
AMANDA Let me look— (*She rises prettily and looks through portieres*) Oh, lovely!—But where is Sister?
TOM Laura is not feeling well and she says that she thinks she'd better not come to the table.
AMANDA What?—Nonsense!—Laura? Oh, Laura!
LAURA (*Off stage, faintly*) Yes, Mother.
AMANDA You really must come to the table. We won't be seated until you come to the table!
Come in, Mr. O'Connor. You sit over there, and I'll—

Laura? Laura Wingfield!
You're keeping us waiting, honey! We can't say grace until you come to the table!

(*The back door is pushed weakly open and* LAURA *comes in. She is obviously quite faint, her lips trembling, her eyes wide and staring. She moves unsteadily toward the table*)

(LEGEND: "TERROR!")

(*Outside a summer storm is coming abruptly. The white curtains billow inward at the windows and there is a sorrowful murmur and deep blue dusk*) (LAURA *suddenly stumbles—she catches at a chair with a faint moan*)

TOM   Laura!
AMANDA   Laura!

(*There is a clap of thunder*)

(LEGEND: "AH!")

(*Despairingly*)

Why, Laura, you *are* sick, darling! Tom, help your sister into the living room, dear!
Sit in the living room, Laura—rest on the sofa.
Well!

(*To the gentleman caller*)

Standing over the hot stove made her ill!—I told her that it was just too warm this evening, but—

(TOM *comes back in.* LAURA *is on the sofa*)

Is Laura all right now?
TOM   Yes.
AMANDA   What *is* that? Rain? A nice cool rain has come up!

(*She gives the gentleman caller a frightened look*)

I think we may—have grace—now. . . .

(TOM *looks at her stupidly*)

Tom, honey—you say grace!
TOM   Oh . . .
"For these and all thy mercies—"

(*They bow their heads,* AMANDA *stealing a nervous glance at* JIM. *In the living room* LAURA, *stretched on the sofa, clenches her hand to her lips, to hold back a shuddering sob*)

God's Holy Name be praised—

(*The Scene Dims Out*)

Scene Seven

A Souvenir.

Half an hour later. Dinner is just being finished in the upstage area which is concealed by the drawn portieres.

As the curtain rises LAURA is still huddled upon the sofa, her feet drawn under her, her head resting on a pale blue pillow, her eyes wide and mysteriously watchful. The new floor lamp with its shade of rose-colored silk gives a soft, becoming light to her face, bringing out the fragile, unearthly prettiness which usually escapes attention. There is a steady murmur of rain, but it is slackening and stops soon after the scene begins; the air outside becomes pale and luminous as the moon breaks out.

A moment after the curtain rises, the lights in both rooms flicker and go out.

JIM Hey, there, Mr. Light Bulb!

(AMANDA *laughs nervously*)

(LEGEND: "SUSPENSION OF A PUBLIC SERVICE")

AMANDA Where was Moses when the lights went out? Ha-ha. Do you know the answer to that one, Mr. O'Connor?
JIM No, Ma'am, what's the answer?
AMANDA In the dark!

(JIM *laughs appreciatively*)

Everybody sit still. I'll light the candles. Isn't it lucky we have them on the table? Where's a match? Which of you gentlemen can provide a match?

JIM   Here.
AMANDA   Thank you, sir.
JIM   Not at all, Ma'am!
AMANDA   I guess the fuse has burnt out. Mr. O'Connor, can you tell a burnt-out fuse? I know I can't and Tom is a total loss when it comes to mechanics.

(SOUND: GETTING UP: VOICES RECEDE A LITTLE TO KITCHENETTE)

Oh, be careful you don't bump into something. We don't want our gentleman caller to break his neck. Now wouldn't that be a fine howdy-do?

JIM   Ha-ha!
Where is the fuse-box?
AMANDA   Right here next to the stove. Can you see anything?
JIM   Just a minute.
AMANDA   Isn't electricity a mysterious thing?
Wasn't it Benjamin Franklin who tied a key to a kite?
We live in such a mysterious universe, don't we? Some people say that science clears up all the mysteries for us. In my opinion it only creates more!
Have you found it yet?
JIM   No, Ma'am. All these fuses look okay to me.
AMANDA   Tom!
TOM   Yes, Mother?
AMANDA   That light bill I gave you several days ago. The one I told you we got the notices about?

(LEGEND: "HA!")

TOM   Oh—Yeah.
AMANDA   You didn't neglect to pay it by any chance?
TOM   Why, I—
AMANDA   Didn't! I might have known it!
JIM   Shakespeare probably wrote a poem on that light bill, Mrs. Wingfield.
AMANDA   I might have known better than to trust him with it! There's such a high price for negligence in this world!
JIM   Maybe the poem will win a ten-dollar prize.
AMANDA   We'll just have to spend the remainder of the evening in the nineteenth century, before Mr. Edison made the Mazda lamp!
JIM   Candlelight is my favorite kind of light.
AMANDA   That shows you're romantic! But that's no excuse for Tom.
Well, we got through dinner. Very considerate of them to let us get

through dinner before they plunged us into everlasting darkness, wasn't it, Mr O'Connor?
JIM Ha-ha!
AMANDA Tom, as a penalty for your carelessness you can help me with the dishes.
JIM Let me give you a hand.
AMANDA Indeed you will not!
JIM I ought to be good for something.
AMANDA Good for something? (*Her tone is rhapsodic*) You? Why, Mr. O'Connor, nobody, *nobody's* given me this much entertainment in years—as you have!
JIM Aw, now, Mrs. Wingfield!
AMANDA I'm not exaggerating, not one bit! But Sister is all by her lonesome. You go keep her company in the parlor!
  I'll give you this lovely old candelabrum that used to be on the altar at the Church of the Heavenly Rest. It was melted a little out of shape when the church burnt down. Lightning struck it one spring. Gypsy Jones was holding a revival at the time and he intimated that the church was destroyed because the Episcopalians gave card parties.
JIM Ha-ha!
AMANDA And how about you coaxing Sister to drink a little wine? I think it would be good for her! Can you carry both at once?
JIM Sure. I'm Superman!
AMANDA Now, Thomas, get into this apron!

(*The door of kitchenette swings closed on* AMANDA'S *gay laughter; the flickering light approaches the portieres*)

(LAURA *sits up nervously as he enters. Her speech at first is low and breathless from the almost intolerable strain of being alone with a stranger*)

(THE LEGEND: "I DON'T SUPPOSE YOU REMEMBER ME AT ALL!")

(*In her first speeches in this scene, before Jim's warmth overcomes her paralyzing shyness,* LAURA'S *voice is thin and breathless as though she has just run up a steep flight of stairs*)

(JIM'S *attitude is gently humorous. In playing this scene it should be stressed that while the incident is apparently unimportant, it is to* LAURA *the climax of her secret life*)

JIM Hello, there, Laura.
LAURA (*Faintly*) Hello. (*She clears her throat*)
JIM How are you feeling now? Better?
LAURA Yes. Yes, thank you.

JIM   This is for you. A little dandelion wine. (*He extends it toward her with extravagant gallantry*)
LAURA   Thank you.
JIM   Drink it—but don't get drunk!

(*He laughs heartily.* LAURA *takes the glass uncertainly; laughs shyly*)

Where shall I set the candles?
LAURA   Oh—oh, anywhere . . .
JIM   How about here on the floor? Any objections?
LAURA   No.
JIM   I'll spread a newspaper under to catch the drippings. I like to sit on the floor. Mind if I do?
LAURA   Oh, no.
JIM   Give me a pillow?
LAURA   What?
JIM   A pillow!
LAURA   Oh . . . (*Hands him one quickly*)
JIM   How about you? Don't you like to sit on the floor?
LAURA   Oh—yes.
JIM   Why don't you, then?
LAURA   I—will.
JIM   Take a pillow! (LAURA *does. Sits on the other side of the candelabrum.* JIM *crosses his legs and smiles engagingly at her*) I can't hardly see you sitting way over there.
LAURA   I can—see you.
JIM   I know, but that's not fair, I'm in the limelight. (LAURA *moves her pillow closer*) Good! Now I can see you! Comfortable?
LAURA   Yes.
JIM   So am I. Comfortable as a cow! Will you have some gum?
LAURA   No, thank you.
JIM   I think that I will indulge, with your permission. (*Musingly unwraps it and holds it up*) Think of the fortune made by the guy that invented the first piece of chewing gum. Amazing, huh? The Wrigley Building is one of the sights of Chicago—I saw it summer before last when I went up to the Century of Progress.[11] Did you take in the Century of Progress?
LAURA   No, I didn't.
JIM   Well, it was quite a wonderful exposition. What impressed me most was the Hall of Science. Gives you an idea of what the future

---

[11] Chicago World's Fair, 1933–1934.

will be in America, even more wonderful than the present time is! (*Pause. Smiling at her*) Your brother tells me you're shy. Is that right, Laura?

LAURA I—don't know.

JIM I judge you to be an old-fashioned type of girl. Well, I think that's a pretty good type to be. Hope you don't think I'm being too personal—do you?

LAURA (*Hastily, out of embarrassment*) I believe I *will* take a piece of gum, if you—don't mind. (*Clearing her throat*) Mr. O'Connor, have you—kept up with your singing?

JIM Singing? Me?

LAURA Yes. I remember what a beautiful voice you had.

JIM When did you hear me sing?

(VOICE OFF STAGE IN THE PAUSE)

VOICE (*Off stage*)

> O blow, ye winds, heigh-ho,
> A-roving I will go!
> I'm off to my love
> With a boxing glove—
> Ten thousand miles away!

JIM You say you've heard me sing?

LAURA Oh, yes! Yes, very often. . . . I—don't suppose—you remember me—at all?

JIM (*Smiling doubtfully*) You know I have an idea I've seen you before. I had that idea soon as you opened the door. It seemed almost like I was about to remember your name. But the name that I started to call you—wasn't a name! And so I stopped myself before I said it.

LAURA Wasn't it—Blue Roses?

JIM (*Springs up. Grinning*) Blue Roses!—My gosh, yes—Blue Roses! That's what I had on my tongue when you opened the door!

Isn't it funny what tricks your memory plays? I didn't connect you with high school somehow or other.

But that's where it was; it was high school. I didn't even know you were Shakespeare's sister!

Gosh, I'm sorry.

LAURA I didn't expect you to. You—barely knew me!

JIM But we did have a speaking acquaintance, huh?

LAURA Yes, we—spoke to each other.

JIM When did you recognize me?

LAURA Oh, right away!

JIM   Soon as I came in the door?
LAURA   When I heard your name I thought it was probably you. I knew that Tom used to know you a little in high school. So when you came in the door—Well, then I was—sure.
JIM   Why didn't you *say* something, then?
LAURA   (*Breathlessly*)   I didn't know what to say, I was—too surprised!
JIM   For goodness' sakes! You know, this sure is funny!
LAURA   Yes! Yes, isn't it, though . . .
JIM   Didn't we have a class in something together?
LAURA   Yes, we did.
JIM   What class was that?
LAURA   It was—singing—Chorus!
JIM   Aw!
LAURA   I sat across the aisle from you in the Aud.
JIM   Aw.
LAURA   Mondays, Wednesdays, and Fridays.
JIM   Now I remember—you always came in late.
LAURA   Yes, it was so hard for me, getting upstairs. I had that brace on my leg—it clumped so loud!
JIM   I never heard any clumping.
LAURA   (*Wincing at the recollection*)   To me it sounded like—thunder!
JIM   Well, well, well, I never even noticed.
LAURA   And everybody was seated before I came in. I had to walk in front of all those people. My seat was in the back row. I had to go clumping all the way up the aisle with everyone watching!
JIM   You shouldn't have been self-conscious.
LAURA   I know, but I was. It was always such a relief when the singing started.
JIM   Aw, yes, I've placed you now! I used to call you Blue Roses. How was it that I got started calling you that?
LAURA   I was out of school a little while with pleurosis. When I came back you asked me what was the matter. I said I had pleurosis—you thought I said Blue Roses. That's what you always called me after that!
JIM   I hope you didn't mind.
LAURA   Oh, no—I liked it. You see, I wasn't acquainted with many—people. . . .
JIM   As I remember you sort of stuck by yourself.
LAURA   I—I—never have had much luck at—making friends.
JIM   I don't see why you wouldn't.
LAURA   Well, I—started out badly.
JIM   You mean being—
LAURA   Yes, it sort of—stood between me—

JIM You shouldn't have let it!
LAURA I know, but it did, and—
JIM You were shy with people!
LAURA I tried not to be but never could—
JIM Overcome it?
LAURA No, I—I never could!
JIM I guess being shy is something you have to work out of kind of gradually.
LAURA (*Sorrowfully*) Yes—I guess it—
JIM Takes time!
LAURA Yes.
JIM People are not so dreadful when you know them. That's what you have to remember! And everybody has problems, not just you, but practically everybody has got some problems.
 You think of yourself as having the only problems, as being the only one who is disappointed. But just look around you and you will see lots of people as disappointed as you are. For instance, I hoped when I was going to high school that I would be further along at this time, six years later, than I am now—You remember that wonderful write-up I had in *The Torch*?
LAURA Yes! (*She rises and crosses to table*)
JIM It said I was bound to succeed in anything I went into! (*Laura returns with the annual*) Holy Jeez! *The Torch*! (*He accepts it reverently. They smile across it with mutual wonder.* LAURA *crouches beside him and they begin to turn through it.* LAURA's *shyness is dissolving in his warmth*)
LAURA Here you are in *The Pirates of Penzance*!
JIM (*Wistfully*) I sang the baritone lead in that operetta.
LAURA (*Raptly*) So—beautifully!
JIM (*Protesting*) Aw—
LAURA Yes, yes—beautifully—beautifully!
JIM You heard me?
LAURA All three times!
JIM No!
LAURA Yes!
JIM All three performances?
LAURA (*Looking down*) Yes.
JIM Why?
LAURA I—wanted to ask you to—autograph my program.
JIM Why didn't you ask me to?
LAURA You were always surrounded by your own friends so much that I never had a chance to.

JIM   You should have just—
LAURA   Well, I—thought you might think I was—
JIM   Thought I might think you was—what?
LAURA   Oh—
JIM   (*With reflective relish*)   I was beleaguered by females in those days.
LAURA   You were terribly popular!
JIM   Yeah—
LAURA   You had such a—friendly way—
JIM   I was spoiled in high school.
LAURA   Everybody—liked you!
JIM   Including you?
LAURA   I—yes, I—I did, too— (*She gently closes the book in her lap*)
JIM   Well, well, well!—Give me that program, Laura. (*She hands it to him. He signs it with a flourish*) There you are—better late than never!
LAURA   Oh, I—what a—surprise!
JIM   My signature isn't worth very much right now.
But some day—maybe—it will increase in value!
Being disappointed is one thing and being discouraged is something else. I am disappointed but I am not discouraged.
I'm twenty-three years old.
How old are you?
LAURA   I'll be twenty-four in June.
JIM   That's not old age!
LAURA   No, but—
JIM   You finished high school?
LAURA   (*With difficulty*)   I didn't go back.
JIM   You mean you dropped out?
LAURA   I made bad grades in my final examinations. (*She rises and replaces the book and the program. Her voice strained*)   How is—Emily Meisenbach getting along?
JIM   Oh, that kraut-head!
LAURA   Why do you call her that?
JIM   That's what she was.
LAURA   You're not still—going with her?
JIM   I never see her.
LAURA   It said in the Personal Section that you were—engaged!
JIM   I know, but I wasn't impressed by that—propaganda!
LAURA   It wasn't—the truth?
JIM   Only in Emily's optimistic opinion!
LAURA   Oh—

(LEGEND: "WHAT HAVE YOU DONE SINCE HIGH SCHOOL?")

(JIM *lights a cigarette and leans indolently back on his elbows, smiling at* LAURA *with a warmth and charm which lights her inwardly with altar candles. She remains by the table and turns in her hands a piece of glass to cover her tumult*)

JIM (*After several reflective puffs on a cigarette*) What have you done since high school? (*She seems not to hear him*) Huh? (LAURA *looks up*) I said what have you done since high school, Laura?
LAURA Nothing much.
JIM You must have been doing something these six long years.
LAURA Yes.
JIM Well, then, such as what?
LAURA I took a business course at business college—
JIM How did that work out?
LAURA Well, not very—well—I had to drop out, it gave me—indigestion—

(JIM *laughs gently*)

JIM What are you doing now?
LAURA I don't do anything—much. Oh, please don't think I sit around doing nothing! My glass collection takes up a good deal of time. Glass is something you have to take good care of.
JIM What did you say—about glass?
LAURA Collection I said—I have one—(*She clears her throat and turns away again, acutely shy*)
JIM (*Abruptly*) You know what I judge to be the trouble with you? Inferiority complex! Know what that is? That's what they call it when someone low-rates himself!

I understand it because I had it, too. Although my case was not so aggravated as yours seems to be. I had it until I took up public speaking, developed my voice, and learned that I had an aptitude for science. Before that time I never thought of myself as being outstanding in any way whatsoever!

Now I've never made a regular study of it, but I have a friend who says I can analyze people better than doctors that make a profession of it. I don't claim that to be necessarily true, but I can sure guess a person's psychology. Laura! (*Takes out his gum*) Excuse me, Laura. I always take it out when the flavor is gone. I'll use this scrap of paper to wrap it in. I know how it is to get it stuck on a shoe.

Yep—that's what I judge to be your principal trouble. A lack of confidence in yourself as a person. You don't have the proper amount of faith in yourself. I'm basing that fact on a number of your remarks and also on certain observations I've made. For instance that clumping you thought was so awful in high school. You say that you even dreaded to walk into class. You see what you did? You dropped out of school, you gave up an education because of a clump, which as far as I know was practically nonexistent! A little physical defect is what you have. Hardly noticeable even! Magnified thousands of times by imagination!

You know what my strong advice to you is? Think of yourself as *superior* in some way!

LAURA In what way would I think?

JIM Why, man alive, Laura! Just look about you a little. What do you see? A world full of common people! All of 'em born and all of 'em going to die!

Which of them has one-tenth of your good points! Or mine! Or anyone else's, as far as that goes—Gosh!

Everybody excels in some one thing. Some in many!

(*Unconsciously glances at himself in the mirror*)

All you've got to do is discover in *what!*
Take me, for instance.

(*He adjusts his tie at the mirror*)

My interest happens to lie in electro-dynamics. I'm taking a course in radio engineering at night school, Laura, on top of a fairly responsible job at the warehouse. I'm taking that course and studying public speaking.

LAURA Ohhhh.

JIM Because I believe in the future of television.

(*Turning back to her*)

I wish to be ready to go up right along with it. Therefore I'm planning to get in on the ground floor. In fact I've already made the right connections and all that remains is for the industry itself to get under way! Full steam—

(*His eyes are starry*)

Knowledge—Zzzzzp! Money—Zzzzzzp!—Power!
That's the cycle democracy is built on!

(*His attitude is convincingly dynamic.* LAURA *stares at him, even her shyness eclipsed in her absolute wonder. He suddenly grins*)

I guess you think I think a lot of myself!

LAURA No—o-o-o, I—

JIM Now how about you? Isn't there something you take more interest in than anything else?
LAURA Well, I do—as I said—have my—glass collection—

(*A peal of girlish laughter from the kitchen*)

JIM I'm not right sure I know what you're talking about. What kind of glass is it?
LAURA Little articles of it, they're ornaments mostly! Most of them are little animals made out of glass, the tiniest little animals in the world. Mother calls them a glass menagerie! Here's an example of one, if you'd like to see it! This one is one of the oldest. It's nearly thirteen.

(MUSIC: "THE GLASS MENAGERIE")
(*He stretches out his hand*)

Oh, be careful—if you breathe, it breaks!
JIM I'd better not take it. I'm pretty clumsy with things.
LAURA Go on, I trust you with him!

(*Places it in his palm*)

There now—you're holding him gently! Hold him over the light, he loves the light! You see how the light shines through him?
JIM It sure does shine!
LAURA I shouldn't be partial, but he *is* my favorite one.
JIM What kind of a thing is this one supposed to be?
LAURA Haven't you noticed the single horn on his forehead?
JIM A unicorn, huh?
LAURA Mmm-hmmm!
JIM Unicorns, aren't they extinct in the modern world?
LAURA I know!
JIM Poor little fellow, he must feel sort of lonesome.
LAURA (*Smiling*) Well, if he does he doesn't complain about it. He stays on a shelf with some horses that don't have horns and all of them seem to get along nicely together.
JIM How do you know?
LAURA (*Lightly*) I haven't heard any arguments among them!
JIM (*Grinning*) No arguments, huh? Well, that's a pretty good sign! Where shall I set him?
LAURA Put him on the table. They all like a change of scenery once in a while!
JIM (*Stretching*) Well, well, well, well—

Look how big my shadow is when I stretch!
LAURA Oh, oh, yes—it stretches across the ceiling!
JIM (*Crossing to door*) I think it's stopped raining. (*Opens fire-escape door*) Where does the music come from?
LAURA From the Paradise Dance Hall across the alley.
JIM How about cutting the rug a little, Miss Wingfield?
LAURA Oh, I—
JIM Or is your program filled up? Let me have a look at it. (*Grasps imaginary card*) Why, every dance is taken! I'll just have to scratch some out. (WALTZ MUSIC: "LA GOLONDRINA") Ahhh, a waltz! (*He executes some sweeping turns by himself then holds his arms toward* LAURA)
LAURA (*Breathlessly*) I—can't dance!
JIM There you go, that inferiority stuff!
LAURA I've never danced in my life!
JIM Come on, try!
LAURA Oh, but I'd step on you!
JIM I'm not made out of glass.
LAURA How—how—how do we start?
JIM Just leave it to me. You hold your arms out a little.
LAURA Like this?
JIM A little bit higher. Right. Now don't tighten up, that's the main thing about it—relax.
LAURA (*Laughing breathlessly*) It's hard not to.
JIM Okay.
LAURA I'm afraid you can't budge me.
JIM What do you bet I can't (*He swings her into motion*)
LAURA Goodness, yes, you can!
JIM Let yourself go, now, Laura, just let yourself go.
LAURA I'm—
JIM Come on!
LAURA Trying!
JIM Not so stiff— Easy does it!
LAURA I know but I'm—
JIM Loosen th' backbone! There now, that's a lot better.
LAURA Am I?
JIM Lots, lots better! (*He moves her about the room in a clumsy waltz*)
LAURA Oh, my!
JIM Ha-ha!
LAURA Oh, my goodness!
JIM Ha-ha-ha! (*They suddenly bump into the table.* JIM *stops*) What did we hit on?

LAURA   Table.
JIM   Did something fall off it? I think—
LAURA   Yes.
JIM   I hope it wasn't the little glass horse with the horn!
LAURA   Yes.
JIM   Aw, aw, aw. Is it broken?
LAURA   Now it is just like all the other horses.
JIM   It's lost its—
LAURA   Horn!
   It doesn't matter. Maybe it's a blessing in disguise.
JIM   You'll never forgive me. I bet that that was your favorite piece of glass.
LAURA   I don't have favorites much. It's no tragedy, Freckles. Glass breaks so easily. No matter how careful you are. The traffic jars the shelves and things fall off them.
JIM   Still I'm awfully sorry that I was the cause.
LAURA   (*Smiling*)   I'll just imagine he had an operation. The horn was removed to make him feel less—freakish!

   (*They both laugh*)

   Now he will feel more at home with the other horses, the ones that don't have horns. . . .
JIM   Ha-ha, that's very funny!

   (*Suddenly serious*)

   I'm glad to see that you have a sense of humor.
   You know—you're—well—very different!
   Surprisingly different from anyone else I know!

   (*His voice becomes soft and hesitant with a genuine feeling*)

   Do you mind me telling you that?

   (LAURA *is abashed beyond speech*)

   I mean it in a nice way. . . .

   (LAURA *nods shyly, looking away*)

   You make me feel sort of—I don't know how to put it!
   I'm usually pretty good at expressing things, but—
   This is something that I don't know how to say!

   (LAURA *touches her throat and clears it—turns the broken unicorn in her hands*)

(*Even softer*)

Has anyone ever told you that you were pretty?

(PAUSE: MUSIC)

(LAURA *looks up slowly, with wonder, and shakes her head*)

Well, you are! In a very different way from anyone else.
And all the nicer because of the difference, too.

(*His voice becomes low and husky.* LAURA *turns away, nearly faint with the novelty of her emotions*)

I wish that you were my sister. I'd teach you to have some confidence in yourself. The different people are not like other people, but being different is nothing to be ashamed of. Because other people are not such wonderful people. They're one hundred times one thousand. You're one times one! They walk all over the earth. You just stay here. They're common as—weeds, but—you—well, you're—*Blue Roses!*

(IMAGE ON SCREEN: BLUE ROSES)

(MUSIC CHANGES)

LAURA But blue is wrong for—roses. . . .
JIM It's right for you!—You're—pretty!
LAURA In what respect am I pretty?
JIM In all respects—believe me! Your eyes—your hair—are pretty! Your hands are pretty!

(*He catches hold of her hand*)

You think I'm making this up because I'm invited to dinner and have to be nice. Oh, I could do that! I could put on an act for you, Laura, and say lots of things without being very sincere. But this time I am. I'm talking to you sincerely. I happened to notice you had this inferiority complex that keeps you from feeling comfortable with people. Somebody needs to build your confidence up and make you proud instead of shy and turning away and—blushing—
Somebody—ought to—
Ought to—*kiss* you, Laura!

(*His hand slips slowly up her arm to her shoulder*)

(MUSIC SWELLS TUMULTUOUSLY)

(*He suddenly turns her about and kisses her on the lips*)

The Glass Menagerie [Scene Seven]

(*When he releases her,* LAURA *sinks on the sofa with a bright, dazed look*)

(JIM *backs away and fishes in his pocket for a cigarette*)

(LEGEND ON SCREEN: "SOUVENIR")

Stumble-john!

(*He lights the cigarette, avoiding her look*)

(*There is a peal of girlish laughter from* AMANDA *in the kitchen*)

(LAURA *slowly raises and opens her hand. It still contains the little broken glass animal. She looks at it with a tender, bewildered expression*)

Stumble-john!
I shouldn't have done that— That was way off the beam. You don't smoke, do you?

(*She looks up, smiling, not hearing the question*)

(*He sits beside her a little gingerly. She looks at him speechlessly—waiting*)

(*He coughs decorously and moves a little farther aside as he considers the situation and senses her feelings, dimly, with perturbation*)

(*Gently*)

Would you—care for a—mint?

(*She doesn't seem to hear him but her look grows brighter even*)

Peppermint—Life-Saver?
My pocket's a regular drug store—wherever I go . . .

(*He pops a mint in his mouth. Then gulps and decides to make a clean breast of it. He speaks slowly and gingerly*)

Laura, you know, if I had a sister like you, I'd do the same thing as Tom. I'd bring out fellows and—introduce her to them. The right type of boys of a type to—appreciate her.
Only—well—he made a mistake about me.
Maybe I've got no call to be saying this. That may not have been the idea in having me over. But what if it was?
There's nothing wrong about that. The only trouble is that in my case—I'm not in a situation to—do the right thing.
I can't take down your number and say I'll phone.

I can't call up next week and—ask for a date.
I thought I had better explain the situation in case you—misunderstood it and—hurt your feelings. . . .

(*Pause*)

(*Slowly, very slowly, LAURA's look changes, her eyes returning slowly from his to the ornament in her palm*)

(AMANDA *utters another gay laugh in the kitchen*)

LAURA (*Faintly*) You—won't—call again?
JIM No, Laura, I can't.

(*He rises from the sofa*)

As I was just explaining, I've—got strings on me.
Laura, I've—been going steady!
I go out all of the time with a girl named Betty.
She's a home-girl like you, and Catholic, and Irish, and in a great many ways we—get along fine.
I met her last summer on a moonlight boat trip up the river to Alton, on the *Majestic*.
Well—right away from the start it was—love!

(LEGEND: LOVE!)

(LAURA *sways slightly forward and grips the arm of the sofa. He fails to notice, now enrapt in his own comfortable being*)

Being in love has made a new man of me!

(*Leaning stiffly forward, clutching the arm of the sofa,* LAURA *struggles visibly with her storm. But* JIM *is oblivious, she is a long way off*)

The power of love is really pretty tremendous!
Love is something that—changes the whole world, Laura!

(*The storm abates a little and* LAURA *leans back. He notices her again*)

It happened that Betty's aunt took sick, she got a wire and had to go to Centralia. So Tom—when he asked me to dinner—I naturally just accepted the invitation, not knowing that you—that he—that I—

(*He stops awkwardly*)

Huh—I'm a stumble-john!

(*He flops back on the sofa*)

(*The holy candles in the altar of* LAURA's *face have been snuffed out. There is a look of almost infinite desolation*)

(JIM *glances at her uneasily*)

I wish that you would—say something.

(*She bites her lip which was trembling and then bravely smiles. She opens her hand again on the broken glass ornament. Then she gently takes his hand and raises it level with her own. She carefully places the unicorn in the palm of his hand, then pushes his fingers closed upon it*)

What are you—doing that for? You want me to have him?—Laura?

(*She nods*)

What for?

LAURA   A—souvenir . . .

(*She rises unsteadily and crouches beside the victrola to wind it up*)

(LEGEND ON SCREEN: "THINGS HAVE A WAY OF TURNING OUT SO BADLY!")

(OR IMAGE: "GENTLEMAN CALLER WAVING GOOD-BYE!—GAILY")

(*At this moment* AMANDA *rushes brightly back in the front room. She bears a pitcher of fruit punch in an old-fashioned cut-glass pitcher and a plate of macaroons. The plate has a gold border and poppies painted on it*)

AMANDA   Well, well, well! Isn't the air delightful after the shower? I've made you children a little liquid refreshment.

(*Turns gaily to the gentleman caller*)

Jim, do you know that song about lemonade?

"Lemonade, lemonade
Made in the shade and stirred with a spade—
Good enough for any old maid!"

JIM (*Uneasily*)   Ha-ha! No—I never heard it.
AMANDA   Why, Laura! You look so serious!
JIM   We were having a serious conversation.
AMANDA   Good! Now you're better acquainted!
JIM (*Uncertainly*)   Ha-ha! Yes.

AMANDA You modern young people are much more serious-minded than my generation. I was so gay as a girl!
JIM You haven't changed, Mrs. Wingfield.
AMANDA Tonight I'm rejuvenated! The gaiety of the occasion, Mr. O'Connor!

(*She tosses her head with a peal of laughter. Spills lemonade*)

Oooo! I'm baptizing myself!
JIM Here—let me—
AMANDA (*Setting the pitcher down*) There now. I discovered we had some maraschino cherries. I dumped them in, juice and all!
JIM You shouldn't have gone to that trouble, Mrs. Wingfield.
AMANDA Trouble, trouble? Why, it was loads of fun!
  Didn't you hear me cutting up in the kitchen? I bet your ears were burning! I told Tom how outdone with him I was for keeping you to himself so long a time! He should have brought you over much, much sooner! Well, now that you've found your way, I want you to be a very frequent caller! Not just occasional but all the time.
  Oh, we're going to have a lot of gay times together! I see them coming!
  Mmm, just breathe that air! So fresh, and the moon's so pretty!
  I'll skip back out—I know where my place is when young folks are having a—serious conversation!
JIM Oh, don't go out, Mrs. Wingfield. The fact of the matter is I've got to be going.
AMANDA Going, now? You're joking! Why, it's only the shank of the evening, Mr. O'Connor!
JIM Well, you know how it is.
AMANDA You mean you're a young workingman and have to keep workingmen's hours. We'll let you off early tonight. But only on the condition that next time you stay later.
  What's the best night for you? Isn't Saturday night the best night for you workingmen?
JIM I have a couple of time-clocks to punch, Mrs. Wingfield. One at morning, another one at night!
AMANDA My, but you *are* ambitious! You work at night, too?
JIM No, Ma'am, not work but—Betty! (*He crosses deliberately to pick up his hat. The band at the Paradise Dance Hall goes into a tender waltz*)
AMANDA Betty? Betty? Who's—Betty!

(*There is an ominous cracking sound in the sky*)

JIM   Oh, just a girl. The girl I go steady with! (*He smiles charmingly. The sky falls*)

(LEGEND: "THE SKY FALLS")

AMANDA   (*A long-drawn exhalation*)   Ohhhh . . . Is it a serious romance, Mr. O'Connor?
JIM   We're going to be married the second Sunday in June.
AMANDA   Ohhhh—how nice!
Tom didn't mention that you were engaged to be married.
JIM   The cat's not out of the bag at the warehouse yet.
You know how they are. They call you Romeo and stuff like that.

(*He stops at the oval mirror to put on his hat. He carefully shapes the brim and the crown to give a discreetly dashing effect*)

It's been a wonderful evening, Mrs. Wingfield. I guess this is what they mean by Southern hospitality.
AMANDA   It really wasn't anything at all.
JIM   I hope it don't seem like I'm rushing off. But I promised Betty I'd pick her up at the Wabash depot, an' by the time I get my jalopy down there her train'll be in. Some women are pretty upset if you keep 'em waiting.
AMANDA   Yes, I know— The tyranny of women!

(*Extends her hand*)

Good-bye, Mr. O'Connor.
I wish you luck—and happiness—and success! All three of them, and so does Laura!—Don't you, Laura?
LAURA   Yes!
JIM   (*Taking her hand*)   Good-bye, Laura. I'm certainly going to treasure that souvenir. And don't you forget the good advice I gave you.

(*Raises his voice to a cheery shout*)

So long, Shakespeare!
Thanks again, ladies—Good night!

(*He grins and ducks jauntily out*)

(*Still bravely grimacing,* AMANDA *closes the door on the gentleman caller. Then she turns back to the room with a puzzled expression. She and* LAURA *don't dare to face each other.* LAURA *crouches beside the victrola to wind it*)

AMANDA   (*Faintly*)   Things have a way of turning out so badly.

I don't believe that I would play the victrola.
Well, well—well—
Our gentleman caller was engaged to be married!
Tom!

TOM (*From back*) Yes, Mother?

AMANDA Come in here a minute. I want to tell you something awfully funny.

TOM (*Enters with macaroon and a glass of the lemonade*) Has the gentleman caller gotten away already?

AMANDA The gentleman caller has made an early departure. What a wonderful joke you played on us!

TOM How do you mean?

AMANDA You didn't mention that he was engaged to be married.

TOM Jim? Engaged?

AMANDA That's what he just informed us.

TOM I'll be jiggered! I didn't know about that.

AMANDA That seems very peculiar.

TOM What's peculiar about it?

AMANDA Didn't you call him your best friend down at the warehouse?

TOM He is, but how did I know?

AMANDA It seems extremely peculiar that you wouldn't know your best friend was going to be married!

TOM The warehouse is where I work, not where I know things about people!

AMANDA You don't know things anywhere! You live in a dream; you manufacture illusions!

(*He crosses to door*)

Where are you going?

TOM I'm going to the movies.

AMANDA That's right, now that you've had us make such fools of ourselves. The effort, the preparations, all the expense! The new floor lamp, the rug, the clothes for Laura! All for what? To entertain some other girl's fiancé!

Go to the movies, go! Don't think about us, a mother deserted, an unmarried sister who's crippled and has no job! Don't let anything interfere with your selfish pleasure!

Just go, go, go—to the movies!

TOM All right, I will! The more you shout about my selfishness to me the quicker I'll go, and I won't go to the movies!

AMANDA Go, then! Then go to the moon—you selfish dreamer!

(TOM *smashes his glass on the floor. He plunges out on the fire escape, slamming the door.* LAURA *screams—cut by door*)

(*Dance-hall music up.* TOM *goes to the rail and grips it desperately, lifting his face in the chill white moonlight penetrating the narrow abyss of the alley*)

(LEGEND ON SCREEN: "AND SO GOOD-BYE . . .")

(TOM's *closing speech is timed with the interior pantomime. The interior scene is played as though viewed through soundproof glass.* AMANDA *appears to be making a comforting speech to* LAURA *who is huddled upon the sofa. Now that we cannot hear the mother's speech, her silliness is gone and she has dignity and tragic beauty.* LAURA's *dark hair hides her face until at the end of the speech she lifts it to smile at her mother.* AMANDA's *gestures are slow and graceful, almost dancelike, as she comforts the daughter. At the end of her speech she glances a moment at the father's picture—then withdraws through the portieres. At close of* TOM's *speech,* LAURA *blows out the candles, ending the play*)

TOM I didn't go to the moon, I went much further—for time is the longest distance between two places—
 Not long after that I was fired for writing a poem on the lid of a shoe-box.
 I left Saint Louis. I descended the steps of this fire escape for a last time and followed, from then on, in my father's footsteps, attempting to find in motion what was lost in space—
 I traveled around a great deal. The cities swept about me like dead leaves, leaves that were brightly colored but torn away from the branches.
 I would have stopped, but I was pursued by something.
 It always came upon me unawares, taking me altogether by surprise. Perhaps it was a familiar bit of music. Perhaps it was only a piece of transparent glass—
 Perhaps I am walking along a street at night, in some strange city, before I have found companions. I pass the lighted window of a shop where perfume is sold. The window is filled with pieces of colored glass, tiny transparent bottles in delicate colors, like bits of a shattered rainbow.
 Then all at once my sister touches my shoulder. I turn around and look into her eyes . . .
 Oh, Laura, Laura, I tried to leave you behind me, but I am more faithful than I intended to be!

I reach for a cigarette, I cross the street, I run into the movies or a bar, I buy a drink, I speak to the nearest stranger—anything that can blow your candles out!

(LAURA *bends over the candles*)

—for nowadays the world is lit by lightning! Blow out your candles, Laura—and so good-bye. . . .

(*She blows the candles out*)

(*The Scene Dissolves*)

EUGENE O'NEILL
[1888 – 1953]

❧ *The Man*

OF HIS CHILDHOOD, O'Neill has written:

> My first seven years were spent mainly in the larger towns all over the United States—my mother accompanying my father on his road tours in *Monte Cristo* and repertoire, although she was never an actress and had rather an aversion for the stage in general. A child has a regular, fixed home, but you might say I started in as a trouper. I knew only actors and the stage. My mother nursed me in the wings and in dressing rooms.

Eugene O'Neill's father was actor-producer James O'Neill, an Irish immigrant who became famous for playing the title role in *The Count of Monte Cristo*. He and Ella Quinlan, daughter of a Midwestern merchant, had three sons, born while James O'Neill was on tour. During the birth of their third son, Eugene Gladstone, Ella O'Neill was given morphine and subsequently became a drug addict.

Alternately touring with the company and attending boarding schools, Eugene's formal schooling ended after a few months at Princeton. Slow to develop, he was supported by a complaining father until he was twenty-five. By the time he tried his hand at plays, he had been married, a father (of Eugene, Jr.), divorced, a Bohemian, a seaman, a hanger-on in his father's touring company, and a tuberculosis patient in a sanitorium. In 1914, having decided to become a playwright, he enrolled in Professor George Pierce Baker's Theater Workshop at Harvard. Although O'Neill was invited to return for a second year, he stayed in Greenwich Village with writers and tramps, and wrote one-act plays based on his adventures at sea. Largely because of the efforts of George Cram Cook and Susan Glaspell, a little theater was formed in rebellion against the commercial theater. Called the Provincetown Players after their makeshift theater in Provincetown, Massachusetts, the group gave O'Neill his first production, *Bound East for Cardiff*, in summer, 1916. Moving to Greenwich Village in the fall, the Provincetown Players continued to produce O'Neill one-acters, but it was with the 1920 Broadway production of *Beyond the Horizon* that the serious professional American theater was born.

From 1920 to 1934, O'Neill endured three marriages, three children, frequent domestic battles, and occasional destructive drinking bouts with his old saloon companions, but all the while he continued to write plays. Much of his personal life, like that of Strindberg whom he admired, is reflected in his work. For the last ten years of his life, he was too ill for sustained effort. He was awarded the Nobel Prize in 1936—and received it in the hospital. Toward the end, he and his wife lived in a hotel, because he required day-and-night service. Almost his last words were, "Born in a hotel room—and God damn it—died in a hotel room!"

❦ *The Work*

EUGENE O'NEILL wrote about forty produced plays, at least as many that are unproduced, and he left elaborate plans for a cycle of dramas about an American family. Though he was constantly experimenting in technique, O'Neill started and ended his dramatic career in realism—fidelity to everyday life. When he began to write in this mode, modern realistic drama was new to the American stage; by the time of his last plays, it was a stale tradition, and yet his last plays are generally recognized to be his finest. Before he ever heard of Expressionism, O'Neill used Expressionistic techniques in *The Hairy Ape* and *Emperor Jones*. In *Strange Interlude*, he adapted the Elizabethan soliloquy and aside, and he flouted the unwritten law that a play may last no longer than two-and-a-half hours. Like the Greeks, he used masks in *Great God Brown* and *Lazarus Laughed*, and he turned even more openly to Greek inspiration in *Mourning Becomes Electra*. Though he ranged over Aeschylus,

Shakespeare, and Strindberg, all his important plays depict a tragic vision of America. Some dozen violent deaths and over two dozen nonviolent deaths, as well as cases of insanity in his drama are an indication of the consistency of his tragic vision. When America was close to victory in World War II, O'Neill told his countrymen: "I'm going on the theory that the United States, instead of being the most successful country in the world, is the greatest failure." Going on to speak of the last play whose rehearsals he attended, *The Iceman Cometh*, O'Neill commented on his mixture of modes: "I think I'm aware of comedy more than I ever was before; a big kind of comedy that doesn't stay funny very long. I've made some use of it in *The Iceman*. The first act is hilarious comedy, *I think*, but then some people may not even laugh. At any rate, the comedy breaks up and the tragedy comes on."

❧ *The Play*

THE TITLE *The Iceman Cometh* suggests several of the play's resonances. O'Neill's friend, Dudley Nichols, wrote:

> The iceman of the title is, of course, death. I don't think O'Neill ever explained, publicly, what he meant by the use of the archaic word, "cometh," but he told me at the time he was writing the play that he meant a combination of the poetic and biblical "Death cometh"— that is, cometh to all the living—and the old bawdy story, a typical Hickey story, of the man who calls upstairs, "Has the iceman come yet?" and his wife calls back, "No, but he's breathin' hard." . . . It is a strange and poetic intermingling of the exalted and the vulgar, that title.

The entire play similarly intermingles the exalted and the vulgar, with tragedy finally emerging from colloquial comedy.

In this late play (1946) O'Neill returns to the saloon-bar setting of his early experiences. Harry Hope's saloon is recognizably Jimmy-the-Priest's on Fulton Street near the New York waterfront, where O'Neill lived after being at sea. Several of the characters are modeled on habitués of this low dive to which, as O'Neill said later, "Gorky's *Night's Lodgings* was an ice cream parlor in comparison." There, in 1912, the date of the play, O'Neill had been close to suicide. He confessed to a newspaper reporter, "In writing *The Iceman Cometh*, I felt I had locked myself in with my memories." And yet, the play is less candidly autobiographical than *Long Day's Journey*, reflecting a broader spectrum of experience than any other O'Neill play.

For all its prolixity and complexity the central conflict is simple—illusion *vs.* reality. In treating this subject, O'Neill followed some of the masterpieces of modern drama—Ibsen's *Wild Duck*, Gorky's *Lower Depths*, Synge's *Playboy of the Western World*, Williams' *Glass Menagerie*. Such later plays as Beckett's *Waiting for Godot* and Gelber's *Connection* indicate that the subject is still viable dramatic material. O'Neill's play deals with a broad spectrum of illusion: the sentimental nostalgia of Harry Hope, the status consciousness of Mosher, McGloin, the bartender-pimps and the whores, the intellectual pride of Willie Oban, the racial denial of Joe Mott, the military memories of the Boer War veterans, the inverted radicalism of Hugo Kalmar, and the cowardly cynicism of Larry Slade. In this curious Utopia, good will is nurtured with cheap whiskey; each citizen is wise to and tolerant of his neighbor's illusions. To himself alone he is blind, until Hickey comes, a diabolical angel bearing harsh light. Hickey's last word in the first three acts is "happy," and yet misery increases steadily.

Though realistic on the surface, the drama is enriched with symbolic suggestion. O'Neill's theme of illusion is an extension of his preoccupation with masks in earlier plays; occasionally the habitués of the saloon function like a Greek chorus, and there are hints of an Apollonian-Dionysiac conflict. In stage grouping, Harry Hope's birthday party suggests the Last Supper, with Hickey as an anti-Christ, a nonredeemer.

In *The Iceman Cometh* O'Neill uses a double plot in the manner of the Elizabethans, emphasizing his theme through separate subplots. Hickey's unacknowledged hatred for his wife is reflected in Harry Hope's hatred for *his* dead wife, and in Parritt's hatred for his mother. Parritt's confession is virtually an echo of Hickey's confession, up to the very moment of emotional revelation. Parritt's "It was because I hated her," is almost immediately followed by Hickey's "Well, you know what you can do with your pipe dream now, you damned bitch!" But Parritt has the courage of his confession, whereas Hickey immediately withdraws into another pipe dream—that of insanity.

After Hickey's arrest, the saloon occupants slowly return to their whiskey-soaked hopes, but Larry, who is sometimes viewed as the tragic protagonist, muses, "I'm the only real convert to death Hickey made here." However even this self-recognition contains a measure of illusion, for it is Parritt who commits suicide, and not Larry, the convert to death. Hickey, through murder, preaches a gospel of new life; Larry, through encouraging Parritt's suicide, preaches the gospel of death. As the final curtain falls, Larry is oblivious to the hilarity that surrounds him, and yet it *is* hilarity, bursting forth from illusion.

❧ *Dramatic Works*

Thirst, 1914.
The Web, 1914.
Warnings, 1914.
Fog, 1914.
Recklessness, 1914.
Bound East for Cardiff, 1916.
Before Breakfast, 1916.
The Long Voyage Home, 1917.
Ile, 1918.
The Moon of the Caribbees, 1918.
In the Zone, 1919.
Where the Cross Is Made, 1919.
The Rope, 1919.
The Dreamy Kid, 1920.
Beyond the Horizon, 1920.
The Emperor Jones, 1921.
Gold, 1921.
Diff'rent, 1922.
The Straw, 1922.
The Hairy Ape, 1922.
Anna Christie, 1922.
The First Man, 1922.
Desire Under the Elms, 1923.

All God's Chillun Got Wings, 1924.
Welded, 1924.
The Great God Brown, 1926.
The Fountain, 1926.
Marco Millions, 1927.
Lazarus Laughed, 1928.
Strange Interlude, 1928.
Dynamo, 1929.
Mourning Becomes Electra, 1931.
Ah, Wilderness!, 1933.
Days Without End, 1934.
The Iceman Cometh, 1946.
Abortion, 1950.
The Movie Man, 1950.
The Sniper, 1950.
Servitude, 1950.
A Wife for a Life, 1950.
A Moon for the Misbegotten, 1953.
Long Day's Journey into Night, 1955.
A Touch of the Poet, 1957.
Hughie, 1959.
More Stately Mansions, 1962.

❦ Selective Bibliography

Brustein, Robert. *The Theatre of Revolt*. Boston: Little, Brown, 1964.
Cargill, Oscar, Fagin, N. Bryllion, and Fisher, William J., eds. *O'Neill and His Plays*. New York: N.Y.U. Press, 1961.
Engle, Edwin A. *The Haunted Heroes of Eugene O'Neill*. Cambridge, Mass.: Harvard University Press, 1953.
Falk, Doris V. *Eugene O'Neill and the Tragic Tension*. New Brunswick, N.J.: Rutgers University Press, 1958.
Gassner, John, ed. *O'Neill: A Collection of Critical Essays*. Englewood Cliffs, N.J.: Prentice-Hall, 1964.
Gelb, Arthur and Barbara. *O'Neill: A Biography*. New York: Harper & Row, 1962.
Leech, Clifford. *Eugene O'Neill*. New York: Grove Press, 1963.
Raleigh, John Henry. *Eugene O'Neill*. Carbondale: Southern Illinois University Press, 1965.
Winther, Sophus K. *Eugene O'Neill: A Critical Study*. New York: Russell & Russell, 1961.
Wright, Robert C. "O'Neill's Universalizing Technique in *The Iceman Cometh*," *Modern Drama*, VIII (May, 1965).

The Iceman Cometh

CHARACTERS

HARRY HOPE, *proprietor of a saloon and rooming house*

ED MOSHER, *Hope's brother-in-law, one-time circus man**

PAT MCGLOIN, *one-time Police Lieutenant**

WILLIE OBAN, *a Harvard Law School alumnus**

JOE MOTT, *one-time proprietor of a Negro gambling house*

PIET WETJOEN ("THE GENERAL"), *one-time leader of a Boer commando**

CECIL LEWIS ("THE CAPTAIN"), *one-time Captain of British infantry**

JAMES CAMERON ("JIMMY TOMORROW"), *one-time Boer War correspondent**

HUGO KALMAR, *one-time editor of Anarchist periodicals**

LARRY SLADE, *one-time Syndicalist-Anarchist**

ROCKY PIOGGI, *night bartender**

DON PARRITT*

PEARL*
MARGIE* } *street walkers*
CORA*

CHUCK MORELLO, *day bartender**

THEODORE HICKMAN (HICKEY), *a hardware salesman*

MORAN

LIEB

* Roomers at Harry Hope's

SCENES

Act One

SCENE   *Back room and a section of the bar at Harry Hope's—early morning in summer, 1912.*

Act Two

SCENE   *Back room, around midnight of the same day.*

Act Three

SCENE   *Bar and a section of the back room—morning of the following day.*

Act Four

SCENE   *Same as Act One. Back room and a section of the bar—around 1:30 A.M. of the next day.*

HARRY HOPE'S *is a Raines-Law hotel*[1] *of the period, a cheap gin-mill of the five-cent whiskey, last-resort variety situated on the downtown West Side of New York. The building, owned by* HOPE, *is a narrow five-story structure of the tenement type, the second floor a flat occupied by the proprietor. The renting of rooms on the upper floors, under the Raines-Law loopholes, makes the establishment legally a hotel and gives it the privilege of serving liquor in the back room of the bar after closing hours and on Sundays, provided a meal is served with the booze, thus making a back room legally a hotel restaurant. This food provision was generally circumvented by putting a property sandwich in the middle of each table, an old desiccated ruin of dust-laden bread and mummified ham or cheese which only the drunkest yokel from the sticks ever regarded as anything but a noisome table decoration. But at* HARRY HOPE'S, HOPE *being a former minor Tammanyite*[2] *and still possessing friends, this food technicality is ignored as irrelevant, except during the fleeting alarms of reform agitation. Even* HOPE'S *back room is not a separate room, but simply the rear of the barroom divided from the bar by drawing a dirty black curtain across the room.*

---

[1] Since the New York Raines Law restricted Sunday liquor sales to hotels, a Raines-Law hotel was a saloon with a few nominal sleeping rooms.

[2] Member of a New York City Democratic political machine.

Act One

SCENE The back room and a section of the bar of HARRY HOPE'S saloon on an early morning in summer, 1912. The right wall of the back room is a dirty black curtain which separates it from the bar. At rear, this curtain is drawn back from the wall so the bartender can get in and out. The back room is crammed with round tables and chairs placed so close together that it is a difficult squeeze to pass between them. In the middle of the rear wall is a door opening on a hallway. In the left corner, built out into the room, is the toilet with a sign "This is it" on the door. Against the middle of the left wall is a nickel-in-the-slot phonograph. Two windows, so glazed with grime one cannot see through them, are in the left wall, looking out on a backyard. The walls and ceiling once were white, but it was a long time ago, and they are now so splotched, peeled, stained and dusty that their color can best be described as dirty. The floor, with iron spittoons placed here and there, is covered with sawdust. Lighting comes from single wall brackets, two at left and two at rear.

There are three rows of tables, from front to back. Three are in the front line. The one at left-front has four chairs; the one at center-front, four; the one at right-front, five. At rear of, and half between, front tables one and two is a table of the second row with five chairs. A table, similarly placed at rear of front tables two and three, also has five chairs. The third row of tables, four chairs to one and six to the other, is against the rear wall on either side of the door.

At right of this dividing curtain is a section of the barroom, with the end of the bar seen at rear, a door to the hall at left of it. At front is a table with four chairs. Light comes from the street windows off right, the gray subdued light of early morning in a narrow street. In the back room, LARRY SLADE and HUGO KALMAR are at the table at left-front, HUGO in a chair facing right, LARRY at rear of table facing front, with an empty chair between them. A fourth chair is at right of table, facing left. HUGO is a small man in his late fifties. He has a head much too big for his body, a high forehead, crinkly long black hair streaked with gray, a *square face with a pug nose, a walrus mustache, black eyes which peer near-sightedly from behind thick-lensed spectacles, tiny hands and feet. He is dressed in threadbare black clothes and his white shirt is frayed at collar and cuffs, but everything about him is fastidiously clean. Even his flowing Windsor tie is neatly tied. There is a foreign atmosphere about him, the stamp of an alien radical, a strong resemblance to the type Anarchist as portrayed, bomb in hand, in newspaper cartoons. He is asleep now, bent forward in his chair, his arms folded on the table, his head resting sideways on his arms.*

LARRY SLADE *is sixty. He is tall, raw-boned, with coarse straight white hair, worn long and raggedly cut. He has a gaunt Irish face with a big nose, high cheekbones, a lantern jaw with a week's stubble of beard, a mystic's meditative pale-blue eyes with a gleam of sharp sardonic humor in them. As slovenly as* HUGO *is neat, his clothes are dirty and much slept in. His gray flannel shirt, open at the neck, has the appearance of having never been washed. From the way he methodically scratches himself with his long-fingered, hairy hands, he is lousy and reconciled to being so. He is the only occupant of the room who is not asleep. He stares in front of him, an expression of tired tolerance giving his face the quality of a pitying but weary old priest's.*

All four chairs at the middle table, front, are occupied. JOE MOTT *sits at left-front of the table, facing front. Behind him, facing right-front, is* PIET WETJOEN *("The General"). At center of the table, rear,* JAMES CAMERON *("Jimmy Tomorrow") sits facing front. At right of table, opposite* JOE, *is* CECIL LEWIS *("The Captain").*

JOE MOTT *is a Negro, about fifty years old, brown-skinned, stocky, wearing a light suit that had once been flashily sporty but is now about to fall apart. His pointed tan buttoned shoes, faded pink shirt and bright tie belong to the same vintage. Still, he manages to preserve an atmosphere of nattiness and there is nothing dirty about his appearance. His face is only mildly negroid in type. The nose is thin and his lips are not noticeably thick. His hair is crinkly and he is beginning to get bald. A scar from a knife slash runs from his left cheekbone to jaw. His face would be hard and tough if it were not for its good nature and lazy humor. He is asleep, his nodding head supported by his left hand.*

PIET WETJOEN, *the Boer, is in his fifties, a huge man with a bald head and a long grizzled beard. He is slovenly dressed in a dirty* shapeless patched suit, spotted by food. A Dutch farmer type, his once great muscular strength has been debauched into flaccid tallow. But despite his blubbery mouth and sodden bloodshot blue eyes, there is still a suggestion of old authority lurking in him like a memory of the drowned. He is hunched forward, both elbows on the table, his hand on each side of his head for support.

JAMES CAMERON ("Jimmy Tomorrow") is about the same size and age as HUGO, a small man. Like HUGO, he wears threadbare black, and everything about him is clean. But the resemblance ceases there. JIMMY has a face like an old well-bred, gentle bloodhound's, with folds of flesh hanging from each side of his mouth, and big brown friendly guileless eyes, more bloodshot than any bloodhound's ever were. He has mouse-colored thinning hair, a little bulbous nose, buck teeth in a small rabbit mouth. But his forehead is fine, his eyes are intelligent and there once was a competent ability in him. His speech is educated, with the ghost of a Scotch rhythm in it. His manners are those of a gentleman. There is a quality about him of a prim, Victorian old maid, and at the same time of a likeable, affectionate boy who has never grown up. He sleeps, chin on chest, hands folded in his lap.

CECIL LEWIS ("The Captain") is as obviously English as Yorkshire pudding and just as obviously the former army officer. He is going on sixty. His hair and military mustache are white, his eyes bright blue, his complexion that of a turkey. His lean figure is still erect and square-shouldered. He is stripped to the waist, his coat, shirt, undershirt, collar and tie crushed up into a pillow on the table in front of him, his head sideways on this pillow, facing front, his arms dangling toward the floor. On his lower left shoulder is the big ragged scar of an old wound.

At the table at right, front, HARRY HOPE, the proprietor, sits in the middle, facing front, with PAT MCGLOIN on his right and ED MOSHER on his left, the other two chairs being unoccupied.

Both MCGLOIN and MOSHER are big paunchy men. MCGLOIN has his old occupation of policeman stamped all over him. He is in his fifties, sandy-haired, bullet-headed, jowly, with protruding ears and little round eyes. His face must once have been brutal and greedy, but time and whiskey have melted it down into a good-humored, parasite's characterlessness. He wears old clothes and is slovenly. He is slumped sideways on his chair, his head drooping jerkily toward one shoulder.

ED MOSHER *is going on sixty. He has a round kewpie's face—
a kewpie who is an unshaven habitual drunkard. He looks like
an enlarged, elderly, bald edition of the village fat boy—a sly
fat boy, congenitally indolent, a practical joker, a born grafter
and con merchant. But amusing and essentially harmless, even
in his most enterprising days, because always too lazy to carry
crookedness beyond petty swindling. The influence of his old
circus career is apparent in his get-up. His worn clothes are
flashy; he wears phony rings and a heavy brass watch-chain (not
connected to a watch). Like* MCGLOIN, *he is slovenly. His head
is thrown back, his big mouth open.*

HARRY HOPE *is sixty, white-haired, so thin the description "bag
of bones" was made for him. He has the face of an old family
horse, prone to tantrums, with balkiness always smoldering in its
wall eyes, waiting for any excuse to shy and pretend to take the
bit in its teeth.* HOPE *is one of those men whom everyone likes
on sight, a softhearted slob, without malice, feeling superior to
no one, a sinner among sinners, a born easy mark for every appeal. He attempts to hide his defenselessness behind a testy
truculent manner, but this has never fooled anyone. He is a little
deaf, but not half as deaf as he sometimes pretends. His sight is
failing but is not as bad as he complains it is. He wears five-and-
ten-cent-store spectacles which are so out of alignment that one
eye at times peers half over one glass while the other eye looks
half under the other. He has badly fitting store teeth, which click
like castanets when he begins to fume. He is dressed in an old
coat from one suit and pants from another.*

*In a chair facing right at the table in the second line, between
the first two tables, front, sits* WILLIE OBAN, *his head on his left
arm outstretched along the table edge. He is in his late thirties,
of average height, thin. His haggard, dissipated face has a small
nose, a pointed chin, blue eyes with colorless lashes and brows.
His blond hair, badly in need of a cut, clings in a limp part to his
skull. His eyelids flutter continually as if any light were too
strong for his eyes. The clothes he wears belong on a scarecrow.
They seem constructed of an inferior grade of dirty blotting
paper. His shoes are even more disreputable, wrecks of imitation
leather, one laced with twine, the other with a bit of wire. He
has no socks, and his bare feet show through holes in the soles,
with his big toes sticking out of the uppers. He keeps muttering
and twitching in his sleep.*

As the curtain rises, ROCKY, *the night bartender, comes from the
bar through the curtain and stands looking over the back room.
He is a Neapolitan-American in his late twenties, squat and*

muscular, with a flat, swarthy face and beady eyes. *The sleeves of his collarless shirt are rolled up on his thick, powerful arms and he wears a soiled apron.* A tough guy but sentimental, in his way, and good-natured. *He signals to* LARRY *with a cautious "Sstt" and motions him to see if* HOPE *is asleep.* LARRY *rises from his chair to look at* HOPE *and nods to* ROCKY. ROCKY *goes back in the bar but immediately returns with a bottle of bar whiskey and a glass. He squeezes between the tables to* LARRY.

ROCKY (*In a low voice out of the side of his mouth*) Make it fast. (LARRY *pours a drink and gulps it down.* ROCKY *takes the bottle and puts it on the table where* WILLIE OBAN *is*) Don't want de Boss to get wise when he's got one of his tightwad buns on. (*He chuckles with an amused glance at* HOPE) Jees, ain't de old bastard a riot when he starts dat bull about turnin' over a new leaf? "Not a damned drink on de house," he tells me, "and all dese bums got to pay up deir room rent. Beginnin' tomorrow," he says. Jees, yuh'd tink he meant it! (*He sits down in the chair at* LARRY'S *left*)

LARRY (*Grinning*) I'll be glad to pay up—tomorrow. And I know my fellow inmates will promise the same. They've all a touching credulity concerning tomorrows. (*A half-drunken mockery in his eyes*) It'll be a great day for them, tomorrow—the Feast of All Fools, with brass bands playing! Their ships will come in, loaded to the gunwales with canceled regrets and promises fulfilled and clean slates and new leases!

ROCKY (*Cynically*) Yeah, and a ton of hop!

LARRY (*Leans toward him, a comical intensity in his low voice*) Don't mock the faith! Have you no respect for religion, you unregenerate Wop? What's it matter if the truth is that their favoring breeze has the stink of nickel whiskey on its breath, and their sea is a growler of lager and ale, and their ships are long since looted and scuttled and sunk on the bottom? To hell with the truth! As the history of the world proves, the truth has no bearing on anything. It's irrelevant and immaterial, as the lawyers say. The lie of a pipe dream is what gives life to the whole misbegotten mad lot of us, drunk or sober. And that's enough philosophic wisdom to give you for one drink of rot-gut.

ROCKY (*Grins kiddingly*) De old Foolosopher, like Hickey calls yuh, ain't yuh? I s'pose you don't fall for no pipe dream?

LARRY (*A bit stiffly*) I don't, no. Mine are all dead and buried behind me. What's before me is the comforting fact that death is a fine long sleep, and I'm damned tired, and it can't come too soon for me.

ROCKY Yeah, just hangin' around hopin' you'll croak, ain't yuh? Well, I'm bettin' you'll have a good long wait. Jees, somebody'll have to take an axe to croak you!

LARRY (*Grins*) Yes, it's my bad luck to be cursed with an iron constitution that even Harry's booze can't corrode.

ROCKY De old anarchist wise guy dat knows all de answers! Dat's you, huh?

LARRY (*Frowns*) Forget the anarchist part of it. I'm through with the Movement long since. I saw men didn't want to be saved from themselves, for that would mean they'd have to give up greed, and they'll never pay that price for liberty. So I said to the world, God bless all here, and may the best man win and die of gluttony! And I took a seat in the grandstand of philosophical detachment to fall asleep observing the cannibals do their death dance. (*He chuckles at his own fancy—reaches over and shakes* HUGO'S *shoulder*) Ain't I telling him the truth, Comrade Hugo?

ROCKY Aw, fer Chris' sake, don't get dat bughouse bum started!

HUGO (*Raises his head and peers at* ROCKY *blearily through his thick spectacles—in a guttural declamatory tone*) Capitalist swine! Bourgeois stool pigeons! Have the slaves no right to sleep even? (*Then he grins at* ROCKY *and his manner changes to a giggling, wheedling playfulness, as though he were talking to a child*) Hello, leedle Rocky! Leedle monkey-face! Vere is your leedle slave girls? (*With an abrupt change to a bullying tone*) Don't be a fool! Loan me a dollar! Damned bourgeois Wop! The great Malatesta is my good friend! Buy me a trink! (*He seems to run down, and is overcome by drowsiness. His head sinks to the table again and he is at once fast asleep*)

ROCKY He's out again. (*More exasperated than angry*) He's lucky no one don't take his cracks serious or he'd wake up every mornin' in a hospital.

LARRY (*Regarding* HUGO *with pity*) No. No one takes him seriously. That's his epitaph. Not even the comrades any more. If I've been through with the Movement long since, it's been through with him, and, thanks to whiskey, he's the only one doesn't know it.

ROCKY I've let him get by wid too much. He's goin' to pull dat slave-girl stuff on me once too often. (*His manner changes to defensive argument*) Hell, yuh'd tink I wuz a pimp or somethin'. Everybody knows me knows I ain't. A pimp don't hold no job. I'm a bartender. Dem tarts, Margie and Poil, dey're just a side line to pick up some extra dough. Strictly business, like dey was fighters and I was deir manager, see? I fix the cops for dem so's dey can hustle widout gettin' pinched. Hell, dey'd be on de Island most of de time if it wasn't fer me. And I don't beat dem up like a pimp would. I treat dem fine. Dey like me. We're pals, see? What if I do take deir dough? Dey'd on'y trow it away. Tarts can't hang on to dough. But I'm a bartender and I work hard for my livin' in dis dump. You know dat, Larry.

LARRY (*With inner sardonic amusement—flatteringly*) A shrewd business man, who doesn't miss any opportunity to get on in the world. That's what I'd call you.
ROCKY (*Pleased*) Sure ting. Dat's me. Grab another ball, Larry. (LARRY *pours a drink from the bottle on* WILLIE'S *table and gulps it down.* ROCKY *glances around the room*) Yuh'd never tink all dese bums had a good bed upstairs to go to. Scared if dey hit the hay dey wouldn't be here when Hickey showed up, and dey'd miss a coupla drinks. Dat's what kept you up too, ain't it?
LARRY It is. But not so much the hope of booze, if you can believe that. I've got the blues and Hickey's a great one to make a joke of everything and cheer you up.
ROCKY Yeah, some kidder! Remember how he woiks up dat gag about his wife, when he's cockeyed, cryin' over her picture and den springin' it on yuh all of a sudden dat he left her in de hay wid de iceman? (*He laughs*) I wonder what's happened to him. Yuh could set your watch by his periodicals before dis. Always got here a coupla days before Harry's birthday party, and now he's on'y got till tonight to make it. I hope he shows soon. Dis dump is like de morgue wid all dese bums passed out. (WILLIE OBAN *jerks and twitches in his sleep and begins to mumble. They watch him*)
WILLIE (*Blurts from his dream*) It's a lie! (*Miserably*) Papa! Papa!
LARRY Poor devil. (*Then angry with himself*) But to hell with pity! It does no good. I'm through with it!
ROCKY Dreamin' about his old man. From what de old-timers say, de old gent sure made a pile of dough in de bucket-shop game before de cops got him. (*He considers* WILLIE *frowningly*) Jees, I've seen him bad but never dis bad. Look at dat get-up. Been playin' de old reliever game. Sold his suit and shoes at Solly's two days ago. Solly give him two bucks and a bum outfit. Yesterday he sells de bum one back to Solly for four bits and gets dese rags to put on. Now he's through. Dat's Solly's final edition he wouldn't take back for nuttin'. Willie sure is on de bottom. I ain't never seen no one so bad, except Hickey on de end of a coupla his bats.
LARRY (*Sardonically*) It's a great game, the pursuit of happiness.
ROCKY Harry don't know what to do about him. He called up his old lady's lawyer like he always does when Willie gets licked. Yuh remember dey used to send down a private dick to give him the rush to a cure, but de lawyer tells Harry nix, de old lady's off of Willie for keeps dis time and he can go to hell.
LARRY (*Watches* WILLIE, *who is shaking in his sleep like an old dog*) There's the consolation that he hasn't far to go! (*As if replying to this,*

WILLIE *comes to a crisis of jerks and moans.* LARRY *adds in a comically intense, crazy whisper*) Be God, he's knocking on the door right now!
WILLIE (*Suddenly yells in his nightmare*) It's a God-damned lie! (*He begins to sob*) Oh, Papa! Jesus! (*All the occupants of the room stir on their chairs but none of them wakes up except* HOPE)
ROCKY (*Grabs his shoulder and shakes him*) Hey, you! Nix! Cut out de noise! (WILLIE *opens his eyes to stare around him with a bewildered horror*)
HOPE (*Opens one eye to peer over his spectacles—drowsily*) Who's that yelling?
ROCKY Willie, Boss. De Brooklyn boys is after him.
HOPE (*Querulously*) Well, why don't you give the poor feller a drink and keep him quiet? Bejees, can't I get a wink of sleep in my own back room?
ROCKY (*Indignantly to* LARRY) Listen to that blind-eyed, deef old bastard, will yuh? He give me strict orders not to let Willie hang up no more drinks, no matter—
HOPE (*Mechanically puts a hand to his ear in the gesture of deafness*) What's that? I can't hear you. (*Then drowsily irascible*) You're a cockeyed liar. Never refused a drink to anyone needed it bad in my life! Told you to use your judgment. Ought to know better. You're too busy thinking up ways to cheat me. Oh, I ain't as blind as you think. I can still see a cash register, bejees!
ROCKY (*Grins at him affectionately now—flatteringly*) Sure, Boss. Swell chance of foolin' you!
HOPE I'm wise to you and your sidekick, Chuck. Bejees, you're burglars, not barkeeps! Blind-eyed, deef old bastard, am I? Oh, I heard you! Heard you often when you didn't think. You and Chuck laughing behind my back, telling people you throw the money up in the air and whatever sticks to the ceiling is my share! A fine couple of crooks! You'd steal the pennies off your dead mother's eyes!
ROCKY (*Winks at* LARRY) Aw, Harry, me and Chuck was on'y kiddin'.
HOPE (*More drowsily*) I'll fire both of you. Bejees, if you think you can play me for an easy mark, you've come to the wrong house. No one ever played Harry Hope for a sucker!
ROCKY (*To* LARRY) No one but everybody.
HOPE (*His eyes shut again—mutters*) Least you could do—keep things quiet— (*He falls asleep*)
WILLIE (*Pleadingly*) Give me a drink, Rocky. Harry said it was all right. God, I need a drink.
ROCKY Den grab it. It's right under your nose.
WILLIE (*Avidly*) Thanks. (*He takes the bottle with both twitching*

hands and tilts it to his lips and gulps down the whiskey in big swallows)
ROCKY (Sharply) When! When! (He grabs the bottle) I didn't say, take a bath! (Showing the bottle to LARRY—indignantly) Jees, look! He's killed a half pint or more! (He turns on WILLIE angrily, but WILLIE has closed his eyes and is sitting quietly, shuddering, waiting for the effect)
LARRY (With a pitying glance) Leave him be, the poor devil. A half pint of that dynamite in one swig will fix him for a while—if it doesn't kill him.
ROCKY (Shrugs his shoulders and sits down again) Aw right by me. It ain't my booze. (Behind him, in the chair at left of the middle table, JOE MOTT, the Negro, has been waking up)
JOE (His eye blinking sleepily) Whose booze? Gimme some. I don't care whose. Where's Hickey? Ain't he come yet? What time's it, Rocky?
ROCKY Gettin' near time to open up. Time you begun to sweep up in de bar.
JOE (Lazily) Never mind de time. If Hickey ain't come, it's time Joe goes to sleep again. I was dreamin' Hickey come in de door, crackin' one of dem drummer's jokes, wavin' a big bankroll and we was all goin' be drunk for two weeks. Wake up and no luck. (Suddenly his eyes open wide) Wait a minute, dough. I got idea. Say, Larry, how 'bout dat young guy, Parritt, came to look you up last night and rented a room? Where's he at?
LARRY Up in his room, asleep. No hope in him, anyway, Joe. He's broke.
JOE Dat what he told you? Me and Rocky knows different. Had a roll when he paid you his room rent, didn't he, Rocky? I seen it.
ROCKY Yeah. He flashed it like he forgot and den tried to hide it quick.
LARRY (Surprised and resentful) He did, did he?
ROCKY Yeah, I figgered he don't belong, but he said he was a friend of yours.
LARRY He's a liar. I wouldn't know him if he hadn't told me who he was. His mother and I were friends years ago on the Coast. (He hesitates—then lowering his voice) You've read in the papers about that bombing on the Coast when several people got killed? Well, the one woman they pinched, Rosa Parritt, is his mother. They'll be coming up for trial soon, and there's no chance for them. She'll get life, I think. I'm telling you this so you'll know why if Don acts a bit queer, and not jump on him. He must be hard hit. He's her only kid.
ROCKY (Nods—then thoughtfully) Why ain't he out dere stickin' by her?

LARRY (*Frowns*) Don't ask questions. Maybe there's a good reason.
ROCKY (*Stares at him—understandingly*) Sure. I get it. (*Then wonderingly*) But den what kind of a sap is he to hang on to his right name?
LARRY (*Irritably*) I'm telling you I don't know anything and I don't want to know. To hell with the Movement and all connected with it! I'm out of it, and everything else, and damned glad to be.
ROCKY (*Shrugs his shoulders—indifferently*) Well, don't tink I'm interested in dis Parritt guy. He's nuttin' to me.
JOE Me neider. If dere's one ting more'n anudder I cares nuttin' about, it's de sucker game you and Hugo call de Movement. (*He chuckles—reminiscently*) Reminds me of damn fool argument me and Mose Porter has de udder night. He's drunk and I'm drunker. He says, "Socialist and Anarchist, we ought to shoot dem dead. Dey's all no-good sons of bitches." I says, "Hold on, you talk 's if Anarchists and Socialists was de same." "Dey is," he says. "Dey's both no-good bastards." "No, dey ain't," I says. "I'll explain the difference. De Anarchist he never works. He drinks but he never buys, and if he do ever git a nickel, he blows it in on bombs, and he wouldn't give you nothin'. So go ahead and shoot him. But de Socialist, sometimes, he's got a job, and if he gets ten bucks, he's bound by his religion to split fifty-fifty wid you. You say—how about my cut, Comrade? And you gets de five. So you don't shoot no Socialists while I'm around. Dat is, not if dey got anything. Of course, if dey's broke, den dey's no-good bastards, too." (*He laughs, immensely tickled*)
LARRY (*Grins with sardonic appreciation*) Be God, Joe, you've got all the beauty of human nature and the practical wisdom of the world in that little parable.
ROCKY (*Winks at* JOE) Sure, Larry ain't de on'y wise guy in dis dump, hey, Joe? (*At a sound from the hall he turns as* DON PARRITT *appears in the doorway.* ROCKY *speaks to* LARRY *out of the side of his mouth*) Here's your guy. (PARRITT *comes forward. He is eighteen, tall and broad-shouldered but thin, gangling and awkward. His face is good-looking, with blond curly hair and large regular features, but his personality is unpleasant. There is a shifting defiance and ingratiation in his light-blue eyes and an irritating aggressiveness in his manner. His clothes and shoes are new, comparatively expensive, sporty in style. He looks as though he belonged in a pool room patronized by would-be sports. He glances around defensively, sees* LARRY *and comes forward*)
PARRITT Hello, Larry. (*He nods to* ROCKY *and* JOE) Hello. (*They nod and size him up with expressionless eyes*)
LARRY (*Without cordiality*) What's up? I thought you'd be asleep.
PARRITT Couldn't make it. I got sick of lying awake. Thought I might as well see if you were around.

LARRY (*Indicates the chair on the right of table*) Sit down and join the bums then. (PARRITT *sits down.* LARRY *adds meaningfully*) The rules of the house are that drinks may be served at all hours.
PARRITT (*Forcing a smile*) I get you. But, hell, I'm just about broke. (*He catches* ROCKY's *and* JOE's *contemptuous glances—quickly*) Oh, I know you guys saw— You think I've got a roll. Well, you're all wrong. I'll show you. (*He takes a small wad of dollar bills from his pocket*) It's all ones. And I've got to live on it till I get a job. (*Then with defensive truculence*) You think I fixed up a phony, don't you? Why the hell would I? Where would I get a real roll? You don't get rich doing what I've been doing. Ask Larry. You're lucky in the Movement if you have enough to eat. (LARRY *regards him puzzledly*)
ROCKY (*Coldly*) What's de song and dance about? We ain't said nuttin'.
PARRITT (*Lamely—placating them now*) Why, I was just putting you right. But I don't want you to think I'm a tightwad. I'll buy a drink if you want one.
JOE (*Cheering up*) If? Man, when I don't want a drink, you call de morgue, tell dem come take Joe's body away, 'cause he's sure enuf dead. Gimme de bottle quick, Rocky, before he changes his mind! (ROCKY *passes him the bottle and glass. He pours a brimful drink and tosses it down his throat, and hands the bottle and glass to* LARRY)
ROCKY I'll take a cigar when I go in de bar. What're you havin'?
PARRITT Nothing. I'm on the wagon. What's the damage? (*He holds out a dollar bill*)
ROCKY Fifteen cents. (*He makes change from his pocket*)
PARRITT Must be some booze!
LARRY It's cyanide cut with carbolic acid to give it a mellow flavor. Here's luck! (*He drinks*)
ROCKY Guess I'll get back in de bar and catch a coupla winks before opening-up time. (*He squeezes through the tables and disappears, right-rear, behind the curtain. In the section of bar at right, he comes forward and sits at the table and slumps back, closing his eyes and yawning*)
JOE (*Stares calculatingly at* PARRITT *and then looks away—aloud to himself, philosophically*) One-drink guy. Dat well done run dry. No hope till Harry's birthday party. 'Less Hickey shows up. (*He turns to* LARRY) If Hickey comes, Larry, you wake me up if you has to bat me wid a chair. (*He settles himself and immediately falls asleep*)
PARRITT Who's Hickey?
LARRY A hardware drummer.[3] An old friend of Harry Hope's and all the gang. He's a grand guy. He comes here twice a year regularly on

---

[3] A salesman of hardware.

a periodical drunk and blows in all his money.

PARRITT (*With a disparaging glance around*) Must be hard up for a place to hang out.

LARRY It has its points for him. He never runs into anyone he knows in his business here.

PARRITT (*Lowering his voice*) Yes, that's what I want, too. I've got to stay under cover, Larry, like I told you last night.

LARRY You did a lot of hinting. You didn't tell me anything.

PARRITT You can guess, can't you? (*He changes the subject abruptly*) I've been in some dumps on the Coast, but this is the limit. What kind of joint is it, anyway?

LARRY (*With a sardonic grin*) What is it? It's the No Chance Saloon. It's Bedrock Bar, The End of the Line Café, The Bottom of the Sea Rathskeller! Don't you notice the beautiful calm in the atmosphere? That's because it's the last harbor. No one here has to worry about where they're going next, because there is no farther they can go. It's a great comfort to them. Although even here they keep up the appearances of life with a few harmless pipe dreams about their yesterdays and tomorrows, as you'll see for yourself if you're here long.

PARRITT (*Stares at him curiously*) What's your pipe dream, Larry?

LARRY (*Hiding resentment*) Oh, I'm the exception. I haven't any left, thank God. (*Shortly*) Don't complain about this place. You couldn't find a better for lying low.

PARRITT I'm glad of that, Larry. I don't feel any too damned good. I was knocked off my base by that business on the Coast, and since then it's been no fun dodging around the country, thinking every guy you see might be a dick.

LARRY (*Sympathetically now*) No, it wouldn't be. But you're safe here. The cops ignore this dump. They think it's as harmless as a graveyard. (*He grins sardonically*) And, be God, they're right.

PARRITT It's been lonely as hell. (*Impulsively*) Christ, Larry, I was glad to find you. I kept saying to myself, "If I can only find Larry. He's the one guy in the world who can understand—" (*He hesitates, staring at* LARRY *with a strange appeal*)

LARRY (*Watching him puzzledly*) Understand what?

PARRITT (*Hastily*) Why, all I've been through. (*Looking away*) Oh, I know you're thinking, This guy has a hell of a nerve. I haven't seen him since he was a kid. I'd forgotten he was alive. But I've never forgotten you, Larry. You were the only friend of Mother's who ever paid attention to me, or knew I was alive. All the others were too busy with the Movement. Even Mother. And I had no Old Man. You used to take me on your knee and tell me stories and crack jokes and make me laugh. You'd ask me questions and take what I said seriously. I guess I got to feel in the years you lived with us that you'd taken the place of my Old Man. (*Embarrassedly*) But, hell, that sounds like a lot of mush. I suppose you don't remember a damned thing about it.

LARRY (*Moved in spite of himself*) I remember well. You were a serious lonely little shaver. (*Then resenting being moved, changes the subject*) How is it they didn't pick you up when they got your mother and the rest?

PARRITT (*In a lowered voice but eagerly, as if he wanted this chance to tell about it*) I wasn't around, and as soon as I heard the news I went under cover. You've noticed my glad rags. I was staked to them—as a disguise, sort of. I hung around pool rooms and gambling joints and hooker shops, where they'd never look for a Wobblie,[4] pretending I was a sport. Anyway, they'd grabbed everyone important, so I suppose they didn't think of me until afterward.

LARRY The papers say the cops got them all dead to rights, that the Burns dicks knew every move before it was made, and someone inside the Movement must have sold out and tipped them off.

PARRITT (*Turns to look* LARRY *in the eyes—slowly*) Yes, I guess that must be true, Larry. It hasn't come out who it was. It may never come out. I suppose whoever it was made a bargain with the Burns men to keep him out of it. They won't need his evidence.

LARRY (*Tensely*) By God, I hate to believe it of any of the crowd, even if I am through long since with any connection with them. I know they're damned fools, most of them, as stupidly greedy for power as the worst capitalist they attack, but I'd swear there couldn't be a yellow stool pigeon among them.

PARRITT Sure. I'd have sworn that, too, Larry.

LARRY I hope his soul rots in hell, whoever it is!

PARRITT Yes, so do I.

LARRY (*After a pause—shortly*) How did you locate me? I hoped I'd found a place of retirement here where no one in the Movement would ever come to disturb my peace.

PARRITT I found out through Mother.

LARRY I asked her not to tell anyone.

PARRITT She didn't tell me, but she'd kept all your letters and I found where she'd hidden them in the flat. I sneaked up there one night after she was arrested.

LARRY I'd never have thought she was a woman who'd keep letters.

PARRITT No, I wouldn't, either. There's nothing soft or sentimental about Mother.

LARRY I never answered her last letters. I haven't written her in a couple

---

[4] Slang for a member of the I.W.W. (Industrial Workers of the World).

of years—or anyone else. I've gotten beyond the desire to communicate with the world—or, what's more to the point, let it bother me any more with its greedy madness.

PARRITT It's funny Mother kept in touch with you so long. When she's finished with anyone, she's finished. She's always been proud of that. And you know how she feels about the Movement. Like a revivalist preacher about religion. Anyone who loses faith in it is more than dead to her; he's a Judas who ought to be boiled in oil. Yet she seemed to forgive you.

LARRY (*Sardonically*) She didn't, don't worry. She wrote to denounce me and try to bring the sinner to repentance and a belief in the One True Faith again.

PARRITT What made you leave the Movement, Larry? Was it on account of Mother?

LARRY (*Starts*) Don't be a damned fool! What the hell put that in your head?

PARRITT Why, nothing—except I remember what a fight you had with her before you left.

LARRY (*Resentfully*) Well, if you do, I don't. That was eleven years ago. You were only seven. If we did quarrel, it was because I told her I'd become convinced the Movement was only a beautiful pipe dream.

PARRITT (*With a strange smile*) I don't remember it that way.

LARRY Then you can blame your imagination—and forget it. (*He changes the subject abruptly*) You asked me why I quit the Movement. I had a lot of good reasons. One was myself, and another was my comrades, and the last was the breed of swine called men in general. For myself, I was forced to admit, at the end of thirty years' devotion to the Cause, that I was never made for it. I was born condemned to be one of those who has to see all sides of a question. When you're damned like that, the questions multiply for you until in the end it's all question and no answer. As history proves, to be a worldly success at anything, especially revolution, you have to wear blinders like a horse and see only straight in front of you. You have to see, too, that this is all black, and that is all white. As for my comrades in the Great Cause, I felt as Horace Walpole did about England, that he could love it if it weren't for the people in it. The material the ideal free society must be constructed from is men themselves and you can't build a marble temple out of a mixture of mud and manure. When man's soul isn't a sow's ear, it will be time enough to dream of silk purses. (*He chuckles sardonically—then irritably as if suddenly provoked at himself for talking so much*) Well, that's why I quit the Movement, if it leaves you any wiser. At any rate, you see it had nothing to do with your mother.

PARRITT (*Smiles almost mockingly*) Oh, sure, I see. But I'll bet Mother has always thought it was on her account. You know her, Larry. To hear her go on sometimes, you'd think she was the Movement.

LARRY (*Stares at him, puzzled and repelled—sharply*) That's a hell of a way for you to talk, after what happened to her!

PARRITT (*At once confused and guilty*) Don't get me wrong. I wasn't sneering, Larry. Only kidding. I've said the same thing to her lots of times to kid her. But you're right. I know I shouldn't now. I keep forgetting she's in jail. It doesn't seem real. I can't believe it about her. She's always been so free. I— But I don't want to think of it. (LARRY *is moved to a puzzled pity in spite of himself.* PARRITT *changes the subject*) What have you been doing all the years since you left—the Coast, Larry?

LARRY (*Sardonically*) Nothing I could help doing. If I don't believe in the Movement, I don't believe in anything else either, especially not the State. I've refused to become a useful member of its society. I've been a philosophical drunken bum, and proud of it. (*Abruptly his tone sharpens with resentful warning*) Listen to me. I hope you've deduced that I've my own reason for answering the impertinent questions of a stranger, for that's all you are to me. I have a strong hunch you've come here expecting something of me. I'm warning you, at the start, so there'll be no misunderstanding, that I've nothing left to give, and I want to be left alone, and I'll thank you to keep your life to yourself. I feel you're looking for some answer to something. I have no answer to give anyone, not even myself. Unless you can call what Heine wrote in his poem to morphine an answer. (*He quotes a translation of the closing couplet sardonically*)

> "Lo, sleep is good; better is death; in sooth,
> The best of all were never to be born."

PARRITT (*Shrinks a bit frightenedly*) That's the hell of an answer. (*Then with a forced grin of bravado*) Still, you never know when it might come in handy. (*He looks away.* LARRY *stares at him puzzledly, interested in spite of himself and at the same time vaguely uneasy*)

LARRY (*Forcing a casual tone*) I don't suppose you've had much chance to hear news of your mother since she's been in jail?

PARRITT No. No chance. (*He hesitates—then blurts out*) Anyway, I don't think she wants to hear from me. We had a fight just before that business happened. She bawled me out because I was going around with tarts. That got my goat, coming from her. I told her, "You've always acted the free woman, you've never let anything stop you from—" (*He checks himself—goes on hurriedly*) That made her sore. She said she wouldn't give a damn what I did except she'd begun to suspect I was too interested in outside things and losing interest in the Movement.

LARRY (*Stares at him*) And were you?

PARRITT (*Hesitates—then with intensity*) Sure I was! I'm no damned fool! I couldn't go on believing forever that gang was going to change the world by shooting off their loud traps on soapboxes and sneaking around blowing up a lousy building or a bridge! I got wise it was all a crazy pipe dream! (*Appealingly*) The same as you did, Larry. That's why I came to you. I knew you'd understand. What finished me was this last business of someone selling out. How can you believe anything after a thing like that happens? It knocks you cold! You don't know what the hell is what! You're through! (*Appealingly*) You know how I feel, don't you, Larry? (LARRY *stares at him, moved by sympathy and pity in spite of himself, disturbed, and resentful at being disturbed, and puzzled by something he feels about* PARRITT *that isn't right. But before he can reply,* HUGO *suddenly raises his head from his arms in a half-awake alcoholic daze and speaks*)

HUGO (*Quotes aloud to himself in a guttural declamatory style*) "The days grow hot, O Babylon! 'Tis cool beneath thy villow trees!" (PARRITT *turns startledly as* HUGO *peers muzzily without recognition at him.* HUGO *exclaims automatically in his tone of denunciation*) Gottammed stool pigeon!

PARRITT (*Shrinks away—stammers*) What? Who do you mean? (*Then furiously*) You lousy bum, you can't call me that! (*He draws back his fist*)

HUGO (*Ignores this—recognizing him now, bursts into his childish teasing giggle*) Hello, leedle Don! Leedle monkey-face. I did not recognize you. You have grown big boy. How is your mother? Where you come from? (*He breaks into his wheedling, bullying tone*) Don't be a fool! Loan me a dollar! Buy me a trink! (*As if this exhausted him, he abruptly forgets it and plumps his head down on his arms again and is asleep*)

PARRITT (*With eager relief*) Sure, I'll buy you a drink, Hugo. I'm broke, but I can afford one for you. I'm sorry I got sore. I ought to have remembered when you're soused you call everyone a stool pigeon. But it's no damned joke right at this time. (*He turns to* LARRY, *who is regarding him now fixedly with an uneasy expression as if he suddenly were afraid of his own thoughts—forcing a smile*) Gee, he's passed out again. (*He stiffens defensively*) What are you giving me the hard look for? Oh, I know. You thought I was going to hit him?

What do you think I am? I've always had a lot of respect for Hugo. I've always stood up for him when people in the Movement panned him for an old drunken has-been. He had the guts to serve ten years in the can in his own country and get his eyes ruined in solitary. I'd like to see some of them here stick that. Well, they'll get a chance now to show— (*Hastily*) I don't mean— But let's forget that. Tell me some more about this dump. Who are all these tanks? Who's that guy trying to catch pneumonia? (*He indicates* LEWIS)

LARRY (*Stares at him almost frightenedly—then looks away and grasps eagerly this chance to change the subject. He begins to describe the sleepers with sardonic relish but at the same time showing his affection for them*) That's Captain Lewis, a one-time hero of the British Army. He strips to display that scar on his back he got from a native spear whenever he's completely plastered. The bewhiskered bloke opposite him is General Wetjoen, who led a commando in the War. The two of them met when they came here to work in the Boer War spectacle at the St. Louis Fair and they've been bosom pals ever since. They dream the hours away in happy dispute over the brave days in South Africa when they tried to murder each other. The little guy between them was in it, too, as correspondent for some English paper. His nickname here is Jimmy Tomorrow. He's the leader of our Tomorrow Movement.

PARRITT What do they do for a living?

LARRY As little as possible. Once in a while one of them makes a successful touch somewhere, and some of them get a few dollars a month from connections at home who pay it on condition they never come back. For the rest, they live on free lunch and their old friend, Harry Hope, who doesn't give a damn what anyone does or doesn't do, as long as he likes you.

PARRITT It must be a tough life.

LARRY It's not. Don't waste your pity. They wouldn't thank you for it. They manage to get drunk, by hook or crook, and keep their pipe dreams, and that's all they ask of life. I've never known more contented men. It isn't often that men attain the true goal of their heart's desire. The same applies to Harry himself and his two cronies at the far table. He's so satisfied with life he's never set foot out of this place since his wife died twenty years ago. He has no need of the outside world at all. This place has a fine trade from the Market people across the street and the waterfront workers, so in spite of Harry's thirst and his generous heart, he comes out even. He never worries in hard times because there's always old friends from the days when he was a jitney Tammany politician, and a friendly brewery to tide him over. Don't ask me what his two pals work at because they don't. Except at being his lifetime guests. The one facing this way is his brother-in-law, Ed Mosher, who once worked for a circus in the ticket wagon. Pat McGloin, the other one, was a police lieutenant back in the flush times of graft when everything went. But he got too greedy and when the usual reform investigation came he was caught redhanded and thrown off the Force. (*He nods at* JOE) Joe here has a yesterday in the same flush period. He ran a colored gambling house then and was a hell of a sport, so they say. Well, that's our whole family circle of inmates, except the two barkeeps and their girls, three ladies of the pavement that room on the third floor.

PARRITT (*Bitterly*) To hell with them! I never want to see a whore again! (*As* LARRY *flashes him a puzzled glance, he adds confusedly*) I mean, they always get you in dutch. (*While he is speaking* WILLIE OBAN *has opened his eyes. He leans toward them, drunk now from the effect of the huge drink he took, and speaks with a mocking suavity*)

WILLIE Why omit me from your Who's Who in Dypsomania, Larry? An unpardonable slight, especially as I am the only inmate of royal blood. (*To* PARRITT—*ramblingly*) Educated at Harvard, too. You must have noticed the atmosphere of culture here. My humble contribution. Yes, Generous Stranger—I trust you're generous—I was born in the purple, the son, but unfortunately not the heir, of the late world-famous Bill Oban, King of the Bucket Shops. A revolution deposed him, conducted by the District Attorney. He was sent into exile. In fact, not to mince matters, they locked him in the can and threw away the key. Alas, his was an adventurous spirit that pined in confinement. And so he died. Forgive these reminiscences. Undoubtedly all this is well known to you. Everyone in the world knows.

PARRITT (*Uncomfortably*) Tough luck. No, I never heard of him.

WILLIE (*Blinks at him incredulously*) Never heard? I thought everyone in the world— Why, even at Harvard I discovered my father was well known by reputation, although that was some time before the District Attorney gave him so much unwelcome publicity. Yes, even as a freshman I was notorious. I was accepted socially with all the warm cordiality that Henry Wadsworth Longfellow would have shown a drunken Negress dancing the can can at high noon on Brattle Street. Harvard was my father's idea. He was an ambitious man. Dictatorial, too. Always knowing what was best for me. But I did make myself a brilliant student. A dirty trick on my classmates, inspired by revenge, I fear. (*He quotes*) "Dear college days, with pleasure rife! The grandest gladdest days of life!" But, of course, that is a Yale hymn, and they're given to rah-rah exaggeration at New Haven. I was a brilliant student at Law School, too. My father wanted a lawyer in the family. He was a calculating man. A thorough knowledge of the law close at hand in the house to help him find fresh ways to evade it. But I discovered the loophole of whiskey and escaped his jurisdiction. (*Abruptly to* PARRITT) Speaking of whiskey, sir, reminds me—and, I hope, reminds you—that when meeting a Prince the customary salutation is "What'll you have?"

PARRITT (*With defensive resentment*) Nix! All you guys seem to think I'm made of dough. Where would I get the coin to blow everyone?

WILLIE (*Skeptically*) Broke? You haven't the thirsty look of the impecunious. I'd judge you to be a plutocrat, your pockets stuffed with ill-gotten gains. Two or three dollars, at least. And don't think we will question how you got it. As Vespasian remarked, the smell of all whiskey is sweet.

PARRITT What do you mean, how I got it? (*To* LARRY, *forcing a laugh*) It's a laugh, calling me a plutocrat, isn't it, Larry, when I've been in the Movement all my life. (LARRY *gives him an uneasy suspicious glance, then looks away, as if avoiding something he does not wish to see*)

WILLIE (*Disgustedly*) Ah, one of those, eh? I believe you now, all right! Go away and blow yourself up, that's a good lad. Hugo is the only licensed preacher of that gospel here. A dangerous terrorist, Hugo! He would as soon blow the collar off a schooner of beer as look at you! (*To* LARRY) Let us ignore this useless youth, Larry. Let us join in prayer that Hickey, the Great Salesman, will soon arrive bringing the blessed bourgeois long green! Would that Hickey or Death would come! Meanwhile, I will sing a song. A beautiful old New England folk ballad which I picked up at Harvard amid the debris of education. (*He sings in a boisterous baritone, rapping on the table with his knuckles at the indicated spots in the song*)

> "Jack, oh, Jack, was a sailor lad
> And he came to a tavern for gin
> He rapped and he rapped with a (*Rap, rap, rap*)
> But never a soul seemed in."

(*The drunks at the tables stir.* ROCKY *gets up from his chair in the bar and starts back for the entrance to the back room.* HOPE *cocks one irritable eye over his specs.* JOE MOTT *opens both of his and grins.* WILLIE *interposes some drunken whimsical exposition to* LARRY) The origin of this beautiful ditty is veiled in mystery, Larry. There was a legend bruited about in Cambridge lavatories that Waldo Emerson composed it during his uninformative period as a minister, while he was trying to write a sermon. But my own opinion is, it goes back much further, and Jonathan Edwards was the author of both words and music. (*He sings*)

"He rapped and rapped, and tapped and tapped
Enough to wake the dead
Till he heard a damsel (*Rap, rap, rap*)
On a window right over his head."

(*The drunks are blinking their eyes now, grumbling and cursing.* ROCKY *appears from the bar at rear, right, yawning*)

HOPE (*With fuming irritation*) Rocky! Bejees, can't you keep that crazy bastard quiet? (ROCKY *starts for* WILLIE)

WILLIE And now the influence of a good woman enters our mariner's life. Well, perhaps "good" isn't the word. But very, very kind. (*He sings*)

"Oh, come up," she cried, "my sailor lad,
And you and I'll agree,
And I'll show you the prettiest (*Rap, rap, rap*)
That ever you did see."

(*He speaks*) You see, Larry? The lewd Puritan touch, obviously, and it grows more marked as we go on. (*He sings*)

"Oh, he put his arm around her waist,
He gazed in her bright blue eyes
And then he—"

(*But here* ROCKY *shakes him roughly by the shoulder*)

ROCKY Piano![5] What d'yuh tink dis dump is, a dump?

HOPE Give him the bum's rush upstairs! Lock him in his room!

ROCKY (*Yanks* WILLIE *by the arm*) Come on, Bum.

WILLIE (*Dissolves into pitiable terror*) No! Please, Rocky! I'll go crazy up in that room alone! It's haunted! I— (*He calls to* HOPE) Please, Harry! Let me stay here! I'll be quiet!

HOPE (*Immediately relents—indignantly*) What the hell you doing to him, Rocky? I didn't tell you to beat up the poor guy. Leave him alone, long as he's quiet. (ROCKY *lets go of* WILLIE *disgustedly and goes back to his chair in the bar*)

WILLIE (*Huskily*) Thanks, Harry. You're a good scout. (*He closes his eyes and sinks back in his chair exhaustedly, twitching and quivering again*)

HOPE (*Addressing* MCGLOIN *and* MOSHER, *who are sleepily awake—ac-*

[5] Quiet! (Italian).

cusingly) Always the way. Can't trust nobody. Leave it to that Dago to keep order and it's like bedlam in a cathouse, singing and everything. And you two big barflies are a hell of a help to me, ain't you? Eat and sleep and get drunk! All you're good for, bejees! Well, you can take that "I'll-have-the-same" look off your maps! There ain't going to be no more drinks on the house till hell freezes over! (*Neither of the two is impressed either by his insults or his threats. They grin hangover grins of tolerant affection at him and wink at each other.* HARRY *fumes*) Yeah, grin! Wink, bejees! Fine pair of sons of bitches to have glued on me for life! (*But he can't get a rise out of them and he subsides into a fuming mumble. Meanwhile, at the middle table,* CAPTAIN LEWIS *and* GENERAL WETJOEN *are as wide awake as heavy hangovers permit.* JIMMY TOMORROW *nods, his eyes blinking.* LEWIS *is gazing across the table at* JOE MOTT, *who is still chuckling to himself over* WILLIE's *song. The expression on* LEWIS's *face is that of one who can't believe his eyes*)

LEWIS (*Aloud to himself, with a muzzy wonder*) Good God! Have I been drinking at the same table with a bloody Kaffir?

JOE (*Grinning*) Hello, Captain. You comin' up for air? Kaffir? Who's he?

WETJOEN (*Blurrily*) Kaffir, dot's a nigger, Joe. (JOE *stiffens and his eyes narrow.* WETJOEN *goes on with heavy jocosity*) Dot's joke on him, Joe. He don't know you. He's still plind drunk, the ploody Limey chentleman! A great mistake I missed him at the pattle of Modder River.[6] Vit mine rifle I shoot damn fool Limey officers py the dozen, but him I miss. De pity of it! (*He chuckles and slaps* LEWIS *on his bare shoulder*) Hey, wake up, Cecil, you ploody fool! Don't you know your old friend, Joe? He's no damned Kaffir! He's white, Joe is!

LEWIS (*Light dawning—contritely*) My profound apologies, Joseph, old chum. Eyesight a trifle blurry, I'm afraid. Whitest colored man I ever knew. Proud to call you my friend. No hard feelings, what? (*He holds out his hand*)

JOE (*At once grins good-naturedly and shakes his hand*) No, Captain, I know it's mistake. Youse regular, if you is a Limey. (*Then his face hardening*) But I don't stand for "nigger" from nobody. Never did. In de old days, people calls me "nigger" wakes up in de hospital. I was de leader ob de Dirty Half-Dozen Gang. All six of us colored boys, we was tough and I was de toughest.

WETJOEN (*Inspired to boastful reminiscence*) Me, in old days in Transvaal, I vas so tough and strong I grab axle of ox wagon mit full load and lift like feather.

---

[6] Battle of the Boer War

LEWIS (*Smiling amiably*) As for you, my balmy Boer that walks like a man, I say again it was a grave error in our foreign policy ever to set you free, once we nabbed you and your commando with Cronje.[7] We should have taken you to the London Zoo and incarcerated you in the baboons' cage. With a sign: "Spectators may distinguish the true baboon by his blue behind."

WETJOEN (*Grins*) Gott! To dink, ten better Limey officers, at least, I shoot clean in the mittle of forehead at Spion Kopje,[8] and you I miss! I neffer forgive myself! (JIMMY TOMORROW *blinks benignantly from one to the other with a gentle drunken smile*)

JIMMY (*Sentimentally*) Now, come, Cecil, Piet! We must forget the War. Boer and Briton, each fought fairly and played the game till the better man won and then we shook hands. We are all brothers within the Empire united beneath the flag on which the sun never sets. (*Tears come to his eyes. He quotes with great sentiment, if with slight application*) "Ship me somewhere east of Suez—"[9]

LARRY (*Breaks in sardonically*) Be God, you're there already, Jimmy. Worst is best here, and East is West, and tomorrow is yesterday. What more do you want?

JIMMY (*With bleary benevolence, shaking his head in mild rebuke*) No, Larry, old friend, you can't deceive me. You pretend a bitter, cynic philosophy, but in your heart you are the kindest man among us.

LARRY (*Disconcerted—irritably*) The hell you say!

PARRITT (*Leans toward him—confidentially*) What a bunch of cuckoos!

JIMMY (*As if reminded of something—with a pathetic attempt at a brisk, no-more-nonsense air*) Tomorrow, yes. It's high time I straightened out and got down to business again. (*He brushes his sleeve fastidiously*) I must have this suit cleaned and pressed. I can't look like a tramp when I—

JOE (*Who has been brooding—interrupts*) Yes, suh, white folks always said I was white. In de days when I was flush, Joe Mott's de only colored man dey allows in de white gamblin' houses. "You're all right, Joe, you're white," dey says. (*He chuckles*) Wouldn't let me play craps, dough. Dey know I could make dem dice behave. "Any odder game and any limit you like, Joe," dey says. Man, de money I lost! (*He chuckles—then with an underlying defensiveness*) Look at de Big Chief in dem days. He knew I was white. I'd saved my dough so I could start my own gamblin' house. Folks in de know tells me, see de man at de top, den you never has trouble. You git Harry Hope

---

[7] Boer leader.
[8] Boer War battle.
[9] From Rudyard Kipling's "Road to Mandalay."

give you a letter to de Chief. And Harry does. Don't you, Harry?
HOPE (*Preoccupied with his own thoughts*) Eh? Sure. Big Bill was a good friend of mine. I had plenty of friends high up in those days. Still could have if I wanted to go out and see them. Sure, I gave you a letter. I said you was white. What the hell of it?
JOE (*To* CAPTAIN LEWIS *who has relapsed into a sleepy daze and is listening to him with an absurd strained attention without comprehending a word*) Dere. You see, Captain. I went to see de Chief, shakin' in my boots, and dere he is sittin' behind a big desk, lookin' as big as a freight train. He don't look up. He keeps me waitin' and waitin', and after 'bout an hour, seems like to me, he says slow and quiet like dere wasn't no harm in him, "You want to open a gamblin' joint, does you, Joe?" But he don't give me no time to answer. He jumps up, lookin' as big as two freight trains, and he pounds his fist like a ham on de desk, and he shouts, "You black son of a bitch, Harry says you're white and you better be white or dere's a little iron room up de river waitin' for you!" Den he sits down and says quiet again, "All right. You can open. Git de hell outa here!" So I opens, and he finds out I'se white, sure 'nuff, 'cause I run wide open for years and pays my sugar on de dot, and de cops and I is friends. (*He chuckles with pride*) Dem old days! Many's de night I come in here. Dis was a first-class hangout for sports in dem days. Good whiskey, fifteen cents, two for two bits. I t'rows down a fifty-dollar bill like it was trash paper and says, "Drink it up, boys, I don't want no change." Ain't dat right, Harry?
HOPE (*Caustically*) Yes, and bejees, if I ever seen you throw fifty cents on the bar now, I'd know I had delirium tremens! You've told that story ten million times and if I have to hear it again, that'll give me D.T.s anyway!
JOE (*Chuckling*) Gittin' drunk every day for twenty years ain't give you de Brooklyn boys. You needn't be scared of me!
LEWIS (*Suddenly turns and beams on* HOPE) Thank you, Harry, old chum. I will have a drink, now you mention it, seeing it's so near your birthday. (*The others laugh*)
HOPE (*Puts his hand to his ear—angrily*) What's that? I can't hear you.
LEWIS (*Sadly*) No, I fancied you wouldn't.
HOPE I don't have to hear, bejees! Booze is the only thing you ever talk about!
LEWIS (*Sadly*) True. Yet there was a time when my conversation was more comprehensive. But as I became burdened with years, it seemed rather pointless to discuss my other subject.
HOPE You can't joke with me! How much room rent do you owe me, tell me that?

LEWIS   Sorry. Adding has always baffled me. Subtraction is my forte.
HOPE (*Snarling*)   Arrh! Think you're funny! Captain, bejees! Showing off your wounds! Put on your clothes, for Christ's sake! This ain't no Turkish bath! Lousy Limey army! Took 'em years to lick a gang of Dutch hayseeds!
WETJOEN   Dot's right, Harry. Gif him hell!
HOPE   No lip out of you, neither, you Dutch spinach! General, hell! Salvation Army, that's what you'd ought t'been General in! Bragging what a shot you were, and, bejees, you missed him! And he missed you, that's just as bad! And now the two of you bum on me! (*Threateningly*) But you've broke the camel's back this time, bejees! You pay up tomorrow or out you go!
LEWIS (*Earnestly*)   My dear fellow, I give you my word of honor as an officer and a gentleman, you shall be paid tomorrow.
WETJOEN   Ve swear it, Harry! Tomorrow vidout fail!
MCGLOIN (*A twinkle in his eye*)   There you are, Harry. Sure, what could be fairer?
MOSHER (*With a wink at* MCGLOIN)   Yes, you can't ask more than that, Harry. A promise is a promise—as I've often discovered.
HOPE (*Turns on them*)   I mean the both of you, too! An old grafting flatfoot[10] and a circus bunco steerer![11] Fine company for me, bejees! Couple of con men living in my flat since Christ knows when! Getting fat as hogs, too! And you ain't even got the decency to get me upstairs where I got a good bed! Let me sleep on a chair like a bum! Kept me down here waitin' for Hickey to show up, hoping I'd blow you to more drinks!
MCGLOIN   Ed and I did our damnedest to get you up, didn't we, Ed?
MOSHER   We did. But you said you couldn't bear the flat because it was one of those nights when memory brought poor old Bessie back to you.
HOPE (*His face instantly becoming long and sad and sentimental—mournfully*)   Yes, that's right, boys. I remember now. I could almost see her in every room just as she used to be—and it's twenty years since she— (*His throat and eyes fill up. A suitable sentimental hush falls on the room*)
LARRY (*In a sardonic whisper to* PARRITT)   Isn't a pipe dream of yesterday a touching thing? By all accounts, Bessie nagged the hell out of him.
JIMMY (*Who has been dreaming, a look of prim resolution on his face, speaks aloud to himself*)   No more of this sitting around and loafing.

---

[10] A policeman who accepts bribes.
[11] A decoy who "steers" the victim in a swindling operation.

Time I took hold of myself. I must have my shoes soled and heeled and shined first thing tomorrow morning. A general spruce-up. I want to have a well-groomed appearance when I— (*His voice fades out as he stares in front of him. No one pays any attention to him except* LARRY *and* PARRITT)

LARRY (*As before, in a sardonic aside to* PARRITT) The tomorrow movement is a sad and beautiful thing, too!

MCGLOIN (*With a huge sentimental sigh—and a calculating look at* HOPE) Poor old Bessie! You don't find her like in these days. A sweeter woman never drew breath.

MOSHER (*In a similar calculating mood*) Good old Bess. A man couldn't want a better sister than she was to me.

HOPE (*Mournfully*) Twenty years, and I've never set foot out of this house since the day I buried her. Didn't have the heart. Once she'd gone, I didn't give a damn for anything. I lost all my ambition. Without her, nothing seemed worth the trouble. You remember, Ed, you, too, Mac—the boys was going to nominate me for Alderman. It was all fixed. Bessie wanted it and she was so proud. But when she was taken, I told them, "No, boys, I can't do it. I simply haven't the heart. I'm through." I would have won the election easy, too. (*He says this a bit defiantly*) Oh, I know there was jealous wise guys said the boys was giving me the nomination because they knew they couldn't win that year in this ward. But that's a damned lie! I knew every man, woman and child in the ward, almost. Bessie made me make friends with everyone, helped me remember all their names. I'd have been elected easy.

MCGLOIN You would, Harry. It was a sure thing.

MOSHER A dead cinch, Harry. Everyone knows that.

HOPE Sure they do. But after Bessie died, I didn't have the heart. Still, I know while she'd appreciate my grief, she wouldn't want it to keep me cooped up in here all my life. So I've made up my mind I'll go out soon. Take a walk around the ward, see all the friends I used to know, get together with the boys and maybe tell 'em I'll let 'em deal me a hand in their game again. Yes, bejees, I'll do it. My birthday, tomorrow, that'd be the right time to turn over a new leaf. Sixty. That ain't too old.

MCGLOIN (*Flatteringly*) It's the prime of life, Harry.

MOSHER Wonderful thing about you, Harry, you keep young as you ever was.

JIMMY (*Dreaming aloud again*) Get my things from the laundry. They must still have them. Clean collar and shirt. If I wash the ones I've got on any more, they'll fall apart. Socks, too. I want to make a good appearance. I met Dick Trumbull on the street a year or two ago. He said, "Jimmy, the publicity department's never been the same since you got—resigned. It's dead as hell." I said, "I know. I've heard rumors the management were at their wits' end and would be only too glad to have me run it for them again. I think all I'd have to do would be go and see them and they'd offer me the position. Don't you think so, Dick?" He said, "Sure, they would, Jimmy. Only take my advice and wait a while until business conditions are better. Then you can strike them for a bigger salary than you got before, do you see?" I said, "Yes, I do see, Dick, and many thanks for the tip." Well, conditions must be better by this time. All I have to do is get fixed up with a decent front tomorrow, and it's as good as done.

HOPE (*Glances at* JIMMY *with a condescending affectionate pity—in a hushed voice*) Poor Jimmy's off on his pipe dream again. Bejees, he takes the cake! (*This is too much for* LARRY. *He cannot restrain a sardonic guffaw. But no one pays any attention to him*)

LEWIS (*Opens his eyes, which are drowsing again—dreamily to* WETJOEN) I'm sorry we had to postpone our trip again this April, Piet. I hoped the blasted old estate would be settled up by then. The damned lawyers can't hold up the settlement much longer. We'll make it next year, even if we have to work and earn our passage money, eh? You'll stay with me at the old place as long as you like, then you can take the *Union Castle* from Southampton to Cape Town. (*Sentimentally, with real yearning*) England in April. I want you to see that, Piet. The old veldt has its points, I'll admit, but it isn't home—especially home in April.

WETJOEN (*Blinks drowsily at him—dreamily*) Ja, Cecil, I know how beautiful it must be, from all you tell me many times. I vill enjoy it. But I shall enjoy more ven I am home, too. The veldt, ja! You could put England on it, and it would look like a farmer's small garden. Py Gott, there is space to be free, the air like vine is, you don't need booze to be drunk! My relations vill so surprised be. They vill not know me, it is so many years. Dey vill be so glad I haf come home at last.

JOE (*Dreamily*) I'll make my stake and get my new gamblin' house open before you boys leave. You got to come to de openin'. I'll treat you white. If you're broke, I'll stake you to buck any game you chooses. If you wins, dat's velvet for you. If you loses, it don't count. Can't treat you no whiter dan dat, can I?

HOPE (*Again with condescending pity*) Bejees, Jimmy's started them off smoking the same hop. (*But the three are finished, their eyes closed again in sleep or a drowse*)

LARRY (*Aloud to himself—in his comically tense, crazy whisper*) Be God, this bughouse will drive me stark, raving loony yet!
HOPE (*Turns on him with fuming suspicion*) What? What d'you say?
LARRY (*Placatingly*) Nothing, Harry. I had a crazy thought in my head.
HOPE (*Irascibly*) Crazy is right! Jah! The old wise guy! Wise, hell! A damned old fool Anarchist I-Won't-Worker![12] I'm sick of you and Hugo, too. Bejees, you'll pay up tomorrow, or I'll start a Harry Hope Revolution! I'll tie a dispossess bomb to your tails that'll blow you out in the street! Bejees, I'll make your Movement move! (*The witticism delights him and he bursts into a shrill cackle. At once* MCGLOIN *and* MOSHER *guffaw enthusiastically*)
MOSHER (*Flatteringly*) Harry, you sure say the funniest things! (*He reaches on the table as if he expected a glass to be there—then starts with well-acted surprise*) Hell, where's my drink? That Rocky is too damned fast cleaning tables. Why, I'd only take one sip of it.
HOPE (*His smiling face congealing*) No, you don't! (*Acidly*) Any time you only take one sip of a drink, you'll have lockjaw and paralysis! Think you can kid me with those old circus con games?—me, that's known you since you was knee-high, and, bejees, you was a crook even then!
MCGLOIN (*Grinning*) It's not like you to be so hard-hearted, Harry. Sure, it's hot, parching work laughing at your jokes so early in the morning on an empty stomach!
HOPE Yah! You, Mac! Another crook! Who asked you to laugh? We was talking about poor old Bessie, and you and her no-good brother start to laugh! A hell of a thing! Talking mush about her, too! "Good old Bess." Bejees, she'd never forgive me if she knew I had you two bums living in her flat, throwing ashes and cigar butts on her carpet. You know her opinion of you, Mac. "That Pat McGloin is the biggest drunken grafter that ever disgraced the police force," she used to say to me. "I hope they send him to Sing Sing for life."
MCGLOIN (*Unperturbed*) She didn't mean it. She was angry at me because you used to get me drunk. But Bess had a heart of gold underneath her sharpness. She knew I was innocent of all the charges.
WILLIE (*Jumps to his feet drunkenly and points a finger at* MCGLOIN—*imitating the manner of a cross-examiner—coldly*) One moment, please. Lieutenant McGloin! Are you aware you are under oath? Do you realize what the penalty for perjury is? (*Purringly*) Come now, Lieutenant, isn't it a fact that you're as guilty as hell? No, don't say, "How about your old man?" I am asking the questions. The fact that

[12] A member of the I.W.W.

he was a crooked old bucket-shop bastard has no bearing on your case. (*With a change to maudlin joviality*) Gentlemen of the Jury, court will now recess while the D.A. sings out a little ditty he learned at Harvard. It was composed in a wanton moment by the Dean of the Divinity School on a moonlight night in July, 1776, while sobering up in a Turkish bath. (*He sings*)

> "Oh, come up," she cried, "my sailor lad,
> And you and I'll agree.
> And I'll show you the prettiest (*Rap, rap, rap on table*)
> That ever you did see."

(*Suddenly he catches* HOPE's *eyes fixed on him condemningly, and sees* ROCKY *appearing from the bar. He collapses back on his chair, pleading miserably*) Please, Harry! I'll be quiet! Don't make Rocky bounce me upstairs! I'll go crazy alone! (*To* MCGLOIN) I apologize, Mac. Don't get sore. I was only kidding you. (ROCKY, *at a relenting glance from* HOPE, *returns to the bar*)

MCGLOIN (*Good-naturedly*) Sure, kid all you like, Willie. I'm hardened to it. (*He pauses—seriously*) But I'm telling you some day before long I'm going to make them reopen my case. Everyone knows there was no real evidence against me, and I took the fall for the ones higher up. I'll be found innocent this time and reinstated. (*Wistfully*) I'd like to have my old job on the Force back. The boys tell me there's fine pickings these days, and I'm not getting rich here, sitting with a parched throat waiting for Harry Hope to buy a drink. (*He glances reproachfully at* HOPE)

WILLIE Of course, you'll be reinstated, Mac. All you need is a brilliant young attorney to handle your case. I'll be straightened out and on the wagon in a day or two. I've never practiced but I was one of the most brilliant students in Law School, and your case is just the opportunity I need to start. (*Darkly*) Don't worry about my not forcing the D.A. to reopen your case. I went through my father's papers before the cops destroyed them, and I remember a lot of people, even if I can't prove— (*Coaxingly*) You will let me take your case, won't you, Mac?

MCGLOIN (*Soothingly*) Sure I will and it'll make your reputation, Willie. (MOSHER *winks at* HOPE, *shaking his head, and* HOPE *answers with identical pantomime, as though to say,* "Poor dopes, they're off again!")

LARRY (*Aloud to himself more than to* PARRITT—*with irritable wonder*) Ah, be damned! Haven't I heard their visions a thousand times? Why should they get under my skin now? I've got the blues, I guess. I wish to hell Hickey'd turn up.

MOSHER (*Calculatingly solicitous—whispering to* HOPE) Poor Willie needs a drink bad, Harry—and I think if we all joined him it'd make him feel he was among friends and cheer him up.
HOPE More circus con tricks! (*Scathingly*) You talking of your dear sister! Bessie had you sized up. She used to tell me, "I don't know what you can see in that worthless, drunken, petty-larceny brother of mine. If I had my way," she'd say, "he'd get booted out in the gutter on his fat behind." Sometimes she didn't say behind, either.
MOSHER (*Grins genially*) Yes, dear old Bess had a quick temper, but there was no real harm in her. (*He chuckles reminiscently*) Remember the time she sent me down to the bar to change a ten-dollar bill for her?
HOPE (*Has to grin himself*) Bejees, do I! She coulda bit a piece out of a stove lid, after she found it out. (*He cackles appreciatively*)
MOSHER I was sure surprised when she gave me the ten spot. Bess usually had better sense, but she was in a hurry to go to church. I didn't really mean to do it, but you know how habit gets you. Besides, I still worked then, and the circus season was going to begin soon, and I needed a little practice to keep my hand in. Or, you never can tell, the first rube that came to my wagon for a ticket might have left with the right change and I'd be disgraced. (*He chuckles*) I said, "I'm sorry, Bess, but I had to take it all in dimes. Here, hold out your hands and I'll count it out for you, so you won't kick afterwards I short-changed you." (*He begins a count which grows more rapid as he goes on*) Ten, twenty, thirty, forty, fifty, sixty, seventy, eighty, ninety, a dollar. Ten, twenty, thirty, forty, fifty, sixty— You're counting with me, Bess, aren't you?—eighty, ninety, two dollars. Ten, twenty— Those are pretty shoes you got on, Bess—forty, fifty, seventy, eighty, ninety, three dollars. Ten, twenty, thirty— What's on at the church tonight, Bess?—fifty, sixty, seventy, ninety, four dollars. Ten, twenty, thirty, fifty, seventy, eighty, ninety— That's a swell new hat, Bess, looks very becoming—six dollars. (*He chuckles*) And so on. I'm bum at it now for lack of practice, but in those days I could have short-changed the Keeper of the Mint.
HOPE (*Grinning*) Stung her for two dollars and a half, wasn't it, Ed?
MOSHER Yes. A fine percentage, if I do say so, when you're dealing to someone who's sober and can count. I'm sorry to say she discovered my mistakes in arithmetic just after I beat it around the corner. She counted it over herself. Bess somehow never had the confidence in me a sister should. (*He sighs tenderly*) Dear old Bess.
HOPE (*Indignant now*) You're a fine guy bragging how you short-changed your own sister! Bejees, if there was a war and you was in it,

they'd have to padlock the pockets of the dead!

MOSHER (*A bit hurt at this*) That's going pretty strong, Harry. I always gave a sucker some chance. There wouldn't be no fun robbing the dead. (*He becomes reminiscently melancholy*) Gosh, thinking of the old ticket wagon brings those days back. The greatest life on earth with the greatest show on earth! The grandest crowd of regular guys ever gathered under one tent! I'd sure like to shake their hands again!

HOPE (*Acidly*) They'd have guns in theirs. They'd shoot you on sight. You've touched every damned one of them. Bejees, you've even borrowed fish from the trained seals and peanuts from every elephant that remembered you! (*This fancy tickles him and he gives a cackling laugh*)

MOSHER (*Overlooking this—dreamily*) You know, Harry, I've made up my mind I'll see the boss in a couple of days and ask for my old job. I can get back my magic touch with change easy, and I can throw him a line of bull that'll kid him I won't be so unreasonable about sharing the profits next time. (*With insinuating complaint*) There's no percentage in hanging around this dive, taking care of you and shooing away your snakes, when I don't even get an eye-opener for my trouble.

HOPE (*Implacably*) No! (MOSHER *sighs and gives up and closes his eyes. The others, except* LARRY *and* PARRITT, *are all dozing again now.* HOPE *goes on grumbling*) Go to hell or the circus, for all I care. Good riddance, bejees! I'm sick of you! (*Then worriedly*) Say, Ed, what the hell you think's happened to Hickey? I hope he'll turn up. Always got a million funny stories. You and the other bums have begun to give me the graveyard fantods. I'd like a good laugh with old Hickey. (*He chuckles at a memory*) Remember that gag he always pulls about his wife and the iceman? He'd make a cat laugh! (ROCKY *appears from the bar. He comes front, behind* MOSHER's *chair, and begins pushing the black curtain along the rod to the rear wall*)

ROCKY Openin' time, Boss. (*He pushes a button at rear which switches off the lights. The back room becomes drabber and dingier than ever in the gray daylight that comes from the street windows, off right, and what light can penetrate the grime of the two backyard windows at left.* ROCKY *turns back to* HOPE—*grumpily*) Why don't you go up to bed, Boss? Hickey'd never turn up dis time of de mornin'!

HOPE (*Starts and listens*) Someone's coming now.

ROCKY (*Listens*) Aw, dat's on'y my two pigs. It's about time dey showed. (*He goes back toward the door at left of the bar*)

HOPE (*Sourly disappointed*) You keep them dumb broads quiet. I don't want to go to bed. I'm going to catch a couple more winks here and I don't want no damn-fool laughing and screeching. (*He settles himself in his chair, grumbling*) Never thought I'd see the day when Harry Hope's would have tarts rooming in it. What'd Bessie think? But I don't let 'em use my rooms for business. And they're good kids. Good as anyone else. They got to make a living. Pay their rent, too, which is more than I can say for— (*He cocks an eye over his specs at* MOSHER *and grins with satisfaction*) Bejees, Ed, I'll bet Bessie is doing somersaults in her grave! (*He chuckles. But* MOSHER'S *eyes are closed, his head nodding, and he doesn't reply, so* HOPE *closes his eyes.* ROCKY *has opened the barroom door at rear and is standing in the hall beyond it, facing right. A girl's laugh is heard*)

ROCKY (*Warningly*) Nix! Piano! (*He comes in, beckoning them to follow. He goes behind the bar and gets a whiskey bottle and glasses and chairs.* MARGIE *and* PEARL *follow him, casting a glance around. Everyone except* LARRY *and* PARRITT *is asleep or dozing. Even* PARRITT *has his eyes closed. The two girls, neither much over twenty, are typical dollar street walkers, dressed in the usual tawdry get-up.* PEARL *is obviously Italian with black hair and eyes.* MARGIE *has brown hair and hazel eyes, a slum New Yorker of mixed blood. Both are plump and have a certain prettiness that shows even through their blobby make-up. Each retains a vestige of youthful freshness, although the game is beginning to get them and give them hard, worn expressions. Both are sentimental, feather-brained, giggly, lazy, good-natured and reasonably contented with life. Their attitude toward* ROCKY *is much that of two maternal, affectionate sisters toward a bullying brother whom they like to tease and spoil. His attitude toward them is that of the owner of two performing pets he has trained to do a profitable act under his management. He feels a proud proprietor's affection for them, and is tolerantly lax in his discipline*)

MARGIE (*Glancing around*) Jees, Poil, it's de Morgue wid all de stiffs on deck. (*She catches* LARRY'S *eye and smiles affectionately*) Hello, Old Wise Guy, ain't you died yet?

LARRY (*Grinning*) Not yet, Margie. But I'm waiting impatiently for the end. (PARRITT *opens his eyes to look at the two girls, but as soon as they glance at him he closes them again and turns his head away*)

MARGIE (*As she and* PEARL *come to the table at right, front, followed by* ROCKY) Who's de new guy? Friend of yours, Larry? (*Automatically she smiles seductively at* PARRITT *and addresses him in a professional chant*) Wanta have a good time, kid?

PEARL Aw, he's passed out. Hell wid him!

HOPE (*Cocks an eye over his specs at them—with drowsy irritation*) You dumb broads cut the loud talk. (*He shuts his eye again*)

ROCKY (*Admonishing them good-naturedly*) Sit down before I knock yuh down. (MARGIE *and* PEARL *sit at left, and rear, of table,* ROCKY *at right of it. The girls pour drinks.* ROCKY *begins in a brisk, businesslike manner but in a lowered voice with an eye on* HOPE) Well, how'd you tramps do?

MARGIE   Pretty good. Didn't we, Poil?

PEARL   Sure. We nailed a coupla all-night guys.

MARGIE   On Sixth Avenoo. Boobs from de sticks.

PEARL   Stinko, de bot' of 'em.

MARGIE   We thought we was in luck. We steered dem to a real hotel. We figgered dey was too stinko to bother us much and we could cop a good sleep in beds that ain't got cobble stones in de mattress like de ones in dis dump.

PEARL   But we was outa luck. Dey didn't bother us much dat way, but dey wouldn't go to sleep either, see? Jees, I never hoid such gabby guys.

MARGIE   Dey got onta politics, drinkin' outa de bottle. Dey forgot we was around. "De Bull Moosers is de on'y reg'lar guys," one guy says. And de other guy says, "You're a God-damned liar! And I'm a Republican!" Den dey'd laugh.

PEARL   Den dey'd get mad and make a bluff dey was goin' to scrap, and den dey'd make up and cry and sing "School Days." Jees, imagine tryin' to sleep wid dat on de phonograph!

MARGIE   Maybe you tink we wasn't glad when de house dick come up and told us all to git dressed and take de air!

PEARL   We told de guys we'd wait for dem 'round de corner.

MARGIE   So here we are.

ROCKY (*Sententiously*)   Yeah. I see you. But I don't see no dough yet.

PEARL (*With a wink at* MARGIE—*teasingly*) Right on de job, ain't he, Margie?

MARGIE   Yeah, our little business man! Dat's him!

ROCKY   Come on! Dig! (*They both pull up their skirts to get the money from their stockings.* ROCKY *watches this move carefully*)

PEARL (*Amused*)   Pipe him keepin' cases, Margie.

MARGIE (*Amused*)   Scared we're holdin' out on him.

PEARL   Way he grabs, yuh'd tink it was him done de woik. (*She holds out a little roll of bills to* ROCKY) Here y'are, Grafter!

MARGIE (*Holding hers out*)   We hope it chokes yuh. (ROCKY *counts the money quickly and shoves it in his pocket*)

ROCKY (*Genially*) You dumb baby dolls gimme a pain. What would you do wid money if I wasn't around? Give it all to some pimp.

PEARL (*Teasingly*)   Jees, what's the difference—? (*Hastily*) Aw, I don't mean dat, Rocky.

ROCKY (*His eyes growing hard—slowly*) A lotta difference, get me?
PEARL Don't get sore. Jees, can't yuh take a little kiddin'?
MARGIE Sure, Rocky, Poil was on'y kiddin'. (*Soothingly*) We know yuh got a reg'lar job. Dat's why we like yuh, see? Yuh don't live offa us. Yuh're a bartender.
ROCKY (*Genially again*) Sure, I'm a bartender. Everyone knows me knows dat. And I treat you goils right, don't I? Jees, I'm wise yuh hold out on me, but I know it ain't much, so what the hell, I let yuh get away wid it. I tink yuh're a coupla good kids. Yuh're aces wid me, see?
PEARL You're aces wid us, too. Ain't he, Margie?
MARGIE Sure, he's aces. (ROCKY *beams complacently and takes the glasses back to the bar.* MARGIE *whispers*) Yuh sap, don't yuh know enough not to kid him on dat? Serve yuh right if he beat yuh up!
PEARL (*Admiringly*) Jees, I'll bet he'd give yuh an awful beatin', too, once he started. Ginnies[13] got awful tempers.
MARGIE Anyway, we wouldn't keep no pimp, like we was reg'lar old whores. We ain't dat bad.
PEARL No. We're tarts, but dat's all.
ROCKY (*Rinsing glasses behind the bar*) Cora got back around three o'clock. She woke up Chuck and dragged him outa de hay to go to a chop suey joint. (*Disgustedly*) Imagine him standin' for dat stuff!
MARGIE (*Disgustedly*) I'll bet dey been sittin' around kiddin' demselves wid dat old pipe dream about gettin' married and settlin' down on a farm. Jees, when Chuck's on de wagon, dey never lay off dat dope! Dey give yuh an earful every time yuh talk to 'em!
PEARL Yeah. Chuck wid a silly grin on his ugly map, de big boob, and Cora gigglin' like she was in grammar school and some tough guy'd just told her babies wasn't brung down de chimney by a boid!
MARGIE And her on de turf long before me and you was! And bot' of 'em arguin' all de time, Cora sayin' she's scared to marry him because he'll go on drunks again. Just as dough any drunk could scare Cora!
PEARL And him swearin', de big liar, he'll never go on no more periodicals! An' den her pretendin'— But it gives me a pain to talk about it. We ought to phone de booby hatch to send round de wagon for 'em.
ROCKY (*Comes back to the table—disgustedly*) Yeah, of all de pipe dreams in dis dump, dey got de nuttiest! And nuttin' stops dem. Dey been dreamin' it for years, every time Chuck goes on de wagon. I never could figger it. What would gettin' married get dem? But de farm stuff is de sappiest part. When bot' of 'em was dragged up in

[13] Slang term for Italians or Americans of Italian extraction.

dis ward and ain't never been nearer a farm dan Coney Island! Jees, dey'd tink dey'd gone deef if dey didn't hear de El[14] rattle! Dey'd get D.T.s if dey ever hoid a cricket choip! I hoid crickets once on my cousin's place in Joisey. I couldn't sleep a wink. Dey give me de heebie-jeebies. (*With deeper disgust*) Jees, can yuh picture a good barkeep like Chuck diggin' spuds? And imagine a whore hustlin' de cows home! For Christ sake! Ain't dat a sweet picture!

MARGIE (*Rebukingly*) Yuh oughtn't to call Cora dat, Rocky. She's a good kid. She may be a tart, but—

ROCKY (*Considerately*) Sure, dat's all I meant, a tart.

PEARL (*Giggling*) But he's right about de damned cows, Margie. Jees, I bet Cora don't know which end of de cow has de horns! I'm goin' to ask her. (*There is the noise of a door opening in the hall and the sound of a man's and woman's arguing voices*)

ROCKY Here's your chance. Dat's dem two nuts now. (CORA *and* CHUCK *look in from the hallway and then come in.* CORA *is a thin peroxide blonde, a few years older than* PEARL *and* MARGIE, *dressed in similar style, her round face showing more of the wear and tear of her trade than theirs, but still with traces of a doll-like prettiness.* CHUCK *is a tough, thick-necked, barrel-chested Italian-American, with a fat, amiable, swarthy face. He has on a straw hat with a vivid band, a loud suit, tie and shirt, and yellow shoes. His eyes are clear and he looks healthy and strong as an ox*)

CORA (*Gaily*) Hello, bums. (*She looks around*) Jees, de Morgue on a rainy Sunday night! (*She waves to* LARRY—*affectionately*) Hello, Old Wise Guy! Ain't you croaked yet?

LARRY (*Grins*) Not yet, Cora. It's damned tiring, this waiting for the end.

CORA Aw, gwan, you'll never die! Yuh'll have to hire someone to croak yuh wid an axe.

HOPE (*Cocks one sleepy eye at her—irritably*) You dumb hookers, cut the loud noise! This ain't a cat-house!

CORA (*Teasingly*) My, Harry! Such language!

HOPE (*Closes his eyes—to himself with a gratified chuckle*) Bejees, I'll bet Bessie's turning over in her grave! (CORA *sits down between* MARGIE *and* PEARL. CHUCK *takes an empty chair from* HOPE's *table and puts it by hers and sits down. At* LARRY's *table,* PARRITT *is glaring resentfully toward the girls*)

PARRITT If I'd known this dump was a hooker hangout, I'd never have come here.

---

[14] Elevated train.

LARRY (*Watching him*) You seem down on the ladies.
PARRITT (*Vindictively*) I hate every bitch that ever lived. They're all alike! (*Catching himself guiltily*) You can understand how I feel, can't you, when it was getting mixed up with a tart that made me have that fight with Mother? (*Then with a resentful sneer*) But what the hell does it matter to you? You're in the grandstand. You're through with life.
LARRY (*Sharply*) I'm glad you remember it. I don't want to know a damned thing about your business. (*He closes his eyes and settles on his chair as if preparing for sleep.* PARRITT *stares at him sneeringly. Then he looks away and his expression becomes furtive and frightened*)
CORA Who's de guy wid Larry?
ROCKY A tightwad. To hell wid him.
PEARL Say, Cora, wise me up. Which end of a cow is de horns on?
CORA (*Embarrassed*) Aw, don't bring dat up. I'm sick of hearin' about dat farm.
ROCKY You got nuttin' on us!
CORA (*Ignoring this*) Me and dis overgrown tramp has been scrappin' about it. He says Joisey's de best place, and I says Long Island because we'll be near Coney. And I tells him, How do I know yuh're off of periodicals for life? I don't give a damn how drunk yuh get, the way we are, but I don't want to be married to no soak.
CHUCK And I tells her I'm off de stuff for life. Den she beefs we won't be married a month before I'll trow it in her face she was a tart. "Jees, Baby," I tells her. "Why should I? What de hell yuh tink I tink I'm marryin', a voigin? Why should I kick as long as yuh lay off it and don't do no cheatin' wid iceman or nobody? (*He gives her a rough hug*) Dat's on de level, Baby. (*He kisses her*)
CORA (*Kissing him*) Aw, yuh big tramp!
ROCKY (*Shakes his head with profound disgust*) Can yuh tie it? I'll buy a drink. I'll do anything. (*He gets up*)
CORA No, dis round's on me. I run into luck. Dat's why I dragged Chuck outa bed to celebrate. It was a sailor. I rolled him. (*She giggles*) Listen, it was a scream. I've run into some nutty souses, but dis guy was de nuttiest. De booze dey dish out around de Brooklyn Navy Yard must be as turrible bug-juice as Harry's. My dogs was givin' out when I seen dis guy holdin' up a lamppost, so I hurried to get him before a cop did. I says, "Hello, Handsome, wanta have a good time?" Jees, he was paralyzed! One of dem polite jags. He tries to bow to me, imagine, and I had to prop him up or he'd fell on his nose. And what d'yuh tink he said? "Lady," he says, "can yuh kindly tell me de nearest way to de Museum of Natural History?" (*They all*

laugh) Can yuh imagine! At two A.M. As if I'd know where de dump was anyway. But I says, "Sure ting, Honey Boy, I'll be only too glad." So I steered him into a side street where it was dark and propped him against a wall and give him a frisk. (*She giggles*) And what d'yuh tink he does? Jees, I ain't lyin', he begins to laugh, de big sap! He says, "Quit ticklin' me." While I was friskin' him for his roll! I near died! Den I toined him 'round and give him a push to start him. "Just keep goin'," I told him. "It's a big white building on your right. You can't miss it." He must be swimmin' in de North River yet! (*They all laugh*)

CHUCK Ain't Uncle Sam de sap to trust guys like dat wid dough!

CORA (*With a business-like air*) I picked twelve bucks offa him. Come on, Rocky. Set 'em up. (ROCKY *goes back to the bar.* CORA *looks around the room*) Say, Chuck's kiddin' about de iceman a minute ago reminds me. Where de hell's Hickey?

ROCKY Dat's what we're all wonderin'.

CORA He oughta be here. Me and Chuck seen him.

ROCKY (*Excited, comes back from the bar, forgetting the drinks*) You seen Hickey? (*He nudges* HOPE) Hey, Boss, come to! Cora's seen Hickey. (HOPE *is instantly wide awake and everyone in the place, except* HUGO *and* PARRITT, *begins to rouse up hopefully, as if a mysterious wireless message had gone round*)

HOPE Where'd you see him, Cora?

CORA Right on de next corner. He was standin' dere. We said, "Welcome to our city. De gang is expectin' yuh wid deir tongues hangin' out a yard long." And I kidded him, "How's de iceman, Hickey? How's he doin' at your house?" He laughs and says, "Fine." And he says, "Tell de gang I'll be along in a minute. I'm just finishin' figurin' out de best way to save dem and bring dem peace."

HOPE (*Chuckles*) Bejees, he's thought up a new gag! It's a wonder he didn't borry a Salvation Army uniform and show up in that! Go out and get him, Rocky. Tell him we're waitin' to be saved! (ROCKY *goes out, grinning*)

CORA Yeah, Harry, he was only kiddin'. But he was funny, too, somehow. He was different, or somethin'.

CHUCK Sure, he was sober, Baby. Dat's what made him different. We ain't never seen him when he wasn't on a drunk, or had de willies gettin' over it.

CORA Sure! Gee, ain't I dumb?

HOPE (*With conviction*) The dumbest broad I ever seen! (*Then puzzledly*) Sober? That's funny. He's always lapped up a good starter on his way here. Well, bejees, he won't be sober long! He'll be good and ripe for my birthday party tonight at twelve. (*He chuckles with excited anticipation—addressing all of them*) Listen! He's fixed some new gag to pull on us. We'll pretend to let him kid us, see? And we'll kid the pants off him. (*They all say laughingly, "Sure, Harry," "Righto," "That's the stuff," "We'll fix him," etc., etc., their faces excited with the same eager anticipation.* ROCKY *appears in the doorway at the end of the bar with* HICKEY, *his arm around* HICKEY'S *shoulders*)

ROCKY (*With an affectionate grin*) Here's the old son of a bitch! (*They all stand up and greet him with affectionate acclaim, "Hello, Hickey!" etc. Even* HUGO *comes out of his coma to raise his head and blink through his thick spectacles with a welcoming giggle*)

HICKEY (*Jovially*) Hello, Gang! (*He stands a moment, beaming around at all of them affectionately. He is about fifty, a little under medium height, with a stout, roly-poly figure. His face is round and smooth and big-boyish with bright blue eyes, a button nose, a small, pursed mouth. His head is bald except for a fringe of hair around his temples and the back of his head. His expression is fixed in a salesman's winning smile of self-confident affability and hearty good fellowship. His eyes have the twinkle of a humor which delights in kidding others but can also enjoy equally a joke on himself. He exudes a friendly, generous personality that makes everyone like him on sight. You get the impression, too, that he must have real ability in his line. There is an efficient, business-like approach in his manner, and his eyes can take you in shrewdly at a glance. He has the salesman's mannerisms of speech, an easy flow of glib, persuasive convincingness. His clothes are those of a successful drummer whose territory consists of minor cities and small towns—not flashy but conspicuously spic and span. He immediately puts on an entrance act, places a hand affectedly on his chest, throws back his head, and sings in a falsetto tenor*) "It's always fair feather, when good fellows get together!" (*Changing to a comic bass and another tune*) "And another little drink won't do us any harm!" (*They all roar with laughter at this burlesque which his personality makes really funny. He waves his hand in a lordly manner to* ROCKY) Do your duty, Brother Rocky. Bring on the rat poison! (ROCKY *grins and goes behind the bar to get drinks amid an approving cheer from the crowd.* HICKEY *comes forward to shake hands with* HOPE—*with affectionate heartiness*) How goes it, Governor!

HOPE (*Enthusiastically*) Bejees, Hickey, you old bastard, it's good to see you! (HICKEY *shakes hands with* MOSHER *and* MCGLOIN; *leans right to shake hands with* MARGIE *and* PEARL; *moves to the middle table to shake hands with* LEWIS, JOE MOTT, WETJOEN *and* JIMMY; *waves to*

WILLIE, LARRY and HUGO. *He greets each by name with the same affectionate heartiness and there is an interchange of "How's the kid?" "How's the old scout?" "How's the boy?" "How's everything?" etc., etc.* ROCKY *begins setting out drinks, whiskey glasses with chasers, and a bottle for each table, starting with* LARRY's *table.* HOPE *says:*) Sit down, Hickey. Sit down. (HICKEY *takes the chair, facing front, at the front of the table in the second row which is half between* HOPE's *table and the one where* JIMMY TOMORROW *is.* HOPE *goes on with excited pleasure*) Bejees, Hickey, it seems natural to see your ugly, grinning map. (*With a scornful nod to* CORA) This dumb broad was tryin' to tell us you'd changed, but you ain't a damned bit. Tell us about yourself. How've you been doin'? Bejees, you look like a million dollars.

ROCKY (*Coming to* HICKEY's *table, puts a bottle of whiskey, a glass and a chaser on it—then hands* HICKEY *a key*) Here's your key, Hickey. Same old room.

HICKEY (*Shoves the key in his pocket*) Thanks, Rocky. I'm going up in a little while and grab a snooze. Haven't been able to sleep lately and I'm tired as hell. A couple of hours good kip will fix me.

HOPE (*As* ROCKY *puts drinks on his table*) First time I ever heard you worry about sleep. Bejees, you never would go to bed. (*He raises his glass, and all the others except* PARRITT *do likewise*) Get a few slugs under your belt and you'll forget sleeping. Here's mud in your eye, Hickey. (*They all join in with the usual humorous toasts*)

HICKEY (*Heartily*) Drink hearty, boys and girls! (*They all drink, but* HICKEY *drinks only his chaser*)

HOPE Bejees, is that a new stunt, drinking your chaser first?

HICKEY No, I forgot to tell Rocky— You'll have to excuse me, boys and girls, but I'm off the stuff. For keeps. (*They stare at him in amazed incredulity*)

HOPE What the hell— (*Then with a wink at the others, kiddingly*) Sure! Joined the Salvation Army, ain't you? Been elected President of the W.C.T.U.? Take that bottle away from him, Rocky. We don't want to tempt him into sin. (*He chuckles and the others laugh*)

HICKEY (*Earnestly*) No, honest, Harry. I know it's hard to believe but— (*He pauses—then adds simply*) Cora was right, Harry. I have changed. I mean, about booze. I don't need it any more. (*They all stare, hoping it's a gag, but impressed and disappointed and made vaguely uneasy by the change they now sense in him*)

HOPE (*His kidding a bit forced*) Yeah, go ahead, kid the pants off us! Bejees, Cora said you was coming to save us! Well, go on. Get this joke off your chest! Start the service! Sing a God-damned hymn if you like. We'll all join in the chorus. "No drunkard can enter this beautiful home." That's a good one. (*He forces a cackle*)

HICKEY (*Grinning*) Oh, hell, Governor! You don't think I'd come around here peddling some brand of temperance bunk, do you? You know me better than that! Just because I'm through with the stuff don't mean I'm going Prohibition. Hell, I'm not that ungrateful! It's given me too many good times. I feel exactly the same as I always did. If anyone wants to get drunk, if that's the only way they can be happy, and feel at peace with themselves, why the hell shouldn't they? They have my full and entire sympathy. I know all about that game from soup to nuts. I'm the guy that wrote the book. The only reason I've quit is— Well, I finally had the guts to face myself and throw overboard the damned lying pipe dream that'd been making me miserable, and do what I had to do for the happiness of all concerned—and then all at once I found I was at peace with myself and I didn't need booze any more. That's all there was to it. (*He pauses. They are staring at him, uneasy and beginning to feel defensive.* HICKEY *looks round and grins affectionately—apologetically*) But what the hell! Don't let me be a wet blanket, making fool speeches about myself. Set 'em up again, Rocky. Here. (*He pulls a big roll from his pocket and peels off a ten-dollar bill. The faces of all brighten*) Keep the balls coming until this is killed. Then ask for more.

ROCKY Jees, a roll dat'd choke a hippopotamus! Fill up, youse guys. (*They all pour out drinks*)

HOPE That sounds more like you, Hickey. That water-wagon bull— Cut out the act and have a drink, for Christ's sake.

HICKEY It's no act, Governor. But don't get me wrong. That don't mean I'm a teetotal grouch and can't be in the party. Hell, why d'you suppose I'm here except to have a party, same as I've always done, and help celebrate your birthday tonight? You've all been good pals to me, the best friends I've ever had. I've been thinking about you ever since I left the house—all the time I was walking over here—

HOPE Walking? Bejees, do you mean to say you walked?

HICKEY I sure did. All the way from the wilds of darkest Astoria. Didn't mind it a bit, either. I seemed to get here before I knew it. I'm a bit tired and sleepy but otherwise I feel great. (*Kiddingly*) That ought to encourage you, Governor—show you a little walk around the ward is nothing to be so scared about. (*He winks at the others.* HOPE *stiffens resentfully for a second.* HICKEY *goes on*) I didn't make such bad time either for a fat guy, considering it's a hell of a ways, and I sat in the park a while thinking. It was going on twelve when I went in the bedroom to tell Evelyn I was leaving. Six hours, say. No, less than that. I'd been standing on the corner some time before Cora and Chuck came along, thinking about all of you. Of course, I was only kidding Cora with that stuff about saving you. (*Then seriously*) No,

I wasn't either. But I didn't mean booze. I meant save you from pipe dreams. I know now, from my experience, they're the things that really poison and ruin a guy's life and keep him from finding any peace. If you knew how free and contented I feel now. I'm like a new man. And the cure for them is so damned simple, once you have the nerve. Just the old dope of honesty is the best policy—honesty with yourself, I mean. Just stop lying about yourself and kidding yourself about tomorrows. (*He is staring ahead of him now as if he were talking aloud to himself as much as to them. Their eyes are fixed on him with uneasy resentment. His manner becomes apologetic again*) Hell, this begins to sound like a damned sermon on the way to lead the good life. Forget that part of it. It's in my blood, I guess. My old man used to whale salvation into my heinie with a birch rod. He was a preacher in the sticks of Indiana, like I've told you. I got my knack of sales gab from him, too. He was the boy who could sell those Hoosier hayseeds building lots along the Golden Street! (*Taking on a salesman's persuasiveness*) Now listen, boys and girls, don't look at me as if I was trying to sell you a goldbrick. Nothing up my sleeve, honest. Let's take an example. Any one of you. Take you, Governor. That walk around the ward you never take—

HOPE (*Defensively sharp*) What about it?

HICKEY (*Grinning affectionately*) Why, you know as well as I do, Harry. Everything about it.

HOPE (*Defiantly*) Bejees, I'm going to take it!

HICKEY Sure, you're going to—this time. Because I'm going to help you. I know it's the thing you've got to do before you'll ever know what real peace means. (*He looks at* JIMMY TOMORROW) Same thing with you, Jimmy. You've got to try and get your old job back. And no tomorrow about it! (*As* JIMMY *stiffens with a pathetic attempt at dignity—placatingly*) No, don't tell me, Jimmy. I know all about tomorrow. I'm the guy that wrote the book.

JIMMY I don't understand you. I admit I've foolishly delayed, but as it happens, I'd just made up my mind that as soon as I could get straightened out—

HICKEY Fine! That's the spirit! And I'm going to help you. You've been damned kind to me, Jimmy, and I want to prove how grateful I am. When it's all over and you don't have to nag at yourself any more, you'll be grateful to me, too! (*He looks around at the others*) And all the rest of you, ladies included, are in the same boat, one way or another.

LARRY (*Who has been listening with sardonic appreciation—in his comically intense, crazy whisper*) Be God, you've hit the nail on the head, Hickey! This dump is the Palace of Pipe Dreams!

HICKEY (*Grins at him with affectionate kidding*) Well, well! The Old Grandstand Foolosopher speaks! You think you're the big exception, eh? Life doesn't mean a damn to you any more, does it? You're retired from the circus. You're just waiting impatiently for the end—the good old Long Sleep! (*He chuckles*) Well, I think a lot of you, Larry, you old bastard. I'll try and make an honest man of you, too!

LARRY (*Stung*) What the devil are you hinting at, anyway?

HICKEY You don't have to ask me, do you, a wise old guy like you? Just ask yourself. I'll bet you know.

PARRITT (*Is watching* LARRY's *face with a curious sneering satisfaction*) He's got your number all right, Larry! (*He turns to* HICKEY) That's the stuff, Hickey. Show the old faker up! He's got no right to sneak out of everything.

HICKEY (*Regards him with surprise at first, then with a puzzled interest*) Hello. A stranger in our midst. I didn't notice you before, Brother.

PARRITT (*Embarrassed, his eyes shifting away*) My name's Parritt. I'm an old friend of Larry's. (*His eyes come back to* HICKEY *to find him still sizing him up—defensively*) Well? What are you staring at?

HICKEY (*Continuing to stare—puzzledly*) No offense, Brother. I was trying to figure— Haven't we met before some place?

PARRITT (*Reassured*) No. First time I've ever been East.

HICKEY No, you're right. I know that's not it. In my game, to be a shark at it, you teach yourself never to forget a name or a face. But still I know damned well I recognized something about you. We're members of the same lodge—in some way.

PARRITT (*Uneasy again*) What are you talking about? You're nuts.

HICKEY (*Dryly*) Don't try to kid me, Little Boy. I'm a good salesman—so damned good the firm was glad to take me back after every drunk—and what made me good was I could size up anyone. (*Frowningly puzzled again*) But I don't see— (*Suddenly breezily good-natured*) Never mind. I can tell you're having trouble with yourself and I'll be glad to do anything I can to help a friend of Larry's.

LARRY Mind your own business, Hickey. He's nothing to you—or to me, either. (HICKEY *gives him a keen inquisitive glance.* LARRY *looks away and goes on sarcastically*) You're keeping us all in suspense. Tell us more about how you're going to save us.

HICKEY (*Good-naturedly but seeming a little hurt*) Hell, don't get sore, Larry. Not at me. We've always been good pals, haven't we? I know I've always liked you a lot.

LARRY (*A bit shamefaced*) Well, so have I liked you. Forget it, Hickey.

HICKEY (*Beaming*) Fine! That's the spirit! (*Looking around at the others, who have forgotten their drinks*) What's the matter, everybody? What is this, a funeral? Come on and drink up! A little action! (*They all drink*) Have another. Hell, this is a celebration! Forget it, if anything I've said sounds too serious. I don't want to be a pain in the neck. Any time you think I'm talking out of turn, just tell me to go chase myself! (*He yawns with growing drowsiness and his voice grows a bit muffled*) No, boys and girls, I'm not trying to put anything over on you. It's just that I know now from experience what a lying pipe dream can do to you—and how damned relieved and contented with yourself you feel when you're rid of it. (*He yawns again*) God, I'm sleepy all of a sudden. That long walk is beginning to get me. I better go upstairs. Hell of a trick to go dead on you like this. (*He starts to get up but relaxes again. His eyes blink as he tries to keep them open*) No, boys and girls, I've never known what real peace was until now. It's a grand feeling, like when you're sick and suffering like hell and the Doc gives you a shot in the arm, and the pain goes, and you drift off. (*His eyes close*) You can let go of yourself at last. Let yourself sink down to the bottom of the sea. Rest in peace. There's no farther you have to go. Not a single damned hope or dream left to nag you. You'll all know what I mean after you— (*He pauses—mumbles*) Excuse—all in—got to grab forty winks— Drink up, everybody—on me— (*The sleep of complete exhaustion overpowers him. His chin sags to his chest. They stare at him with puzzled uneasy fascination*)

HOPE (*Forcing a tone of irritation*) Bejees, that's a fine stunt, to go to sleep on us! (*Then fumingly to the crowd*) Well, what the hell's the matter with you bums? Why don't you drink up? You're always crying for booze, and now you've got it under your nose, you sit like dummies! (*They start and gulp down their whiskies and pour another.* HOPE *stares at* HICKEY) Bejees, I can't figure Hickey. I still say he's kidding us. Kid his own grandmother, Hickey would. What d'you think, Jimmy?

JIMMY (*Unconvincingly*) It must be another of his jokes, Harry, although— Well, he does appear changed. But he'll probably be his natural self again tomorrow— (*Hastily*) I mean, when he wakes up.

LARRY (*Staring at* HICKEY *frowningly—more aloud to himself than to them*) You'll make a mistake if you think he's only kidding.

PARRITT (*In a low confidential voice*) I don't like that guy, Larry. He's too damned nosy. I'm going to steer clear of him. (LARRY *gives him a suspicious glance, then looks hastily away*)

JIMMY (*With an attempt at open-minded reasonableness*) Still, Harry, I have to admit there was some sense in his nonsense. It is time I got my job back—although I hardly need him to remind me.

HOPE (*With an air of frankness*) Yes, and I ought to take a walk around the ward. But I don't need no Hickey to tell me, seeing I got it all set for my birthday tomorrow.

LARRY (*Sardonically*) Ha! (*Then in his comically intense, crazy whisper*) Be God, it looks like he's going to make two sales of his peace at least! But you'd better make sure first its the real McCoy and not poison.

HOPE (*Disturbed—angrily*) You bughouse I-Won't-Work harp, who asked you to shove in an oar? What the hell d'you mean, poison? Just because he has your number— (*He immediately feels ashamed of this taunt and adds apologetically*) Bejees, Larry, you're always croaking about something to do with death. It gets my nanny. Come on, fellers, let's drink up. (*They drink.* HOPE's *eyes are fixed on* HICKEY *again*) Stone cold sober and dead to the world! Spilling that business about pipe dreams! Bejees, I don't get it. (*He bursts out again in angry complaint*) He ain't like the old Hickey! He'll be a fine wet blanket to have around at my birthday party! I wish to hell he'd never turned up!

MOSHER (*Who has been the least impressed by* HICKEY's *talk and is the first to recover and feel the effect of the drinks on top of his hangover—genially*) Give him time, Harry, and he'll come out of it. I've watched many cases of almost fatal teetotalism, but they all came out of it completely cured and as drunk as ever. My opinion is the poor sap is temporarily bughouse from overwork. (*Musingly*) You can't be too careful about work. It's the deadliest habit known to science, a great physician once told me. He practiced on street corners under a torchlight. He was positively the only doctor in the world who claimed that rattlesnake oil, rubbed on the prat, would cure heart failure in three days. I remember well his saying to me, "You are naturally delicate, Ed, but if you drink a pint of bad whiskey before breakfast every evening, and never work if you can help it, you may live to a ripe old age. It's staying sober and working that cuts men off in their prime." (*While he is talking, they turn to him with eager grins. They are longing to laugh, and as he finishes they roar. Even* PARRITT *laughs.* HICKEY *sleeps on like a dead man, but* HUGO, *who had passed into his customary coma again, head on table, looks up through his thick spectacles and giggles foolishly*)

HUGO (*Blinking around at them. As the laughter dies he speaks in his giggling, wheedling manner, as if he were playfully teasing children*) Laugh, leedle bourgeois monkey-faces! Laugh like fools, leedle stupid people! (*His tone suddenly changes to one of guttural soapbox denunciation and he pounds on the table with a small fist*) I vill laugh, too! But I vill laugh last! I vill laugh at you! (*He declaims his favorite quotation*) "The days grow hot, O Babylon! 'Tis cool beneath thy villow trees!" (*They all hoot him down in a chorus of amused jeering.* HUGO *is not offended. This is evidently their customary reaction. He giggles good-naturedly.* HICKEY *sleeps on. They have all forgotten their uneasiness about him now and ignore him*)

LEWIS (*Tipsily*) Well, now that our little Robespierre has got the daily bit of guillotining off his chest, tell me more about your doctor friend, Ed. He strikes me as the only bloody sensible medico I ever heard of. I think we should appoint him house physician here without a moment's delay. (*They all laughingly assent*)

MOSHER (*Warming to his subject, shakes his head sadly*) Too late! The old Doc has passed on to his Maker. A victim of overwork, too. He didn't follow his own advice. Kept his nose to the grindstone and sold one bottle of snake oil too many. Only eighty years old when he was taken. The saddest part was that he knew he was doomed. The last time we got paralyzed together he told me: "This game will get me yet, Ed. You see before you a broken man, a martyr to medical science. If I had any nerves I'd have a nervous breakdown. You won't believe me, but this last year there was actually one night I had so many patients, I didn't even have time to get drunk. The shock to my system brought on a stroke which, as a doctor, I recognized was the beginning of the end." Poor old Doc! When he said this he started crying. "I hate to go before my task is completed, Ed," he sobbed. "I'd hoped I'd live to see the day when, thanks to my miraculous cure, there wouldn't be a single vacant cemetery lot left in this glorious country." (*There is a roar of laughter. He waits for it to die and then goes on sadly*) I miss Doc. He was a gentleman of the old school. I'll bet he's standing on a street corner in hell right now, making suckers of the damned, telling them there's nothing like snake oil for a bad burn. (*There is another roar of laughter. This time it penetrates* HICKEY's *exhausted slumber. He stirs on his chair, trying to wake up, managing to raise his head a little and force his eyes half open. He speaks with a drowsy, affectionately encouraging smile. At once the laughter stops abruptly and they turn to him startledly*)

HICKEY That's the spirit—don't let me be a wet blanket—all I want is to see you happy— (*He slips back into heavy sleep again. They all stare at him, their faces again puzzled, resentful and uneasy*)

Curtain

Act Two

SCENE   The back room only. The black curtain dividing it from the bar is the right wall of the scene. It is getting on toward midnight of the same day.

The back room has been prepared for a festivity. At center, front, four of the circular tables are pushed together to form one long table with an uneven line of chairs behind it, and chairs at each end. This improvised banquet table is covered with old table cloths, borrowed from a neighboring beanery, and is laid with glasses, plates and cutlery before each of the seventeen chairs. Bottles of bar whiskey are placed at intervals within reach of any sitter. An old upright piano and stool have been moved in and stand against the wall at left, front.

At right, front, is a table without chairs. The other tables and chairs that had been in the room have been moved out, leaving a clear floor space at rear for dancing. The floor has been swept clean of sawdust and scrubbed. Even the walls show evidence of having been washed, although the result is only to heighten their splotchy leprous look. The electric light brackets are adorned with festoons of red ribbon. In the middle of the separate table at right, front, is a birthday cake with six candles. Several packages, tied with ribbon, are also on the table. There are two necktie boxes, two cigar boxes, a fifth containing a half dozen handkerchiefs, the sixth is a square jeweler's watch box.

As the curtain rises, CORA, CHUCK, HUGO, LARRY, MARGIE, PEARL and ROCKY are discovered. CHUCK, ROCKY and the three girls have dressed up for the occasion. CORA is arranging a bouquet of flowers in a vase, the vase being a big schooner glass from the bar, on top of the piano. CHUCK sits in a chair at the foot (left) of the banquet table. He has turned it so he can watch her. Near the middle of the row of chairs behind the table, LARRY sits, facing front, a drink of whiskey before him. He is staring before him in frowning, disturbed meditation. Next to him, on his left, HUGO is in his habitual position, passed out, arms on table, head on arms, a full whiskey glass by his head. By the separate table at right, front, MARGIE and PEARL are arranging *the cake and presents, and* ROCKY *stands by them. All of them, with the exception of* CHUCK *and* ROCKY, *have had plenty to drink and show it, but no one, except* HUGO, *seems to be drunk. They are trying to act up in the spirit of the occasion but there is something forced about their manner, an undercurrent of nervous irritation and preoccupation.*

CORA (*Standing back from the piano to regard the flower effect*) How's dat, Kid?

CHUCK (*Grumpily*) What de hell do I know about flowers?

CORA Yuh can see dey're pretty, can't yuh, yuh big dummy?

CHUCK (*Mollifyingly*) Yeah, Baby, sure. If yuh like 'em, dey're aw right wid me. (CORA *goes back to give the schooner of flowers a few more touches*)

MARGIE (*Admiring the cake*) Some cake, huh, Poil? Lookit! Six candles. Each for ten years.

PEARL When do we light de candles, Rocky?

ROCKY (*Grumpily*) Ask dat bughouse Hickey. He's elected himself boss of dis boithday racket. Just before Harry comes down, he says. Den Harry blows dem out wid one breath, for luck. Hickey was goin' to have sixty candles, but I says, Jees, if de old guy took dat big a breath, he'd croak himself.

MARGIE (*Challengingly*) Well, anyways, it's some cake, ain't it?

ROCKY (*Without enthusiasm*) Sure, it's aw right by me. But what de hell is Harry goin' to do wid a cake? If he ever et a hunk, it'd croak him.

PEARL Jees, yuh're a dope! Ain't he, Margie?

MARGIE A dope is right!

ROCKY (*Stung*) You broads better watch your step or—

PEARL (*Defiantly*) Or what?

MARGIE Yeah! Or what? (*They glare at him truculently*)

ROCKY Say, what de hell's got into youse? It'll be twelve o'clock and Harry's boithday before long. I ain't lookin' for no trouble.

PEARL (*Ashamed*) Aw, we ain't neider, Rocky. (*For the moment this argument subsides*)

CORA (*Over her shoulder to* CHUCK—*acidly*) A guy what can't see flowers is pretty must be some dumbbell.

CHUCK Yeah? Well, if I was as dumb as you—(*Then mollifyingly*) Jees, yuh got your scrappin' pants on, ain't yuh? (*Grins good-naturedly*) Hell, Baby, what's eatin' yuh? All I'm tinkin' is, flowers is dat louse Hickey's stunt. We never had no flowers for Harry's boithday before. What de hell can Harry do wid flowers? He don't know a cauliflower from a geranium.

ROCKY Yeah, Chuck, it's like I'm tellin' dese broads about de cake. Dat's Hickey's wrinkle, too. (*Bitterly*) Jees, ever since he woke up,

yuh can't hold him. He's taken on de party like it was his boithday.
MARGIE Well, he's payin' for everything, ain't he?
ROCKY Aw, I don't mind de boithday stuff so much. What gets my goat is de way he's tryin' to run de whole dump and everyone in it. He's buttin' in all over de place, tellin' everybody where dey get off. On'y he don't really tell yuh. He just keeps hintin' around.
PEARL Yeah. He was hintin' to me and Margie.
MARGIE Yeah, de lousy drummer.
ROCKY He just gives yuh an earful of dat line of bull about yuh got to be honest wid yourself and not kid yourself, and have de guts to be what yuh are. I got sore. I told him dat's aw right for de bums in dis dump. I hope he makes dem wake up. I'm sick of listenin' to dem hop demselves up. But it don't go wid me, see? I don't kid myself wid no pipe dream. (PEARL *and* MARGIE *exchange a derisive look. He catches it and his eyes narrow*) What are yuh grinnin' at?
PEARL (*Her face hard—scornfully*) Nuttin'.
MARGIE Nuttin'.
ROCKY It better be nuttin'! Don't let Hickey put no ideas in your nuts if you wanta stay healthy! (*Then angrily*) I wish de louse never showed up! I hope he don't come back from de delicatessen. He's gettin' everyone nuts. He's ridin' someone every minute. He's got Harry and Jimmy Tomorrow run ragged, and de rest is hidin' in deir rooms so dey won't have to listen to him. Dey're all actin' cagey wid de booze, too, like dey was scared if dey get too drunk, dey might spill deir guts, or somethin'. And everybody's gettin' a prize grouch on.
CORA Yeah, he's been hintin' around to me and Chuck, too. Yuh'd tink he suspected me and Chuck hadn't no real intention of gettin' married. Yuh'd tink he suspected Chuck wasn't goin' to lay off periodicals— or maybe even didn't want to.
CHUCK He didn't say it right out or I'da socked him one. I told him, "I'm on de wagon for keeps and Cora knows it."
CORA I told him, "Sure, I know it. And Chuck ain't never goin' to trow it in my face dat I was a tart, neider. And if yuh tink we're just kiddin' ourselves, we'll show yuh!"
CHUCK We're goin' to show him!
CORA We got it all fixed. We've decided Joisey is where we want de farm, and we'll get married dere, too, because yuh don't need no license. We're goin' to get married tomorrow. Ain't we, Honey?
CHUCK You bet, Baby.
ROCKY (*Disgusted*) Christ, Chuck, are yuh lettin' dat bughouse louse Hickey kid yuh into—
CORA (*Turns on him angrily*) Nobody's kiddin' him into it, nor me neider! And Hickey's right. If dis big tramp's goin' to marry me, he

ought to do it, and not just shoot off his old bazoo about it.
ROCKY (*Ignoring her*) Yuh can't be dat dumb, Chuck.
CORA You keep outa dis! And don't start beefin' about crickets on de farm drivin' us nuts. You and your crickets! Yuh'd tink dey was elephants!
MARGIE (*Coming to* ROCKY'S *defense—sneeringly*) Don't notice dat broad, Rocky. Yuh heard her say "tomorrow," didn't yuh? It's de same old crap.
CORA (*Glares at her*) Is dat so?
PEARL (*Lines up with* MARGIE—*sneeringly*) Imagine Cora a bride! Dat's a hot one! Jees, Cora, if all de guys you've stayed wid was side by side, yuh could walk on 'em from here to Texas!
CORA (*Starts moving toward her threateningly*) Yuh can't talk like dat to me, yuh fat Dago hooker! I may be a tart, but I ain't a cheap old whore like you!
PEARL (*Furiously*) I'll show yuh who's a whore! (*They start to fly at each other, but* CHUCK *and* ROCKY *grab them from behind*)
CHUCK (*Forcing* CORA *onto a chair*) Sit down and cool off, Baby.
ROCKY (*Doing the same to* PEARL) Nix on de rough stuff, Poil.
MARGIE (*Glaring at* CORA) Why don't you leave Poil alone, Rocky? She'll fix dat blonde's clock! Or if she don't, I will!
ROCKY Shut up, you! (*Disgustedly*) Jees, what dames! D'yuh wanta gum Harry's party?
PEARL (*A bit shamefaced—sulkily*) Who wants to? But nobody can't call me a —.
ROCKY (*Exasperatedly*) Aw, bury it! What are you, a voigin? (PEARL *stares at him, her face growing hard and bitter. So does* MARGIE)
PEARL Yuh mean you tink I'm a whore, too, huh?
MARGIE Yeah, and me?
ROCKY Now don't start nuttin'!
PEARL I suppose it'd tickle you if me and Margie did what dat louse, Hickey, was hintin' and come right out and admitted we was whores.
ROCKY Aw right! What of it? It's de truth, ain't it?
CORA (*Lining up with* PEARL *and* MARGIE—*indignantly*). Jees, Rocky, dat's a fine hell of a ting to say to two goils dat's been as good to yuh as Poil and Margie! (*To* PEARL) I didn't mean to call yuh dat, Poil. I was on'y mad.
PEARL (*Accepts the apology gratefully*) Sure, I was mad, too, Cora. No hard feelin's.
ROCKY (*Relieved*) Dere. Dat fixes everything, don't it?
PEARL (*Turns on him—hard and bitter*) Aw right, Rocky. We're whores. You know what dat makes you, don't you?

ROCKY (*Angrily*) Look out, now!
MARGIE A lousy little pimp, dat's what!
ROCKY I'll loin yuh! (*He gives her a slap on the side of the face*)
PEARL A dirty little Ginny pimp, dat's what!
ROCKY (*Gives her a slap too*) And dat'll loin you! (*But they only stare at him with hard sneering eyes*)
MARGIE He's provin' it to us, Poil.
PEARL Yeah! Hickey's convoited him. He's give up his pipe dream!
ROCKY (*Furious and at the same time bewildered by their defiance*) Lay off me or I'll beat de hell—
CHUCK (*Growls*) Aw, lay off dem. Harry's party ain't no time to beat up your stable.
ROCKY (*Turns to him*) Whose stable? Who d'yuh tink yuh're talkin' to? I ain't never beat dem up! What d'yuh tink I am? I just give dem a slap, like any guy would his wife, if she got too gabby. Why don't yuh tell dem to lay off me? I don't want no trouble on Harry's boithday party.
MARGIE (*A victorious gleam in her eye—tauntingly*) Aw right, den, yuh poor little Ginny. I'll lay off yuh till de party's over if Poil will.
PEARL (*Tauntingly*) Sure, I will. For Harry's sake, not yours, yuh little Wop!
ROCKY (*Stung*) Say, listen, youse! Don't get no wrong idea—(*But an interruption comes from* LARRY *who bursts into a sardonic laugh. They all jump startledly and look at him with unanimous hostility.* ROCKY *transfers his anger to him*) Who de hell yuh laughin' at, yuh half-dead old stew bum?
CORA (*Sneeringly*) At himself, he ought to be! Jees, Hickey's sure got his number!
LARRY (*Ignoring them, turns to* HUGO *and shakes him by the shoulder—in his comically intense, crazy whisper*) Wake up, Comrade! Here's the Revolution starting on all sides of you and you're sleeping through it! Be God, it's not to Bakunin's[15] ghost you ought to pray in your dreams, but to the great Nihilist, Hickey! He's started a movement that'll blow up the world!
HUGO (*Blinks at him through his thick spectacles—with guttural denunciation*) You, Larry! Renegade! Traitor! I vill have you shot! (*He giggles*) Don't be a fool! Buy me a trink! (*He sees the drink in front of him, and gulps it down. He begins to sing the Carmagnole*[16] *in a guttural basso, pounding on the table with his glass*) "Dansons

---

[15] Nineteenth-century Russian Revolutionary.
[16] A song popularized during the French Revolution; see end of play.

la Carmagnole! Vive le son! Vive le son! Dansons la Carmagnole! Vive le son des canons!"

ROCKY   Can dat noise!

HUGO (*Ignores this—to* LARRY, *in a low tone of hatred*)   That bourgeois svine, Hickey! He laughs like good fellow, he makes jokes, he dares make hints to me so I see what he dares to think. He thinks I am finish, it is too late, and so I do not vish the Day come because it vill not be my Day. Oh, I see what he thinks! He thinks lies even vorse, dat I— (*He stops abruptly with a guilty look, as if afraid he was letting something slip—then revengefully*) I vill have him hanged the first one of all on de first lamppost! (*He changes his mood abruptly and peers around at* ROCKY *and the others—giggling again*) Vhy you so serious, leedle monkey-faces? It's all great joke, no? So ve get drunk, and ve laugh like hell, and den ve die, and de pipe dream vanish! (*A bitter mocking contempt creeps into his tone*) But be of good cheer, leedle stupid peoples! "The days grow hot, O Babylon!" Soon, leedle proletarians, ve vill have free picnic in the cool shade, ve vill eat hot dogs and trink free beer beneath the villow trees! Like hogs, yes! Like beautiful leedle hogs! (*He stops startledly, as if confused and amazed at what he has heard himself say. He mutters with hatred*) Dot Gottamned liar, Hickey. It is he who makes me sneer. I want to sleep. (*He lets his head fall forward on his folded arms again and closes his eyes.* LARRY *gives him a pitying look, then quickly drinks his drink*)

CORA (*Uneasily*)   Hickey ain't overlookin' no bets, is he? He's even give Hugo de woiks.

LARRY   I warned you this morning he wasn't kidding.

MARGIE (*Sneering*)   De old wise guy!

PEARL   Yeah, still pretendin' he's de one exception, like Hickey told him. He don't do no pipe dreamin'! Oh, no!

LARRY (*Sharply resentful*)   I—! (*Then abruptly he is drunkenly good-natured, and you feel this drunken manner is an evasive exaggeration*) All right, take it out on me, if it makes you more content. Sure, I love every hair of your heads, my great big beautiful baby dolls, and there's nothing I wouldn't do for you!

PEARL (*Stiffly*)   De old Irish bunk, huh? We ain't big. And we ain't your baby dolls. (*Suddenly she is mollified and smiles*) But we admit we're beautiful. Huh, Margie?

MARGIE (*Smiling*)   Sure ting! But what would he do wid beautiful dolls, even if he had de price, de old goat? (*She laughs teasingly—then pats* LARRY *on the shoulder affectionately*) Aw, yuh're aw right at dat, Larry, if yuh are full of bull!

PEARL   Sure. Yuh're aces wid us. We're noivous, dats's all. Dat lousy

drummer—why can't he be like he's always been? I never seen a guy change so. You pretend to be such a fox, Larry. What d'yuh tink's happened to him?
LARRY I don't know. With all his gab I notice he's kept that to himself so far. Maybe he's saving the great revelation for Harry's party. (*Then irritably*) To hell with him! I don't want to know. Let him mind his own business and I'll mind mine.
CHUCK Yeah, dat's what I say.
CORA Say, Larry, where's dat young friend of yours disappeared to?
LARRY I don't care where he is, except I wish it was a thousand miles away! (*Then, as he sees they are surprised at his vehemence, he adds hastily*) He's a pest.
ROCKY (*Breaks in with his own preoccupation*) I don't give a damn what happened to Hickey, but I know what's gonna happen if he don't watch his step. I told him, "I'll take a lot from you, Hickey, like everyone else in dis dump, because yuh've always been a grand guy. But dere's tings I don't take from you nor nobody, see? Remember dat, or you'll wake up in a hospital—or maybe worse, wid your wife and de iceman walkin' slow behind yuh."
CORA Aw, yuh shouldn't make dat iceman crack, Rocky. It's aw right for him to kid about it but—I notice Hickey ain't pulled dat old iceman gag dis time. (*Excitedly*) D'yuh suppose dat he did catch his wife cheatin'? I don't mean wid no iceman, but wid some guy.
ROCKY Aw, dat's de bunk. He ain't pulled dat gag or showed her photo around because he ain't drunk. And if he'd caught her cheatin' he'd be drunk, wouldn't he? He'd have beat her up and den gone on de woist drunk he'd ever staged. Like any other guy'd do. (*The girls nod, convinced by this reasoning*)
CHUCK Sure! Rocky's got de right dope, Baby. He'd be paralyzed. (*While he is speaking, the Negro,* JOE, *comes in from the hallway. There is a noticeable change in him. He walks with a tough, truculent swagger and his good-natured face is set in sullen suspicion*)
JOE (*To* ROCKY—*defiantly*) I's stood tellin' people dis dump is closed for de night all I's goin' to. Let Harry hire a doorman, pay him wages, if he wants one.
ROCKY (*Scowling*) Yeah? Harry's pretty damned good to you.
JOE (*Shamefaced*) Sure he is. I don't mean dat. Anyways, it's all right. I told Schwartz, de cop, we's closed for de party. He'll keep folks away. (*Aggressively again*) I want a big drink, dat's what!
CHUCK Who's stoppin' yuh? Yuh can have all yuh want on Hickey.
JOE (*Has taken a glass from the table and has his hand on a bottle when* HICKEY's *name is mentioned. He draws his hand back as if he were*

going to refuse—then grabs it defiantly and pours a big drink) All right, I's earned all de drinks on him I could drink in a year for listenin' to his crazy bull. And here's hopin' he gets de lockjaw! (*He drinks and pours out another*) I drinks on him but I don't drink wid him. No, suh, never no more!

ROCKY Aw, bull! Hickey's aw right. What's he done to you?

JOE (*Sullenly*) Dat's my business. I ain't buttin' in yours, is I? (*Bitterly*) Sure, you think he's all right. He's a white man, ain't he? (*His tone becomes aggressive*) Listen to me, you white boys! Don't you get it in your heads I's pretendin' to be what I ain't, or dat I ain't proud to be what I is, get me? Or you and me's goin' to have trouble! (*He picks up his drink and walks left as far away from them as he can get and slumps down on the piano stool*)

MARGIE (*In a low angry tone*) What a noive! Just because we act nice to him, he gets a swelled nut! If dat ain't a coon all over!

CHUCK Talkin' fight talk, huh? I'll moider de nigger! (*He takes a threatening step toward* JOE, *who is staring before him guiltily now*)

JOE (*Speaks up shamefacedly*) Listen, boys, I's sorry. I didn't mean dat. You been good friends to me. I's nuts, I guess. Dat Hickey, he gets my head all mixed up wit' craziness. (*Their faces at once clear of resentment against him*)

CORA Aw, dat's aw right, Joe. De boys wasn't takin' yuh serious. (*Then to the others, forcing a laugh*) Jees, what'd I say, Hickey ain't overlookin' no bets. Even Joe. (*She pauses—then adds puzzledly*) De funny ting is, yuh can't stay sore at de bum when he's around. When he forgets de bughouse preachin', and quits tellin' yuh where yuh get off, he's de same old Hickey. Yuh can't help likin' de louse. And yuh got to admit he's got de right dope—(*She adds hastily*) I mean, on some of de bums here.

MARGIE (*With a sneering look at* ROCKY) Yeah, he's coitinly got one guy I know sized up right! Huh, Poil?

PEARL He coitinly has!

ROCKY Cut it out, I told yuh!

LARRY (*Is staring before him broodingly. He speaks more aloud to himself than to them*) It's nothing to me what happened to him. But I have a feeling he's dying to tell us, inside him, and yet he's afraid. He's like that damned kid. It's strange the queer way he seemed to recognize him. If he's afraid, it explains why he's off booze. Like that damned kid again. Afraid if he got drunk, he'd tell— (*While he is speaking,* HICKEY *comes in the doorway at rear. He looks the same as in the previous act, except that now his face beams with the excited expectation of a boy going to a party. His arms are piled with packages*)

HICKEY (*Booms in imitation of a familiar Polo Grounds*[17] *bleacherite cry—with rising volume*) Well! Well!! Well!!! (*They all jump startledly. He comes forward, grinning*) Here I am in the nick of time. Give me a hand with these bundles, somebody. (MARGIE *and* PEARL *start taking them from his arms and putting them on the table. Now that he is present, all their attitudes show the reaction* CORA *has expressed. They can't help liking him and forgiving him*)
MARGIE Jees, Hickey, yuh scared me outa a year's growth, sneakin' in like dat.
HICKEY Sneaking? Why, me and the taxi man made enough noise getting my big surprise in the hall to wake the dead. You were all so busy drinking in words of wisdom from the Old Wise Guy here, you couldn't hear anything else. (*He grins at* LARRY) From what I heard, Larry, you're not so good when you start playing Sherlock Holmes. You've got me all wrong. I'm not afraid of anything now—not even myself. You better stick to the part of Old Cemetery, the Barker for the Big Sleep—that is, if you can still let yourself get away with it! (*He chuckles and gives* LARRY *a friendly slap on the back.* LARRY *gives him a bitter angry look*)
CORA (*Giggles*) Old Cemetery! That's him, Hickey. We'll have to call him dat.
HICKEY (*Watching* LARRY *quizzically*) Beginning to do a lot of puzzling about me, aren't you, Larry? But that won't help you. You've got to think of yourself. I couldn't give you my peace. You've got to find your own. All I can do is help you, and the rest of the gang, by showing you the way to find it. (*He has said this with a simple persuasive earnestness. He pauses, and for a second they stare at him with fascinated resentful uneasiness*)
ROCKY (*Breaks the spell*) Aw, hire a church!
HICKEY (*Placatingly*) All right! All right! Don't get sore, boys and girls. I guess that did sound too much like a lousy preacher. Let's forget it and get busy on the party. (*They look relieved*)
CHUCK Is dose bundles grub, Hickey? You bought enough already to feed an army.
HICKEY (*With boyish excitement again*) Can't be too much! I want this to be the biggest birthday Harry's ever had. You and Rocky go in the hall and get the big surprise. My arms are busted lugging it. (*They catch his excitement.* CHUCK *and* ROCKY *go out, grinning expectantly. The three girls gather around* HICKEY, *full of thrilled curiosity*)
PEARL Jees, yuh got us all het up! What is it, Hickey?

[17] Baseball playing field of what were the New York Giants.

HICKEY Wait and see. I got it as a treat for the three of you more than anyone. I thought to myself, I'll bet this is what will please those whores more than anything. (*They wince as if he had slapped them, but before they have a chance to be angry, he goes on affectionately*) I said to myself, I don't care how much it costs, they're worth it. They're the best little scouts in the world, and they've been damned kind to me when I was down and out! Nothing is too good for them. (*Earnestly*) I mean every word of that, too—and then some! (*Then, as if he noticed the expression on their faces for the first time*) What's the matter? You look sore. What—? (*Then he chuckles*) Oh, I see. But you know how I feel about that. You know I didn't say it to offend you. So don't be silly now.

MARGIE (*Lets out a tense breath*) Aw right, Hickey. Let it slide.

HICKEY (*Jubilantly, as* CHUCK *and* ROCKY *enter carrying a big wicker basket*) Look! There it comes! Unveil it, boys. (*They pull off a covering burlap bag. The basket is piled with quarts of champagne*)

PEARL (*With childish excitement*) It's champagne! Jees, Hickey, if you ain't a sport! (*She gives him a hug, forgetting all animosity, as do the other girls*)

MARGIE I never been soused on champagne. Let's get stinko, Poil.

PEARL You betcha my life! De bot' of us! (*A holiday spirit of gay festivity has seized them all. Even* JOE MOTT *is standing up to look at the wine with an admiring grin, and* HUGO *raises his head to blink at it*)

JOE You sure is hittin' de high spots, Hickey. (*Boastfully*) Man, when I runs my gamblin' house, I drinks dat old bubbly water in steins! (*He stops guiltily and gives* HICKEY *a look of defiance*) I's goin' to drink it dat way again, too, soon's I make my stake! And dat ain't no pipe dream, neider! (*He sits down where he was, his back turned to them*)

ROCKY What'll we drink it outa, Hickey? Dere ain't no wine glasses.

HICKEY (*Enthusiastically*) Joe has the right idea! Schooners! That's the spirit for Harry's birthday! (ROCKY *and* CHUCK *carry the basket of wine into the bar. The three girls go back and stand around the entrance to the bar, chatting excitedly among themselves and to* CHUCK *and* ROCKY *in the bar*)

HUGO (*With his silly giggle*) Ve vill trink vine beneath the villow trees!

HICKEY (*Grins at him*) That's the spirit, Brother—and let the lousy slaves drink vinegar! (HUGO *blinks at him startledly, then looks away*)

HUGO (*Mutters*) Gottamned liar! (*He puts hs head back on his arms and closes his eyes, but this time his habitual pass-out has a quality of hiding*)

LARRY (*Gives* HUGO *a pitying glance—in a low tone of anger*) Leave

Hugo be! He rotted ten years in prison for his faith! He's earned his dream! Have you no decency or pity?

HICKEY (*Quizzically*) Hello, what's this? I thought you were in the grandstand. (*Then with a simple earnestness, taking a chair by* LARRY, *and putting a hand on his shoulder*) Listen, Larry, you're getting me all wrong. Hell, you ought to know me better. I've always been the best-natured slob in the world. Of course, I have pity. But now I've seen the light, it isn't my old kind of pity—the kind yours is. It isn't the kind that lets itself off easy by encouraging some poor guy to go on kidding himself with a lie—the kind that leaves the poor slob worse off because it makes him feel guiltier than ever—the kind that makes his lying hopes nag at him and reproach him until he's a rotten skunk in his own eyes. I know all about that kind of pity. I've had a bellyful of it in my time, and it's all wrong! (*With a salesman's persuasiveness*) No, sir. The kind of pity I feel now is after final results that will really save the poor guy, and make him contented with what he is, and quit battling himself, and find peace for the rest of his life. Oh, I know how you resent the way I have to show you up to yourself. I don't blame you. I know from my own experience it's bitter medicine, facing yourself in the mirror with the old false whiskers off. But you forget that, once you're cured. You'll be grateful to me when all at once you find you're able to admit, without feeling ashamed, that all the grandstand foolosopher bunk and the waiting for the Big Sleep stuff is a pipe dream. You'll say to yourself, I'm just an old man who is scared of life, but even more scared of dying. So I'm keeping drunk and hanging on to life at any price, and what of it? Then you'll know what real peace means, Larry, because you won't be scared of either life or death any more. You simply won't give a damn! Any more than I do!

LARRY (*Has been staring into his eyes with a fascinated wondering dread*) Be God, if I'm not beginning to think you've gone mad! (*With a rush of anger*) You're a liar!

HICKEY (*Injuredly*) Now listen, that's no way to talk to an old pal who's trying to help you. Hell, if you really wanted to die, you'd just take a hop off your fire escape, wouldn't you? And if you really were in the grandstand, you wouldn't be pitying everyone. Oh, I know the truth is tough at first. It was for me. All I ask is for you to suspend judgment and give it a chance. I'll absolutely guarantee— Hell, Larry, I'm no fool. Do you suppose I'd deliberately set out to get under everyone's skin and put myself in dutch[18] with all my old pals, if I

---

[18] In disfavor.

wasn't certain, from my own experience, that it means contentment in the end for all of you? (LARRY *again is staring at him fascinatedly.* HICKEY *grins*) As for my being bughouse, you can't crawl out of it that way. Hell, I'm too damned sane. I can size up guys, and turn 'em inside out, better than I ever could. Even where they're strangers like that Parritt kid. He's licked, Larry. I think there is only one possible way out you can help him to take. That is, if you have the right kind of pity for him.

LARRY (*Uneasily*) What do you mean? (*Attempting indifference*) I'm not advising him, except to leave me out of his troubles. He's nothing to me.

HICKEY (*Shakes his head*) You'll find he won't agree to that. He'll keep after you until he makes you help him. Because he has to be punished, so he can forgive himself. He's lost all his guts. He can't manage it alone, and you're the only one he can turn to.

LARRY For the love of God, mind your own business! (*With forced scorn*) A lot you know about him! He's hardly spoken to you!

HICKEY No, that's right. But I do know a lot about him just the same. I've had hell inside me. I can spot it in others. (*Frowning*) Maybe that's what gives me the feeling there's something familiar about him, something between us. (*He shakes his head*) No, it's more than that. I can't figure it. Tell me about him. For instance, I don't imagine he's married, is he?

LARRY No.

HICKEY Hasn't he been mixed up with some woman? I don't mean trollops. I mean the old real love stuff that crucifies you.

LARRY (*With a calculating relieved look at him—encouraging him along this line*) Maybe you're right. I wouldn't be surprised.

HICKEY (*Grins at him quizzically*) I see. You think I'm on the wrong track and you're glad I am. Because then I won't suspect whatever he did about the Great Cause. That's another lie you tell yourself, Larry, that the good old Cause means nothing to you any more. (LARRY *is about to burst out in denial but* HICKEY *goes on*) But you're all wrong about Parritt. That isn't what's got him stopped. It's what's behind that. And it's a woman. I recognize the symptoms.

LARRY (*Sneeringly*) And you're the boy who's never wrong! Don't be a damned fool. His trouble is he was brought up a devout believer in the Movement and now he's lost his faith. It's a shock, but he's young and he'll soon find another dream just as good. (*He adds sardonically*) Or as bad.

HICKEY All right. I'll let it go at that, Larry. He's nothing to me except I'm glad he's here because he'll help me make you wake up to yourself.

I don't even like the guy, or the feeling there's anything between us. But you'll find I'm right just the same, when you get to the final showdown with him.

LARRY There'll be no showdown! I don't give a tinker's damn—

HICKEY Sticking to the old grandstand, eh? Well, I knew you'd be the toughest to convince of all the gang, Larry. And, along with Harry and Jimmy Tomorrow, you're the one I want most to help. (*He puts an arm around* LARRY's *shoulder and gives him an affectionate hug*) I've always liked you a lot, you old bastard! (*He gets up and his manner changes to his bustling party excitement—glancing at his watch*) Well, well, not much time before twelve. Let's get busy, boys and girls. (*He looks over the table where the cake is*) Cake all set. Good. And my presents, and yours, girls, and Chuck's, and Rocky's. Fine. Harry'll certainly be touched by your thought of him. (*He goes back to the girls*) You go in the bar, Pearl and Margie, and get the grub ready so it can be brought right in. There'll be some drinking and toasts first, of course. My idea is to use the wine for that, so get it all set. I'll go upstairs now and root everyone out. Harry the last. I'll come back with him. Somebody light the candles on the cake when you hear us coming, and you start playing Harry's favorite tune, Cora. Hustle now, everybody. We want this to come off in style. (*He bustles into the hall.* MARGIE *and* PEARL *disappear in the bar.* CORA *goes to the piano.* JOE *gets off the stool sullenly to let her sit down*)

CORA I got to practice. I ain't laid my mits on a box in Gawd knows when. (*With the soft pedal down, she begins gropingly to pick out "The Sunshine of Paradise Alley"*) Is dat right, Joe? I've forgotten dat hasbeen tune. (*She picks out a few more notes*) Come on, Joe, hum de tune so I can follow. (JOE *begins to hum and sing in a low voice and correct her. He forgets his sullenness and becomes his old self again*)

LARRY (*Suddenly gives a laugh—in his comically intense, crazy tone*) Be God, it's a second feast of Belshazzar, with Hickey to do the writing on the wall![19]

CORA Aw, shut up, Old Cemetery! Always beefin'! (WILLIE *comes in from the hall. He is in a pitiable state, his face pasty, haggard with sleeplessness and nerves, his eyes sick and haunted. He is sober.* CORA *greets him over her shoulder kiddingly*) If it ain't Prince Willie! (*Then kindly*) Gee, kid, yuh look sick. Git a coupla shots in yuh.

WILLIE (*Tensely*) No, thanks. Not now. I'm tapering off. (*He sits down weakly on* LARRY's *right*)

---

[19] Book of Daniel, V.

CORA (*Astonished*) What d'yuh know? He means it!

WILLIE (*Leaning toward* LARRY *confidentially—in a low shaken voice*) It's been hell up in that damned room, Larry! The things I've imagined! (*He shudders*) I thought I'd go crazy. (*With pathetic boastful pride*) But I've got it beat now. By tomorrow morning I'll be on the wagon. I'll get back my clothes the first thing. Hickey's loaning me the money. I'm going to do what I've always said—go to the D.A.'s office. He was a good friend of my Old Man's. He was only assistant, then. He was in on the graft, but my Old Man never squealed on him. So he certainly owes it to me to give me a chance. And he knows that I really was a brilliant law student (*Self-reassuringly*) Oh, I know I can make good, now I'm getting off the booze forever. (*Moved*) I owe a lot to Hickey. He's made me wake up to myself—see what a fool—it wasn't nice to face but— (*With bitter resentment*) It isn't what he says. It's what you feel behind—what he hints— Christ, you'd think all I really wanted to do with my life was sit here and stay drunk. (*With hatred*) I'll show him!

LARRY (*Masking pity behind a sardonic tone*) If you want my advice, you'll put the nearest bottle to your mouth until you don't give a damn for Hickey!

WILLIE (*Stares at a bottle greedily, tempted for a moment—then bitterly*) That's fine advice! I thought you were my friend! (*He gets up with a hurt glance at* LARRY, *and moves away to take a chair in back of the left end of the table, where he sits in dejected, shaking misery, his chin on his chest*)

JOE (*To* CORA) No, like dis. (*He beats time with his finger and sings in a low voice*) "She is the sunshine of Paradise Alley." (*She plays*) Dat's more like it. Try it again. (*She begins to play through the chorus again.* DON PARRITT *enters from the hall. There is a frightened look on his face. He slinks in furtively, as if he were escaping from someone. He looks relieved when he sees* LARRY *and comes and slips into the chair on his right.* LARRY *pretends not to notice his coming, but he instinctively shrinks with repulsion.* PARRITT *leans toward him and speaks ingratiatingly in a low secretive tone*)

PARRITT Gee, I'm glad you're here, Larry. That damned fool, Hickey, knocked on my door. I opened up because I thought it must be you, and he came busting in and made me come downstairs. I don't know what for. I don't belong in this birthday celebration. I don't know this gang and I don't want to be mixed up with them. All I came here for was to find you.

LARRY (*Tensely*) I've warned you—

PARRITT (*Goes on as if he hadn't heard*) Can't you make Hickey mind his own business? I don't like that guy, Larry. The way he acts, you'd think he had something on me. Why, just now he pats me on the shoulder, like he was sympathizing with me, and says, "I know how it is, Son, but you can't hide from yourself, not even here on the bottom of the sea. You've got to face the truth and then do what must be done for your own peace and the happiness of all concerned." What did he mean by that, Larry?

LARRY How the hell would I know?

PARRITT Then he grins and says, "Never mind, Larry's getting wise to himself. I think you can rely on his help in the end. He'll have to choose between living and dying, and he'll never choose to die while there is a breath left in the old bastard!" And then he laughs like it was a joke on you. (*He pauses.* LARRY *is rigid on his chair, staring before him.* PARRITT *asks him with a sudden taunt in his voice*) Well, what do you say to that, Larry?

LARRY I've nothing to say. Except you're a bigger fool than he is to listen to him.

PARRITT (*With a sneer*) Is that so? He's no fool where you're concerned. He's got your number, all right! (LARRY'S *face tightens but he keeps silent.* PARRITT *changes to a contrite, appealing air*) I don't mean that. But you keep acting as if you were sore at me, and that gets my goat. You know what I want most is to be friends with you, Larry. I haven't a single friend left in the world. I hoped you— (*Bitterly*) And you could be, too, without it hurting you. You ought to, for Mother's sake. She really loved you. You loved her, too, didn't you?

LARRY (*Tensely*) Leave what's dead in its grave.

PARRITT I suppose, because I was only a kid, you didn't think I was wise about you and her. Well, I was. I've been wise, ever since I can remember, to all the guys she's had, although she'd tried to kid me along it wasn't so. That was a silly stunt for a free Anarchist woman, wasn't it, being ashamed of being free?

LARRY Shut your damned trap!

PARRITT (*Guiltily but with a strange undertone of satisfaction*) Yes, I know I shouldn't say that now. I keep forgetting she isn't free any more. (*He pauses*) Do you know, Larry, you're the one of them all she cared most about? Anyone else who left the Movement would have been dead to her, but she couldn't forget you. She'd always make excuses for you. I used to try and get her goat about you. I'd say, "Larry's got brains and yet he thinks the Movement is just a crazy pipe dream." She'd blame it on booze getting you. She'd kid herself that you'd give up booze and come back to the Movement—tomorrow! She'd say, "Larry can't kill in himself a faith he's given his life to, not without killing himself." (*He grins sneeringly*) How about it, Larry? Was she right? (LARRY *remains silent. He goes on insistently*) I suppose what she really meant was, come back to her. She was always getting the Movement mixed up with herself. But I'm sure she really must have loved you, Larry. As much as she could love anyone besides herself. But she wasn't faithful to you, even at that, was she? That's why you finally walked out on her, isn't it? I remember that last fight you had with her. I was listening. I was on your side, even if she was my mother, because I liked you so much; you'd been so good to me—like a father. I remember her putting on her high-and-mighty free-woman stuff, saying you were still a slave to bourgeois morality and jealousy and you thought a woman you loved was a piece of private property you owned. I remember that you got mad and you told her, "I don't like living with a whore, if that's what you mean!"

LARRY (*Bursts out*) You lie! I never called her that!

PARRITT (*Goes on as if* LARRY *hadn't spoken*) I think that's why she still respects you, because it was you who left her. You were the only one to beat her to it. She got sick of the others before they did of her. I don't think she ever cared much about them, anyway. She just had to keep on having lovers to prove to herself how free she was. (*He pauses—then with a bitter repulsion*) It made home a lousy place. I felt like you did about it. I'd get feeling it was like living in a whorehouse—only worse, because she didn't have to make her living—

LARRY You bastard! She's your mother! Have you no shame?

PARRITT (*Bitterly*) No! She brought me up to believe that family-respect stuff is all bourgeois, property-owning crap. Why should I be ashamed?

LARRY (*Making a move to get up*) I've had enough!

PARRITT (*Catches his arm—pleadingly*) No! Don't leave me! Please! I promise I won't mention her again! (LARRY *sinks back in his chair*) I only did it to make you understand better. I know this isn't the place to— Why didn't you come up to my room, like I asked you? I kept waiting. We could talk everything over there.

LARRY There's nothing to talk over!

PARRITT But I've got to talk to you. Or I'll talk to Hickey. He won't let me alone! I feel he knows, anyway! And I know he'd understand, all right—in his way. But I hate his guts! I don't want anything to do with him! I'm scared of him, honest. There's something not human behind his damned grinning and kidding.

LARRY (*Starts*) Ah! You feel that, too?

PARRITT (*Pleadingly*) But I can't go on like this. I've got to decide what I've got to do. I've got to tell you, Larry!

LARRY (*Again starts up*) I won't listen!
PARRITT (*Again holds him by the arm*) All right! I won't. Don't go! (LARRY *lets himself be pulled down on his chair.* PARRITT *examines his face and becomes insultingly scornful*) Who do you think you're kidding? I know damned well you've guessed—
LARRY I've guessed nothing!
PARRITT But I want you to guess now! I'm glad you have! I know now, since Hickey's been after me, that I meant you to guess right from the start. That's why I came to you. (*Hurrying on with an attempt at a plausible frank air that makes what he says seem doubly false*) I want you to understand the reason. You see, I began studying American history. I got admiring Washington and Jefferson and Jackson and Lincoln. I began to feel patriotic and love this country. I saw it was the best government in the world, where everybody was equal and had a chance. I saw that all the ideas behind the Movement came from a lot of Russians like Bakunin and Kropotkin and were meant for Europe, but we didn't need them here in a democracy where we were free already. I didn't want this country to be destroyed for a damned foreign pipe dream. After all, I'm from old American pioneer stock. I began to feel I was a traitor for helping a lot of cranks and bums and free women plot to overthrow our government. And then I saw it was my duty to my country—
LARRY (*Nauseated—turns on him*) You stinking rotten liar! Do you think you can fool me with such hypocrite's cant! (*Then turning away*) I don't give a damn what you did! It's on your head—whatever it was! I don't want to know—and I won't know!
PARRITT (*As if* LARRY *had never spoken—falteringly*) But I never thought Mother would be caught. Please believe that, Larry. You know I never would have—
LARRY (*His face haggard, drawing a deep breath and closing his eyes—as if he were trying to hammer something into his own brain*) All I know is I'm sick of life! I'm through! I've forgotten myself! I'm drowned and contented on the bottom of a bottle. Honor or dishonor, faith or treachery are nothing to me but the opposites of the same stupidity which is ruler and king of life, and in the end they rot into dust in the same grave. All things are the same meaningless joke to me, for they grin at me from the one skull of death. So go away. You're wasting breath. I've forgotten your mother.
PARRITT (*Jeers angrily*) The old foolosopher, eh? (*He spits out contemptuously*) You lousy old faker!
LARRY (*So distracted he pleads weakly*) For the love of God, leave me in peace the little time that's left to me!

PARRITT Aw, don't pull that pitiful old-man junk on me! You old bastard, you'll never die as long as there's a free drink of whiskey left!
LARRY (*Stung—furiously*) Look out how you try to taunt me back into life, I warn you! I might remember the thing they call justice there, and the punishment for—(*He checks himself with an effort—then with a real indifference that comes from exhaustion*) I'm old and tired. To hell with you! You're as mad as Hickey, and as big a liar. I'd never let myself believe a word you told me.
PARRITT (*Threateningly*) The hell you won't! Wait till Hickey gets through with you! (PEARL *and* MARGIE *come in from the bar. At the sight of them,* PARRITT *instantly subsides and becomes self-conscious and defensive, scowling at them and then quickly looking away*)
MARGIE (*Eyes him jeeringly*) Why, hello, Tightwad Kid. Come to join de party? Gee, don't he act bashful, Poil?
PEARL Yeah. Especially wid his dough. (PARRITT *slinks to a chair at the left end of the table, pretending he hasn't heard them. Suddenly there is a noise of angry, cursing voices and a scuffle from the hall.* PEARL *yells*) Hey, Rocky! Fight in de hall! (ROCKY *and* CHUCK *run from behind the bar curtain and rush into the hall.* ROCKY'S *voice is heard in irritated astonishment,* "What de hell?" *and then the scuffle stops and* ROCKY *appears holding* CAPTAIN LEWIS *by the arm, followed by* CHUCK *with a similar hold on* GENERAL WETJOEN. *Although these two have been drinking they are both sober, for them. Their faces are sullenly angry, their clothes disarranged from the tussle*)
ROCKY (*Leading* LEWIS *forward—astonished, amused and irritated*) Can yuh beat it? I've heard youse two call each other every name yuh could think of but I never seen you— (*Indignantly*) A swell time to stage your first bout, on Harry's boithday party! What started de scrap?
LEWIS (*Forcing a casual tone*) Nothing, old chap. Our business, you know. That bloody ass, Hickey, made some insinuation about me, and the boorish Boer had the impertinence to agree with him.
WETJOEN Dot's a lie! Hickey made joke about me, and this Limey said yes, it was true!
ROCKY Well, sit down, de bot' of yuh, and cut out de rough stuff. (*He and* CHUCK *dump them down in adjoining chairs toward the left end of the table, where, like two sulky boys, they turn their backs on each other as far as possible in chairs which both face front*)
MARGIE (*Laughs*) Jees, lookit de two bums! Like a coupla kids! Kiss and make up, for Gawd's sakes!
ROCKY Yeah. Harry's party begins in a minute and we don't want no soreheads around.

LEWIS (*Stiffly*) Very well. In deference to the occasion, I apologize, General Wetjoen—provided that you do also.
WETJOEN (*Sulkily*) I apologize, Captain Lewis—because Harry is my goot friend.
ROCKY Aw, hell! If yuh can't do better'n dat—! (MOSHER *and* MCGLOIN *enter together from the hall. Both have been drinking but are not drunk*)
PEARL Here's de star boarders. (*They advance, their heads together, so interested in a discussion they are oblivious to everyone*)
MCGLOIN I'm telling you, Ed, it's serious this time. That bastard, Hickey, has got Harry on the hip. (*As he talks,* MARGIE, PEARL, ROCKY *and* CHUCK *prick up their ears and gather round.* CORA, *at the piano, keeps running through the tune, with soft pedal, and singing the chorus half under her breath, with* JOE *still correcting her mistakes. At the table,* LARRY, PARRITT, WILLIE, WETJOEN *and* LEWIS *sit motionless, staring in front of them.* HUGO *seems asleep in his habitual position*) And you know it isn't going to do us no good if he gets him to take that walk tomorrow.
MOSHER You're damned right. Harry'll mosey around the ward, dropping in on everyone who knew him when. (*Indignantly*) And they'll all give him a phony glad hand and a ton of good advice about what a sucker he is to stand for us.
MCGLOIN He's sure to call on Bessie's relations to do a little cryin' over dear Bessie. And you know what that bitch and all her family thought of me.
MOSHER (*With a flash of his usual humor—rebukingly*) Remember, Lieutenant, you are speaking of my sister! Dear Bessie wasn't a bitch. She was a God-damned bitch! But if you think my loving relatives will have time to discuss you, you don't know them. They'll be too busy telling Harry what a drunken crook I am and saying he ought to have me put in Sing Sing!
MCGLOIN (*Dejectedly*) Yes, once Bessie's relations get their hooks in him, it'll be as tough for us as if she wasn't gone.
MOSHER (*Dejectedly*) Yes, Harry has always been weak and easily influenced, and now he's getting old he'll be an easy mark for those grafters. (*Then with forced reassurance*) Oh, hell, Mac, we're saps to worry. We've heard Harry pull that bluff about taking a walk every birthday he's had for twenty years.
MCGLOIN (*Doubtfully*) But Hickey wasn't sicking him on those times. Just the opposite. He was asking Harry what he wanted to go out for when there was plenty of whiskey here.
MOSHER (*With a change to forced carelessness*) Well, after all, I don't care whether he goes out or not. I'm clearing out tomorrow morning

anyway. I'm just sorry for you, Mac.

MCGLOIN (*Resentfully*) You needn't be, then. Ain't I going myself? I was only feeling sorry for you.

MOSHER Yes, my mind is made up. Hickey may be a lousy, interfering pest, now he's gone teetotal on us, but there's a lot of truth in some of his bull. Hanging around here getting plastered with you, Mac, is pleasant, I won't deny, but the old booze gets you in the end, if you keep lapping it up. It's time I quit for a while. (*With forced enthusiasm*) Besides, I feel the call of the old carefree circus life in my blood again. I'll see the boss tomorrow. It's late in the season but he'll be glad to take me on. And won't all the old gang be tickled to death when I show up on the lot!

MCGLOIN Maybe—if they've got a rope handy!

MOSHER (*Turns on him—angrily*) Listen! I'm damned sick of that kidding!

MCGLOIN You are, are you? Well, I'm sicker of your kidding me about getting reinstated on the Force. And whatever you'd like, I can't spend my life sitting here with you, ruining my stomach with rotgut. I'm tapering off, and in the morning I'll be fresh as a daisy. I'll go and have a private chin with the Commissioner. (*With forced enthusiasm*) Man alive, from what the boys tell me, there's sugar galore these days, and I'll soon be ridin' around in a big red automobile—

MOSHER (*Derisively—beckoning an imaginary Chinese*) Here, One Lung Hop! Put fresh peanut oil in the lamp and cook the Lieutenant another dozen pills! It's his gowed-up night!

MCGLOIN (*Stung—pulls back a fist threateningly*) One more crack like that and I'll—!

MOSHER (*Putting up his fists*) Yes? Just start—! (CHUCK *and* ROCKY *jump between them*)

ROCKY Hey! Are you guys nuts? Jees, it's Harry's boithday party! (*They both look guilty*) Sit down and behave.

MOSHER (*Grumpily*) All right. Only tell him to lay off me. (*He lets* ROCKY *push him in a chair, at the right end of the table, rear*)

MCGLOIN (*Grumpily*) Tell him to lay off me. (*He lets* CHUCK *push him into the chair on* MOSHER's *left. At this moment* HICKEY *bursts in from the hall, bustling and excited*)

HICKEY Everything all set? Fine! (*He glances at his watch*) Half a minute to go. Harry's starting down with Jimmy. I had a hard time getting them to move! They'd rather stay hiding up there, kidding each other along. (*He chuckles*) Harry don't even want to remember it's his birthday now! (*He hears a noise from the stairs*) Here they come! (*Urgently*) Light the candles! Get ready to play, Cora! Stand up, everybody! Get that wine ready, Chuck and Rocky! (MARGIE *and* PEARL *light the candles on the cake.* CORA *gets her hands set over the piano keys, watching over her shoulder.* ROCKY *and* CHUCK *go in the bar. Everybody at the table stands up mechanically.* HUGO *is the last, suddenly coming to and scrambling to his feet.* HARRY HOPE *and* JIMMY TOMORROW *appear in the hall outside the door.* HICKEY *looks up from his watch*) On the dot! It's twelve! (*Like a cheer leader*) Come on now, everybody, with a Happy Birthday, Harry! (*With his voice leading they all shout "Happy Birthday, Harry!" in a spiritless chorus.* HICKEY *signals to* CORA, *who starts playing and singing in a whiskey soprano "She's the Sunshine of Paradise Alley."* HOPE *and* JIMMY *stand in the doorway. Both have been drinking heavily. In* HOPE *the effect is apparent only in a bristling, touchy, pugnacious attitude. It is entirely different from the usual irascible beefing he delights in and which no one takes seriously. Now he really has a chip on his shoulder.* JIMMY, *on the other hand, is plainly drunk, but it has not had the desired effect, for beneath a pathetic assumption of gentlemanly poise, he is obviously frightened and shrinking back within himself.* HICKEY *grabs* HOPE'S *hand and pumps it up and down. For a moment* HOPE *appears unconscious of this handshake. Then he jerks his hand away angrily*)

HOPE Cut out the glad hand, Hickey. D'you think I'm a sucker? I know you, bejees, you sneaking, lying drummer! (*With rising anger, to the others*) And all you bums! What the hell you trying to do, yelling and raising the roof? Want the cops to close the joint and get my license taken away? (*He yells at* CORA *who has stopped singing but continues to play mechanically with many mistakes*) Hey, you dumb tart, quit banging that box! Bejees, the least you could do is learn the tune!

CORA (*Stops—deeply hurt*) Aw, Harry! Jees, ain't I— (*Her eyes begin to fill*)

HOPE (*Glaring at the other girls*) And you two hookers, screaming at the top of your lungs! What d'you think this is, a dollar cathouse? Bejees, that's where you belong!

PEARL (*Miserably*) Aw, Harry— (*She begins to cry*)

MARGIE Jees, Harry, I never thought you'd say that—like yuh meant it. (*She puts her arm around* PEARL—*on the verge of tears herself*) Aw, don't bawl, Poil. He don't mean it.

HICKEY (*Reproachfully*) Now, Harry! Don't take it out on the gang because you're upset about yourself. Anyway, I've promised you you'll come through all right, haven't I? So quit worrying. (*He slaps* HOPE *on the back encouragingly.* HOPE *flashes him a glance of hate*) Be

yourself, Governor. You don't want to bawl out the old gang just when they're congratulating you on your birthday, do you? Hell, that's no way!
HOPE (*Looking guilty and shamefaced now—forcing an unconvincing attempt at his natural tone*) Bejees, they ain't as dumb as you. They know I was only kidding them. They know I appreciate their congratulations. Don't you, fellers? (*There is a listless chorus of "Sure, Harry," "Yes," "Of course we do," etc. He comes forward to the two girls, with* JIMMY *and* HICKEY *following him, and pats them clumsily*) Bejees, I like you broads. You know I was only kidding. (*Instantly they forgive him and smile affectionately*)
MARGIE Sure we know, Harry.
PEARL Sure.
HICKEY (*Grinning*) Sure. Harry's the greatest kidder in this dump and that's saying something! Look how he's kidded himself for twenty years! (*As* HOPE *gives him a bitter, angry glance, he digs him in the ribs with his elbow playfully*) Unless I'm wrong, Governor, and I'm betting I'm not. We'll soon know, eh? Tomorrow morning. No, by God, it's *this* morning now!
JIMMY (*With a dazed dread*) This morning?
HICKEY Yes, it's today at last, Jimmy. (*He pats him on the back*) Don't be so scared! I've promised I'll help you.
JIMMY (*Trying to hide his dread behind an offended, drunken dignity*) I don't understand you. Kindly remember I'm fully capable of settling my own affairs!
HICKEY (*Earnestly*) Well, isn't that exactly what I want you to do, settle with yourself once and for all? (*He speaks in his ear in confidential warning*) Only watch out on the booze, Jimmy. You know, not too much from now on. You've had a lot already, and you don't want to let yourself duck out of it by being too drunk to move—not this time! (JIMMY *gives him a guilty, stricken look and turns away and slumps into the chair on* MOSHER'S *right*)
HOPE (*To* MARGIE—*still guiltily*) Bejees, Margie, you know I didn't mean it. It's that lousy drummer riding me that's got my goat.
MARGIE I know.(*She puts a protecting arm around* HOPE *and turns him to face the table with the cake and presents*) Come on. You ain't noticed your cake yet. Ain't it grand?
HOPE (*Trying to brighten up*) Say, that's pretty. Ain't ever had a cake since Bessie— Six candles. Each for ten years, eh? Bejees, that's thoughtful of you.
PEARL It was Hickey got it.
HOPE (*His tone forced*) Well, it was thoughtful of him. He means

well, I guess. (*His eyes, fixed on the cake, harden angrily*) To hell with his cake. (*He starts to turn away.* PEARL *grabs his arm*)

PEARL Wait, Harry. Yuh ain't seen de presents from Margie and me and Cora and Chuck and Rocky. And dere's a watch all engraved wid your name and de date from Hickey.

HOPE To hell with it! Bejees, he can keep it! (*This time he does turn away*)

PEARL Jees, he ain't even goin' to look at our presents.

MARGIE (*Bitterly*) Dis is all wrong. We gotta put some life in dis party or I'll go nuts! Hey, Cora, what's de matter wid dat box? Can't yuh play for Harry? Yuh don't have to stop just because he kidded yuh!

HOPE (*Rouses himself—with forced heartiness*) Yes, come on, Cora. You was playing it fine. (CORA *begins to play half-heartedly.* HOPE *suddenly becomes almost tearfully sentimental*) It was Bessie's favorite tune. She was always singing it. It brings her back. I wish— (*He chokes up*)

HICKEY (*Grins at him—amusedly*) Yes, we've all heard you tell us you thought the world of her, Governor.

HOPE (*Looks at him with frightened suspicion*) Well, so I did, bejees! Everyone knows I did! (*Threateningly*) Bejees, if you say I didn't—

HICKEY (*Soothingly*) Now, Governor. I didn't say anything. You're the only one knows the truth about that. (HOPE *stares at him confusedly.* CORA *continues to play. For a moment there is a pause, broken by* JIMMY TOMORROW *who speaks with muzzy, self-pitying melancholy out of a sentimental dream*)

JIMMY Marjorie's favorite song was "Loch Lomond." She was beautiful and she played the piano beautifully and she had a beautiful voice. (*With gentle sorrow*) You were lucky, Harry. Bessie died. But there are more bitter sorrows than losing the woman one loves by the hand of death—

HICKEY (*With an amused wink at* HOPE) Now, listen, Jimmy, you needn't go on. We've all heard the story about how you came back to Cape Town and found her in the hay with a staff officer. We know you like to believe that was what started you on the booze and ruined your life.

JIMMY (*Stammers*) I—I'm talking to Harry. Will you kindly keep out of— (*With a pitiful defiance*) My life is not ruined!

HICKEY (*Ignoring this—with a kidding grin*) But I'll bet when you admit the truth to youself, you'll confess you were pretty sick of her hating you for getting drunk. I'll bet you were really damned relieved when she gave you such a good excuse. (JIMMY *stares at him strickenly.* HICKEY *pats him on the back again—with sincere sympathy*) I know how it is, Jimmy. I— (*He stops abruptly and for a second he seems to lose his self-assurance and become confused*)

LARRY (*Seizing on this with vindictive relish*) Ha! So that's what happened to you, is it? Your iceman joke finally came home to roost, did it? (*He grins tauntingly*) You should have remembered there's truth in the old superstition that you'd better look out what you call because in the end it comes to you!

HICKEY (*Himself again—grins to* LARRY *kiddingly*) Is that a fact, Larry? Well, well! Then you'd better watch out how you keep calling for that old Big Sleep! (LARRY *starts and for a second looks superstitiously frightened. Abruptly* HICKEY *changes to his jovial, bustling, master-of-ceremonies manner*) But what are we waiting for, boys and girls? Let's start the party rolling! (*He shouts to the bar*) Hey, Chuck and Rocky! Bring on the big surprise! Governor, you sit at the head of the table here. (*He makes* HARRY *sit down on the chair at the end of the table, right. To* MARGIE *and* PEARL) Come on, girls, sit down. (*They sit side by side on* JIMMY'S *right.* HICKEY *bustles down to the left end of table*) I'll sit here at the foot. (*He sits, with* CORA *on his left and* JOE *on her left.* ROCKY *and* CHUCK *appear from the bar, each bearing a big tray laden with schooners of champagne which they start shoving in front of each member of the party*)

ROCKY (*With forced cheeriness*) Real champagne, bums! Cheer up! What is dis, a funeral? Jees, mixin' champagne wid Harry's redeye will knock yuh paralyzed! Ain't yuh never satisfied? (*He and* CHUCK *finish serving out the schooners, grab the last two themselves and sit down in the two vacant chairs remaining near the middle of the table. As they do so,* HICKEY *rises, a schooner in his hand*)

HICKEY (*Rapping on the table for order when there is nothing but a dead silence*) Order! Order, Ladies and Gents! (*He catches* LARRY'S *eyes on the glass in his hand*) Yes, Larry, I'm going to drink with you this time. To prove I'm not teetotal because I'm afraid booze would make me spill my secrets, as you think. (LARRY *looks sheepish.* HICKEY *chuckles and goes on*) No, I gave you the simple truth about that. I don't need booze or anything else any more. But I want to be sociable and propose a toast in honor of our old friend, Harry, and drink it with you. (*His eyes fix on* HUGO, *who is out again, his head on his plate— To* CHUCK, *who is on* HUGO'S *left*) Wake up our demon bomb-tosser, Chuck. We don't want corpses at this feast.

CHUCK (*Gives* HUGO *a shake*) Hey Hugo, come up for air! Don't yuh see de champagne? (HUGO *blinks around and giggles foolishly*)

HUGO Ve vill eat birthday cake and trink champagne beneath the villow tree! (*He grabs his schooner and takes a greedy gulp—then sets it back on the table with a grimace of distaste—in a strange, arrogantly disdainful tone, as if he were rebuking a butler*) Dis vine is unfit to trink. It has not properly been iced.

HICKEY (*Amusedly*)   Always a high-toned swell at heart, eh, Hugo? God help us poor bums if you'd ever get to telling us where to get off! You'd have been drinking our blood beneath those willow trees! (*He chuckles,* HUGO *shrinks back in his chair, blinking at him, but* HICKEY *is now looking up the table at* HOPE. *He starts his toast, and as he goes on he becomes more moved and obviously sincere*) Here's the toast, Ladies and Gents! Here's to Harry Hope, who's been a friend in need to every one of us! Here's to the old Governor, the best sport and the kindest, biggest-hearted guy in the world! Here's wishing you all the luck there is, Harry, and long life and happiness! Come on, everybody! To Harry! Bottoms up! (*They have all caught his sincerity with eager relief. They raise their schooners with an enthusiastic chorus of* "Here's how, Harry!" "Here's luck, Harry!" *etc., and gulp half the wine down,* HICKEY *leading them in this*)

HOPE (*Deeply moved—his voice husky*)   Bejees, thanks, all of you. Bejees, Hickey, you old son of a bitch, that's white of you! Bejees, I know you meant it, too.

HICKEY (*Moved*)   Of course I meant it, Harry, old friend! And I mean it when I say I hope today will be the biggest day in your life, and in the lives of everyone here, the beginning of a new life of peace and contentment where no pipe dreams can ever nag at you again. Here's to that, Harry! (*He drains the remainder of his drink, but this time he drinks alone. In an instant the attitude of everyone has reverted to uneasy, suspicious defensiveness*)

ROCKY (*Growls*)   Aw, forget dat bughouse line of bull for a minute, can't yuh?

HICKEY (*Sitting down—good-naturedly*)   You're right, Rocky, I'm talking too much. It's Harry we want to hear from. Come on, Harry! (*He pounds his schooner on the table*) Speech! Speech! (*They try to recapture their momentary enthusiasm, rap their schooners on the table, call* "Speech," *but there is a hollow ring in it.* HOPE *gets to his feet reluctantly, with a forced smile, a smoldering resentment beginning to show in his manner*)

HOPE (*Lamely*)   Bejees, I'm no good at speeches. All I can say is thanks to everybody again for remembering me on my birthday. (*Bitterness coming out*) Only don't think because I'm sixty I'll be a bigger damned fool easy mark than ever! No, bejees! Like Hickey says, it's going to be a new day! This dump has got to be run like other dumps, so I can make some money and not just split even. People has got to pay what they owe me! I'm not running a damned orphan asylum for bums and crooks! Nor a God-damned hooker shanty, either! Nor an Old Men's Home for lousy Anarchist tramps that ought to be in jail! I'm sick of being played for a sucker! (*They stare at him with stunned, bewildered hurt. He goes on in a sort of furious desperation, as if he hated himself for every word he said, and yet couldn't stop*) And don't think you're kidding me right now, either! I know damned well you're giving me the laugh behind my back, thinking to yourselves, The old, lying, pipe-dreaming faker, we've heard his bull about taking a walk around the wards for years, he'll never make it! He's yellow, he ain't got the guts, he's scared he'll find out— (*He glares around at them almost with hatred*) But I'll show you, bejees! (*He glares at* HICKEY) I'll show you, too, you son of a bitch of a frying-pan-peddling bastard!

HICKEY (*Heartily encouraging*) That's the stuff, Harry! Of course you'll try to show me! That's what I want you to do! (HARRY *glances at him with helpless dread—then drops his eyes and looks furtively around the table. All at once he becomes miserably contrite*)

HOPE (*His voice catching*) Listen, all of you! Bejees, forgive me. I lost my temper! I ain't feeling well! I got a hell of a grouch on! Bejees, you know you're all as welcome here as the flowers in May! (*They look at him with eager forgiveness.* ROCKY *is the first one who can voice it*)

ROCKY Aw, sure, Boss, you're always aces wid us, see?

HICKEY (*Rises to his feet again. He addresses them now with the simple, convincing sincerity of one making a confession of which he is genuinely ashamed*) Listen, everybody! I know you are sick of my gabbing, but I think this is the spot where I owe it to you to do a little explaining and apologize for some of the rough stuff I've had to pull on you. I know how it must look to you. As if I was a damned busybody who was not only interfering in your private business, but even sicking some of you on to nag at each other. Well, I have to admit that's true, and I'm damned sorry about it. But it simply had to be done! You must believe that! You know old Hickey. I was never one to start trouble. But this time I had to—for your own good! I had to make you help me with each other. I saw I couldn't do what I was after alone. Not in the time at my disposal. I knew when I came here I wouldn't be able to stay with you long. I'm slated to leave on a trip. I saw I'd have to hustle and use every means I could. (*With a joking boastfulness*) Why, if I had enough time, I'd get a lot of sport out of selling my line of salvation to each of you all by my lonesome. Like it was fun in the old days, when I traveled house to house, to convince some dame, who was sicking the dog on me, her house wouldn't be properly furnished unless she bought another wash boiler. And I could do it with you, all right. I know every one of you, inside and out, by heart. I may have been drunk when I've been here before, but old Hickey could never be so drunk he didn't have to see through people. I mean, everyone except himself. And, finally, he had to see through himself, too. (*He pauses. They stare at him, bitter, uneasy and fascinated. His manner changes to deep earnestness*) But here's the point to get. I swear I'd never act like I have if I wasn't absolutely sure it will be worth it to you in the end, after you're rid of the damned guilt that makes you lie to yourselves you're something you're not, and the remorse that nags at you and makes you hide behind lousy pipe dreams about tomorrow. You'll be in a today where there is no yesterday or tomorrow to worry you. You won't give a damn what you are any more. I wouldn't say this unless I knew, Brothers and Sisters. This peace is real! It's a fact! I know! Because I've got it! Here! Now! Right in front of you! You see the difference in me! You remember how I used to be! Even when I had two quarts of rotgut under my belt and joked and sang "Sweet Adeline," I still felt like a guilty skunk. But you can all see that I don't give a damn about anything now. And I promise you, by the time this day is over, I'll have every one of you feeling the same way! (*He pauses. They stare at him fascinatedly. He adds with a grin*) I guess that'll be about all from me, boys and girls—for the present. So let's get on with the party. (*He starts to sit down*)

LARRY (*Sharply*) Wait! (*Insistently—with a sneer*) I think it would help us poor pipe-dreaming sinners along the sawdust trail to salvation if you told us now what it was happened to you that converted you to this great peace you've found. (*More and more with a deliberate, provocative taunting*) I notice you didn't deny it when I asked you about the iceman. Did this great revelation of the evil habit of dreaming about tomorrow come to you after you found your wife was sick of you? (*While he is speaking the faces of the gang have lighted up vindictively, as if all at once they saw a chance to revenge themselves. As he finishes, a chorus of sneering taunts begins, punctuated by nasty, jeering laughter*)

HOPE Bejees, you've hit it, Larry! I've noticed he hasn't shown her picture around this time!
MOSHER He hasn't got it! The iceman took it away from him!
MARGIE Jees, look at him! Who could blame her?
PEARL She must be hard up to fall for an iceman!
CORA Imagine a sap like him advisin' me and Chuck to git married!
CHUCK Yeah! He done so good wid it!
JIMMY At least I can say Marjorie chose an officer and a gentleman.

LEWIS Come to look at you, Hickey, old chap, you've sprouted horns like a bloody antelope!
WETJOEN Pigger, py Gott! Like a water buffalo's!
WILLIE (*Sings to his Sailor Lad tune*)

"Come up," she cried, "my iceman lad,
And you and I'll agree—"

(*They all join in a jeering chorus, rapping with knuckles or glasses on the table at the indicated spot in the lyric*)

"And I'll show you the prettiest (*Rap, rap, rap*)
That ever you did see!"

(A *roar of derisive, dirty laughter. But* HICKEY *has remained unmoved by all this taunting. He grins good-naturedly, as if he enjoyed the poke at his expense, and joins in the laughter*)

HICKEY Well, boys and girls, I'm glad to see you getting in good spirits for Harry's party, even if the joke is on me. I admit I asked for it by always pulling that iceman gag in the old days. So laugh all you like. (*He pauses. They do not laugh now. They are again staring at him with baffled uneasiness. He goes on thoughtfully*) Well, this forces my hand, I guess, your bringing up the subject of Evelyn. I didn't want to tell you yet. It's hardly an appropriate time. I meant to wait until the party was over. But you're getting the wrong idea about poor Evelyn, and I've got to stop that. (*He pauses again. There is a tense stillness in the room. He bows his head a little and says quietly*) I'm sorry to tell you my dearly beloved wife is dead. (A *gasp comes from the stunned company. They look away from him, shocked and miserably ashamed of themselves, except* LARRY *who continues to stare at him*)

LARRY (*Aloud to himself with a superstitious shrinking*) Be God, I felt he'd brought the touch of death on him! (*Then suddenly he is even more ashamed of himself than the others and stammers*) Forgive me, Hickey, I'd like to cut my dirty tongue out! (*This releases a chorus of shamefaced mumbles from the crowd.* "Sorry, Hickey." "I'm sorry, Hickey." "We're sorry, Hickey")

HICKEY (*Looking around at them—in a kindly, reassuring tone*) Now look here, everybody. You mustn't let this be a wet blanket on Harry's party. You're still getting me all wrong. There's no reason— You'll see, I don't feel any grief. (*They gaze at him startledly. He goes on with convincing sincerity*) I've got to feel glad, for her sake. Because she's at peace. She's rid of me at last. Hell, I don't have to tell you—you all know what I was like. You can imagine what she went through, married to a no-good cheater and drunk like I was. And there was no way out of it for her. Because she loved me. But now she is at peace like she always longed to be. So why should I feel sad? She wouldn't want me to feel sad. Why, all that Evelyn ever wanted out of life was to make me happy. (*He stops, looking around at them with a simple, gentle frankness. They stare at him in bewildered, incredulous confusion*)

Curtain

Act Three

SCENE *Barroom of* HARRY HOPE'S, *including a part of what had been the back room in Acts One and Two. In the right wall are two big windows, with the swinging doors to the street between them. The bar itself is at rear. Behind it is a mirror, covered with mosquito netting to keep off the flies, and a shelf on which are barrels of cheap whiskey with spiggots and a small show case of bottled goods. At left of the bar is the doorway to the hall. There is a table at left, front, of barroom proper, with four chairs. At right, front, is a small free-lunch counter, facing left, with a space between it and the window for the dealer to stand when he dishes out soup at the noon hour. Over the mirror behind the bar are framed photographs of Richard Croker and Big Tim Sullivan,*[20] *flanked by framed lithographs of John L. Sullivan and Gentleman Jim Corbett in ring costume.*

At left, in what had been the back room, with the dividing curtain drawn, the banquet table of Act Two has been broken up, and the tables are again in the crowded arrangement of Act One. Of these, we see one in the front row with five chairs at left of the barroom table, another with five chairs at left-rear of it, a third back by the rear wall with five chairs, and finally, at extreme left-front, one with four chairs, partly on and partly off stage, left.

---

[20] Influential Tammanyites of the turn of the century.

It is around the middle of the morning of HOPE's *birthday, a hot summer day. There is sunlight in the street outside, but it does not hit the windows and the light in the back-room section is dim.*

JOE MOTT *is moving around, a box of sawdust under his arm, strewing it over the floor. His manner is sullen, his face set in gloom. He ignores everyone. As the scene progresses, he finishes his sawdusting job, goes behind the lunch counter and cuts loaves of bread.* ROCKY *is behind the bar, wiping it, washing glasses, etc. He wears his working clothes, sleeves rolled up. He looks sleepy, irritable, and worried. At the barroom table, front,* LARRY *sits in a chair, facing right-front. He has no drink in front of him. He stares ahead, deep in harried thought. On his right, in a chair facing right,* HUGO *sits sprawled forward, arms and head on the table as usual, a whiskey glass beside his limp hand. At rear of the front table at left of them, in a chair facing left,* PARRITT *is sitting. He is staring in front of him in a tense, strained immobility.*

As the curtain rises, ROCKY *finishes his work behind the bar. He comes forward and drops wearily in the chair at right of* LARRY's *table, facing left.*

ROCKY Nuttin' now till de noon rush from de Market. I'm goin' to rest my fanny. (*Irritably*) If I ain't a sap to let Chuck kid me into workin' his time so's he can take de mornin' off. But I got sick of arguin' wid 'im. I says, "Aw right, git married! What's it to me?" Hickey's got de bot' of dem bugs. (*Bitterly*) Some party last night, huh? Jees, what a funeral! It was jinxed from de start, but his tellin' about his wife croakin' put de K.O. on it.

LARRY Yes, it turned out it wasn't a birthday feast but a wake!

ROCKY Him promisin' he'd cut out de bughouse bull about peace—and den he went on talkin' and talkin' like he couldn't stop! And all de gang sneakin' upstairs, leavin' free booze and eats like dey was poison! It didn't do dem no good if dey thought dey'd shake him. He's been hoppin' from room to room all night. Yuh can't stop him. He's got his Reform Wave goin' strong dis mornin'! Did yuh notice him drag Jimmy out de foist ting to get his laundry and his clothes pressed so he wouldn't have no excuse? And he give Willie de dough to buy his his stuff back from Solly's. And all de rest been brushin' and shavin' demselves wid de shakes—

LARRY (*Defiantly*) He didn't come to my room! He's afraid I might ask him a few questions.

ROCKY (*Scornfully*) Yeah? It don't look to me he's scared of yuh. I'd say you was scared of him.
LARRY (*Stung*) You'd lie, then!
PARRITT (*Jerks round to look at* LARRY—*sneeringly*) Don't let him kid you, Rocky. He had his door locked. I couldn't get in, either.
ROCKY Yeah, who d'yuh tink yuh're kiddin', Larry? He's showed you up, aw right. Like he says, if yuh was so anxious to croak, why wouldn't yuh hop off your fire escape long ago?
LARRY (*Defiantly*) Because it'd be a coward's quitting, that's why!
PARRITT He's all quitter, Rocky. He's a yellow old faker!
LARRY (*Turns on him*) You lying punk! Remember what I warned you—!
ROCKY (*Scowls at* PARRITT) Yeah, keep outta dis, you! Where d'yuh get a license to butt in? Shall I give him de bum's rush, Larry? If you don't want him around, nobody else don't.
LARRY (*Forcing an indifferent tone*) No. Let him stay. I don't mind him. He's nothing to me. (ROCKY *shrugs his shoulders and yawns sleepily*)
PARRITT You're right, I have nowhere to go now. You're the only one in the world I can turn to.
ROCKY (*Drowsily*) Yuh're a soft old sap, Larry. He's a no-good louse like Hickey. He don't belong. (*He yawns*) I'm all in. Not a wink of sleep. Can't keep my peepers open. (*His eyes close and his head nods.* PARRITT *gives him a glance and then gets up and slinks over to slide into the chair on* LARRY's *left, between him and* ROCKY. LARRY *shrinks away, but determinedly ignores him*)
PARRITT (*Bending toward him—in a low, ingratiating, apologetic voice*) I'm sorry for riding you, Larry. But you get my goat when you act as if you didn't care a damn what happened to me, and keep your door locked so I can't talk to you. (*Then hopefully*) But that was to keep Hickey out, wasn't it? I don't blame you. I'm getting to hate him. I'm getting more and more scared of him. Especially since he told us his wife was dead. It's that queer feeling he gives me that I'm mixed up with him some way. I don't know why, but it started me thinking about Mother—as if she was dead. (*With a strange undercurrent of something like satisfaction in his pitying tone*) I suppose she might as well be. Inside herself, I mean. It must kill her when she thinks of me—I know she doesn't want to, but she can't help it. After all, I'm her only kid. She used to spoil me and made a pet of me. Once in a great while, I mean. When she remembered me. As if she wanted to make up for something. As if she felt guilty. So she must have loved me a little, even if she never let it interfere with her freedom. (*With a*

strange pathetic wistfulness) Do you know, Larry, I once had a sneaking suspicion that maybe, if the truth was known, you were my father.

LARRY (*Violently*) You damned fool! Who put that insane idea in your head? You know it's a lie! Anyone in the Coast crowd could tell you I never laid eyes on your mother till after you were born.

PARRITT Well, I'd hardly ask them, would I? I know you're right, though, because I asked her. She brought me up to be frank and ask her anything, and she'd always tell me the truth. (*Abruptly*) But I was talking about how she must feel now about me. My getting through with the Movement. She'll never forgive that. The Movement is her life. And it must be the final knockout for her if she knows I was the one who sold—

LARRY Shut up, damn you!

PARRITT It'll kill her. And I'm sure she knows it must have been me. (*Suddenly with desperate urgency*) But I never thought the cops would get her! You've got to believe that! You've got to see what my only reason was! I'll admit what I told you last night was a lie—that bunk about getting patriotic and my duty to my country. But here's the true reason, Larry—the only reason! It was just for money! I got stuck on a whore and wanted dough to blow in on her and have a good time! That's all I did it for! Just money! Honest! (*He has the terrible grotesque air, in confessing his sordid baseness, of one who gives an excuse which exonerates him from any real guilt*)

LARRY (*Grabs him by the shoulder and shakes him*) God damn you, shut up! What the hell is it to me? (ROCKY *starts awake*)

ROCKY What's comin' off here?

LARRY (*Controlling himself*) Nothing. This gabby young punk was talking my ear off, that's all. He's a worse pest than Hickey.

ROCKY (*Drowsily*) Yeah, Hickey— Say, listen, what d'yuh mean about him bein' scared you'd ask him questions? What questions?

LARRY Well, I feel he's hiding something. You notice he didn't say what his wife died of.

ROCKY (*Rebukingly*) Aw, lay off dat. De poor guy— What are yuh gettin' at, anyway? Yuh don't tink it's just a gag of his?

LARRY I don't. I'm damned sure he's brought death here with him. I feel the cold touch of it on him.

ROCKY Aw, bunk! You got croakin' on de brain, Old Cemetery. (*Suddenly* ROCKY's *eyes widen*) Say! D'yuh mean yuh tink she committed suicide, 'count of his cheatin' or someting?

LARRY (*Grimly*) It wouldn't surprise me. I'd be the last to blame her.

ROCKY (*Scornfully*) But dat's crazy! Jees, if she'd done dat, he wouldn't tell us he was glad about it, would he? He ain't dat big a bastard.

PARRITT (*Speaks up from his own preoccupation—strangely*) You know better than that, Larry. You know she'd never commit suicide. She's like you. She'll hang on to life even when there's nothing left but—
LARRY (*Stung—turns on him viciously*) And how about you? Be God, if you had any guts or decency—! (*He stops guiltily*)
PARRITT (*Sneeringly*) I'd take that hop off your fire escape you're too yellow to take, I suppose?
LARRY (*As if to himself*) No! Who am I to judge? I'm done with judging.
PARRITT (*Tauntingly*) Yes, I suppose you'd like that, wouldn't you?
ROCKY (*Irritably mystified*) What de hell's all dis about? (*To* PARRITT) What d'you know about Hickey's wife? How d'yuh know she didn't—?
LARRY (*With forced belittling casualness*) He doesn't. Hickey's addled the little brains he's got. Shove him back to his own table, Rocky. I'm sick of him.
ROCKY (*To* PARRITT, *threateningly*) Yuh heard Larry? I'd like an excuse to give yuh a good punch in de snoot. So move quick!
PARRITT (*Gets up—to* LARRY) If you think moving to another table will get rid of me! (*He moves away—then adds with bitter reproach*) Gee, Larry, that's a hell of a way to treat me, when I've trusted you, and I need your help. (*He sits down in his old place and sinks into a wounded, self-pitying brooding*)
ROCKY (*Going back to his train of thought*) Jees, if she committed suicide, yuh got to feel sorry for Hickey, huh? Yuh can understand how he'd go bughouse and not be responsible for all de crazy stunts he's stagin' here. (*Then puzzledly*) But how can yuh be sorry for him when he says he's glad she croaked, and yuh can tell he means it? (*With weary exasperation*) Aw, nuts! I don't get nowhere tryin' to figger his game. (*His face hardening*) But I know dis. He better lay off me and my stable! (*He pauses—then sighs*) Jees, Larry, what a night dem two pigs give me! When de party went dead, dey pinched a coupla bottles and brung dem up deir room and got stinko. I don't get a wink of sleep, see? Just as I'd drop off on a chair here, dey'd come down lookin' for trouble. Or else dey'd raise hell upstairs, laughin' and singin', so I'd get scared dey'd get de joint pinched and go up to tell dem to can de noise. And every time dey'd crawl my frame wid de same old argument. Dey'd say, "So yuh agreed wid Hickey, do yuh, yuh dirty little Ginny? We're whores, are we? Well, we agree wid Hickey about you, see! Yuh're nuttin' but a lousy pimp!" Den I'd slap dem. Not beat 'em up, like a pimp would. Just slap dem. But it don't do no good. Dey'd keep at it over and over. Jees, I get de earache just thinkin'

of it! "Listen," dey'd say, "if we're whores we gotta right to have a reg'lar pimp and not stand for no punk imitation! We're sick of wearin' out our dogs poundin' sidewalks for a double-crossin' bartender, when all de thanks we get is he looks down on us. We'll find a guy who really needs us to take care of him and ain't ashamed of it. Don't expect us to work tonight, 'cause we won't, see? Not if de streets was blocked wid sailors! We're goin' on strike and yuh can like it or lump it!" (*He shakes his head*) Whores goin' on strike! Can yuh tie dat? (*Going on with his story*) Dey says, "We're takin' a holiday. We're goin' to beat it down to Coney Island and shoot the chutes and maybe we'll come back and maybe we won't. And you can go to hell!" So dey put on deir lids and beat it, de bot' of dem stinko. (*He sighs dejectedly. He seems grotesquely like a harried family man, henpecked and browbeaten by a nagging wife.* LARRY *is deep in his own bitter preoccupation and hasn't listened to him.* CHUCK *enters from the hall at rear. He has his straw hat with the gaudy band in his hand and wears a Sunday-best blue suit with a high stiff collar. He looks sleepy, hot, uncomfortable and grouchy*)

CHUCK (*Glumly*) Hey, Rocky. Cora wants a sherry flip. For her noives.

ROCKY (*Turns indignantly*) Sherry flip! Christ, she don't need nuttin' for her noive! What's she tink dis is, de Waldorf?

CHUCK Yeah, I told her, what would we use for sherry, and dere wasn't no egg unless she laid one. She says, "Is dere a law yuh can't go out and buy de makings, yuh big tramp?" (*Resentfully puts his straw hat on his head at a defiant tilt*) To hell wid her! She'll drink booze or nuttin'! (*He goes behind the bar to draw a glass of whiskey from a barrel*)

ROCKY (*Sarcastically*) Jees, a guy oughta give his bride anything she wants on de weddin' day, I should tink! (*As* CHUCK *comes from behind the bar,* ROCKY *surveys him derisively*) Pipe de bridegroom, Larry! All dolled up for de killin'! (LARRY *pays no attention*)

CHUCK Aw, shut up!

ROCKY One week on dat farm in Joisey, dat's what I give yuh! Yuh'll come runnin' in here some night yellin' for a shot of booze 'cause de crickets is after yuh! (*Disgustedly*) Jees, Chuck, dat louse Hickey's coitinly made a prize coupla suckers outa youse.

CHUCK (*Unguardedly*) Yeah. I'd like to give him one sock in de puss—just one! (*Then angrily*) Aw, can dat! What's he got to do wid it? Ain't we always said we was goin' to? So we're goin' to, see? And don't give me no argument! (*He stares at* ROCKY *truculently. But* ROCKY *only shrugs his shoulders with weary disgust and* CHUCK *subsides into complaining gloom*) If on'y Cora'd cut out de beefin'. She don't gimme a minute's rest all night. De same old stuff over and over! Do I really want to marry her? I says, "Sure, Baby, why not?" She says, "Yeah, but after a week yuh'll be tinkin' what a sap you was. Yuh'll make dat an excuse to go off on a periodical, and den I'll be tied for life to a no-good soak, and de foist ting I know yuh'll have me out hustlin' again, your own wife!" Den she'd bust out cryin', and I'd get sore. "Yuh're a liar," I'd say. "I ain't never taken your dough 'cept when I was drunk and not workin'!" "Yeah," she'd say, "and how long will yuh stay sober now? Don't tink yuh can kid me wid dat water-wagon bull! I've heard it too often." Dat'd make me sore and I'd say, "Don't call me a liar. But I wish I was drunk right now, because if I was, yuh wouldn't be keepin' me awake all night beefin'. If yuh opened your yap, I'd knock de stuffin' outa yuh!" Den she'd yell, "Dat's a sweet way to talk to de goil yuh're goin' to marry." (*He sighs explosively*) Jees, she's got me hangin' on de ropes! (*He glances with vengeful yearning at the drink of whiskey in his hand*) Jees, would I like to get a quart of dis redeye under my belt!

ROCKY Well, why de hell don't yuh?

CHUCK (*Instantly suspicious and angry*) Sure! You'd like dat, wouldn't yuh? I'm wise to you! Yuh don't wanta see me get married and settle down like a reg'lar guy! Yuh'd like me to stay paralyzed all de time, so's I'd be like you, a lousy pimp!

ROCKY (*Springs to his feet, his face hardened viciously*) Listen! I don't take dat even from you, see!

CHUCK (*Puts his drink on the bar and clenches his fists*) Yeah? Wanta make sometin' of it? (*Jeeringly*) Don't make me laugh! I can lick ten of youse wid one mit!

ROCKY (*Reaching for his hip pocket*) Not wid lead in your belly, yuh won't!

JOE (*Has stopped cutting when the quarrel started—expostulating*) Hey, you, Rocky and Chuck! Cut it out! You's ole friends! Don't let dat Hickey make you crazy!

CHUCK (*Turns on him*) Keep outa our business, yuh black bastard!

ROCKY (*Like* CHUCK, *turns on* JOE, *as if their own quarrel was forgotten and they became natural allies against an alien*) Stay where yuh belong, yuh doity nigger!

JOE (*Snarling with rage, springs from behind the lunch counter with the bread knife in his hand*) You white sons of bitches! I'll rip your guts out! (CHUCK *snatches a whiskey bottle from the bar and raises it above his head to hurl at* JOE. ROCKY *jerks a short-barreled, nickel-plated revolver from his hip pocket. At this moment* LARRY *pounds on the table with his fist and bursts into a sardonic laugh*)

LARRY That's it! Murder each other, you damned loons, with Hickey's blessing! Didn't I tell you he'd brought death with him? (*His inter-*

ruption startles them. They pause to stare at him, their fighting fury suddenly dies out and they appear deflated and sheepish)

ROCKY (*To* JOE) Aw right, you. Leggo dat shiv and I'll put dis gat away. (JOE *sullenly goes back behind the counter and slaps the knife on top of it.* ROCKY *slips the revolver back in his pocket.* CHUCK *lowers the bottle to the bar.* HUGO, *who has awakened and raised his head when* LARRY *pounded on the table, now giggles foolishly*)

HUGO Hello, leedle peoples! Neffer mind! Soon you vill eat hot dogs beneath the villow trees and trink free vine— (*Abruptly in a haughty fastidious tone*) The champagne vas not properly iced. (*With guttural anger*) Gottamned liar, Hickey! Does that prove I vant to be aristocrat? I love only the proletariat! I vill lead them! I vill be like a Gott to them! They vill be my slaves! (*He stops in bewildered self-amazement—to* LARRY *appealingly*) I am very trunk, no, Larry? I talk foolishness. I am so trunk, Larry, old friend, am I not, I don't know vhat I say?

LARRY (*Pityingly*) You're raving drunk, Hugo. I've never seen you so paralyzed. Lay your head down now and sleep it off.

HUGO (*Gratefully*) Yes. I should sleep. I am too crazy trunk. (*He puts his head on his arms and closes his eyes*)

JOE (*Behind the lunch counter—brooding superstitiously*) You's right, Larry. Bad luck come in de door when Hickey come. I's an ole gamblin' man and I knows bad luck when I feels it! (*Then defiantly*) But it's white man's bad luck. He can't jinx me! (*He comes from behind the counter and goes to the bar—addressing* ROCKY *stiffly*) De bread's cut and I's finished my job. Do I get de drink I's earned? (ROCKY *gives him a hostile look but shoves a bottle and glass at him.* JOE *pours a brimful drink—sullenly*) I's finished wid dis dump for keeps. (*He takes a key from his pocket and slaps it on the bar*) Here's de key to my room. I ain't comin' back. I's goin' to my own folks where I belong. I don't stay where I's not wanted. I's sick and tired of messin' round wid white men. (*He gulps down his drink—then looking around defiantly he deliberately throws his whiskey glass on the floor and smashes it*)

ROCKY Hey! What de hell—!

JOE (*With a sneering dignity*) I's on'y savin' you de trouble, White Boy. Now you don't have to break it, soon's my back's turned, so's no white man kick about drinkin' from de same glass. (*He walks stiffly to the street door—then turns for a parting shot—boastfully*) I's tired of loafin' 'round wid a lot of bums. I's a gamblin' man. I's gonna get in a big crap game and win me a big bankroll. Den I'll get de okay to open up my old gamblin' house for colored men. Den maybe I comes back here sometime to see de bums. Maybe I throw a twenty-dollar bill on de bar and say, "Drink it up," and listen when dey all pat me on de back and say, "Joe, you sure is white." But I'll say, "No, I'm black and my dough is black man's dough, and you's proud to drink wid me or you don't get no drink!" Or maybe I just says, "You can all go to hell. I don't lower myself drinkin' wid no white trash!" (*He opens the door to go out—then turns again*) And dat ain't no pipe dream! I'll git de money for my stake today, somehow, somewheres! If I has to borrow a gun and stick up some white man, I gets it! You wait and see! (*He swaggers out through the swinging doors*)

CHUCK (*Angrily*) Can yuh beat de noive of dat dinge! Jees, if I wasn't dressed up, I'd go out and mop up de street wid him!

ROCKY Aw, let him go, de poor old dope! Him and his gamblin' house! He'll be back tonight askin' Harry for his room and bummin' me for a ball. (*Vengefully*) Den I'll be de one to smash de glass. I'll loin him his place! (*The swinging doors are pushed open and* WILLIE OBAN *enters from the street. He is shaved and wears an expensive, well-cut suit, good shoes and clean linen. He is absolutely sober, but his face is sick, and his nerves in a shocking state of shakes*)

CHUCK Another guy all dolled up! Got your clothes from Solly's, huh, Willie? (*Derisively*) Now yuh can sell dem back to him again tomorrow.

WILLIE (*Stiffly*) No, I—I'm through with that stuff. Never again. (*He comes to the bar*)

ROCKY (*Sympathetically*) Yuh look sick, Willie. Take a ball to pick yuh up. (*He pushes a bottle toward him*)

WILLIE (*Eyes the bottle yearningly but shakes his head—determinedly*) No, thanks. The only way to stop is to stop. I'd have no chance if I went to the D.A.'s office smelling of booze.

CHUCK Yuh're really goin' dere?

WILLIE (*Stiffly*) I said I was, didn't I? I just came back here to rest a few minutes, not because I needed any booze. I'll show that cheap drummer I don't have to have any Dutch courage— (*Guiltily*) But he's been very kind and generous staking me. He can't help his insulting manner, I suppose. (*He turns away from the bar*) My legs are a bit shaky yet. I better sit down a while. (*He goes back and sits at the left of the second table, facing* PARRITT, *who gives him a scowling, suspicious glance and then ignores him.* ROCKY *looks at* CHUCK *and taps his head disgustedly.* CAPTAIN LEWIS *appears in the doorway from the hall*)

CHUCK (*Mutters*) Here's anudder one. (LEWIS *looks spruce and cleanshaven. His ancient tweed suit has been brushed and his frayed linen is clean. His manner is full of a forced, jaunty self-assurance. But he is sick and beset by katzenjammer*[21])

LEWIS Good morning, gentlemen all. (*He passes along the front of bar*

[21] A bad hangover.

to look out in the street) A jolly fine morning, too. (*He turns back to the bar*) An eyeopener? I think not. Not required, Rocky, old chum. Feel extremely fit, as a matter of fact. Though can't say I slept much, thanks to that interfering ass, Hickey, and that stupid bounder of a Boer. (*His face hardens*) I've had about all I can take from that fellow. It's my own fault, of course, for allowing a brute of a Dutch farmer to become familiar. Well, it's come to a parting of the ways now, and good riddance. Which reminds me, here's my key. (*He puts it on the bar*) I shan't be coming back. Sorry to be leaving good old Harry and the rest of you, of course, but I can't continue to live under the same roof with that fellow. (*He stops, stiffening into hostility as* WETJOEN *enters from the hall, and pointedly turns his back on him.* WETJOEN *glares at him sneeringly. He, too, has made an effort to spruce up his appearance, and his bearing has a forced swagger of conscious physical strength. Behind this, he is sick and feebly holding his booze-sodden body together*)

ROCKY (*To* LEWIS—*disgustedly putting the key on the shelf in back of the bar*) So Hickey's kidded the pants offa you, too? Yuh tink yuh're leavin' here, huh?

WETJOEN (*Jeeringly*) Ja! Dot's vhat he kids himself.

LEWIS (*Ignores him—airily*) Yes, I'm leaving, Rocky. But that ass, Hickey, has nothing to do with it. Been thinking things over. Time I turned over a new leaf, and all that.

WETJOEN He's going to get a job! Dot's what he says!

ROCKY What at, for Chris' sake?

LEWIS (*Keeping his airy manner*) Oh, anything. I mean, not manual labor, naturally, but anything that calls for a bit of brains and education. However humble. Beggars can't be choosers. I'll see a pal of mine at the Consulate. He promised any time I felt an energetic fit he'd get me a post with the Cunard—clark in the office or something of the kind.

WETJOEN Ja! At Limey Consulate they promise anything to get rid of him vhen he comes there tronk! They're scared to call the police and have him pinched because it vould scandal in the papers make about a Limey officer and chentleman!

LEWIS As a matter of fact, Rocky, I only wish a post temporarily. Means to an end, you know. Save up enough for a first-class passage home, that's the bright idea.

WETJOEN He's sailing back to home, sveet home! Dot's biggest pipe dream of all. What leetle brain the poor Limey has left, dot isn't in whiskey pickled, Hickey has made crazy! (LEWIS' *fists clench, but he manages to ignore this*)

CHUCK (*Feels sorry for* LEWIS *and turns on* WETJOEN—*sarcastically*) Hickey ain't made no sucker outa you, huh? You're too foxy, huh? But I'll bet you tink yuh're goin' out and land a job, too.
WETJOEN (*Bristles*) I am, ja. For me, it is easy. Because I put on no airs of chentleman. I am not ashamed to vork with my hands. I vas a farmer before the war ven ploody Limey thieves steal my country. (*Boastfully*) Anyone I ask for job can see vith one look I have the great strength to do work of ten ordinary mens.
LEWIS (*Sneeringly*) Yes, Chuck, you remember he gave a demonstration of his extraordinary muscles last night when he helped to move the piano.
CHUCK Yuh couldn't even hold up your corner. It was your fault de damned box almost fell down de stairs.
WETJOEN My hands vas sweaty! Could I help dot my hands slip? I could de whole veight of it lift! In old days in Transvaal, I lift loaded oxcart by the axle! So vhy shouldn't I get job? Dot longshoreman boss, Dan, he tell me any time I like, he take me on. And Benny from de Market he promise me same.
LEWIS You remember, Rocky, it was one of those rare occasions when the Boer that walks like a man—spelled with a double o, by the way—was buying drinks and Dan and Benny were stony. They'd bloody well have promised him the moon.
ROCKY Yeah, yuh big boob, dem boids was on'y kiddin' yuh.
WETJOEN (*Angrily*) Dot's lie! You vill see dis morning I get job! I'll show dot bloody Limey chentleman, and dot liar, Hickey! And I need vork only lettle vhile to save money for my passage home. I need not much money because I am not ashamed to travel steerage. I don't put on first-cabin airs! (*Tauntingly*) Und *I can* go home to my country! Vhen I get there, they vill let *me* come in!
LEWIS (*Grows rigid—his voice trembling with repressed anger*) There was a rumor in South Africa, Rocky, that a certain Boer officer—if you call the leaders of a rabble of farmers officers—kept advising Cronje to retreat and not stand and fight—
WETJOEN And I vas right! I vas right! He got surrounded at Paardeberg![22]
He had to surrender!
LEWIS (*Ignoring him*) Good strategy, no doubt, but a suspicion grew afterwards into a conviction among the Boers that the officer's caution was prompted by a desire to make his personal escape. His countrymen felt extremely savage about it, and his family disowned him. So I

[22] Boer war battle.

imagine there would be no welcoming committee waiting on the dock, nor delighted relatives making the veldt ring with their happy cries—

WETJOEN (*With guilty rage*) All lies! You Gottamned Limey— (*Trying to control himself and copy* LEWIS' *manner*) I also haf heard rumors of a Limey officer who, after the war, lost all his money gambling vhen he vas tronk. But they found out it vas regiment money, too, he lost—

LEWIS (*Loses his control and starts for him*) You bloody Dutch scum!

ROCKY (*Leans over the bar and stops* LEWIS *with a straight-arm swipe on the chest*) Cut it out! (*At the same moment* CHUCK *grabs* WETJOEN *and yanks him back*)

WETJOEN (*Struggling*) Let him come! I saw them come before—at Modder River, Magersfontein, Spion Kopje—waving their silly swords, so afraid they couldn't show off how brave they vas!—and I kill them vith my rifle so easy! (*Vindictively*) Listen to me, you Cecil! Often vhen I am tronk and kidding you I say I am sorry I missed you, but now, py Gott, I am sober, and I don't joke, and I say it!

LARRY (*Gives a sardonic guffaw—with his comically crazy, intense whisper*) Be God, you can't say Hickey hasn't the miraculous touch to raise the dead, when he can start the Boer War raging again! (*This interruption acts like a cold douche on* LEWIS *and* WETJOEN. *They subside, and* ROCKY *and* CHUCK *let go of them.* LEWIS *turns his back on the Boer*)

LEWIS (*Attempting a return of his jaunty manner, as if nothing had happened*) Well, time I was on my merry way to see my chap at the Consulate. The early bird catches the job, what? Good-bye and good luck, Rocky, and everyone. (*He starts for the street door*)

WETJOEN Py Gott, if dot Limey can go, I can go! (*He hurries after* LEWIS. *But* LEWIS, *his hand about to push the swinging doors open, hesitates, as though struck by a sudden paralysis of the will, and* WETJOEN *has to jerk back to avoid bumping into him. For a second they stand there, one behind the other, staring over the swinging doors into the street*)

ROCKY Well, why don't yuh beat it?

LEWIS (*Guiltily casual*) Eh? Oh, just happened to think. Hardly the decent thing to pop off without saying good-bye to old Harry. One of the best, Harry. And good old Jimmy, too. They ought to be down any moment. (*He pretends to notice* WETJOEN *for the first time and steps away from the door—apologizing as to a stranger*) Sorry. I seem to be blocking your way out.

WETJOEN (*Stiffly*) No. I vait to say good-bye to Harry and Jimmy, too. (*He goes to right of door behind the lunch counter and looks through the window, his back to the room.* LEWIS *takes up a similar stand at the window on the left of door*)

CHUCK Jees, can yuh beat dem simps! (*He picks up* CORA's *drink at the end of the bar*) Hell, I'd forgot Cora. She'll be trowin' a fit. (*He goes into the hall with the drink*)

ROCKY (*Looks after him disgustedly*) Dat's right, wait on her and spoil her, yuh poor sap! (*He shakes his head and begins to wipe the bar mechanically*)

WILLIE (*Is regarding* PARRITT *across the table from him with an eager, calculating eye. He leans over and speaks in a low confidential tone*) Look here, Parritt. I'd like to have a talk with you.

PARRITT (*Starts—scowling defensively*) What about?

WILLIE (*His manner becoming his idea of a crafty criminal lawyer's*) About the trouble you're in. Oh, I know. You don't admit it. You're quite right. That's my advice. Deny everything. Keep your mouth shut. Make no statements whatever without first consulting your attorney.

PARRITT Say! What the hell—?

WILLIE But you can trust me. I'm a lawyer, and it's just occurred to me you and I ought to co-operate. Of course I'm going to see the D.A. this morning about a job on his staff. But that may take time. There may not be an immediate opening. Meanwhile it would be a good idea for me to take a case or two, on my own, and prove my brilliant record in law school was no flash in the pan. So why not retain me as your attorney?

PARRITT You're crazy! What do I want with a lawyer?

WILLIE That's right. Don't admit anything. But you can trust me, so let's not beat about the bush. You got in trouble out on the Coast, eh? And now you're hiding out. Any fool can spot that. (*Lowering his voice still more*) You feel safe here, and maybe you are, for a while. But remember, they get you in the end. I know from my father's experience. No one could have felt safer than he did. When anyone mentioned the law to him, he nearly died laughing. But—

PARRITT You crazy mutt! (*Turning to* LARRY *with a strained laugh*) Did you get that, Larry? This damned fool thinks the cops are after me!

LARRY (*Bursts out with his true reaction before he thinks to ignore him*) I wish to God they were! And so should you, if you had the honor of a louse! (PARRITT *stares into his eyes guiltily for a second. Then he smiles sneeringly*)

PARRITT And you're the guy who kids himself he's through with the Movement! You old lying faker, you're still in love with it! (LARRY *ignores him again now*)

WILLIE (*Disappointedly*) Then you're not in trouble, Parritt? I was hoping— But never mind. No offense meant. Forget it.

PARRITT (*Condescendingly—his eyes on* LARRY) Sure. That's all right,

Willie. I'm not sore at you. It's that damned old faker that gets my goat. (*He slips out of his chair and goes quietly over to sit in the chair beside* LARRY *he had occupied before—in a low, insinuating, intimate tone*) I think I understand, Larry. It's really Mother you still love—isn't it?—in spite of the dirty deal she gave you. But hell, what did you expect? She was never true to anyone but herself and the Movement. But I understand how you can't help still feeling—because I still love her, too. (*Pleading in a strained, desperate tone*) You know I do, don't you? You must! So you see I couldn't have expected they'd catch her! You've got to believe me that I sold them out just to get a few lousy dollars to blow in on a whore. No other reason, honest! There couldn't possibly be any other reason! (*Again he has a strange air of exonerating himself from guilt by this shameless confession*)

LARRY (*Trying not to listen, has listened with increasing tension*) For the love of Christ will you leave me in peace! I've told you you can't make me judge you! But if you don't keep still, you'll be saying something soon that will make you vomit your own soul like a drink of nickel rotgut that won't stay down! (*He pushes back his chair and springs to his feet*) To hell with you! (*He goes to the bar*)

PARRITT (*Jumps up and starts to follow him—desperately*) Don't go, Larry! You've got to help me! (*But* LARRY *is at the bar, back turned, and* ROCKY *is scowling at him. He stops, shrinking back into himself helplessly, and turns away. He goes to the table where he had been before, and this time he takes the chair at rear facing directly front. He puts his elbows on the table, holding his head in his hands as if he had a splitting headache*)

LARRY Set 'em up, Rocky. I swore I'd have no more drinks on Hickey, if I died of drought, but I've changed my mind! Be God, he owes it to me, and I'd get blind to the world now if it was the Iceman of Death himself treating! (*He stops, startledly, a superstitious awe coming into his face*) What made me say that, I wonder. (*With a sardonic laugh*) Well, be God, it fits, for Death was the Iceman Hickey called to his home!

ROCKY Aw, forget dat iceman gag! De poor dame is dead. (*Pushing a bottle and glass at* LARRY) Gwan and get paralyzed! I'll be glad to see one bum in dis dump act natural. (LARRY *downs a drink and pours another*)

(ED MOSHER *appears in the doorway from the hall. The same change which is apparent in the manner and appearance of the others shows in him. He is sick, his nerves are shattered, his eyes are apprehensive, but he, too, puts on an exaggeratedly self-con-*

fident bearing. He saunters to the bar between LARRY *and the street entrance*)

MOSHER Morning, Rocky. Hello, Larry. Glad to see Brother Hickey hasn't corrupted you to temperance. I wouldn't mind a shot myself. (*As* ROCKY *shoves a bottle toward him he shakes his head*) But I remember the only breath-killer in this dump is coffee beans. The boss would never fall for that. No man can run a circus successfully who believes guys chew coffee beans because they like them. (*He pushes the bottle away*) No, much as I need one after the hell of a night I've had— (*He scowls*) That drummer son of a drummer! I had to lock him out. But I could hear him through the wall doing his spiel to someone all night long. Still at it with Jimmy and Harry when I came down just now. But the hardest to take was that flannel-mouth, flatfoot Mick trying to tell me where I got off! I had to lock him out, too. (*As he says this,* MCGLOIN *comes in the doorway from the hall. The change in his appearance and manner is identical with that of* MOSHER *and the others*)

MCGLOIN He's a liar, Rocky! It was me locked him out! (MOSHER *starts to flare up—then ignores him. They turn their backs on each other.* MCGLOIN *starts into the back-room section*)

WILLIE Come and sit here, Mac. You're just the man I want to see. If I'm to take your case, we ought to have a talk before we leave.

MCGLOIN (*Contemptuously*) We'll have no talk. You damned fool, do you think I'd have your father's son for my lawyer? They'd take one look at you and bounce us both out on our necks! (WILLIE *winces and shrinks down in his chair.* MCGLOIN *goes to the first table beyond him and sits with his back to the bar*) I don't need a lawyer, anyway. To hell with the law! All I've got to do is see the right ones and get them to pass the word. They will, too. They know I was framed. And once they've passed the word, it's as good as done, law or no law.

MOSHER God, I'm glad I'm leaving this madhouse! (*He pulls his key from his pocket and slaps it on the bar*) Here's my key, Rocky.

MCGLOIN (*Pulls his from his pocket*) And here's mine. (*He tosses it to* ROCKY) I'd rather sleep in the gutter than pass another night under the same roof with that loon, Hickey, and a lying circus grifter! (*He adds darkly*) And if that hat fits anyone here, let him put it on! (MOSHER *turns toward him furiously but* ROCKY *leans over the bar and grabs his arm*)

ROCKY Nix! Take it easy! (MOSHER *subsides.* ROCKY *tosses the keys on the shelf—disgustedly*) You boids gimme a pain. It'd soive you right if I wouldn't give de keys back to yuh tonight. (*They both turn on him resentfully, but there is an interruption as* CORA *appears in the doorway from the hall with* CHUCK *behind her. She is drunk, dressed in her gaudy best, her face plastered with rouge and mascara, her hair a bit disheveled, her hat on anyhow*)

CORA (*Comes a few steps inside the bar—with a strained bright giggle*) Hello, everybody! Here we go! Hickey just told us, ain't it time we beat it, if we're really goin'. So we're showin' de bastard, ain't we, Honey? He's comin' right down wid Harry and Jimmy. Jees, dem two look like dey was goin' to de electric chair! (*With frightened anger*) If I had to listen to any more of Hickey's bunk, I'd brain him. (*She puts her hand on* CHUCK'S *arm*) Come on, Honey. Let's get started before he comes down.

CHUCK (*Sullenly*) Sure, anyting yuh say, Baby.

CORA (*Turns on him truculently*) Yeah? Well, I say we stop at de foist reg'lar dump and yuh gotta blow me to a sherry flip—or four or five, if I want 'em!—or all bets is off!

CHUCK Aw, yuh got a fine bun on now!

CORA Cheap skate! I know what's eatin' you, Tightwad! Well, use my dough, den, if yuh're so stingy. Yuh'll grab it all, anyway, right after de ceremony. I know you! (*She hikes her skirt up and reaches inside the top of her stocking*) Here, yuh big tramp!

CHUCK (*Knocks her hand away—angrily*) Keep your lousy dough! And don't show off your legs to dese bums when yuh're goin' to be married, if yuh don't want a sock in de puss!

CORA (*Pleased—meekly*) Aw right, Honey. (*Looking around with a foolish laugh*) Say, why don't all you barflies come to de weddin'? (*But they are all sunk in their own apprehensions and ignore her. She hesitates, miserably uncertain*) Well, we're goin', guys. (*There is no comment. Her eyes fasten on* ROCKY—*desperately*) Say, Rocky, yuh gone deef? I said me and Chuck was goin' now.

ROCKY (*Wiping the bar—with elaborate indifference*) Well, good-bye. Give my love to Joisey.

CORA (*Tearfully indignant*) Ain't yuh goin' to wish us happiness, yuh doity little Ginny?

ROCKY Sure. Here's hopin' yuh don't moider each odder before next week.

CHUCK (*Angrily*) Aw, Baby, what d'we care for dat pimp? (ROCKY *turns on him threateningly, but* CHUCK *hears someone upstairs in the hall and grabs* CORA'S *arm*) Here's Hickey comin'! Let's get outa here! (*They hurry into the hall. The street door is heard slamming behind them*)

ROCKY (*Gloomily pronounces an obituary*) One regular guy and one all-right tart gone to hell! (*Fiercely*) Dat louse Hickey oughta be croaked! (*There is a muttered growl of assent from most of the gathering. Then*

· *The Iceman Cometh* [ACT THREE]

HARRY HOPE *enters from the hall, followed by* JIMMY TOMORROW, *with* HICKEY *on his heels.* HOPE *and* JIMMY *are both putting up a front of self-assurance, but* CORA'S *description of them was apt. There is a desperate bluff in their manner as they walk in, which suggests the last march of the condemned.* HOPE *is dressed in an old black Sunday suit, black tie, shoes, socks, which give him the appearance of being in mourning.* JIMMY'S *clothes are pressed, his shoes shined, his white linen immaculate. He has a hangover and his gently appealing dog's eyes have a boiled look.* HICKEY'S *face is a bit drawn from lack of sleep and his voice is hoarse from continual talking, but his bustling energy appears nervously intensified, and his beaming expression is one of triumphant accomplishment*)

HICKEY Well, here we are! We've got this far, at least! (*He pats* JIMMY *on the back*) Good work, Jimmy. I told you you weren't half as sick as you pretended. No excuse whatever for postponing—

JIMMY I'll thank you to keep your hands off me! I merely mentioned I would feel more fit tomorrow. But it might as well be today, I suppose.

HICKEY Finish it now, so it'll be dead forever, and you can be free! (*He passes him to clap* HOPE *encouragingly on the shoulder*) Cheer up, Harry. You found your rheumatism didn't bother you coming downstairs, didn't you? I told you it wouldn't. (*He winks around at the others. With the exception of* HUGO *and* PARRITT, *all their eyes are fixed on him with bitter animosity. He gives* HOPE *a playful nudge in the ribs*) You're the damnedest one for alibis, Governor! As bad as Jimmy!

HOPE (*Putting on his deaf manner*) Eh? I can't hear— (*Defiantly*) You're a liar! I've had rheumatism on and off for twenty years. Ever since Bessie died. Everybody knows that.

HICKEY Yes, we know it's the kind of rheumatism you turn on and off! We're on to you, you old faker! (*He claps him on the shoulder again, chuckling*)

HOPE (*Looks humiliated and guilty—by way of escape he glares around at the others*) Bejees, what are all you bums hanging round staring at me for? Think you was watching a circus! Why don't you get the hell out of here and 'tend to your own business, like Hickey's told you? (*They look at him reproachfully, their eyes hurt. They fidget as if trying to move*)

HICKEY Yes, Harry, I certainly thought they'd have had the guts to be gone by this time. (*He grins*) Or maybe I did have my doubts. (*Abruptly he becomes sincerely sympathetic and earnest*) Because I know exactly what you're up against, boys. I know how damned yellow a man can be when it comes to making himself face the truth. I've been through the mill, and I had to face a worse bastard in myself than any of you will have to in yourselves. I know you become such a coward you'll grab at any lousy excuse to get out of killing your pipe dreams. And yet, as I've told you over and over, it's exactly those damned tomorrow dreams which keep you from making peace with yourself. So you've got to kill them like I did mine. (*He pauses. They glare at him with fear and hatred. They seem about to curse him, to spring at him. But they remain silent and motionless. His manner changes and he becomes kindly bullying*) Come on, boys! Get moving! Who'll start the ball rolling? You, Captain, and you, General. You're nearest the door. And besides, you're old war heroes! You ought to lead the forlorn hope! Come on, now, show us a little of that good old battle of Modder River spirit we've heard so much about! You can't hang around all day looking as if you were scared the street outside would bite you!

LEWIS (*Turns with humiliated rage—with an attempt at jaunty casualness*) Right you are, Mister Bloody Nosey Parker! Time I pushed off. Was only waiting to say good-bye to you, Harry, old chum.

HOPE (*Dejectedly*) Good-bye, Captain. Hope you have luck.

LEWIS Oh, I'm bound to, Old Chap, and the same to you. (*He pushes the swinging doors open and makes a brave exit, turning to his right and marching off outside the window at right of door*)

WETJOEN Py Gott, if dot Limey can, I can! (*He pushes the door open and lumbers through it like a bull charging an obstacle. He turns left and disappears off rear, outside the farthest window*)

HICKEY (*Exhortingly*) Next? Come on, Ed. It's a fine summer's day and the call of the old circus lot must be in your blood! (MOSHER *glares at him, then goes to the door.* MCGLOIN *jumps up from his chair and starts moving toward the door.* HICKEY *claps him on the back as he passes*) That's the stuff, Mac.

MOSHER Good-bye, Harry. (*He goes out, turning right outside*)

MCGLOIN (*Glowering after him*) If that crooked grifter has the guts— (*He goes out, turning left outside.* HICKEY *glances at* WILLIE *who, before he can speak, jumps from his chair*)

WILLIE Good-bye, Harry, and thanks for all the kindness.

HICKEY (*Claps him on the back*) That's the way, Willie! The D.A.'s a busy man. He can't wait all day for you, you know. (WILLIE *hurries to the door*)

HOPE (*Dully*) Good luck, Willie. (WILLIE *goes out and turns right outside. While he is doing so,* JIMMY, *in a sick panic, sneaks to the bar and furtively reaches for* LARRY's *glass of whiskey*)

HICKEY And now it's your turn, Jimmy, old pal. (*He sees what* JIMMY *is at and grabs his arm just as he is about to down the drink*) Now, now,

Jimmy! You can't do that to yourself. One drink on top of your hangover and an empty stomach and you'll be orey-eyed. Then you'll tell yourself you wouldn't stand a chance if you went up soused to get your old job back.

JIMMY (*Pleads abjectly*) Tomorrow! I will tomorrow! I'll be in good shape tomorrow! (*Abruptly getting control of himself—with shaken firmness*) All right. I'm going. Take your hands off me.

HICKEY That's the ticket! You'll thank me when it's all over.

JIMMY (*In a burst of futile fury*) You dirty swine! (*He tries to throw the drink in* HICKEY's *face, but his aim is poor and it lands on* HICKEY's *coat.* JIMMY *turns and dashes through the door, disappearing outside the window at right of door*)

HICKEY (*Brushing the whiskey off his coat—humorously*) All set for an alcohol rub! But no hard feelings. I know how he feels. I wrote the book. I've seen the day when if anyone forced me to face the truth about my pipe dreams, I'd have shot them dead. (*He turns to* HOPE—*encouragingly*) Well, Governor, Jimmy made the grade. It's up to you. If he's got the guts to go through with the test, then certainly you—

LARRY (*Bursts out*) Leave Harry alone, damn you!

HICKEY (*Grins at him*) I'd make up my mind about myself if I was you, Larry, and not bother over Harry. He'll come through all right. I've promised him that. He doesn't need anyone's bum pity. Do you, Governor?

HOPE (*With a pathetic attempt at his old fuming assertiveness*) No, bejees! Keep your nose out of this, Larry. What's Hickey got to do with it? I've always been going to take this walk, ain't I? Bejees, you bums want to keep me locked up in here 's if I was in jail! I've stood it long enough! I'm free, white and twenty-one, and I'll do as I damned please, bejees! You keep your nose out, too, Hickey! You'd think you was boss of this dump, not me. Sure, I'm all right! Why shouldn't I be? What the hell's to be scared of, just taking a stroll around my own ward? (*As he talks he has been moving toward the door. Now he reaches it*) What's the weather like outside, Rocky?

ROCKY Fine day, Boss.

HOPE What's that? Can't hear you. Don't look fine to me. Looks 's if it'd pour down cats and dogs any minute. My rheumatism— (*He catches himself*) No, must be my eyes. Half blind, bejees. Makes things look black. I see now it's a fine day. Too damned hot for a walk, though, if you ask me. Well, do me good to sweat the booze out of me. But I'll have to watch out for the damned automobiles. Wasn't none of them around the last time, twenty years ago. From what I've seen of 'em through the window, they'd run over you as soon as look at you.

Not that I'm scared of 'em. I can take care of myself. (*He puts a reluctant hand on the swinging door*) Well, so long— (*He stops and looks back—with frightened irascibility*) Bejees, where are you, Hickey? It's time we got started.

HICKEY (*Grins and shakes his head*) No, Harry. Can't be done. You've got to keep a date with yourself alone.

HOPE (*With forced fuming*) Hell of a guy, you are! Thought you'd be willing to help me across the street, knowing I'm half blind. Half deaf, too. Can't bear those damned automobiles. Hell with you! Bejees, I've never needed no one's help and I don't now! (*Egging himself on*) I'll take a good long walk now I've started. See all my old friends. Bejees, they must have given me up for dead. Twenty years is a long time. But they know it was grief over Bessie's death that made me— (*He puts his hand on the door*) Well, the sooner I get started— (*Then he drops his hand—with sentimental melancholy*) You know, Hickey, that's what gets me. Can't help thinking the last time I went out was to Bessie's funeral. After she'd gone, I didn't feel life was worth living. Swore I'd never go out again. (*Pathetically*) Somehow, I can't feel it's right for me to go, Hickey, even now. It's like I was doing wrong to her memory.

HICKEY Now, Governor, you can't let yourself get away with that one any more!

HOPE (*Cupping his hand to his ear*) What's that? Can't hear you. (*Sentimentally again but with desperation*) I remember now clear as day the last time before she— It was a fine Sunday morning. We went out to church together. (*His voice breaks on a sob*)

HICKEY (*Amused*) It's a great act, Governor. But I know better, and so do you. You never did want to go to church or any place else with her. She was always on your neck, making you have ambition and go out and do things, when all you wanted was to get drunk in peace.

HOPE (*Falteringly*) Can't hear a word you're saying. You're a Goddamned liar, anyway! (*Then in a sudden fury, his voice trembling with hatred*) Bejees, you son of a bitch, if there was a mad dog outside I'd go and shake hands with it rather than stay here with you! (*The momentum of his fit of rage does it. He pushes the door open and strides blindly out into the street and as blindly past the window behind the free-lunch counter*)

ROCKY (*In amazement*) Jees, he made it! I'd give yuh fifty to one he'd never— (*He goes to the end of the bar to look through the window— disgustedly*) Aw, he's stopped. I'll bet yuh he's comin' back.

HICKEY Of course, he's coming back. So are all the others. By tonight they'll all be here again. You dumbbell, that's the whole point.

ROCKY (*Excitedly*) No, he ain't neider! He's gone to de coib. He's lookin' up and down. Scared stiff of automobiles. Jees, dey ain't more'n two an hour comes down dis street, de old boob! (*He watches excitedly, as if it were a race he had a bet on, oblivious to what happens in the bar*)

LARRY (*Turns on* HICKEY *with bitter defiance*) And now it's my turn, I suppose? What is it I'm to do to achieve this blessed peace of yours?

HICKEY (*Grins at him*) Why, we've discussed all that, Larry. Just stop lying to yourself—

LARRY You think when I say I'm finished with life, and tired of watching the stupid greed of the human circus, and I'll welcome closing my eyes in the long sleep of death—you think that's a coward's lie?

HICKEY (*Chuckling*) Well, what do you think, Larry?

LARRY (*With increasing bitter intensity, more as if he were fighting with himself than with* HICKEY) I'm afraid to live, am I?—and even more afraid to die! So I sit here, with my pride drowned on the bottom of a bottle, keeping drunk so I won't see myself shaking in my britches with fright, or hear myself whining and praying: Beloved Christ, let me live a little longer at any price! If it's only for a few days more, or a few hours even, have mercy, Almighty God, and let me still clutch greedily to my yellow heart this sweet treasure, this jewel beyond price, the dirty, stinking bit of withered old flesh which is my beautiful little life! (*He laughs with a sneering, vindictive self-loathing, staring inward at himself with contempt and hatred. Then abruptly he makes* HICKEY *again the antagonist*) You think you'll make me admit that to myself?

HICKEY (*Chuckling*) But you just did admit it, didn't you?

PARRITT (*Lifts his head from his hands to glare at* LARRY—*jeeringly*) That's the stuff, Hickey! Show the old yellow faker up! He can't play dead on me like this! He's got to help me!

HICKEY Yes, Larry, you've got to settle with him. I'm leaving you entirely in his hands. He'll do as good a job as I could at making you give up that old grandstand bluff.

LARRY (*Angrily*) I'll see the two of you in hell first!

ROCKY (*Calls excitedly from the end of the bar*) Jees, Harry's startin' across de street! He's goin' to fool yuh, Hickey, yuh bastard! (*He pauses, watching—then worriedly*) What de hell's he stoppin' for? Right in de middle of de street! Yuh'd tink he was paralyzed or somethin'! (*Disgustedly*) Aw, he's quittin'! He's turned back! Jees, look at de old bastard travel! Here he comes! (HOPE *passes the window outside the free-lunch counter in a shambling, panic-stricken run. He comes lurching blindly through the swinging doors and stumbles to the bar at* LARRY's *right*)

HOPE Bejees, give me a drink quick! Scared me out of a year's growth! Bejees, that guy ought to be pinched! Bejees, it ain't safe to walk in the streets! Bejees, that ends me! Never again! Give me that bottle! (*He slops a glass full and drains it and pours another*— *To* ROCKY, *who is regarding him with scorn—appealingly*) You seen it, didn't you, Rocky?

ROCKY Seen what?

HOPE That automobile, you dumb Wop! Feller driving it must be drunk or crazy. He'd run right over me if I hadn't jumped. (*Ingratiatingly*) Come on, Larry, have a drink. Everybody have a drink. Have a cigar, Rocky. I know you hardly ever touch it.

ROCKY (*Resentfully*) Well, dis is de time I do touch it! (*Pouring a drink*) I'm goin' to get stinko, see! And if yuh don't like it, yuh know what yuh can do! I gotta good mind to chuck my job, anyways. (*Disgustedly*) Jees, Harry, I thought yuh had some guts! I was bettin' yuh'd make it and show dat four-flusher up. (*He nods at* HICKEY—*then snorts*) Automobile, hell! Who d'yuh tink yuh're kiddin'? Dey wasn' no automobile! Yuh just quit cold!

HOPE (*Feebly*) Guess I ought to know! Bejees, it almost killed me!

HICKEY (*Comes to the bar between him and* LARRY, *and puts a hand on his shoulder—kindly*) Now, now, Governor. Don't be foolish. You've faced the test and come through. You're rid of all that nagging dream stuff now. You know you can't believe it any more.

HOPE (*Appeals pleadingly to* LARRY) Larry, you saw it, didn't you? Drink up! Have another! Have all you want! Bejees, we'll go on a grand old souse together! You saw that automobile, didn't you?

LARRY (*Compassionately, avoiding his eyes*) Sure, I saw it, Harry. You had a narrow escape. Be God, I thought you were a goner!

HICKEY (*Turns on him with a flash of sincere indignation*) What the hell's the matter with you, Larry? You know what I told you about the wrong kind of pity. Leave Harry alone! You'd think I was trying to harm him, the fool way you act! My oldest friend! What kind of a louse do you think I am? There isn't anything I wouldn't do for Harry, and he knows it! All I've wanted to do is fix it so he'll be finally at peace with himself for the rest of his days! And if you'll only wait until the final returns are in, you'll find that's exactly what I've accomplished! (*He turns to* HOPE *and pats his shoulder—coaxingly*) Come now, Governor. What's the use of being stubborn, now when it's all over and dead? Give up that ghost automobile.

HOPE (*Beginning to collapse within himself—dully*) Yes, what's the use —now? All a lie! No automobile. But, bejees, something ran over me! Must have been myself, I guess. (*He forces a feeble smile—then wearily*)

Guess I'll sit down. Feel all in. Like a corpse, bejees. (*He picks a bottle and glass from the bar and walks to the first table and slumps down in the chair, facing left-front. His shaking hand misjudges the distance and he sets the bottle on the table with a jar that rouses* HUGO, *who lifts his head from his arms and blinks at him through his thick spectacles.* HOPE *speaks to him in a flat, dead voice*) Hello, Hugo. Coming up for air? Stay passed out, that's the right dope. There ain't any cool willow trees—except you grow your own in a bottle. (*He pours a drink and gulps it down*)

HUGO (*With his silly giggle*) Hello, Harry, stupid proletarian monkey-face! I vill trink champagne beneath the villow— (*With a change to aristocratic fastidiousness*) But the slaves must ice it properly! (*With guttural rage*) Gottamned Hickey! Peddler pimp for nouveau-riche capitalism! Vhen I lead the jackass mob to the sack of Babylon, I vill make them hang him to a lamppost the first one!

HOPE (*Spiritlessly*) Good work. I'll help pull on the rope. Have a drink, Hugo.

HUGO (*Frightenedly*) No, thank you. I am too trunk now. I hear myself say crazy things. Do not listen, please. Larry vill tell you I haf never been so crazy trunk. I must sleep it off. (*He starts to put his head on his arms but stops and stares at* HOPE *with growing uneasiness*) Vhat's matter, Harry? You look funny. You look dead. Vhat's happened? I don't know you. Listen, I feel I am dying, too. Because I am so crazy trunk! It is very necessary I sleep. But I can't sleep here with you. You look dead. (*He scrambles to his feet in a confused panic, turns his back on* HOPE *and settles into the chair at the next table which faces left. He thrusts his head down on his arms like an ostrich hiding its head in the sand. He does not notice* PARRITT, *nor* PARRITT *him*)

LARRY (*To* HICKEY *with bitter condemnation*) Another one who's begun to enjoy your peace!

HICKEY Oh, I know it's tough on him right now, the same as it is on Harry. But that's only the first shock. I promise you they'll both come through all right.

LARRY And you believe that! I see you do! You mad fool!

HICKEY Of course, I believe it! I tell you I know from my own experience!

HOPE (*Spiritlessly*) Close that big clam of yours, Hickey. Bejees, you're a worse gabber than that nagging bitch, Bessie, was. (*He drinks his drink mechanically and pours another*)

ROCKY (*In amazement*) Jees, did yuh hear dat?

HOPE (*Dully*) What's wrong with this booze? There's no kick in it.

ROCKY (*Worriedly*) Jees, Larry, Hugo had it right. He does look like he'd croaked.

HICKEY (*Annoyed*) Don't be a damned fool! Give him time. He's coming along all right. (*He calls to* HOPE *with a first trace of underlying uneasiness*) You're all right, aren't you, Harry?

HOPE (*Dully*) I want to pass out like Hugo.

LARRY (*Turns to* HICKEY—*with bitter anger*) It's the peace of death you've brought him.

HICKEY (*For the first time loses his temper*) That's a lie! (*But he controls this instantly and grins*) Well, well, you did manage to get a rise out of me that time. I think such a hell of a lot of Harry— (*Impatiently*) You know that's damned foolishness. Look at me. I've been through it. Do I look dead? Just leave Harry alone and wait until the shock wears off and you'll see. He'll be a new man. Like I am. (*He calls to* HOPE *coaxingly*) How's it coming, Governor? Beginning to feel free, aren't you? Relieved and not guilty any more?

HOPE (*Grumbles spiritlessly*) Bejees, you must have been monkeying with the booze, too, you interfering bastard! There's no life in it now. I want to get drunk and pass out. Let's all pass out. Who the hell cares?

HICKEY (*Lowering his voice—worriedly to* LARRY) I admit I didn't think he'd be hit so hard. He's always been a happy-go-lucky slob. Like I was. Of course, it hit me hard, too. But only for a minute. Then I felt as if a ton of guilt had been lifted off my mind. I saw what had happened was the only possible way for the peace of all concerned.

LARRY (*Sharply*) What was it happened? Tell us that! And don't try to get out of it! I want a straight answer! (*Vindictively*) I think it was something you drove someone else to do!

HICKEY (*Puzzled*) Someone else?

LARRY (*Accusingly*) What did your wife die of? You've kept that a deep secret, I notice—for some reason!

HICKEY (*Reproachfully*) You're not very considerate, Larry. But, if you insist on knowing now, there's no reason you shouldn't. It was a bullet through the head that killed Evelyn. (*There is a second's tense silence*)

HOPE (*Dully*) Who the hell cares? To hell with her and that nagging old hag, Bessie.

ROCKY Christ. You had de right dope, Larry.

LARRY (*Revengefully*) You drove your poor wife to suicide? I knew it! Be God, I don't blame her! I'd almost do as much myself to be rid of you! It's what you'd like to drive us all to— (*Abruptly he is ashamed of himself and pitying*) I'm sorry, Hickey. I'm a rotten louse to throw that in your face.

HICKEY (*Quietly*) Oh, that's all right, Larry. But don't jump at conclusions. I didn't say poor Evelyn committed suicide. It's the last thing she'd ever have done, as long as I was alive for her to take care of and forgive. If you'd known her at all, you'd never get such a crazy suspicion. (*He pauses—then slowly*) No, I'm sorry to have to tell you my poor wife was killed. (LARRY *stares at him with growing horror and shrinks back along the bar away from him.* PARRITT *jerks his head up from his hands and looks around frightenedly, not at* HICKEY, *but at* LARRY. ROCKY'S *round eyes are popping.* HOPE *stares dully at the table top.* HUGO, *his head hidden in his arms, gives no sign of life*)

LARRY (*Shakenly*) Then she—was murdered.

PARRITT (*Springs to his feet—stammers defensively*) You're a liar, Larry! You must be crazy to say that to me! You know she's still alive! (*But no one pays any attention to him*)

ROCKY (*Blurts out*) Moidered? Who done it?

LARRY (*His eyes fixed with fascinated horror on* HICKEY—*frightenedly*) Don't ask questions, you dumb Wop! It's none of our damned business! Leave Hickey alone!

HICKEY (*Smiles at him with affectionate amusement*) Still the old grandstand bluff, Larry? Or is it some more bum pity? (*He turns to* ROCKY—*matter-of-factly*) The police don't know who killed her yet, Rocky. But I expect they will before very long. (*As if that finished the subject, he comes forward to* HOPE *and sits beside him, with an arm around his shoulder—affectionately coaxing*) Coming along fine now, aren't you, Governor? Getting over the first shock? Beginning to feel free from guilt and lying hopes and at peace with yourself?

HOPE (*With a dull callousness*) Somebody croaked your Evelyn, eh? Bejees, my bets are on the iceman! But who the hell cares? Let's get drunk and pass out. (*He tosses down his drink with a lifeless, automatic movement—complainingly*) Bejees, what did you do to the booze, Hickey? There's no damned life left in it.

PARRITT (*Stammers, his eyes on* LARRY, *whose eyes in turn remain fixed on* HICKEY) Don't look like that, Larry! You've got to believe what I told you! It had nothing to do with her! It was just to get a few lousy dollars!

HUGO (*Suddenly raises his head from his arms and, looking straight in front of him, pounds on the table frightenedly with his small fists*) Don't be a fool! Buy me a trink! But no more vine! It is not properly iced! (*With guttural rage*) Gottamned stupid proletarian slaves! Buy me a trink or I vill have you shot! (*He collapses into abject begging*) Please, for Gott's sake! I am not trunk enough! I cannot sleep! Life is a crazy monkey-face! Always there is blood beneath the villow trees! I hate it and I am afraid! (*He hides his face on his arms, sobbing muffledly*) Please, I am crazy trunk! I say crazy things! For Gott's sake, do not listen to me! (*But no one pays any attention to him.* LARRY *stands shrunk back against the bar.* ROCKY *is leaning over it. They stare at* HICKEY. PARRITT *stands looking pleadingly at* LARRY)

HICKEY (*Gazes with worried kindliness at* HOPE) You're beginning to worry me, Governor. Something's holding you up somewhere. I don't see why— You've faced the truth about yourself. You've done what you had to do to kill your nagging pipe dreams. Oh, I know it knocks you cold. But only for a minute. Then you see it was the only possible way to peace. And you feel happy. Like I did. That's what worries me about you, Governor. It's time you began to feel happy—

Curtain

Act Four

SCENE *Same as Act One—the back room with the curtain separating it from the section of the barroom with its single table at right of curtain, front. It is around half past one in the morning of the following day.*

The tables in the back room have a new arrangement. The one at left, front, before the window to the yard, is in the same position. So is the one at the right, rear, of it in the second row. But this table now has only one chair. This chair is at right of it, facing directly front. The two tables on either side of the door at rear are unchanged. But the table which was at center, front, has been pushed toward right so that it and the table at right, rear, of it in the second row, and the last table at right in the front row, are now jammed so closely together that they form one group.

LARRY, HUGO *and* PARRITT *are at the table at left, front.* LARRY *is at left of it, beside the window, facing front.* HUGO *sits at rear, facing front, his head on his arms in his habitual position, but he is not asleep. On* HUGO's *left is* PARRITT, *his chair facing left, front. At right of table, an empty chair, facing left.* LARRY's *chin is on his chest, his eyes fixed on the floor. He will not look at* PARRITT, *who keeps staring at him with a sneering, pleading challenge.*

Two bottles of whiskey are on each table, whiskey and chaser glasses, a pitcher of water.

The one chair by the table at right, rear, of them is vacant. At the first table at right of center, CORA sits at left, front, of it, facing front. Around the rear of this table are four empty chairs. Opposite CORA, in a sixth chair, is CAPTAIN LEWIS, also facing front. On his left, MCGLOIN is facing front in a chair before the middle table of his group. At right, rear, of him, also at this table, GENERAL WETJOEN sits facing front. In back of this table are three empty chairs.

At right, rear, of WETJOEN, but beside the last table of the group, sits WILLIE. On WILLIE's left, at rear of table, is HOPE. On HOPE's left, at right, rear, of table, is MOSHER. Finally, at right of table is JIMMY TOMORROW. All of the four sit facing front.

There is an atmosphere of oppressive stagnation in the room, and a quality of insensibility about all the people in this group at right. They are like wax figures, set stiffly on their chairs, carrying out mechanically the motions of getting drunk but sunk in a numb stupor which is impervious to stimulation.

In the bar section, JOE is sprawled in the chair at right of table, facing left. His head rolls forward in a sodden slumber. ROCKY is standing behind his chair, regarding him with dull hostility. ROCKY's face is set in an expression of tired, callous toughness. He looks now like a minor Wop gangster.

ROCKY (*Shakes* JOE *by the shoulder*) Come on, yuh damned nigger! Beat it in de back room! It's after hours. (*But* JOE *remains inert.* ROCKY *gives up*) Aw, to hell wid it. Let de dump get pinched. I'm through wid dis lousy job, anyway! (*He hears someone at rear and calls*) Who's dat? (CHUCK *appears from rear. He has been drinking heavily, but there is no lift to his jag; his manner is grouchy and sullen. He has evidently been brawling. His knuckles are raw and there is a mouse under one eye. He has lost his straw hat, his tie is awry, and his blue suit is dirty.* ROCKY *eyes him indifferently*) Been scrappin', huh? Started off on your periodical, ain't yuh? (*For a second there is a gleam of satisfaction in his eyes*)

CHUCK Yeah, ain't yuh glad? (*Truculently*) What's it to yuh?

ROCKY Not a damn ting. But dis is someting to me. I'm out on my feet holdin' down your job. Yuh said if I'd take your day, yuh'd relieve me at six, and here it's half past one A.M. Well, yuh're takin' over now, get me, no matter how plastered yuh are!

CHUCK Plastered, hell! I wisht I was. I've lapped up a gallon, but it don't hit me right. And to hell wid de job. I'm goin' to tell Harry I'm quittin'.

ROCKY Yeah? Well, I'm quittin', too.
CHUCK I've played sucker for dat crummy blonde long enough, lettin' her kid me into woikin'. From now on I take it easy.
ROCKY I'm glad yuh're gettin' some sense.
CHUCK And I hope yuh're gettin' some. What a prize sap you been, tendin' bar when yuh got two good hustlers in your stable!
ROCKY Yeah, but I ain't no sap now. I'll loin dem, when dey get back from Coney. (*Sneeringly*) Jees, dat Cora sure played you for a dope, feedin' yuh dat marriage-on-de-farm hop!
CHUCK (*Dully*) Yeah. Hickey got it right. A lousy pipe dream. It was her pulling sherry flips on me woke me up. All de way walkin' to de ferry, every ginmill we come to she'd drag me in to blow her. I got tinkin', Christ, what won't she want when she gets de ring on her finger and I'm hooked? So I tells her at de ferry, "Kiddo, yuh can go to Joisey, or to hell, but count me out."
ROCKY She says it was her told you to go to hell, because yuh'd started hittin' de booze.
CHUCK (*Ignoring this*) I got tinkin', too, Jees, won't I look sweet wid a wife dat if yuh put all de guys she's stayed wid side by side, dey'd reach to Chicago. (*He sighs gloomily*) Dat kind of dame, yuh can't trust 'em. De minute your back is toined, dey're cheatin' wid de iceman or someone. Hickey done me a favor, makin' me wake up. (*He pauses—then adds pathetically*) On'y it was fun, kinda, me and Cora kiddin' ourselves— (*Suddenly his face hardens with hatred*) Where is dat son of a bitch, Hickey? I want one good sock at dat guy—just one!—and de next buttin' in he'll do will be in de morgue! I'll take a chance on goin' to de Chair—!
ROCKY (*Starts—in a low warning voice*) Piano! Keep away from him, Chuck! He ain't here now, anyway. He went out to phone, he said. He wouldn't call from here. I got a hunch he's beat it. But if he does come back, yuh don't know him, if anyone asks yuh, get me? (*As* CHUCK *looks at him with dull surprise he lowers his voice to a whisper*) De Chair, maybe dat's where he's goin'. I don't know nuttin, see, but it looks like he croaked his wife.
CHUCK (*With a flash of interest*) Yuh mean she really was cheatin' on him? Den I don't blame de guy—
ROCKY Who's blamin' him? When a dame asks for it—But I don't know nuttin' about it, see?
CHUCK Is any of de gang wise?
ROCKY Larry is. And de boss ought to be. I tried to wise de rest of dem up to stay clear of him, but dey're all so licked, I don't know if dey got it. (*He pauses—vindictively*) I don't give a damn what he done to

his wife, but if he gets de Hot Seat I won't go into no mournin'!
CHUCK Me, neider!
ROCKY Not after his trowin' it in my face I'm a pimp. What if I am? Why de hell not? And what he's done to Harry. Jees, de poor old slob is so licked he can't even get drunk. And all de gang. Dey're all licked. I couldn't help feelin' sorry for de poor bums when dey showed up tonight, one by one, lookin' like pooches wid deir tails between deir legs, dat everyone'd been kickin' till dey was too punch-drunk to feel it no more. Jimmy Tomorrow was de last. Schwartz, de copper, brung him in. Seen him sittin' on de dock on West Street, lookin' at de water and cryin'! Schwartz thought he was drunk and I let him tink it. But he was cold sober. He was tryin' to jump in and didn't have de noive, I figured it. Noive! Jees, dere ain't enough guts left in de whole gang to battle a mosquito!
CHUCK Aw, to hell wid 'em! Who cares? Gimme a drink. (ROCKY *pushes the bottle toward him apathetically*) I see you been hittin' de redeye, too.
ROCKY Yeah. But it don't do no good. I can't get drunk right. (CHUCK *drinks.* JOE *mumbles in his sleep.* CHUCK *regards him resentfully*) Dis doity dinge was able to get his snootful and pass out. Jees, even Hickey can't faze a nigger! Yuh'd tink he was fazed if yuh'd seen him come in. Stinko, and he pulled a gat and said he'd plug Hickey for insultin' him. Den he dropped it and begun to cry and said he wasn't a gamblin' man or a tough guy no more; he was yellow. He'd borrowed de gat to stick up someone, and den didn't have de guts. He got drunk panhandlin' drinks in nigger joints, I s'pose. I guess dey felt sorry for him.
CHUCK He ain't got no business in de bar after hours. Why don't yuh chuck him out?
ROCKY (*Apathetically*) Aw, to hell wid it. Who cares?
CHUCK (*Lapsing into the same mood*) Yeah. I don't.
JOE (*Suddenly lunges to his feet dazedly—mumbles in humbled apology*) Scuse me, White Boys. Scuse me for livin'. I don't want to be where I's not wanted. (*He makes his way swayingly to the opening in the curtain at rear and tacks down to the middle table of the three at right, front. He feels his way around it to the table at its left and gets to the chair in back of* CAPTAIN LEWIS)
CHUCK (*Gets up—in a callous, brutal tone*) My pig's in de back room, ain't she? I wanna collect de dough I wouldn't take dis mornin', like a sucker, before she blows it. (*He goes rear*)
ROCKY (*Getting up*) I'm comin', too. I'm trough woikin'. I ain't no lousy bartender. (CHUCK *comes through the curtain and looks for* CORA *as* JOE *flops down in the chair in back of* CAPTAIN LEWIS)

JOE (*Taps* LEWIS *on the shoulder—servilely apologetic*) If you objects to my sittin' here, Captain, just tell me and I pulls my freight.
LEWIS No apology required, old chap. Anybody could tell you I should feel honored a bloody Kaffir would lower himself to sit beside me. (JOE *stares at him with sodden perplexity—then closes his eyes.* CHUCK *comes forward to take the chair behind* CORA'S, *as* ROCKY *enters the back room and starts over toward* LARRY's *table*)
CHUCK (*His voice hard*) I'm waitin', Baby. Dig!
CORA (*With apathetic obedience*) Sure. I been expectin' yuh. I got it all ready. Here. (*She passes a small roll of bills she has in her hand over her shoulder, without looking at him. He takes it, glances at it suspiciously, then shoves it in his pocket without a word of acknowledgment.* CORA *speaks with a tired wonder at herself rather than resentment toward him*) Jees, imagine me kiddin' myself I wanted to marry a drunken pimp.
CHUCK Dat's nuttin', Baby. Imagine de sap I'da been, when I can get your dough just as easy widout it!
ROCKY (*Takes the chair on* PARRITT's *left, facing* LARRY—*dully*) Hello, Old Cemetery. (LARRY *doesn't seem to hear. To* PARRITT) Hello, Tightwad. You still around?
PARRITT (*Keeps his eyes on* LARRY—*in a jeeringly challenging tone*) Ask Larry! He knows I'm here, all right, although he's pretending not to! He'd like to forget I'm alive! He's trying to kid himself with that grandstand philosopher stuff! But he knows he can't get away with it now! He kept himself locked in his room until a while ago, alone with a bottle of booze, but he couldn't make it work! He couldn't even get drunk! He had to come out! There must have been something there he was even more scared to face than he is Hickey and me! I guess he got looking at the fire escape and thinking how handy it was, if he was really sick of life and only had the nerve to die! (*He pauses sneeringly.* LARRY's *face has tautened, but he pretends he doesn't hear.* ROCKY *pays no attention. His head has sunk forward, and he stares at the table top, sunk in the same stupor as the other occupants of the room.* PARRITT *goes on, his tone becoming more insistent*) He's been thinking of me, too, Rocky. Trying to figure a way to get out of helping me! He doesn't want to be bothered understanding. But he does understand all right! He used to love her, too. So he thinks I ought to take a hop off the fire escape! (*He pauses.* LARRY's *hands on the table have clinched into fists, as his nails dig into his palms, but he remains silent.* PARRITT *breaks and starts pleading*) For God's sake, Larry, can't you say something? Hickey's got me all balled up. Thinking of what he must have done has got me so I don't know any more what I did or why. I can't go on

like this! I've got to know what I ought to do—
LARRY (*In a stifled tone*) God damn you! Are you trying to make me your executioner?
PARRITT (*Starts frightenedly*) Execution? Then you do think—?
LARRY I don't think anything!
PARRITT (*With forced jeering*) I suppose you think I ought to die because I sold out a lot of loud-mouthed fakers, who were cheating suckers with a phony pipe dream, and put them where they ought to be, in jail? (*He forces a laugh*) Don't make me laugh! I ought to get a medal! What a damned old sap you are! You must still believe in the Movement! (*He nudges* ROCKY *with his elbow*) Hickey's right about him, isn't he, Rocky? An old no-good drunken tramp, as dumb as he is, ought to take a hop off the fire escape!
ROCKY (*Dully*) Sure. Why don't he? Or you? Or me? What de hell's de difference? Who cares? (*There is a faint stir from all the crowd, as if this sentiment struck a responsive chord in their numbed minds. They mumble almost in chorus as one voice, like sleepers talking out of a dully irritating dream, "The hell with it!" "Who cares?" Then the sodden silence descends again on the room.* ROCKY *looks from* PARRITT *to* LARRY *puzzledly. He mutters*) What am I doin' here wid youse two? I remember I had someting on my mind to tell yuh. What—? Oh, I got it now. (*He looks from one to the other of their oblivious faces with a strange, sly, calculating look—ingratiatingly*) I was tinking how you was bot' reg'lar guys. I tinks, ain't two guys like dem saps to be hangin' round like a coupla stew bums and wastin' demselves. Not dat I blame yuh for not woikin'. On'y suckers woik. But dere's no percentage in bein' broke when yuh can grab good jack for yourself and make someone else woik for yuh, is dere? I mean, like I do. So I tinks, Dey're my pals and I ought to wise up two good guys like dem to play my system, and not be lousy barflies, no good to demselves or nobody else. (*He addresses* PARRITT *now—persuasively*) What yuh tink, Parritt? Ain't I right? Sure, I am. So don't be a sucker, see? Yuh ain't a bad-lookin' guy. Yuh could easy make some gal who's a good hustler, an' start a stable. I'd help yuh and wise yuh up to de inside dope on de game. (*He pauses inquiringly.* PARRITT *gives no sign of having heard him.* ROCKY *asks impatiently*) Well, what about it? What if dey do call yuh a pimp? What de hell do you care—any more'n I do.
PARRITT (*Without looking at him—vindictively*) I'm through with whores. I wish they were all in jail—or dead!
ROCKY (*Ignores this—disappointedly*) So yuh won't touch it, huh? Aw right, stay a bum! (*He turns to* LARRY) Jees, Larry, he's sure one dumb boob, ain't he? Dead from de neck up! He don't know a good

ting when he sees it. (*Oily, even persuasive again*) But how about you, Larry? You ain't dumb. So why not, huh? Sure, yuh're old, but dat don't matter. All de hustlers tink yuh're aces. Dey fall for yuh like yuh was deir uncle or old man or someting. Dey'd like takin' care of yuh. And de cops 'round here, dey like yuh, too. It'd be a pipe for yuh, 'specially wid me to help yuh and wise yuh up. Yuh wouldn't have to worry where de next drink's comin' from, or wear doity clothes. (*Hopefully*) Well, don't it look good to yuh?

LARRY (*Glances at him—for a moment he is stirred to sardonic pity*) No, it doesn't look good, Rocky. I mean, the peace Hickey's brought you. It isn't contented enough, if you have to make everyone else a pimp, too.

ROCKY (*Stares at him stupidly—then pushes his chair back and gets up, grumbling*) I'm a sap to waste time on yuh. A stew bum is a stew bum and yuh can't change him. (*He turns away—then turns back for an afterthought*) Like I was sayin' to Chuck, yuh better keep away from Hickey. If anyone asks yuh, yuh don't know nuttin', get me? Yuh never even hoid he had a wife. (*His face hardens*) Jees, we all ought to git drunk and stage a celebration when dat bastard goes to de Chair.

LARRY (*Vindictively*) Be God, I'll celebrate with you and drink long life to him in hell! (*Then guiltily and pityingly*) No! The poor mad devil— (*Then with angry self-contempt*) Ah, pity again! The wrong kind! He'll welcome the Chair!

PARRITT (*Contemptuously*) Yes, what are you so damned scared of death for? I don't want your lousy pity.

ROCKY Christ, I hope he don't come back, Larry. We don't know nuttin' now. We're on'y guessin', see? But if de bastard keeps on talkin'—

LARRY (*Grimly*) He'll come back. He'll keep on talking. He's got to. He's lost his confidence that the peace he's sold us is the real McCoy, and it's made him uneasy about his own. He'll have to prove to us— (*As he is speaking* HICKEY *appears silently in the doorway at rear. He has lost his beaming salesman's grin. His manner is no longer self-assured. His expression is uneasy, baffled and resentful. It has the stubborn set of an obsessed determination. His eyes are on* LARRY *as he comes in. As he speaks, there is a start from all the crowd, a shrinking away from him*)

HICKEY (*Angrily*) That's a damned lie, Larry! I haven't lost confidence a damned bit! Why should I? (*Boastfully*) By God, whenever I made up my mind to sell someone something I knew they ought to want, I've sold 'em! (*He suddenly looks confused—haltingly*) I mean— It isn't kind of you, Larry, to make that kind of crack when I've been doing my best to help—

ROCKY (*Moving away from him toward right—sharply*) Keep away from me! I don't know nuttin' about yuh, see? (*His tone is threatening but his manner as he turns his back and ducks quickly across to the bar entrance is that of one in flight. In the bar he comes forward and slumps in a chair at the table, facing front*)

HICKEY (*Comes to the table at right, rear, of* LARRY'S *table and sits in the one chair there, facing front. He looks over the crowd at right, hopefully and then disappointedly. He speaks with a strained attempt at his old affectionate jollying manner*) Well, well! How are you coming along, everybody? Sorry I had to leave you for a while, but there was something I had to get finally settled. It's all fixed now.

HOPE (*In the voice of one reiterating mechanically a hopeless complaint*) When are you going to do something about this booze, Hickey? Bejees, we all know you did something to take the life out of it. It's like drinking dishwater! We can't pass out! And you promised us peace. (*His group all join in in a dull, complaining chorus,* "We can't pass out! You promised us peace!")

HICKEY (*Bursts into resentful exasperation*) For God's sake, Harry, are you still harping on that damned nonsense! You've kept it up all afternoon and night! And you've got everybody else singing the same crazy tune! I've had about all I can stand— That's why I phoned— (*He controls himself*) Excuse me, boys and girls. I don't mean that. I'm just worried about you, when you play dead on me like this. I was hoping by the time I got back you'd be like you ought to be! I thought you were deliberately holding back, while I was around, because you didn't want to give me the satisfaction of showing me I'd had the right dope. And I did have! I know from my own experience. (*Exasperatedly*) But I've explained that a million times! And you've all done what you needed to do! By rights you should be contented now, without a single damned hope or lying dream left to torment you! But here you are, acting like a lot of stiffs cheating the undertaker! (*He looks around accusingly*) I can't figure it—unless it's just your damned pig-headed stubbornness! (*He breaks—miserably*) Hell, you oughtn't to act this way with me! You're my old pals, the only friends I've got. You know the one thing I want is to see you all happy before I go— (*Rousing himself to his old brisk, master-of-ceremonies manner*) And there's damned little time left now. I've made a date for two o'clock. We've got to get busy right away and find out what's wrong. (*There is a sodden silence. He goes on exasperatedly*) Can't you appreciate what you've got, for God's sake? Don't you know you're free now to be yourselves, without having to feel remorse or guilt, or lie to yourselves about reforming tomorrow? Can't you see there is no tomorrow now? You're rid of it forever! You've killed it! You don't have to care a damn about anything any more! You've finally got the game of life licked, don't you see that? (*Angrily exhorting*) Then why the hell don't you get pie-eyed and celebrate? Why don't you laugh and sing "Sweet Adeline"? (*With bitterly hurt accusation*) The only reason I can think of is, you're putting on this rotten half-dead act just to get back at me! Because you hate my guts! (*He breaks again*) God, don't do that, gang! It makes me feel like hell to think you hate me. It makes me feel you suspect I must have hated you. But that's a lie! Oh, I know I used to hate everyone in the world who wasn't as rotten a bastard as I was! But that was when I was still living in hell—before I faced the truth and saw the one possible way to free poor Evelyn and give her the peace she'd always dreamed about. (*He pauses. Everyone in the group stirs with awakening dread and they all begin to grow tense on their chairs*)

CHUCK (*Without looking at* HICKEY—*with dull, resentful viciousness*) Aw, put a bag over it! To hell wid Evelyn! What if she was cheatin'? And who cares what yuh did to her? Dat's your funeral. We don't give a damn, see? (*There is a dull, resentful chorus of assent, "We don't give a damn."* CHUCK *adds dully*) All we want outa you is keep de hell away from us and give us a rest. (*A muttered chorus of assent*)

HICKEY (*As if he hadn't heard this—an obsessed look on his face*) The one possible way to make up to her for all I'd made her go through, and get her rid of me so I couldn't make her suffer any more, and she wouldn't have to forgive me again! I saw I couldn't do it by killing myself, like I wanted to for a long time. That would have been the last straw for her. She'd have died of a broken heart to think I could do that to her. She'd have blamed herself for it, too. Or I couldn't just run away from her. She'd have died of grief and humiliation if I'd done that to her. She'd have thought I'd stopped loving her. (*He adds with a strange impressive simplicity*) You see, Evelyn loved me. And I loved her. That was the trouble. It would have been easy to find a way out if she hadn't loved me so much. Or if I hadn't loved her. But as it was, there was only one possible way. (*He pauses—then adds simply*) I had to kill her. (*There is a second's dead silence as he finishes—then a tense indrawn breath like a gasp from the crowd, and a general shrinking movement*)

LARRY (*Bursts out*) You mad fool, can't you keep your mouth shut! We may hate you for what you've done here this time, but we remember the old times, too, when you brought kindness and laughter with you instead of death! We don't want to know things that will make us help send you to the Chair!

PARRITT (*With angry scorn*) Ah, shut up, you yellow faker! Can't you face anything? Wouldn't I deserve the Chair, too, if I'd— It's worse if you kill someone and they have to go on living. I'd be glad of the Chair! It'd wipe it out! It'd square me with myself!

HICKEY (*Disturbed—with a movement of repulsion*) I wish you'd get rid of that bastard, Larry. I can't have him pretending there's something in common between him and me. It's what's in your heart that counts. There was love in my heart, not hate.

PARRITT (*Glares at him in angry terror*) You're a liar! I don't hate her! I couldn't! And it had nothing to do with her, anyway! You ask Larry!

LARRY (*Grabs his shoulder and shakes him furiously*) God damn you, stop shoving your rotten soul in my lap! (PARRITT *subsides, hiding his face in his hands and shuddering*)

HICKEY (*Goes on quietly now*) Don't worry about the Chair, Larry. I know it's still hard for you not to be terrified by death, but when you've made peace with yourself, like I have, you won't give a damn. (*He addresses the group at right again—earnestly*) Listen, everybody. I've made up my mind the only way I can clear things up for you, so you'll realize how contented and carefree you ought to feel, now I've made you get rid of your pipe dreams, is to show you what a pipe dream did to me and Evelyn. I'm certain if I tell you about it from the beginning, you'll appreciate what I've done for you and why I did it, and how damned grateful you ought to be—instead of hating me. (*He begins eagerly in a strange running narrative manner*) You see, even when we were kids, Evelyn and me—

HOPE (*Bursts out, pounding with his glass on the table*) No! who the hell cares? We don't want to hear it. All we want is to pass out and get drunk and a little peace! (*They are all, except* LARRY *and* PARRITT, *seized by the same fit and pound with their glasses, even* HUGO, *and* ROCKY *in the bar, and shout in chorus, "Who the hell cares? We want to pass out!"*)

HICKEY (*With an expression of wounded hurt*) All right, if that's the way you feel. I don't want to cram it down your throats. I don't need to tell anyone. I don't feel guilty. I'm only worried about you.

HOPE What did you do to this booze? That's what we'd like to hear. Bejees, you done something. There's no life or kick in it now. (*He appeals mechanically to* JIMMY TOMORROW) Ain't that right, Jimmy?

JIMMY (*More than any of them, his face has a wax-figure blankness that makes it look embalmed. He answers in a precise, completely lifeless voice, but his reply is not to* HARRY's *question, and he does not look at him or anyone else*) Yes. Quite right. It was all a stupid lie—my nonsense about tomorrow. Naturally, they would never give me my position back. I would never dream of asking them. It would be hopeless. I didn't resign. I was fired for drunkenness. And that was years ago. I'm much worse now. And it was absurd of me to excuse my drunkenness by pretending it was my wife's adultery that ruined my life. As Hickey guessed, I was a drunkard before that. Long before. I discovered early in life that living frightened me when I was sober. I have forgotten why I married Marjorie. I can't even remember now if she was pretty. She was a blonde, I think, but I couldn't swear to it. I had some idea of wanting a home, perhaps. But, of course, I much preferred the nearest pub. Why Marjorie married me, God knows. It's impossible to believe she loved me. She soon found I much preferred drinking all night with my pals to being in bed with her. So, naturally, she was unfaithful. I didn't blame her. I really didn't care. I was glad to be free—even grateful to her, I think, for giving me such a good tragic excuse to drink as much as I damned well pleased. (*He stops like a mechanical doll that has run down. No one gives any sign of having heard him. There is a heavy silence. Then* ROCKY, *at the table in the bar, turns grouchily as he hears a noise behind him. Two men come quietly forward. One,* MORAN, *is middle-aged. The other,* LIEB, *is in his twenties. They look ordinary in every way, without anything distinctive to indicate what they do for a living*)

ROCKY (*Grumpily*) In de back room if yuh wanta drink. (MORAN *makes a peremptory sign to be quiet. All of a sudden* ROCKY *senses they are detectives and springs up to face them, his expression freezing into a wary blankness.* MORAN *pulls back his coat to show his badge*)

MORAN (*In a low voice*) Guy named Hickman in the back room?

ROCKY Tink I know de names of all de guys—?

MORAN Listen, you! This is murder. And don't be a sap. It was Hickman himself phoned in and said we'd find him here around two.

ROCKY (*Dully*) So dat's who he phoned to. (*He shrugs his shoulders*) Aw right, if he asked for it. He's de fat guy sittin' alone. (*He slumps down in his chair again*) And if yuh want a confession all yuh got to do is listen. He'll be tellin' all about it soon. Yuh can't stop de bastard talkin'. (MORAN *gives him a curious look, then whispers to* LIEB, *who disappears rear and a moment later appears in the hall doorway of the back room. He spots* HICKEY *and slides into a chair at the left of the doorway, cutting off escape by the hall.* MORAN *goes back and stands in the opening in the curtain leading to the back room. He sees* HICKEY *and stands watching him and listening*)

HICKEY (*Suddenly bursts out*) I've got to tell you! Your being the way you are now gets my goat! It's all wrong! It puts things in my mind—about myself. It makes me think, if I got balled up about you, how do I know I wasn't balled up about myself? And that's plain damned foolishness. When you know the story of me and Evelyn, you'll see there wasn't any other possible way out of it, for her sake. Only I've got to start way back at the beginning or you won't understand. (*He starts his story, his tone again becoming musingly reminiscent*) You see, even as a kid I was always restless. I had to keep on the go. You've heard the old saying, "Ministers' sons are sons of guns." Well, that was me, and then some. Home was like a jail. I didn't fall for the religious bunk. Listening to my old man whooping up hell fire and scaring those Hoosier suckers into shelling out their dough only handed me a laugh, although I had to hand it to him, the way he sold them nothing for something. I guess I take after him, and that's what made me a good salesman. Well, anyway, as I said, home was like jail, and so was school, and so was that damned hick town. The only place I liked was the pool rooms, where I could smoke Sweet Caporals, and mop up a couple of beers, thinking I was a hell-on-wheels sport. We had one hooker shop in town, and, of course, I liked that, too. Not that I hardly ever had entrance money. My old man was a tight old bastard. But I liked to sit around in the parlor and joke with the girls, and they liked me because I could kid 'em along and make 'em laugh. Well, you know what a small town is. Everyone got wise to me. They all said I was a no-good tramp. I didn't give a damn what they said. I hated everybody in the place. That is, except Evelyn. I loved Evelyn. Even as a kid. And Evelyn loved me. (*He pauses. No one moves or gives any sign except by the dread in their eyes that they have heard him. Except* PARRITT, *who takes his hands from his face to look at* LARRY *pleadingly*)

PARRITT   I loved Mother, Larry! No matter what she did! I still do! Even though I know she wishes now I was dead! You believe that, don't you? Christ, why can't you say something?

HICKEY (*Too absorbed in his story now to notice this—goes on in a tone of fond, sentimental reminiscence*)   Yes, sir, as far back as I can remember, Evelyn and I loved each other. She always stuck up for me. She wouldn't believe the gossip—or she'd pretend she didn't. No one could convince her I was no good. Evelyn was stubborn as all hell once she'd made up her mind. Even when I'd admit things and ask her forgiveness, she'd make excuses for me and defend me against myself. She'd kiss me and say she knew I didn't mean it and I wouldn't do it again. So I'd promise I wouldn't. I'd have to promise, she was so sweet and good, though I knew darned well— (*A touch of strange bitterness comes into his voice for a moment*) No, sir, you couldn't stop Evelyn. Nothing on earth could shake her faith in me. Even I couldn't. She was a sucker for a pipe dream. (*Then quickly*) Well, naturally, her family forbid her seeing me. They were one of the town's best, rich for that hick burg, owned the trolley line and lumber company. Strict Methodists, too. They hated my guts. But they couldn't stop Evelyn. She'd sneak notes to me and meet me on the sly. I was getting more restless. The town was getting more like a jail. I made up my mind to beat it. I knew exactly what I wanted to be by that time. I'd met a lot of drummers around the hotel and liked 'em. They were always telling jokes. They were sports. They kept moving. I liked their life. And I knew I could kid people and sell things. The hitch was how to get the railroad fare to the Big Town. I told Mollie Arlington my trouble. She was the madame of the cathouse. She liked me. She laughed and said, "Hell, I'll stake you, Kid! I'll bet on you. With that grin of yours and that line of bull, you ought to be able to sell skunks for good ratters!" (*He chuckles*) Mollie was all right. She gave me confidence in myself. I paid her back, the first money I earned. Wrote her a kidding letter, I remember, saying I was peddling baby carriages and she and the girls had better take advantage of our bargain offer. (*He chuckles*) But that's ahead of my story. The night before I left town, I had a date with Evelyn. I got all worked up, she was so pretty and sweet and good. I told her straight, "You better forget me, Evelyn, for your own sake. I'm no good and never will be. I'm not worthy to wipe your shoes." I broke down and cried. She just said, looking white and scared, "Why, Teddy? Don't you still love me?" I said, "Love you? God, Evelyn, I love you more than anything in the world. And I always will!" She said, "Then nothing else matters, Teddy, because nothing but death could stop my loving you. So I'll wait, and when you're ready you send for me and we'll be married. I know I can make you happy, Teddy, and once you're happy you won't want to do any of the bad things you've done any more." And I said, "Of course, I won't, Evelyn!" I meant it, too. I believed it. I loved her so much she could make me believe anything. (*He sighs. There is a suspended, waiting silence. Even the two detectives are drawn into it. Then* HOPE *breaks into dully exasperated, brutally callous protest*)

HOPE Get it over, you long-winded bastard! You married her, and you caught her cheating with the iceman, and you croaked her, and who the hell cares? What's she to us? All we want is to pass out in peace, bejees! (*A chorus of dull, resentful protest from all the group. They mumble, like sleepers who curse a person who keeps awakening them,* "What's it to us? We want to pass out in peace!" HOPE *drinks and they mechanically follow his example. He pours another and they do the same. He complains with a stupid, nagging insistence*) No life in the booze! No kick! Dishwater. Bejees, I'll never pass out!

HICKEY (*Goes on as if there had been no interruption*) So I beat it to the Big Town. I got a job easy, and it was a cinch for me to make good. I had the knack. It was like a game, sizing people up quick, spotting what their pet pipe dreams were, and then kidding 'em along that line, pretending you believed what they wanted to believe about themselves. Then they liked you, they trusted you, they wanted to buy something to show their gratitude. It was fun. But still, all the while I felt guilty, as if I had no right to be having such a good time away from Evelyn. In each letter I'd tell her how I missed her, but I'd keep warning her, too. I'd tell her all my faults, how I liked my booze every once in a while, and so on. But there was no shaking Evelyn's belief in me, or her dreams about the future. After each letter of hers, I'd be as full of faith as she was. So as soon as I got enough saved to start us off, I sent for her and we got married. Christ, wasn't I happy for a while! And wasn't she happy! I don't care what anyone says, I'll bet there never was two people who loved each other more than me and Evelyn. Not only then but always after, in spite of everything I did— (*He pauses—then sadly*) Well, it's all there, at the start, everything that happened afterwards. I never could learn to handle temptation. I'd want to reform and mean it. I'd promise Evelyn, and I'd promise myself, and I'd believe it. I'd tell her, it's the last time. And she'd say, "I know it's the last time, Teddy. You'll never do it again." That's what made it so hard. That's what made me feel such a rotten skunk—her always forgiving me. My playing around with women, for instance. It was only a harmless good time to me. Didn't mean anything. But I'd know what it meant to Evelyn. So I'd say to myself, never again. But you know how it is, traveling around. The damned hotel rooms. I'd get seeing things in the wall paper. I'd get bored as hell. Lonely and homesick. But at the same time sick of home. I'd feel free and I'd want to celebrate a little. I never drank on the job, so it had to be dames. Any tart. What I'd want was some tramp I could be myself with without being ashamed—someone I could tell a dirty joke to and she'd laugh.

CORA (*With a dull, weary bitterness*) Jees, all de lousy jokes I've had to listen to and pretend was funny!

HICKEY (*Goes on obliviously*) Sometimes I'd try some joke I thought was a corker on Evelyn. She'd always make herself laugh. But I could tell she thought it was dirty, not funny. And Evelyn always knew about the tarts I'd been with when I came home from a trip. She'd kiss me and look in my eyes, and she'd know. I'd see in her eyes how she was trying not to know, and then telling herself even if it was true, he couldn't help it, they tempt him, and he's lonely, he hasn't got me, it's only his body, anyway, he doesn't love them, I'm the only one he loves. She was right, too. I never loved anyone else. Couldn't if I wanted

to. (*He pauses*) She forgave me even when it all had to come out in the open. You know how it is when you keep taking chances. You may be lucky for a long time, but you get nicked in the end. I picked up a nail from some tart in Altoona.
CORA (*Dully, without resentment*) Yeah. And she picked it up from some guy. It's all in de game. What de hell of it?
HICKEY I had to do a lot of lying and stalling when I got home. It didn't do any good. The quack I went to got all my dough and then told me I was cured and I took his word. But I wasn't, and poor Evelyn— But she did her best to make me believe she fell for my lie about how traveling men get things from drinking cups on trains. Anyway, she forgave me. The same way she forgave me every time I'd turn up after a periodical drunk. You all know what I'd be like at the end of one. You've seen me. Like something lying in the gutter that no alley cat would lower itself to drag in—something they threw out of the D.T. ward in Bellevue along with the garbage, something that ought to be dead and isn't! (*His face is convulsed with self-loathing*) Evelyn wouldn't have heard from me in a month or more. She'd have been waiting there alone, with the neighbors shaking their heads and feeling sorry for her out loud. That was before she got me to move to the outskirts, where there weren't any next-door neighbors. And then the door would open and in I'd stumble—looking like what I've said—into her home, where she kept everything so spotless and clean. And I'd sworn it would never happen again, and now I'd have to start swearing again this was the last time. I could see disgust having a battle in her eyes with love. Love always won. She'd make herself kiss me, as if nothing had happened, as if I'd just come home from a business trip. She'd never complain or bawl me out. (*He bursts out in a tone of anguish that has anger and hatred beneath it*) Christ, can you imagine what a guilty skunk she made me feel! If she'd only admitted once she didn't believe any more in her pipe dream that some day I'd behave! But she never would. Evelyn was stubborn as hell. Once she'd set her heart on anything, you couldn't shake her faith that it had to come true—tomorrow! It was the same old story, over and over, for years and years. It kept piling up, inside her and inside me. God, can you picture all I made her suffer, and all the guilt she made me feel, and how I hated myself! If she only hadn't been so damned good—if she'd been the same kind of wife I was a husband. God, I used to pray sometimes she'd—I'd even say to her, "Go on, why don't you, Evelyn? It'd serve me right. I wouldn't mind. I'd forgive you." Of course, I'd pretend I was kidding— the same way I used to joke here about her being in the hay with the iceman. She'd have been so hurt if I'd said it seriously. She'd have

thought I'd stopped loving her. (*He pauses—then looking around at them*) I suppose you think I'm a liar, that no woman could have stood all she stood and still loved me so much—that it isn't human for any woman to be so pitying and forgiving. Well, I'm not lying, and if you'd ever seen her, you'd realize I wasn't. It was written all over her face, sweetness and love and pity and forgiveness. (*He reaches mechanically for the inside pocket of his coat*) Wait! I'll show you. I always carry her picture. (*Suddenly he looks startled. He stares before him, his hand falling back—quietly*) No, I'm forgetting I tore it up—afterwards. I didn't need it any more. (*He pauses. The silence is like that in the room of a dying man where people hold their breath, waiting for him to die*)

CORA (*With a muffled sob*) Jees, Hickey! Jees! (*She shivers and puts her hands over her face*)

PARRITT (*To* LARRY *in a low insistent tone*) I burnt up Mother's picture, Larry. Her eyes followed me all the time. They seemed to be wishing I was dead!

HICKEY It kept piling up, like I've said. I got so I thought of it all the time. I hated myself more and more, thinking of all the wrong I'd done to the sweetest woman in the world who loved me so much. I got so I'd curse myself for a lousy bastard every time I saw myself in the mirror. I felt such pity for her it drove me crazy. You wouldn't believe a guy like me, that's knocked around so much, could feel such pity. It got so every night I'd wind up hiding my face in her lap, bawling and begging her forgiveness. And, of course, she'd always comfort me and say, "Never mind, Teddy, I know you won't ever again." Christ, I loved her so, but I began to hate that pipe dream! I began to be afraid I was going bughouse, because sometimes I couldn't forgive her for forgiving me. I even caught myself hating her for making me hate myself so much. There's a limit to the guilt you can feel and the forgiveness and the pity you can take! You have to begin blaming someone else, too. I got so sometimes when she'd kiss me it was like she did it on purpose to humiliate me, as if she'd spit in my face! But all the time I saw how crazy and rotten of me that was, and it made me hate myself all the more. You'd never believe I could hate so much, a good-natured, happy-go-lucky slob like me. And as the time got nearer to when I was due to come here for my drunk around Harry's birthday, I got nearly crazy. I kept swearing to her every night that this time I really wouldn't, until I'd made it a real final test to myself—and to her. And she kept encouraging me and saying, "I can see you really mean it now, Teddy. I know you'll conquer it this time, and we'll be so happy, dear." When she'd say that and kiss me, I'd believe it, too. Then she'd go to bed, and I'd stay up alone because I couldn't sleep and I didn't want to disturb her, tossing and rolling around. I'd get so damned lonely. I'd get thinking how peaceful it was here, sitting around with the old gang, getting drunk and forgetting love, joking and laughing and singing and swapping lies. And finally I knew I'd have to come. And I knew if I came this time, it was the finish. I'd never have the guts to go back and be forgiven again, and that would break Evelyn's heart because to her it would mean I didn't love her any more. (*He pauses*) That last night I'd driven myself crazy trying to figure some way out for her. I went in the bedroom. I was going to tell her it was the end. But I couldn't do that to her. She was sound asleep. I thought, God, if she'd only never wake up, she'd never know! And then it came to me—the only possible way out, for her sake. I remembered I'd given her a gun for protection while I was away and it was in the bureau drawer. She'd never feel any pain, never wake up from her dream. So I—

HOPE (*Tries to ward this off by pounding with his glass on the table—with brutal, callous exasperation*) Give us a rest, for the love of Christ! Who the hell cares? We want to pass out in peace! (*They all, except* PARRITT *and* LARRY, *pound with their glasses and grumble in chorus:* "Who the hell cares? We want to pass out in peace!" MORAN, *the detective, moves quietly from the entrance in the curtain across the back of the room to the table where his companion,* LIEB, *is sitting.* ROCKY *notices his leaving and gets up from the table in the rear and goes back to stand and watch in the entrance.* MORAN *exchanges a glance with* LIEB, *motioning him to get up. The latter does so. No one notices them. The clamor of banging glasses dies out as abruptly as it started.* HICKEY *hasn't appeared to hear it*)

HICKEY (*Simply*) So I killed her. (*There is a moment of dead silence. Even the detectives are caught in it and stand motionless*)

PARRITT (*Suddenly gives up and relaxes limply in his chair—in a low voice in which there is a strange exhausted relief*) I may as well confess, Larry. There's no use lying any more. You know, anyway. I didn't give a damn about the money. It was because I hated her.

HICKEY (*Obliviously*) And then I saw I'd always known that was the only possible way to give her peace and free her from the misery of loving me. I saw it meant peace for me, too, knowing she was at peace. I felt as though a ton of guilt was lifted off my mind. I remember I stood by the bed and suddenly I had to laugh. I couldn't help it, and I knew Evelyn would forgive me. I remember I heard myself speaking to her, as if it was something I'd always wanted to say: "Well, you know what you can do with your pipe dream now, you damned bitch!" (*He stops with a horrified start, as if shocked out of a nightmare, as if he couldn't believe he heard what he had just said. He stammers*) No! I never—!

PARRITT (*To* LARRY—*sneeringly*) Yes, that's it! Her and the damned old Movement pipe dream! Eh, Larry?

HICKEY (*Bursts into frantic denial*) No! That's a lie! I never said—! Good God, I couldn't have said that! If I did, I'd gone insane! Why, I loved Evelyn better than anything in life! (*He appeals brokenly to the crowd*) Boys, you're all my old pals! You've known old Hickey for years! You know I'd never— (*His eyes fix on* HOPE) You've known me longer than anyone, Harry. You know I must have been insane, don't you, Governor?

HOPE (*At first with the same defensive callousness—without looking at him*) Who the hell cares? (*Then suddenly he looks at* HICKEY *and there is an extraordinary change in his expression. His face lights up, as if he were grasping at some dawning hope in his mind. He speaks with a groping eagerness*) Insane? You mean—you went really insane? (*At the tone of his voice, all the group at the tables by him start and stare at him as if they caught his thought. Then they all look at* HICKEY *eagerly, too*)

HICKEY Yes! Or I couldn't have laughed! I couldn't have said that to her! (MORAN *walks up behind him on one side, while the second detective,* LIEB, *closes in on him from the other*)

MORAN (*Taps* HICKEY *on the shoulder*) That's enough, Hickman. You know who we are. You're under arrest. (*He nods to* LIEB, *who slips a pair of handcuffs on* HICKEY's *wrists.* HICKEY *stares at them with stupid incomprehension.* MORAN *takes his arm*) Come along and spill your guts where we can get it on paper.

HICKEY No, wait, Officer! You owe me a break! I phoned and made it easy for you, didn't I? Just a few minutes! (*To* HOPE—*pleadingly*) You know I couldn't say that to Evelyn, don't you, Harry—unless—

HOPE (*Eagerly*) And you've been crazy ever since? Everything you've said and done here—

HICKEY (*For a moment forgets his own obsession and his face takes on its familiar expression of affectionate amusement and he chuckles*) Now, Governor! Up to your old tricks, eh? I see what you're driving at, but I can't let you get away with— (*Then, as* HOPE's *expression turns to resentful callousness again and he looks away, he adds hastily with pleading desperation*) Yes, Harry, of course, I've been out of my mind ever since! All the time I've been here! You saw I was insane, didn't you?

MORAN (*With cynical disgust*) Can it! I've had enough of your act. Save it for the jury. (*Addressing the crowd, sharply*) Listen, you guys. Don't fall for his lies. He's starting to get foxy now and thinks he'll plead insanity. But he can't get away with it. (*The crowd at the grouped tables are grasping at hope now. They glare at him resentfully*)

HOPE (*Begins to bristle in his old-time manner*) Bejees, you dumb dick, you've got a crust trying to tell us about Hickey! We've known him for years, and every one of us noticed he was nutty the minute he showed up here! Bejees, if you'd heard all the crazy bull he was pulling about bringing us peace—like a bughouse preacher escaped from an asylum! If you'd seen all the damned-fool things he made us do! We only did them because— (*He hesitates—then defiantly*) Because we hoped he'd come out of it if we kidded him along and humored him. (*He looks around at the others*) Ain't that right, fellers? (*They burst into a chorus of eager assent: "Yes, Harry!" "That's it, Harry!" "That's why!" "We knew he was crazy!" "Just to humor him!"*)

MORAN A fine bunch of rats! Covering up for a dirty, cold-blooded murderer.

HOPE (*Stung into recovering all his old fuming truculence*) Is that so? Bejees, you know the old story, when Saint Patrick drove the snakes out of Ireland they swam to New York and joined the police force! Ha! (*He cackles insultingly*) Bejees, we can believe it now when we look at you, can't we, fellers? (*They all growl assent, glowering defiantly at* MORAN. MORAN *glares at them, looking as if he'd like to forget his prisoner and start cleaning out the place.* HOPE *goes on pugnaciously*) You stand up for your rights, bejees, Hickey! Don't let this smart-aleck dick get funny with you. If he pulls any rubber-hose tricks, you let me know! I've still got friends at the Hall! Bejees, I'll have him back in uniform pounding a beat where the only graft he'll get will be stealing tin cans from the goats!

MORAN (*Furiously*) Listen, you cockeyed old bum, for a plugged nickel I'd— (*Controlling himself, turns to* HICKEY, *who is oblivious to all this, and yanks his arm*) Come on, you!

HICKEY (*With a strange mad earnestness*) Oh, I want to go, Officer. I can hardly wait now. I should have phoned you from the house right afterwards. It was a waste of time coming here. I've got to explain to Evelyn. But I know she's forgiven me. She knows I was insane. You've got me all wrong, Officer. I want to go to the Chair.

MORAN Crap!

HICKEY (*Exasperatedly*) God, you're a dumb dick! Do you suppose I give a damn about life now? Why, you bonehead, I haven't got a single damned lying hope or pipe dream left!

MORAN (*Jerks him around to face the door to the hall*) Get a move on!

HICKEY (*As they start walking toward rear—insistently*) All I want you to see is I was out of my mind afterwards, when I laughed at her! I was a raving rotten lunatic or I couldn't have said— Why, Evelyn was the only thing on God's earth I ever loved! I'd have killed myself before

I'd ever have hurt her! (*They disappear in the hall.* HICKEY's *voice keeps on protesting*)

HOPE (*Calls after him*)   Don't worry, Hickey! They can't give you the Chair! We'll testify you was crazy! Won't we, fellers? (*They all assent. Two or three echo* HOPE's "*Don't worry, Hickey.*" *Then from the hall comes the slam of the street door.* HOPE's *face falls—with genuine sorrow*) He's gone. Poor crazy son of a bitch! (*All the group around him are sad and sympathetic, too.* HOPE *reaches for his drink*) Bejees, I need a drink. (*They grab their glasses.* HOPE *says hopefully*) Bejees, maybe it'll have the old kick, now he's gone. (*He drinks and they follow suit*)

ROCKY (*Comes forward from where he has stood in the bar entrance— hopefully*)   Yeah, Boss, maybe we can get drunk now. (*He sits in the chair by* CHUCK *and pours a drink and tosses it down. Then they all sit still, waiting for the effect, as if this drink were a crucial test, so absorbed in hopeful expectancy that they remain oblivious to what happens at* LARRY's *table*)

LARRY (*His eyes full of pain and pity—in a whisper, aloud to himself*)   May the Chair bring him peace at last, the poor tortured bastard!

PARRITT (*Leans toward him—in a strange low insistent voice*)   Yes, but he isn't the only one who needs peace, Larry. I can't feel sorry for him. He's lucky. He's through, now. It's all decided for him. I wish it was decided for me. I've never been any good at deciding things. Even about selling out, it was the tart the detective agency got after me who put it in my mind. You remember what Mother's like, Larry. She makes all the decisions. She's always decided what I must do. She doesn't like anyone to be free but herself. (*He pauses, as if waiting for comment, but* LARRY *ignores him*) I suppose you think I ought to have made those dicks take me away with Hickey. But how could I prove it, Larry? They'd think I was nutty. Because she's still alive. You're the only one who can understand how guilty I am. Because you know her and what I've done to her. You know I'm really much guiltier than he is. You know what I did is a much worse murder. Because she is dead and yet she has to live. For a while. But she can't live long in jail. She loves freedom too much. And I can't kid myself like Hickey, that she's at peace. As long as she lives, she'll never be able to forget what I've done to her even in her sleep. She'll never have a second's peace. (*He pauses —then bursts out*) Jesus, Larry, can't you say something? (LARRY *is at the breaking point.* PARRITT *goes on*) And I'm not putting up any bluff, either, that I was crazy afterwards when I laughed to myself and thought, "You know what you can do with your freedom pipe dream now, don't you, you damned old bitch!"

LARRY (*Snaps and turns on him, his face convulsed with detestation. His quivering voice has a condemning command in it*) Go! Get the hell out of life, God damn you, before I choke it out of you! Go up—!
PARRITT (*His manner is at once transformed. He seems suddenly at peace with himself. He speaks simply and gratefully*) Thanks, Larry. I just wanted to be sure. I can see now it's the only possible way I can ever get free from her. I guess I've really known that all my life. (*He pauses—then with a derisive smile*) It ought to comfort Mother a little, too. It'll give her the chance to play the great incorruptible Mother of the Revolution, whose only child is the Proletariat. She'll be able to say: "Justice is done! So may all traitors die!" She'll be able to say: "I am glad he's dead! Long live the Revolution!" (*He adds with a final implacable jeer*) You know her, Larry! Always a ham!
LARRY (*Pleads distractedly*) Go, for the love of Christ, you mad tortured bastard, for your own sake! (HUGO *is roused by this. He lifts his head and peers uncomprehendingly at* LARRY. *Neither* LARRY *nor* PARRITT *notices him*)
PARRITT (*Stares at* LARRY. *His face begins to crumble as if he were going to break down and sob. He turns his head away, but reaches out fumblingly and pats* LARRY's *arm and stammers*) Jesus, Larry, thanks. That's kind. I knew you were the only one who could understand my side of it. (*He gets to his feet and turns toward the door*)
HUGO (*Looks at* PARRITT *and bursts into his silly giggle*) Hello, leedle Don, leedle monkey-face! Don't be a fool! Buy me a trink!
PARRITT (*Puts on an act of dramatic bravado—forcing a grin*) Sure, I will, Hugo! Tomorrow! Beneath the willow trees! (*He walks to the door with a careless swagger and disappears in the hall. From now on,* LARRY *waits, listening for the sound he knows is coming from the backyard outside the window, but trying not to listen, in an agony of horror and cracking nerve*)
HUGO (*Stares after* PARRITT *stupidly*) Stupid fool! Hickey make you crazy, too. (*He turns to the oblivious* LARRY—*with a timid eagerness*) I'm glad, Larry, they take the crazy Hickey avay to asylum. He makes me have bad dreams. He makes me tell lies about myself. He makes me want to spit on all I have ever dreamed. Yes, I am glad they take him to asylum. I don't feel I am dying now. He vas selling death to me, that crazy salesman. I think I have a trink now, Larry. (*He pours a drink and gulps it down*)
HOPE (*Jubilantly*) Bejees, fellers, I'm feeling the old kick, or I'm a liar! It's putting life back in me! Bejees, if all I've lapped up begins to hit me, I'll be paralyzed before I know it! It was Hickey kept it from— Bejees, I know that sounds crazy, but he was crazy, and he'd got all of

us as bughouse as he was. Bejees, it does queer things to you, having to listen day and night to a lunatic's pipe dreams—pretending you believe them, to kid him along and doing any crazy thing he wants to humor him. It's dangerous, too. Look at me pretending to start for a walk just to keep him quiet. I knew damned well it wasn't the right day for it. The sun was broiling and the streets full of automobiles. Bejees, I could feel myself getting sunstroke, and an automobile damn near ran over me. (*He appeals to* ROCKY, *afraid of the result, but daring it*) Ask Rocky. He was watching. Didn't it, Rocky?

ROCKY (*A bit tipsily*) What's dat, Boss? Jees, all de booze I've mopped up is beginning to get to me. (*Earnestly*) De automobile, Boss? Sure, I seen it! Just missed yuh! I thought yuh was a goner. (*He pauses—then looks around at the others, and assumes the old kidding tone of the inmates, but hesitantly, as if still a little afraid*) On de woid of a honest bartender! (*He tries a wink at the others. They all respond with smiles that are still a little forced and uneasy*)

HOPE (*Flashes him a suspicious glance. Then he understands—with his natural testy manner*) You're a bartender, all right. No one can say different. (ROCKY *looks grateful*) But, bejees, don't pull that honest junk! You and Chuck ought to have cards in the Burglars' Union! (*This time there is an eager laugh from the group.* HOPE *is delighted*) Bejees, it's good to hear someone laugh again! All the time that bas—poor old Hickey was here, I didn't have the heart— Bejees, I'm getting drunk and glad of it! (*He cackles and reaches for the bottle*) Come on, fellers. It's on the house. (*They pour drinks. They begin rapidly to get drunk now.* HOPE *becomes sentimental*) Poor old Hickey! We mustn't hold him responsible for anything he's done. We'll forget that and only remember him the way we've always known him before—the kindest, biggest-hearted guy ever wore shoe leather. (*They all chorus hearty sentimental assent:* "That's right, Harry!" "That's all!" "Finest fellow!" "Best scout!" *etc.* HOPE *goes on*) Good luck to him in Matteawan![23] Come on, bottoms up! (*They all drink. At the table by the window* LARRY's *hands grip the edge of the table. Unconsciously his head is inclined toward the window as he listens*)

LARRY (*Cannot hold back an anguished exclamation*) Christ! Why don't he—!

HUGO (*Beginning to be drunk again—peers at him*) Vhy don't he what? Don't be a fool! Hickey's gone. He vas crazy. Have a trink. (*Then as he receives no reply—with vague uneasiness*) What's matter with you, Larry? You look funny. What you listen to out in backyard, Larry?

[23] A New York State hospital for the criminally insane.

(CORA *begins to talk in the group at right*)

CORA (*Tipsily*) Well, I thank Gawd now me and Chuck did all we could to humor de poor nut. Jees, imagine us goin' off like we really meant to git married, when we ain't even picked out a farm yet!

CHUCK (*Eagerly*) Sure ting, Baby. We kidded him we was serious.

JIMMY (*Confidently—with a gentle, drunken unction*) I may as well say I detected his condition almost at once. All that talk of his about tomorrow, for example. He had the fixed idea of the insane. It only makes them worse to cross them.

WILLIE (*Eagerly*) Same with me, Jimmy. Only I spent the day in the park. I wasn't such a damned fool as to—

LEWIS (*Getting jauntily drunk*) Picture my predicament if I *had* gone to the Consulate. The pal of mine there is a humorous blighter. He would have got me a job out of pure spite. So I strolled about and finally came to roost in the park. (*He grins with affectionate kidding at* WETJOEN) And lo and behold, who was on the neighboring bench but my old battlefield companion, the Boer that walks like a man—who, if the British Government had taken my advice, would have been removed from his fetid kraal on the veldt straight to the baboon's cage at the London Zoo, and little children would now be asking their nurses: "Tell me, Nana, is that the Boer General, the one with the blue behind?" (*They all laugh uproariously.* LEWIS *leans over and slaps* WETJOEN *affectionately on the knee*) No offense meant, Piet, old chap.

WETJOEN (*Beaming at him*) No offense taken, you tamned Limey! (WETJOEN *goes on—grinningly*) About a job, I felt the same as you, Cecil.

(*At the table by the window* HUGO *speaks to* LARRY *again*)

HUGO (*With uneasy insistence*) What's matter, Larry? You look scared. What you listen for out there? (*But* LARRY *doesn't hear, and* JOE *begins talking in the group at right*)

JOE (*With drunken self-assurance*) No, suh, I wasn't fool enough to git in no crap game. Not while Hickey's around. Crazy people puts a jinx on you.

(MCGLOIN *is now heard. He is leaning across in front of* WETJOEN *to talk to* ED MOSHER *on* HOPE'S *left*)

MCGLOIN (*With drunken earnestness*) I know you saw how it was, Ed. There was no good trying to explain to a crazy guy, but it ain't the right time. You know how getting reinstated is.

MOSHER (*Decidedly*) Sure, Mac. The same way with the circus. The boys tell me the rubes are wasting all their money buying food and

times never was so hard. And I never was one to cheat for chicken feed.
HOPE (*Looks around him in an ecstasy of bleary sentimental content*) Bejees, I'm cockeyed! Bejees, you're all cockeyed! Bejees, we're all all right! Let's have another! (*They pour out drinks. At the table by the window* LARRY *has unconsciously shut his eyes as he listens.* HUGO *is peering at him frightenedly now*)
HUGO (*Reiterates stupidly*) What's matter, Larry? Why you keep eyes shut? You look dead. What you listen for in backyard? (*Then, as* LARRY *doesn't open his eyes or answer, he gets up hastily and moves away from the table, mumbling with frightened anger*) Crazy fool! You vas crazy like Hickey! You give me bad dreams, too. (*He shrinks quickly past the table where* HICKEY *had sat to the rear of the group at right*)
ROCKY (*Greets him with boisterous affection*) Hello, dere, Hugo! Welcome to de party!
HOPE Yes, bejees, Hugo! Sit down! Have a drink! Have ten drinks, bejees!
HUGO (*Forgetting* LARRY *and bad dreams, gives his familiar giggle*) Hello, leedle Harry! Hello, nice, leedle, funny monkey-faces! (*Warming up, changes abruptly to his usual declamatory denunciation*) Gottamned stupid bourgeois! Soon comes the Day of Judgment! (*They make derisive noises and tell him to sit down. He changes again, giggling good-naturedly, and sits at rear of the middle table*) Give me ten trinks, Harry. Don't be a fool. (*They laugh.* ROCKY *shoves a glass and bottle at him. The sound of* MARGIE'S *and* PEARL'S *voices is heard from the hall, drunkenly shrill. All of the group turn toward the door as the two appear. They are drunk and look blowsy and disheveled. Their manner as they enter hardens into a brazen defensive truculence*)
MARGIE (*Stridently*) Gangway for two good whores!
PEARL Yeah! and we want a drink quick!
MARGIE (*Glaring at* ROCKY) Shake de lead outa your pants, Pimp! A little soivice!
ROCKY (*His black bullet eyes sentimental, his round Wop face grinning welcome*) Well, look who's here! (*He goes to them unsteadily, opening his arms*) Hello, dere, Sweethearts! Jees, I was beginnin' to worry about yuh, honest! (*He tries to embrace them. They push his arms away, regarding him with amazed suspicion*)
PEARL What kind of a gag is dis?
HOPE (*Calls to them effusively*) Come on and join the party, you broads! Bejees, I'm glad to see you! (*The girls exchange a bewildered glance, taking in the party and the changed atmosphere*)
MARGIE Jees, what's come off here?
PEARL Where's dat louse, Hickey?
ROCKY De cops got him. He'd gone crazy and croaked his wife. (*The*

girls exclaim, "Jees!" But there is more relief than horror in it.
ROCKY goes on) He'll get Matteawan. He ain't responsible. What he's pulled don't mean nuttin'. So forget dat whore stuff. I'll knock de block off anyone calls you whores! I'll fill de bastard full of lead! Yuh're tarts, and what de hell of it? Yuh're as good as anyone! So forget it, see? (*They let him get his arms around them now. He gives them a hug. All the truculence leaves their faces. They smile and exchange maternally amused glances*)

MARGIE (*With a wink*)   Our little bartender, ain't he, Poil?

PEARL   Yeah, and a cute little Ginny at dat! (*They laugh*)

MARGIE   And is he stinko!

PEARL   Stinko is right. But he ain't got nuttin' on us. Jees, Rocky, did we have a big time at Coney!

HOPE   Bejees, sit down, you dumb broads! Welcome home! Have a drink! Have ten drinks, bejees! (*They take the empty chairs on* CHUCK's *left, warmly welcomed by all.* ROCKY *stands in back of them, a hand on each of their shoulders, grinning with proud proprietorship.* HOPE *beams over and under his crooked spectacles with the air of a host whose party is a huge success, and rambles on happily*) Bejees, this is all right! We'll make this my birthday party, and forget the other. We'll get paralyzed! But who's missing? Where's the Old Wise Guy? Where's Larry?

ROCKY   Over by de window, Boss. Jees, he's got his eyes shut. De old bastard's asleep. (*They turn to look.* ROCKY *dismisses him*) Aw, to hell wid him. Let's have a drink. (*They turn away and forget him*)

LARRY (*Torturedly arguing to himself in a shaken whisper*)   It's the only way out for him! For the peace of all concerned, as Hickey said! (*Snapping*) God damn his yellow soul, if he doesn't soon, I'll go up and throw him off!—like a dog with its guts ripped out you'd put out of misery! (*He half rises from his chair just as from outside the window comes the sound of something hurtling down, followed by a muffled, crunching thud.* LARRY *gasps and drops back on his chair, shuddering, hiding his face in his hands. The group at right hear it but are too preoccupied with drinks to pay much attention*)

HOPE (*Wonderingly*)   What the hell was that?

ROCKY   Aw, nuttin'. Someting fell off de fire escape. A mattress, I'll bet. Some of dese bums been sleepin' on de fire escapes.

HOPE (*His interest diverted by this excuse to beef—testily*)   They've got to cut it out! Bejees, this ain't a fresh-air cure. Mattresses cost money.

MOSHER   Now don't start crabbing at the party, Harry. Let's drink up. (HOPE *forgets it and grabs his glass, and they all drink*)

LARRY (*In a whisper of horrified pity*)   Poor devil! (*A long-forgotten faith returns to him for a moment and he mumbles*) God rest his soul in peace. (*He opens his eyes—with a bitter self-derision*) Ah, the damned pity—the wrong kind, as Hickey said! Be God, there's no hope! I'll never be a success in the grandstand—or anywhere else! Life is too much for me! I'll be a weak fool looking with pity at the two sides of everything till the day I die! (*With an intense bitter sincerity*) May that day come soon! (*He pauses startledly, surprised at himself —then with a sardonic grin*) Be God, I'm the only real convert to death Hickey made here. From the bottom of my coward's heart I mean that now!

HOPE (*Calls effusively*)   Hey there, Larry! Come over and get paralyzed! What the hell you doing, sitting there? (*Then as* LARRY *doesn't reply he immediately forgets him and turns to the party. They are all very drunk now, just a few drinks ahead of the passing-out stage, and hilariously happy about it*) Bejees, let's sing! Let's celebrate! It's my birthday party! Bejees, I'm oreyeyed! I want to sing! (*He starts the chorus of* "She's the Sunshine of Paradise Alley," *and instantly they all burst into song. But not the same song. Each starts the chorus of his or her choice.* JIMMY TOMORROW'S *is* "A Wee Dock and Doris"; ED MOSHER'S, "Break the News to Mother"; WILLIE OBAN'S, *the Sailor Lad ditty he sang in Act One;* GENERAL WETJOEN'S, "Waiting at the Church"; MCGLOIN'S, "Tammany"; CAPTAIN LEWIS'S, "The Old Kent Road"; JOE'S, "All I Got Was Sympathy"; PEARL'S *and* MARGIE'S, "Everybody's Doing It"; ROCKY'S, "You Great Big Beautiful Doll"; CHUCK'S, "The Curse of an Aching Heart"; CORA'S, "The Oceana Roll"; *while* HUGO *jumps to his feet and, pounding on the table with his fist, bellows in his guttural basso the French Revolutionary* "Carmagnole." *A weird cacophony results from this mixture and they stop singing to roar with laughter. All but* HUGO, *who keeps on with drunken fervor*)

HUGO   Dansons la Carmagnole!
Vive le son! Vive le son!
Dansons la Carmagnole!
Vive le son des canons!

(*They all turn on him and howl him down with amused derision. He stops singing to denounce them in his most fiery style*) Capitalist swine! Stupid bourgeois monkeys! (*He declaims*) "The days grow hot, O Babylon!" (*They all take it up and shout in enthusiastic jeering chorus*) " 'Tis cool beneath thy willow trees!" (*They pound their glasses on the table, roaring with laughter, and* HUGO *giggles with them. In his chair by the window,* LARRY *stares in front of him, oblivious to their racket*)

Curtain

ARTHUR MILLER
[1915 –   ]

❦ *The Man*

THE SECOND SON of a middle-class Jewish clothing manufacturer, Arthur Miller was born and raised in New York City. During his school years, his chief interest was football, in which he suffered an injury that disqualified him from the armed forces during World War II; he was not, he recalls, "encumbered by anything resembling a thought." Upon graduation from high school in 1932, he worked in an auto parts warehouse for fifteen dollars a week (an experience drawn upon for *A Memory of Two Mondays*); by the fall of 1934, he had saved enough money to attend the University of Michigan. During his sophomore and junior years, he won Hopwood awards for playwriting and, upon graduation in 1938, won a playwriting contest sponsored by the Theater Guild. The following year he joined the W.P.A. Federal Theater Project as a dramatist. After the project ended, he did radio and film work, and wrote a moderately successful novel, *Focus*, about antisemitism.

Miller's first produced play, *The Man Who Had All the Luck*—about the American success myth—lasted only four performances on Broadway; his next play, *All My Sons*, not only ran for over three hundred performances, but also won a Drama Critics' Circle Award. Two years later, *Death of a Salesman*, held by some critics to be one of the more significant modern tragedies, ran more than seven hundred performances and won both the Drama Critics' Circle Award and the Pulitzer Prize. Four years later, *The Crucible* won an Antoinette Perry Award (a "Tony").

The twin sobriquets "witch-hunting" and "McCarthyism"—the former inspired by the Salem trials which were the source of *The Crucible*, the latter by the notorious senator from Wisconsin—describe an aspect of American political life in the 1950's. Although *The Crucible* has an importance beyond the immediate political events of its day, it is also relevant to these events. Miller's liberal political views made him the target of congressional un-American investigators. Life imitated art when Miller was subpoenaed in 1956, for he emulated the actions of John Proctor, protagonist of *The Crucible*: the playwright agreed to talk about himself but refused to discuss any of his acquaintances. He was indicted for contempt, found guilty the following year, and had his conviction reversed by the Appeals Court in 1958.

During these stormy political years, Miller's first marriage ended. In 1956 he married the actress Marilyn Monroe, for whom he wrote a motion picture, *The Misfits* (filmed in 1960). That same year, they were divorced. Two years later, she committed suicide. Miller's play, *After the Fall*, reflects both political and personal aspects of his life, though the play is not an autobiography.

❧ *The Work*

MORAL PASSION and an attitude of social responsibility form an important aspect of Arthur Miller's plays. In *All My Sons*, a war profiteer who has sold defective airplane parts to the government, choosing wealth and security for his sons at the possible cost of the lives of other people's sons, accepts his guilt and commits suicide. In *A View from the Bridge*, a longshoreman who had taken under his protection illegal immigrants from Italy forgoes his responsibility in neurotic frenzy and informs on them to the immigration authorities. Miller's adaptation of Ibsen's *An Enemy of the People* concerns integrity and responsibility to the community, as does *Incident at Vichy*, in which an Austrian aristocrat atones for a life of social irresponsibility by taking the place of a Jew marked for death by the Nazis. *After the Fall* dramatizes a quest by the leading character, Quentin, who seeks to uncover his responsibility in the fates of those whose lives he touched closely, notably his suicidal second wife.

Integrity and responsibility are connected to a search for identity. Quentin's search is for himself, taking place in his past and within his mind. Willy Loman, in *Death of a Salesman*, clings to the American dream of success through personality (a myth cherished by the Gentleman

Caller in *Glass Menagerie*), never understanding himself or his real needs. "The man didn't know who he was," his older son accurately comments; he, on the other hand, finds himself and rejects his father's false dream. However, though Miller dramatizes the individual in a moment of self-confrontation and potential self-understanding, he does not overlook his role in the social fabric. His characters are clearly related to family, community, and nation.

❧ *The Play*

LIKE THE PROBLEMS of social responsibility and self-knowledge, that of integrity has been a major concern not only in the plays of Arthur Miller but in the modern drama generally, including works as diverse as *Peer Gynt* and *The Iceman Cometh*. These questions dominate *The Crucible*, and as each of the characters enters his own crucible, an aspect of the subject of integrity is revealed. The fate of the principal character, Proctor, exemplifies the conflict between integrity and self-preservation; it dramatizes the theme that one should preserve one's integrity at any cost—even one's life. At the opposite pole is Abigail, who has no integrity and who, to save herself, destroys others. Elizabeth insists upon the integrity of her marriage to the point that this virtue becomes a vice, an uncompromising and unyielding attitude to her husband; but in the midst of her ordeal she faces the truth about herself. Hale—who perhaps undergoes a more radical change than any other character—begins with complete integrity as he resolves to keep an open mind about the presence of witches; when he realizes that his life is based on false foundations, he goes to the extreme of advising the condemned persons to perjure themselves to save their lives.

The subject has heroic implications, and the play's hero-victims have stature. They do not expire with a whimper but endure their trials and ultimately go to their deaths with dignity. When huge stones are placed upon the chest of old Giles Corey to coerce him into talking, he says but two words, "More weight." Proctor, like Joan of Arc, tears up his confession, and advises his wife as he goes to his death, "Give them no tear. Show them a heart of stone and sink them with it." Unlike Willy Loman, who did not know who he was, and unlike his counterparts who find it difficult to articulate what they stand for, the people of Salem—and

Miller himself has pointed this out—were aware of who they were, recognized the moral forces in conflict, and knew precisely "where they stood" in relation to these forces. They could articulate their feelings and beliefs. Moreover, they could use language more flavorful and rhetorical than that of ordinary people today. Such a passage as "Now Hell and Heaven grapple on our backs, and all our old pretense is ripped away. . . . It is a Providence and no great change. We are what we always were, but naked now. Aye, naked. And the wind, God's icy wind, will blow" may not possess the lyric beauty of Synge's dialogue, but it is richer than the prosaic dialogue that dominates our stage.

The Crucible presents an intermingling of social and psychological motifs characteristic of its author. After the play's Broadway opening, Miller felt that the relationship between Proctor and Abigail needed expansion, and he added a scene in which the two confront each other in the forest after his wife's arrest. The scene provides a transition from the frightened, improvising vixen of the sick-bed scene to the psychotic demon of the trial scene, who aims at becoming Proctor's second wife. Unfortunately, there is a corresponding loss in dramatic momentum in the averted movement from arrest to trial, and a shift in emphasis toward the psychological aspect. One of the major production questions concerns the scene's inclusion or exclusion, and a factor to be weighed is the opportunity it provides for emotional acting. Miller's skill in giving actors powerful roles and in presenting directors with highly charged scenes—such as this forest scene and the hallucination scene at the end of the trial—are among the more striking characteristics of *The Crucible* in particular and of his plays in general.

❧ *Dramatic Works*

The Man Who Had All the Luck, 1944.
All My Sons, 1947.
Death of a Salesman, 1949.
An Enemy of the People (adaptation of the play by Henrik Ibsen), 1950.
The Crucible, 1953.
A Memory of Two Mondays, 1955.
A View from the Bridge, 1955.
After the Fall, 1964.
Incident at Vichy, 1964.

❧ Selective Bibliography

Bentley, Eric. *The Dramatic Event*. New York: Horizon, 1954.

Ganz, Arthur. "The Silence of Arthur Miller," *Drama Survey*, III (Fall, 1963).

Gassner, John. *Theatre at the Crossroads*. New York: Holt, Rinehart & Winston, 1960.

Miller, Arthur. "A Note on the Historical Accuracy of *The Crucible*," in *Theatre and Drama in the Making*, eds. John Gassner and Ralph G. Allen. New York: Houghton Mifflin, 1964, Vol. II.

Weales, Gerald. *American Drama Since World War II*. New York: Harcourt, Brace, 1962.

Welland, Dennis. *Arthur Miller*. New York: Grove Press, 1961.

JOHN OSBORNE
[1929 –]

❧ *The Man*

JOHN JAMES OSBORNE was born in the year of the stockmarket crash and was raised during the Depression. Although Osborne, unlike Jimmy Porter (the protagonist of *Look Back in Anger*), did not attend a university, he did receive a general certificate of education from Belmont College. A small-part actor for a time, his playwriting career was established with *Look Back in Anger*. In addition to stage and television plays, he wrote the award-winning film, *Tom Jones*.

❧ *The Work*

THE PREMIERE OF *Look Back in Anger* at the Royal Court Theatre (one hundred years after Shaw's birth and fifty years after the Vedrenne-Barker seasons at the same theater) was a milestone in modern English drama. There is a pressing contemporaneity about Osborne's subjects and characters that one does not find in earlier plays, such as those of Eliot. Eliot abstracts and consistently attempts to universalize the particulars with which he deals. Osborne does the reverse: even when he portrays an historical figure, Martin Luther, one feels a relevance to today's rebels; and one finds striking similarities between Osborne's treatment of the Established Catholic Church of the sixteenth century and today's Establishment. Osborne's world is one of nuclear explosions, of a shrinking

British Empire, and of class distinctions as seen from below.

Less than three months before *Look Back in Anger* opened, the British government sent Archbishop Makarios of Cyprus into exile. Before the end of the year, the United States tested the first aerial H Bomb on Bikini Atoll, the Russians crushed the Hungarian uprising, and the Suez Crisis occurred. Such writers as Kingsley Amis, John Wain, and Colin Wilson were at this time questioning or attacking various aspects or attitudes of the Establishment. *Look Back in Anger* became not only the focal point but virtually the Bible of the under-thirty generation in England; it was, in fact, responsible for the label "Angry Young Man." Osborne attacked the Establishment as "inept deceivers . . . who rule our lives. . . . they are not merely dangerous, they are murderous." He satirized such sacred cows as religion, the royal family, the class system, journalism, and public taste.

It might appear that Osborne is a latter-day Odets in an England that is lagging behind the United States. Although it is true that there is still a strong caste system in England and that despite the medical benefits of the English Welfare State the British worker has a lower standard of living than his American counterpart, Osborne's plays are considerably different from those of Odets. They present no such pat solutions as those in *Waiting for Lefty. Awake and Sing!* prophesied Utopia, whereas *Look Back in Anger* portrays the progeny of anti-Utopia. Odets' naïvely hopeful heroes represent the fighting optimism of the Depression era, whereas Osborne's represent the raging despair of the more materially comfortable atomic era.

❧ *The Play*

IN *Man and Superman*, written in 1903, Bernard Shaw created an automobile driver-mechanic named Enry Straker, whom he called "the New Man." Straker is proud of his lower-class origins; John Tanner, his employer, remarks that he takes more trouble to drop the letter *h* from his speech than his father did to acquire it. He is also proud that he is a skilled worker, and states with polite condescension that at Oxford one is taught to be a gentleman while at the Polytechnic School, which he attended, one is taught to be an engineer. Straker is outspoken even before his employer. When Tanner remarks that he would have given a sovereign to Straker's more deferential grandfather, the mechanic corrects him, "Five shillins, more likely." And when Tanner proclaims himself to be a Socialist, Straker adds, "(*drily*) Most rich men are, I notice." Shaw's New Man represents proletarian pride in his skills, education without breeding, and a socialist outlook. Enry Straker looks forward to the man Osborne describes as looking back. Jimmy Porter is Enry Straker's grandson, living in a world that Enry helped create.

Porter, too, comes from working-class people, feels at home with them, and is continually berating the upper and middle classes. What was disdain in Straker becomes contempt in Porter. Although the latter is not a skilled laborer, he attended a university—not Oxford or Cambridge, but one of the state-supported institutions. It is probably no more than a coincidence, but Porter's patroness, the woman who started him off in the sweet stall, has the same surname as Straker's employer, Tanner.

Just as Straker is the New Man of the start of the century, Porter is the New Man of midcentury, a member of what English critic Kenneth Tynan calls the "new intelligentsia created by free education and state scholarships." The attitude of the Establishment toward these people has been summarized by Somerset Maugham: "They are scum."

Jimmy Porter looks about him into a void. He sees the dreary mechanized materialism of what he calls "the American Age." The Brave New World has become "the Brave New-nothing-very-much-thank-you." Looking forward only to more of the same, he angrily looks back and sees the Edwardian values exposed as hypocritical and fraudulent, the Socialist ideals betrayed. His values begin "on the far side of despair." All that remains to him is the animal affection and warmth of squirrel and bear.

Osborne's vigorous prose is not merely grafted onto a leading character; rather, the author has created a character who delights in flamboyant rhetoric. Jimmy's verbal lashes use different images for each target. Alison's father is "one of those sturdy old plants left over from the Edwardian Wilderness that can't understand why the sun isn't shining any more," while the religious Helena is described by such phrases as "genuflecting sin-jobber" and "full of ecstatic wind." Jimmy's language not only describes others but reveals himself; his description of Alison's mother, for example ("as rough as a night in a Bombay brothel, and as tough as a matelot's arm"), shows a character straining for effect as he tries to shock.

The other characters are more than sounding boards for the talkative leading man; each functions dramatically. The proletarian Cliff, unlike Jimmy, accepts his dreary life with calm, good-natured resignation. The Colonel, recently returned from India, is a relic of the attitudes and values of British imperialism. Helena professes belief in traditional codes of conduct while conducting her life in violation of these codes. Instead of changing her morality to suit her needs, she sublimates her needs to reaffirm her morality. Alison, on the other hand, changes her morality and in fact undergoes the most drastic change in the play. Although she has discarded the values of her parents and of Helena before we first see her, she acquires her husband's values only during the course of the play. When she leaves him and loses her child, she experiences insecurity, futility, and the nearness of death. She returns to him, capable of joining him to create a kind of happiness based on shared sorrow, a kind of shelter in a dangerous world.

Osborne's portrait of young people experiencing the social and personal tensions of midcentury England is dramatized in what the author himself has called an old-fashioned play. The opening tableaux of Acts I and III are parallel; first Alison, then Helena, stands at the ironing board while the men sit in armchairs reading newspapers. Following in the footsteps of Shaw, Osborne utilizes a conventional dramatic genre, the adultery play. In the first act The Other Woman arrives; in the second she persuades The Wife to leave and then goes to bed with The Husband; in the third The Wife returns, The Other Woman leaves, and Husband and Wife are reconciled. Osborne, like Shaw, perverts the morality implied in the traditional genre he exploits. The Other Woman, not The Wife, is the incarnation of traditional morality. The Wife states that she "gave up believing in the divine rights of marriage long ago." The Other Woman calls herself "evil" and the situation "wrong and terrible"; she tells The Wife, "You should have been outraged" and confesses, "I feel so—*ashamed.*" The Erring Husband is called "an Eminent Victorian." More important perhaps is the fact that the conventional reunion of husband and wife signals the affirmation not of the conventional but of the unconventional. The representative of traditional morality has left the household, following the departure of the representative of good-natured resignation. Alison's return to her husband implies a bolstering of the forces against the Establishment.

Although Osborne has been called an "Angry Young Man" and has been identified with Jimmy Porter, one should not assume that the author agrees with his antiheroic hero that there are no more good causes or that he shares his despair. To write of despair is not to despair. To write of frustration, heartache, and futility may be an act of affirmation.

❦ *Dramatic Works*

The Devil Inside Him (with Stella Linden), 1949.
Personal Enemy (with Anthony Creighton), 1955
Look Back in Anger, 1956.
The Entertainer, 1957
Epitaph for George Dillon (with Anthony Creighton), 1958 (written earlier than *Look Back in Anger*, but not performed professionally until this date).
The World of Paul Slickey, 1959.
Luther, 1961.
Plays for England: The Blood of the Bambergs and *Under Plain Cover*, 1962.
Inadmissible Evidence, 1964.
A Patriot for Me, 1965.

❦ *Selective Bibliography*

Allsop, Kenneth. *The Angry Decade.* New York: British Book Centre, 1958.
Huss, Roy. "John Osborne's Backward Half-Way Look," *Modern Drama*, VI (May, 1963).
Osborne, John. "They Call It Cricket," *Declaration*, ed. Tom Maschler. London: MacGibbon and Kee, 1959.
Taylor, John Russell. *Anger and After* (also called *The Angry Theatre*). Baltimore: Penguin, 1963.
Tynan, Kenneth. *Tynan on Theatre.* Harmondsworth: Penguin, 1964.
Worth, Katharine J. "The Angry Young Man: John Osborne," *Experimental Drama*, ed. William A. Armstrong. London: Bell, 1963.

Look Back in Anger
A Play in Three Acts

CAST

In Order of Appearance

JIMMY PORTER HELENA CHARLES
CLIFF LEWIS COLONEL REDFERN
ALISON PORTER

The action throughout takes place in the Porters' one-room flat in the Midlands.

TIME *The present* [i.e., 1956]

SCENES

ACT ONE

Early evening, April

ACT TWO

SCENE 1 *Two weeks later*
SCENE 2 *The following evening*

ACT THREE

SCENE 1 *Several months later*
SCENE 2 *A few minutes later*

Act One

The Porters' one-room flat in a large Midland town. Early evening. April.

The scene is a fairly large attic room, at the top of a large Victorian house. The ceiling slopes down quite sharply from L. to R. Down R. are two small low windows. In front of these is a dark oak dressing table. Most of the furniture is simple, and rather old. Up R. is a double bed, running the length of most of the back wall, the rest of which is taken up with a shelf of books. Down R. below the bed is a heavy chest of drawers, covered with books, neckties, and odds and ends, including a large, tattered toy teddy bear and soft, woolly squirrel. Up L. is a door. Below this a small wardrobe. Most of the wall L. is taken up with a high, oblong window. This looks out on to the landing, but light comes through it from a skylight beyond. Below the wardrobe is a gas stove, and, beside this, a, wooden food cupboard, on which is a small, portable radio. Down C. is a sturdy dining table and three chairs, and, below this, L. and R., two deep, shabby leather armchairs.

At rise of curtain, JIMMY and CLIFF are seated in the two armchairs R. and L., respectively. All that we can see of either of them is two pairs of legs, sprawled way out beyond the newspapers which hide the rest of them from sight. They are both reading. Beside them, and between them, is a jungle of newspapers and weeklies. When we do eventually see them, we find that JIMMY is a tall, thin young man about twenty-five, wearing a very worn tweed jacket and flannels. Clouds of smoke fill the room from the pipe he is smoking. He is a disconcerting mixture of sincerity and cheerful malice, of tenderness and freebooting cruelty; restless, importunate, full of pride, a combination which alienates the sensitive and insensitive alike. Blistering honesty, or apparent honesty, like his, makes few friends. To many he may seem sensitive to the point of vulgarity. To others, he is simply a loudmouth. To be as vehement as he is is to be almost noncommittal. CLIFF is the same age, short, dark, big-boned, wearing a pullover and grey, new, but very creased trousers. He is easy and relaxed, almost to lethargy, with the rather sad, natural intelligence of the self-taught. If JIMMY alienates love, CLIFF *seems to exact it—demonstrations of it, at least, even from the cautious. He is a soothing, natural counterpoint to* JIMMY.

Standing L., below the food cupboard, is ALISON. *She is leaning over an ironing board. Beside her is a pile of clothes. Hers is the most elusive personality to catch in the uneasy polyphony of these three people. She is tuned in a different key, a key of well-bred malaise that is often drowned in the robust orchestration of the other two. Hanging over the grubby, but expensive, skirt she is wearing is a cherry red shirt of* JIMMY's, *but she manages somehow to look quite elegant in it. She is roughly the same age as the men. Somehow, their combined physical oddity makes her beauty more striking than it really is. She is tall, slim, dark. The bones of her face are long and delicate. There is a surprising reservation about her eyes, which are so large and deep they should make equivocation impossible. The room is still, smoke-filled. The only sound is the occasional thud of* ALISON's *iron on the board. It is one of those chilly Spring evenings, all cloud and shadows. Presently,* JIMMY *throws his paper down.*

JIMMY Why do I do this every Sunday? Even the book reviews seem to be the same as last week's. Different books—same reviews. Have you finished that one yet?

CLIFF Not yet.

JIMMY I've just read three whole columns on the English Novel. Half of it's in French. Do the Sunday papers make *you* feel ignorant?

CLIFF Not 'arf.

JIMMY Well, you *are* ignorant. You're just a peasant. (*To* ALISON) What about you? You're not a peasant are you?

ALISON (*Absently*) What's that?

JIMMY I said do the papers make you feel you're not so brilliant after all?

ALISON Oh—I haven't read them yet.

JIMMY I didn't ask you that. I said—

CLIFF Leave the poor girlie alone. She's busy.

JIMMY Well, she can talk, can't she? You can talk, can't you? You can express an opinion. Or does the White Woman's Burden[1] make it impossible to think?

ALISON I'm sorry. I wasn't listening properly.

JIMMY You bet you weren't listening. Old Porter talks, and everyone

[1] In 1899 Rudyard Kipling coined the phrase "White Man's Burden" for the obligation of the white race to manage the affairs of the supposedly backward, nonwhite races in the colonies.

turns over and goes to sleep. And Mrs. Porter gets 'em all going with the first yawn.

CLIFF Leave her alone, I said.

JIMMY (*Shouting*) All right, dear. Go back to sleep. It was only me talking. You know? Talking? Remember? I'm sorry.

CLIFF Stop yelling. I'm trying to read.

JIMMY Why do you bother? You can't understand a word of it.

CLIFF Uh huh.

JIMMY You're too ignorant.

CLIFF Yes, and uneducated. Now shut up, will you?

JIMMY Why don't you get my wife to explain it to you? She's educated. (*To her*) That's right, isn't it?

CLIFF (*Kicking out at him from behind his paper*) Leave her alone, I said.

JIMMY Do that again, you Welsh ruffian, and I'll pull your ears off. (*He bangs* CLIFF's *paper out of his hands*)

CLIFF (*Leaning forward*) Listen—I'm trying to better myself. Let me get on with it, you big, horrible man. Give it me. (*Puts his hand out for paper*)

ALISON Oh, give it to him, Jimmy, for heaven's sake! I can't think!

CLIFF Yes, come on, give me the paper. She can't think.

JIMMY Can't think! (*Throws the paper back at him*) She hasn't had a thought for years! Have you?

ALISON No.

JIMMY (*Picks up a weekly*) I'm getting hungry.

ALISON Oh, no, not already!

CLIFF He's a bloody pig.

JIMMY I'm not a pig. I just like food—that's all.

CLIFF Like it! You're like a sexual maniac—only with you it's food. You'll end up in the *News of the World*,[2] boyo, you wait. James Porter, aged twenty-five, was bound over last week after pleading guilty to interfering with a small cabbage and two tins of beans on his way home from "The Builder's Arms." The accused said he hadn't been feeling well for some time, and had been having black-outs. He asked for his good record as an air-raid warden, second class, to be taken into account.

JIMMY (*Grins*) Oh, yes, yes, yes. I like to eat. I'd like to live too. Do you mind?

CLIFF Don't see any use in your eating at all. You never get any fatter.

JIMMY People like me don't get fat. I've tried to tell you before. We

---

[2] A scandal sheet.

just burn everything up. Now shut up while I read. You can make me some more tea.

CLIFF   Good God, you've just had a great potful! I only had one cup.

JIMMY   Like hell! Make some more.

CLIFF   (*To* ALISON)   Isn't that right? Didn't I only have one cup?

ALISON   (*Without looking up*)   That's right.

CLIFF   There you are. And she only had one cup too. I saw her. You guzzled the lot.

JIMMY   (*Reading his weekly*)   Put the kettle on.

CLIFF   Put it on yourself. You've creased up my paper.

JIMMY   I'm the only one who knows how to treat a paper, or anything else, in this house. (*Picks up another paper*) Girl here wants to know whether her boy friend will lose all respect for her if she gives him what he asks for. Stupid bitch.

CLIFF   Just let me get at her, that's all.

JIMMY   Who buys this damned thing? (*Throws it down*) Haven't you read the other posh[3] paper yet?

CLIFF   Which?

JIMMY   Well, there are only two posh papers on a Sunday[4]—the one you're reading, and this one. Come on, let me have that one, and you take this.

CLIFF   Oh, all right (*They exchange*) I was only reading the Bishop of Bromley. (*Puts out his hand to* ALISON) How are you, dullin'?

ALISON   All right, thank you, dear.

CLIFF   (*Grasping her hand*)   Why don't you leave all that, and sit down for a bit? You look tired.

ALISON   (*Smiling*)   I haven't much more to do.

CLIFF   (*Kisses her hand, and puts her fingers in his mouth*)   She's a beautiful girl, isn't she?

JIMMY   That's what they all tell me.

(*His eyes meet hers*)

CLIFF   It's a lovely, delicious paw you've got. Ummmmm. I'm going to bite it off.

ALISON   Don't! I'll burn his shirt.

JIMMY   Give her her finger back, and don't be so sickening. What's the Bishop of Bromley say?

CLIFF   (*Letting go of* ALISON)   Oh, it says here that he makes a very moving appeal to all Christians to do all they can to assist in the manufacture of the H-Bomb.

---

[3] Elegant, smart; the word would not be used by anyone in that class.
[4] *The Times* and *The Observer*.

JIMMY Yes, well, that's quite moving, I suppose. (*To* ALISON) Are you moved, my darling?

ALISON Well, naturally.

JIMMY There you are: even my wife is moved. I ought to send the Bishop a subscription. Let's see. What else does he say. Dumdidum-didumdidum. Ah, yes. He's upset because someone has suggested that he supports the rich against the poor. He says he denies the difference of class distinctions. "This idea has been persistently and wickedly fostered by—the working classes!" Well!

(*He looks up at both of them for reaction, but* CLIFF *is reading, and* ALISON *is intent on her ironing*)

JIMMY (*To* CLIFF) Did you read that bit?

CLIFF Um?

(*He has lost them, and he knows it, but he won't leave it*)

JIMMY (*To Alison*) You don't suppose your father could have written it, do you?

ALISON Written what?

JIMMY What I just read out, of course.

ALISON Why should my father have written it?

JIMMY Sounds rather like Daddy, don't you think?

ALISON Does it?

JIMMY Is the Bishop of Bromley his nom de plume, do you think?

CLIFF Don't take any notice of him. He's being offensive. And it's so easy for him.

JIMMY (*Quickly*) Did you read about the woman who went to the mass meeting of a certain American evangelist at Earls Court? She went forward, to declare herself for love or whatever it is, and, in the rush of converts to get to the front, she broke four ribs and got kicked in the head. She was yelling her head off in agony, but with 50,000 people putting all they'd got into "Onward Christian Soldiers," nobody even knew she was there. (*He looks up sharply for a response, but there isn't any*) Sometimes, I wonder if there isn't something wrong with me. What about that tea?

CLIFF (*Still behind paper*) What tea?

JIMMY Put the kettle on.

(ALISON *looks up at him*)

ALISON Do you want some more tea?

JIMMY I don't know. No, I don't think so.

ALISON Do you want some, Cliff?

JIMMY No, he doesn't. How much longer will you be doing that?

ALISON   Won't be long.
JIMMY   God, how I hate Sundays! It's always so depressing, always the same. We never seem to get any further, do we? Always the same ritual. Reading the papers, drinking tea, ironing. A few more hours, and another week gone. Our youth is slipping away. Do you know that?
CLIFF   (*Throws down paper*)   What's that?
JIMMY   (*Casually*)   Oh, nothing, nothing. Damn you, damn both of you, damn them all.
CLIFF   Let's go to the pictures. (*To* ALISON)   What do you say, lovely?
ALISON   I don't think I'll be able to. Perhaps Jimmy would like to go. (*To* JIMMY)   Would you like to?
JIMMY   And have my enjoyment ruined by the Sunday night yobs[5] in the front row? No, thank you. (*Pause*) Did you read Priestley's[6] piece this week? Why on earth I ask, I don't know. I know damned well you haven't. Why do I spend ninepence on that damned paper every week? Nobody reads it except me. Nobody can be bothered. No one can raise themselves out of their delicious sloth. You two will drive me round the bend soon—I know it, as sure as I'm sitting here. I know you're going to drive me mad. Oh, heavens, how I long for a little ordinary human enthusiasm. Just enthusiasm—that's all. I want to hear a warm, thrilling voice cry out Hallelujah! (*He bangs his breast theatrically*) Hallelujah! I'm alive! I've an idea. Why don't we have a little game? Let's pretend that we're human beings, and that we're actually alive. Just for a while. What do you say? Let's pretend we're human. (*He looks from one to the other*) Oh, brother, it's such a long time since I was with anyone who got enthusiastic about anything.
CLIFF   What did he say?
JIMMY   (*Resentful of being dragged away from his pursuit of* ALISON) What did who say?
CLIFF   Mr. Priestley.
JIMMY   What he always says, I suppose. He's like Daddy—still casting well-fed glances back to the Edwardian twilight from his comfortable, disenfranchised wilderness. What the devil have you done to those trousers?
CLIFF   Done?
JIMMY   Are they the ones you bought last week-end? Look at them. Do you see what he's done to those new trousers?
ALISON   You are naughty, Cliff. They look dreadful.
JIMMY   You spend good money on a new pair of trousers, and then

[5] Dolts.
[6] J. B. Priestley (1894–   ), English playwright, critic, and essayist.

sprawl about in them like a savage. What do you think you're going to do when I'm not around to look after you? Well, what are you going to do? Tell me?

CLIFF (*Grinning*) I don't know. (*To* ALISON) What am I going to do, lovely?

ALISON You'd better take them off.

JIMMY Yes, go on. Take 'em off. And I'll kick your behind for you.

ALISON I'll give them a press while I've got the iron on.

CLIFF O.K. (*Starts taking them off*) I'll just empty the pockets. (*Takes out keys, matches, handkerchief*)

JIMMY Give me those matches, will you?

CLIFF Oh, you're not going to start up that old pipe again, are you? It stinks the place out. (*To* ALISON) Doesn't it smell awful?

(*Jimmy grabs the matches, and lights up*)

ALISON I don't mind it. I've got used to it.

JIMMY She's a great one for getting used to things. If she were to die, and wake up in paradise—after the first five minutes, she'd have got used to it.

CLIFF (*Hands her the trousers*) Thank you, lovely. Give me a cigarette, will you?

JIMMY Don't give him one.

CLIFF I can't stand the stink of that old pipe any longer. I must have a cigarette.

JIMMY I thought the doctor said no cigarettes?

CLIFF Oh, why doesn't he shut up?

JIMMY All right. They're your ulcers. Go ahead, and have a bellyache, if that's what you want. I give up. I give up. I'm sick of doing things for people. And all for what?

(ALISON *gives* CLIFF *a cigarette. They both light up, and she goes on with her ironing*)

Nobody thinks, nobody cares. No beliefs, no convictions and no enthusiasm. Just another Sunday evening.

(CLIFF *sits down again, in his pullover and shorts*)

Perhaps there's a concert on. (*Picks up* Radio Times) Ah. (*Nudges* CLIFF *with his foot*) Make some more tea.

(CLIFF *grunts. He is reading again*)

Oh, yes. There's a Vaughan Williams.[7] Well, that's something, anyway.

[7] (Ralph) Vaughan Williams (1872–1958), English composer.

Something strong, something simple, something English. I suppose people like me aren't supposed to be very patriotic. Somebody said—what was it—we get our cooking from Paris (that's a laugh), our politics from Moscow, and our morals from Port Said.[8] Something like that, anyway. Who was it? (*Pause*) Well, you wouldn't know anyway. I hate to admit it, but I think I can understand how her Daddy must have felt when he came back from India, after all those years away. The old Edwardian brigade do make their brief little world look pretty tempting. All homemade cakes and croquet, bright ideas, bright uniforms. Always the same picture: high summer, the long days in the sun, slim volumes of verse, crisp linen, the smell of starch. What a romantic picture. Phony, too, of course. It must have rained sometimes. Still, even I regret it somehow, phony or not. If you've no world of your own, it's rather pleasant to regret the passing of someone else's. I must be getting sentimental. But I must say it's pretty dreary living in the American Age—unless you're an American, of course. Perhaps all our children will be Americans. That's a thought, isn't it? (*He gives* CLIFF *a kick, and shouts at him*) I said that's a thought!

CLIFF You did?

JIMMY You sit there like a lump of dough. I thought you were going to make me some tea.

(CLIFF *groans.* JIMMY *turns to* ALISON)

Is your friend Webster coming tonight?

ALISON He might drop in. You know what he is.

JIMMY Well, I hope he doesn't. I don't think I could take Webster tonight.

ALISON I thought you said he was the only person who spoke your language.

JIMMY So he is. Different dialect but same language. I like him. He's got bite, edge, drive——

ALISON Enthusiasm.

JIMMY You've got it. When he comes here, I begin to feel exhilarated. He doesn't like me, but he gives me something, which is more than I get from most people. Not since——

ALISON Yes, we know. Not since you were living with Madeline. (*She folds some of the clothes she has already ironed, and crosses to the bed with them*)

CLIFF (*Behind paper again*) Who's Madeline?

---

[8] In "England Your England" George Orwell wrote, "the English intelligentsia . . . take their cookery from Paris and their opinions from Moscow."

ALISON Oh, wake up, dear. You've heard about Madeline enough times. She was his mistress. Remember? When he was fourteen. Or was it thirteen?
JIMMY Eighteen.
ALISON He owes just about everything to Madeline.
CLIFF I get mixed up with all your women. Was she the one all those years older than you?
JIMMY Ten years.
CLIFF Proper little Marchbanks,[9] you are!
JIMMY What time's that concert on? (*Checks paper*)
CLIFF (*Yawns*) Oh, I feel so sleepy. Don't feel like standing behind that blinking sweet-stall[10] again tomorrow. Why don't you do it on your own, and let me sleep in?
JIMMY I've got to be at the factory first thing, to get some more stock, so you'll have to put it up on your own. Another five minutes.

(ALISON *has returned to her ironing board. She stands with her arms folded, smoking, staring thoughtfully*)

She had more animation in her little finger than you two put together.
CLIFF Who did?
ALISON Madeline.
JIMMY Her curiosity about things, and about people was staggering. It wasn't just a naïve nosiness. With her, it was simply the delight of being awake, and watching.

(ALISON *starts to press* CLIFF's *trousers*)

CLIFF (*Behind paper*) Perhaps I will make some tea, after all.
JIMMY (*Quietly*) Just to be with her was an adventure. Even to sit on the top of a bus with her was like setting out with Ulysses.
CLIFF Wouldn't have said Webster was much like Ulysses. He's an ugly little devil.
JIMMY I'm not talking about Webster, stupid. He's all right though, in his way. A sort of female Emily Brontë. He's the only one of your friends (*To* ALISON) who's worth tuppence, anyway. I'm surprised you get on with him.
ALISON So is he, I think.
JIMMY (*Rising to window R., and looking out*) He's not only got guts, but sensitivity as well. That's about the rarest combination I can think of. None of your other friends have got either.

[9] Eugene Marchbanks, the eighteen-year-old poet in Shaw's *Candida*, falls in love with thirty-three-year-old Candida.
[10] Candy stand.

ALISON (*Very quietly and earnestly*) Jimmy, please—don't go on.

(*He turns and looks at her. The tired appeal in her voice has pulled him up suddenly. But he soon gathers himself for a new assault. He walks C., behind* CLIFF, *and stands, looking down at his head*)

JIMMY Your friends—there's a shower for you.

CLIFF (*Mumbling*) Dry up. Let her get on with my trousers.

JIMMY (*Musingly*) Don't think I could provoke her. Nothing I could do would provoke her. Not even if I were to drop dead.

CLIFF Then drop dead.

JIMMY They're either militant like her Mummy and Daddy. Militant, arrogant, and full of malice. Or vague. She's somewhere between the two.

CLIFF Why don't you listen to that concert of yours? And don't stand behind me. That blooming droning on behind me gives me a funny feeling down the spine.

(JIMMY *gives his ears a twist and* CLIFF *roars with pain.* JIMMY *grins back at him*)

That hurt, you rotten sadist! (*To* ALISON) I wish you'd kick his head in for him.

JIMMY (*Moving in between them*) Have you ever seen her brother? Brother Nigel? The straight-backed, chinless wonder from Sandhurst?[11] I only met him once myself. He asked me to step outside when I told his mother she was evil minded.

CLIFF And did you?

JIMMY Certainly not. He's a big chap. Well, you've never heard so many well-bred commonplaces come from beneath the same bowler hat. The Platitude from Outer Space—that's brother Nigel. He'll end up in the Cabinet one day, make no mistake. But somewhere at the back of that mind is the vague knowledge that he and his pals have been plundering and fooling everybody for generations. (*Going upstage, and turning*) Now Nigel is just about as vague as you can get without being actually invisible. And invisible politicians aren't much use to anyone—not even to *his* supporters! And nothing is more vague about Nigel than his knowledge. His knowledge of life and ordinary human beings is so hazy, he really deserves some sort of decoration for it—a medal inscribed "For Vaguery in the Field." But it wouldn't do for him to be troubled by any stabs of conscience, however vague. (*Moving down again*) Besides, he's a patriot and an Englishman, and he doesn't

---

[11] The Royal Military College is located at Sandhurst.

like the idea that he may have been selling out his countrymen all these years, so what does he do? The only thing he *can* do—seek sanctuary in his own stupidity. The only way to keep things as much like they always have been as possible, is to make any alternative too much for your poor, tiny brain to grasp. It takes some doing nowadays. It really does. But they knew all about character building at Nigel's school, and he'll make it all right. Don't you worry, he'll make it. And, what's more, he'll do it better than anybody else!

(*There is no sound, only the plod of* ALISON's *iron. Her eyes are fixed on what she is doing.* CLIFF *stares at the floor. His cheerfulness has deserted him for the moment.* JIMMY *is rather shakily triumphant. He cannot allow himself to look at either of them to catch their response to his rhetoric, so he moves across to the window, to recover himself, and look out*)

It's started to rain. That's all it needs. This room and the rain. (*He's been cheated out of his response, but he's got to draw blood somehow. Conversationally*) Yes, that's the little woman's family. You know Mummy and Daddy, of course. And don't let the Marquess of Queensberry manner[12] fool you. They'll kick you in the groin while you're handing your hat to the maid. As for Nigel and Alison——(*In a reverent, Stuart Hibberd*[13] *voice*) Nigel and Alison. They're what they sound like: sycophantic, phlegmatic, and pusillanimous.

CLIFF I'll bet that concert's started by now. Shall I put it on?
JIMMY I looked up that word the other day. It's one of those words I've never been quite sure of, but always thought I knew.
CLIFF What was that?
JIMMY I told you—pusillanimous. Do you know what it means?

(CLIFF *shakes his head*)

Neither did I really. All this time, I have been married to this woman, this monument to non-attachment, and suddenly I discover that there is actually a word that sums her up. Not just an adjective in the English language to describe her with—it's her name! Pusillanimous! It sounds like some fleshy Roman matron, doesn't it? The Lady Pusillanimous seen here with her husband Sextus, on their way to the Games.

(CLIFF *looks troubled, and glances uneasily at* ALISON)

---

[12] In 1867 the Marquess of Queensberry drew up rules for boxing, which have since been known as "the Marquess of Queensberry Rules."

[13] A BBC news commentator.

Poor old Sextus! If he were put into a Hollywood film, he's so unimpressive, they'd make some poor British actor play the part. He doesn't know it, but those beefcake Christians will make off with his wife in the wonder of stereophonic sound before the picture's over.

(ALISON *leans against the board, and closes her eyes*)

The Lady Pusillanimous has been promised a brighter easier world than old Sextus can ever offer her. Hi, Pusey! What say we get the hell down to the Arena, and maybe feed ourselves to a couple of lions, huh?

ALISON God help me, if he doesn't stop, I'll go out of my mind in a minute.

JIMMY Why don't you? That would be something, anyway. (*Crosses to chest of drawers R.*) But I haven't told you what it means yet, have I? (*Picks up dictionary*) I don't have to tell her—she knows. In fact, if my pronunciation is at fault, she'll probably wait for a suitably public moment to correct it. Here it is. I quote: Pusillanimous. Adjective. Wanting of firmness of mind, of small courage, having a little mind, mean-spirited, cowardly, timid of mind. From the Latin *pusillus*, very little, and *animus*, the mind. (*Slams the book shut*) That's my wife! That's *her*, isn't it? Behold the Lady Pusillanimous. (*Shouting hoarsely*) Hi, Pusey! When's your next picture?

(JIMMY *watches her, waiting for her to break. For no more than a flash,* ALISON's *face seems to contort, and it looks as though she might throw her head back, and scream. But it passes in a moment. She is used to these carefully rehearsed attacks, and it doesn't look as though he will get his triumph tonight. She carries on with her ironing.* JIMMY *crosses, and switches on the radio. The Vaughan Williams concert has started. He goes back to his chair, leans back in it, and closes his eyes*)

ALISON (*Handing* CLIFF *his trousers*) There you are, dear. They're not very good, but they'll do for now.

(CLIFF *gets up and puts them on*)

CLIFF Oh, that's lovely.

ALISON Now try and look after them. I'll give them a real press later on.

CLIFF Thank you, you beautiful, darling girl.

(*He puts his arms round her waist, and kisses her. She smiles, and gives his nose a tug.* JIMMY *watches from his chair*)

ALISON (*To* CLIFF) Let's have a cigarette, shall we?

CLIFF That's a good idea. Where are they?

ALISON On the stove. Do you want one, Jimmy?
JIMMY No, thank you, I'm trying to listen. Do you mind?
CLIFF Sorry, your lordship.

(*He puts a cigarette in* ALISON's *mouth, and one in his own, and lights up.* CLIFF *sits down, and picks up his paper.* ALISON *goes back to her board.* CLIFF *throws down paper, picks up another, and thumbs through that*)

JIMMY Do you have to make all that racket?
CLIFF Oh, sorry.
JIMMY It's quite a simple thing, you know—turning over a page. Anyway, that's my paper. (*Snatches it away*)
CLIFF Oh, don't be so mean!
JIMMY Price ninepence, obtainable from any news-agent's. Now let me hear the music, for God's sake. (*Pause. To* ALISON) Are you going to be much longer doing that?
ALISON Why?
JIMMY Perhaps you haven't noticed it, but it's interfering with the radio.
ALISON I'm sorry. I shan't be much longer.

(*A pause. The iron mingles with the music.* CLIFF *shifts restlessly in his chair,* JIMMY *watches* ALISON, *his foot beginning to twitch dangerously. Presently, he gets up quickly, crossing below* ALISON *to the radio, and turns it off*)

What did you do that for?
JIMMY I wanted to listen to the concert, that's all.
ALISON Well, what's stopping you?
JIMMY Everyone's making such a din—that's what's stopping me.
ALISON Well, I'm very sorry, but I can't just stop everything because you want to listen to music.
JIMMY Why not?
ALISON Really, Jimmy, you're like a child.
JIMMY Don't try and patronize me. (*Turning to* CLIFF) She's so clumsy. I watch for her to do the same things every night. The way she jumps on the bed, as if she were stamping on someone's face, and draws the curtains back with a great clatter, in that casually destructive way of hers. It's like someone launching a battleship. Have you ever noticed how noisy women are? (*Crosses below chairs to L.C.*) Have you? The way they kick the floor about, simply walking over it? Or have you watched them sitting at their dressing tables, dropping their weapons and banging down their bits of boxes and brushes and lip-

sticks? (*He faces her dressing table*) I've watched her doing it night after night. When you see a woman in front of her bedroom mirror, you realise what a refined sort of a butcher she is. (*Turns in*) Did you ever see some dirty old Arab, sticking his fingers into some mess of lamb fat and gristle? Well, she's just like that. Thank God they don't have many women surgeons! Those primitive hands would have your guts out in no time. Flip! Out it comes, like the powder out of its box. Flop! Back it goes, like the powder puff on the table.

CLIFF (*Grimacing cheerfully*) Ugh! Stop it!

JIMMY (*Moving upstage*) She'd drop your guts like hair clips and fluff all over the floor. You've got to be fundamentally insensitive to be as noisy and as clumsy as that. (*He moves C., and leans against the table*) I had a flat underneath a couple of girls once. You heard every damned thing those bastards did, all day and night. The most simple, everyday actions were a sort of assault course on your sensibilities. I used to plead with them. I even got to screaming the most ingenious obscenities I could think of, up the stairs at them. But nothing, nothing, would move them. With those two, even a simple visit to the lavatory sounded like a medieval siege. Oh, they beat me in the end—I had to go. I expect they're still at it. Or they're probably married by now, and driving some other poor devils out of their minds. Slamming their doors, stamping their high heels, banging their irons and saucepans—the eternal flaming racket of the female.

(*Church bells start ringing outside*)

JIMMY Oh, hell! Now the bloody bells have started! (*He rushes to the window*) Wrap it up, will you? Stop ringing those bells! There's somebody going crazy in here! I don't want to hear them!

ALISON Stop shouting! (*Recovering immediately*) You'll have Miss Drury up here.

JIMMY I don't give a damn about Miss Drury—that mild old gentlewoman doesn't fool me, even if she takes in you two. She's an old robber. She gets more than enough out of us for this place every week. Anyway, she's probably in church, (*Points to the window*) swinging on those bloody bells!

(CLIFF *goes to the window, and closes it*)

CLIFF Come on, now, be a good boy. I'll take us all out, and we'll have a drink.

JIMMY They're not open yet. It's Sunday. Remember? Anyway, it's raining.

CLIFF Well, shall we dance? (*He pushes* JIMMY *round the floor, who is*

past the mood for this kind of fooling) Do you come here often?
JIMMY Only in the mating season. All right, all right, very funny. (*He tries to escape, but* CLIFF *holds him like a vise*) Let me go.
CLIFF Not until you've apologized for being nasty to everyone. Do you think bosoms will be in or out, this year?
JIMMY Your teeth will be out in a minute, if you don't let go!

(*He makes a great effort to wrench himself free, but* CLIFF *hangs on. They collapse to the floor C., below the table, struggling.* ALISON *carries on with her ironing. This is routine, but she is getting close to breaking point, all the same.* CLIFF *manages to break way, and finds himself in front of the ironing board.* JIMMY *springs up. They grapple*)

ALISON Look out, for heaven's sake! Oh, it's more like a zoo every day!

(JIMMY *makes a frantic, deliberate effort, and manages to push* CLIFF *on to the ironing board, and into* ALISON. *The board collapses.* CLIFF *falls against her, and they end up in a heap on the floor.* ALISON *cries out in pain.* JIMMY *looks down at them, dazed and breathless*)

CLIFF (*Picking himself up*) She's hurt. Are you all right?
ALISON Well, does it look like it!
CLIFF She's burnt her arm on the iron.
JIMMY Darling, I'm sorry.
ALISON Get out!
JIMMY I'm sorry, believe me. You think I did it on pur——
ALISON (*Her head shaking helplessly*) Clear out of my sight!

(*He stares at her uncertainly.* CLIFF *nods to him, and he turns and goes out of the door*)

CLIFF Come and sit down. (*He leads her to the armchair R.*) You look a bit white. Are you all right?
ALISON Yes. I'm all right now.
CLIFF Let's have a look at your arm. (*Examines it*) Yes, it's quite red. That's going to be painful. What should I do with it?
ALISON Oh, it's nothing much. A bit of soap on it will do. I never can remember what you do with burns.
CLIFF I'll just pop down to the bathroom and get some. Are you sure you're all right?
ALISON Yes.
CLIFF (*Crossing to door*) Won't be a minute. (*Exit*)

(*She leans back in the chair, and looks up at the ceiling. She breathes in deeply, and brings her hands up to her face. She winces as she feels the pain in her arm, and she lets it fall. She runs her hand through her hair)*

ALISON (*In a clenched whisper*) Oh, God!

(CLIFF *re-enters with a bar of soap*)

CLIFF It's this scented muck. Do you think it'll be all right?

ALISON That'll do.

CLIFF Here we are then. Let's have your arm. (*He kneels down beside her, and she holds out her arm*) I've put it under the tap. It's quite soft. I'll do it ever so gently. (*Very carefully, he rubs the soap over the burn*) All right? (*She nods*) You're a brave girl.

ALISON I don't feel very brave. (*Tears harshening her voice*) I really don't, Cliff. I don't think I can take much more. (*Turns her head away*) I think I feel rather sick.

CLIFF All over now. (*Puts the soap down*) Would you like me to get you something? (*She shakes her head. He sits on the arm of the chair, and puts his arm round her. She leans her head back on to him*) Don't upset yourself, lovely. (*He massages the back of her neck, and she lets her head fall forward*)

ALISON Where is he?

CLIFF In my room.

ALISON What's he doing?

CLIFF Lying on the bed. Reading, I think. (*Stroking her neck*) That better?

(*She leans back, and closes her eyes again*)

ALISON Bless you.

(*He kisses the top of her head*)

CLIFF I don't think I'd have the courage to live on my own again—in spite of everything. I'm pretty rough, and pretty ordinary really, and I'd seem worse on my own. And you get fond of people too, worse luck.

ALISON I don't think I want anything more to do with love. Any more. I can't take it on.

CLIFF You're too young to start giving up. Too young, and too lovely. Perhaps I'd better put a bandage on that—do you think so?

ALISON There's some on my dressing table.

(CLIFF *crosses to the dressing table* R.)

I keep looking back, as far as I remember, and I can't think what it was to feel young, really young. Jimmy said the same thing to me the other day. I pretended not to be listening—because I knew that would hurt him, I suppose. And—of course—he got savage, like tonight. But I knew just what he meant. I suppose it would have been so easy to say, "Yes, darling, I know just what you mean. I know what you're feeling." (*Shrugs*) It's those easy things that seem to be so impossible with us.

(CLIFF *stands down R., holding the bandage, his back to her*)

CLIFF I'm wondering how much longer I can go on watching you two tearing the insides out of each other. It looks pretty ugly sometimes.
ALISON You wouldn't seriously think of leaving us, would you?
CLIFF I suppose not. (*Crosses to her*)
ALISON I think I'm frightened. If only I knew what was going to happen.
CLIFF (*Kneeling on the arm of her chair*) Give it here. (*She holds out her arm*) Yell out if I hurt you. (*He bandages it for her*)
ALISON (*Staring at her outstretched arm*) Cliff——
CLIFF Um? (*Slight pause*) What is it, lovely?
ALISON Nothing.
CLIFF I said: what is it?
ALISON You see——(*Hesitates*) I'm pregnant.
CLIFF (*After a few moments*) I'll need some scissors.
ALISON They're over there.
CLIFF (*Crossing to the dressing table*) That is something, isn't it? When did you find this out?
ALISON Few days ago. It was a bit of a shock.
CLIFF Yes, I dare say.
ALISON After three years of married life, I have to get caught out now.
CLIFF None of us infallible, I suppose. (*Crosses to her*) Must say I'm surprised, though.
ALISON It's always been out of the question. What with—this place, and no money, and oh—everything. He's resented it, I know. What can you do?
CLIFF You haven't told him yet.
ALISON Not yet.
CLIFF What are you going to do?
ALISON I've no idea.
CLIFF (*Having cut her bandage, he starts tying it*) That too tight?
ALISON Fine, thank you. (*She rises, goes to the ironing board, folds it up, and leans it against the food cupboard R.*)
CLIFF Is it . . . Is it . . . ?
ALISON Too late to avert the situation? (*Places the iron on the rack of the stove*) I'm not certain yet. Maybe not. If not, there won't be any problem, will there?
CLIFF And if it is too late?

(*Her face is turned away from him. She simply shakes her head*)

Why don't you tell him now?

(*She kneels down to pick up the clothes on the floor, and folds them up*)

After all, he does love you. You don't need me to tell you that.

ALISON   Can't you see? He'll suspect my motives at once. He never stops telling himself that I know how vulnerable he is. Tonight it might be all right—we'd make love. But later, we'd both lie awake, watching for the light to come through that little window, and dreading it. In the morning, he'd feel hoaxed, as if I were trying to kill him in the worst way of all. He'd watch me growing bigger every day, and I wouldn't dare to look at him.

CLIFF   You may have to face it, lovely.

ALISON   Jimmy's got his own private morality, as you know. What my mother calls "loose." It is pretty free, of course, but it's very harsh too. You know, it's funny, but we never slept together before we were married.

CLIFF   It certainly is—knowing him!

ALISON   We knew each other such a short time, everything moved at such a pace, we didn't have much opportunity. And, afterwards, he actually taunted me with my virginity. He was quite angry about it, as if I had deceived him in some strange way. He seemed to think an untouched woman would defile him.

CLIFF   I've never heard you talking like this about him. He'd be quite pleased.

ALISON   Yes, he would. (*She gets up, the clothes folded over her arm*) Do you think he's right?

CLIFF   What about?

ALISON   Oh—everything.

CLIFF   Well, I suppose he and I think the same about a lot of things, because we're alike in some ways. We both come from working people, if you like. Oh, I know some of his mother's relatives are pretty posh, but he hates them as much as he hates yours. Don't quite know why. Anyway, he gets on with me because I'm common. (*Grins*) Common as dirt, that's me.

(*She puts her hand on his head, and strokes it thoughtfully*)

ALISON   You think I should tell him about the baby?

(*He gets up, and puts his arm round her*)

CLIFF   It'll be all right—you see. Tell him.

(He kisses her. Enter JIMMY. *He looks at them curiously, but without surprise. They are both aware of him, but make no sign of it. He crosses to the armchair L., and sits down next to them. He picks up a paper, and starts looking at it.* CLIFF *glances at him,* ALISON's *head against his cheek)*

There you are, you old devil, you! Where have you been?
JIMMY   You know damn well where I've been. (*Without looking at her*) How's your arm?
ALISON   Oh, it's all right. It wasn't much.
CLIFF   She's beautiful, isn't she?
JIMMY   You seem to think so.

(CLIFF *and* ALISON *still have their arms round one another*)

CLIFF   Why the hell she married you, I'll never know.
JIMMY   You think she'd have been better off with you?
CLIFF   I'm not her type. Am I, dullin'?
ALISON   I'm not sure what my type is.
JIMMY   Why don't you both get into bed, and have done with it.
ALISON   You know, I think he really means that.
JIMMY   I do. I can't concentrate with you two standing there like that.
CLIFF   He's just an old Puritan at heart.
JIMMY   Perhaps I am, at that. Anyway, you both look pretty silly slobbering over each other.
CLIFF   I think she's beautiful. And so do you, only you're too much of a pig to say so.
JIMMY   You're just a sexy little Welshman, and you know it! Mummy and Daddy turn pale, and face the east every time they remember she's married to me. But if they saw all this going on, they'd collapse. Wonder what they *would* do, incidentally. Send for the police I expect. (*Genuinely friendly*) Have you got a cigarette?
ALISON (*Disengaging*)   I'll have a look. (*She goes to her handbag on the table C.*)
JIMMY (*Pointing at* CLIFF)   He gets more like a little mouse every day, doesn't he? (*He is trying to re-establish himself*) He really does look like one. Look at those ears, and that face, and the little short legs.
ALISON (*Looking through her bag*)   That's because he *is* a mouse.
CLIFF   Eek! Eek! I'm a mouse.
JIMMY   A randy little mouse.
CLIFF (*Dancing round the table, and squeaking*)   I'm a mouse, I'm a mouse, I'm a randy little mouse. That's a mourris dance.

JIMMY A what?
CLIFF A *Mourris Dance*. That's a Morris Dance strictly for mice.
JIMMY You stink. You really do. Do you know that?
CLIFF Not as bad as you, you horrible old bear. (*Goes over to him, and grabs his foot*) You're a stinking old bear, you hear me?
JIMMY Let go of my foot, you whimsy little half-wit. You're making my stomach heave. I'm resting! If you don't let go, I'll cut off your nasty, great, slimy tail!

(CLIFF *gives him a tug, and* JIMMY *falls to the floor.* ALISON *watches them, relieved and suddenly full of affection*)

ALISON I've run out of cigarettes.

(CLIFF *is dragging* JIMMY *along the floor by his feet*)

JIMMY (*Yelling*) Go out and get me some cigarettes, and stop playing the fool!
CLIFF O.K. (*He lets go of* JIMMY's *legs suddenly, who yells again as his head bangs on the floor*)
ALISON Here's half a crown. (*Giving it him*) The shop on the corner will be open.
CLIFF Right you are. (*Kisses her on the forehead quickly*) Don't forget. (*Crosses upstage to door*)
JIMMY Now get to hell out of here!
CLIFF (*At door*) Hey, shorty!
JIMMY What do you want?
CLIFF Make a nice pot of tea.
JIMMY (*Getting up*) I'll kill you first.
CLIFF (*Grinning*) That's my boy! (*Exit*)

(JIMMY *is now beside* ALISON, *who is still looking through her handbag. She becomes aware of his nearness, and, after a few moments, closes it. He takes hold of her bandaged arm*)

JIMMY How's it feeling?
ALISON Fine. It wasn't anything.
JIMMY All this fooling about can get a bit dangerous. (*He sits on the edge of the table, holding her hand*) I'm sorry.
ALISON I know.
JIMMY I mean it.
ALISON There's no need.
JIMMY I did it on purpose.
ALISON Yes.
JIMMY There's hardly a moment when I'm not—watching and wanting you. I've got to hit out somehow. Nearly four years of being in the

same room with you, night and day, and I still can't stop my sweat breaking out when I see you doing—something as ordinary as leaning over an ironing board.

(*She strokes his head, not sure of herself yet*)

(*Sighing*) Trouble is— Trouble is you get used to people. Even their trivialities become indispensable to you. Indispensable, and a little mysterious. (*He slides his head forward, against her, trying to catch his thoughts*) I think . . . I must have a lot of—old stock. . . . Nobody wants it. . . . (*He puts his face against her belly. She goes on stroking his head, still on guard a little. Then he lifts his head, and they kiss passionately*) What are we going to do tonight?

ALISON   What would you like to do? Drink?

JIMMY   I know what I want now.

(*She takes his head in her hands and kisses him*)

ALISON   Well, you'll have to wait till the proper time.

JIMMY   There's no such thing.

ALISON   Cliff will be back in a minute.

JIMMY   What did he mean by "don't forget"?

ALISON   Something I've been meaning to tell you.

JIMMY   (*Kissing her again*)   You're fond of him, aren't you?

ALISON   Yes, I am.

JIMMY   He's the only friend I seem to have left now. People go away. You never see them again. I can remember lots of names—men and women. When I was at school—Watson, Roberts, Davies. Jenny, Madeline, Hugh . . . (*Pause*) And there's Hugh's mum, of course. I'd almost forgotten her. She's been a good friend to us, if you like. She's even letting me buy the sweet-stall off her in my own time. She only bought it for us, anyway. She's so fond of you. I can never understand why you're so—distant with her.

ALISON   (*Alarmed at this threat of a different mood*)   Jimmy—please no!

JIMMY   (*Staring at her anxious face*)   You're very beautiful. A beautiful, great-eyed squirrel.

(*She nods brightly, relieved*)

Hoarding, nut-munching squirrel. (*She mimes this delightedly*) With highly polished, gleaming fur, and an ostrich feather of a tail.

ALISON   Wheeeeeeeeee!

JIMMY   How I envy you. (*He stands, her arms around his neck*)

ALISON   Well, you're a jolly super bear, too. A really sooooooooooooooooper, marvelous bear.

JIMMY   Bears and squirrels *are* marvelous.

ALISON Marvelous and beautiful. (*She jumps up and down excitedly, making little "paw gestures"*) Oooooooh! Oooooooh!
JIMMY What the hell's that?
ALISON That's a dance squirrels do when they're happy.

(*They embrace again*)

JIMMY What makes you think you're happy?
ALISON Everything just seems all right suddenly. That's all. Jimmy——
JIMMY Yes?
ALISON You know I told you I'd something to tell you?
JIMMY Well?

(CLIFF *appears in the doorway*)

CLIFF Didn't get any further than the front door. Miss Drury hadn't gone to church after all. I couldn't get away from her. (*To* ALISON) Someone on the phone for you.
ALISON On the phone? Who on earth is it?
CLIFF Helena something.

(JIMMY *and* ALISON *look at each other quickly*)

JIMMY (*To* CLIFF) Helena Charles?
CLIFF That's it.
ALISON Thank you, Cliff. (*Moves upstage*) I won't be a minute.
CLIFF You will. Old Miss Drury will keep you down there forever. She doesn't think we keep this place clean enough. (*Comes and sits in the armchair down R.*) Thought you were going to make me some tea, you rotter.

(JIMMY *makes no reply*)

What's the matter, boyo?
JIMMY (*Slowly*) That bitch.
CLIFF Who?
JIMMY (*To himself*) Helena Charles.
CLIFF Who is this Helena?
JIMMY One of her old friends. And one of my natural enemies. You're sitting on my chair.
CLIFF Where are we going for a drink?
JIMMY I don't know.
CLIFF Well, you were all for it earlier on.
JIMMY What does she want? What would make her ring up? It can't be for anything pleasant. Oh, well, we shall soon know. (*He settles on the table*) Few minutes ago things didn't seem so bad either. I've just

about had enough of this "expense of spirit"[14] lark, as far as women are concerned. Honestly, it's enough to make you become a scoutmaster or something, isn't it? Sometimes I almost envy old Gide and the Greek Chorus boys. Oh, I'm not saying that it mustn't be hell for them a lot of the time. But, at least, they do seem to have a cause— not a particularly good one, it's true. But plenty of them do seem to have a revolutionary fire about them, which is more than you can say for the rest of us. Like Webster, for instance. He doesn't like me— they hardly ever do. (*He is talking for the sake of it, only half listening to what he is saying*) I dare say he suspects me because I refuse to treat him either as a clown or as a tragic hero. He's like a man with a strawberry mark—he keeps thrusting it in your face because he can't believe it doesn't interest or horrify you particularly. (*Picks up* ALISON's *handbag thoughtfully, and starts looking through it*) As if I give a damn which way he likes his meat served up. I've got my own strawberry mark—only it's in a different place. No, as far as the Michaelangelo Brigade's concerned, I must be a sort of right-wing deviationist. If the Revolution ever comes, I'll be the first to be put up against the wall, with all the other poor old liberals.

CLIFF (*Indicating* ALISON's *handbag*) Wouldn't you say that that was her private property?

JIMMY You're quite right. But do you know something? Living night and day with another human being has made me predatory and suspicious. I know that the only way of finding out exactly what's going on is to catch them when they don't know you're looking. When she goes out, I go through everything—trunks, cases, drawers, bookcase, everything. Why? To see if there is something of me somewhere, a reference to me. I want to know if I'm being betrayed.

CLIFF You look for trouble, don't you?

JIMMY Only because I'm pretty certain of finding it. (*Brings out a letter from the handbag*) Look at that! Oh, I'm such a fool. This is happening every five minutes of the day. She gets letters. (*He holds it up*) Letters from her mother, letters in which I'm not mentioned at all because my name is a dirty word. And what does she do?

(*Enter* ALISON. *He turns to look at her*)

She writes long letters back to Mummy, and never mentions me at all, because I'm just a dirty word to her too. (*He throws the letter down at her feet*) Well, what did your friend want?

ALISON She's at the station. She's—coming over.

---

[14] Shakespeare's Sonnet 129.

JIMMY I see. She said, "Can I come over?" And you said, "My husband, Jimmy—if you'll forgive me using such a dirty word, will be delighted to see you. He'll kick your face in!" (*He stands up, unable to sustain his anger, poised on the table*)

ALISON (*Quietly*) She's playing with the company at the Hippodrome this week, and she's got no digs. She can't find anywhere to stay——

JIMMY That I don't believe!

ALISON So I said she could come here until she fixes something else. Miss Drury's got a spare room downstairs.

JIMMY Why not have her in here? Did you tell her to bring her armor? Because she's going to need it!

ALISON (*Vehemently*) Oh, why don't you shut up, please!

JIMMY Oh, my dear wife, you've got so much to learn. I only hope you learn it one day. If only something—something would happen to you, and wake you out of your beauty sleep! (*Coming in close to her*) If you could have a child, and it would die. Let it grow, let a recognizable human face emerge from that little mass of indiarubber and wrinkles. (*She retreats away from him*) Please—if only I could watch you face that. I wonder if you might even become a recognizable human being yourself. But I doubt it.

(*She moves away, stunned, and leans on the gas stove down L. He stands rather helplessly on his own*)

Do you know I have never known the great pleasure of lovemaking when I didn't desire it myself? Oh, it's not that she hasn't her own kind of passion. She has the passion of a python. She just devours me whole every time, as if I were some over-large rabbit. That's me. That bulge around her navel—if you're wondering what it is—it's me. Me, buried alive down there, and going mad, smothered in that peaceful looking coil. Not a sound, not a flicker from her—she doesn't even rumble a little. You'd think that this indigestible mess would stir up some kind of tremor in those distended, overfed tripes—but not her! (*Crosses up to the door*) She'll go on sleeping and devouring until there's nothing left of me. (*Exit*)

(ALISON's *head goes back as if she were about to make some sound. But her mouth remains open and trembling, as* CLIFF *looks on*)

Curtain

Act Two / SCENE ONE

Two weeks later. Evening.

ALISON *is standing over the gas stove, pouring water from the kettle into a large teapot. She is only wearing a slip, and her feet are bare. In the room across the hall,* JIMMY *is playing on his jazz trumpet, in intermittent bursts.* ALISON *takes the pot to the table C., which is laid for four people. The Sunday paper jungle around the two armchairs is as luxuriant as ever. It is late afternoon, the end of a hot day. She wipes her forehead. She crosses to the dressing table R., takes out a pair of stockings from one of the drawers, and sits down on the small chair beside it to put them on. While she is doing this, the door opens and* HELENA *enters. She is the same age as* ALISON, *medium height, carefully and expensively dressed. Now and again, when she allows her rather judicial expression of alertness to soften, she is very attractive. Her sense of matriarchal authority makes most men who meet her anxious, not only to please but impress, as if she were the gracious representative of visiting royalty. In this case, the royalty of that middle-class womanhood, which is so eminently secure in its divine rights, that it can afford to tolerate the parliament, and reasonably free assembly of its menfolk. Even from other young women, like* ALISON, *she receives her due of respect and admiration. In* JIMMY, *as one would expect, she arouses all the rabble-rousing instincts of his spirit. And she is not accustomed to having to defend herself against catcalls. However, her sense of modestly exalted responsibility enables her to behave with an impressive show of strength and dignity, although the strain of this is beginning to tell on her a little. She is carrying a large salad colander.*

ALISON Did you manage all right?
HELENA Of course. I've prepared most of the meals in the last week, you know.
ALISON Yes, you have. It's been wonderful having someone to help. Another woman, I mean.
HELENA (*Crossing down L.*) I'm enjoying it. Although I don't think I shall ever get used to having to go down to the bathroom every time I want some water for something.

ALISON It is primitive, isn't it?
HELENA Yes. It is rather. (*She starts tearing up green salad on to four plates, which she takes from the food cupboard*) Looking after one man is really enough, but two is rather an undertaking.
ALISON Oh, Cliff looks after himself, more or less. In fact, he helps me quite a lot.
HELENA Can't say I'd noticed it.
ALISON You've been doing it instead, I suppose.
HELENA I see.
ALISON You've settled in so easily somehow.
HELENA Why shouldn't I?
ALISON It's not exactly what you're used to, is it?
HELENA And are you used to it?
ALISON Everything seems very different here now—with you here.
HELENA Does it?
ALISON Yes. I was on my own before——
HELENA Now you've got me. So you're not sorry you asked me to stay?
ALISON Of course not. Did you tell him his tea was ready?
HELENA I banged on the door of Cliff's room, and yelled. He didn't answer, but he must have heard. I don't know where Cliff is.
ALISON (*Leaning back in her chair*) I thought I'd feel cooler after a bath, but I feel hot again already. God, I wish he'd lose that damned trumpet.
HELENA I imagine that's for my benefit.
ALISON Miss Drury will ask us to go soon, I know it. Thank goodness, she isn't in. Listen to him.
HELENA Does he drink?
ALISON Drink? (*Rather startled*) He's not an alcoholic, if that's what you mean. (*They both pause, listening to the trumpet*) He'll have the rest of the street banging on the door next.
HELENA (*Pondering*) It's almost as if he wanted to kill someone with it. And me in particular. I've never seen such hatred in someone's eyes before. It's slightly horrifying. Horrifying (*Crossing to food cupboard for tomatoes, beetroot, and cucumber*) and oddly exciting.

  (ALISON *faces her dressing mirror, and brushes her hair*)

ALISON He had his own jazz band once. That was when he was still a student, before I knew him. I rather think he'd like to start another, and give up the stall altogether.
HELENA Is Cliff in love with you?
ALISON (*Stops brushing for a moment*) No . . . I don't think so.
HELENA And what about you? You look as though I've asked you a rather peculiar question. The way things are, you might as well be

frank with me. I only want to help. After all, your behaviour together is a little strange—by most people's standards, to say the least.
ALISON You mean you've seen us embracing each other?
HELENA Well, it doesn't seem to go on as much as it did, I admit. Perhaps he finds my presence inhibiting—even if Jimmy's isn't.
ALISON We're simply fond of each other—there's no more to it than that.
HELENA Darling, really! It can't be as simple as that.
ALISON You mean there must be something physical too? I suppose there is, but it's not exactly a consuming passion with either of us. It's just a relaxed, cheerful sort of thing, like being warm in bed. You're too comfortable to bother about moving for the sake of some other pleasure.
HELENA I find it difficult to believe anyone's that lazy!
ALISON I think *we* are.
HELENA And what about Jimmy? After all, he is your husband. Do you mean to say he actually approves of it?
ALISON It isn't easy to explain. It's what he would call a question of allegiances, and he expects you to be pretty literal about them. Not only about himself and all the things he believes in, his present and his future, but his past as well. All the people he admires and loves, and has loved. The friends he used to know, people I've never even known —and probably wouldn't have liked. His father, who died years ago. Even the other women he's loved. Do you understand?
HELENA Do you?
ALISON I've tried to. But I still can't bring myself to feel the way he does about things. I can't believe that he's right somehow.
HELENA Well, that's something, anyway.
ALISON If things have worked out with Cliff, it's because he's kind and lovable, and I've grown genuinely fond of him. But it's been a fluke. It's worked because Cliff is such a nice person anyway. With Hugh, it was quite different.
HELENA Hugh?
ALISON Hugh Tanner. He and Jimmy were friends almost from childhood. Mrs. Tanner is his mother——
HELENA Oh yes—the one who started him off in the sweet business.
ALISON That's right. Well, after Jimmy and I were married, we'd no money—about eight pounds ten in actual fact—and no home. He didn't even have a job. He'd only left the university about a year. (*Smiles*) No—left. I don't think one "comes down" from Jimmy's university. According to him, it's not even red brick, but white tile.[15] Anyway, we

---

[15] "To come down" is "to graduate" and is used for Oxford and Cambridge. The "red brick" schools are state supported; Jimmy's description, "white tile," derives from the lavatories.

went off to live in Hugh's flat. It was over a warehouse in Poplar.
HELENA   Yes. I remember seeing the postmark on your letters.
ALISON   Well, that was where I found myself on my wedding night. Hugh and I disliked each other on sight, and Jimmy knew it. He was so proud of us both, so pathetically anxious that we should take to each other. Like a child showing off his toys. We had a little wedding celebration, and the three of us tried to get tight on some cheap port they'd brought in. Hugh got more and more subtly insulting—he'd a rare talent for that. Jimmy got steadily depressed, and I just sat there, listening to their talk, looking and feeling very stupid. For the first time in my life, I was cut off from the kind of people I'd always known, my family, my friends, everybody. And I'd burnt my boats. After all those weeks of brawling with Mummy and Daddy about Jimmy, I knew I couldn't appeal to them without looking foolish and cheap. It was just before the General Election, I remember, and Nigel was busy getting himself into Parliament. He didn't have time for anyone but his constituents. Oh, he'd have been sweet and kind, I know.
HELENA   (*Moving in C.*)   Darling, why didn't you come to me?
ALISON   You were away on tour in some play, I think.
HELENA   So I was.
ALISON   Those next few months at the flat in Poplar were a nightmare. I suppose I must be soft and squeamish, and snobbish, but I felt as though I'd been dropped in a jungle. I couldn't believe that two people, two educated people could be so savage, and so—so uncompromising. Mummy has always said that Jimmy is utterly ruthless, but she hasn't met Hugh. He takes the first prize for ruthlessness—from all comers. Together, they were frightening. They both came to regard me as a sort of hostage from those sections of society they had declared war on.
HELENA   How were you living all this time?
ALISON   I had a tiny bit coming in from a few shares I had left, but it hardly kept us. Mummy had made me sign everything else over to her, in trust, when she knew I was really going to marry Jimmy.
HELENA   Just as well, I imagine.
ALISON   They soon thought of a way out of that. A brilliant campaign. They started inviting themselves—through me—to people's houses, friends of Nigel's and mine, friends of Daddy's, oh everyone: the Arksdens, the Tarnatts, the Wains——
HELENA   Not the Wains?
ALISON   Just about everyone I'd ever known. Your people must have been among the few we missed out. It was just enemy territory to them, and, as I say, they used me as a hostage. We'd set out from headquarters in Poplar, and carry out our raids on the enemy in W.1, S.W.1, S.W.3,

and W.8.[16] In my name, we'd gatecrash everywhere—cocktails, weekends, even a couple of houseparties. I used to hope that one day, somebody would have the guts to slam the door in our faces, but they didn't. They were too well-bred, and probably sorry for me as well. Hugh and Jimmy despised them for it. So we went on plundering them, wolfing their food and drinks, and smoking their cigars like ruffians. Oh, they enjoyed themselves.

HELENA Apparently.

ALISON Hugh fairly revelled in the role of the barbarian invader. Sometimes I thought he might even dress the part—you know, furs, spiked helmet, sword. He even got a fiver out of Old Man Wain once. Blackmail, of course. People would have signed almost anything to get rid of us. He told him that we were about to be turned out of our flat for not paying the rent. At least it was true.

HELENA I don't understand you. You must have been crazy.

ALISON Afraid more than anything.

HELENA But letting them do it! Letting them get away with it! You managed to stop them stealing the silver, I suppose?

ALISON Oh, they knew their guerrilla warfare better than that. Hugh tried to seduce some fresh-faced young girl at the Arksdens' once, but that was the only time we were more or less turned out.

HELENA It's almost unbelievable. I don't understand your part in it all. Why? That's what I don't see. Why did you——

ALISON Marry him? There must be about six different answers. When the family came back from India, everything seemed, I don't know—unsettled? Anyway, Daddy seemed remote and rather irritable. And Mummy—well, you know Mummy. I didn't have much to worry about. I didn't know I was born as Jimmy says. I met him at a party. I remember it so clearly. I was almost twenty-one. The men there all looked as though they distrusted him, and as for the women, they were all intent on showing their contempt for this rather odd creature, but no one seemed quite sure how to do it. He'd come to the party on a bicycle, he told me, and there was oil all over his dinner jacket. It had been such a lovely day, and he'd been in the sun. Everything about him seemed to burn, his face, the edges of his hair glistened and seemed to spring off his head, and his eyes were so blue and full of the sun. He looked so young and frail, in spite of the tired line of his mouth. I knew I was taking on more than I was ever likely to be capable of bearing, but there never seemed to be any choice. Well, the

---

[16] Postal-zone designations (West 1, Southwest 1, etc.) for fashionable sections of London.

howl of outrage and astonishment went up from the family, and that did it. Whether or no he was in love with me, that did it. He made up his mind to marry me. They did just about everything they could think of to stop us.

HELENA Yes, it wasn't a very pleasant business. But you can see their point.

ALISON Jimmy went into battle with his axe swinging round his head—frail, and so full of fire. I had never seen anything like it. The old story of the knight in shining armor—except that his armor didn't really shine very much.

HELENA And what about Hugh?

ALISON Things got steadily worse between us. He and Jimmy even went to some of Nigel's political meetings. They took bunches of their Poplar cronies with them, and broke them up for him.

HELENA He's really a savage, isn't he?

ALISON Well, Hugh was writing some novel or other, and he made up his mind he must go abroad—to China, or some God-forsaken place. He said that England was finished for us, anyway. All the old gang was back—Dame Alison's Mob, as he used to call it. The only real hope was to get out, and try somewhere else. He wanted us to go with him, but Jimmy refused to go. There was a terrible, bitter row over it. Jimmy accused Hugh of giving up, and he thought it was wrong of him to go off forever, and leave his mother all on her own. He was upset by the whole idea. They quarrelled for days over it. I almost wished they'd both go, and leave me behind. Anyway, they broke up. A few months later we came up here, and Hugh went off to find the New Millennium on his own. Sometimes, I think Hugh's mother blames me for it all. Jimmy, too, in a way, although he's never said so. He never mentions it. But whenever that woman looks at me, I can feel her thinking, "If it hadn't been for you, everything would have been all right. We'd have all been happy." Not that I dislike her—I don't. She's very sweet, in fact. Jimmy seems to adore her principally because she's been poor almost all her life, and she's frankly ignorant. I'm quite aware how snobbish that sounds, but it happens to be the truth.

HELENA Alison, listen to me. You've got to make up your mind what you're going to do. You're going to have a baby, and you have a new responsibility. Before, it was different—there was only yourself at stake. But you can't go on living in this way any longer. (*To her*)

ALISON I'm so tired. I dread him coming into the room.

HELENA Why haven't you told him you're going to have a child?

ALISON I don't know. (*Suddenly anticipating* HELENA's *train of thought*) Oh, it's his, all right. There couldn't be any doubt of that. You

see——(*She smiles*) I've never really wanted anyone else.
HELENA Listen, darling—you've got to tell him. Either he learns to behave like anyone else, and looks after you——
ALISON Or?
HELENA Or you must get out of this mad-house. (*Trumpet crescendo*) This menagerie. He doesn't seem to know what love or anything else means.
ALISON (*Pointing to chest of drawers up R.*) You see that bear, and that squirrel? Well, that's him, and that's me.
HELENA Meaning?
ALISON The game we play: bears and squirrels, squirrels and bears.

(HELENA *looks rather blank*)

Yes, it's quite mad, I know. Quite mad. (*Picks up the two animals*) That's him. . . . And that's me. . . .
HELENA I didn't realise he was a bit fey, as well as everything else!
ALISON Oh, there's nothing fey about Jimmy. It's just all we seem to have left. Or had left. Even bears and squirrels seem to have gone their own ways now.
HELENA Since I arrived?
ALISON It started during those first months we had alone together—after Hugh went abroad. It was the one way of escaping from everything—a sort of unholy priest-hole of being animals to one another. We could become little furry creatures with little furry brains. Full of dumb, uncomplicated affection for each other. Playful, careless creatures in their own cosy zoo for two. A silly symphony for people who couldn't bear the pain of being human beings any longer. And now, even they are dead, poor little silly animals. They were all love, and no brains. (*Puts them back*)
HELENA (*Gripping her arm*) Listen to me. You've got to fight him. Fight, or get out. Otherwise, he *will* kill you.

(*Enter* CLIFF)

CLIFF There you are, dullin'. Hullo, Helena. Tea ready?
ALISON Yes, dear, it's all ready. Give Jimmy a call, will you?
CLIFF Right. (*Yelling back through door*) Hey, you horrible man! Stop that bloody noise, and come and get your tea! (*Coming in C.*) Going out?
HELENA (*Crossing to L.*) Yes.
CLIFF Pictures?
HELENA No. (*Pause*) Church.
CLIFF (*Really surprised*) Oh! I see. Both of you?

HELENA Yes. Are you coming?
CLIFF Well. . . . I—I haven't read the papers properly yet. Tea, tea, tea! Let's have some tea, shall we?

>(*He sits at the upstage end of the table.* HELENA *puts the four plates of salad on it, sits down L., and they begin the meal.* ALISON *is making up her face at her dressing table. Presently,* JIMMY *enters. He places his trumpet on the bookcase, and comes above the table*)

Hullo, boyo. Come and have your tea. That blinkin' trumpet—why don't you stuff it away somewhere?
JIMMY You like it all right. Anyone who doesn't like real jazz, hasn't any feeling either for music or people. (*He sits R. end of table*)
HELENA Rubbish.
JIMMY (*To* CLIFF) That seems to prove my point for you. Did you know that Webster played the banjo?
CLIFF No, does he really?
HELENA He said he'd bring it along next time he came.
ALISON (*Muttering*) Oh, no!
JIMMY Why is it that nobody knows how to treat the papers in this place? Look at them. I haven't even glanced at them yet—not the posh ones, anyway.
CLIFF By the way, can I look at your *New*——
JIMMY No, you can't! (*Loudly*) You want anything, you pay for it. Like I have to. Price——
CLIFF Price ninepence, obtainable from any bookstall! You're a mean old man, that's what you are.
JIMMY What do you want to read it for, anyway? You've no intellect, no curiosity. It all just washes over you. Am I right?
CLIFF Right.
JIMMY What are you, you Welsh trash?
CLIFF Nothing, that's what I am.
JIMMY Nothing, are you? Blimey, you ought to be Prime Minister. You must have been talking to some of my wife's friends. They're a very intellectual set, aren't they? I've seen 'em.

>(CLIFF *and* HELENA *carry on with their meal*)

They all sit around feeling very spiritual, with their mental hands on each other's knees, discussing sex as if it were the Art of Fugue. If you don't want to be an emotional old spinster, just you listen to your dad! (*He starts eating. The silent hostility of the two women has set him off on the scent, and he looks quite cheerful, although the occasional*

579 · *Look Back in Anger* [ACT TWO, *Scene One*]

thick edge of his voice belies it) You know your trouble, son? Too anxious to please.
HELENA Thank heavens somebody is!
JIMMY You'll end up like one of those chocolate meringues my wife is so fond of. My wife—that's the one on the tom-toms behind me, sweet and sticky on the outside, and sink your teeth in it, (*Savoring every word*) inside, all white, messy, and disgusting. (*Offering teapot sweetly to* HELENA) Tea?
HELENA Thank you.

(*He smiles, and pours out a cup for her*)

JIMMY That's how you'll end up, my boy—black hearted, evil minded, and vicious.
HELENA (*Taking cup*) Thank you.
JIMMY And those old favorites, your friends and mine: sycophantic, phlegmatic, and, of course, top of the bill—pusillanimous.
HELENA (*To* ALISON) Aren't you going to have your tea?
ALISON Won't be long.
JIMMY Thought of the title for a new song today. It's called "You can quit hanging round my counter, Mildred, 'cos you'll find my position is closed."[17] (*Turning to* ALISON *suddenly*) Good?
ALISON Oh, very good.
JIMMY Thought you'd like it. If I can slip in a religious angle, it should be a big hit. (*To* HELENA) Don't you think so? I was thinking you might help me there. (*She doesn't reply*) It might help you if I recite the lyrics. Let's see now, it's something like this:

    I'm so tired of necking,
    Of pecking, home wrecking,
    Of empty bed blues—
    Just pass me the booze.
    I'm tired of being hetero,
    Rather ride on the metero,
    Just pass me the booze.
    This perpetual whoring
    Gets quite dull and boring,
    So avoid that old python coil,
    And pass me the celibate oil.
    You can quit, etc.

No?

[17] The English notice, "Position Closed," corresponds to the American "Next window please," when a clerk is temporarily absent from his post.

CLIFF Very good, boyo.
JIMMY Oh, yes, and I know what I meant to tell you—I wrote a poem while I was at the market yesterday. If you're interested, which you obviously are. (*To* HELENA) It should appeal to you, in particular. It's soaked in the theology of Dante, with a good slosh of Eliot as well. It starts off "There are no dry cleaners in Cambodia!"
CLIFF What do you call it?
JIMMY "The Cess Pool." Myself being a stone dropped in it, you see——
CLIFF You should be dropped in it, all right.
HELENA (*To* JIMMY) Why do you try so hard to be unpleasant?

(*He turns very deliberately, delighted that she should rise to the bait so soon—he's scarcely in his stride yet*)

JIMMY What's that?
HELENA Do you have to be so offensive?
JIMMY You mean now? You think I'm being offensive? You underestimate me. (*Turning to* ALISON) Doesn't she?
HELENA I think you're a very tiresome young man.

(*A slight pause as his delight catches up with him. He roars with laughter*)

JIMMY Oh dear, oh dear! My wife's friends! Pass Lady Bracknell the cucumber sandwiches,[18] will you? (*He returns to his meal, but his curiosity about* ALISON'S *preparations at the mirror won't be denied any longer. He turns round casually, and speaks to her*) Going out?
ALISON That's right.
JIMMY On a Sunday evening in this town? Where on earth are you going?
ALISON (*Rising*) I'm going out with Helena.
JIMMY That's not a direction—that's an affliction. (*She crosses to the table, and sits down C. He leans forward, and addresses her again*) I didn't ask you what was the matter with you. I asked you where you were going.
HELENA (*Steadily*) She's going to church.

(*He has been prepared for some plot, but he is as genuinely surprised by this as* CLIFF *was a few minutes earlier*)

JIMMY You're doing what? (*Silence*) Have you gone out of your mind or something? (*To* HELENA) You're determined to win her, aren't

---

[18] Gwendolyn's guardian in Oscar Wilde's *The Importance of Being Earnest*; she likes cucumber sandwiches.

you? So it's come to this now! How feeble can you get? (*His rage mounting within*) When I think of what I did, what I endured, to get you out——

ALISON (*Recognizing an onslaught on the way, starts to panic*) Oh yes, we all know what you did for me! You rescued me from the wicked clutches of my family, and all my friends! I'd still be rotting away at home, if you hadn't ridden up on your charger, and carried me off!

(*The wild note in her voice has reassured him. His anger cools and hardens. His voice is quite calm when he speaks*)

JIMMY The funny thing is, you know, I really did have to ride up on a white charger—off-white, really. Mummy locked her up in their eight-bedroomed castle, didn't she? There is no limit to what the middle-aged mummy will do in the holy crusade against ruffians like me. Mummy and I took one quick look at each other, and, from then on, the age of chivalry was dead. I knew that, to protect her innocent young, she wouldn't hesitate to cheat, lie, bully, and blackmail. Threatened with me, a young man without money, background, or even looks, she'd bellow like a rhinoceros in labor—enough to make every male rhino for miles turn white, and pledge himself to celibacy. But even I under-estimated her strength. Mummy may look over-fed and a bit flabby on the outside, but don't let that well-bred guzzler fool you. Underneath all that, she's armor-plated—— (*He clutches wildly for something to shock* HELENA *with*) She's as rough as a night in a Bombay brothel, and as tough as a matelot's arm. She's probably in that bloody cistern, taking down every word we say. (*Kicks cistern*) Can you 'ear me, mother. (*Sits on it, beats like bongo drums*) Just about get her in there. Let me give you an example of this lady's tactics. You may have noticed that I happen to wear my hair rather long. Now, if my wife is honest, or concerned enough to explain, she could tell you that this is not due to any dark, unnatural instincts I possess, but because (a) I can usually think of better things than a haircut to spend two bob on, and (b) I prefer long hair. But that obvious, innocent explanation didn't appeal to Mummy at all. So she hires detectives to watch me, to see if she can't somehow get me into the *News of the World*. All so that I shan't carry off her daughter on that poor old charger of mine, all tricked out and caparisoned in discredited passions and ideals! The old grey mare that actually once led the charge against the old order—well, she certainly ain't what she used to be. It was all she could do to carry me, but your weight (*To* ALISON) was too much for her. She just dropped dead on the way.

CLIFF (*Quietly*) Don't let's brawl, boyo. It won't do any good.

JIMMY Why *don't* we brawl? It's the only thing left I'm any good at.
CLIFF Jimmy, boy——
JIMMY (*To* ALISON) You've let this genuflecting sin-jobber win you over, haven't you? She's got you back, hasn't she?
HELENA Oh, for heaven's sake, don't be such a bully! You've no right to talk about her mother like that!
JIMMY (*Capable of anything now*) I've got every right. That old bitch should be dead! (*To* ALISON) Well? Aren't I right?

(CLIFF *and* HELENA *look at* ALISON *tensely, but she just gazes at her plate*)

I said she's an old bitch, and should be dead! What's the matter with you? Why don't you leap to her defence!

(CLIFF *gets up quickly, and takes his arm*)

CLIFF Jimmy, don't!

(JIMMY *pushes him back savagely, and he sits down helplessly, turning his head away on to his hand*)

JIMMY If someone said something like that about me, she'd react soon enough—she'd spring into her well-known lethargy, and say nothing! I say she ought to be dead. (*He brakes for a fresh spurt later. He's saving his strength for the knock-out*) My God, those worms will need a good dose of salts the day they get through her! Oh what a bellyache you've got coming to you, my little wormy ones! Alison's mother is on the way! (*In what he intends to be a comic declamatory voice*) She will pass away, my friends, leaving a trail of worms gasping for laxatives behind her—from purgatives to purgatory.

(*He smiles down at* ALISON, *but still she hasn't broken.* CLIFF *won't look at them. Only* HELENA *looks at him. Denied the other two, he addresses her*)

Is anything the matter?
HELENA I feel rather sick, that's all. Sick with contempt and loathing.

(*He can feel her struggling on the end of his line, and he looks at her rather absently*)

JIMMY One day, when I'm no longer spending my days running a sweet-stall, I may write a book about us all. It's all here. (*Slapping his forehead*) Written in flames a mile high. And it won't be recollected in tranquillity either, picking daffodils with Auntie Wordsworth. It'll be recollected in fire, and blood. My blood.

HELENA (*Thinking patient reasonableness may be worth a try*) She simply said that she's going to church with me. I don't see why that calls for this incredible outburst.
JIMMY Don't you? Perhaps you're not as clever as I thought.
HELENA You think the world's treated you pretty badly, don't you?
ALISON (*Turning her face away L.*) Oh, don't try and take his suffering away from him—he'd be lost without it.

(*He looks at her in surprise, but he turns back to* HELENA. ALISON *can have her turn again later*)

JIMMY I thought this play you're touring in finished up on Saturday week?
HELENA That's right.
JIMMY Eight days ago, in fact.
HELENA Alison wanted me to stay.
JIMMY What are you plotting?
HELENA Don't you think we've had enough of the heavy villain?
JIMMY (*To* ALISON) You don't believe in all that stuff. Why you don't believe in anything. You're just doing it to be vindictive, aren't you? Why—why are you letting her influence you like this?
ALISON (*Starting to break*) Why, why, why, why! (*Putting her hands over her ears*) That word's pulling my head off!
JIMMY And as long as you're around, I'll go on using it. (*He crosses down to the armchair, and seats himself on the back of it. He addresses* HELENA'S *back*) The last time she was in a church was when she was married to me. I expect that surprises you, doesn't it? It was expediency, pure and simple. We were in a hurry, you see. (*The comedy of this strikes him at once, and he laughs*) Yes, we were actually in a hurry! Lusting for the slaughter! Well, the local registrar was a particular pal of Daddy's, and we knew he'd spill the beans to the Colonel like a shot. So we had to seek out some local vicar who didn't know him quite so well. But it was no use. When my best man—a chap I'd met in the pub that morning—and I turned up, Mummy and Daddy were in the church already. They'd found out at the last moment, and had come to watch the execution carried out. How I remember looking down at them, full of beer for breakfast, and feeling a bit buzzed. Mummy was slumped over her pew in a heap—the noble, female rhino, pole-axed at last! And Daddy sat beside her, upright and unafraid, dreaming of his days among the Indian Princes, and unable to believe he'd left his horsewhip at home. Just the two of them in that empty church—them and me. (*Coming out of his remembrance suddenly*) I'm not sure what happened after that. We must have been

married, I suppose. I think I remember being sick in the vestry. (*To* ALISON) Was I?

HELENA   Haven't you finished?

(*He can smell blood again, and he goes on calmly, cheerfully*)

JIMMY (*To* ALISON)   Are you going to let yourself be taken in by this saint in Dior's clothing?[19] I will tell you the simple truth about her. (*Articulating with care*) She is a cow. I wouldn't mind that so much, but she seems to have become a sacred cow as well!

CLIFF   You've gone too far, Jimmy. Now dry up!

HELENA   Oh, let him go on.

JIMMY (*To* CLIFF)   I suppose you're going over to that side as well. Well, why don't you? Helena will help to make it pay off for you. She's an expert in the New Economics—the Economics of the Supernatural. It's all a simple matter of payments and penalties. (*Rises*) She's one of those apocalyptic share pushers who are spreading all those rumours about a transfer of power. (*His imagination is racing, and the words pour out*) Reason and Progress, the old firm, is selling out! Everyone get out while the going's good. Those forgotten shares you had in the old traditions, the old beliefs are going up—up and up and up. (*Moves up L.*) There's going to be a change over. A new Board of Directors, who are going to see that the dividends are always attractive, and that they go to the right people. (*Facing them*) Sell out everything you've got: all those stocks in the old, free inquiry. (*Crosses to above table*) The Big Crash is coming, you can't escape it, so get in on the ground floor with Helena and her friends while there's still time. And there isn't much of it left. Tell me, what could be more gilt-edged than the next world! It's a capital gain, and it's all yours. (*He moves round the table, back to his chair R.*) You see, I know Helena and her kind so very well. In fact, her kind are everywhere, you can't move for them. They're a romantic lot. They spend their time mostly looking forward to the past. The only place they can see the light is the Dark Ages. She's moved long ago into a lovely little cottage of the soul, cut right off from the ugly problems of the twentieth century altogether. She prefers to be cut off from all the conveniences we've fought to get for centuries. She'd rather go down to the ecstatic little shed at the bottom of the garden to relieve her sense of guilt. Our Helena is full of ecstatic wind—(*He leans across the table at her*) aren't you? (*He waits for her to reply*)

HELENA (*Quite calmly*)   It's a pity you've been so far away all this time. I would probably have slapped your face.

---

[19] Christian Dior, fashionable Paris dress designer.

(*They look into each other's eyes across the table. He moves slowly up, above* CLIFF, *until he is beside her*)

You've behaved like this ever since I first came.

JIMMY   Helena, have you ever watched somebody die?

(*She makes a move to rise*)

No, don't move away.

(*She remains seated, and looks up at him*)

It doesn't look dignified enough for you.

HELENA   (*Like ice*)   If you come any nearer, I will slap your face.

(*He looks down at her, a grin smouldering round his mouth*)

JIMMY   I hope you won't make the mistake of thinking for one moment that I am a gentleman.

HELENA   I'm not very likely to do that.

JIMMY   (*Bringing his face close to hers*)   I've no public school scruples about hitting girls. (*Gently*) If you slap my face—by God, I'll lay you out!

HELENA   You probably would. You're the type.

JIMMY   You bet I'm the type. I'm the type that detests physical violence. Which is why, if I find some woman trying to cash in on what she thinks is my defenseless chivalry by lashing out with her frail little fists, I lash back at her.

HELENA   Is that meant to be subtle, or just plain Irish?

(*His grin widens*)

JIMMY   I think you and I understand one another all right. But you haven't answered my question. I said: have you watched somebody die?

HELENA   No, I haven't.

JIMMY   Anyone who's never watched somebody die is suffering from a pretty bad case of virginity. (*His good humor of a moment ago deserts him, as he begins to remember*) For twelve months, I watched my father dying—when I was ten years old. He'd come back from the war in Spain,[20] you see. And certain god-fearing gentlemen there had made such a mess of him, he didn't have long left to live. Everyone knew it—even I knew it. (*He moves R.*) But, you see, I was the only one who cared. (*Turns to the window*) His family were embarrassed by the whole business. Embarrassed and irritated. (*Looking*

[20] Spanish Civil War, 1936–1939.

out) As for my mother, all she could think about was the fact that she had allied herself to a man who seemed to be on the wrong side in all things. My mother was all for being associated with minorities, provided they were the smart, fashionable ones. (*He moves up C. again*) We all of us waited for him to die. The family sent him a cheque every month, and hoped he'd get on with it quietly, without too much vulgar fuss. My mother looked after him without complaining, and that was about all. Perhaps she pitied him. I suppose she was capable of that. (*With a kind of appeal in his voice*) But I was the only one who cared! (*He moves L., behind the armchair*) Every time I sat on the edge of his bed, to listen to him talking or reading to me, I had to fight back my tears. At the end of twelve months, I was a veteran. (*He leans forward on the back of the armchair*) All that that feverish failure of a man had to listen to him was a small, frightened boy. I spent hour upon hour in that tiny bedroom. He would talk to me for hours, pouring out all that was left of his life to one, lonely, bewildered little boy, who could barely understand half of what he said. All he could feel was the despair and the bitterness, the sweet, sickly smell of a dying man. (*He moves around the chair*) You see, I learnt at an early age what it was to be angry—angry and helpless. And I can never forget it. (*Sits*) I knew more about— love . . . betrayal . . . and death, when I was ten years old than you will probably ever know all your life.

(*They all sit silently. Presently,* HELENA *rises*)

HELENA Time we went.

(ALISON *nods*)

I'll just get my things together. (*Crosses to door*) I'll see you downstairs. (*Exit. A slight pause*)

JIMMY (*Not looking at her, almost whispering*) Doesn't it matter to you—what people do to me? What are you trying to do to me? I've given you just everything. Doesn't it mean *anything* to you?

(*Her back stiffens. His axe-swinging bravado has vanished, and his voice crumples in disabled rage*)

JIMMY You Judas! You phlegm! She's taking you with her, and you're so bloody feeble, you'll let her do it!

(ALISON *suddenly takes hold of her cup, and hurls it on the floor. He's drawn blood at last. She looks down at the pieces on the floor, and then at him. Then she crosses R., takes out a dress on a hanger, and slips it on. As she is zipping up the side, she feels giddy, and she has to lean against the wardrobe for support. She closes her eyes)*

ALISON *(Softly)* All I want is a little peace.
JIMMY Peace! God! She wants peace! *(Hardly able to get his words out)* My heart is so full, I feel ill—and she wants peace!

(She crosses to the bed to put on her shoes. CLIFF *gets up from the table, and sits in the armchair R. He picks up a paper, and looks at that.* JIMMY *has recovered slightly, and manages to sound almost detached)*

I rage, and shout my head off, and everyone thinks "poor chap!" or "what an objectionable young man!" But that girl there can twist your arm off with her silence. I've sat in this chair in the dark for hours. And, although she knows I'm feeling as I feel now, she's turned over, and gone to sleep. *(He gets up and faces* CLIFF, *who doesn't look up from his paper)* One of us is crazy. One of us is mean and stupid and crazy. Which is it? Is it me? Is it me, standing here like an hysterical girl, hardly able to get my words out? Or is it her? Sitting there, putting on her shoes to go out with that—— *(But inspiration has deserted him by now)* Which is it?

*(*CLIFF *is still looking down at his paper)*

I wish to heaven you'd try loving her, that's all. *(He moves up C., watching her look for her gloves)* Perhaps, one day, you may want to come back. I shall wait for that day. I want to stand up in your tears, and splash about in them, and sing. I want to be there when you grovel. I want to be there, I want to watch it, I want the front seat.

*(*HELENA *enters, carrying two prayer books)*

I want to see your face rubbed in the mud—that's all I can hope for. There's nothing else I want any longer.
HELENA *(After a moment)* There's a phone call for you.
JIMMY *(Turning)* Well, it can't be anything good, can it? *(Exit)*
HELENA All ready?
ALISON Yes—I think so.
HELENA You feel all right, don't you? *(She nods)* What's he been raving about now? Oh, what does it matter? He makes me want to claw his hair out by the roots. When I think of what you will be going through in a few months' time—and all for him! It's as if you'd done *him* wrong! These *men!* *(Turning on* CLIFF*)* And all the time you just sit there, and do nothing!
CLIFF *(Looking up slowly)* That's right—I just sit here.

HELENA What's the matter with you? What sort of a man are you?
CLIFF I'm not the District Commissioner, you know. Listen, Helena—I don't feel like Jimmy does about you, but I'm not exactly on your side, either. And since you've been here, everything's certainly been worse than it's ever been. This has always been a battlefield, but I'm pretty certain that if I hadn't been here, everything would have been over between these two long ago. I've been a—a no-man's land between them. Sometimes, it's been still and peaceful, no incidents, and we've all been reasonably happy. But most of the time, it's simply a very narrow strip of plain hell. But where I come from, we're used to brawling and excitement. Perhaps I even enjoy being in the thick of it. I love these two people very much. (*He looks at her steadily, and adds simply*) And I pity all of us.
HELENA Are you including me in that? (*But she goes on quickly to avoid his reply*) I don't understand him, you, or any of it. All I know is that none of you seems to know how to behave in a decent, civilized way. (*In command now*) Listen, Alison—I've sent your father a wire.
ALISON (*Numbed and vague by now*) Oh?

(HELENA *looks at her, and realizes quickly that everything now will have to depend on her own authority. She tries to explain patiently*)

HELENA Look, dear—he'll get it first thing in the morning. I thought it would be better than trying to explain the situation over the phone. I asked him to come up, and fetch you home tomorrow.
ALISON What did you say?
HELENA Simply that you wanted to come home, and would he come up for you.
ALISON I see.
HELENA I knew that would be quite enough. I told him there was nothing to worry about, so they won't worry and think there's been an accident or anything. I had to do something, dear. (*Very gently*) You didn't mind, did you?
ALISON No, I don't mind. Thank you.
HELENA And you will go when he comes for you?
ALISON (*Pause*) Yes. I'll go.
HELENA (*Relieved*) I expect he'll drive up. He should be here about tea-time. It'll give you plenty of time to get your things together. And, perhaps, after you've gone—Jimmy (*Saying the word almost with difficulty*) will come to his senses, and face up to things.
ALISON Who was on the phone?
HELENA I didn't catch it properly. It rang after I'd sent the wire off—

just as soon as I put the receiver down almost. I had to go back down the stairs again. Sister somebody, I think.

ALISON Must have been a hospital or something. Unless he knows someone in a convent—*that* doesn't seem very likely, does it? Well, we'll be late, if we don't hurry.

(*She puts down one of the prayer books on the table. Enter* JIMMY. *He comes down C., between the two women*)

CLIFF All right, boyo?
JIMMY (*To* ALISON) It's Hugh's mum. She's—had a stroke. (*Slight pause*)
ALISON I'm sorry.

(JIMMY *sits on the bed*)

CLIFF How bad is it?
JIMMY They didn't say much. But I think she's dying.
CLIFF Oh dear. . . .
JIMMY (*Rubbing his fist over his face*) It doesn't make any sense at all. Do you think it does?
ALISON I'm sorry—I really am.
CLIFF Anything I can do?
JIMMY The London train goes in half an hour. You'd better order me a taxi.
CLIFF Right. (*He crosses to the door, and stops*) Do you want me to come with you, boy?
JIMMY No thanks. After all, you hardly knew her. It's not for you to go.

(HELENA *looks quickly at* ALISON)

She may not even remember me, for all I know.
CLIFF O.K. (*Exit*)
JIMMY I remember the first time I showed her your photograph—just after we were married. She looked at it, and the tears just welled up in her eyes, and she said: "But she's so beautiful! She's so beautiful!" She kept repeating it as if she couldn't believe it. Sounds a bit simple and sentimental when you repeat it. But it was pure gold the way she said it.

(*He looks at her. She is standing by the dressing table, her back to him*)

She got a kick out of you, like she did out of everything else. Hand me my shoes, will you?

(*She kneels down, and hands them to him*)

(*Looking down at his feet*) You're coming with me, aren't you? She (*He shrugs*) hasn't got anyone else now. I . . . need you . . . to come with me.

(*He looks into her eyes, but she turns away, and stands up. Outside, the church bells start ringing.* HELENA *moves up to the door and waits, watching them closely.* ALISON *stands quite still,* JIMMY'S *eyes burning into her. Then, she crosses in front of him to the table where she picks up the prayer book, her back to him. She wavers, and seems about to say something, but turns upstage instead, and walks quickly to the door*)

ALISON (*Hardly audible*)   Let's go.

(*She goes out,* HELENA *following.* JIMMY *gets up, looks about him unbelievingly, and leans against the chest of drawers. The teddy bear is close to his face, and he picks it up gently, looks at it quickly, and throws it downstage. It hits the floor with a thud, and it makes a rattling, groaning sound—as guaranteed in the advertisement.* JIMMY *falls forward on to the bed, his face buried in the covers*)

Quick Curtain

Act Two / SCENE TWO

The following evening. When the curtain rises, ALISON *is discovered R., going from her dressing table to the bed, and packing her things into a suitcase. Sitting down L. is her father,* COLONEL REDFERN, *a large handsome man, about sixty. Forty years of being a soldier sometimes conceals the essentially gentle, kindly man underneath. Brought up to command respect, he is often slightly withdrawn and uneasy now that he finds himself in a world where his authority has lately become less and less unquestionable. His wife would relish the present situation, but he is only disturbed and bewildered by it. He looks around him, discreetly scrutinizing everything.*

COLONEL (*Partly to himself*)   I'm afraid it's all beyond me. I suppose it always will be. As for Jimmy—he just speaks a different language from any of us. Where did you say he'd gone?

ALISON He's gone to see Mrs. Tanner.
COLONEL Who?
ALISON Hugh Tanner's mother.
COLONEL Oh, I see.
ALISON She's been taken ill—a stroke. Hugh's abroad, as you know, so Jimmy's gone to London to see her.

(*He nods*)

He wanted me to go with him.
COLONEL Didn't she start him off in this sweet-stall business?
ALISON Yes.
COLONEL What is she like? Nothing like her son, I trust?
ALISON Not remotely. Oh—how can you describe her? Rather—ordinary. What Jimmy insists on calling "working class." A charwoman who married an actor, worked hard all her life, and spent most of it struggling to support her husband and her son. Jimmy and she are very fond of each other.
COLONEL So you didn't go with him?
ALISON No
COLONEL Who's looking after the sweet-stall?
ALISON Cliff. He should be in soon.
COLONEL Oh, yes, of course—Cliff. Does he live here, too?
ALISON Yes. His room is just across the landing.
COLONEL Sweet-stall. It does seem an extraordinary thing for an educated young man to be occupying himself with. Why should he want to do that, of all things? I've always thought he must be quite clever in his way.
ALISON (*No longer interested in this problem*) Oh, he tried so many things—journalism, advertising, even vacuum cleaners for a few weeks. He seems to have been as happy doing this as anything else.
COLONEL I've often wondered what it was like—where you were living, I mean. You didn't tell us very much in your letters.
ALISON There wasn't a great deal to tell you. There's not much social life here.
COLONEL Oh, I know what you mean. You were afraid of being disloyal to your husband.
ALISON Disloyal! (*She laughs*) He thought it was high treason of me to write to you at all! I used to have to dodge downstairs for the post, so that he wouldn't see I was getting letters from home. Even then I had to hide them.
COLONEL He really does hate us, doesn't he?
ALISON Oh, yes—don't have any doubts about that. He hates all of us.

COLONEL (*Sighs*) It seems a great pity. It was all so unfortunate—unfortunate and unnecessary. I'm afraid I can't help feeling that he must have had a certain amount of right on his side.
ALISON (*Puzzled by this admission*) Right on his side?
COLONEL It's a little late to admit it, I know, but your mother and I weren't entirely free from blame. I have never said anything—there was no point afterwards—but I have always believed that she went too far over Jimmy. Of course, she was extremely upset at the time—we both were—and that explains a good deal of what happened. I did my best to stop her, but she was in such a state of mind, there was simply nothing I could do. She seemed to have made up her mind that if he was going to marry you, he must be a criminal, at the very least. All those inquiries, the private detectives—the accusations. I hated every moment of it.
ALISON I suppose she was trying to protect me—in a rather heavy-handed way, admittedly.
COLONEL I must confess I find that kind of thing rather horrifying. Anyway, I try to think now that it never happened. I didn't approve of Jimmy at all, and I don't suppose I ever should, but, looking back on it, I think it would have been better, for all concerned, if we had never attempted to interfere. At least, it would have been a little more dignified.
ALISON It wasn't your fault.
COLONEL I don't know. We were all to blame, in our different ways. No doubt Jimmy acted in good faith. He's honest enough, whatever else he may be. And your mother—in her heavy-handed way, as you put it—acted in good faith as well. Perhaps you and I were the ones most to blame.
ALISON You and I!
COLONEL I think you may take after me a little, my dear. You like to sit on the fence because it's comfortable and more peaceful.
ALISON Sitting on the fence! I married him, didn't I?
COLONEL Oh, yes, you did.
ALISON In spite of all the humiliating scenes and the threats! What did you say to me at the time? Wasn't I letting you down, turning against you, how could I do this to you, etcetera?
COLONEL Perhaps it might have been better if you hadn't written letters to us—knowing how we felt about your husband, and after everything that had happened. (*He looks at her uncomfortably*) Forgive me, I'm a little confused, what with everything—the telegram, driving up here suddenly. . . . (*He trails off rather helplessly. He looks tired. He glances at her nervously, a hint of accusation in his eyes, as if he*

expected her to defend herself further. She senses this, and is more confused than ever)

ALISON Do you know what he said about Mummy? He said she was an overfed, overprivileged old bitch. "A good blow-out for the worms" was his expression, I think.

COLONEL I see. And what does he say about me?

ALISON Oh, he doesn't seem to mind you so much. In fact, I think he rather likes you. He likes you because he can feel sorry for you. (*Conscious that what she says is going to hurt him*) "Poor old Daddy—just one of those sturdy old plants left over from the Edwardian Wilderness that can't understand why the sun isn't shining any more." (*Rather lamely*) Something like that, anyway.

COLONEL He has quite a turn of phrase, hasn't he? (*Simply, and without malice*) Why did you ever have to meet this young man?

ALISON Oh, Daddy, please don't put me on trial now. I've been on trial every day and night of my life for nearly four years.

COLONEL But why should he have married you, feeling as he did about everything?

ALISON That is the famous American question—you know, the sixty-four dollar one! Perhaps it was revenge.

(*He looks up uncomprehendingly*)

Oh, yes. Some people do actually marry for revenge. People like Jimmy, anyway. Or perhaps he should have been another Shelley, and can't understand now why I'm not another Mary, and you're not William Godwin. He thinks he's got a sort of genius for love and friendship—on his own terms. Well, for twenty years, I'd lived a happy, uncomplicated life, and suddenly, this—this spiritual barbarian—throws down the gauntlet at me. Perhaps only another woman could understand what a challenge like that means—although I think Helena was as mystified as you are.

COLONEL I am mystified. (*He rises, and crosses to the window R.*) Your husband has obviously taught you a great deal, whether you realize it or not. What any of it means, I don't know. I always believed that people married each other because they were in love. That always seemed a good enough reason to me. But apparently, that's too simple for young people nowadays. They have to talk about challenges and revenge. I just can't believe that love between men and women is really like that.

ALISON Only some men and women.

COLONEL But why you? My daughter. . . . No. Perhaps Jimmy is right. Perhaps I am a—what was it? an old plant left over from the Edwardian

Wilderness. And I can't understand why the sun isn't shining any more. You can see what he means, can't you? It was March, 1914, when I left England, and, apart from leaves every ten years or so, I didn't see much of my own country until we all came back in '47. Oh, I knew things had changed, of course. People told you all the time the way it was going—going to the dogs, as the Blimps[21] are supposed to say. But it seemed very unreal to me, out there. The England I remembered was the one I left in 1914, and I was happy to go on remembering it that way. Beside, I had the Maharajah's army to command—that was my world, and I loved it, all of it. At the time, it looked like going on forever. When I think of it now, it seems like a dream. If only it could have gone on forever. Those long, cool evenings up in the hills, everything purple and golden. Your mother and I were so happy then. It seemed as though we had everything we could ever want. I think the last day the sun shone was when that dirty little train steamed out of that crowded, suffocating Indian station, and the battalion band playing for all it was worth. I knew in my heart it was all over then. Everything.

ALISON You're hurt because everything is changed. Jimmy is hurt because everything is the same. And neither of you can face it. Something's gone wrong somewhere, hasn't it?

COLONEL It looks like it, my dear.

(She picks up the squirrel from the chest of drawers, is about to put it in her suitcase, hesitates, and then puts it back. The COLONEL turns and looks at her. She moves down toward him, her head turned away. For a few moments, she seems to be standing on the edge of choice. The choice made, her body wheels round suddenly, and she is leaning against him, weeping softly)

(After a pause) This is a big step you're taking. You've made up your mind to come back with me? Is that really what you want?

(Enter HELENA)

HELENA I'm sorry. I came in to see if I could help you pack, Alison. Oh, you look as though you've finished.

(ALISON leaves her father, and moves to the bed, pushing down the lid of her suitcase)

ALISON All ready.

HELENA Have you got everything?

[21] British upper classes.

ALISON Well, no. But Cliff can send the rest on sometime, I expect. He should have been back by now. Oh, of course, he's had to put the stall away on his own today.
COLONEL (*Crossing and picking up the suitcase*) Well, I'd better put this in the car then. We may as well get along. Your mother will be worried, I know. I promised her I'd ring her when I got here. She's not very well.
HELENA I hope my telegram didn't upset her too much. Perhaps I shouldn't have—
COLONEL Not at all. We were very grateful that you did. It was very kind of you, indeed. She tried to insist on coming with me, but I finally managed to talk her out of it. I thought it would be best for everyone. What about your case, Helena? If you care to tell me where it is, I'll take it down with this one.
HELENA I'm afraid I shan't be coming tonight.
ALISON (*Very surprised*) Aren't you coming with us?

(*Enter* CLIFF)

HELENA I'd like to, but the fact is I've an appointment tomorrow in Birmingham—about a job. They've just sent me a script. It's rather important, and I don't want to miss it. So it looks as though I shall have to stay here tonight.
ALISON Oh, I see. Hullo, Cliff.
CLIFF Hullo, there.
ALISON Daddy—this is Cliff.
COLONEL How do you do, Cliff.
CLIFF How do you do, sir. (*Slight pause*)
COLONEL Well, I'd better put this in the car, hadn't I? Don't be long, Alison. Good-bye, Helena. I expect we shall be seeing you again soon, if you're not busy.
HELENA Oh, yes, I shall be back in a day or two.

(CLIFF *takes off his jacket*)

COLONEL Well, then—good-bye, Cliff.
CLIFF Good-bye, sir.

(*The* COLONEL *goes out.* CLIFF *comes down* L. HELENA *moves* C.)

You're really going then?
ALISON Really going.
CLIFF I should think Jimmy would be back pretty soon. You won't wait?

ALISON No, Cliff.
CLIFF Who's going to tell him?
HELENA I can tell him. That is, if I'm here when he comes back.
CLIFF (*Quietly*) You'll be here. (*To* ALISON) Don't you think you ought to tell him yourself?

(*She hands him an envelope from her handbag. He takes it*)

Bit conventional, isn't it?
ALISON I'm a conventional girl.

(*He crosses to her, and puts his arms round her*)

CLIFF (*Back over his shoulder, to* HELENA) I hope you're right, that's all.
HELENA What do you mean? You hope *I'm* right?
CLIFF (*To* ALISON) The place is going to be really cock-eyed now. You know that, don't you?
ALISON Please, Cliff——

(*He nods. She kisses him*)

I'll write to you later.
CLIFF Good-bye, lovely.
ALISON Look after him.
CLIFF We'll keep the old nut-house going somehow.

(*She crosses C., in between the two of them, glances quickly at the two armchairs, the papers still left around them from yesterday.* HELENA *kisses her on the cheek, and squeezes her hand*)

HELENA See you soon.

(ALISON *nods, and goes out quickly.* CLIFF *and* HELENA *are left looking at each other*)

Would you like me to make you some tea?
CLIFF No, thanks.
HELENA Think I might have some myself, if you don't mind.
CLIFF So you're staying?
HELENA Just for tonight. Do you object?
CLIFF Nothing to do with me. (*Against the table C.*) Of course, he may not be back until later on.

(*She crosses L., to the window, and lights a cigarette*)

HELENA What do you think he'll do? Perhaps he'll look out one of his

old girl friends. What about this Madeline?
CLIFF   What about her?
HELENA   Isn't she supposed to have done a lot for him? Couldn't he go back to her?
CLIFF   I shouldn't think so.
HELENA   What happened?
CLIFF   She was nearly old enough to be his mother. I expect that's something to do with it! Why the hell should I know!

(*For the first time in the play, his good humor has completely deserted him. She looks surprised*)

HELENA   You're his friend, aren't you? Anyway, he's not what you'd call reticent about himself, is he? I've never seen so many souls stripped to the waist since I've been here.

(*He turns to go*)

HELENA   Aren't you staying?
CLIFF   No, I'm not. There was a train in from London about five minutes ago. And, just in case he may have been on it, I'm going out.
HELENA   Don't you think you ought to be here when he comes?
CLIFF   I've had a hard day, and I don't think I want to see anyone hurt until I've had something to eat first, and perhaps a few drinks as well. I think I might pick up some nice, pleasant little tart in a milk bar, and sneak her in past old mother Drury. Here! (*Tossing the letter at her*) You give it to him! (*Crossing to door*) He's all yours. (*At door*) And I hope he rams it up your nostrils! (*Exit*)

(*She crosses to the table, and stubs out her cigarette. The front door downstairs is heard to slam. She moves to the wardrobe, opens it idly. It is empty, except for one dress, swinging on a hanger. She goes over to the dressing table, now cleared but for a framed photograph of* JIMMY. *Idly, she slams the empty drawers open and shut. She turns upstage to the chest of drawers, picks up the toy bear, and sits on the bed, looking at it. She lays her head back on the pillow, still holding the bear. She looks up quickly as the door crashes open, and* JIMMY *enters. He stands looking at her, then moves down C., taking off his raincoat, and throwing it over the table. He is almost giddy with anger, and has to steady himself on the chair. He looks up*)

JIMMY   That old bastard nearly ran me down in his car! Now, if he'd killed me, that really would have been ironical. And how right and fitting that my wife should have been a passenger. A passenger! What's the matter with everybody? (*Crossing up to her*) Cliff practically walked into me, coming out of the house. He belted up the other way, and pretended not to see me. Are you the only one who's not afraid to stay?

(*She hands him* ALISON's *note. He takes it*)

Oh, it's one of these, is it? (*He rips it open. He reads a few lines, and almost snorts with disbelief*) Did you write this for her! Well, listen to this then! (*Reading*) "My dear—I must get away. I don't suppose you will understand, but please try. I need peace so desperately, and, at the moment, I am willing to sacrifice everything just for that. I don't know what's going to happen to us. I know you will be feeling wretched and bitter, but try to be a little patient with me. I shall always have a deep, loving need of you—Alison." Oh, how could she be so bloody wet! "Deep loving need!" That makes me puke! (*Crossing to R.*) She couldn't say, "You rotten bastard! I hate your guts, I'm clearing out, and I hope you rot!" No, she has to make a polite, emotional mess out of it! (*Seeing the dress in the wardrobe, he rips it out, and throws it in the corner up L.*) "Deep, loving need!" I never thought she was capable of being as phony as that! What is that—a line from one of those plays you've been in? What are you doing here anyway? You'd better keep out of my way, if you don't want your head kicked in.

HELENA (*Calmly*) If you'll stop thinking about yourself for one moment, I'll tell you something I think you ought to know. Your wife is going to have a baby.

(*He just looks at her*)

Well? Doesn't that mean anything? Even to you?

(*He is taken aback, but not so much by the news, as by her*)

JIMMY All right—yes. I am surprised. I give you that. But, tell me. Did you honestly expect me to go soggy at the knees, and collapse with remorse! (*Leaning nearer*) Listen, if you'll stop breathing your female wisdom all over me, I'll tell you something: I don't care. (*Beginning quietly*) I don't care if she's going to have a baby. I don't care if it has two heads! (*He knows her fingers are itching*) Do I disgust you? Well, go on—slap my face. But remember what I told you before, will you? For eleven hours, I have been watching someone I love very much going through the sordid process of dying. She was alone, and I was the only one with her. And when I have to walk behind that coffin on Thursday, I'll be on my own again. Because that bitch won't even send her a bunch of flowers—I know! She made the great mistake of all her kind. She thought that because Hugh's mother was a deprived and ignorant old woman, who said all the wrong things in all the wrong places, she couldn't be taken seriously. And you think I should be overcome with awe because that cruel, stupid girl is going to have a baby! (*Anguish in his voice*) I can't believe it! I can't. (*Grabbing her shoulder*) Well, the performance is over. Now leave me alone, and *get out*, you evil-minded little virgin.

(*She slaps his face savagely. An expression of horror and disbelief floods his face. But it drains away, and all that is left is pain. His hand goes up to his head, and a muffled cry of despair escapes him.* HELENA *tears his hand away, and kisses him passionately, drawing him down beside her*)

Curtain

Act Three / SCENE ONE

Several months later. A Sunday evening. ALISON's *personal belongings, such as her make-up things on the dressing table, for example, have been replaced by* HELENA's.

At rise of curtain, we find JIMMY and CLIFF *sprawled in their respective armchairs, immersed in the Sunday newspapers.* HELENA *is standing down L. leaning over the ironing board, a small pile of clothes beside her. She looks more attractive than before, for the setting of her face is more relaxed. She still looks quite smart, but in an unpremeditated, careless way; she wears an old shirt of* JIMMY's.

CLIFF   That stinking old pipe! (*Pause*)
JIMMY   Shut up.
CLIFF   Why don't you do something with it?
JIMMY   Why do I spend half of Sunday reading the papers?
CLIFF   (*Kicks him without lowering his paper*)   It stinks!
JIMMY   So do you, but I'm not singing an aria about it. (*Turns to the next page*) The dirty ones get more and more wet round the mouth, and the posh ones are more pompous than ever. (*Lowering paper, and waving pipe at* HELENA) Does this bother you?
HELENA   No. I quite like it.
JIMMY   (*To* CLIFF)   There you are—she likes it! (*He returns to his*

paper. CLIFF *grunts*) Have you read about the grotesque and evil practices going on in the Midlands?
CLIFF Read about the what?
JIMMY Grotesque and evil practices going on in the Midlands?
CLIFF No, what about 'em?
JIMMY Seems we don't know the old place. It's all in here. Startling Revelations this week! Pictures too. Reconstructions of midnight invocations to the Coptic Goddess of fertility.
HELENA Sounds madly depraved.
JIMMY Yes, it's rather us, isn't it? My gosh, look at 'em! Snarling themselves silly. Next week a well-known debutante relates how, during an evil orgy in Market Harborough, she killed and drank the blood of a white cockerel. Well—I'll bet Fortnums[22] must be doing a roaring line in sacrificial cocks! (*Thoughtful*) Perhaps that's what Miss Drury does on Sunday evenings. She puts in a stint as evil high priestess down at the Y.W.—probably having a workout at this very moment. (*To* HELENA) You never dabbled in this kind of thing, did you?
HELENA (*Laughs*) Not lately!
JIMMY Sounds rather your cup of tea—cup of blood, I should say. (*In an imitation of a Midlands accent*) Well, I mean, it gives you something to do, doesn't it? After all, it wouldn't do if we was all alike, would it? It'd be a funny world if we was all the same, that's what *I* always say! (*Resuming in his normal voice*) All I know is that somebody's been sticking pins into *my* wax image for years. (*Suddenly*) Of course: Alison's mother! Every Friday, the wax arrives from Harrods,[22] and all through the week-end, she's stabbing away at it with a hatpin! Ruined her bridge game, I dare say.
HELENA Why don't *you* try it?
JIMMY Yes, it's an idea. (*Pointing to* CLIFF) Just for a start, we could roast him over the gas stove. Have we got enough shillings for the meter? It seems to be just the thing for these autumn evenings. After all, the whole point of a sacrifice is that you give up something you never really wanted in the first place. You know what I mean? People are doing it around you all the time. They give up their careers, say —or their beliefs—or sex. And everyone thinks to themselves: how wonderful to be able to do that. If only I were capable of doing that! But the truth of it is that they've been kidding themselves, and they've been kidding you. It's not awfully difficult—giving up something you were incapable of ever really wanting. We shouldn't be admiring them. We should feel rather sorry for them. (*Coming back from this*

---

[22] Fortnums and Harrods are fashionable London department stores.

sudden, brooding excursion, and turning to CLIFF) You'll make an admirable sacrifice.

CLIFF (*Mumbling*) Dry up! I'm trying to read.

JIMMY Afterwards, we can make a loving cup from his blood. Can't say I fancy that so much. I've seen it—it looks like cochineal, ever so common. (*To* HELENA) Yours would be much better—pale Cambridge blue, I imagine. No? And afterwards, we could make invocations to the Coptic Goddess of fertility. Got any idea how you do that? (*To* CLIFF) Do you know?

CLIFF Shouldn't have thought *you* needed to make invocations to the Coptic whatever-she-is!

JIMMY Yes, I see what you mean. (*To* HELENA) Well, we don't want to *ask* for trouble, do we? Perhaps it might appeal to the lady here— she's written a long letter all about artificial insemination. It's headed: Haven't we tried God's patience enough! (*Throws the paper down*) Let's see the other posh one.

CLIFF Haven't finished yet.

JIMMY Well, hurry up. I'll have to write and ask them to put hyphens in between the syllables for you. There's a particularly savage correspondence going on in there about whether Milton wore braces[23] or not. I just want to see who gets shot down this week.

CLIFF Just read that. Don't know what it was about, but a Fellow of All Souls seems to have bitten the dust, and the Athenaeum's going up in flames, so the Editor declares that this correspondence is now closed.

JIMMY I think you're actually acquiring yourself a curiosity, my boy. Oh, yes, and then there's an American professor from Yale or somewhere, who believes that when Shakespeare was writing *The Tempest*, he changed his sex. Yes, he was obliged to go back to Stratford because the other actors couldn't take him seriously any longer. This professor chap is coming over here to search for certain documents which will prove that poor old W.S. ended up in someone else's second best bed—a certain Warwickshire farmer's, whom he married after having three children by him.

(HELENA *laughs.* JIMMY *looks up quizzically*)

Is anything the matter?

HELENA No, nothing. I'm only beginning to get used to him. I never (*This is to* CLIFF) used to be sure when he was being serious, or when he wasn't.

---

[23] Suspenders.

CLIFF Don't think he knows himself half the time. When in doubt, just mark it down as an insult.
JIMMY Hurry up with that paper, and shut up! What are we going to do tonight? There isn't even a decent concert on. (*To* HELENA) Are you going to church?
HELENA (*Rather taken aback*) No. I don't think so. Unless you want to.
JIMMY Do I detect a growing, satanic glint in her eyes lately? Do you think it's living in sin with me that does it? (*To* HELENA) Do you feel very sinful, my dear? Well? Do you?

(*She can hardly believe that this is an attack, and she can only look at him, uncertain of herself*)

Do you feel sin crawling out of your ears, like stored up wax or something? Are you wondering whether I'm joking or not? Perhaps I ought to wear a red nose and funny hat. I'm just curious, that's all.

(*She is shaken by the sudden coldness in his eyes, but before she has time to fully realize how hurt she is, he is smiling at her, and shouting cheerfully at Cliff*)

Let's have that paper, stupid!
CLIFF Why don't you drop dead!
JIMMY (*To* HELENA) Will you be much longer doing that?
HELENA Nearly finished.
JIMMY Talking of sin, wasn't that Miss Drury's Reverend friend I saw you chatting with yesterday? Helena darling, I said wasn't that. . . .
HELENA Yes, it was.
JIMMY My dear, you don't have to be on the defensive you know.
HELENA I'm not on the defensive.
JIMMY After all, there's no reason why we shouldn't have the parson to tea up here. Why don't we? Did you find that you had much in common?
HELENA No, I don't think so.
JIMMY Do you think that some of this spiritual beefcake would make a man of me? Should I go in for this moral weight lifting and get myself some overdeveloped muscle? I was a liberal skinny weakling. I too was afraid to strip down to my soul, but now everyone looks at my superb physique in envy. I can perform any kind of press there is without betraying the least sign of passion or kindliness.
HELENA All right, Jimmy.
JIMMY Two years ago I couldn't even lift up my head—now I have more uplift than a film starlet.
HELENA Jimmy, can we have one day, just one day, without tumbling over religion or politics?

603 · Look Back in Anger [ACT THREE, Scene One]

CLIFF Yes, change the record, old boy, or pipe down.
JIMMY (*Rising*) Thought of the title for a new song today. It's called "My mother's in the madhouse—that's why I'm in love with you." The lyrics are catchy, too. I was thinking we might work it into the act.
HELENA Good idea.
JIMMY I was thinking we'd scrub Jock and Day, and call ourselves something else. "And jocund day stands tiptoed on the misty mountain tops."[24] It's too intellectual! Anyway, I shouldn't think people will want to be reminded of that peculiar man's plays after Harvard and Yale have finished with him. How about something bright and snappy? I know—— What about—T.S. Eliot and Pam!
CLIFF (*Casually falling in with this familiar routine*) Mirth, mellerdy, and madness!
JIMMY (*Sitting at the table R. and "strumming" it*) Bringing quips and strips for you!

(*They sing together*)

"For we may be guilty, darling. . . .
But we're both insane as well!"

(JIMMY *stands up, and rattles his lines off at almost unintelligible speed*)

Ladies and gentlemen, as I was coming to the theater tonight, I was passing through the stage door, and a man comes up to me, and 'e says:
CLIFF 'Ere! Have you seen nobody?
JIMMY Have I seen who?
CLIFF Have you seen nobody?
JIMMY Of course, I haven't seen nobody! Kindly don't waste my time! Ladies and gentlemen, a little recitation entitled "She said she was called a little Gidding[25] but she was more like a gelding iron!" Thank you. "She said she was called little Gidding——"
CLIFF Are you quite sure you haven't seen nobody?
JIMMY Are you still here?
CLIFF I'm looking for nobody!
JIMMY W*ill* you kindly go away! "She said she was called little Gidding——"
CLIFF Well, I can't find nobody anywhere, and I'm supposed to give him this case!

[24] *Romeo and Juliet*, Act III, Scene 5, lines 9–10.
[25] "Little Gidding" is the last of T. S. Eliot's *Four Quartets*.

JIMMY   Will you kindly stop interrupting per*lease!* Can't you see I'm trying to entertain these ladies and gentlemen? Who is this nobody you're talking about?
CLIFF   I was told to come here and give this case to nobody.
JIMMY   You were told to come here and give this case to nobody.
CLIFF   That's right. And when I gave it to him, nobody would give me a shilling.
JIMMY   And when you gave it to him, nobody would give you a shilling.
CLIFF   That's right.
JIMMY   Well, what about it?
CLIFF   Nobody's not here!
JIMMY   Now, let me get this straight: when you say nobody's here, you don't mean nobody's here?
CLIFF   No.
JIMMY   You mean—nobody's here.
CLIFF   That's right.
JIMMY   Well, why didn't you say so before?
HELENA (*Not quite sure if this is really her cue*)   Hey! You down there!
JIMMY   Oh, it goes on for hours yet, but never mind. What is it, sir?
HELENA (*Shouting*)   I think your sketch stinks! I say—I think your sketch stinks!
JIMMY   He thinks it stinks. And, who, pray, might you be?
HELENA Me? Oh— (*With mock modesty*) I'm nobody.
JIMMY   Then here's your bloody case! (*He hurls a cushion at her, which hits the ironing board*)
HELENA My ironing board!

(*The two men do a Flanagan and Allen,*[26] *moving slowly in step, as they sing*)

JIMMY AND CLIFF   Now there's a certain little lady, and you all know who I mean.
She may have been to Roedean,[27] but to me she's still a queen.
Someday I'm goin' to marry her,
When times are not so bad,
Her mother doesn't care for me
So I'll 'ave to ask 'er dad.
We'll build a little home for two,
And have some quiet menage,
We'll send our kids to public school

[26] Music hall song-and-dance team.
[27] A fashionable girls' school; a "Roedean girl" is caricatured as a tweedy Amazon and sports enthusiast.

And live on bread and marge.
Don't be afraid to sleep with your sweetheart,
Just because she's better than you.
Those forgotten middle-classes may have fallen on their noses,
But a girl who's true blue,
Will still have something left for you,
The angels up above, will know that you're in love
So don't be afraid to sleep with your sweetheart,
Just because she's better than you. . . .
   They call me Sydney,
Just because she's better than you.

 (*But* JIMMY *has had enough of this gag by now, and he pushes* CLIFF *away*)

JIMMY Your damned great feet! That's the second time you've kicked my ankle! It's no good—Helena will have to do it. Go on, go and make some tea, and we'll decide what we're going to do.
CLIFF Make some yourself!

 (*He pushes him back violently,* JIMMY *loses his balance, and falls over*)

JIMMY You rough bastard! (*He leaps up, and they grapple, falling on to the floor with a crash. They roll about, grunting and gasping.* CLIFF *manages to kneel on* JIMMY's *chest*)
CLIFF (*Breathing heavily*) I want to read the papers!
JIMMY You're a savage, a hooligan! You really are! Do you know that! You don't deserve to live in the same house with decent, sensitive people!
CLIFF Are you going to dry up, or do I read the papers down here?

 (JIMMY *makes a supreme effort, and* CLIFF *topples to the floor*)

JIMMY You've made me wrench my guts! (*He pushes the struggling* CLIFF *down*)
CLIFF Look what you're doing! You're ripping my shirt. Get off!
JIMMY Well, what do you want to wear a shirt for? (*Rising*) A tough character like you! Now go and make me some tea.
CLIFF It's the only clean one I've got. Oh, you big oaf! (*Getting up from the floor, and appealing to* HELENA) Look! It's filthy!
HELENA Yes, it is. He's stronger than he looks. If you like to take it off now, I'll wash it through for you. It'll be dry by the time we want to go out.

 (CLIFF *hesitates*)

What's the matter, Cliff?
CLIFF Oh, it'll be all right.
JIMMY Give it to her, and quit moaning!
CLIFF Oh, all right. (*He takes it off, and gives it to her*) Thanks Helena.
HELENA (*Taking it*) Right. I won't be a minute with it.

(*She goes out.* JIMMY *flops into his armchair R.*)

JIMMY (*Amused*) You look like Marlon Brando or something. (*Slight pause*) You don't care for Helena, do you?
CLIFF You didn't seem very keen yourself once. (*Hesitating, then quickly*) It's not the same, is it?
JIMMY (*Irritably*) No, of course it's not the same, you idiot! It never is! Today's meal is always different from yesterday's and the last woman isn't the same as the one before. If you can't accept that, you're going to be pretty unhappy, my boy.
CLIFF (*Sits on the arm of his chair, and rubs his feet*) Jimmy—I don't think I shall stay here much longer.
JIMMY (*Rather casually*) Oh, why not?
CLIFF (*Picking up his tone*) Oh, I don't know. I've just thought of trying somewhere different. The sweetstall's all right, but I think I'd like to try something else. You're highly educated, and it suits you, but I need something a bit better.
JIMMY Just as you like, my dear boy. It's your business, not mine.
CLIFF And another thing—I think Helena finds it rather a lot of work to do with two chaps about the place. It won't be so much for her if there's just the two of you. Anyway, I think I ought to find some girl who'll just look after me.
JIMMY Sounds like a good idea. Can't think who'd be stupid enough to team themselves up with you though. Perhaps Helena can think of somebody for you—one of her posh girl friends with lots of money, and no brains. That's what you want.
CLIFF Something like that.
JIMMY Any idea what you're going to do?
CLIFF Not much.
JIMMY That sounds like you, all right! Shouldn't think you'll last five minutes without me to explain the score to you.
CLIFF (*Grinning*) Don't suppose so.
JIMMY You're such a scruffy little beast—I'll bet some respectable little madam from Pinner or Guildford[28] gobbles you up in six

[28] Midlands towns that suggest respectability.

607 · Look Back in Anger [ACT THREE, Scene One]

months. She'll marry you, send you out to work, and you'll end up as clean as a new pin.

CLIFF (*Chuckling*) Yes, I'm stupid enough for that, too!

JIMMY (*To himself*) I seem to spend my life saying good-bye. (*Slight pause*)

CLIFF My feet hurt.

JIMMY Try washing your socks. (*Slowly*) It's a funny thing. You've been loyal, generous, and a good friend. But I'm quite prepared to see you wander off, find a new home, and make out on your own. And all because of something I want from that girl downstairs, something I know in my heart she's incapable of giving. You're worth a half a dozen Helenas to me or to anyone. And, if you were in my place, you'd do the same thing. Right?

CLIFF Right.

JIMMY Why, why, why, why do we let these women bleed us to death? Have you ever had a letter, and on it is franked "Please Give Your Blood Generously"? Well, the Postmaster-General does that, on behalf of all the women of the world. I suppose people of our generation aren't able to die for good causes any longer. We had all that done for us, in the thirties and the forties, when we were still kids. (*In his familiar, semi-serious mood*) There aren't any good, brave causes left. If the big bang does come, and we all get killed off, it won't be in aid of the old-fashioned, grand design. It'll just be for the Brave New-nothing-very-much-thank-you. About as pointless and inglorious as stepping in front of a bus. No, there's nothing left for it, me boy, but to let yourself be butchered by the women.

(*Enter* HELENA)

HELENA Here you are, Cliff. (*Handing him the shirt*)

CLIFF Oh, thanks, Helena, very much. That's decent of you.

HELENA Not at all. I should dry it over the gas—the fire in your room would be better. There won't be much room for it over that stove.

CLIFF Right, I will. (*Crosses to door*)

JIMMY And hurry up about it, stupid. We'll all go out, and have a drink soon. (*To* HELENA) O.K.?

HELENA O.K.

JIMMY (*Shouting to* CLIFF *on his way out*) But make me some tea first, you madcap little Charlie.

(*She crosses down L.*)

Darling, I'm sick of seeing you behind that damned ironing board!

HELENA (*Wryly*) Sorry.

JIMMY Get yourself glammed up, and we'll hit the town. See you've put a shroud over Mummy, I think you should have laid a Union Jack over it.
HELENA Is anything wrong?
JIMMY Oh, don't frown like that—you look like the presiding magistrate!
HELENA How should I look?
JIMMY As if your heart stirred a little when you looked at me.
HELENA Oh, it does that, all right.
JIMMY Cliff tells me he's leaving us.
HELENA I know. He told me last night.
JIMMY Did he? I always seem to be at the end of the queue when they're passing information out.
HELENA I'm sorry he's going.
JIMMY Yes, so am I. He's a sloppy, irritating bastard, but he's got a big heart. You can forgive somebody almost anything for that. He's had to learn how to take it, and he knows how to hand it out. Come here.

(*He is sitting on the arm of his chair. She crosses to him, and they look at each other. Then she puts out her hand, and runs it over his head, fondling his ear and neck*)

Right from that first night, you have always put out your hand to me first. As if you expected nothing, or worse than nothing, and didn't care. You made a good enemy, didn't you? What they call a worthy opponent. But then, when people put down their weapons, it doesn't mean they've necessarily stopped fighting.
HELENA (*Steadily*) I love you.
JIMMY I think perhaps you do. Yes, I think perhaps you do. Perhaps it means something to lie with your victorious general in your arms. Especially, when he's heartily sick of the whole campaign, tired out, hungry, and dry. (*His lips find her fingers, and he kisses them. She presses his head against her*) You stood up, and came out to meet me. Oh, Helena— (*His face comes up to her, and they embrace fiercely*) Don't let anything go wrong!
HELENA (*Softly*) Oh, my darling——
JIMMY Either you're with me or against me.
HELENA I've always wanted you—always!

(*They kiss again*)

JIMMY T. S. Eliot and Pam, we'll make a good double. If you'll help me. I'll close that damned sweetstall, and we'll start everything

from scratch. What do you say? We'll get away from this place.
HELENA (*Nodding happily*)   I say that's wonderful.
JIMMY (*Kissing her quickly*)   Put all that junk away, and we'll get out. We'll get pleasantly, joyfully tiddly, we'll gaze at each other tenderly and lecherously in "The Builder's Arms," and then we'll come back here, and I'll make such love to you, you'll not care about anything else at all.

(*She moves away L., after kissing his hand*)

HELENA   I'll just change out of your old shirt. (*Folding ironing board*)
JIMMY (*Moving to door*)   Right. I'll hurry up the little man.

(*But before he reaches the door, it opens and* ALISON *enters. She wears a raincoat, her hair is untidy, and she looks rather ill. There is a stunned pause*)

ALISON (*Quietly*)   Hullo.
JIMMY (*To* HELENA, *after a moment*)   Friend of yours to see you.

(*He goes out quickly, and the two women are left looking at each other*)

Quick Curtain

Act Three / SCENE TWO

It is a few minutes later. From CLIFF's *room, across the landing, comes the sound of* JIMMY's *jazz trumpet.*

At rise of the Curtain, HELENA *is standing L. of the table, pouring out a cup of tea.* ALISON *is sitting on the armchair R. She bends down and picks up* JIMMY's *pipe. Then she scoops up a little pile of ash from the floor, and drops it in the ashtray on the arm of the chair.*

ALISON   He still smokes this foul old stuff. I used to hate it at first, but you get used to it.
HELENA   Yes.
ALISON   I went to the pictures last week, and some old man was smok-

ing it in front, a few rows away. I actually got up, and sat right behind him.

HELENA (*Coming down with cup of tea*) Here, have this. It usually seems to help.

ALISON (*Taking it*) Thanks.

HELENA Are you sure you feel all right now?

ALISON (*Nods*) It was just—oh, everything. It's my own fault—entirely. I must be mad, coming here like this. I'm sorry, Helena.

HELENA Why should you be sorry—you of all people?

ALISON Because it was unfair and cruel of me to come back. I'm afraid a sense of timing is one of the things I seem to have learnt from Jimmy. But it's something that can be in very bad taste. (*Sips her tea*) So many times, I've just managed to stop myself coming here—right at the last moment. Even today, when I went to the booking office at St. Pancras, it was like a charade, and I never believed that I'd let myself walk on to that train. And when I was on it, I got into a panic. I felt like a criminal. I told myself I'd turn round at the other end, and come straight back. I couldn't even believe that this place existed any more. But once I got here, there was nothing I could do. I had to convince myself that everything I remembered about this place had really happened to me once. (*She lowers her cup, and her foot plays with the newspapers on the floor*) How many times in these past few months I've thought of the evenings we used to spend here in this room. Suspended and rather remote. You make a good cup of tea.

HELENA (*Sitting L. of table*) Something Jimmy taught *me*.

ALISON (*Covering her face*) Oh, why am I here! You must all wish me a thousand miles away!

HELENA I don't wish anything of the kind. You've more right to be here than I.

ALISON Oh, Helena, don't bring out the book of rules——

HELENA You are his wife, aren't you? Whatever I have done, I've never been able to forget that fact. You have all the rights——

ALISON Helena—even I gave up believing in the divine rights of marriage long ago. Even before I met Jimmy. They've got something different now—constitutional monarchy. You are where you are by consent. And if you start trying any strong arm stuff, you're out. And I'm out.

HELENA Is that something you learnt from him?

ALISON Don't make me feel like a blackmailer or something, please! I've done something foolish, and rather vulgar in coming here tonight. I regret it, and I detest myself for doing it. But I did not come here in order to gain anything. Whatever it was—hysteria or just macabre curiosity, I'd certainly no intention of making any kind of breach between you and Jimmy. You must believe that.

HELENA Oh, I believe it all right. That's why everything seems more wrong and terrible than ever. You didn't even reproach me. You should have been outraged, but you weren't. (*She leans back, as if she wanted to draw back from herself*) I feel so—ashamed.

ALISON You talk as though he were something you'd swindled me out of——

HELENA (*Fiercely*) And you talk as if he were a book or something you pass around to anyone who happens to want it for five minutes. What's the matter with you? You sound as though you were quoting *him* all the time. I thought you told me once you couldn't bring yourself to believe in him.

ALISON I don't think I ever believed in your way either.

HELENA At least, I still believe in right and wrong! Not even the months in this madhouse have stopped me doing that. Even though everything I have done is wrong, at least I have known it was wrong.

ALISON You loved him, didn't you? That's what you wrote, and told me.

HELENA And it was true.

ALISON It was pretty difficult to believe at the time. I couldn't understand it.

HELENA I could hardly believe it myself.

ALISON Afterwards, it wasn't quite so difficult. You used to say some pretty harsh things about him. Not that I was sorry to hear them—they were rather comforting then. But you even shocked me sometimes.

HELENA I suppose I was a little over-emphatic. There doesn't seem much point in trying to explain everything, does there?

ALISON Not really.

HELENA Do you know—I have discovered what is wrong with Jimmy? It's very simple really. He was born out of his time.

ALISON Yes. I know.

HELENA There's no place for people like that any longer—in sex, or politics, or anything. That's why he's so futile. Sometimes, when I listen to him, I feel he thinks he's still in the middle of the French Revolution. And that's where he ought to be, of course. He doesn't know where he is, or where he's going. He'll never do anything, and he'll never amount to anything.

ALISON I suppose he's what you'd call an Eminent Victorian.[29] Slightly comic—in a way.... We seem to have had this conversation before.

---

[29] Title of Lytton Strachey's irreverent biographical studies.

HELENA Yes, I remember everything you said about him. It horrified me. I couldn't believe that you could have married someone like that. Alison—it's all over between Jimmy and me. I can see it now. I've got to get out. No—listen to me. When I saw you standing there tonight, I knew that it was all utterly wrong. That I didn't believe in any of this, and not Jimmy or anyone could make me believe otherwise. (*Rising*) How could I have ever thought I could get away with it! He wants one world and I want another, and lying in that bed won't ever change it! I believe in good and evil, and I don't have to apologize for that. It's quite a modern, scientific belief now, so they tell me. And, by everything I have ever believed in, or wanted, what I have been doing is wrong and evil.

ALISON Helena—you're not going to leave him?

HELENA Yes, I am. (*Before* ALISON *can interrupt, she goes on*) Oh, I'm not stepping aside to let you come back. You can do what you like. Frankly, I think you'd be a fool—but that's your own business. I think I've given you enough advice.

ALISON But he—he'll have no one.

HELENA Oh, my dear, he'll find somebody. He'll probably hold court here like one of the Renaissance popes. Oh, I know I'm throwing the book of rules at you, as you call it, but, believe me, you're never going to be happy without it. I tried throwing it away all these months, but I know now it just doesn't work. When you came in at that door, ill and tired and hurt, it was all over for me. You see—I didn't know about the baby. It was such a shock. It's like a judgment on us.

ALISON You saw me, and I had to tell you what had happened. I lost the child. It's a simple fact. There is no judgment, there's no blame——

HELENA Maybe not. But I feel it just the same.

ALISON But don't you see? It isn't logical!

HELENA No, it isn't. (*Calmly*) But I know it's right.

(*The trumpet gets louder*)

ALISON Helena (*Going to her*), you mustn't leave him. He needs you, I know he needs you——

HELENA Do you think so?

ALISON Maybe you're not the right one for him—we're neither of us right——

HELENA (*Moving upstage*) Oh, why doesn't he stop that damned noise!

ALISON He wants something quite different from us. What it is exactly I don't know—a kind of cross between a mother and a Greek courtesan, a henchwoman, a mixture of Cleopatra and Boswell. But give him a little longer——

613 · Look Back in Anger [ACT THREE, Scene Two]

HELENA (*Wrenching the door open*) Please! Will you stop that! I can't think!

(*There is a slight pause, and the trumpet goes on. She puts her hands to her head*)

Jimmy, for God's sake!

(*It stops*)

Jimmy, I want to speak to you.
JIMMY (*Off*) Is your friend still with you?
HELENA Oh, don't be an idiot, and come in here! (*She moves down L.*)
ALISON (*Rising*) He doesn't want to see me.
HELENA Stay where you are, and don't be silly. I'm sorry. It won't be very pleasant, but I've made up my mind to go, and I've got to tell him now.

(*Enter* JIMMY)

JIMMY Is this another of your dark plots? (*He looks at* ALISON) Hadn't she better sit down? She looks a bit ghastly.
HELENA I'm so sorry, dear. Would you like some more tea, or an aspirin or something?

(ALISON *shakes her head, and sits. She can't look at either of them*)

(*To* JIMMY, *the old authority returning*) It's not very surprising, is it? She's been very ill, she's——
JIMMY (*Quietly*) You don't have to draw a diagram for me—I can see what's happened to her.
HELENA And doesn't it mean anything to you?
JIMMY I don't exactly relish the idea of anyone being ill, or in pain. It was my child, too, you know. But (*He shrugs*) it isn't my first loss.
ALISON (*On her breath*) It was mine.

(*He glances at her, but turns back to* HELENA *quickly*)

JIMMY What are you looking so solemn about? What's she doing here?
ALISON I'm sorry, I'm—— (*Presses her hand over her mouth*)

(HELENA *crosses to* JIMMY *C., and grasps his hand*)

HELENA Don't, please. Can't you see the condition she's in? She's done nothing, she's said nothing, none of it's her fault.

(*He takes his hand away, and moves away a little downstage*)

JIMMY What isn't her fault?

HELENA   Jimmy—I don't want a brawl, so please——
JIMMY   Let's hear it, shall we?
HELENA   Very well, I'm going downstairs to pack my things. If I hurry, I shall just catch the 7:15 to London.

(*They both look at him, but he simply leans forward against the table, not looking at either of them*)

This is not Alison's doing—you must understand that. It's my own decision entirely. In fact, she's just been trying to talk me out of it. It's just that suddenly, tonight, I see what I have really known all along. That you can't be happy when what you're doing is wrong, or is hurting someone else. I suppose it could never have worked, anyway, but I do love you, Jimmy. I shall never love anyone as I have loved you. (*Turns away L.*) But I can't go on. (*Passionately and sincerely*) I can't take part—in all this suffering. I can't! (*She appeals to him for some reaction, but he only looks down at the table, and nods.* HELENA *recovers, and makes an effort to regain authority. To* ALISON) You probably won't feel up to making that journey again tonight, but we can fix you up at an hotel before I go. There's about half an hour. I'll just make it. (*She turns up to the door, but* JIMMY's *voice stops her*)

JIMMY   (*In a low, resigned voice*)   They all want to escape from the pain of being alive. And, most of all, from love. (*Crosses to the dressing table*) I always knew something like this would turn up—some problem, like an ill wife—and it would be too much for those delicate, hot-house feelings of yours. (*He sweeps up* HELENA's *things from the dressing table, and crosses over to the wardrobe. Outside, the church bells start ringing*) It's no good trying to fool yourself about love. You can't fall into it like a soft job, without dirtying up your hands. (*Hands her the make-up things, which she takes. He opens the wardrobe*) It takes muscle and guts. And if you can't bear the thought (*Takes out a dress on a hanger*) of messing up your nice, clean soul, (*Crossing back to her*) you'd better give up the whole idea of life, and become a saint. (*Puts the dress in her arms*) Because you'll never make it as a human being. It's either this world or the next.

(*She looks at him for a moment, and then goes out quickly. He is shaken, and he avoids* ALISON's *eyes, crossing to the window. He rests against it, then bangs his fist against the frame*)

Oh, those bells!

(*The shadows are growing around them.* JIMMY *stands, his head against the window pane.* ALISON *is huddled forward in the armchair R. Presently, she breaks the stillness, and rises to above the table*)

ALISON I'm . . . sorry. I'll go now. (*She starts to move upstage. But his voice pulls her up*)

JIMMY You never even sent any flowers to the funeral. Not—a little bunch of flowers. You had to deny me that, too, didn't you?

(*She starts to move, but again he speaks*)

The injustice of it is almost perfect! The wrong people going hungry, the wrong people being loved, the wrong people dying!

(*She moves to the gas stove. He turns to face her*)

Was I really wrong to believe that there's a—a kind of—burning virility of mind and spirit that looks for something as powerful as itself? The heaviest, strongest creatures in this world seem to be the loneliest. Like the old bear, following his own breath in the dark forest. There's no warm pack, no herd to comfort him. That voice that cries out doesn't *have* to be a weakling's, does it? (*He moves in a little*) Do you remember that first night I saw you at that grisly party? You didn't really notice me, but I was watching you all the evening. You seemed to have a wonderful relaxation of spirit. I knew that was what I wanted. You've got to be really brawny to have that kind of strength—the strength to relax. It was only after we were married that I discovered that it wasn't relaxation at all. In order to relax, you've first got to sweat your guts out. And, as far as you were concerned, you'd never had a hair out of place, or a bead of sweat anywhere.

(*A cry escapes from her, and her fist flies to her mouth. She moves down to below the table, leaning on it*)

I may be a lost cause, but I thought if you loved me, it needn't matter.

(*She is crying silently. He moves down to face her*)

ALISON It doesn't matter! I was wrong, I was wrong! I don't want to be neutral. I don't want to be a saint. I want to be a lost cause. I want to be corrupt and futile!

(*All he can do is watch her helplessly. Her voice takes on a little strength, and rises*)

Don't you understand? It's gone! It's gone! That—that helpless human being inside my body. I thought it was so safe, and secure in there. Nothing could take it from me. It was mine, my responsibility. But it's lost. (*She slides down against the leg of the table to the floor*) All I wanted was to die. I never knew what it was like. I didn't know it could be like that! I was in pain, and all I could think of was you, and what I'd lost. (*Scarcely able to speak*) I thought: if only—if only he could see me now, so stupid, and ugly, and ridiculous. This is what he's been longing for me to feel. This is what he wants to splash about in! I'm in the fire, and I'm burning, and all I want is to die! It's cost him his child, and any others I might have had! But what does it matter—this is what he wanted from me! (*She raises her face to him*) Don't you see! I'm in the mud at last! I'm groveling! I'm crawling! Oh, God——

(*She collapses at his feet. He stands, frozen for a moment, then he bends down and takes her shaking body in his arms. He shakes his head, and whispers*)

JIMMY   Don't. Please, don't. . . . I can't——

(*She gasps for her breath against him*)

You're all right. You're all right now. Please, I—I. . . . Not any more. . . .

(*She relaxes suddenly. He looks down at her, full of fatigue, and says with a kind of mocking, tender irony*)

We'll be together in our bear's cave, and our squirrel's drey, and we'll live on honey, and nuts—lots and lots of nuts. And we'll sing songs about ourselves—about warm trees and snug caves, and lying in the sun. And you'll keep those big eyes on my fur, and help me keep my claws in order, because I'm a bit of a soppy, scruffy sort of a bear. And I'll see that you keep that sleek, bushy tail glistening as it should, because you're a very beautiful squirrel, but you're none too bright either, so we've got to be careful. There are cruel steel traps lying about everywhere, just waiting for rather mad, slightly satanic, and very timid little animals. Right?

(ALISON *nods*)

(*Pathetically*) Poor squirrels!

ALISON   (*With the same comic emphasis*)   Poor bears! (*She laughs a little. Then she looks at him very tenderly, and adds very, very softly*) Oh, poor, poor bears! (*Slides her arms around him*)

Curtain

HAROLD PINTER

[1930   ]

❧ *The Man*

SON OF AN EAST END TAILOR, Harold Pinter has been connected with theater all his adult life. He left school at the age of sixteen to study acting at the Royal Academy of Dramatic Art and at the Central School of Speech and Drama. In 1949 he became a professional actor under the name of David Baron. While playing in repertory, he began to write—poetry, short prose pieces, an unfinished novel *The Dwarfs*. In 1957 he turned to drama, and has written little else since that date.

❧ *The Work*

IN LESS THAN A DECADE of dramatic writing, Pinter has produced nine plays, seven review sketches, and four movies. At first classified with the Kitchen Sink dramatists, who write of life in the lower classes, Pinter is now generally assigned to the Theater of the Absurd, which reflects metaphysical absurdity. But he himself rejects all labels, aesthetic or political.

However Pinter may react against labels, he does admit to being influenced by Kafka and Beckett; and willy-nilly, he is a contemporary and a countryman of the Angry Young Englishmen who have been raising strident voices against the Establishment. Thus, his dramas take place in drab *English* rooms, but many of these dramas express a far more generalized anguish. Pinter himself is acutely aware of the importance of the claustrophobic room in his plays. He says, "I write a play with a particular thing in mind, a particular set of characters, possibly two characters in a room, and the circumstances grow, and of course, the characters grow. . . . Obviously they are scared of what is outside the room. Outside the room there is a world bearing upon them which is frightening. I am sure it is frightening to you and me as well." So frightening are some of Pinter's plays that one of his reviewers coined the apt phrase for his work, "comedy of menace," indicating how Pinter joins comic to serious, how he explores the threatening through the comic. Like the Vice of the old Morality plays, Pinter's immoral and impersonal Establishment is characterized by comic clichés whose cumulative effect is a kind of damnation.

Pinter's Establishment is recognizable by its commonplaces. The victims of Pinter's Establishment, scapegoat clowns, may themselves be cogs in the Establishment wheel, until that wheel runs over them. Living their stage life in boxlike rooms, Pinter's characters use a stylized conversational idiom that starts in comedy and often finishes in pity and terror. But Pinter is no Hitchcock. Like Kafka and Beckett, Pinter finds both comedy and menace in the ambiguity of the universe.

In his plays, much of the comedy arises from the inarticulateness and incoherence of his characters. They furnish us with partial explanations and incomplete expositions; they express themselves in monosyllables, stammering, clichés, repetition, contradiction, and laborious, spurious logic. The rhythm of their idiom probes more deeply into reality than does the everyday speech it seems to echo, for Pinter implies that there can be no articulate certainty about the world. Thus, the impossibility of verification becomes the only verity. To quote Pinter, "I'd say that what goes on in my plays is realistic, but what I'm doing is not realism."

At the realistic level, his drama is often climaxed in violence. Thus, Bert Hudd attacks a blind Negro in *The Room*; Goldberg and McCann take Stanley Webber for "special treatment" in *The Birthday Party*; Ben is about to shoot Gus in *The Dumb Waiter*; a half-crazed Len is tortured by the titular dwarfs of *The Dwarfs*. And yet, these murderous villains are only surrogates for mysterious, malevolent forces, who seem bent on destruction.

In Pinter's later plays, sex is the prime force in the breakdown of the individual. Like the earlier metaphysical dramas, the later group presents a realistic surface, though the milieu is on a higher social plane. In none of these realistically set plays can the meaning be realistically explained.

❧ The Play

PINTER'S PLAYS usually begin with two characters in a stage room, but *The Dumb Waiter* is distinctive in that there are only two characters, Ben and Gus, who remain in the room for most of the play. The room is sparsely but realistically furnished with two beds, and between them a serving-hatch, a dumbwaiter, through which menace will enter.

The one-act play begins with a long comic pantomime scene; Ben lies on a bed, newspaper in hand, while Gus plays the clown, removing from one shoe a flattened matchbox, from the other a flattened cigarette pack, shaking each one to point up their emptiness. He goes off stage, and we hear the lavatory chain being pulled, but the toilet does not flush. When Gus returns on stage, he scratches his head.

Ben reads the sensational newspaper items to Gus, who replies with English cliché phrases for which Pinter has an extraordinarily accurate ear: "Go on!" "Get away," "It's unbelievable," "Incredible." Gus's comments are so innocuous that we may fail to notice that all the newspaper items deal with death. As Ben continues to read, Gus begins to complain about the room in which they are waiting to do a job—the toilet tank fills too slowly, there are no windows, the bed linen is dirty, there should have been another blanket. The only thing Gus likes is the crockery, which is incongruously but ominously striped with black—our first hint that their "job" has to do with death. When Gus describes their job, we catch echoes of Kafka: "I mean, you come into a place when it's still dark, you come into a room you've never seen before, you sleep all day, you do your job, and then you go away in the night again."

During the course of the brief play Gus asks many questions, but his most insistent line is about the questions he *meant* to ask—as insistent as Beckett's well-known line about waiting for Godot. Through questions, quarrels, and a mysterious envelope, menace seeps into the windowless room. The envelope proves to contain twelve matches, and these reflect ironically on the flattened matchbox and cigarette packet that Gus removed from his shoe in the opening pantomime. Close upon the discovery of the matches, we first see the revolvers that establish menace concretely. When Gus and Ben argue fiercely about whether to say "light the kettle" or "light the gas," we realize that the grotesque linguistic dispute cloaks a far deeper hostility.

By the middle of the play, Pinter has built a symbolic world on his realistic foundation; the dumbwaiter begins to function as an altar and an oracle. The increasingly exotic food commands are as obscure as Delphic pronouncements, and, humble mortals that they are, Ben and Gus offer their meager foodstuffs in ritualistic sacrifice. Authority from above even settles their language problems, but Ben and Gus still can have no tea since they still have no shilling for the gas meter, and Gus asks pointedly, "Why did he send us matches if he knew there was no gas?" The routine rehearsal for their "job" is followed by a crescendo of questions from Gus. No longer a dumb waiter, he screams into the speaking-tube, "WE'VE GOT NOTHING LEFT! NOTHING! DO YOU UNDERSTAND?" It is evident that "NOTHING" refers to all their resources—material and spiritual.

In the last few minutes, as in the first few minutes of the play, Ben lies down with his newspaper. Though he does not read aloud this time, the two men exchange the same clichés as in the opening scene. The death-centered news items no longer need be read aloud, for death is virtually in the room. While Gus goes off stage, Ben receives the order to do his job. An unarmed, dishevelled Gus enters the room through a different door, and the curtain falls. Ben and the dumbwaiter remain in the room, but Gus will be destroyed because he refuses to continue as a dumb waiter. In Pinter's stage world, they only serve who meekly stand and wait.

❧ *Dramatic Works*

The Room, 1957.
The Birthday Party, 1957.
The Dumb Waiter, 1957.
A Slight Ache, 1959.
The Caretaker, 1960.
A Night Out, 1960.

Night School, 1960 (unpublished).
The Dwarfs, 1960.
The Collection, 1961.
The Lover, 1963.
The Homecoming, 1965.

❦ Selective Bibliography

Cohn, Ruby. "Avatars of Godot," *Comparative Literature Studies*, II (Summer, 1965).

———. "The World of Harold Pinter," *Tulane Drama Review*, VI (March, 1962).

Dukore, Bernard. "The Theatre of Harold Pinter," *Tulane Drama Review*, VI (March, 1962).

Dick, Kay. "Mr. Pinter and the Fearful Matter," *Texas Quarterly*, IV (Autumn, 1961).

Esslin, Martin. "Godot and His Children," *Experimental Drama*, ed. William Armstrong. Chester Springs, Pa.: Dufour Editions, 1963.

Taylor, John Russell. *Anger and After*. Baltimore: Penguin, 1963.

The Dumb Waiter

SCENE A *basement room. Two beds, flat against the back wall. A serving hatch, closed, between the beds. A door to the kitchen and lavatory, left. A door to a passage, right.*

BEN *is lying on a bed, left, reading a paper.* GUS *is sitting on a bed, right, tying his shoelaces, with difficulty. Both are dressed in shirts, trousers and braces.*[1]
  Silence.
  GUS *ties his laces, rises, yawns and begins to walk slowly to the door, left. He stops, looks down, and shakes his foot.*
  BEN *lowers his paper and watches him.* GUS *kneels and unties his shoe-lace and slowly takes off the shoe. He looks inside it and brings out a flattened matchbox. He shakes it and examines it. Their eyes meet.* BEN *rattles his paper and reads.* GUS *puts the matchbox in his pocket and bends down to put on his shoe. He ties his lace, with difficulty.* BEN *lowers his paper and watches him.* GUS *walks to the door, left, stops, and shakes the other foot. He kneels, unties his shoe-lace, and slowly takes off the shoe. He looks inside it and brings out a flattened cigarette packet. He shakes it and examines it. Their eyes meet.* BEN *rattles his paper and reads.* GUS *puts the packet in his pocket, bends down, puts on his shoe and ties the lace.*
  He wanders off, left.
  BEN *slams the paper down on the bed and glares after him. He picks up the paper and lies on his back, reading.*
  Silence.
  A lavatory chain is pulled twice off, left, but the lavatory does not flush.
  Silence.

[1] Suspenders.

GUS *re-enters, left, and halts at the door, scratching his head.*
BEN *slams down the paper*

BEN Kaw! (*He picks up the paper*) What about this? Listen to this! (*He refers to the paper*) A man of eighty-seven wanted to cross the road. But there was a lot of traffic, see? He couldn't see how he was going to squeeze through. So he crawled under a lorry.
GUS He what?
BEN He crawled under a lorry. A stationary lorry.
GUS No?
BEN The lorry started and ran over him.
GUS Go on!
BEN That's what it says here.
GUS Get away.
BEN It's enough to make you want to puke, isn't it?
GUS Who advised him to do a thing like that?
BEN A man of eighty-seven crawling under a lorry!
GUS It's unbelievable.
BEN It's down here in black and white.
GUS Incredible.

(*Silence.* GUS *shakes his head and exits.* BEN *lies back and reads. The lavatory chain is pulled once off left, but the lavatory does not flush.* BEN *whistles at an item in the paper.* GUS *re-enters*)

I want to ask you something.
BEN What are you doing out there?
GUS Well, I was just—
BEN What about the tea?
GUS I'm just going to make it.
BEN Well, go on, make it.
GUS Yes, I will. (*He sits in a chair. Ruminatively*) He's laid on some very nice crockery this time, I'll say that. It's sort of striped. There's a white stripe.

(BEN *reads*)

It's very nice. I'll say that.

(BEN *turns the page*)

You know, sort of round the cup. Round the rim. All the rest of it's black, you see. Then the saucer's black, except for right in the middle, where the cup goes, where it's white.

(BEN *reads*)

Then the plates are the same, you see. Only they've got a black stripe—the plates—right across the middle. Yes, I'm quite taken with the crockery.

BEN (*Still reading*)   What do you want plates for? You're not going to eat.

GUS   I've brought a few biscuits.

BEN   Well, you'd better eat them quick.

GUS   I always bring a few biscuits. Or a pie. You know I can't drink tea without anything to eat.

BEN   Well, make the tea then, will you? Time's getting on.

(GUS *brings out the flattened cigarette packet and examines it*)

GUS   You got any cigarettes? I think I've run out. (*He throws the packet high up and leans forward to catch it*) I hope it won't be a long job, this one. (*Aiming carefully, he flips the packet under his bed*) Oh, I wanted to ask you something.

BEN   (*Slamming his paper down*)   Kaw!

GUS   What's that?

BEN   A child of eight killed a cat!

GUS   Get away.

BEN   It's a fact. What about that, eh? A child of eight killing a cat!

GUS   How did he do it?

BEN   It was a girl.

GUS   How did she do it?

BEN   She—

(*He picks up the paper and studies it*)

It doesn't say.

GUS   Why not?

BEN   Wait a minute. It just says—Her brother, aged eleven, viewed the incident from the toolshed.

GUS   Go on!

BEN   That's bloody ridiculous.

(*Pause*)

GUS   I bet he did it.

BEN   Who?

GUS   The brother.

BEN   I think you're right.

(*Pause*)

(*Slamming down the paper*) What about that, eh? A kid of eleven killing a cat and blaming it on his little sister of eight! It's enough to—

(*He breaks off in disgust and seizes the paper.* GUS *rises*)

GUS What time is he getting in touch?

(BEN *reads*)

What time is he getting in touch?
BEN What's the matter with you? It could be any time. Any time.
GUS (*moves to the foot of* BEN'S *bed*). Well, I was going to ask you something.
BEN What?
GUS Have you noticed the time that tank takes to fill?
BEN What tank?
GUS In the lavatory.
BEN No. Does it?
GUS Terrible.
BEN Well, what about it?
GUS What do you think's the matter with it?
BEN Nothing.
GUS Nothing?
BEN It's got a deficient ballcock, that's all.
GUS A deficient what?
BEN Ballcock.
GUS No? Really?
BEN That's what I should say.
GUS Go on! That didn't occur to me. (GUS *wanders to his bed and presses the mattress*) I didn't have a very restful sleep today, did you? It's not much of a bed. I could have done with another blanket too. (*He catches sight of a picture on the wall*) Hello, what's this? (*Peering at it*) "The First Eleven." Cricketeers. You seen this, Ben?
BEN (*Reading*) What?
GUS The first eleven.
BEN What?
GUS There's a photo here of the first eleven.
BEN What first eleven?
GUS (*Studying the photo*) It doesn't say.
BEN What about that tea?
GUS They all look a bit old to me. (GUS *wanders downstage, looks out front, then all about the room*) I wouldn't like to live in this dump. I wouldn't mind if you had a window, you could see what it looked like outside.
BEN What do you want a window for?

GUS Well, I like to have a bit of a view, Ben. It whiles away the time. (*He walks about the room*) I mean, you come into a place when it's still dark, you come into a room you've never seen before, you sleep all day, you do your job, and then you go away in the night again. (*Pause*) I like to get a look at the scenery. You never get the chance in this job.
BEN You get your holidays, don't you?
GUS Only a fortnight.
BEN (*Lowering the paper*) You kill me. Anyone would think you're working every day. How often do we do a job? Once a week? What are you complaining about?
GUS Yes, but we've got to be on tap though, haven't we? You can't move out of the house in case a call comes.
BEN You know what your trouble is?
GUS What?
BEN You haven't got any interests.
GUS I've got interests.
BEN What? Tell me one of your interests. (*Pause*)
GUS I've got interests.
BEN Look at me. What have I got?
GUS I don't know. What?
BEN I've got my woodwork. I've got my model boats. Have you ever seen me idle? I'm never idle. I know how to occupy my time, to its best advantage. Then when a call comes, I'm ready.
GUS Don't you ever get a bit fed up?
BEN Fed up? What with? (*Silence*)

(BEN *reads.* GUS *feels in the pocket of his jacket, which hangs on the bed*)

GUS You got any cigarettes? I've run out.

(*The lavatory flushes off left*)

There she goes. (GUS *sits on his bed*) No, I mean, I say the crockery's good. It is. It's very nice. But that's about all I can say for this place. It's worse than the last one. Remember that last place we were in? Last time, where was it? At least there was a wireless there. No, honest. He doesn't seem to bother much about our comfort these days.
BEN When are you going to stop jabbering?
GUS You'd get rheumatism in a place like this, if you stay long.
BEN We're not staying long. Make the tea, will you? We'll be on the job in a minute.

(GUS *picks up a small bag by his bed and brings out a packet of tea. He examines it and looks up*)

GUS Eh, I've been meaning to ask you.
BEN What the hell is it now?
GUS Why did you stop the car this morning, in the middle of that road?
BEN (*Lowering the paper*) I thought you were asleep.
GUS I was, but I woke up when you stopped. You did stop, didn't you? (*Pause*) In the middle of that road. It was still dark, don't you remember? I looked out. It was all misty. I thought perhaps you wanted to kip, but you were sitting up dead straight, like you were waiting for something.
BEN I wasn't waiting for anything.
GUS I must have fallen asleep again. What was all that about then? Why did you stop?
BEN (*Picking up the paper*) We were too early.
GUS Early? (*He rises*) What do you mean? We got the call, didn't we, saying we were to start right away. We did. We shoved out on the dot. So how could we be too early?
BEN (*Quietly*) Who took the call, me or you?
GUS You.
BEN We were too early.
GUS Too early for what? (*Pause*) You mean someone had to get out before we got in? (*He examines the bedclothes*) I thought these sheets didn't look too bright. I thought they ponged[2] a bit. I was too tired to notice when I got in this morning. Eh, that's taking a bit of a liberty, isn't it? I don't want to share my bed-sheets. I told you things were going down the drain. I mean, we've always had clean sheets laid on up till now. I've noticed it.
BEN How do you know those sheets weren't clean?
GUS What do you mean?
BEN How do you know they weren't clean? You've spent the whole day in them haven't you?
GUS What, you mean it might be my pong? (*He sniffs sheets*) Yes. (*He sits slowly on bed*) It could be my pong, I suppose. It's difficult to tell. I don't really know what I pong like, that's the trouble.
BEN (*Referring to the paper*) Kaw!
GUS Eh, Ben.
BEN Kaw!
GUS Ben.
BEN What?

[2] Stank.

GUS What town are we in? I've forgotten.
BEN I've told you. Birmingham.
GUS Go on! (*He looks with interest about the room*) That's in the Midlands. The second biggest city in Great Britain. I'd never have guessed. (*He snaps his fingers*) Eh, it's Friday today, isn't it? It'll be Saturday tomorrow.
BEN What about it?
GUS (*Excited*) We could go and watch the Villa.[3]
BEN They're playing away.
GUS No, are they? Caarr! What a pity.
BEN Anyway, there's no time. We've got to get straight back.
GUS Well, we have done in the past, haven't we? Stayed over and watched a game, haven't we? For a bit of relaxation.
BEN Things have tightened up, mate. They've tightened up.

(GUS *chuckles to himself*)

GUS I saw the Villa get beat in a cup tie once. Who was it against now? White shirts. It was one-all at half-time. I'll never forget it. Their opponents won by a penalty. Talk about drama. Yes, it was a disputed penalty. Disputed. They got beat two–one, anyway, because of it. You were there yourself.
BEN Not me.
GUS Yes, you were there. Don't you remember that disputed penalty?
BEN No.
GUS He went down just inside the area. Then they said he was just acting. I didn't think the other bloke touched him myself. But the referee had the ball on the spot.
BEN Didn't touch him! What are you talking about? He laid him out flat!
GUS Not the Villa. The Villa don't play that sort of game.
BEN Get out of it. (*Pause*)
GUS Eh, that must have been here, in Birmingham.
BEN What must?
GUS The Villa. That must have been here.
BEN They were playing away.
GUS Because you know who the other team was? It was the Spurs. It was Tottenham Hotspur.
BEN Well, what about it?
GUS We've never done a job in Tottenham.
BEN How do you know?
GUS I'd remember Tottenham.

---

[3] A soccer team; English football is American soccer.

(BEN *turns on his bed to look at him*)
BEN Don't make me laugh, will you?

(BEN *turns back and reads.* GUS *yawns and speaks through his yawn*)

GUS When's he going to get in touch? (*Pause*) Yes, I'd like to see another football match. I've always been an ardent football fan. Here, what about coming to see the Spurs tomorrow?
BEN (*Tonelessly*) They're playing away.
GUS Who are?
BEN The Spurs.
GUS Then they might be playing here.
BEN Don't be silly.
GUS If they're playing away they might be playing here. They might be playing the Villa.
BEN (*Tonelessly*) But the Villa are playing away.

(*Pause. An envelope slides under the door, right.* GUS *sees it. He stands, looking at it*)

GUS Ben.
BEN Away. They're all playing away.
GUS Ben, look here.
BEN What?
GUS Look.

(BEN *turns his head and sees the envelope. He stands*)

BEN What's that?
GUS I don't know.
BEN Where did it come from?
GUS Under the door.
BEN Well, what is it?
GUS I don't know.

(*They stare at it*)

BEN Pick it up.
GUS What do you mean?
BEN Pick it up!

(GUS *slowly moves towards it, bends and picks it up*)

  What is it?
GUS An envelope.
BEN Is there anything on it?
GUS No.

BEN   Is it sealed?
GUS   Yes.
BEN   Open it.
GUS   What?
BEN   Open it!

(GUS *opens it and looks inside*)

What's in it?

(GUS *empties twelve matches into his hand*)

GUS   Matches.
BEN   Matches?
GUS   Yes.
BEN   Show it to me.

(GUS *passes the envelope.* BEN *examines it*)

Nothing on it. Not a word.
GUS   That's funny, isn't it?
BEN   It came under the door?
GUS   Must have done.
BEN   Well, go on.
GUS   Go on where?
BEN   Open the door and see if you can catch anyone outside.
GUS   Who, me?
BEN   Go on!

(GUS *stares at him, puts the matches in his pocket, goes to his bed and brings a revolver from under the pillow. He goes to the door, opens it, looks out and shuts it*)

GUS   No one. (*He replaces the revolver*)
BEN   What did you see?
GUS   Nothing.
BEN   They must have been pretty quick.

(GUS *takes the matches from pocket and looks at them*)

GUS   Well, they'll come in handy.
BEN   Yes.
GUS   Won't they?
BEN   Yes, you're always running out, aren't you?
GUS   All the time.
BEN   Well, they'll come in handy then.
GUS   Yes.
BEN   Won't they?

GUS Yes, I could do with them. I could do with them too.
BEN You could, eh?
GUS Yes.
BEN Why?
GUS We haven't got any.
BEN Well, you've got some now, haven't you?
GUS I can light the kettle now.
BEN Yes, you're always cadging[4] matches. How many have you got there?
GUS About a dozen.
BEN Well, don't lose them. Red too. You don't even need a box.

(GUS *probes his ear with a match*)

(*Slapping his hand*) Don't waste them! Go on, go and light it.
GUS Eh?
BEN Go and light it.
GUS Light what?
BEN The kettle.
GUS You mean the gas.
BEN Who does?
GUS You do.
BEN (*His eyes narrowing*)   What do you mean, I mean the gas?
GUS Well, that's what you mean, don't you? The gas.
BEN (*Powerfully*)   If I say go and light the kettle I mean go and light the kettle.
GUS How can you light a kettle?
BEN It's a figure of speech! Light the kettle. It's a figure of speech!
GUS I've never heard it.
BEN Light the kettle! It's common usage!
GUS I think you've got it wrong.
BEN (*Menacing*)   What do you mean?
GUS They say put on the kettle.
BEN (*Taut*) Who says?

(*They stare at each other, breathing hard*)

(*Deliberately*) I have never in all my life heard anyone say put on the kettle.
GUS I bet my mother used to say it.
BEN Your mother? When did you last see your mother?
GUS I don't know, about—
BEN Well, what are you talking about your mother for?

---

[4] Slang for borrowing; as in American "bumming a cigarette."

(*They stare*)

Gus, I'm not trying to be unreasonable. I'm just trying to point out something to you.

GUS Yes, but—
BEN Who's the senior partner here, me or you?
GUS You.
BEN I'm only looking after your interests, Gus. You've got to learn, mate.
GUS Yes, but I've never heard—
BEN (*Vehemently*) Nobody says light the gas! What does the gas light?
GUS What does the gas—?
BEN (*Grabbing him with two hands by the throat, at arm's length*) THE KETTLE, YOU FOOL!

(GUS *takes the hands from his throat*)

GUS All right, all right. (*Pause*)
BEN Well, what are you waiting for?
GUS I want to see if they light.
BEN What?
GUS The matches. (*He takes out the flattened box and tries to strike*) No. (*He throws the box under the bed*)

(BEN *stares at him*)

(GUS *raises his foot*) Shall I try it on here?

(BEN *stares*. GUS *strikes a match on his shoe. It lights*)

Here we are.
BEN (*Wearily*) Put on the bloody kettle, for Christ's sake.

> BEN *goes to his bed, but, realising what he has said, stops and half turns. They look at each other.* GUS *slowly exits, left.* BEN *slams his paper down on the bed and sits on it, head in hands*)

GUS (*Entering*) It's going.
BEN What?
GUS The stove. (GUS *goes to his bed and sits*) I wonder who it'll be tonight. (*Silence*) Eh, I've been wanting to ask you something.
BEN (*Putting his legs on the bed*) Oh, for Christ's sake.
GUS No. I was going to ask you something. (*He rises and sits on* BEN'S *bed*)
BEN What are you sitting on my bed for?

(GUS *sits*)

What's the matter with you? You're always asking me questions. What's the matter with you?
BEN   Nothing.
BEN   You never used to ask me so many damn questions. What's come over you?
GUS   No, I was just wondering.
BEN   Stop wondering. You've got a job to do. Why don't you just do it and shut up?
GUS   That's what I was wondering about.
BEN   What?
GUS   The job.
BEN   What job?
GUS   (*Tentatively*)   I thought perhaps you might know something.

(BEN *looks at him*)

I thought perhaps you—I mean—have you got any idea—who it's going to be tonight?
BEN   Who what's going to be?

(*They look at each other*)

GUS   (*At length*)   Who it's going to be. (*Silence*)
BEN   Are you feeling all right?
GUS   Sure.
BEN   Go and make the tea.
GUS   Yes, sure.

(GUS *exits, left,* BEN *looks after him. He then takes his revolver from under the pillow and checks it for ammunition.* GUS *re-enters*)

The gas has gone out.
BEN   Well, what about it?
GUS   There's a meter.
BEN   I haven't got any money.
GUS   Nor have I.
BEN   You'll have to wait.
GUS   What for?
BEN   For Wilson.
GUS   He might not come. He might just send a message. He doesn't always come.
BEN   Well, you'll have to do without it, won't you?

GUS Blimey.
BEN You'll have a cup of tea afterwards. What's the matter with you?
GUS I like to have one before.

(BEN *holds the revolver up to the light and polishes it*)

BEN You'd better get ready anyway.
GUS Well, I don't know, that's a bit much, you know, for my money. (*He picks up a packet of tea from the bed and throws it into the bag*) I hope he's got a shilling, anyway, if he comes. He's entitled to have. After all, it's his place, he could have seen there was enough gas for a cup of tea.
BEN What do you mean, it's his place?
GUS Well, isn't it?
BEN He's probably only rented it. It doesn't have to be his place.
GUS I know it's his place. I bet the whole house is. He's not even laying on any gas now either. (GUS *sits on his bed*) It's his place all right. Look at all the other places. You go to this address, there's a key there, there's a teapot, there's never a soul in sight—(*He pauses*) Eh, nobody ever hears a thing, have you ever thought of that? We never get any complaints, do we, too much noise or anything like that? You never see a soul, do you?—except the bloke who comes. You ever noticed that? I wonder if the walls are sound-proof. (*He touches the wall above his bed*) Can't tell. All you do is wait, eh? Half the time he doesn't even bother to put in an appearance, Wilson.
BEN Why should he? He's a busy man.
GUS (*Thoughtfully*) I find him hard to talk to, Wilson. Do you know that, Ben?
BEN Scrub round it, will you? (*Pause*)
GUS There are a number of things I want to ask him. But I can never get round to it, when I see him. (*Pause*) I've been thinking about the last one.
BEN What last one?
GUS That girl.

(BEN *grabs the paper, which he reads*)

(*Rising, looking down at* BEN) How many times have you read that paper?

(BEN *slams the paper down and rises*)

BEN (*Angrily*) What do you mean?
GUS I was just wondering how many times you'd—
BEN What are you doing, criticising me?

GUS No, I was just—
BEN You'll get a swipe round your earhole if you don't watch your step.
GUS Now look here, Ben—
BEN I'm not looking anywhere! (*He addresses the room*) How many times have I—! A bloody liberty!
GUS I didn't mean that.
BEN You just get on with it, mate. Get on with it, that's all. (BEN *gets back on the bed*)
GUS I was just thinking about that girl, that's all. (GUS *sits on his bed*) She wasn't much to look at, I know, but still. It was a mess though, wasn't it? What a mess. Honest, I can't remember a mess like that one. They don't seem to hold together like men, women. A looser texture, like. Didn't she spread, eh? She didn't half spread. Kaw! But I've been meaning to ask you.

(BEN *sits up and clenches his eyes*)

Who clears up after we've gone? I'm curious about that. Who does the clearing up? Maybe they don't clear up. Maybe they just leave them there, eh? What do you think? How many jobs have we done? Blimey, I can't count them. What if they never clear anything up after we've gone.

BEN (*Pityingly*) You mutt. Do you think we're the only branch of this organisation? Have a bit of common. They got departments for everything.
GUS What cleaners and all?
BEN You birk!
GUS No, it was that girl made me start to think—

(*There is a loud clatter and racket in the bulge of wall between the beds, of something descending. They grab their revolvers, jump up and face the wall. The noise comes to a stop. Silence. They look at each other.* BEN *gestures sharply towards the wall.* GUS *approaches the wall slowly. He bangs it with his revolver. It is hollow.* BEN *moves to the head of his bed, his revolver cocked.* GUS *puts his revolver on his bed and pats along the bottom of the centre panel. He finds a rim. He lifts the panel. Disclosed is a serving-hatch, a "dumb waiter." A wide box is held by pulleys.* GUS *peers into the box. He brings out a piece of paper*)

BEN What is it?
GUS You have a look at it.
BEN Read it.

GUS (*Reading*)   Two braised steak and chips. Two sago puddings. Two teas without sugar.
BEN   Let me see that. (*He takes the paper*)
GUS (*To himself*)   Two teas without sugar.
BEN   Mmmm.
GUS   What do you think of that?
BEN   Well—

(*The box goes up.* BEN *levels his revolver*)

GUS   Give us a chance! They're in a hurry, aren't they?

(BEN *re-reads the note.* GUS *looks over his shoulder*)

That's a bit—that's a bit funny, isn't it?
BEN (*Quickly*)   No. It's not funny. It probably used to be a café here, that's all. Upstairs. These places change hands very quickly.
GUS   A café?
BEN   Yes.
GUS   What, you mean this was the kitchen, down here?
BEN   Yes, they change hands overnight, these places. Go into liquidation. The people who run it, you know, they don't find it a going concern, they move out.
GUS   You mean the people who ran this place didn't find it a going concern and moved out?
BEN   Sure.
GUS   WELL, WHO'S GOT IT NOW? (*Silence*)
BEN   What do you mean, who's got it now?
GUS   Who's got it now? If they moved out, who moved in?
BEN   Well, that all depends—

(*The box descends with a clatter and bang.* BEN *levels his revolver.* GUS *goes to the box and brings out a piece of paper*)

GUS (*Reading*)   Soup of the day. Liver and onions. Jam tart.

(*A pause.* GUS *looks at* BEN. BEN *takes the note and reads it. He walks slowly to the hatch.* GUS *follows.* BEN *looks into the hatch but not up it.* GUS *puts his hand on* BEN's *shoulder.* BEN *throws it off.* GUS *puts his finger to his mouth. He leans on the hatch and swiftly looks up it.* BEN *flings him away in alarm.* BEN *looks at the note. He throws his revolver on the bed and speaks with decision*)

BEN   We'd better send something up.
GUS   Eh?

BEN We'd better send something up.
GUS Oh! Yes. Yes. Maybe you're right.

   (*They are both relieved at the decision*)

BEN (*Purposefully*)   Quick! What have you got in that bag?
GUS Not much. (GUS *goes to the hatch and shouts up it*) Wait a minute!
BEN Don't do that!

   (GUS *examines the contents of the bag and brings them out, one by one*)

GUS Biscuits. A bar of chocolate. Half a pint of milk.
BEN That all?
GUS Packet of tea.
BEN Good.
GUS We can't send the tea. That's all the tea we've got.
BEN Well, there's no gas. You can't do anything with it, can you?
GUS Maybe they can send us down a bob.
BEN What else is there?
GUS (*Reaching into bag*)   One Eccles[5] cake.
BEN One Eccles cake?
GUS Yes.
BEN You never told me you had an Eccles cake.
GUS Didn't I?
BEN Why only one? Didn't you bring one for me?
GUS I didn't think you'd be keen.
BEN Well, you can't send up one Eccles cake, anyway.
GUS Why not?
BEN Fetch one of those plates.
GUS All right. (GUS *goes towards the door, left, and stops*) Do you mean I can keep the Eccles cake then?
BEN Keep it?
GUS Well, they don't know we've got it, do they?
BEN That's not the point.
GUS Can't I keep it?
BEN No, you can't. Get the plate.

   (GUS *exits, left.* BEN *looks in the bag. He brings out a packet of crisps. Enter* GUS *with a plate*)

   (*Accusingly, holding up the crisps*) Where did these come from?
GUS What?

   [5] English brand name.

BEN   Where did these crisps come from?
GUS   Where did you find them?
BEN   (*Hitting him on the shoulder*)   You're playing a dirty game, my lad!
GUS   I only eat those with beer!
BEN   Well, where were you going to get the beer?
GUS   I was saving them till I did.
BEN   I'll remember this. Put everything on the plate.

(*They pile everything on to the plate. The box goes up without the plate*)

Wait a minute!

(*They stand*)

GUS   It's gone up.
BEN   It's all your stupid fault, playing about!
GUS   What do we do now?
BEN   We'll have to wait till it comes down. (BEN *puts the plate on the bed, puts on his shoulder holster, and starts to put on his tie*) You'd better get ready.

(GUS *goes to his bed, puts on his tie, and starts to fix his holster*)

GUS   Hey, Ben.
BEN   What?
GUS   What's going on here? (*Pause*)
BEN   What do you mean?
GUS   How can this be a café?
BEN   It used to be a café.
GUS   Have you seen the gas stove?
BEN   What about it?
GUS   It's only got three rings.
BEN   So what?
GUS   Well, you couldn't cook much on three rings, not for a busy place like this.
BEN (*Irritably*)   That's why the service is slow! (BEN *puts on his waistcoat*)
GUS   Yes, but what happens when we're not here? What do they do then? All these menus coming down and nothing going up. It might have been going on like this for years.

(BEN *brushes his jacket*)

What happens when we go?

(BEN *puts on his jacket*)

They can't do much business.

(*The box descends. They turn about.* GUS *goes to the hatch and brings out a note*)

GUS (*Reading*) Macaroni Pastitsio. Ormitha Macarounada.
BEN What was that?
GUS Macaroni Pastitsio. Ormitha Macarounada.
BEN Greek dishes.
GUS No.
BEN That's right.
GUS That's pretty high class.
BEN Quick before it goes up.

(GUS *puts the plate in the box*)

GUS (*Calling up the hatch*) Three McVitie and Price! One Lyons Red Label! One Smith's Crisps! One Eccles cake![6] One Fruit and Nut!
BEN Cadbury's.
GUS (*Up the hatch*) Cadbury's!
BEN (*Handing the milk*) One bottle of milk.
GUS (*Up the hatch*) One bottle of milk! Half a pint! (*He looks at the label*) Express Dairy! (*He puts the bottle in the box*)

(*The box goes up*)

Just did it.
BEN You shouldn't shout like that.
GUS Why not?
BEN It isn't done. (BEN *goes to his bed*) Well, that should be all right, anyway, for the time being.
GUS You think so, eh?
BEN Get dressed, will you? It'll be any minute now.

(GUS *puts on his waistcoat.* BEN *lies down and looks up at the ceiling*)

GUS This is some place. No tea and no biscuits.
BEN Eating makes you lazy, mate. You're getting lazy, you know that? You don't want to get slack on your job.
GUS Who me?
BEN Slack, mate, slack.
GUS Who me? Slack?
BEN Have you checked your gun? You haven't even checked your gun. It looks disgraceful, anyway. Why don't you ever polish it?

[6] Common English brand names.

(GUS *rubs his revolver on the sheet.* BEN *takes out a pocket mirror and straightens his tie*)

GUS   I wonder where the cook is. They must have had a few, to cope with that. Maybe they had a few more gas stoves. Eh! Maybe there's another kitchen along the passage.

BEN   Of course there is! Do you know what it takes to make an Ormitha Macarounada?

GUS   No, what?

BEN   An Ormitha—! Buck your ideas up, will you?

GUS   Takes a few cooks, eh? (GUS *puts his revolver in its holster*) The sooner we're out of this place the better. (*He puts on his jacket*) Why doesn't he get in touch? I feel like I've been here years. (*He takes his revolver out of its holster to check the ammunition*) We've never let him down though, have we? We've never let him down. I was thinking only the other day, Ben. We're reliable, aren't we? (*He puts his revolver back in its holster*) Still, I'll be glad when it's over tonight. (*He brushes his jacket*) I hope the bloke's not going to get excited tonight, or anything. I'm feeling a bit off. I've got a splitting headache. (*Silence*)

(*The box descends.* BEN *jumps up.* GUS *collects the note*)

(*Reading*) One Bamboo Shoots, Water Chestnuts and Chicken. One Char Siu and Beansprouts.

BEN   Beansprouts?

GUS   Yes.

BEN   Blimey.

GUS   I wouldn't know where to begin. (*He looks back at the box. The packet of tea is inside it. He picks it up*) They've sent back the tea.

BEN   (*Anxious*)   What'd they do that for?

GUS   Maybe it isn't tea-time.

(*The box goes up. Silence*)

BEN   (*Throwing the tea on the bed, and speaking urgently*)   Look here. We'd better tell them.

GUS   Tell them what?

BEN   That we can't do it, we haven't got it.

GUS   All right then.

BEN   Lend us your pencil. We'll write a note.

(GUS, *turning for a pencil, suddenly discovers the speaking-tube, which hangs on the right wall of the hatch facing his bed*)

GUS   What's this?

BEN What?
GUS This.
BEN (*Examining it*) This? It's a speaking-tube.
GUS How long has that been there?
BEN Just the job. We should have used it before, instead of shouting up there.
GUS Funny I never noticed it before.
BEN Well, come on.
GUS What do you do?
BEN See that? That's a whistle.
GUS What, this?
BEN Yes, take it out. Pull it out.

(GUS *does so*)

That's it.
GUS What do we do now?
BEN Blow into it.
GUS Blow?
BEN It whistles up there if you blow. Then they know you want to speak. Blow.

(GUS *blows. Silence*)

GUS (*Tube at mouth*) I can't hear a thing.
BEN Now you speak! Speak into it!

(GUS *looks at* BEN, *then speaks into the tube*)

GUS The larder's bare!
BEN Give me that! (*He grabs the tube and puts it to his mouth. Speaking with great deference*) Good evening. I'm sorry to—bother you, but we just thought we'd better let you know that we haven't got anything left. We sent up all we had. There's no more food down here. (*He brings the tube slowly to his ear*) What? (*To mouth*) What? (*To ear. He listens. To mouth*) No, all we had we sent up. (*To ear. He listens. To mouth*) Oh, I'm very sorry to hear that. (*To ear. He listens. To* GUS) The Eccles cake was stale. (*He listens. To* GUS) The chocolate was melted. (*He listens. To* GUS) The milk was sour.
GUS What about the crisps?
BEN (*Listening*) The biscuits were mouldy. (*He glares at* GUS. *Tube to mouth*) Well, we're very sorry about that. (*Tube to ear*) What? (*To mouth*) What? (*To ear*) Yes. Yes. (*To mouth*) Yes certainly. Certainly. Right away. (*To ear. The voice has ceased. He hangs up the tube. Excitedly*) Did you hear that?
GUS What?

BEN You know what he said? Light the kettle! Not put on the kettle! Not light the gas! But light the kettle!
GUS How can we light the kettle?
BEN What do you mean?
GUS There's no gas.
BEN (*Clapping hand to head*) Now what do we do?
GUS What did he want us to light the kettle for?
BEN For tea. He wanted a cup of tea.
GUS *He* wanted a cup of tea! What about me? I've been wanting a cup of tea all night!
BEN (*Despairingly*) What do we do now?
GUS What are we supposed to drink?

(BEN *sits on his bed, staring*)

What about us?

(BEN *sits*)

I'm thirsty too. I'm starving. And he wants a cup of tea. That beats the band, that does.

(BEN *lets his head sink on to his chest*)

I could do with a bit of sustenance myself. What about you? You look as if you could with something too. (GUS *sits on his bed*) We send him up all we've got and he's not satisfied. No, honest, it's enough to make the cat laugh. Why did you send him up all that stuff? (*Thoughtfully*) Why did I send it up? (*Pause*) Who knows what he's got upstairs? He's probably got a salad bowl. They must have something up there. They won't get much from down here. You notice they didn't ask for any salads? They've probably got a salad bowl up there. Cold meat, radishes, cucumbers. Watercress. Roll mops. (*Pause*) Hardboiled eggs. (*Pause*) The lot. They've probably got a crate of beer too. Probably eating my crisps with a pint of beer now. Didn't have anything to say about those crisps, did he? They do all right, don't worry about that. You don't think they're just going to sit there and wait for stuff to come up from down here, do you? That'll get them nowhere. (*Pause*) They do all right. (*Pause*) And he wants a cup of tea. (*Pause*) That's past a joke, in my opinion. (*He looks over at* BEN, *rises, and goes to him*) What's the matter with you? You don't look too bright. I feel like an Alka-Seltzer myself.

(BEN *sits up*)

BEN (*In a low voice*) Time's getting on.

GUS I know. I don't like doing a job on an empty stomach.
BEN (*Wearily*) Be quiet a minute. Let me give you your instructions.
GUS What for? We always do it the same way, don't we?
BEN Let me give you your instructions.

(GUS *sighs and sits next to* BEN *on the bed. The instructions are stated and repeated automatically*)

When we get the call, you go over and stand behind the door.
GUS Stand behind the door.
BEN If there's a knock on the door you don't answer it.
GUS If there's a knock on the door I don't answer it.
BEN But there won't be a knock on the door.
GUS So I won't answer it.
BEN When the bloke comes in—
GUS When the bloke comes in—
BEN Shut the door behind him.
GUS Shut the door behind him.
BEN Without divulging your presence.
GUS Without divulging my presence.
BEN He'll see me and come towards me.
GUS He'll see you and come towards you.
BEN He won't see you.
GUS (*Absently*) Eh?
BEN He won't see you.
GUS He won't see me.
BEN But he'll see me.
GUS He'll see you.
BEN He won't know you're there.
GUS He won't know you're there.
BEN He won't know *you're* there.
GUS He won't know I'm there.
BEN I take out my gun.
GUS You take out your gun.
BEN He stops in his tracks.
GUS He stops in his tracks.
BEN If he turns round—
GUS If he turns round—
BEN You're there.
GUS I'm here.

(BEN *frowns and presses his forehead*)

You've missed something out.

BEN I know. What?
GUS I haven't taken my gun out, according to you.
BEN You take your gun out—
GUS After I've closed the door.
BEN After you've closed the door.
GUS You've never missed that out before, you know that?
BEN When he sees you behind him—
GUS Me behind him—
BEN And me in front of him—
GUS And you in front of him—
BEN He'll feel uncertain—
GUS Uneasy.
BEN He won't know what to do.
GUS So what will he do?
BEN He'll look at me and he'll look at you.
GUS We won't say a word.
BEN We'll look at him.
GUS He won't say a word.
BEN He'll look at us.
GUS And we'll look at him.
BEN Nobody says a word. (*Pause*)
GUS What do we do if it's a girl?
BEN We do the same.
GUS Exactly the same?
BEN Exactly. (*Pause*)
GUS We don't do anything different?
BEN We do exactly the same.
GUS Oh. (GUS *rises, and shivers*) Excuse me.

(*He exits through the door on the left.* BEN *remains sitting on the bed, still. The lavatory chain is pulled once off left, but the lavatory does not flush. Silence.* GUS *re-enters and stops inside the door, deep in thought. He looks at* BEN, *then walks slowly across to his own bed. He is troubled. He stands, thinking. He turns and looks at* BEN. *He moves a few paces towards him*)

(*Slowly in a low, tense voice*) Why did he send us matches if he knew there was no gas?

(*Silence.* BEN *stares in front of him.* GUS *crosses to the left side of* BEN, *to the foot of his bed, to get to his other ear*)

Ben. Why did he send us matches if he knew there was no gas?

(BEN *looks up*)

Why did he do that?
BEN Who?
GUS Who sent us those matches?
BEN What are you talking about?

(GUS *stares down at him*)

GUS (*Thickly*) Who is it upstairs?
BEN (*Nervously*) What's one thing to do with another?
GUS Who is it, though?
BEN What's one thing to do with another? (BEN *fumbles for his paper on the bed*)
GUS I asked you a question.
BEN Enough!
GUS (*With growing agitation*) I asked you before. Who moved in? I asked you. You said the people who had it before moved out. Well, who moved in?
BEN (*Hunched*) Shut up.
GUS I told you, didn't I?
BEN (*Standing*) Shut up!
GUS (*Feverishly*) I told you before who owned this place, didn't I? I told you.

(BEN *hits him viciously on the shoulder*)

I told you who ran this place, didn't I?

(BEN *hits him viciously on the shoulder*)

(*Violently*) Well, what's he playing all these games for? That's what I want to know. What's he doing it for?
BEN What games?
GUS (*Passionately, advancing*) What's he doing it for? We've been through our tests, haven't we? We got right through our tests, years ago, didn't we? We took them together, don't you remember, didn't we? We've proved ourselves before now, haven't we? We've always done our job. What's he doing all this for? What's the idea? What's he playing these games for?

(*The box in the shaft comes down behind them. The noise is this time accompanied by a shrill whistle, as it falls.* GUS *rushes to the hatch and seizes the note*)

(*Reading*) Scampi![7] (*He crumbles the note, picks up the tube, takes*

---

[7] Italian for "shrimp"; pun on English "scamp."

out the whistle, blows and speaks) WE'VE GOT NOTHING LEFT! NOTHING! DO YOU UNDERSTAND?

(BEN *seizes the tube and flings* GUS *away. He follows* GUS *and slaps him hard, back-handed, across the chest*)

BEN Stop it! You maniac!
GUS But you heard!
BEN (*Savagely*) That's enough! I'm warning you!

(*Silence.* BEN *hangs the tube. He goes to his bed and lies down. He picks up his paper and reads. Silence. The box goes up. They turn quickly, their eyes meet.* BEN *turns to his paper. Slowly* GUS *goes back to his bed, and sits. Silence. The hatch falls back into place. They turn quickly, their eyes meet.* BEN *turns back to his paper. Silence.* BEN *throws his paper down*)

BEN Kaw! (*He picks up the paper and looks at it*) Listen to this! (*Pause*) What about that, eh? (*Pause*) Kaw! (*Pause*) Have you ever heard such a thing?
GUS (*Dully*) Go on!
BEN It's true.
GUS Get away.
BEN It's down here in black and white.
GUS (*Very low*) Is that a fact?
BEN Can you imagine it.
GUS It's unbelievable.
BEN It's enough to make you want to puke, isn't it?
GUS (*Almost inaudible*) Incredible.

(BEN *shakes his head. He puts the paper down and rises. He fixes the revolver in his holster*)

(GUS *stands up. He goes towards the door on the left*)

BEN Where are you going?
GUS I'm going to have a glass of water.

(*He exits.* BEN *brushes dust off his clothes and shoes. The whistle in the speaking-tube blows. He goes to it, takes the whistle out and puts the tube to his ear. He listens. He puts it to his mouth*)

BEN Yes. (*To ear. He listens. To mouth*) Straight away. Right. (*To ear. He listens. To mouth*) Sure we're ready. (*To ear. He listens. To mouth*) Understood. Repeat. He has arrived and will be coming in straight away. The normal method to be employed. Understood. (*To ear. He listens.*

To mouth) Sure we're ready. (*To ear. He listens. To mouth*) Right. (*He hangs the tube up*) Gus! (*He takes out a comb and combs his hair, adjusts his jacket to diminish the bulge of the revolver. The lavatory flushes off left.* BEN *goes quickly to the door, left*) Gus!

(*The door right opens sharply.* BEN *turns, his revolver levelled at the door.* GUS *stumbles in. He is stripped of his jacket, waistcoat, tie, holster and revolver. He stops, body stooping, his arms at his sides. He raises his head and looks at* BEN. *A long silence. They stare at each other*)

Curtain

EDWARD ALBEE

[1928 –]

❦ *The Man*

EDWARD ALBEE was abandoned by his natural parents and was adopted, at the age of two, by Reed and Frances Albee, the former the millionaire heir to the Keith-Albee chain of theaters. Albee's youth was apparently that of the "poor little rich boy"—rich in material possessions but poor in parental understanding. He went from one expensive prep school to another, possibly in the manner of Salinger's Holden Caulfield. At Choate, he began to write poetry and fiction.

According to Albee, it was Thornton Wilder, whom he met in 1953, who advised him to write plays. He did not follow this advice until shortly before his thirtieth birthday, when he wrote *The Zoo Story*. While it was being refused by New York producers, he sent a copy to a composer friend in Italy, who liked the play, and sent it from Florence to Zurich, where it was forwarded to Frankfurt and then to Berlin, where it was first produced in German. In January, 1960, it was produced off-Broadway on a double bill with *Krapp's Last Tape* by Samuel Beckett. Enthusiastically received, it launched Albee's playwriting career.

❦ The Work

IN HIS PREFACE TO *The American Dream,* Albee writes, "This play is an examination of the American Scene, an attack on the substitution of artificial for real values in our society, a condemnation of complacency, cruelty, emasculation and vacuity; it is a stand against the fiction that everything in this slipping land of ours is peachy-keen." While the statement is naïve—since the targets are "safe" (acceptable) and few would maintain that everything is "peachy-keen"—the first part of the statement is an accurate description of Albee's work. His more simplistic plays—such as *The American Dream* and its offshoot, *The Sandbox,* which uses characters from the former play and is, in effect, *The American Dream* outdoors—have caricatures of emasculating mothers, emasculated fathers, machine-made young men who are empty-headed and muscle-bound, and lovable grandmothers of "pioneer stock," who are dying. These figures, attitudes, and relationships exist in all of his plays. The main character of *The Death of Bessie Smith,* for example, is not the blues singer but an emasculating white nurse who is related to the matrons of *Sandbox, American Dream,* and *Virginia Woolf.* Albee's plays contain alienated children, an adoption agency in *American Dream,* a false pregnancy and a nonexistent child in *Virginia Woolf,* and an orphaned outcast in *Zoo Story,* who describes his parents in Keith-Albee jargon: "That particular vaudeville act is playing the cloud circuit now . . ."

❦ The Play

THE TITLE of Albee's first play suggests several of its facets. On the literal level, Jerry has just come from the zoo, where he decided to do what we see him doing. The title also suggests the animalistic violence that lies beneath our thin veneer of civilization and which surfaces at the end of the play. And it symbolizes the caged isolation of modern man. Isolation, loneliness, and frustration are, in fact, major subjects in this realistic and symbolic drama of a lonely outcast who tries to make contact with another human being and who finally binds himself to that other in death.

One of Albee's impressive achievements in this play is his soldering of the realistic and the symbolic. Classical mythology is evoked by Jerry's reference to his landlady and her dog as "the gatekeepers of my dwelling," and to the latter as "a descendant of the puppy that guarded the gates of hell or some such resort." Biblical parallels are suggested by such utterances of Jerry as "So be it" and "It came to pass"; the Bible is again evoked when the dying Jerry says, "you have comforted me. Dear Peter," and Peter replies, "Oh my God!" Several critics have commented on the biblical references, interpreting Peter as the rock on which institutions are built and seeing Jerry as, variously, a Christ figure, a Christ parody, and a Jeremiah who denounces false gods.

At the surface level, there are evident differences between Jerry and Peter. Although they live in the same city, they live in different worlds, and Albee emphasizes their differences. Jerry is an orphan and an outcast, describing himself as "a *permanent transient.*" Peter, on the other hand, is a conformist, a respectable middle-class citizen who has established values and tastes. Peter lives with a wife and two children; Jerry lives alone and has two empty picture frames. Their very language proclaims their different social spheres: Peter the bourgeois square, Jerry the hipster-drifter. Their language also reflects their imaginations: Peter's stories are factual, Jerry's parabolic. However, each is associated with a prop that is partly ironic: the materialist, conformist Peter has a book and the imaginative, sensitive Jerry has a knife.

While the differences between Peter and Jerry are evident, there are striking similarities which are more subtly delineated. Although a cat is associated with Peter and a dog with Jerry, the latter at one point says that he called the dog his "PUSSY-CAT." Peter's wife apparently has refused to have more children, while Jerry's landlady "has some foul parody of sexual desire" of which he is the object. Jerry had just visited a zoo; Peter lives with a pair of parakeets and a pair of cats in what Jerry calls "[his] own little zoo." However, beneath the similarities linking Jerry to Peter are the differences which separate the outsider from the insider: Jerry stays outside his landlady's apartment, while Peter has a conventional marriage; Jerry is a visitor at the literal zoo, observing the animals from outside their cages, whereas Peter lives inside his metaphorical zoo. Nevertheless, they are different sides of the *same* coin, for both are emasculated products of American society. While Peter has lost his manhood by domesticity, Jerry's life is sterile. If no male children issue from Peter's loins, nothing at all issues from Jerry's. The latter's relationship with his landlady involves a parody of sex. He immaturely uses pornographic playing cards. He can love women only once ("For about an hour"). And he not only had a homosexual experience when he was fifteen, but it is implied that he currently practices homosexuality; he is immolated by a knife, symbol of an erect phallus, inserted by a man whose name has a phallic connotation.

This knife, hidden by Jerry, represents the violence that lies beneath the surface of our lives and is the fang of the human animal who has just come from the zoo and who tells a story of a savage dog; he gives this knife to the domesticated animal he meets on the park bench. The violence that erupts at the end of the play is cunningly prepared. Jerry has walked not due north but in a northerly direction, and comments that "sometimes a person has to go a very long distance out of his way to come back a short distance correctly." While Jerry's story of the dog is apparently a digression, it is really circular for he forces Peter into the same relationship with him (enmity) that the dog had, persuades him to defend his territory as the dog did, and makes Peter stab him as the dog bit at him. Following the stabbing, Jerry pointedly tells Peter that he is not a vegetable but an animal. Again, however, there is a vital difference within the similarity: whereas the dog tried to prevent Jerry from entering "the gates of hell," Peter releases Jerry from his hell.

Albee has called *The Zoo Story* a "novice work" and has humbly expressed gratitude for its favorable reception. Although Albee's statement is sincere, one need not agree with him but may regard his first work as a mature piece of art and "novice" only in point of time.

❧ *Dramatic Works*

The Zoo Story, 1958.
The Sandbox, 1959.
The Death of Bessie Smith, 1959.
Fam and Yam, 1960.
The American Dream, 1960.
Bartleby (with William Flanagan and James Hinton, Jr.), 1961.

Who's Afraid of Virginia Woolf?, 1962.
The Ballad of the Sad Café, 1963.
Tiny Alice, 1964.
Malcolm, 1965.

❧ Selective Bibliography

"Albee: Odd Man In on Broadway," *Newsweek*, LXI (February 4, 1963).
Baxandall, Lee. "The Theatre of Edward Albee," *Tulane Drama Review*, IX (Summer, 1965).
Esslin, Martin. *The Theatre of the Absurd*. New York: Doubleday Anchor, 1961.
Goodman, Henry. "The New Dramatists: 4. Edward Albee," *Drama Survey*, II (June, 1962).
Zimbardo, Rose A. "Symbolism and Naturalism in Edward Albee's *The Zoo Story*," *Twentieth Century Literature*, VIII (April, 1962).

The Zoo Story

A Play in One Scene

FOR WILLIAM FLANAGAN

THE PLAYERS

PETER, *a man in his early forties, neither fat nor gaunt, neither handsome nor homely. He wears tweeds, smokes a pipe, carries horn-rimmed glasses. Although he is moving into middle age, his dress and manner would suggest a man younger.*

JERRY, *a man in his late thirties, not poorly dressed, but carelessly. What was once a trim and lightly muscled body has begun to go to fat; and while he is no longer handsome, it is evident that he once was. His fall from physical grace should not suggest debauchery; he has, to come closest to it, a great weariness.*

SCENE *It is Central Park; a Sunday afternoon in summer; the present. There are two park benches, one toward either side of the stage; they both face the audience. Behind them: foliage, trees, sky. At the beginning, Peter is seated on one of the benches.*

As the curtain rises, PETER *is seated on the bench stage-right. He is reading a book. He stops reading, cleans his glasses, goes back to reading.* JERRY *enters.*

JERRY I've been to the zoo. (PETER *doesn't notice*) I said, I've been to the zoo. MISTER, I'VE BEEN TO THE ZOO!

PETER Hm? . . . What? . . . I'm sorry, were you talking to me?

JERRY I went to the zoo, and then I walked until I came here. Have I been walking north?

PETER (*Puzzled*) North? Why . . . I . . . I think so. Let me see.
JERRY (*Pointing past the audience*) Is that Fifth Avenue?
PETER Why yes; yes, it is.
JERRY And what is that cross street there; that one, to the right?
PETER That? Oh, that's Seventy-fourth Street.
JERRY And the zoo is around Sixty-fifth Street; so, I've been walking north.
PETER (*Anxious to get back to his reading*) Yes; it would seem so.
JERRY Good old north.
PETER (*Lightly, by reflex*) Ha, ha.
JERRY (*After a slight pause*) But not due north.
PETER I . . . well, no, not due north; but, we . . . call it north. It's northerly.
JERRY (*Watches as* PETER, *anxious to dismiss him, prepares his pipe*) Well, boy; you're not going to get lung cancer, are you?
PETER (*Looks up, a little annoyed, then smiles*) No, sir. Not from this.
JERRY No, sir. What you'll probably get is cancer of the mouth, and then you'll have to wear one of those things Freud wore after they took one whole side of his jaw away. What do they call those things?
PETER (*Uncomfortable*) A prosthesis?
JERRY The very thing! A prosthesis. You're an educated man, aren't you? Are you a doctor?
PETER Oh, no; no. I read about it somewhere; *Time* magazine, I think. (*He turns to his book*)
JERRY Well, *Time* magazine isn't for blockheads.
PETER No, I suppose not.
JERRY (*After a pause*) Boy, I'm glad that's Fifth Avenue there.
PETER (*Vaguely*) Yes.
JERRY I don't like the west side of the park much.
PETER Oh? (*Then, slightly wary, but interested*) Why?
JERRY (*Offhand*) I don't know.
PETER Oh. (*He returns to his book*)
JERRY (*He stands for a few seconds, looking at* PETER, *who finally looks up again, puzzled*) Do you mind if we talk?
PETER (*Obviously minding*) Why . . . no, no.
JERRY Yes you do; you do.
PETER (*Puts his book down, his pipe out and away, smiling*) No, really; I don't mind.
JERRY Yes you do.
PETER (*Finally decided*) No; I don't mind at all, really.
JERRY It's . . . it's a nice day.
PETER (*Stares unnecessarily at the sky*) Yes. Yes, it is; lovely.

JERRY I've been to the zoo.
PETER Yes, I think you said so ... didn't you?
JERRY You'll read about it in the papers tomorrow, if you don't see it on your TV tonight. You have TV, haven't you?
PETER Why yes, we have two; one for the children.
JERRY You're married!
PETER (*With pleased emphasis*) Why, certainly.
JERRY It isn't a law, for God's sake.
PETER No ... no, of course not.
JERRY And you have a wife.
PETER (*Bewildered by the seeming lack of communication*) Yes!
JERRY And you have children.
PETER Yes; two.
JERRY Boys?
PETER No, girls ... both girls.
JERRY But you wanted boys.
PETER Well ... naturally, every man wants a son, but ...
JERRY (*Lightly mocking*) But that's the way the cookie crumbles?
PETER (*Annoyed*) I wasn't going to say that.
JERRY And you're not going to have any more kids, are you?
PETER (*A bit distantly*) No. No more. (*Then back, and irksome*) Why did you say that? How would you know about that?
JERRY The way you cross your legs, perhaps; something in the voice. Or maybe I'm just guessing. Is it your wife?
PETER (*Furious*) That's none of your business! (*A silence*) Do you understand? (JERRY *nods.* PETER *is quiet now*) Well, you're right. We'll have no more children.
JERRY (*Softly*) That *is* the way the cookie crumbles.
PETER (*Forgiving*) Yes ... I guess so.
JERRY Well, now; what else?
PETER What were you saying about the zoo ... that I'd read about it, or see ... ?
JERRY I'll tell you about it, soon. Do you mind if I ask you questions?
PETER Oh, not really.
JERRY I'll tell you why I do it; I don't talk to many people—except to say like: give me a beer, or where's the john, or what time does the feature go on, or keep your hands to yourself, buddy. You know —things like that.
PETER I must say I don't ...
JERRY But every once in a while I like to talk to somebody, really *talk*; like to get to know somebody, know all about him.

PETER (*Lightly laughing, still a little uncomfortable*) And am I the guinea pig for today?
JERRY On a sun-drenched Sunday afternoon like this? Who better than a nice married man with two daughters and . . . uh . . . a dog? (PETER *shakes his head*) No? Two dogs. (PETER *shakes his head again*) Hm. No dogs? (PETER *shakes his head, sadly*) Oh, that's a shame. But you look like an animal man. CATS? (PETER *nods his head, ruefully*) Cats! But, that can't be your idea. No, sir. Your wife and daughters? (PETER *nods his head*) Is there anything else I should know?
PETER (*He has to clear his throat*) There are . . . there are two parakeets. One . . . uh . . . one for each of my daughters.
JERRY Birds.
PETER My daughters keep them in a cage in their bedroom.
JERRY Do they carry disease? The birds.
PETER I don't believe so.
JERRY That's too bad. If they did you could set them loose in the house and the cats could eat them and die, maybe. (PETER *looks blank for a moment, then laughs*) And what else? What do you do to support your enormous household?
PETER I . . . uh . . . I have an executive position with a . . . a small publishing house. We . . . uh . . . we publish textbooks.
JERRY That sounds nice; very nice. What do you make?
PETER (*Still cheerful*) Now look here!
JERRY Oh, come on.
PETER Well, I make around eighteen thousand a year, but I don't carry more than forty dollars at any one time . . . in case you're a . . . holdup man . . . ha, ha, ha.
JERRY (*Ignoring the above*) Where do you live? (PETER *is reluctant*) Oh, look; I'm not going to rob you, and I'm not going to kidnap your parakeets, your cats, or your daughters.
PETER (*Too loud*) I live between Lexington and Third Avenue, on Seventy-fourth Street.
JERRY That wasn't so hard, was it?
PETER I didn't mean to seem . . . ah . . . it's that you don't really carry on a conversation; you just ask questions. And I'm . . . I'm normally . . . uh . . . reticent. Why do you just stand there?
JERRY I'll start walking around in a little while, and eventually I'll sit down. (*Recalling*) Wait until you see the expression on his face.
PETER What? Whose face? Look here; is this something about the zoo?
JERRY (*Distantly*) The what?
PETER The zoo; the zoo. Something about the zoo.

JERRY The zoo?
PETER You've mentioned it several times.
JERRY (*Still distant, but returning abruptly*) The zoo? Oh, yes; the zoo. I was there before I came here. I told you that. Say, what's the dividing line between upper-middle-middle-class and lower-upper-middle-class?
PETER My dear fellow, I . . .
JERRY Don't my dear fellow me.
PETER (*Unhappily*) Was I patronizing? I believe I was; I'm sorry. But, you see, your question about the classes bewildered me.
JERRY And when you're bewildered you become patronizing?
PETER I . . . I don't express myself too well, sometimes. (*He attempts a joke on himself*) I'm in publishing, not writing.
JERRY (*Amused, but not at the humor*) So be it. The truth *is*: I was being patronizing.
PETER Oh, now; you needn't say that.

(*It is at this point that Jerry may begin to move about the stage with slowly increasing determination and authority, but pacing himself, so that the long speech about the dog comes at the high point of the arc*)

JERRY All right. Who are your favorite writers? Baudelaire and J. P. Marquand?
PETER (*Wary*) Well, I like a great many writers; I have a considerable . . . catholicity of taste, if I may say so. Those two men are fine, each in his way. (*Warming up*) Baudelaire, of course . . . uh . . . is by far the finer of the two, but Marquand has a place . . . in our . . . uh . . . national . . .
JERRY Skip it.
PETER I . . . sorry.
JERRY Do you know what I did before I went to the zoo today? I walked all the way up Fifth Avenue from Washington Square; all the way.
PETER Oh; you live in the Village![1] (*This seems to enlighten* PETER)
JERRY No, I don't. I took the subway down to the Village so I could walk all the way up Fifth Avenue to the zoo. It's one of those things a person has to do; sometimes a person has to go a very long distance out of his way to come back a short distance correctly.
PETER (*Almost pouting*) Oh, I thought you lived in the Village.
JERRY What were you trying to do? Make sense out of things? Bring order? The old pigeonhole bit? Well, that's easy; I'll tell you. I live

[1] Greenwich Village, a section of lower Manhattan, traditionally associated with artists, bohemians, and social and sexual rebels.

in a four-story brownstone rooming-house on the upper West Side between Columbus Avenue and Central Park West. I live on the top floor; rear; west. It's a laughably small room, and one of my walls is made of beaverboard; this beaverboard separates my room from another laughably small room, so I assume that the two rooms were once one room, a small room, but not necessarily laughable. The room beyond my beaverboard wall is occupied by a colored queen[2] who always keeps his door open; well, not always but *always* when he's plucking his eyebrows, which he does with Buddhist concentration. This colored queen has rotten teeth, which is rare, and he has a Japanese kimono, which is also pretty rare; and he wears this kimono to and from the john in the hall, which is pretty frequent. I mean, he goes to the john a lot. He never bothers me, and he never brings anyone up to his room. All he does is pluck his eyebrows, wear his kimono and go to the john. Now, the two front rooms on my floor are a little larger, I guess; but they're pretty small, too. There's a Puerto Rican family in one of them, a husband, a wife, and some kids; I don't know how many. These people entertain a lot. And in the other front room, there's somebody living there, but I don't know who it is. I've never seen who it is. Never. Never ever.

PETER (*Embarrassed*) Why . . . why do you live there?

JERRY (*From a distance again*) I don't know.

PETER It doesn't sound like a very nice place . . . where you live.

JERRY Well, no; it isn't an apartment in the East Seventies. But, then again, I don't have one wife, two daughters, two cats and two parakeets. What I do have, I have toilet articles, a few clothes, a hot plate that I'm not supposed to have, a can opener, one that works with a key, you know; a knife, two forks, and two spoons, one small, one large; three plates, a cup, a saucer, a drinking glass, two picture frames, both empty, eight or nine books, a pack of pornographic playing cards, regular deck, an old Western Union typewriter that prints nothing but capital letters, and a small strongbox without a lock which has in it . . . what? Rocks! Some rocks . . . sea-rounded rocks I picked up on the beach when I was a kid. Under which . . . weighed down . . . are some letters . . . please letters . . . please why don't you do this, and please when will you do that letters. And when letters, too. When will you write? When will you come? When? These letters are from more recent years.

PETER (*Stares glumly at his shoes, then*) About those two empty picture frames . . . ?

JERRY I don't see why they need any explanation at all. Isn't it clear?

---

[2] A male homosexual.

I don't have pictures of anyone to put in them.

PETER Your parents . . . perhaps . . . a girl friend . . .

JERRY You're a very sweet man, and you're possessed of a truly enviable innocence. But good old Mom and good old Pop are dead . . . you know? . . . I'm broken up about it, too . . . I mean really. BUT. That particular vaudeville act is playing the cloud circuit now, so I don't see how I can look at them, all neat and framed. Besides, or, rather, to be pointed about it, good old Mom walked out on good old Pop when I was ten and a half years old; she embarked on an adulterous turn of our southern states . . . a journey of a year's duration . . . and her most constant companion . . . among others, among many others . . . was a Mr. Barleycorn. At least, that's what good old Pop told me after he went down . . . came back . . . brought her body north. We'd received the news between Christmas and New Year's, you see, that good old Mom had parted with the ghost in some dump in Alabama. And, without the ghost . . . she was less welcome. I mean, what was she? A stiff . . . a northern stiff. At any rate, good old Pop celebrated the New Year for an even two weeks and then slapped into the front of a somewhat moving city omnibus, which sort of cleaned things out family-wise. Well no; then there was Mom's sister, who was given neither to sin nor the consolations of the bottle. I moved in on her, and my memory of her is slight excepting I remember still that she did all things dourly: sleeping, eating, working, praying. She dropped dead on the stairs to her apartment, my apartment then, too, on the afternoon of my high school graduation. A terribly middle-European joke, if you ask me.

PETER Oh, my; oh, my.

JERRY Oh, your what? But that was a long time ago, and I have no feeling about any of it that I care to admit to myself. Perhaps you can see, though, why good old Mom and good old Pop are frameless. What's your name? Your first name?

PETER I'm Peter.

JERRY I'd forgotten to ask you. I'm Jerry.

PETER (*With a slight, nervous laugh*) Hello, Jerry.

JERRY (*Nods his hello*) And let's see now; what's the point of having a girl's picture, especially in two frames? I have two picture frames, you remember. I never see the pretty little ladies more than once, and most of them wouldn't be caught in the same room with a camera. It's odd, and I wonder if it's sad.

PETER The girls?

JERRY No. I wonder if it's sad that I never see the little ladies more than once. I've never been able to have sex with, or, how is it put? . . .

make love to anybody more than once. Once; that's it. . . . Oh, wait; for a week and a half, when I was fifteen . . . and I hang my head in shame that puberty was late . . . I was a h-o-m-o-s-e-x-u-a-l. I mean, I was queer . . . (Very fast) . . . queer, queer, queer . . . with bells ringing, banners snapping in the wind. And for those eleven days, I met at least twice a day with the park superintendent's son . . . a Greek boy, whose birthday was the same as mine, except he was a year older. I think I was very much in love . . . maybe just with sex. But that was the jazz of a very special hotel, wasn't it? And now; oh, do I love the little ladies; really, I love them. For about an hour.

PETER Well, it seems perfectly simple to me. . . .
JERRY (Angry) Look! Are you going to tell me to get married and have parakeets?
PETER (Angry himself) Forget the parakeets! And stay single if you want to. It's no business of mine. I didn't start this conversation in the . . .
JERRY All right, all right. I'm sorry. All right? You're not angry?
PETER (Laughing) No, I'm not angry.
JERRY (Relieved) Good. (Now back to his previous tone) Interesting that you asked me about the picture frames. I would have thought that you would have asked me about the pornographic playing cards.
PETER (With a knowing smile) Oh, I've seen those cards.
JERRY That's not the point. (Laughs) I suppose when you were a kid you and your pals passed them around, or you had a pack of your own.
PETER Well, I guess a lot of us did.
JERRY And you threw them away just before you got married.
PETER Oh, now; look here. I didn't *need* anything like that when I got older.
JERRY No?
PETER (Embarrassed) I'd rather not talk about these things.
JERRY So? Don't. Besides, I wasn't trying to plumb your post-adolescent sexual life and hard times; what I wanted to get at is the value difference between pornographic playing cards when you're a kid, and pornographic playing cards when you're older. It's that when you're a kid you use the cards as a substitute for a real experience, and when you're older you use real experience as a substitute for the fantasy. But I imagine you'd rather hear about what happened at the zoo.
PETER (Enthusiastic) Oh, yes; the zoo. (Then, awkward) That is . . . if you. . . .
JERRY Let me tell you about why I went . . . well, let me tell you some things. I've told you about the fourth floor of the roominghouse where I live. I think the rooms are better as you go down, floor by floor. I guess

they are; I don't know. I don't know any of the people on the third and second floors. Oh, wait! I do know that there's a lady living on the third floor, in the front. I know because she cries all the time. Whenever I go out or come back in, whenever I pass her door, I always hear her crying, muffled, but . . . very determined. Very determined indeed. But the one I'm getting to, and all about the dog, is the landlady. I don't like to use words that are too harsh in describing people. I don't like to. But the landlady is a fat, ugly, mean, stupid, unwashed, misanthropic, cheap, drunken bag of garbage. And you may have noticed that I very seldom use profanity, so I can't describe her as well as I might.

PETER You describe her . . . vividly.

JERRY Well, thanks. Anyway, she has a dog, and I will tell you about the dog, and she and her dog are the gatekeepers of my dwelling. The woman is bad enough; she leans around in the entrance hall, spying to see that I don't bring in things or people, and when she's had her midafternoon pint of lemon-flavored gin she always stops me in the hall, and grabs ahold of my coat or my arm, and she presses her disgusting body up against me to keep me in a corner so she can talk to me. The smell of her body and her breath . . . you can't imagine it . . . and somewhere, somewhere in the back of that pea-sized brain of hers, an organ developed just enough to let her eat, drink, and emit, she has some foul parody of sexual desire. And I, Peter, I am the object of her sweaty lust.

PETER That's disgusting. That's . . . horrible.

JERRY But I have found a way to keep her off. When she talks to me, when she presses herself to my body and mumbles about her room and how I should come there, I merely say: but, Love; wasn't yesterday enough for you, and the day before? Then she puzzles, she makes slits of her tiny eyes, she sways a little, and then, Peter . . . and it is at this moment that I think I might be doing some good in that tormented house . . . a simple-minded smile begins to form on her unthinkable face, and she giggles and groans as she thinks about yesterday and the day before; as she believes and relives what never happened. Then, she motions to that black monster of a dog she has, and she goes back to her room. And I am safe until our next meeting.

PETER It's so . . . unthinkable. I find it hard to believe that people such as that really *are*.

JERRY (*Lightly mocking*) It's for reading about, isn't it?

PETER (*Seriously*) Yes.

JERRY And fact is better left to fiction. You're right, Peter. Well, what I have been meaning to tell you about is the dog; I shall, now.

PETER (*Nervously*) Oh, yes; the dog.
JERRY Don't go. You're not thinking of going, are you?
PETER Well . . . no, I don't think so.
JERRY (*As if to a child*) Because after I tell you about the dog, do you know what then? Then . . . then I'll tell you about what happened at the zoo.
PETER (*Laughing faintly*) You're . . . you're full of stories, aren't you?
JERRY You don't *have* to listen. Nobody is holding you here; remember that. Keep that in your mind.
PETER (*Irritably*) I know that.
JERRY You do? Good.

(*The following long speech, it seems to me, should be done with a great deal of action, to achieve a hypnotic effect on Peter, and on the audience, too. Some specific actions have been suggested, but the director and the actor playing Jerry might best work it out for themselves*)

ALL RIGHT. (*As if reading from a huge billboard*) THE STORY OF JERRY AND THE DOG! (*Natural again*) What I am going to tell you has something to do with how sometimes it's necessary to go a long distance out of the way in order to come back a short distance correctly; or, maybe I only think that it has something to do with that. But, it's why I went to the zoo today, and why I walked north . . . northerly, rather . . . until I came here. All right. The dog, I think I told you, is a black monster of a beast: an oversized head, tiny, tiny ears, and eyes . . . bloodshot, infected, maybe; and a body you can see the ribs through the skin. The dog is black, all black; all black except for the bloodshot eyes, and . . . yes . . . and an open sore on its . . . *right* forepaw; that is red, too. And, oh yes; the poor monster, and I do believe it's an old dog . . . it's certainly a misused one . . . almost always has an erection . . . of sorts. That's red, too. And . . . what else? . . . oh, yes; there's a gray-yellow-white color, too, when he bares his fangs. Like this: Grrrrrrr! Which is what he did when he saw me for the first time . . . the day I moved in. I worried about that animal the very first minute I met him. Now, animals don't take to me like Saint Francis had birds hanging off him all the time. What I mean is: animals are indifferent to me . . . like people (*He smiles slightly*) . . . most of the time. But this dog wasn't indifferent. From the very beginning he'd snarl and then go for me, to get one of my legs. Not like he was rabid, you know; he was sort of a stumbly dog, but he wasn't half-assed, either. It was a good, stumbly run; but I always got away. He got a piece of my trouser leg, look, you can see right here, where it's mended; he got that the second day I lived there; but, I kicked free and got upstairs fast, so that was that. (*Puzzles*) I still don't know to this day how the other roomers manage it, but you know what I *think*: I think it had to do only with me. Cozy. So. Anyway, this went on for over a week, whenever I came in; but never when I went out. That's funny. Or, it *was* funny. I could pack up and live in the street for all the dog cared. Well, I thought about it up in my room one day, one of the times after I'd bolted upstairs, and I made up my mind. I decided: First, I'll kill the dog with kindness, and if that doesn't work . . . I'll just kill him. (PETER *winces*) Don't react, Peter; just listen. So, the next day I went out and bought a bag of hamburgers, medium rare, no catsup, no onion; and on the way home I threw away all the rolls and kept just the meat. (*Action for the following, perhaps*) When I got back to the rooming-house the dog was waiting for me. I half opened the door that led into the entrance hall, and there he was; waiting for me. It figured. I went in, very cautiously, and I had the hamburgers, you remember; I opened the bag, and I set the meat down about twelve feet from where the dog was snarling at me. Like so! He snarled; stopped snarling; sniffed; moved slowly; then faster; then faster toward the meat. Well, when he got to it he stopped, and he looked at me. I smiled; but tentatively, you understand. He turned his face back to the hamburgers, smelled, sniffed some more, and then . . . RRRAAAAGGGGHHHH, like that . . . he tore into them. It was as if he had never eaten anything in his life before, except like garbage. Which might very well have been the truth. I don't think the landlady ever eats anything but garbage. But. He ate all the hamburgers, almost all at once, making sounds in his throat like a woman. *Then*, when he'd finished the meat, the hamburger, and tried to eat the paper, too, he sat down and smiled. I think he smiled; I know cats do. It was a very gratifying few moments. Then, BAM, he snarled and made for me again. He didn't get me this time, either. So, I got upstairs, and I lay down on my bed and started to think about the dog again. To be truthful, I was offended, and I was damn mad, too. It was six perfectly good hamburgers with not enough pork in them to make it disgusting. I was offended. But, after a while, I decided to try it for a few more days. If you think about it, this dog had what amounted to an antipathy toward me; really. And, I wondered if I mightn't overcome this antipathy. So, I tried it for five more days, but it was always the same: snarl, sniff; move; faster; stare; gobble; RAAGGGHHH; smile; snarl; BAM. Well, now; by this time Columbus Avenue was strewn with hamburger rolls and I was less offended than disgusted. So, I decided to kill the dog.

(PETER *raises a hand in protest*)

Oh, don't be so alarmed, Peter; I didn't succeed. The day I tried to kill the dog I bought only one hamburger and what I thought was a murderous portion of rat poison. When I bought the hamburger I asked the man not to bother with the roll, all I wanted was the meat. I expected some reaction from him, like: we don't sell no hamburgers without rolls; or, wha' d'ya wanna do, eat it out'a ya han's? But no; he smiled benignly, wrapped up the hamburger in waxed paper, and said: A bite for ya pussy-cat? I wanted to say: No, not really; it's part of a plan to poison a dog I know. But, you can't say "a dog I know" without sounding funny; so I said, a little too loud, I'm afraid, and too formally: YES, A BITE FOR MY PUSSY-CAT. People looked up. It always happens when I try to simplify things; people look up. But that's neither hither nor thither. So. On my way back to the roominghouse, I kneaded the hamburger and the rat poison together between my hands, at that point feeling as much sadness as disgust. I opened the door to the entrance hall, and there the monster was, waiting to take the offering and then jump me. Poor bastard; he never learned that the moment he took to smile before he went for me gave me time enough to get out of range. BUT, there he was; malevolence with an erection, waiting. I put the poison patty down, moved toward the stairs and watched. The poor animal gobbled the food down as usual, smiled, which made me almost sick, and then, BAM. But, I sprinted up the stairs, as usual, and the dog didn't get me, as usual. AND IT CAME TO PASS THAT THE BEAST WAS DEATHLY ILL. I knew this because he no longer attended me, and because the landlady sobered up. She stopped me in the hall the same evening of the attempted murder and confided the information that God had struck her puppy-dog a surely fatal blow. She had forgotten her bewildered lust, and her eyes were wide open for the first time. They looked like the dog's eyes. She sniveled and implored me to pray for the animal. I wanted to say to her: Madam, I have myself to pray for, the colored queen, the Puerto Rican family, the person in the front room whom I've never seen, the woman who cries deliberately behind her closed door, and the rest of the people in all roominghouses, everywhere; besides, Madam, I don't understand how to pray. But . . . to simplify things . . . I told her I would pray. She looked up. She said that I was a liar, and that I probably wanted the dog to die. I told her, and there was so much truth here, that I didn't want the dog to die. I didn't, and not just because I'd poisoned him. I'm afraid that I must tell you I wanted the dog to live so that I could see what our new relationship might come to.

(PETER *indicates his increasing displeasure and slowly growing antagonism*)

Please understand, Peter; that sort of thing is important. You must believe me; it *is* important. We have to know the effect of our actions. (*Another deep sigh*) Well, anyway; the dog recovered. I have no idea why, unless he was a descendant of the puppy that guarded the gates of hell or some such resort. I'm not up on my mythology. (*He pronounces the word myth-o-logy*) Are you?

(PETER *sets to thinking, but* JERRY *goes on*)

At any rate, and you've missed the eight-thousand-dollar question, Peter; at any rate, the dog recovered his health and the landlady recovered her thirst, in no way altered by the bow-wow's deliverance. When I came home from a movie that was playing on Forty-second Street, a movie I'd seen, or one that was very much like one or several I'd seen, after the landlady told me puppykins was better, I was so hoping for the dog to be waiting for me. I was . . . well, how would you put it . . . enticed? . . . fascinated? . . . no, I don't think so . . . heart-shatteringly anxious, that's it; I was heart-shatteringly anxious to confront my friend again.

(PETER *reacts scoffingly*)

Yes, Peter; friend. That's the only word for it. I was heart-shatteringly et cetera to confront my doggy friend again. I came in the door and advanced, unafraid, to the center of the entrance hall. The beast was there . . . looking at me. And, you know, he looked better for his scrape with the nevermind. I stopped; I looked at him; he looked at me. I think . . . I think we stayed a long time that way . . . still, stone-statue . . . just looking at one another. I looked more into his face than he looked into mine. I mean, I can concentrate longer at looking into a dog's face than a dog can concentrate at looking into mine, or into anybody else's face, for that matter. But during that twenty seconds or two hours that we looked into each other's face, we made contact. Now, here is what I had wanted to happen: I loved the dog now, and I wanted him to love me. I had tried to love, and I had tried to kill, and both had been unsuccessful by themselves. I hoped . . . and I don't really know why I expected the dog to understand anything, much less my motivations . . . I hoped that the dog would understand.

(PETER *seems to be hypnotized*)

It's just . . . it's just that . . . (JERRY *is abnormally tense, now*) . . . it's just that if you can't deal with people, you have to make a start somewhere. WITH ANIMALS! (*Much faster now, and like a conspirator*) Don't you see? A person has to have some way of dealing with SOMETHING. If not with people . . . if not with people . . . SOMETHING. With a bed, with a cockroach, with a mirror . . . no, that's too hard, that's one of the last steps. With a cockroach, with a . . . with a . . . with a carpet, a roll of toilet paper . . . no, not that, either . . . that's a mirror, too; always check bleeding. You see how hard it is to find things? With a street corner, and too many lights, all colors reflecting on the oily-wet streets . . . with a wisp of smoke, a wisp . . . of smoke . . . with . . . with pornographic playing cards, with a strongbox . . . WITHOUT A LOCK . . . with love, with vomiting, with crying, with fury because the pretty little ladies aren't pretty little ladies, with making money with your body which is an act of love and I could prove it, with howling because you're alive; with God. How about that? WITH GOD WHO IS A COLORED QUEEN WHO WEARS A KIMONO AND PLUCKS HIS EYEBROWS, WHO IS A WOMAN WHO CRIES WITH DETERMINATION BEHIND HER CLOSED DOOR . . . with God who, I'm told, turned his back on the whole thing some time ago . . . with . . . some day, with people. (JERRY *sighs the next word heavily*) People. With an idea; a concept. And where better, where ever better in this humiliating excuse for a jail, where better to communicate one single, simple-minded idea than in an entrance hall? Where? It would be A START! Where better to make a beginning . . . to understand and just possibly be understood . . . a beginning of an understanding, than with . . . (*Here* JERRY *seems to fall into almost grotesque fatigue*) . . . than with A DOG. Just that; a dog. (*Here there is a silence that might be prolonged for a moment or so; then* JERRY *wearily finishes his story*) A dog. It seemed like a perfectly sensible idea. Man is a dog's best friend, remember. So: the dog and I looked at each other. I longer than the dog. And what I saw then has been the same ever since. Whenever the dog and I see each other we both stop where we are. We regard each other with a mixture of sadness and suspicion, and then we feign indifference. We walk past each other safely; we have an understanding. It's very sad, but you'll have to admit that it is an understanding. We had made many attempts at contact, and we had failed. The dog has returned to garbage, and I to solitary but free passage. I have not returned. I mean to say, I have *gained* solitary free passage, if that much further loss can be said to be gain. I have learned that neither kindness nor cruelty by themselves, independent of each other, creates any effect beyond themselves; and I have learned that the two combined, together, at the same time, are the teaching emotion. And what is gained is loss. And what has been the result: the dog and I have attained a compromise; more of a bargain, really.

We neither love nor hurt because we do not try to reach each other. And, *was* trying to feed the dog an act of love? And, perhaps, was the dog's attempt to bite me *not* an act of love? If we can so misunderstand, well then, why have we invented the word love in the first place? (*There is silence.* JERRY *moves to* PETER'S *bench and sits down beside him. This is the first time* JERRY *has sat down during the play*) The Story of Jerry and the Dog: the end.

(PETER *is silent*)

Well, Peter? (JERRY *is suddenly cheerful*) Well, Peter? Do you think I could sell that story to the *Reader's Digest* and make a couple of hundred bucks for *The Most Unforgettable Character I've Ever Met*? Huh? (JERRY *is animated, but* PETER *is disturbed*) Oh, come on now, Peter; tell me what you think.

PETER (*Numb*) I ... I don't understand what ... I don't think I ... (*Now, almost tearfully*) Why did you tell me all of this?

JERRY Why not?

PETER I DON'T UNDERSTAND!

JERRY (*Furious, but whispering*) That's a lie.

PETER No. No, it's not.

JERRY (*Quietly*) I tried to explain it to you as I went along. I went slowly; it all has to do with ...

PETER I DON'T WANT TO HEAR ANY MORE. I don't understand you, or your landlady, or her dog....

JERRY Her dog! I thought it was my ... No. No, you're right. It *is* her dog. (*Looks at* PETER *intently, shaking his head*) I don't know what I was thinking about; of course you don't understand. (*In a monotone, wearily*) I don't live in your block; I'm not married to two parakeets, or whatever your setup is. I am a *permanent transient,* and my home is the sickening roominghouses on the West Side of New York City, which is the greatest city in the world. Amen.

PETER I'm ... I'm sorry; I didn't mean to ...

JERRY Forget it. I suppose you don't quite know what to make of me, eh?

PETER (*A joke*) We get all kinds in publishing. (*Chuckles*)

JERRY You're a funny man. (*He forces a laugh*) You know that? You're a very ... a richly comic person.

PETER (*Modestly, but amused*) Oh, now, not really. (*Still chuckling*)

JERRY Peter, do I annoy you, or confuse you?

PETER (*Lightly*) Well, I must confess that this wasn't the kind of afternoon I'd anticipated.

JERRY You mean, I'm not the gentleman you were expecting.

PETER I wasn't expecting anybody.

JERRY   No, I don't imagine you were. But I'm here, and I'm not leaving.
PETER   (*Consulting his watch*)   Well, you may not be, but I must be getting home soon.
JERRY   Oh, come on; stay a while longer.
PETER   I really should get home; you see . . .
JERRY   (*Tickles* PETER's *ribs with his fingers*)   Oh, come on.
PETER   (*He is very ticklish; as* JERRY *continues to tickle him his voice becomes falsetto*)   No, I . . . OHHHHH! Don't do that. Stop, Stop. Ohhh, no, no.
JERRY   Oh, come on.
PETER   (*As* JERRY *tickles*)   Oh, hee, hee, hee. I must go. I . . . hee, hee, hee. After all, stop, stop, hee, hee, hee, after all, the parakeets will be getting dinner ready soon. Hee, hee. And the cats are setting the table. Stop, stop, and, and . . . (PETER *is beside himself now*) . . . and we're having . . . hee, hee . . . uh . . . ho, ho, ho.

(JERRY *stops tickling* PETER, *but the combination of the tickling and his own mad whimsy has* PETER *laughing almost hysterically. As his laughter continues, then subsides,* JERRY *watches him, with a curious fixed smile*)

JERRY   Peter?
PETER   Oh, ha, ha, ha, ha, ha. What? What?
JERRY   Listen, now.
PETER   Oh, ho, ho. What . . . what is it, Jerry? Oh, my.
JERRY   (*Mysteriously*)   Peter, do you want to know what happened at the zoo?
PETER   Ah, ha, ha. The what? Oh, yes; the zoo. Oh, ho, ho. Well, I had my own zoo there for a moment with . . . hee, hee, the parakeets getting dinner ready, and the . . . ha, ha, whatever it was, the . . .
JERRY   (*Calmly*)   Yes, that was very funny, Peter. I wouldn't have expected it. But do you want to hear about what happened at the zoo, or not?
PETER   Yes. Yes, by all means; tell me what happened at the zoo. Oh, my. I don't know what happened to me.
JERRY   Now I'll let you in on what happened at the zoo; but first, I should tell you why I went to the zoo. I went to the zoo to find out more about the way people exist with animals, and the way animals exist with each other, and with people too. It probably wasn't a fair test, what with everyone separated by bars from everyone else, the animals for the most part from each other, and always the people from the animals. But, if it's a zoo, that's the way it is. (*He pokes* PETER *on the arm*)   Move over.

PETER (*Friendly*) I'm sorry, haven't you enough room? (*He shifts a little*)
JERRY (*Smiling slightly*) Well, all the animals are there, and all the people are there, and it's Sunday and all the children are there. (*He pokes* PETER *again*) Move over.
PETER (*Patiently, still friendly*) All right. (*He moves some more, and* JERRY *has all the room he might need*)
JERRY And it's a hot day, so all the stench is there, too, and all the balloon sellers, and all the ice cream sellers, and all the seals are barking, and all the birds are screaming. (*Pokes* PETER *harder*) Move over!
PETER (*Beginning to be annoyed*) Look here, you have more than enough room! (*But he moves more, and is now fairly cramped at one end of the bench*)
JERRY And I am there, and it's feeding time at the lions' house, and the lion keeper comes into the lion cage, one of the lion cages, to feed one of the lions. (*Punches* PETER *on the arm, hard*) MOVE OVER!
PETER (*Very annoyed*) I can't move over any more, and stop hitting me. What's the matter with you?
JERRY Do you want to hear the story? (*Punches* PETER'S *arm again*)
PETER (*Flabbergasted*) I'm not so sure! I certainly don't want to be punched in the arm.
JERRY (*Punches* PETER'S *arm again*) Like that?
PETER Stop it! What's the matter with you?
JERRY I'm crazy, you bastard.
PETER That isn't funny.
JERRY Listen to me, Peter. I want this bench. You go sit on the bench over there, and if you're good I'll tell you the rest of the story.
PETER (*Flustered*) But . . . whatever for? What *is* the matter with you? Besides, I see no reason why I should give up this bench. I sit on this bench almost every Sunday afternoon, in good weather. It's secluded here; there's never anyone sitting here, so I have it all to myself.
JERRY (*Softly*) Get off this bench, Peter; I want it.
PETER (*Almost whining*) No.
JERRY I said I want this bench, and I'm going to have it. Now get over there.
PETER People can't have everything they want. You should know that; it's a rule; people can have some of the things they want, but they can't have everything.
JERRY (*Laughs*) Imbecile! You're slow-witted!
PETER Stop that!

JERRY You're a vegetable! Go lie down on the ground.
PETER (*Intense*) Now *you* listen to me. I've put up with you all afternoon.
JERRY Not really.
PETER LONG ENOUGH. I've put up with you long enough. I've listened to you because you seemed . . . well, because I thought you wanted to talk to somebody.
JERRY You put things well; economically, and, yet . . . oh, what is the word I want to put justice to your . . . JESUS, you make me sick . . . get off here and give me my bench.
PETER MY BENCH!
JERRY (*Pushes* PETER *almost, but not quite, off the bench*) Get out of my sight.
PETER (*Regaining his position*) God da . . . mn you. That's enough! I've had enough of you. I will not give up this bench; you can't have it, and that's that. Now, go away.

(JERRY *snorts but does not move*)

Go away, I said.

(JERRY *does not move*)

Get away from here. If you don't move on . . . you're a bum . . . that's what you are. . . . If you don't move on, I'll get a policeman here and make you go.

(JERRY *laughs, stays*)

I warn you, I'll call a policeman.
JERRY (*Softly*) You won't find a policeman around here; they're all over on the west side of the park chasing fairies[3] down from trees or out of the bushes. That's all they do. That's their function. So scream your head off; it won't do you any good.
PETER POLICE! I warn you, I'll have you arrested. POLICE! (*Pause*) I said POLICE! (*Pause*) I feel ridiculous.
JERRY You look ridiculous: a grown man screaming for the police on a bright Sunday afternoon in the park with nobody harming you. If a policeman *did* fill his quota and come sludging over this way he'd probably take you in as a nut.
PETER (*With disgust and impotence*) Great God, I just came here to read, and now you want me to give up the bench. You're mad.

---

[3] A pun referring to both supernatural beings and homosexuals, who apparently frequent the west side of Central Park.

JERRY Hey, I got news for you, as they say. I'm on your precious bench, and you're never going to have it for yourself again.

PETER (*Furious*) Look, you; get off my bench. I don't care if it makes any sense or not. I want this bench to myself; I want you OFF IT!

JERRY (*Mocking*) Aw . . . look who's mad.

PETER GET OUT!

JERRY No.

PETER I WARN YOU!

JERRY Do you know how ridiculous you look *now*?

PETER (*His fury and self-consciousness have possessed him*) It doesn't matter. (*He is almost crying*) GET AWAY FROM MY BENCH!

JERRY Why? You have everything in the world you want; you've told me about your home, and your family, and *your own* little zoo. You have everything, and now you want this bench. Are these the things men fight for? Tell me, Peter, is this bench, this iron and this wood, is this your honor? Is this the thing in the world you'd fight for? Can you think of anything more absurd?

PETER Absurd? Look, I'm not going to talk to you about honor, or even try to explain it to you. Besides, it isn't a question of honor; but even if it were, you wouldn't understand.

JERRY (*Contemptuously*) You don't even know what you're saying, do you? This is probably the first time in your life you've had anything more trying to face than changing your cats' toilet box. Stupid! Don't you have any idea, not even the slightest, what other people *need*?

PETER Oh, boy, listen to you; well, you don't need this bench. That's for sure.

JERRY Yes; yes, I do.

PETER (*Quivering*) I've come here for years; I have hours of great pleasure, great satisfaction, right here. And that's important to a man. I'm a responsible person, and I'm a GROWNUP. This is my bench, and you have no right to take it away from me.

JERRY Fight for it, then. Defend yourself; defend your bench.

PETER You've *pushed* me to it. Get up and fight.

JERRY Like a man?

PETER (*Still angry*) Yes, like a man, if you insist on mocking me even further.

JERRY I'll have to give you credit for one thing: you *are* a vegetable, and a slightly nearsighted one, I think . . .

PETER THAT'S ENOUGH. . . .

JERRY . . . but, you know, as they say on TV all the time—you know—and I mean this, Peter, you have a certain dignity; it surprises me. . . .

PETER STOP!

JERRY (*Rises lazily*) Very well, Peter, we'll battle for the bench, but we're not evenly matched. (*He takes out and clicks open an ugly-looking knife*)

PETER (*Suddenly awakening to the reality of the situation*) You *are* mad! You're stark raving mad! YOU'RE GOING TO KILL ME!

(*But before* PETER *has time to think what to do,* JERRY *tosses the knife at* PETER'S *feet*)

JERRY There you go. Pick it up. You have the knife and we'll be more evenly matched.

PETER (*Horrified*) No!

JERRY (*Rushes over to* PETER, *grabs him by the collar;* PETER *rises; their faces almost touch*) Now you pick up that knife and you fight with me. You fight for your self-respect; you fight for that goddamned bench.

PETER (*Struggling*) No! Let . . . let go of me! He . . . Help!

JERRY (*Slaps* PETER *on each "fight"*) You fight, you miserable bastard; fight for that bench; fight for your parakeets; fight for your cats, fight for your two daughters; fight for your wife; fight for your manhood, you pathetic little vegetable. (*Spits in* PETER'S *face*) You couldn't even get your wife with a male child.

PETER (*Breaks away, enraged*) It's a matter of genetics, not manhood, you . . . you monster. (*He darts down, picks up the knife and backs off a little; he is breathing heavily*) I'll give you one last chance; get out of here and leave me alone! (*He holds the knife with a firm arm, but far in front of him, not to attack, but to defend*)

JERRY (*Sighs heavily*) So be it!

(*With a rush he charges* PETER *and impales himself on the knife. Tableau: For just a moment, complete silence,* JERRY *impaled on the knife at the end of* PETER's *still firm arm. Then* PETER *screams, pulls away, leaving the knife in* JERRY. JERRY *is motionless, on point. Then he, too, screams, and it must be the sound of an infuriated and fatally wounded animal. With the knife in him, he stumbles back to the bench that* PETER *had vacated. He crumbles there, sitting, facing* PETER, *his eyes wide in agony, his mouth open*)

PETER (*Whispering*) Oh my God, oh my God, oh my God. . . . (*He repeats these words many times, very rapidly*)

JERRY (JERRY *is dying; but now his expression seems to change. His features relax, and while his voice varies, sometimes wrenched with pain, for the most part he seems removed from his dying. He smiles*) Thank you, Peter. I mean that, now; thank you very much.

(PETER's *mouth drops open. He cannot move; he is transfixed*)

Oh, Peter, I was so afraid I'd drive you away. (*He laughs as best he can*) You don't know how afraid I was you'd go away and leave me. And now I'll tell you what happened at the zoo. I think . . . I think this is what happened at the zoo . . . I think. I think that while I was at the zoo I decided that I would walk north . . . northerly, rather . . . until I found you . . . or somebody . . . and I decided that I would talk to you . . . I would tell you things . . . and things that I would tell you would . . . Well, here we are. You see? Here we *are*. But . . . I don't know . . . could I have planned all this? No . . . no, I couldn't have. But I think I did. And now I've told you what you wanted to know, haven't I? And now you know all about what happened at the zoo. And now you know what you'll see in your TV, and the face I told you about . . . you remember . . . the face I told you about . . . my face, the face you see right now. Peter . . . Peter? . . . Peter . . . thank you. I came unto you (*He laughs, so faintly*) and you have comforted me. Dear Peter.

PETER (*Almost fainting*) Oh my God!

JERRY You'd better go now. Somebody might come by, and you don't want to be here when anyone comes.

PETER (*Does not move, but begins to weep*) Oh my God, oh my God.

JERRY (*Most faintly, now; he is very near death*) You won't be coming back here any more, Peter; you've been dispossessed. You've lost your bench, but you've defended your honor. And Peter, I'll tell you something now; you're not really a vegetable; it's all right, you're an animal. You're an animal, too. But you'd better hurry now, Peter. Hurry, you'd better go . . . see? (JERRY *takes a handkerchief and with great effort and pain wipes the knife handle clean of fingerprints*) Hurry away, Peter.

(PETER *begins to stagger away*)

Wait . . . wait, Peter. Take your book . . . book. Right here . . . beside me . . . on your bench . . . my bench, rather. Come . . . take your book.

(PETER *starts for the book, but retreats*)

Hurry . . . Peter.

(PETER *rushes to the bench, grabs the book, retreats*)

Very good, Peter . . . very good. Now . . . hurry away.

(PETER *hesitates for a moment, then flees, stage-left*)

Hurry away.... (*His eyes are closed now*) Hurry away, your parakeets are making the dinner ... the cats ... are setting the table ...
PETER (*Off stage. A pitiful howl*)   OH MY GOD!
JERRY (*His eyes still closed, he shakes his head and speaks; a combination of scornful mimicry and supplication*)   Oh ... my ... God. (*He is dead*)

Curtain

SAMUEL BECKETT
[1906 –]

❦ *The Man*

BORN into a middle-class Irish Protestant family, Samuel Beckett was educated at Portora Royal School and Trinity College, receiving a degree in modern languages in 1927. While still a student, he visited Paris and met James Joyce; soon afterwards, Beckett published an exegetical essay on *Finnegans Wake*, then still *Work in Progress*. After two years at the Ecole Normale Supérieure in Paris, another year as Assistant Professor of French at Trinity, two years in London, and some traveling on the continent, Beckett moved permanently to Paris in 1937.

From his student days, he wrote verse, short stories, and criticism. In Paris when World War II broke out, he worked in the French underground, and fled to unoccupied France hours before the Nazis searched his apartment. While working as an agricultural laborer, he wrote his second and last English novel *Watt*. After the War, Beckett shifted to French for his writing. Critics have seen this expression in a foreign tongue as proof of his own alienation, and that of his characters. Poet, novelist, playwright, translator, Beckett remains an irrepressible Irishman in his comic astringency, and a French Existentialist in his artistic depiction of man's metaphysical situation. Beckett is virtually a prototype of the Absurdist writer, alienated in a world he never made and that defies his efforts to make sense of it.

❧ *The Work*

ALL BECKETT'S WORK, French and English, fiction and drama, imitates the tragicomedy of the human condition in its unreconstructed absurdity. Fiction and drama spurn the traditions of each genre in order to evoke a fragmented world peopled by fragmented beings. His early fiction, written in English, deals with protagonists who are increasingly out of place in society. When Beckett shifted to French, his fiction took the form of first-person monologue. Though the names change in successive works from Molloy to Malone to Worm to Pim, the narrations resemble one another—"A sinecure handed down from generation to generation," in the words of the Unnamable. From volume to volume, plot and characters—those staples of fiction—are successively reduced: Molloy goes in search of his mother, Moran in search of Molloy, but Malone is confined to his bed, waiting for death, and the Unnamable, a nameless and unnamable protagonist, located in an unidentified Limbo, seeks to penetrate behind names, behind words, to whatever might be himself. In his most recent novel-poem *How It Is*, Beckett abandons not only plot and characters, but even sentences; in incantatory free verse, still another Beckett monologuist crawls naked through a world of slimy mud, meeting and perhaps becoming Pim, then Bom; on he crawls after the encounter, none the warmer, none the wiser.

In Beckett's dramatic development, the reduction is not quite so linear. *Eleutheria,* an unpublished play written about 1947, contains a multiple setting, three acts, and about a dozen characters. *Waiting for Godot*, written at about the same period, has a single and spare setting, two repetitive acts, and five characters. Volumes of interpretation have already been written about this slender structure, which is often cited as the first drama of the Absurd.

By Martin Esslin's definition, all Beckett's dramas are Absurdist—dramas that find the situation of man-in-the-world absurd, and which reflect that absurdity by their non sequitur of plot and dialogue. Absurdist man is aware, in Camus' phrase, that "Men die and they are not happy." In *Waiting for Godot* Didi and Gogo eagerly consider hanging themselves, but they lack the will and the power. In *Endgame* the world is dying; Hamm and Clov alternately hope for death, and Nell dies unseen

679 · *Embers*

on stage. In *All That Fall*, the protagonists, looking forward to death, meet after a child has fallen under a train. *Krapp's Last Tape* is set "in the future," and *Embers* evokes the past, though the death that separates past and future remains ambiguous in both these plays. In *Happy Days* an immobile Winnie and a crawling Willie are the last dying couple on a scorched earth, and in Beckett's *Play* the three characters of an eternal triangle are fixed in their funeral urns, eternally recalling their triangularity.

❦ *The Play*

WRITTEN for the British Broadcasting Corporation, the brief radio play *Embers* embodies Beckett's major themes and techniques. Following *Krapp's Last Tape* by less than a year, *Embers*, too, is largely a monologue that emphasizes the absurdity of man-in-the-world. Krapp reminisces into his tape recorder, whereas Henry reminisces in order to drown the sound of the sea, which is audible whenever he stops talking. And like Krapp, Henry may be remembering, or he may be inventing, in a desperate effort to escape from himself.

The name Henry is derived from German *Heimrih*, meaning head of the family, and at first it seems as though Henry is trying to fill this position. Though his father's death has left him technical head of the family, it is soon apparent that he can command no one. The sea drowned his father, and Henry must keep talking to drown out the sea. Like other Beckett protagonists, Henry evokes other characters, who may be fictional or real. The very names of his characters—Bolt-on and Hollow-way—suggest the bleak atmosphere of *Embers*. As in *Endgame*, as in *Krapp's Last Tape*, Beckett depicts a dying world, reduced to embers; only his own babbling stands between Henry and the omnivorous sea.

Even as he builds a narrative between himself and the sea, Henry finds it difficult to commit himself with any definiteness, and constantly contradicts himself in his soliloquies: "shutters . . . no, hangings," "the light, no light," "sitting there in the . . . no, standing," "conversation then on the step, no, in the room," and, finally, "not a sound, only the embers, sound of dying, dying glow, Holloway, Bolton, Bolton, Holloway, old men, great trouble, white world, not a sound." Whenever Henry pauses, he is plagued by the sound of the relentless sea. Again, he calls upon his father, again he returns to his fictions, and, when his father doesn't answer, recalls his wife Ada almost parenthetically, wondering whether his father ever met her.

The implication is strengthened that Henry is head of a dead family —dead wife Ada and dead daughter Addie. In his dialogue with Ada, we learn that Henry's whole life has been a battle against the sea. From Ada, too, we learn that Henry has always talked to himself in this way, and she advises him to see Holloway: "There's something wrong with your brain, you ought to see Holloway, he's alive still, isn't he?" But we never know whether Holloway is "alive still" or living only in Henry's story about Bolton.

The couple listens to the sea, then to their daughter Addie taking music lessons, riding lessons. Ada tells Henry of her recollection of his father, sitting motionless on a rock and looking out to sea, in a position that Henry himself often took. After she leaves him, Henry weaves words about this confrontation of father and wife; he tries to keep his mind on Ada, but his narrative soon dissolves into the story of Bolton and Holloway, whose very eyes suggest the sea: "Not a word, just the look, the old blue eye, very glassy, lids worn thin, lashes gone, whole thing swimming. . . ."

At the end of the play, after calling vainly on "Ada! Father! Christ!" Henry moves to the edge of the sea, and the drama ends as it began— in seemingly disconnected monologue. But there are subtle suggestions of Christ's crucifixion: Christ died at nine on Good Friday, and Henry has noted that a plumber will come at nine on Friday: "Ah yes, the waste." Instead of a resurrection, however, Saturday and Sunday will bring nothing at all. Retrospectively, Henry's pleas to his father recall Christ's words on the cross: "My God, my God, why hast thou forsaken me?" Henry's father and Henry's Christ both forsake him, and his life is thus a crucifixion without hope of relief. With his last words, Henry fights on against the sound of the sea: "Not a sound," he sounds out. But the closing stage direction is "*Sea*," which has always symbolized an ominous mystery for man.

❦ Dramatic Works[*]

Eleutheria, 1947 (unpublished).
Waiting for Godot, 1952.
All That Fall, 1957.
Act Without Words I, 1957.
Endgame, 1957.
Krapp's Last Tape, 1958.
Embers, 1959.

Act Without Words II, 1959.
Happy Days, 1961.
Words and Music, 1962.
Cascando, 1963.
Play, 1963.
Come and Go, 1965.

❦ Selective Bibliography[†]

Coe, Richard. *Samuel Beckett.* New York: Grove, 1964.
Cohn, Ruby. *Samuel Beckett: the Comic Gamut.* New Brunswick, N.J.: Rutgers University Press, 1962.
Esslin, Martin. *The Theatre of the Absurd.* New York: Doubleday Anchor, 1961.
Guicharnaud, Jacques, and Beckelman, June, *Modern French Theatre.* New Haven: Yale University Press, 1961.
Mayoux, Jean-Jacques. "The Theatre of Samuel Beckett," *Perspective*, XI (Autumn, 1959).
Pronko, Leonard C. *Avant-Garde.* Berkeley: University of California Press, 1962.

---

[*] Since some of these were originally written in French, and then translated by the author, dates given are those of first production or publication.

[†] There is almost no detailed criticism of *Embers*, but general criticism of Beckett's drama is listed instead.

Embers[1]

Sea scarcely audible.
HENRY'S *boots on shingle. He halts.*
Sea a little louder.

HENRY On. (*Sea. Voice louder*) On! (*He moves on. Boots on shingle. As he goes*) Stop. (*Boots on shingle. As he goes, louder*) Stop! (*He halts. Sea a little louder*) Down. (*Sea. Voice louder*) Down! (*Slither of shingle as he sits. Sea, still faint, audible throughout what follows whenever pause indicated*) Who is beside me now? (*Pause*) An old man, blind and foolish. (*Pause*) My father, back from the dead, to be with me. (*Pause*) As if he hadn't died. (*Pause*) No, simply back from the dead to be with me, in this strange place. (*Pause*) Can he hear me? (*Pause*) Yes, he must hear me. (*Pause*) To answer me? (*Pause*) No, he doesn't answer me. (*Pause*) Just to be with me. (*Pause*) That sound you hear is the sea. (*Pause. Louder*) I say that sound you hear is the sea, we are sitting on the strand. (*Pause*) I mention it because the sound is so strange, so unlike the sound of the sea, that if you didn't see what it was you wouldn't know what it was. (*Pause*) Hooves! (*Pause. Louder*) Hooves! (*Sound of hooves walking on hard road. They die rapidly away. Pause*) Again! (*Hooves as before. Pause. Excitedly*) Train it to mark time! Shoe it with steel and tie it up in the yard, have it stamp all day! (*Pause*) A ten ton mammoth back from the dead, shoe it with steel and have it tramp the world down! (*Pause*) Listen to it! (*Pause*) Listen to the light now, you always loved light, not long past noon and all the shore in shadow and the sea out as far as the island. (*Pause*) You would never live this side of the bay, you

---

[1] *Embers* was first produced by The British Broadcasting Corporation's Third Programme on June 24, 1959.

wanted the sun on the water for that evening bathe you took once too often. But when I got your money I moved across, as perhaps you may know. (*Pause*) We never found your body, you know, that held up probate an unconscionable time, they said there was nothing to prove you hadn't run away from us all and alive and well under a false name in the Argentine for example, that grieved mother greatly. (*Pause*) I'm like you in that, can't stay away from it, but I never go in, no, I think the last time I went in was with you. (*Pause*) Just be near it. (*Pause*) Today it's calm, but I often hear it above in the house and walking the roads and start talking, oh just loud enough to drown it, nobody notices. (*Pause*) But I'd be talking now no matter where I was, I once went to Switzerland to get away from the cursed thing and never stopped all the time I was there. (*Pause*) I usen't to need anyone, just to myself, stories, there was a great one about an old fellow called Bolton, I never finished it, I never finished anything, everything always went on for ever. (*Pause*) Bolton. (*Pause. Louder*) Bolton! (*Pause*) There before the fire. (*Pause*) Before the fire with all the shutters . . . no, hangings, hangings, all the hangings drawn and the light, no light, only the light of the fire, sitting there in the . . . no, standing, standing there on the hearthrug in the dark before the fire with his arms on the chimney-piece and his head on his arms, standing there waiting in the dark before the fire in his old red dressing-gown and no sound in the house of any kind, only the sound of the fire. (*Pause*) Standing there in his old red dressing-gown might go on fire any minute like when he was a child, no, that was his pyjamas, standing there waiting in the dark, no light, only the light of the fire, and no sound of any kind, only the fire, an old man in great trouble. (*Pause*) Ring then at the door and over he goes to the window and looks out between the hangings, fine old chap, very big and strong, bright winter's night, snow everywhere, bitter cold, white world, cedar boughs bending under load, and then as the arm goes up to ring again recognizes . . . Holloway . . . (*Long pause*) . . . yes, Holloway, recognizes Holloway, goes down and opens. (*Pause*) Outside all still, not a sound, dog's chain maybe or a bough groaning if you stood there listening long enough, white world, Holloway with his little black bag, not a sound, bitter cold, full moon small and white, crooked trail of Holloway's galoshes. Vega in the Lyre[2] very green. (*Pause*) Vega in the Lyre very green. (*Pause*) Following conversation then on the step, no, in the room, back in the room, following conversation then back in the room, Holloway: "My dear Bolton, it is now past midnight,

---

[2] Brightest star in the constellation Lyre.

if you would be good enough—", gets no further, Bolton: "Please! PLEASE!" Dead silence then, not a sound, only the fire, all coal, burning down now. Holloway on the hearthrug trying to toast his arse, Bolton, where's Bolton, no light, only the fire, Bolton at the window, his back to the hangings, holding them a little apart with his hand, looking out, white world, even the spire, white to the vane, most unusual, silence in the house, not a sound, only the fire, no flames now, embers. (*Pause*) Embers. (*Pause*) Shifting, lapsing, furtive like, dreadful sound, Holloway on the rug, fine old chap, six foot, burly, legs apart, hands behind his back holding up the tails of his old macfarlane, Bolton at the window, grand old figure in his old red dressing-gown, back against the hangings, hand stretched out widening the chink, looking out, white world, great trouble, not a sound, only the embers, sound of dying, dying glow, Holloway, Bolton, Bolton, Holloway, old men, great trouble, white world, not a sound. (*Pause*) Listen to it! (*Pause*) Close your eyes and listen to it, what would you think it was? (*Pause. Vehement*) A drip! A drip! (*Sound of drip, rapidly amplified, suddenly cut off*) Again! (*Drip again. Amplification begins*) No! (*Drip cut off. Pause*) Father! (*Pause. Agitated*) Stories, stories, years and years of stories, till the need came on me, for someone, to be with me, anyone, a stranger, to talk to, imagine he hears me, years of that, and then, now, for someone who . . . knew me, in the old days, anyone, to be with me, imagine he hears me, what I am, now. (*Pause*) No good either. (*Pause*) Not there either. (*Pause*) Try again. (*Pause*) White world, not a sound. (*Pause*) Holloway. (*Pause*) Holloway says he'll go, damned if he'll sit up all night before a black grate, doesn't understand, call a man out, an old friend, in the cold and dark, an old friend, urgent need, bring the bag, then not a word, no explanation, no heat, no light, Bolton: "Please! PLEASE!," Holloway, no refreshment, no welcome, chilled to the medulla, catch his death, can't understand, strange treatment, old friend, says he'll go, doesn't move, not a sound, fire dying, white beam from window, ghastly scene, wishes to God he hadn't come, no good, fire out, bitter cold, great trouble, white world, not a sound, no good. (*Pause*) No good. (*Pause*) Can't do it. (*Pause*) Listen to it! (*Pause*) Father! (*Pause*) You wouldn't know me now, you'd be sorry you ever had me, but you were that already, a washout, that's the last I heard from you, a washout. (*Pause. Imitating father's voice*) "Are you coming for a dip?" "No." "Come on, come on." "No." Glare, stump to door, turn, glare. "A washout, that's all you are, a washout!" (*Violent slam of door. Pause*) Again! (*Slam. Pause*) Slam life shut like that! (*Pause*) Washout. (*Pause*) Wish to Christ she had. (*Pause*) Never met Ada, did you, or did you, I can't remember, no matter, no one'd know her now. (*Pause*) What turned her against me do you think, the child I suppose, horrid little creature, wish to God we'd never had her, I used to walk with her in the fields, Jesus that was awful, she wouldn't let go my hand and I mad to talk. "Run along now, Addie, and look at the lambs." (*Imitating* ADDIE's *voice*) "No papa." "Go on now, go on." (*Plaintive*) "No papa." (*Violent*) "Go on with you now when you're told and look at the lambs!" (ADDIE's *loud wail*. *Pause*) Ada too, conversation with her, that was something, that's what hell will be like, small chat to the babbling of Lethe about the good old days when we wished we were dead. (*Pause*) Price of margarine fifty years ago. (*Pause*) And now. (*Pause*. With solemn indignation) Price of blueband[3] now! (*Pause*) Father! (*Pause*) Tired of talking to you. (*Pause*) That was always the way, walk all over the mountains with you talking and talking and then suddenly mum and home in misery and not a word to a soul for weeks, sulky little bastard, better off dead, better off dead. (*Long pause*) Ada. (*Pause. Louder*) Ada!

ADA (*Low remote voice throughout*)   Yes.
HENRY   Have you been there long?
ADA   Some little time. (*Pause*) Why do you stop, don't mind me. (*Pause*) Do you want me to go away? (*Pause*) Where is Addie? (*Pause*)
HENRY   With her music master. (*Pause*) Are you going to answer me today?
ADA   You shouldn't be sitting on the cold stones, they're bad for your growths. Raise yourself up till I slip my shawl under you. (*Pause*) Is that better?
HENRY   No comparison, no comparison. (*Pause*) Are you going to sit down beside me?
ADA   Yes. (*No sound as she sits*) Like that? (*Pause*) Or do you prefer like that? (*Pause*) You don't care. (*Pause*) Chilly enough I imagine, I hope you put on your jaegers.[4] (*Pause*) Did you put on your jaegers, Henry?
HENRY   What happened was this, I put them on and then I took them off again and then I put them on again and then I took them off again and then I took them on again and then I—
ADA   Have you them on now?
HENRY   I don't know. (*Pause*) Hooves! (*Pause. Louder*) Hooves! (*Sound of hooves walking on hard road. They die rapidly away*) Again! (*Hooves as before. Pause*)

[3] A kind of margarine.
[4] Long woolen underwear.

ADA   Did you hear them?
HENRY   Not well.
ADA   Galloping?
HENRY   No. (*Pause*) Could a horse mark time? (*Pause*)
ADA   I'm not sure that I know what you mean.
HENRY   (*Irritably*)   Could a horse be trained to stand still and mark time with its four legs?
ADA   Oh. (*Pause*) The ones I used to fancy all did. (*She laughs. Pause*) Laugh, Henry, it's not every day I crack a joke. (*Pause*) Laugh, Henry, do that for me.
HENRY   You wish *me* to laugh?
ADA   You laughed so charmingly once, I think that's what first attracted me to you. That and your smile. (*Pause*) Come on, it will be like old times.

(*Pause. He tries to laugh, fails*)

HENRY   Perhaps I should begin with the smile. (*Pause for smile*) Did that attract you? (*Pause*) Now I'll try again. (*Long horrible laugh*) Any of the old charm there?
ADA   Oh Henry! (*Pause*)
HENRY   Listen to it![5] (*Pause*) Lips and claws! (*Pause*) Get away from it! Where it couldn't get at me! The Pampas! What?
ADA   Calm yourself.
HENRY   And I live on the brink of it! Why? Professional obligations? (*Brief laugh*) Reasons of health? (*Brief laugh*) Family ties? (*Brief laugh*) A woman? (*Laugh in which she joins*) Some old grave I cannot tear myself away from? (*Pause*) Listen to it! What is it like?
ADA   It is like an old sound I used to hear. (*Pause*) It is like another time, in the same place. (*Pause*) It was rough, the spray came flying over us. (*Pause*) Strange it should have been rough then. (*Pause*) And calm now. (*Pause*)
HENRY   Let us get up and go.
ADA   Go? Where? and Addie? She would be very distressed if she came and found you had gone without her. (*Pause*) What do you suppose is keeping her?

(*Smart blow of cylindrical ruler on piano case. Unsteadily, ascending and descending,* ADDIE *plays scale of A Flat Major, hands first together, then reversed. Pause*)

MUSIC MASTER (*Italian accent*)   Santa Cecilia![6] (*Pause*)

[5] The sea.
[6] Patron saint of music.

Embers

ADDIE Will I play my piece now please?

> (*Pause.* MUSIC MASTER *beats two bars of waltz time with ruler on piano case.* ADDIE *plays opening bars of Chopin's 5th Waltz in A Flat Major.* MUSIC MASTER *beating time lightly with ruler as she plays. In first chord of bass, bar 5, she plays E instead of F. Resounding blow of ruler on piano case.* ADDIE *stops playing*)

MUSIC MASTER (*Violently*) Fa!
ADDIE (*Tearfully*) What?
MUSIC MASTER (*Violently*) Eff! Eff!
ADDIE (*Tearfully*) Where?
MUSIC MASTER (*Violently*) Qua! (*He thumps note*) Fa!

> (*Pause.* ADDIE *begins again,* MUSIC MASTER *beating time lightly with ruler. When she comes to bar 5 she makes same mistake. Tremendous blow of ruler on piano case.* ADDIE *stops playing, begins to wail*)

MUSIC MASTER (*Frenziedly*) Eff! Eff! (*He hammers note*) Eff! (*He hammers note*) Eff!

> (*Hammered note, "eff" and* ADDIE'S *wail amplified to paroxysm, then suddenly cut off. Pause*)

ADA You are silent today.
HENRY It was not enough to drag her into the world, now she must play the piano.
ADA She must learn. She shall learn. That—and riding. (*Hooves walking*)
RIDING MASTER Now Miss! Elbows in Miss! Hands down Miss! (*Hooves trotting*) Now Miss! Back straight Miss! Knees in Miss! (*Hooves cantering*) Now Miss! Tummy in Miss! Chin up Miss! (*Hooves galloping*) Now Miss! Eyes front Miss! (ADDIE *begins to wail*) Now Miss! Now Miss!

> (*Galloping hooves, "now Miss!" and* ADDIE'S *wail amplified to paroxysm, then suddenly cut off. Pause*)

ADA What are you thinking of? (*Pause*) I was never taught, until it was too late. All my life I regretted it.
HENRY What was your strong point, I forget.
ADA Oh . . . geometry I suppose, plane and solid. (*Pause*) First plane, then solid. (*Shingle as he gets up*) Why do you get up?
HENRY I thought I might try and get as far as the water's edge. (*Pause. With a sigh*) And back. (*Pause*) Stretch my old bones. (*Pause*)
ADA Well why don't you? (*Pause*) Don't stand there thinking about it.

(*Pause*) Don't stand there staring. (*Pause. He goes towards sea. Boots on shingle, say ten steps. He halts at water's edge. Pause. Sea a little louder. Distant*) Don't wet your good boots. (*Pause*)
HENRY   Don't, don't . . .

(*Sea suddenly rough*)

ADA   (*Twenty years earlier, imploring*)   Don't! Don't!
HENRY   (*Do.,*[7] *urgent*)   Darling!
ADA   (*Do., more feebly*)   Don't!
HENRY   (*Do., exultantly*)   Darling!

(*Rough sea.* ADA *cries out. Cry and sea amplified, cut off. End of evocation. Pause. Sea calm. He goes back up deeply shelving beach. Boots laborious on shingle. He halts. Pause. He moves on. He halts. Pause. Sea calm and faint*)

ADA   Don't sit there gaping. Sit down. (*Pause. Shingle as he sits*) On the shawl. (*Pause*) Are you afraid we might touch? (*Pause*) Henry.
HENRY   Yes.
ADA   You should see a doctor about your talking, it's worse, what must it be like for Addie? (*Pause*) Do you know what she said to me once, when she was still quite small, she said, Mummy, why does Daddy keep on talking all the time? She heard you in the lavatory. I didn't know what to answer.
HENRY   Daddy! Addie! (*Pause*) I told you to tell her I was praying. (*Pause*) Roaring prayers at God and his saints.
ADA   It's very bad for the child. (*Pause*) It's silly to say it keeps you from hearing it, it doesn't keep you from hearing it and even if it does you shouldn't be hearing it, there must be something wrong with your brain. (*Pause*)
HENRY   That! I shouldn't be hearing that!
ADA   I don't think you are hearing it. And if you are what's wrong with it, it's a lovely peaceful gentle soothing sound, why do you hate it? (*Pause*) And if you hate it why don't you keep away from it? Why are you always coming down here? (*Pause*) There's something wrong with your brain, you ought to see Holloway, he's alive still, isn't he? (*Pause*)
HENRY   (*Wildly*)   Thuds, I want thuds! Like this! (*He fumbles in the shingle, catches up two big stones and starts dashing them together*) Stone! (*Clash*) Stone! (*Clash. "Stone!" and clash amplified, cut off. Pause. He throws one stone away. Sound of its fall*) That's life! (*He

---

[7] Ditto.

throws the other stone away. Sound of its fall) Not this . . . *(Pause)* . . . sucking!
ADA And why life? *(Pause)* Why life, Henry? *(Pause)* Is there anyone about?
HENRY Not a living soul.
ADA I thought as much. *(Pause)* When we longed to have it to ourselves there was always someone. Now that it does not matter the place is deserted.
HENRY Yes, you were always very sensitive to being seen in gallant conversation. The least feather of smoke on the horizon and you adjusted your dress and became immersed in the Manchester Guardian. *(Pause)* The hole is still there, after all these years. *(Pause. Louder)* The hole is still there.
ADA What hole? The earth is full of holes.
HENRY Where we did it at last for the first time.
ADA Ah yes, I think I remember. *(Pause)* The place has not changed.
HENRY Oh yes it has, I can see it. *(Confidentially)* There is a levelling going on! *(Pause)* What age is she now?
ADA I have lost count of time.
HENRY Twelve? Thirteen? *(Pause)* Fourteen?
ADA I really could not tell you, Henry.
HENRY It took us a long time to have her. *(Pause)* Years we kept hammering away at it. *(Pause)* But we did it in the end. *(Pause. Sigh)* We had her in the end. *(Pause)* Listen to it! *(Pause)* It's not so bad when you get out on it. *(Pause)* Perhaps I should have gone into the merchant navy.
ADA It's only on the surface, you know. Underneath all is as quiet as the grave. Not a sound. All day, all night, not a sound. *(Pause)*
HENRY Now I walk about with the gramophone. But I forgot it today.
ADA There is no sense in that. *(Pause)* There is no sense in trying to drown it. *(Pause)* See Holloway. *(Pause)*
HENRY Let us go for a row.
ADA A row? And Addie? She would be very distressed if she came and found you had gone for a row without her. *(Pause)* Who were you with just now? *(Pause)* Before you spoke to me.
HENRY I was trying to be with my father.
ADA Oh. *(Pause)* No difficulty about that.
HENRY I mean I was trying to get him to be with me. *(Pause)* You seem a little cruder than usual today, Ada. *(Pause)* I was asking him if he ever met you, I couldn't remember.
ADA Well?
HENRY He doesn't answer any more.

ADA I suppose you have worn him out. (*Pause*) You wore him out living and now you are wearing him out dead. (*Pause*) The time comes when one cannot speak to you any more. (*Pause*) The time will come when no one will speak to you at all, not even complete strangers. (*Pause*) You will be quite alone with your voice, there will be no other voice in the world but yours. (*Pause*) Do you hear me? (*Pause*)
HENRY I can't remember if he met you.
ADA You know he met me.
HENRY No, Ada, I don't know, I'm sorry, I have forgotten almost everything connected with you.
ADA You weren't there. Just your mother and sister. I had called to fetch you, as arranged. We were to go bathing together. (*Pause*)
HENRY (*Irritably*) Drive on, drive on! Why do people always stop in the middle of what they are saying?
ADA None of them knew where you were. Your bed had not been slept in. They were all shouting at one another. Your sister said she would throw herself off the cliff. Your father got up and went out, slamming the door. I left soon afterwards and passed him on the road. He did not see me. He was sitting on a rock looking out to sea. I never forgot his posture. And yet it was a common one. You used to have it sometimes. Perhaps just the stillness, as if he had been turned to stone. I could never make it out. (*Pause*)
HENRY Keep on, keep on! (*Imploringly*) Keep it going, Ada, every syllable is a second gained.
ADA That's all, I'm afraid. (*Pause*) Go on now with your father or your stories or whatever you were doing, don't mind me any more.
HENRY I can't! (*Pause*) I can't do it any more!
ADA You were doing it a moment ago, before you spoke to me.
HENRY (*Angrily*) I can't do it any more now! (*Pause*) Christ! (*Pause*)
ADA Yes, you know what I mean, there are attitudes remain in one's mind for reasons that are clear, the carriage of a head for example, bowed when one would have thought it should be lifted, and vice versa, or a hand suspended in mid air, as if unowned. That kind of thing. But with your father sitting on the rock that day nothing of the kind, no detail you could put your finger on and say, How very peculiar! No, I could never make it out. Perhaps, as I said, just the great stillness of the whole body, as if all the breath had left it. (*Pause*) Is this rubbish a help to you, Henry? (*Pause*) I can try and go on a little if you wish. (*Pause*) No? (*Pause*) Then I think I'll be getting back.
HENRY Not yet! You needn't speak. Just listen. Not even. Be with me. (*Pause*) Ada! (*Pause. Louder*) Ada! (*Pause*) Christ! (*Pause*) Hooves! (*Pause. Louder*) Hooves! (*Pause*) Christ! (*Long pause*) Left soon

afterwards, passed you on the road, didn't see her, looking out to . . . (*Pause*) Can't have been looking out to sea. (*Pause*) Unless you had gone round the other side. (*Pause*) Had you gone round the cliff side? (*Pause*) Father! (*Pause*) Must have I suppose. (*Pause*) Stands watching you a moment, then on down path to tram, up on open top and sits down in front. (*Pause*) Sits down in front. (*Pause*) Suddenly feels uneasy and gets down again, conductor: "Changed your mind, Miss?", goes back up path, no sign of you. (*Pause*) Very unhappy and uneasy, hangs round a bit, not a soul about, cold wind coming in off sea, goes back down path and takes tram home. (*Pause*) Takes tram home. (*Pause*) Christ! (*Pause*) "My dear Bolton . . ." (*Pause*) "If it's an injection you want, Bolton, let down your trousers and I'll give you one, I have a panhysterectomy at nine," meaning of course the anaesthetic. (*Pause*) Fire out, bitter cold, white world, great trouble, not a sound. (*Pause*) Bolton starts playing with the curtain, no, hanging, difficult to describe, draws it back, no, kind of gathers it towards him and the moon comes flooding in, then lets it fall back, heavy velvet affair, and pitch black in the room, then towards him again, white, black, white, black, Holloway: "Stop that for the love of God, Bolton, do you want to finish me?" (*Pause*) Black, white, black, white, maddening thing. (*Pause*) Then he suddenly strikes a match, Bolton does, lights a candle, catches it up above his head, walks over and looks Holloway full in the eye. (*Pause*) Not a word, just the look, the old blue eye, very glassy, lids worn thin, lashes gone, whole thing swimming, and the candle shaking over his head. (*Pause*) Tears? (*Pause. Long laugh*) Good God no! (*Pause*) Not a word, just the look, the old blue eye, Holloway: "If you want a shot say so and let me get to hell out of here." (*Pause*) "We've had this before, Bolton, don't ask me to go through it again." (*Pause*) Bolton: "Please!" (*Pause*) "Please!" (*Pause*) "Please, Holloway!" (*Pause*) Candle shaking and guttering all over the place, lower now, old arm tired, takes it in the other hand and holds it high again, that's it, that was always it, night, and the embers cold, and the glim shaking in your old fist, saying, Please! Please! (*Pause*) Begging. (*Pause*) Of the poor. (*Pause*) Ada! (*Pause*) Father! (*Pause*) Christ! (*Pause*) Holds it high again, naughty world, fixes Holloway, eyes drowned, won't ask again, just the look, Holloway covers his face, not a sound, white world, bitter cold, ghastly scene, old men, great trouble, no good. (*Pause*) No good. (*Pause*) Christ! (*Pause. Shingle as he gets up. He goes towards sea. Boots on shingle. He halts. Pause. Sea a little louder*) On. (*Pause. He moves on. Boots on shingle. He halts at water's edge. Pause. Sea a little louder*) Little book. (*Pause*) This evening . . . (*Pause*) Nothing this evening. (*Pause*) Tomorrow . . . tomorrow . . .

plumber at nine, then nothing. (*Pause. Puzzled*) Plumber at nine? (*Pause*) Ah, yes, the waste. (*Pause*) Words. (*Pause*) Saturday . . . nothing. Sunday . . . Sunday . . . nothing all day. (*Pause*) Nothing, all day nothing. (*Pause*) All day all night nothing. (*Pause*) Not a sound. (*Sea*)